"From creation to new creation, God [...] center for the whole Bible. With car[...] through the canon, demonstrating [...] understanding how the Bible fits together. This will be essential reading for all courses on biblical theology."

—**David G. Firth**, Trinity College Bristol and University of the Free State

"Duvall and Hays make a clear and convincing case that the relational presence of God is indeed the central theme of biblical theology. The book is full of those 'Well, of course!' and 'Why didn't I think of that?' moments. Just consider the biblical story: Human beings were created to be in relationship with God. That relationship was broken by the fall. The rest of the Bible describes the restoration and renewal of that relationship, climaxing with God dwelling with his people in the book of Revelation. 'Well, of course this is the central theme of the Bible!' With such a simple yet profound thesis, so well written and comprehensively executed, this volume is destined to become a classic."

—**Mark L. Strauss**, Bethel Seminary

"Scott Duvall and Daniel Hays are two of my favorite biblical scholars. I am constantly blessed by their works, and now I can add *God's Relational Presence* to that number. This is a compressive biblical theology that covers the entire canon of Scripture. They make a compelling argument that the relational presence of God is the 'cohesive center' that ties all the major biblical-theological themes together in the great redemptive story. This resource will well serve faithful teachers of the Word of God. It is a volume I will seek out again and again."

—**Daniel L. Akin**, Southeastern Baptist Theological Seminary

"What a wonderful gift to the church! This is great teamwork by an Old Testament and a New Testament scholar. It is the fruit of years of interaction with and meditation on the Scriptures, to which their many published works attest. I had a hard time putting this book down. Duvall and Hays engage in the search for the holy grail of biblical theology—the elusive center. While many scholars will not agree that they have found the center, they have come very close. Beginning in the garden with the uninterrupted communion between God and the first human community and ending in the garden-city with that same communion, Duvall and Hays explore the plotline of the Bible through the fall, the call of the patriarchs, the exodus, Sinai, the conquest and the kingdom, the exile, the prophetic hope and the realization of those hopes in Christ, the church, and the eschaton. They argue that this cohesive center is not like the hub of a wheel, where the spokes perfectly align, but more like the center of a spider web, where the threads are more asymmetrical, connecting sometimes directly and other times more indirectly. Exegetically sound and comprehensive in research, this book becomes essential reading for biblical theology!"

—**Stephen G. Dempster**, Crandall University

GOD'S
RELATIONAL
PRESENCE

GOD'S RELATIONAL PRESENCE

The Cohesive Center of Biblical Theology

J. SCOTT DUVALL
AND J. DANIEL HAYS

B
Baker Academic
a division of Baker Publishing Group
Grand Rapids, Michigan

Published by Baker Academic
a division of Baker Publishing Group
PO Box 6287, Grand Rapids, MI 49516-6287
www.bakeracademic.com

Printed in the United States of America

Library of Congress Cataloging-in-Publication Data
Names: Duvall, J. Scott, author. | Hays, J. Daniel, 1953– author.
Title: God's relational presence : the cohesive center of biblical theology / J. Scott Duvall and J. Daniel Hays.
Description: Grand Rapids, MI : Baker Academic, a division of Baker Publishing Group, [2019] | Includes bibliographical references and index.
Identifiers: LCCN 2019010107 | ISBN 9780801049590 (pbk. : alk. paper)
Subjects: LCSH: Presence of God. | Bible—Theology. | God—Biblical teaching.
Classification: LCC BT180.P6 D88 2019 | DDC 231.7/6—dc23
LC record available at https://lccn.loc.gov/2019010107

ISBN 978-1-5409-6264-5 (casebound)

19   20   21   22   23   24   25   7   6   5   4   3   2   1

We dedicate this book to Jack Kuhatschek, our friend and former editor, who has probably had more positive influence on our writing careers than anyone else. Thanks, Jack, for your friendship, for all the great dinners, for the many thought-provoking theological discussions, and for the opportunity to write for the church, the classroom, and the academy.

CONTENTS

DETAILED CONTENTS

ACKNOWLEDGMENTS

First, we thank James Korsmo, Dave Nelson, and the editorial staff at Baker Academic for making this dream of ours into a reality. We also acknowledge and thank Dylan Watson, Ransey Joiner, and Caleb Collins, undergraduate students at Ouachita Baptist University who helped with research and bibliographic details. Likewise, we give a special word of thanks and recognition to research assistant Adam Jones, who helped us immensely with the bibliography and documentation. Finally, we thank our wives, Judy Duvall and Donna Hays, for their constant support, encouragement, and loving patience.

ABBREVIATIONS

Bible Texts and Versions

CSB	Christian Standard Bible
ESV	English Standard Version
ET	English translation
HCSB	Holman Christian Standard Bible
LXX	Septuagint
MT	Masoretic Text
NASB	New American Standard Bible
NET	The NET Bible (New English Translation)
NETS	New English Translation of the Septuagint
NIV	New International Version
NLT	New Living Translation
NRSV	New Revised Standard Version
NT	New Testament
OT	Old Testament

Secondary Sources

AB	Anchor Bible
ABD	*Anchor Bible Dictionary*. Edited by David Noel Freedman. 6 vols. New York: Doubleday, 1992
AnBib	Analecta Biblica
AOAT	Alter Orient und Altes Testament
ApOTC	Apollos Old Testament Commentary
AYB	Anchor Yale Bible
AYBRL	Anchor Yale Bible Reference Library
BAFCS	The Book of Acts in Its First Century Setting
BBR	*Bulletin for Biblical Research*
BCOTWP	Baker Commentary on the Old Testament Wisdom and Psalms

BDAG	Danker, Frederick W., Walter Bauer, William F. Arndt, and F. Wilbur Gingrich. *Greek-English Lexicon of the New Testament and Other Early Christian Literature*. 3rd ed. Chicago: University of Chicago Press, 2000
BDB	Brown, Francis, S. R. Driver, and Charles A. Briggs. *A Hebrew and English Lexicon of the Old Testament*. Oxford: Clarendon, 1907
BECNT	Baker Exegetical Commentary on the New Testament
BETL	Bibliotheca Ephemeridum Theologicarum Lovaniensium
BHHB	Baylor Handbook on the Hebrew Bible
Bib	*Biblica*
BibInt	*Biblical Interpretation*
BJSUCSD	Biblical and Judaic Studies from the University of California, San Diego
BLS	Bible and Literature Series
BSac	*Bibliotheca Sacra*
BTCB	Brazos Theological Commentary on the Bible
BTL	Biblical Theology for Life
BTNT	Biblical Theology of the New Testament
BTS	Biblical Tools and Studies
BZ	*Biblische Zeitschrift*
BZAW	Beihefte zur Zeitschrift für die alttestamentliche Wissenschaft
CBQ	*Catholic Biblical Quarterly*
CBQMS	Catholic Biblical Quarterly Monograph Series
CC	Continental Commentaries
CNTUOT	*Commentary on the New Testament Use of the Old Testament*. Edited by G. K. Beale and D. A. Carson. Grand Rapids: Baker Academic, 2007
ConBOT	Coniectanea Biblica: Old Testament Series
COQG	Christian Origins and the Question of God
CTJ	*Calvin Theological Journal*
EB	Exploring the Bible
EBS	Encountering Biblical Studies
ECC	Eerdmans Critical Commentary
ExpTim	*Expository Times*
FAT	Forschungen zum Alten Testament
FBBS	Facet Books, Biblical Series
FOTL	Forms of the Old Testament Literature
FRLANT	Forschungen zur Religion und Literatur des Alten und Neuen Testaments
GAOT	The Gospel according to the Old Testament
HAR	*Hebrew Annual Review*
HBT	*Horizons in Biblical Theology*
HCOT	Historical Commentary on the Old Testament
HMSCS	Hearing the Message of Scripture Commentary Series
HSM	Harvard Semitic Monographs
IBC	Interpretation: A Bible Commentary for Teaching and Preaching
IBT	Interpreting Biblical Texts
ICC	International Critical Commentary
IDBSup	*Interpreter's Dictionary of the Bible: Supplementary Volume*. Edited by Keith Crim. Nashville: Abingdon, 1976
Int	*Interpretation*

ITC	International Theological Commentary
IVPNTC	IVP New Testament Commentary Series
JBL	*Journal of Biblical Literature*
JETS	*Journal of the Evangelical Theological Society*
JPTSup	Journal of Pentecostal Theology Supplement
JSNT	*Journal for the Study of the New Testament*
JSNTSup	Journal for the Study of the New Testament Supplement Series
JSOT	*Journal for the Study of the Old Testament*
JSOTSup	Journal for the Study of the Old Testament Supplement Series
JSQ	*Jewish Studies Quarterly*
JTISup	Journal for Theological Interpretation, Supplements
JTS	*Journal of Theological Studies*
KEL	Kregel Exegetical Library
LHBOTS	The Library of Hebrew Bible/Old Testament Studies
LNTS	The Library of New Testament Studies
NAC	New American Commentary
NACSBT	New American Commentary Studies in Bible and Theology
NCB	New Century Bible
NCBC	New Cambridge Bible Commentary
NDBT	*New Dictionary of Biblical Theology.* Edited by T. Desmond Alexander and Brian S. Rosner. Downers Grove, IL: InterVarsity, 2000
NEchtB	Neue Echter Bibel
NIB	*The New Interpreter's Bible.* Edited by Leander E. Keck. 12 vols. Nashville: Abingdon, 1994–2004
NIBC	New International Biblical Commentary
NICNT	New International Commentary on the New Testament
NICOT	New International Commentary on the Old Testament
NIDOTTE	*New International Dictionary of Old Testament Theology and Exegesis.* Edited by Willem A. VanGemeren. 5 vols. Grand Rapids: Zondervan, 1997
NIGTC	New International Greek Testament Commentary
NIVAC	NIV Application Commentary
NSBT	New Studies in Biblical Theology
NTL	New Testament Library
NTT	New Testament Theology
OBS	Oxford Bible Series
OBT	Overtures to Biblical Theology
OTL	Old Testament Library
OTM	Oxford Theological Monographs
OtSt	Oudtestamentische Studiën
PBTM	Paternoster Biblical and Theological Monographs
PNTC	Pillar New Testament Commentary
PSt	Pauline Studies
ResQ	*Restoration Quarterly*
S&I	*Scripture and Interpretation*
SBET	*Scottish Bulletin of Evangelical Theology*
SBJT	*The Southern Baptist Journal of Theology*
SBL	Studies in Biblical Literature

SBLDS	Society of Biblical Literature Dissertation Series
SBLRBS	Society of Biblical Literature Resources for Biblical Study
SBLSymS	Society of Biblical Literature Symposium Series
SBTS	Sources for Biblical and Theological Study
SGBC	The Story of God Bible Commentary
SHBC	Smyth & Helwys Bible Commentary
SNTSMS	Society for New Testament Studies Monograph Series
SOTBT	Studies in Old Testament Biblical Theology
STAR	Studies in Theology and Religion
STDJ	Studies on the Texts of the Desert of Judah
STI	Studies in Theological Interpretation
TBC	Torch Bible Commentaries
TBS	Tools for Biblical Study
TBST	The Bible Speaks Today
TDNT	*Theological Dictionary of the New Testament*. Edited by Gerhard Kittel and Gerhard Friedrich. Translated by Geoffrey W. Bromiley. 10 vols. Grand Rapids: Eerdmans, 1964–76
TDOT	*Theological Dictionary of the Old Testament*. Edited by G. Johannes Botterweck and Helmer Ringgren. Translated by John T. Willis et al. 8 vols. Grand Rapids: Eerdmans, 1974–2006
THOTC	Two Horizons Old Testament Commentary
TLOT	*Theological Lexicon of the Old Testament*. Edited by Ernst Jenni, with assistance from Claus Westermann. Translated by Mark E. Biddle. 3 vols. Peabody, MA: Hendrickson, 1997
TOTC	Tyndale Old Testament Commentaries
TTCS	Teach the Text Commentary Series
TWOT	*Theological Wordbook of the Old Testament*. Edited by R. Laird Harris, Gleason L. Archer Jr., and Bruce K. Waltke. 2 vols. Chicago: Moody, 1980
TynBul	*Tyndale Bulletin*
UBCS	Understanding the Bible Commentary Series
VT	*Vetus Testamentum*
WBC	Word Biblical Commentary
WestBC	Westminster Bible Companion
WTJ	*Westminster Theological Journal*
WUNT	Wissenschaftliche Untersuchungen zum Neuen Testament
WW	*Word and World*
ZAW	*Zeitschrift für die alttestamentliche Wissenschaft*
ZECNT	Zondervan Exegetical Commentary on the New Testament

INTRODUCTION

Our Basic Thesis

Our basic thesis is that the Triune God desires to have a personal, encountering relationship with his people and enters into his creation in order to facilitate that relationship. Thus the Bible begins with God's presence relating to his people in the garden (Genesis) and ends with God's presence relating to his people in the garden (Revelation). This holy, intense, powerful presence of God appears to Moses in the burning bush and on Mount Sinai, and then enters into the tabernacle (and later into the temple) so that God can dwell among his people. Indeed, the presence of God dwelling among his people is foundational to his covenant with them, and Israel's worshiping relationship with God centers on his presence in the tabernacle or temple. Yet because of their sin and disobedience, Israel is banished from God's presence. God departs from the temple (Ezekiel), and Israel is exiled away from the land. The restoration of God's presence is promised throughout the OT prophets and is fulfilled in the Gospels when Jesus, Immanuel (God with us), appears. The incarnation brings to a climax the relational presence of God, the theme that drove the entire OT story. In Acts, after Jesus's ascension, the Holy Spirit comes to dwell within each believer, just as the holy presence of God in the OT dwelt in the tabernacle or temple. Paul explains the broad, far-reaching theological implications of the Triune God's relational presence among his people. Indeed, almost every aspect of Paul's theology connects to the relational presence of God. The entire story culminates at the end of Revelation, where the presence of God is once again in Jerusalem (the *new* Jerusalem) and in the garden, relating to his people. This "megatheme" drives the biblical story, uniting and providing interconnecting cohesion across the canon for all of the other major themes, such as covenant, kingdom, creation, holiness, redemption, law and grace, sin and forgiveness, life and death, worship, and obedient living. It is indeed the cohesive center of biblical theology.

What Do We Mean by "Biblical Theology"?

Within the field of biblical and theological studies, the term "biblical theology" can have a wide range of meanings.[1] In this book we are using the term to refer to theology that is derived from the exegesis of Scripture using the genre and context of the biblical books and that utilizes the theological categories emerging from the biblical story line within each book and connecting across the canon from book to book. Underlying our approach to biblical theology is the presupposition that the Bible is divinely inspired. So while we affirm the complex composition of the Bible, a corollary of our presupposition is that there is a unity within the Bible, a coherence, divinely placed, that ties it all together, including the OT and the NT.

Our methodology for developing biblical theology starts with exegesis and inductive study,[2] while still recognizing that due to the nature of Scripture, exegetical analysis and theological analysis often are inextricably interconnected. Thus throughout the book we will be discussing exegetical details from specific texts and engaging with biblical commentaries and monographs that are primarily exegetical in nature but that also often move into theological analysis. The scope of this book, however—we are covering the entire Bible—limits our exegetical analysis to only the most significant details, and thus we often will move to conclusions quickly while referencing respected commentaries for more thorough discussion and argumentation, especially on controversial passages.

Following inductive exegetical study and the associated theological analysis, we will move to synthesis. Here we attempt to synthesize the exegetical results, first of all employing categories from within each book, paying particular attention to the genre and context of that book. We next attempt to synthesize more broadly, connecting the results from each book into the ongoing plot and the biblical themes across larger units (e.g., the Pentateuch, the Pauline Letters) and likewise attempting to connect each synthesis into an overarching story line or "megastory." In this step we often engage with

---

1. See the survey of the spectrum of biblical theology by Klink and Lockett, *Understanding Biblical Theology*, and the extensive discussion by Barr, *The Concept of Biblical Theology*. For a brief history of biblical theology, see Pate et al., *The Story of Israel*, 11–17.

2. What we are espousing methodologically for developing biblical theology is similar to that presented by Carson, "Systematic Theology and Biblical Theology," esp. 91–92, 100–101; Hafemann, "Biblical Theology."

books on OT and NT theology, since often they are undertaking a similar attempt at synthesis.

Our approach to biblical theology is both "descriptive" and "prescriptive." We seek to identify and synthesize the theology emerging from each book and across the canon, but we do this with the end purpose of applying that theology to Christian living.

We are attempting to develop a "whole-Bible" biblical theology.[3] "Whole-Bible" biblical theology is inherently a Christian endeavor. Likewise, both of us write from within the Protestant tradition. Thus in the OT, rather than follow the Jewish Tanakh canonical order of the biblical books,[4] or the Catholic canonical collection that includes the Apocrypha, we will follow the traditional Protestant canon in our study. In general, variations in canonical ordering (Christian versus Jewish) only affect the development of biblical theology in a few cases (1–2 Chronicles, Ruth, Daniel, etc.), and then usually in only minor ways. None of these variations in canonical location affect the conclusions of our study significantly. For example, placing 1–2 Chronicles at the end of the OT canon, as some suggest, still fits in well with the flow of our argument, perhaps even strengthening the argument slightly. That is, 2 Chronicles ends with a summary of the three-part (tripartite) covenant formulation, a call to rebuild the temple (the place for God's presence to dwell on earth), and a promise regarding God's relational presence with his people.

---

3. Carson has underscored that one of the basic challenges, yet still a critical necessity, to writing biblical theology is the difficult task of dealing in a scholarly and accurate way with the entire Bible (Carson, "Current Issues in Biblical Theology," 20–23, 34–35).

4. We tend to disagree with those fellow Christians who argue that biblical theology should be based on the order of the Jewish canon and not the Christian canon, supposedly because the former is "earlier." These fellow Christians often point to Jesus's references to "the Law and the Prophets" as indicating that he recognized the Jewish canonical order. Yet note, first, that "the Law" and "the Prophets" are very large groupings, not at all indicative, for example, of where the book of Daniel should be located. Second, the Gospels refer to these broad groupings of the Jewish Scriptures in three different ways: (1) "the Law and the Prophets" (Matt. 7:12; 22:40; Luke 16:16); (2) "the Prophets and the Law" (Matt. 11:13); (3) "the Law of Moses, the Prophets, and the Psalms" (Luke 24:44). Third, the significance of specific canonical ordering (e.g., where Ruth was to be located) most likely became much more significant when the Scriptures moved from collections of scrolls to codices (books). Hurtado points out that Christians adopted the codex form for their Scriptures very early in the Christian movement, well in advance of Jewish acceptance of the codex for their Holy Books. In the first few centuries of the Christian era Judaism was still primarily using scrolls, and the Jewish preference for scrolls continued for several centuries after the widespread acceptance of codices by the Christians, and even now scrolls often are preferred in Jewish synagogues over codices (Hurtado, *The Earliest Christian Artifacts*, 43–93). The point here is that specific canonical ordering becomes more theologically significant as the collection of Holy Books moves from numerous individual and separate scrolls to one bound codex. Hurtado posits that the Christian preference for the codex was both a characteristic of early Christianity and "a distinguishing mark" (p. 69).

This provides a powerful connecting theme to the NT.[5] Our conclusions remain the same, whether 2 Chronicles closes the OT canon or Malachi does.

Likewise, our project is a Christian "whole-Bible" biblical theology because we see a plot-like movement throughout the Scriptures that is divinely inspired. Our starting observation is that Genesis is the plot-forming beginning and Revelation is the consummating end, with Jesus Christ at the center of the story. Thus historical movement is an important issue for the methodology that we are proposing, and our approach to biblical theology has a certain diachronic aspect to it. On the other hand, we see very limited benefit to the development of Christian biblical theology from the numerous evolving compositional theories and accompanying historical settings that frequently are being discussed and debated within the broader academy, especially in the field of OT studies.[6] Thus we will primarily presuppose the history that is reflected in the canon and build our biblical theology based on the historical background and movement as the Christian canon presents it.

The Cohesive Center of Biblical Theology

Obviously, there are numerous very important and pervasive themes running throughout the Bible, such as promise and fulfillment, redemption, creation, the kingdom of God, covenant, God's glory, and the sovereignty of God. Over the years many of these have been proposed as the "center" of biblical theology. Yet identifying the center of biblical theology is not just a matter of arguing which theme is the most pervasive or the most frequent. Rather, the center of biblical theology would be the megatheme that provides the cohesion that connects the other pervasive themes, along with the details, into a coherent whole. Furthermore, instead of using the analogy of a wheel, which has a hub (the center) and equally balanced spokes (the central themes) connected to the hub, to describe the center of biblical theology, we prefer the analogy of a spiderweb. The major themes of biblical theology would be like the main threads in the web, connected in one way or another to the center, but not always directly (some go radially and some go in concurrent circles). In the wheel analogy, everything must connect directly to the hub of the wheel, which can result, theologically speaking, in forcing an artificial orderliness onto the diversity of the Bible. The center of a web, on the other

5. Note the similar thematic emphases in Rev. 21–22, which brings the NT canon to a close.

6. One exception will be the book of Psalms, where we will acknowledge that the historical setting (preexilic, exilic, or postexilic) for the composition and collection of the five books of the Psalter probably does impact exegesis, synthesis, and biblical theology.

hand, conveys a sense of interconnectedness that still allows for canonical flexibility.[7] All of the central themes and subthemes in biblical theology would ultimately depend on the center for structural integrity and cohesion, even while the specific manner of interconnection, both historically and theologically, can be complex.

Similarly, from an overall biblical narrative point of view, the cohesive center of biblical theology must be that megatheme that drives the plot of the story from beginning to end. Isolating the center of biblical theology, therefore, involves identifying which central theme is most integrally related to the plot. That is, the center of biblical theology is that prevalent theme that is continually advancing the plot forward and interconnecting the other themes. We will argue that the relational presence of God does this continually throughout Scripture. Likewise, in arguing that the relational presence of God is the "cohesive center" of biblical theology, we are neither ignoring nor downplaying the importance of other prevalent and highly significant biblical themes (e.g., covenant, kingdom of God), but rather suggesting that the cohesive central megatheme of God's relational presence connects all of these other themes into the big overarching plot of the biblical story. In our view, most of these other major biblical themes are actually "subplots" (so to speak), each of which is interconnected and related to the megastory of God's relational presence. Our subtitle for this book, *The Cohesive Center of Biblical Theology*, reflects this argument for the relational presence of God as that "spiderweb-like cohesive center" that ties all of the major biblical themes together as it likewise moves God's story forward from the beginning to the end.

Presence and Omnipresence, Immanence and Transcendence

One of the challenges of Christian theology, both systematic theology and biblical theology, is the interaction—some might even say, tension—between the transcendence of God (his otherness) and the immanence of God (his relatedness to the creation, and especially to his people within the creation). Sometimes there is a tendency, both in systematic theology and even in biblical theology, to acknowledge both immanence and transcendence but to view the transcendent God as the way he *really* is and the immanent God as his (somewhat secondary) accommodation to us. We suspect that this mode of theological understanding is due in part to the underlying assumptions of

7. For the spiderweb analogy, we are indebted to C. Campbell, *Paul and Union with Christ*, 437–39.

Western thought (perhaps some manner of residual Neoplatonic dualism). If we are not careful, this becomes a strong, subtle presupposition that colors our reading and theological understanding of the biblical text.

On the other hand, the goal of theology, especially biblical theology, is to seek to know God *as he has revealed himself to us through the Scriptures.* Thus when Isaiah describes the coming of God with "He tends his flock like a shepherd: He gathers the lambs in his arms and carries them close to his heart" (40:11), should we wave this away as metaphoric accommodation, saying that God in his transcendence is not *really* like that? We definitely should not. God is clearly both transcendent and immanent, and to ignore his self-revelation of either is to construct a golden calf of our own understanding and blasphemously to label it "God." An important part of our understanding of God and our relationship with him is to view him as loving us and caring for us intimately as a shepherd cares for his sheep. This is one of the ways in which he has revealed himself to us through Scripture.

The Bible certainly affirms God's transcendence and does not shirk from the tension between transcendence and immanence,[8] yet as the biblical story unfolds and as God seeks to relate to his people, almost by definition (i.e., this biblical story is a story about relatedness) immanence takes center stage in how God reveals himself (although transcendence still hovers about continuously). This "tension" in our understanding carries over into the important distinction between God's presence and his omnipresence.[9] The OT, for example, certainly does affirm God's omnipresence, but on the other hand, Moses does not remove his sandals and fearfully hide his face in front of *every* bush that he encounters in the wilderness. There is something spectacularly special and unique about *that* particular bush in Exodus 3 because God is present in a very intense way in *that* particular flaming bush. Likewise, while God's omnipresence fills all the mountains of the world, the one in Exodus 19 is quite different: "Mount Sinai was covered with smoke, because the LORD descended on it in fire. The smoke billowed up from it like smoke from a furnace, and the whole mountain trembled violently" (v. 18). Thus when God reveals at Mount Sinai the promise of his presence as the central aspect of the covenant relationship between him and the people of Israel, he is speaking not about some vague concept of omnipresence but of a very real and terrifying holy presence as he comes to actually dwell among them. He instructs Moses, "Have them make me a sanctuary [a holy place], so that I may dwell among them" (Exod. 25:8). This indwelling of God's presence lies at the center of his relationship with

---

8. Clements, *God and Temple*, 136.
9. See the helpful discussion by Moltmann, *The Coming of God*, 302–8.

his people. He states, "I will dwell among the Israelites, and I will be their God. And they shall know that I am the LORD their God who brought them out of the land of Egypt that I might dwell among them" (Exod. 29:45–46). Then after the tabernacle is constructed, God comes into the tabernacle to dwell in the midst of Israel. "Then the cloud covered the tent of meeting, and the glory of the LORD filled the tabernacle" (Exod. 40:34).[10] This is not some "quasi" or "proxy" presence of God but God himself taking up residence for the purpose of relating to his people.[11] It is this relational presence of God that we are tracking through the Scriptures.

Certainly, as mentioned above, one of the central and defining events in the OT is the encounter with God at Mount Sinai. There he establishes his covenant relationship with Israel defined by a three-part formula: "I will be your God; you will be my people; *I will dwell in your midst.*" Climaxing the spectacular events in the book of Exodus, in 40:34 "the glory of the LORD" (the presence of God) enters the tabernacle to dwell with Israel. A continuation of God's presence "in their midst" occurs in 1 Kings 8:10–11 as "the glory of the LORD" fills the new temple that Solomon has constructed. The importance of this reality to the entire flow of the OT story and the theology flowing out of it cannot be overstressed. As R. E. Clements notes, "For Yahweh to be the God of Israel means that he dwells in their midst. . . . Israel only becomes Israel when Yahweh dwells in its midst."[12] Indeed, the immanence of God is a critical component of God's revelation to his people.

Both the OT and the NT present God as both transcendent and immanent, not allowing either to dominate the other.[13] In the OT, as the immanence of God becomes associated with God dwelling with his people on earth in the tabernacle/temple, the Scriptures add "an eschatological hope in which Israel looked to the future for the full manifestation of Yahweh's dwelling with men. . . . A clear path was made for the central assertion of Christianity; the Incarnation of God in Christ. . . . Here divine immanence and transcendence

---

10. The phrase "glory of the LORD" (כְּבוֹד יְהוָה, *kebod Yahweh*) refers to the divine presence, indicating that God himself comes to dwell in the tabernacle. See M. Weinfeld, "כָּבוֹד," *TDOT* 7:29–33; M. Moore, "Divine Presence," 166.

11. Burnett writes, "Throughout the Hebrew Bible, Israel's identity is intimately bound with the memory of its first encounters with its God and an understanding of various relational foundations for continuing divine presence" (Burnett, *Where Is God?*, 5).

12. Clements, *God and Temple*, 115. Likewise, commenting on Exod. 29:45 ("I will dwell among the Israelites; and I will be their God"), Brueggemann states, "Presence is everything," noting the strong connection between "presence" and "being 'their God'" (Brueggemann, *Theology of the Old Testament*, 663).

13. Vriezen notes that "the transcendent God is at the same time the immanent God" (Vriezen, *Outline of Old Testament Theology*, 183).

are reconciled in the person of one who is the perfect union of the human and the divine."[14]

Use of Anthropomorphism and Other Figures of Speech

As part of the introductory matters, we need to address the issue of figurative language. We are well aware of the extensive and often complex use of figurative, poetic, and apocalyptic language throughout the Bible, especially in the OT.[15] In regard to God's actions and feelings, anthropomorphic figures of speech abound. Yet it is important to keep a few things in mind. First, the presence of God dwelling in the tabernacle and then in the temple was a reality and not a metaphor. The cloud surrounding his glory/presence as he entered the tabernacle was real and not figurative. Second, as we explore language that is clearly figurative, it is important to remember that there are always literal realities behind the figures of speech in the Scriptures, areas of similarity to which the figures of speech point.[16] Third, the anthropomorphic figures of speech create images that are part of God's revelation to us. For a good example, let's look again at the text from Isaiah cited above, where the prophet writes, "He tends his flock like a shepherd: He gathers the lambs in his arms and carries them close to his heart" (40:11). The analogy is obvious: God will care for his people and lovingly gather them up just as a shepherd cares for his sheep and lovingly gathers them up. Even though this is a figure of speech, it does convey a very real image of God that he has chosen for his revelation to us, an image in this case that relates tangentially to our theme of presence. God does not simply decree the restoration from his distant throne up in heaven; nor does he simply accomplish the restoration by sending emissaries or angels to do his bidding. One of the central images he has chosen for his role in the future restoration is that of a shepherd personally walking along with those who are being regathered, carrying young lambs lovingly in his arms.

In this book we will track the real and literal presence of God in the midst of Israel as he dwells in the temple, later departs from the temple, and then returns in the incarnation. We will also point to the very frequent anthropomorphic figures of speech that portray God as "up close and personal" in his

---

14. Clements, *God and Temple*, 138.

15. On OT poetry and figurative language, see J. D. Hays, *The Message of the Prophets*, 46–57; Duvall and Hays, *Grasping God's Word*, 373–91.

16. See the helpful discussion on anthropomorphic metaphor in Fretheim, *The Suffering of God*, 5–12.

involvement with his people. We will argue that the two are related, and that the figures of speech about God's close personal relatedness are anchored in the reality of his personal encounter with Israel at Sinai and in his very real and literal presence dwelling in their midst, first in the garden, then in the tabernacle, and then in the temple. These two strands—the very real presence of God in Israel's midst and the anthropomorphic figures of speech about God—merge together climactically in the NT, through the incarnation of Christ, the indwelling of the Holy Spirit, and the ultimate restoration seen in the new Jerusalem at the very end of the Christian canon.

How This Book Came to Be

One of us (J. Scott Duvall) is a NT professor, and one of us (J. Daniel Hays) is an OT professor. We began writing together in 2001, when we produced *Grasping God's Word: A Hands-On Approach to Reading, Interpreting, and Applying the Bible* (Zondervan). We quickly recognized the benefits of working together collaboratively as specialists in NT studies and in OT studies. Indeed, the complexity of biblical studies makes it difficult for one person, normally limited to one area of specialized detailed study, to address the entire Bible academically. Also, as professors (teaching at Ouachita Baptist University), we both regularly encountered the need to explain the entire Bible and the flow of the biblical story to our students. Meeting this challenge has been our passion for the last twenty-five years. In 2004 we formally began writing biblical theology, joining with several other colleagues at Ouachita to produce *The Story of Israel: A Biblical Theology* (InterVarsity), in which we and our colleagues tracked the theme of "sin, exile, and restoration" across the biblical canon. Then the two of us worked together again on two works dealing with the entire Bible, *The Baker Illustrated Bible Handbook* (Baker Books, 2011) and *Living God's Word: Discovering Our Place in the Great Story of Scripture* (Zondervan, 2012). It was at about this time that we both began noticing how frequently the theme of God's presence was occurring. We started having intriguing conversations about what each one of us was discovering in our own discipline of study in regard to God's presence, starting with the observation that the Bible begins with God's presence in the garden (Genesis) and ends with God's presence in a restored garden (Revelation). At this time, in our academic study, Scott was focusing on the book of Revelation (*Revelation*, Baker Books, 2014; *The Heart of Revelation: Understanding the Ten Essential Themes of the Bible's Final Book*, Baker Books, 2016), while Danny was working on the OT prophets (*The Message of the Prophets: A Survey of the Old Testament Prophetic and Apocalyptic Books of the Old Testament*, Zondervan, 2010; *Jeremiah and Lamentations*, Baker Books, 2016). Also, starting to probe more directly into the theme of God's relational presence, Danny wrote the popular-level book *The Temple and the Tabernacle: A Study of God's Dwelling Places from Genesis to Revelation* (Baker Books, 2016). Our separate studies in Revelation and in the OT prophets convinced us both that the relational presence of God was a central theme of biblical theology, spanning across the OT and the NT, and providing unity between the Testaments.

More and more during the years that ensued, once we began looking for it, we were continually struck by the frequency and the centrality of the presence of God throughout the rest of the canon as well.[17] At the exegetical text-by-text level, we were impressed by the number of times that top OT and NT commentaries were noting the significant role that the presence of God was playing in specific texts. For example, commentators on Matthew were observing that the book of Matthew starts with "Immanuel" and ends with "I am with you always." What was missing was a volume that brought together all of these separate exegetical conclusions and synthesized them into an overall biblical theology. This is what we are seeking to do.

We are not the first to argue that the presence of God is a central theme of biblical theology. Over the years, scholars from several different disciplines have been coming to similar, or at least related, conclusions. In 1978 OT scholar Samuel Terrien published *The Elusive Presence: The Heart of Biblical Theology* (Harper & Row). Terrien comes to many of the same conclusions that we do, but his development of the argument is very uneven across the canon, and due to his source-critical presuppositions, he skips over quite a bit of relevant material and tries to synthesize his conclusions back into his source-critical framework. He is helpful but limited in his scope. Without arguing that it is *the* center of biblical or OT theology, nonetheless several other OT scholars, such as R. E. Clements and Tremper Longman,[18] stress the importance of God's presence throughout the OT and into the NT. Likewise, NT scholar G. K. Beale, in pursuing the theme of the cosmic temple, earthly temple, and the mission of God's people, comes to several of the same conclusions that we do, although he is more narrowly focused.[19] From the field of systematics, yet while moving quickly across the canon in a biblical theology

---

17. We are indebted to our friend and former editor Jack Kuhatschek, who participated in several of these early conversations and first suggested to us that the theme is not just the "presence of God" but rather the "*relational* presence of God."

18. Clements, *God and Temple*; Longman, *Immanuel in Our Place*.

19. Beale, *The Temple and the Church's Mission*; Beale and Kim, *God Dwells among Us*.

approach, Ryan Lister likewise comes to conclusions very similar to ours.[20] So to various degrees and from several different fields of study, a number of scholars have concluded that the presence of God is a central theme, perhaps even *the* central theme, in the Bible.

What we seek to do in this volume is to develop a full-blown biblical theology of the relational presence of God, tracking this theme across the entire biblical canon, exegetically establishing the important centrality of this theme in all parts of the canon. In the process, as we show how repeatedly this megatheme occurs and how central this theme is to the story and the plot—indeed, how this megatheme drives the plot and provides cohesion for the story and interconnects the other major themes—we will be arguing that this megatheme, the relational presence of God, is the cohesive center of biblical theology.

---

20. Lister, *The Presence of God*. Likewise noting the centrality of the presence of God and its critical significance for Christian living is Booth, *The Tabernacling Presence of God*.

ONE

The Relational Presence of God in the Pentateuch

Terminology

Although throughout the OT there are numerous terms and idioms that imply the presence of God,[1] the central and most frequent term is *panim* (פָּנִים, plural of פָּנֶה, *paneh*).[2] This term occurs over two thousand times in the OT. The basic meaning of *panim* (פָּנִים/פָּנֶה) is "face" in the anatomical sense, but the term is used in a wide range of idioms and other figures of speech. Because "face" was more expressive than "hand" and more inclusive than "eye," it frequently was used as a synecdoche to represent the entire person.[3] Because of the ability of *panim* to express emotions and reactions, it also carries strong connotations of relationship. In fact, as H. Simian-Yofre explains, "The term *pānîm* describes relationships. . . . Applied to Yahweh,

1. As is well known, the OT uses two primary Hebrew words for God, *Yahweh* (usually translated as "the LORD") and *Elohim* (usually translated as "God"). In keeping with our perspective as a "whole-Bible" biblical theology, and in striving for consistency, we have in general used the word "God" in our discussion throughout the book, even in OT contexts. Exceptions, of course, are occasionally necessary when the specific meaning of the name Yahweh plays a critical role in our exegetical and theological discussion.

2. I. Wilson includes a long list of additional terms and concepts that imply God's presence; these include: to speak from an earthly site, to come, to come down, to be in thick darkness, to go up among, to go with, to go in the midst of, to go before, to pass by, to pass before, to stand with, to be with, to be in the midst of, to appear, and to meet (I. Wilson, *Out of the Midst of the Fire*, 207–8).

3. H. Simian-Yofre, "פָּנִים," *TDOT* 11:607; A. S. van der Woude, "פָּנִים," *TLOT* 2:1001.

pānîm says no more and no less than when applied to human beings." That is, it refers to "real personal presence, relationship, and meeting (or refusing to meet). All the fundamental relationships between God and human beings can be described by *pānîm* and its associated expressions. . . . Insofar as *pānîm* bespeaks presence, its purpose is to underline the positive aspect of the interpersonal relationship. The negative aspect of the relationship is expressed by separation from *pānîm*" (the idiom "to set one's face against" would be an exception, carrying strong negative overtones).[4]

The construct form of *panim* is used with several different prepositions to form idiomatic expressions, many of which are used of God. One of the most frequent forms is *lipne Yahweh* (לִפְנֵי יְהוָה, before the LORD, in the presence of the LORD), which occurs 236 times in the OT.[5] Like the other idioms, while this expression is somewhat fluid, the majority of usages refer to the *spatial* presence of God, often in the tabernacle or in the temple.[6] Indeed, this is one of the most common expressions indicating the very real, spatial presence of God in the tabernacle or in the temple.

Genesis

Many have noted the significance of the fact that the Bible opens with creation (Gen. 1–2) and ends (or climaxes) with the new creation (Rev. 21–22).[7] This observation certainly has suggestive implications for the starting point of a biblical theology.[8] As discussed throughout this book, however, the theme of God's relational presence incorporates both "creation" and "salvation history." This is part of the larger "bookend" phenomena in which Genesis 1–11 is paralleled by many elements in Revelation 19–22.[9] In relational terms

---

4. H. Simian-Yofre, "פָּנִים," *TDOT* 11:606–7. Van der Woude stresses that when used of God, פָּנִים refers not to some kind of representative figure, but to the personal presence of God himself (A. S. van der Woude, "פָּנִים," *TLOT* 2:1004–5).

5. Fowler, "The Meaning of *lipnê* YHWH," 384.

6. Fowler, "The Meaning of *lipnê* YHWH," 387; Simian-Yofre, "פָּנִים," 11:608–10. For discussions on the other prepositional combinations and idioms with פָּנִים, see Simian-Yofre, "פָּנִים," 11:611–14. For usages of פָּנִים with verbs and prepositions that connote concepts of "hiding the face," see Balentine, *The Hidden God*, 1–76.

7. Scobie, *The Ways of Our God*, 149; Fretheim, *God and World*, 9; Dumbrell, *The End of the Beginning*, 189–96; Westermann, *Beginning and End in the Bible*.

8. While for much of the twentieth century many OT scholars dismissed "creation" as a major theme, opting instead for "salvation history" as the dominating center of OT theology, in more recent years more and more scholars are recognizing the importance of "creation" as an important and interrelated theme. For example, Scobie quips, "It needs to be asserted that the Bible does *not* begin with Exodus but with Genesis!" (Scobie, *The Ways of Our God*, 148–49).

9. See the helpful comparative chart in Duvall, "The Beginning and the End."

between God and people, the Bible opens with God and his people in a garden and closes with God and his people once again back in a garden.

The Presence of God in Creation and in the Garden

Throughout the creation account in Genesis, God is depicted as being personally involved. In Genesis 1:2 reference is made to "the Spirit of God . . . hovering over the waters." While there is no consensus regarding the meaning (or even translation—wind, spirit, Spirit) of this phrase, it seems to refer to an activity of God, thus implying his powerful presence or an extension of the power associated with his presence.[10] Yet moving from Genesis 1 to Genesis 2, we notice a shift in names and in stress, from a focus on God's transcendence in Genesis 1 (Elohim as Creator of the universe) to a focus on God's immanence (Yahweh forming people and walking in the garden). Throughout the creation account in Genesis 2, the language and the imagery evoke a spatial presence. That is, God *formed* a man (and animals [2:19]) out of the dust of the ground as a potter shapes a pot (2:7). God also *breathed* into the man's nostrils (2:7), *planted* a garden (2:8), and *took* the man and *put* him in the garden (2:13). Later, God *brought* the animals to the man (2:19) and, after *building* the woman from the man's rib, *brought* the woman to the man (2:22).[11] The imagery in the creation narrative in Genesis 2 does not portray God seated upon his throne in the heavens sending out orders to those below; rather, it portrays him as one who is very much present down in the garden, personally involved in creation.[12]

Continuing this picture of God and stressing his actual presence in the garden is Genesis 3:8, when "the man and his wife heard the sound of the LORD God as he was walking in the garden in the cool of the day." Although a few scholars have suggested alternate translations and correlating alternate

10. Waltke suggests that it describes the "almighty Spirit" preparing the earth for human habitation (Waltke, *Genesis*, 65). J. Walton proposes understanding "spirit/wind of God" as representing an extension of God's power, like his hand (J. Walton, *Genesis*, 77). Routledge notes that "in the OT the presence and activity of the Spirit is identified with presence and activity of God himself" (Routledge, *Old Testament Theology*, 113). Sailhamer argues that the "Spirit of God" doing the work of creation in Gen. 1:2 is paralleled by the "Spirit of God" that fills and empowers Bezalel to build the tabernacle in Exod. 31:1–5 (Sailhamer, *The Pentateuch as Narrative*, 32–33).

11. Fretheim, *God and World*, 39. W. Brown writes, "As both gardener and potter, God works naturally and intimately with creation" (W. Brown, "Manifest Diversity," 23).

12. Averbeck points to several of these actions (shapes, breathes, plants, etc.) and notes that while Gen. 1:1–2:3 stresses the transcendence of God, Gen. 2:4–4:26 stresses his immanence, presenting God as in close intimate relationship with his people (Averbeck, "Tabernacle," 822). Bonhoeffer notes that God's shaping of humankind with his own hands stresses not only God's authority but also his "nearness" (Bonhoeffer, *Creation and Fall*, 46).

understandings,[13] the majority of commentators and translations retain the traditional understanding that God is personally strolling in the garden.[14] Furthermore, the text seems to imply that this was a normal occurrence.[15] Terence Fretheim writes, "The Creator of the universe and all creatures chooses not to relate to the world at a distance, but takes on human form, goes for a walk among the creatures, and personally engages them regarding recent events."[16] This has staggering implications for our understanding of the relationship between God and the first couple. He has graciously placed them in a wonderful garden with everything provided for them. Most important of all, they were blessed by the close, personal fellowship with the very real presence of God himself. In this initial portrayal of how God relates to his people, he is pictured not as the King seated up on the heavenly throne (although his authority is clearly underscored as he forms the first man from the dirt) but as One who is very much here on earth in the garden walking and talking with his people. As John Walton states, "The presence of God was the key to the garden."[17]

The Garden as a Temple Containing the Presence of God

The early chapters of Genesis depict the garden of Eden as the place where God lives and relates to his people. This reality (where God dwells and relates to his people) is something that we will see repeated later in the tabernacle and the temple.[18] The similarities and strong thematic and lexical parallels between the garden of Eden and the tabernacle/temple have led numerous scholars from across the theological spectrum to affirm a strong connection between the garden of Eden in Genesis 2 and the tabernacle/temple later in the OT. Many scholars maintain that the garden of Eden is to be viewed as an archetypal tabernacle/temple.[19] At the heart of this

13. Niehaus has argued that Gen. 3:8 refers not to God strolling in the cool of the day but rather to a terrifying wind/storm theophany (Niehaus, "In the Wind of the Storm"). For a similar view, see Stuart, "'The Cool of the Day.'"

14. For example, V. Hamilton, *The Book of Genesis*, 192–93; Ross, *Creation and Blessing*, 143; Cassuto, *From Adam to Noah*, 150–54; Wenham, *Genesis 1–15*, 76; Westermann, *Genesis 1–11*, 254; Waltke, *Genesis*, 92.

15. Wenham, *Genesis 1–15*, 76; Goldingay, *Old Testament Theology*, 1:136.

16. Fretheim, "The Book of Genesis," 362.

17. J. Walton, *Genesis*, 182.

18. J. D. Hays, *The Temple and the Tabernacle*, 20–21.

19. Wenham, "Sanctuary Symbolism in the Garden of Eden Story"; Wenham, *Genesis 1–15*, 61–62; Waltke, *Genesis*, 85; Longman, *Immanuel in Our Place*, 7, 35–36; Fretheim, *Exodus*, 269; Beale, *The Temple and the Church's Mission*, 66–80; J. Walton, *Genesis*, 181–84; Mathews, *Genesis 1–11:26*, 210, 257; Provan, *Discovering Genesis*, 57–58, 70–71; B. Arnold, *Genesis*, 58–59 (at least noting some of the similarities); Middleton, *A New Heaven and a New*

connection is the presence of God, for it is the "presence" or the "indwelling" of God that defines what a temple is. That is, throughout the ancient Near East, as well as in Israel, temples were regarded as the residences of the gods and not simply as gathering places for worship, as churches often are viewed today.[20]

Relationship, Presence, and the Image of God

Genesis 1:26–27 states, "Let us make man in our image, according to our likeness. They will rule. . . . So God created man in his own image" (CSB). There is no clear consensus regarding the meaning of the phrase "the image of God" (often referred to as the *imago Dei*) among either biblical scholars or systematic theologians, and this issue continues to generate a great deal of scholarly discussion. Earlier views that understood the *imago Dei* as referring to spiritual, mental, or physical similarities have largely been rejected. Claus Westermann argues for a relational understanding: being created in the image of God gives human beings the unique status of being God's counterparts. He writes, "The relationship to God is not something which is added to human existence; humans are created in such a way that their very existence is intended to be their relationship to God."[21] Likewise, more recently Robin Routledge has listed "relationship" as one of the "implications" of the *imago Dei*, stating, "Human beings are made for relationship with God."[22] Although some authors declare that the royal/functional view (discussed below) is the near-consensus majority view of the *imago Dei*, especially for OT scholars, that is simply not the case; numerous scholars, both in OT studies and in other disciplines, concur with Westermann that "relationship" is a critical part of the *imago Dei*. Brevard Childs, for example, in regard to the "image of God," writes, "In spite of its unclarity, at least one can say that it denotes a special relationship between God and mankind."[23]

Earth, 46–49; Brueggemann, *Theology of the Old Testament*, 533; Dumbrell, *The End of the Beginning*, 41; M. Smith, *Where the Gods Are*, 34–36; W. Brown, "Manifest Diversity," 21–24; Booth, *The Tabernacling Presence of God*, 11–13; Morales, *The Tabernacle Pre-Figured*, 83–91; T. D. Alexander, *From Paradise to the Promised Land*, 123–25.

20. J. D. Hays, *The Temple and the Tabernacle*, 13–17.

21. Westermann, *Genesis 1–11*, 158.

22. Routledge, *Old Testament Theology*, 140.

23. Childs, *Old Testament Theology*, 34. Also holding the "relational" view, although with some variation in their understanding of it, are Atkinson, *The Message of Genesis 1–11*, 37; H. W. Wolff, *Anthropology of the Old Testament*, 159; K. Barth, *Church Dogmatics* III/1, 183–97; Brunner, *Man in Revolt*, 94–96; Grenz, *The Social God and the Relational Self*; Fretheim, *God and World*, 13–14, 54–56; House, *Old Testament Theology*, 61; Birch et al., *A Theological Introduction to the Old Testament*, 49; Booth, *The Tabernacling Presence of God*, 14–15.

Popular among OT scholars over the last forty years or so has been an understanding that sees the *imago Dei* in a royal/functional manner. When placed in the context of similar ancient Near Eastern backgrounds, the terms for image and likeness seem to imply that God is designating humans to be his "royal" representatives to rule and to mediate blessings to the world.[24] In this view, people made in the image of God were like small statues that ancient kings would place in their provinces to stress their rule over that area and to project their controlling presence.[25]

More recently some scholars have argued that for understanding the *imago Dei* there is a closer similarity to the use of cult/temple statues that represent the deity itself than to the king/royal statue background.[26] This has led to a current trend that tends to acknowledge that the *imago Dei* in Genesis 1 probably reflects a royal representative view as part of its meaning but also carries a diverse range of other connotations. For example, Catherine McDowell argues for three major connotations of the *imago Dei*. First, based on texts like Genesis 5:1, the image of God implies a "kinship." That is, it denotes God as the father of humanity.[27] This has strong implications for the relational view. Second, as in the royal representative view, it designates humans as God's representatives, especially in law and justice. Finally, the *imago Dei* creates the imagery of a "divine statue," which in the ancient Near East was placed in the temple like a miniature god. The implication of this third aspect is that "humankind was designated to dwell in the divine presence, that is, with God in his most holy place."[28]

Recently J. Gordon McConville has combined the relational view and the royal/functional view. He posits that humans represent the presence of God in the world, a representative capacity that is characterized by the power and privilege of God's presence. But the image also carries a strong aspect of relationality—to God, to fellow humans, and to the creation itself.[29] Bill Arnold, likewise, accepts the royal representative view, but he also notes that

24. For example, Clines, "The Image of God in Man." See also the more recent discussion in Middleton, *The Liberating Image*, 26–29.

25. Von Rad, *Genesis*, 60.

26. McDowell, *The Image of God in the Garden of Eden*; Schuele, "Made in the Image of God"; Middleton, *The Liberating Image*, 27.

27. On this view, see also Mathews, *Genesis 1–11:26*, 170.

28. McDowell, *The Image of God in the Garden of Eden*, 207–8. See also McDowell, "'In the Image of God He Created Them,'" 32–34. Likewise expanding on the range of connotations beyond the royal representative view is R. Peterson, *The* Imago Dei *as Human Identity*, arguing for "human identity" as the primary feature of the *imago Dei* and the royal representation aspect as secondary.

29. McConville, *Being Human in God's World*, 24–29.

"Genesis 1 emphasized the intimate relationship between God and humanity in the 'image of God' concept (1:26–27)."[30]

While there is still no complete consensus in understanding precisely what the "image of God" refers to in Genesis 1, the most widely held views among scholars swirl around the concepts of presence, rule, power, and relationship.

Banishment from the Garden and the Presence of God

After Adam and Eve listen to the serpent, disobey God, and eat of the forbidden fruit, they are banished from the garden of Eden. This event, often referred to theologically as the "fall," plays an important role in Christian theology. Yet the critical consequence of the eviction from the garden is that Adam and Eve loose the great privilege and blessing of direct access to the presence of God.[31] God had told Adam that on the day he ate of the tree of the knowledge of good and evil he certainly would die (Gen. 2:17). Yet what God actually does to Adam and Eve is banish them and separate them from his presence.[32] Thus the banishment from the garden likewise suggests connections to death. Loss of direct access to the tree of life and loss of direct access to the presence of God seem to be inseparable. Routledge writes, "In the OT, physical death also has a spiritual dimension: it brings relationship with God to an end. Similarly life is more than mere existence: it is also about continuing to enjoy the blessings of God's presence."[33]

Cherubim are stationed on the east side of the garden to guard the way back to the tree of life (Gen. 3:24). Throughout the OT, cherubim are closely

30. B. Arnold, *Genesis*, 45, 59. See also Dyrness, *Themes in Old Testament Theology*, 83–84. Similarly, after discussing the "image of God" and OT physiology, Brueggemann qualifies the discussion by noting "what seems to me the central concern of Israel regarding humanity: namely, that the human person is *a person in relation to Yahweh*, who lives in an intense mutuality with Yahweh" (Brueggemann, *Theology of the Old Testament*, 453).

31. Morales, *The Tabernacle Pre-Figured*, 103–4. G. Anderson underscores that the "fall" probably should be understood more as an "exile" (G. Anderson, *Christian Doctrine and the Old Testament*, 59–60).

32. Mathews, *Genesis 1–11:26*, 258. This is stressed by numerous OT scholars. J. Walton, for example, points out that it was not so much "paradise" that is lost but the presence of God (J. Walton, *Genesis*, 231). See also Longman, *How to Read Genesis*, 112; Routledge, *Old Testament Theology*, 152; V. Hamilton, *The Book of Genesis*, 310; Westermann, *Genesis 1–11*, 277; Wenham, *Genesis 1–15*, 90; T. D. Alexander, *From Paradise to the Promised Land*, 127, 163.

33. Routledge, *Old Testament Theology*, 152. Atkinson adds, "Adam's death is a change of place (from within the Garden to outside the Garden) and a change of situation before God (in fellowship with God, to alienated from God). And all death can be so understood" (Atkinson, *The Message of Genesis 1–11*, 37). Wenham writes, "Only in the presence of God did man enjoy fullness of life. . . . The expulsion from the garden of delight where God himself lived would therefore have been regarded by the godly men of ancient Israel as yet more catastrophic than physical death" (Wenham, *Genesis 1–15*, 90).

associated with the tabernacle and the temple, and especially with the very presence of God.[34] In both the future tabernacle of Exodus and the future temple of 1 Kings, the entrances face the east. Thus the mention of cherubim stationed at the eastern entrance to the garden of Eden implies that they are guarding the way back into the garden/temple wherein lies the tree of life and the presence of God.

The continued eastward movement throughout Genesis 3–11 (Gen. 3:24; 4:16; 11:2) perhaps is suggestive of the continuing movement away from the presence of God.[35] Likewise, numerous scholars have noted that the initial banishment in Genesis 3:23–24 foreshadows or parallels the future exile of Israel, who will be driven out of the promised land (paralleling the garden) and away from God's presence.[36]

Thus the basic theological problem ("the inciting incident") that gives rise to the unfolding biblical story is now set.[37] Through disobedience and sin people have lost access to and relationship with God, resulting in the loss of eternal life as well. Yet God in his grace will continue to work outside of the garden to restore humankind to relationship with him. This is the story of the rest of the Bible. At the center of this story about restoring the relationship between God and humanity is God's relational presence.

The Tower of Babel

Movement in Genesis 11 continues to the east, where the people build a city and a tower in Shinar (Babylonia). Most OT scholars concur that the tower is a Babylonian-style "ziggurat," typically a large terraced structure with a central stairway. In the archaeological theology of these structures in the ancient Near East, at the top of these stairways was "the gate of the gods, the entrance into their heavenly abode."[38] Usually there was a temple

---

34. V. Hamilton writes, "All OT references to the cherubim suggest, directly or indirectly, that the cherubim are symbols of God's presence" (V. Hamilton, *The Book of Genesis*, 210). J. D. Hays suggests that it may be better to view them as divine attendants or guardians of the access to God's presence (J. D. Hays, *The Temple and the Tabernacle*, 111–22).

35. Several scholars have noted the "eastward" movement in Gen. 3–11 (3:24; 4:16; 11:2). W. D. Tucker states, "The movement eastward symbolized a distancing from the paradisiacal qualities of Eden and from the presence of God" (W. D. Tucker, "The Pentateuch," 37). See also V. Hamilton, *The Book of Genesis*, 352.

36. Waltke with Yu, *Old Testament Theology*, 150; McKeown, *Genesis*, 38; W. D. Tucker, "The Pentateuch," 33; Fretheim, "The Book of Genesis," 365.

37. Morales concludes, "Exile from the divine Presence, then, is *the* point of tragedy driving the ensuing biblical narrative toward the mediated dénouement of the tabernacle" (Morales, *The Tabernacle Pre-Figured*, 102).

38. J. Walton, *Genesis*, 374.

located nearby on the ground level, but the ziggurat functioned primarily as a means to facilitate access to the gods. That is, the stairway allowed for the gods to descend down to earth. Thus it seems that the construction of this tower is a humanly initiated attempt to regain the presence of God, along with counteracting God's decree for the people to scatter and fill the earth (Gen. 1:28; 9:1). John Goldingay observes, "The builders may not be able to get back to God's garden, but perhaps they can reach God's dwelling some other way."[39] Furthermore, these builders do not want to honor the deity, or call on his name, but rather to make a name for themselves (11:4). The ironic consequence is that they do not achieve the blessings of the relational presence of God, but rather his presence comes down and scatters them in judgment, in essence a continuing of the exile theme that began in Genesis 3:23–24 when Adam and Eve were banished from the garden.[40]

The Patriarchs, the Covenant, and the Presence of God

In his sovereign freedom God's relational presence is not restricted to the garden, and the theme of his presence lies at the heart of the story throughout the patriarchal narratives.[41] Genesis 12–50 recounts the story of the patriarchs Abraham, Isaac, and Jacob, and at the theological center of this section is the account of how God establishes a relationship with this family through his covenant with them. Running throughout this story and inextricably intertwined with the establishment and the continuation of the patriarchal covenant is the theme of God's presence. To each of the patriarchs God not only promises descendants, land, and blessing, but in each case he also includes the promise of his relational presence.[42]

This is seen first of all through the frequent theophanic appearances that occur. That is, in establishing his covenant relationship with the patriarchs, God regularly appears to them.[43] This connection is made in the

---

39. Goldingay, *Old Testament Theology*, 1:189. Also viewing the tower as an attempt to regain God's presence is W. D. Tucker, "The Pentateuch," 37.

40. Morales, *The Tabernacle Pre-Figured*, 45.

41. W. Brown, "Manifest Diversity," 24–25.

42. W. Kaiser stresses the relational aspect of the promise of presence: "God's active presence manifested his character, power, and ability to fulfill the repeated word of promise. It was preeminently a word of personal relationship" (W. Kaiser, *The Promise-Plan of God*, 62).

43. The terminology used in several passages stresses the actual spatial presence of God in his appearances to the patriarchs. Thus *lipne* or related forms are used in Gen. 17:1 ("walk *before* me"); 18:22 ("Abraham remained standing *before* the LORD"); 19:27 ("Abraham . . . returned to the place where he had stood *before* the LORD"). In 32:30 Jacob names the site of his wrestling encounter "Peniel" ("face of God"), explaining, "It is because I saw God face to face, and yet my life was spared." Likewise, verbs of spatial movement are often used of God

following passages: 12:7;[44] 15:17; 17:1; 18:1; 19:27; 26:2–3, 24; 28:12–15; 32:30; 35:9–12.[45]

In addition, although the connection between God's presence and the patriarchal covenant is strongly implied in most of these texts, several of the texts make the connection explicit. For example, in regard to Abraham, Genesis 17:1–2 states, "The LORD appeared to him [Abram] and said, 'I am God Almighty; walk before me faithfully and be blameless. Then I will make my covenant between me and you and will greatly increase your numbers.'" The same tight connection occurs with Isaac (Gen. 26:2–5, 23–24), where the promise of God's presence ("I will be with you")[46] is tied explicitly with the confirmation of God's promise to Abraham. Likewise, in the reaffirmation of the Abrahamic promise to Jacob (Gen. 28:12–15), God restates clearly his promise of presence ("I am with you" [v. 15]).[47] To be in covenant relationship with God meant that the patriarchs would experience his "I am with you" presence.[48]

Another closely related theme, one that will resurface continually throughout the pentateuchal story, is that of "the land." That is, the promises of presence, covenant, and land are all tightly interconnected, seemingly all part of the same "package." Thus in Genesis 28:13–15, for example, God declares, "I will give you and your descendants the land on which you are lying. . . . I am with you and will watch over you wherever you go, and I will bring you back to this land. I will not leave you until I have done what I have promised you."[49] It is the presence of God that drives the fulfillment of the land promise.

---

in the patriarchal narratives: "a smoking firepot with a blazing torch appeared and passed ['abar] between the pieces" (15:17); "When he had finished speaking with Abraham, God went up ['alah] from him" (17:22); "Then God went up ['alah] from him" (35:13); "I will go down [yarad] to Egypt with you" (46:4).

44. Longman states that Abraham built this altar specifically "at a place where God made his special presence known" (Longman, *Immanuel in Our Place*, 19). Also connecting the altar site to the presence of God is Cook, "God's Real Absence and Real Presence," 145.

45. K. Walton tracks the theme of the presence and absence of God throughout the Jacob narrative, arguing that this theme is central and critical to the narrative (K. Walton, *Thou Traveller Unknown*, 220).

46. House notes that this phrase "indicates continual presence" (House, *Old Testament Theology*, 77).

47. God's presence plays a central role in the Joseph narratives as well. See Fritsch, "God Was with Him." Fritsch also notes the later theological understanding of the Joseph story as Stephen in Acts 7:9–10 pointed out that Joseph's brothers sold him as a slave into Egypt, but that "God was with him" (p. 32).

48. The classic tripartite formulation of the covenant throughout the OT is "I will be your God; you will be my people; I will dwell in your midst" (Lev. 26:9–13). Aspects of this formulation occur several times in God's statements to the patriarchs. Not only does he promise his presence, but he also states, "I will be their God" (Gen. 17:8). See W. Kaiser, *The Promise-Plan of God*, 62–63.

49. See Ross, *Creation and Blessing*, 490–91.

Note, however, with the exception perhaps of the smoking firepot of Genesis 15:17, that the divine "I am with you" presence experienced by the patriarchs in Genesis is an "accompanying" presence, which is different, at least in intensity, from the presence of God that will be encountered and experienced by Moses and the Israelites in Exodus. In Genesis, God appears in a form much like a regular human being, while in Exodus, God's presence will be associated with frightening phenomena such as fire, lightning, and smoke—a presence in which holiness is stressed and projected outwardly.[50]

Exodus

In accordance with his promises to the patriarchs in Genesis, in Exodus God reveals himself to Moses and then demonstrates his saving and judging power by delivering Israel from Egypt (Exod. 1–18). From Exodus 19 to Exodus 40, however, the central focus of the story zeroes in on the presence of God as he establishes his covenant with Israel and then actually comes to dwell among his people.[51] Indeed, the climax or high point of the entire book of Exodus is God's taking up residence in the tabernacle to dwell among his people.[52] Commenting on Exodus 29:45, Rolf Rendtorff exclaims, "According to this it is practically the goal of Israel's being led out of Egypt that God should dwell in the midst of them."[53] Likewise, John Durham argues that the presence of God with and in the midst of his people is the central unifying theme of Exodus.[54] Similarly G. Henton Davies concludes, "The book of Exodus is above all else in the OT the book of the Presence of the Lord. This is the thesis and the theme. . . . Indeed this may truly be described as no other than the theme of Israel itself."[55]

Furthermore, T. Desmond Alexander notes that the theme of God's presence in Exodus connects all the way back to Genesis 3. That is, the coming of God to dwell in Israel's midst in Exodus "marks a partial restoration of the broken relationship between God and humanity that resulted from Adam and Eve's action in the Garden of Eden, and it anticipates future developments whereby God's presence will fill a world inhabited by those who are holy as God is holy."[56]

---

50. W. Brown, "Manifest Diversity," 6.
51. Dozeman identifies the two central themes of Exodus as the power of Yahweh (1:1–15:21) and the presence of Yahweh (15:22–40:38) (Dozeman, *Exodus*, 44–45).
52. Schnittjer, *The Torah Story*, 203.
53. Rendtorff, *The Canonical Hebrew Bible*, 65.
54. Durham, *Exodus*, xxi.
55. G. H. Davies, *Exodus*, 48.
56. T. D. Alexander, *Exodus*, 1. Similarly, Dempster writes, "The goal of exodus is the building of the Edenlike sanctuary so that the Lord can dwell with his people" (Dempster, "Geography and Genealogy," 74).

God's Presence and the Meaning of the Name Yahweh

In Exodus 3:1–2 the "angel of the LORD" appears to Moses "in flames of fire from within a bush" on "the mountain of God." As Moses draws near, God himself speaks to him from within the bush (3:4), cautioning Moses about coming any closer. "Take off your sandals," God instructs Moses, "for the place where you are standing is holy ground" (3:5). Moses then hides his face, afraid to look at God (3:6). This action underscores the reality of the presence of God in this encounter.[57] These opening verses of Exodus 3 alert us to the fact that encountering the presence of God in Exodus is going to be different from the encounters with the presence of God observed in Genesis. In contrast to the encounters in Genesis, suddenly now the presence of God is regularly accompanied by fire (and often smoke, a cloud, and/or lightning).[58] Likewise, the presence of God in Exodus now normally includes a projection of holy space that is dangerous for people to violate. These themes usually were absent in the encounters of God's presence experienced by the patriarchs (a possible exception is the firepot in Gen. 15:17), but fire, smoke, and holiness will continue to be part of God's presence throughout Exodus (and into Leviticus, Numbers, and Deuteronomy). Thus from Exodus 3 on into the rest of the Pentateuch the text implies that encounters with the presence of God are different and perhaps more intense than the encounters that the patriarchs had.

In Exodus 3:6 God identifies himself to Moses as "the God of Abraham, the God of Isaac and the God of Jacob." This not only identifies God but also connects back to the covenant and the promises that he made to the patriarchs—the promise of land, descendants, blessing, and the "I will be with you" promise of presence. God explains that he has heard the cry of his people in Egypt and that he has "come down" (יָרַד, *yarad*) to rescue them and to take them to a good land (3:7–9). Then God informs Moses that he is the one to go to Pharaoh and bring the Israelites out of Egypt.

When Moses questions his worthiness for the task, God tells him in 3:12, "I am [or "I will be"] with you" (אֶהְיֶה עִמָּךְ, *'ehyeh 'immak*), a promise similar to the promises made to the patriarchs in association with the covenant in Genesis. God also promises a sign of this promise of presence: Moses and the people will return and worship God on that very mountain.[59] In 3:13 Moses

---

57. Goldingay, *Old Testament Theology*, 1:334.

58. Propp points out the fire "in the Burning Bush (3:2), in the cloud pillar (13:21–22; 14:24), atop Mount Sinai (19:18; 24:17) and upon the Tabernacle (40:38)." Citing M. Greenberg, Propp states, "It is possible to epitomize the entire story of Exodus as the movement of the fiery manifestation of the divine presence" (Propp, *Exodus 1–18*, 16–17).

59. Note that in Exod. 19 the events that take place on "that mountain" in fulfillment of this promise focus on God's fiery presence on the top of the mountain.

asks God for a more definitive name than just "the God of your fathers." Moses is not just curious; to learn someone's name was to enter into a relationship with that person.[60] God answers him by declaring, "I AM WHO I AM [אֶהְיֶה אֲשֶׁר אֶהְיֶה, *'ehyeh 'asher 'ehyeh*]. This is what you are to say to the Israelites: 'I AM [אֶהְיֶה, *'ehyeh*] has sent me'" (3:14). Then God adds, "Say to the Israelites, 'The LORD [יְהוָה, *Yahweh*], the God of your fathers . . . has sent me to you" (3:15).

There is no complete consensus among scholars on the exact meaning or the implications in meaning of the name Yahweh ("the LORD") in this passage. Neither is there a consensus on the related understanding of "I AM WHO I AM" and "I AM has sent me." Yet note that the three declarations "I will be with you" (3:12), "I AM WHO I AM" (3:14a), and "I AM" (3:14b) all have the same imperfect form of the verb "to be" (הָיָה, *hayah*), as illustrated here:

Exodus 3:12	"I am/will be with you"	(אֶהְיֶה עִמָּךְ)
Exodus 3:14a	"I AM WHO I AM"	(אֶהְיֶה אֲשֶׁר אֶהְיֶה)
Exodus 3:14b	"I AM"	(אֶהְיֶה)

Thus most scholars at least conclude that the divine name Yahweh (יְהוָה, the LORD), given in Exodus 3:15, is also related to the verb *hayah* (הָיָה, to be). Furthermore, due to the clear meaning of presence in Exodus 3:12, quite a large number of scholars maintain that the connotations of *hayah* as reflected in the divine name Yahweh imply that there is a promise or an implication of divine presence associated with the very name of Yahweh.[61]

In fact, Thomas Dozeman argues that the progression from 3:12 to 3:14 and the repetition of "I AM" (אֶהְיֶה, *'ehyeh*) is relating the themes of divine presence and the God of the fathers. Furthermore, Dozeman notes, "The aim

---

60. Waltke with Yu, *Old Testament Theology*, 359.

61. Von Rad, for example, states that in this passage הָיָה "is to be understood in the sense of 'being present,' 'being there,' and therefore precisely not in the sense of absolute, but of relative and efficacious, being" (von Rad, *Old Testament Theology*, 1:180). Seitz concludes that the connection to 3:12 "points to an interpretation of the divine name as involving most especially God's presence with Moses and the people *in the events of redemption from bondage*" (Seitz, "The Call of Moses," 153). Preuss notes that the expression "to be with" (*hayah 'et* or *hayah 'im*) "calls to mind the divine name Yahweh" and is "even used to explain its meaning." It is used to "describe Yahweh as a God who leads, accompanies, goes with, and fights for his own, as a shepherd of his flock, etc." (H. Preuss, "אֵת," *TDOT* 1:452–53). See also the extensive discussion of the phrase "I will be with you" and its important connection to the widespread theme of the presence of God in Preuss, ". . . ich will mit dir sein!"

of Exodus 3:14" is "to advance the theme of divine presence through reflection on the meaning of the divine name. . . . The verbal focus emphasizes the theme of divine presence in the divine reassurance to Moses."[62] Likewise, Paul House writes, "The reference to the patriarch and the derivation of Yahweh from the verb 'to be' indicates that God's abiding and relational presence is emphasized in this verse."[63] Edmond Jacob comes to similar conclusions, noting, "It is not the idea of eternity which is primary . . . but that of presence."[64] James Plastaras states that "the name Yahweh 'defines' God in terms of active presence."[65] T. C. Vriezen summarizes it as "the One who is always really present."[66] Commenting on Exodus 3:13–15, Charles Scobie writes, "By far the most convincing explanation is that God reveals himself to Moses as the One *who is* with him and with his people. God is 'I am' in the sense of 'I am present,' or 'I am with you.'"[67] Thus there is a strong case that one of the most core characteristics reflected in the revelation and in the basic meaning of the name Yahweh is his relational presence.[68] This is highly significant, for the name Yahweh is the primary name for God used through-

62. Dozeman, *Exodus*, 134–35.

63. House, *Old Testament Theology*, 93.

64. E. Jacob, *Theology of the Old Testament*, 52.

65. Plastaras, *The God of Exodus*, 95. Plastaras thus suggests translating Exod. 3:14a as "I will be present where (when, to whom) I will be present" (p. 99).

66. Vriezen, *Outline of Old Testament Theology*, 181.

67. Scobie, *The Ways of Our God*, 110.

68. Quite a number of OT scholars underscore the connection between Yahweh's revelation of his name and the promise of his presence in this passage. In addition to those cited above, Waltke and Yu write, "In its function God's name suggests his pragmatic presence" (Waltke with Yu, *Old Testament Theology*, 366). W. Kaiser explains, "It was not so much an ontological designation or a static notion of being . . . it was rather a promise of a dynamic, active *presence*. . . . Moses and Yahweh's son, Israel, would know His presence in a day-to-day experience as it never was known before" (W. Kaiser, *Toward an Old Testament Theology*, 107). Eichrodt concurs, stating, "The deity was demonstrably and immediately present and active" (Eichrodt, *Theology of the Old Testament*, 1:190). Kessler states that "I am who I am" is an "expression of Yahweh's active presence with God's people" (Kessler, *Old Testament Theology*, 210). Hertog stresses the presence context of the passage and suggests translating 3:14a as "I am present as I am present" (Hertog, "The Prophetic Dimension of the Divine Name," 226–27). In regard to the divine name in Exod. 3, V. Hamilton posits that "the dominant idea is presence" (V. Hamilton, *Exodus*, 66). C. Barth writes, "The name of God is a promise of God's presence and help" (C. Barth, *God with Us*, 71). Martens explicates, "YHWH is the name by which God represents himself as present, here and now, to act, especially to deliver" (Martens, *God's Design*, 9–10). Others noting the important connection between the revelation and meaning of the divine name in Exod. 3 and the theme of divine presence include Routledge, *Old Testament Theology*, 84–85; Durham, *Exodus*, 39; Abba, "The Divine Name Yahweh," 325–26; Isbell, "The Divine Name אהיה," 115–17; B. Jacob, *The Second Book of the Bible*, 72–73; Lister, *The Presence of God*, 178–79; Brueggemann, "The Book of Exodus," 714; Terrien, *The Elusive Presence*, 119; G. H. Davies, *Exodus*, 48, 71–72; Saner, *"Too Much to Grasp,"* 163–64; Preuss, ". . . ich will mit dir sein!," 158–59.

out the OT (over 6,800 times), typically also carrying strong connotations of personal, covenantal relationship.[69] It is also perhaps significant to note that, as mentioned above, the phrase "before the LORD" (לִפְנֵי יְהוָה, *lipne Yahweh*, in the presence of the LORD) occurs over two hundred times, while "before God" (*lipne Elohim*) is quite rare, occurring but a handful of times, usually in postexilic literature.[70]

In Exodus 6:2–3 God tells Moses that by his name Yahweh he did not make himself "fully known" to the patriarchs. Many OT scholars understand this statement by God to mean that although the patriarchs were familiar with the actual name of Yahweh (i.e., they called on the name of Yahweh), they did not know or experience the full revelatory nature of the name Yahweh revealed in the spectacular events of the exodus and the encounter with God at Mount Sinai. Our suggested understanding from Exodus 3 that the name Yahweh includes connotations of divine presence fits in with this understanding of Exodus 6, but expands on it to include the intense presence of God as the critical factor in the deliverance that is experienced. That is, although the patriarchs in Genesis experienced the "I am with you" accompanying presence of God, they did not experience the more intensive presence of God as Moses does at the burning bush or as Israel does at Mount Sinai and later in the tabernacle, where fire, smoke, lightning, and holiness create powerful but dangerous situations of encounter that require precautions such as protective veiling, distancing, the removal of shoes, and atonement for sin.

The Presence of God in Judging the Egyptians

The presence of God not only plays a central role in blessing and delivering God's people but also plays a dominant and terrifying role in exacting judgment on God's enemies. In the narrative describing God's punishment of Pharaoh and Egypt, God is depicted in anthropomorphic terms as being right there with his people in Egypt. First, his many conversations with

69. Soulen argues that God's name declaration in Exod. 3 (and throughout Exodus) combines God's uniqueness, his presence, and his blessing. Soulen also notes that the connection between God's name and his presence echoes throughout the OT: "The Old Testament often portrays God's name declaration in conjunction with some account of God coming to be present with God's people. . . . But the Bible links God's name declaration and God's presence in many other ways as well" (Soulen, *Distinguishing the Voices*, 136, 152).

70. Note also, as mentioned above, the shift from using "Elohim" in Gen. 1 to using "Yahweh" in Gen. 2. Rather than attribute this to a change in sources, it seems best to recognize the shift in emphasis from the transcendent God (Elohim) in Gen. 1 to the imminent, covenant God (Yahweh) in Gen. 2.

Moses ("then the LORD said to Moses") in Egypt seem to take place right there. There is no mention of Moses trying to communicate with God up in the heavens or God appearing to him in dreams. Second, the anthropomorphic idiom of God's "mighty/right hand" striking Egypt is frequent (Exod. 3:20; 6:1; 7:4–5; 9:3, 15; 13:3, 9, 14, 16; 15:6, 9, 12), conveying at least a figurative visual image of God personally carrying out this punishment on Egypt. Finally, for the climactic tenth plague (death of the firstborn), God declares, "I will bring one more plague on Pharaoh" (11:1). Then God specifically states, "I will go throughout Egypt. Every firstborn son in Egypt will die. . . . On that same night I will pass through Egypt and strike down every firstborn of both people and animals. . . . I am the LORD" (11:4–5; 12:12, 23). Thus the Egyptians experience the powerful presence of God in judgment.

The Presence of God in the Exodus Event

As the Israelites leave Egypt, God is personally present to lead them (Exod. 13:17–18). "By day the LORD went ahead of them in a pillar of cloud to guide them on their way and by night in a pillar of fire to give them light, so that they could travel by day or night. Neither the pillar of cloud by day nor the pillar of fire by night left its place in front of the people" (13:21–22). The fire recalls the encounter of Moses with God in the burning bush.[71] Both the fire and the cloud will continue to be associated with God's presence and his glory through Israel's spectacular encounter with God on Mount Sinai in Exodus 19. The cloud serves to conceal or to veil the glory of God, in essence protecting the Israelites from God's holiness, a theme that will be developed in the chapters to come.[72] In this sense, the cloud becomes a symbol of God's presence.[73] In Exodus 16:10, because of their grumbling, Moses calls the people to "come [lit. "draw near"] before [*lipne*] the LORD." Recall that the Hebrew construction *lipne* has strong connotations of direct spatial presence. God's presence is affirmed in this passage, as indicated by 16:10: "There was the glory of the LORD appearing in the cloud." This is not some quasi representation of God but rather the powerful and holy presence of God himself.[74]

---

71. Durham, *Exodus*, 186.
72. Niehaus writes, "The easy intimacy in which he [God] spoke his first covenant words to the man and woman (Ge 1:28–30) is gone. . . . When God comes in glory he must conceal that glory in smoke, cloud, and storm in order to protect sinful humanity from the otherwise devastating effects of it" (Niehaus, *God at Sinai*, 179).
73. Clements, *God and Temple*, 22.
74. Houtman, *Exodus*, 2:225.

The Song of Moses and the Purpose of the Exodus

After God demonstrates his great power by delivering the Israelites and destroying the Egyptian chariot army in the Red Sea, Moses praises God with a song. First he praises God's great power in drowning the Egyptian army (Exod. 15:1–12). In 15:13 and 15:17, however, Moses turns to the purpose of the great deliverance that they have just experienced. First he states, "In your unfailing love you will lead the people you have redeemed. In your great strength you will guide them to your holy dwelling" (15:13). Then he declares, "You will bring them in and plant them in the mountain of your inheritance—the place, LORD, you made for your dwelling, the sanctuary, Lord, your hands established" (15:17). This declaration by Moses strongly implies that one of the most important goals of God in delivering the Israelites from Egypt through the exodus was "the settlement of Yahweh in the midst of his special people."[75] Stephen Dempster concludes, "Thus the goal of the exodus is the building of the Edenlike sanctuary so that the Lord can dwell with his people."[76]

The Presence of God at Mount Sinai

Back in Exodus 3 God had appeared to Moses at the mountain of God from within the fire of a burning bush. In that encounter God commissioned Moses to deliver the Israelites. God then promised his enabling and empowering presence to Moses ("I will be with you") and informed him that the sign or proof of this reality would be that after Moses brought the people out of Egypt they would worship God on that same mountain (3:12). God then revealed his name Yahweh to Moses in a context that probably connected the presence of God to the name Yahweh. Now in Exodus 19, in fulfillment of that promise, God has brought the Israelites out of Egypt to Mount Sinai, where he will encounter them with his very real and intense presence, establish a covenant relationship with them, and then actually move into their midst to dwell with them in the tabernacle and to travel with them. This encounter

75. Durham, *Exodus*, 209. Some of the terminology in these two verses regarding the dwelling place of God is ambiguous, and scholars disagree over whether the reference is to Mount Sinai, a temporary camp en route to Mount Sinai, the tabernacle, Mount Zion, or the temple to be located on Mount Zion. Durham (*Exodus*, 209) and Clements (*God and Temple*, 52–55) argue that 15:17 is clearly referring to Mount Zion. The disagreement over the location that is being referenced does not detract from the fact that Israel was being delivered from Egypt in order to come close to God in his dwelling place (here on earth), a fact that Moses sees clearly. Enns concludes, "God is bringing his people out of Egypt in order that he might be present with them" (Enns, *Exodus*, 300).

76. Dempster, "Geography and Genealogy," 72.

with God at Mount Sinai is one of the most central and important events in the entire OT.[77]

In addition to being at the same location (the mountain of God), Israel's encounter with God at Mount Sinai in Exodus 19 and Exodus 24–25 has several contrasting parallels with Moses's encounter with God at the burning bush in Exodus 3. In Exodus 3 God speaks to one man, Moses, and in Exodus 19 he speaks to all the people of Israel through Moses (the word "people" is stressed, occurring eleven times in Exod. 19). In 3:2 the bush is on fire, and in 19:18 the entire mountain is on fire. In 3:5 God tells Moses that the ground he is standing on is holy, and in 19:23 the entire mountain is holy. Dozeman even observes that there is a suggestive wordplay between the Hebrew words for "bush" (סְנֶה, seneh) and "Sinai" (סִינַי, sinay).[78]

In Exodus 19:4 God makes it clear that this encounter is a central part of his plan. Not only has he judged the Egyptians and then "carried [the Israelites] on eagles' wings," but also he has brought them to himself. That is, God is affirming, indeed even stressing, what Moses declared in 15:13–17, that God's central purpose of the exodus is to bring his people into his presence. What this will mean for Israel is explained in the verses that follow: a covenant relationship, a treasured possession, a kingdom of priests, and a holy nation—with God dwelling in their midst. Note the important sequence of Exodus 19:4–6:

1. You have seen what I did to the Egyptians (v. 4)
2. How I carried you on eagles' wings (v. 4)
3. I brought you to myself (v. 4)
4. Now if you keep my covenant (v. 5)
5. You will be my treasured possession (v. 5)
6. You will be for me a kingdom of priests (v. 6)
7. And a holy nation (v. 6)

Note the tight association between God's relational presence and his covenant. The statement "I . . . brought you to myself" (19:4) is followed immediately with "Now . . . if you keep my covenant" (19:5). This connection between God's relational presence and his covenant was seen as well back in the patriarchal narratives of Genesis where the "I am with you" accompanying presence was continually associated with the covenant God made with the patriarchs.

77. Durham, *Exodus*, 265.
78. Dozeman, *Exodus*, 124.

Exodus 24 will drive this point home, centering the entire covenant ratification event on Mount Sinai with God himself on the top of the mountain in the cloud and the fire (vv. 15–17). Moses reads "the Book of the Covenant" to the people (v. 7), and they agree to keep the covenant (v. 7). He sprinkles them with the blood of the covenant (v. 8), leads the elders partway up the mountain to have a fellowship meal with God (vv. 9–11), and then goes up the mountain by himself into the cloud and stays for forty days, receiving the Ten Commandments and the instructions for how to build the tabernacle, the earthly residence of the presence of God.

The encounter with God in Exodus 19 and in Exodus 24 not only connects back with parallels to Exodus 3 and the burning bush but also projects forward with parallels to the tabernacle and the temple. That is, the presence of God on the top of the mountain creates a very "temple-like" setting. Fire, smoke, the glory of God, and the holiness of God are all closely associated with God in the tabernacle and then in the temple. Furthermore, God's relational, yet holy, presence on Mount Sinai creates a three-level gradation of holy space and access just as in the tabernacle and temple. In the tabernacle and temple all Israel could access the first level, the courtyard,[79] while only the priests could access the next level of increased holiness, the holy place. Finally, only the high priest could enter into the very presence of God in the most holy place. At Sinai, all of Israel gathers just beyond the foot of the mountain (19:2). A selected group of seventy elders is allowed to go partway up the holy mountain (24:9–11). Yet Moses alone goes up to the top of the mountain to communicate with God himself (24:12, 15–18). Likewise, just as the altar will be placed right outside the tabernacle and the temple, so Moses builds an altar at the foot of the mountain (24:4), and he makes sacrifices prior to leading the seventy elders halfway up the mountain.[80]

It is within this holy mountain/tabernacle/temple context that God's designation of Israel as a "kingdom of priests" and a "holy nation" should be understood. That is, the fiery presence of God on the top of Mount Sinai has created a very temple-like situation. Recall that throughout the ancient Near East temples served as the residences of the gods. Additionally, throughout the ancient Near East common people almost never entered temples. The norm throughout the region was that only priests actually entered the temple precincts and served the gods. In Exodus it is God's clear intention to come and to dwell right in the midst of Israel, and he is going to invite all of Israel into the courtyard of his dwelling (the tabernacle and then the temple), just as

79. Hartley, *Leviticus*, lvii.
80. J. D. Hays, *The Temple and the Tabernacle*, 33–35.

he allows them in Exodus 19 to camp right at the foot of his holy mountain. This privilege—being able to access the "courtyard" of God's mountain/tabernacle/temple (i.e., where his presence resides)—elevates all of the people to "priesthood" status.[81] The point here is relationship and access rather than function.[82] Peter Gentry concurs with this understanding and then argues that the meaning of the designation "kingdom of priests" is therefore closely interconnected with the meaning of "holy" in the designation of Israel as a "holy nation." What "holy" means in this context is that they are "given access to the presence of Yahweh and devoted solely to the service and worship of the Lord."[83] Likewise, although it will be the priests who have regular access to the presence of God, Exodus 23:14–17 prescribes three annual festivals when all of Israel is to come to the tabernacle.

Several other scholars expand on this concept that "priest" implies access to the presence of God, proposing that the connection between the phrases "kingdom of priests" and "holy nation" implies that the Israelites would be priests who mediate between God and the nations. As within one nation, priests constitute a smaller group that has special mediating access to the temple and the presence of the deity, so here Israel is the small group (among the nations of the world) that has mediating access to the presence of God.[84] In this sense, everything associated with the tabernacle/temple is to be holy, so the people (as priests and mediators) are also declared to be a holy nation.[85]

The Presence of God in the Tabernacle

In Exodus 25:8–9 God tells Moses, "Have the people make a sanctuary for me, and I will dwell among them. Make this tabernacle and all its furnishings

81. Plastaras states, "Israel would be a 'kingdom of priests' serving Yahweh upon his holy mountain" (Plastaras, *The God of Exodus*, 224). See also Gentry and Wellum, *Kingdom through Covenant*, 318–21, arguing that "priesthood" in this context refers to the privilege of access to the divine presence.

82. J. Davies, "A Royal Priesthood," 157.

83. Gentry, "The Meaning of 'Holy,'" 404.

84. Houtman makes this connection but adds that Israel's status as priests was contingent on keeping the covenant, as stated in 19:5 (Houtman, *Exodus*, 2:445–46). Durham suggests that the "kingdom of priests" statement implies that Israel is to be committed to the "extension throughout the world of the ministry of Yahweh's Presence" (Durham, *Exodus*, 263). See also Kessler, *Old Testament Theology*, 269; Routledge, *Old Testament Theology*, 172. T. D. Alexander views this as a restoration of the priest-like status that Adam and Eve had in the garden prior to their expulsion, where they had direct access to God in the temple-like garden (T. D. Alexander, *Exodus*, 97). See also Beale, *The Temple and the Church's Mission*, 117.

85. J. D. Hays, *The Temple and the Tabernacle*, 32–34. Note also the parallel between the ritual cleansing for all the people described in Exod. 19:10–15 and the ritual cleansing described later for the Levitical priests.

exactly like the pattern I will show you." The Hebrew word translated as "sanctuary" (מִקְדָּשׁ, *miqdash*) is from the word normally translated as "holy" and thus could be rendered as "holy place." This emphasizes the ongoing theme of holiness that is associated with the presence of God. Likewise, the word translated as "tabernacle" (מִשְׁכָּן, *mishkan*) is a noun form of the Hebrew verb *shakan*, often translated as "to dwell." That is, the tabernacle will be the dwelling place for God himself. With the exception of the "golden calf" interruption (Exod. 32–34), all of the remaining chapters of Exodus (25–31; 35–40) deal with the construction of the tabernacle, the new dwelling place of God.[86]

In Exodus 29:45–46 God restates his promise to dwell with Israel, declaring, "Then I will dwell [שָׁכַנְתִּי, *shakanti*] among the Israelites and be their God. Then they will know that I am the LORD their God, who brought them out of Egypt so that I might dwell [לְשָׁכְנִי, *leshakeni*] among them. I am the LORD their God." This text states quite straightforwardly that God's purpose behind the exodus is to settle and dwell in the midst of Israel.[87] Note also that the essence of "knowing the LORD" in this passage is a combination of "I brought you out of Egypt" and "I will dwell in your midst."

Also in this passage we see the further development of the important tripartite covenant formulation. Throughout much of the OT, God's covenant relationship with Israel will be defined by a tripartite formula statement: "I will be your God; you will be my people; I will dwell in your midst." All three elements appear in various texts throughout Exodus, but the two aspects "I will be your God" and "I will dwell in your midst" are stressed in this passage (29:45–46) and are tightly interconnected.[88] R. E. Clements writes, "In these verses it is perfectly clear that for Yahweh to be the God of Israel means that he dwells in their midst, and that the means to the realization of this is the building of the tabernacle."[89]

After Moses and the Israelites finish constructing the tabernacle in accordance with God's specific instructions, the climax of the book of Exodus

---

86. Note that most of the special furniture in the holy place of the tabernacle connects in some way to the presence of God: the table for the bread of the presence, the menorah lamp, the altar of incense. See J. D. Hays, *The Temple and the Tabernacle*, 35–58.

87. Dozeman, *Exodus*, 659. See also Sommer, "Conflicting Constructions of Divine Presence," 44.

88. W. Kaiser suggests that Exod. 29:42–46 completes the triad in Exodus (W. Kaiser, *The Promise-Plan of God*, 85–86).

89. Clements, *God and Temple*, 115. Likewise, Brueggemann concludes of Exod. 29:45, "The statement suggests that being 'their God' is equivalent to being available and accessible, and this is the only important evidence given here of being 'their God.' Presence is everything" (Brueggemann, *Theology of the Old Testament*, 663).

occurs,[90] for in 40:34 "the glory of the LORD filled the tabernacle."[91] That is, just as he promised, the presence of God comes to dwell in the tabernacle, in the midst of Israel. In the same manner in which God came to Mount Sinai—in cloud, fire, holiness, and so forth—so God now dwells in the tabernacle and travels with Israel to the promised land. The tabernacle, then, becomes like a mobile Mount Sinai.[92] The significance of this event cannot be overstated, for it is at the heart of the purpose of the entire exodus story,[93] which is, in turn, at the heart of the entire OT.[94] God delivers the Israelites from Egypt so that he can come to dwell in their midst and relate to them.[95]

Throughout the Exodus 19–24 narrative, the people, and primarily Moses, are ascending up to encounter God on the top of the mountain (the theme of up-and-down movement in Exod. 19–24 is significant). After God comes down to dwell in the tabernacle (40:34), people no longer have to go up the mountain to relate to him. Martin Hauge writes, "The parallel movement of divine descent and human ascent is substituted by the divine descent into the human world as the sole means of encounter."[96]

In the larger pentateuchal context, the coming of God in his glory and holiness to dwell in the tabernacle right in the midst of Israel is a move to restore the close intimate relationship that people had with him in the garden—a relationship that was lost in Genesis 3.[97] The "central catastrophe of the biblical drama" was the loss of God's presence in Genesis 3, and God's movement to dwell in the tabernacle in the midst of his people can be understood at least as the "initial resolution" to this problem.[98]

---

90. Niehaus, *God at Sinai*, 202.

91. The phrase "glory of the LORD" frequently is used synonymously with the presence of God, as a "technical term for God's presence with his people" (C. J. Collins, "כבד," *NIDOTTE* 2:579, 581–83). It is used similarly in Exod. 16:7–10; 24:16–17.

92. Averbeck, "Tabernacle," 824; Milgrom, *Leviticus 1–16*, 58.

93. T. D. Alexander, *Exodus*, 186.

94. Plastaras, *The God of Exodus*, 6–7.

95. Rendtorff, *The Canonical Hebrew Bible*, 65.

96. Hauge, *The Descent from the Mountain*, 139–40.

97. House, *Old Testament Theology*, 120; Dozeman, *Exodus*, 417–18. Fretheim argues for a tight connection between the construction of the tabernacle and creation in general, where the tabernacle is to be viewed as a "microcosm of creation," not "fully re-creative of the world," but "a crucial beginning . . . in God's ongoing re-creation of a new world in the present" (Fretheim, *God and World*, 128). This fits into Fretheim's overall understanding of Exodus, which he views as being "shaped in a decisive way by a creation theology" (see Fretheim, *God and World*, 110; *Exodus*, 12–14). Also underscoring the parallels between the tabernacle account in Exodus and creation are Balentine, *The Torah's Vision of Worship*, 138–40; Longman, *Immanuel in Our Place*, 35–36.

98. Morales, *The Tabernacle Pre-Figured*, 248–49. Also viewing the dwelling of God in the tabernacle as a movement toward the reversal of banishment from the garden and the presence of God are Plastaras, *The God of Exodus*, 258–61; Ross, *Recalling the Hope of Glory*, 84–86.

Transcendence, Immanence, and Holiness in Exodus

In the book of Exodus, as people encounter the very presence of God here on earth, the tension between God's transcendence (God's otherness) and his immanence (God's relatedness) becomes stark.[99] God in his glory does indeed come down to earth, but that glory brings with it danger. God comes to dwell among his people so that they can approach him and fellowship with him, but that holy presence normally is accompanied by terrifying and awe-inspiring smoke, fire, clouds, or earthquakes. Wherever God's presence arrives, that space becomes holy[100] and the demands on people for holiness and cleanness become important (and thus the need for Leviticus). In this regard, Exodus further develops an important theme regarding God's presence. As God becomes immanent (here in this world), he remains totally holy. Indeed, his glory and his holiness constitute a danger and hindrance to people who desire to approach him.

Yet God goes to great lengths to provide his people with the means to approach and worship him. Indeed, many of the details regarding the construction of the tabernacle and the rules regarding Israel's manner of worship seem to be given by God to allow people to approach and fellowship with him—indeed, even to allow him to live in their midst—despite his great glory and holiness. Thus the clouds, smoke, and veils/curtains that find such emphasis serve to shield people from the danger stemming from close proximity to God. Likewise, the demarcations of holiness boundaries, the institution of numerous cleansings, and even the entire sacrificial system serve as a means of enablement so that God can indeed dwell in the midst of the people and they can truly worship him. God does not encounter Israel at Mount Sinai just to give them the law. He comes in order to dwell in their midst so that he can fellowship with them and bless them. He gives them the law so that they can approach him in his holiness and his glory, and so that he can continue to live in their midst.[101]

Sin and the Crisis over God's Presence

Exodus 32 presents an almost unimaginable interruption to the story. While Moses is up on the mountain interacting with God about the details of building

99. Averbeck, "Tabernacle," 822.

100. Jensen notes a wide range of concepts often associated with the meaning of "holy" (e.g., separation, power, wholly other, character) but concludes that the most helpful understanding of "holy" is to view it in connection to "space." Jensen writes, "Holiness in this approach is anything that belongs to God's realm or sphere of existence, over against other places that do not have the same direct relation to it." Closely associated with this central ("spatial") concept of holiness, he continues, is the presence of God (Jensen, "Holiness in the Priestly Writings," 97–107).

101. Sommer, *Revelation and Authority*, 57.

the tabernacle, the new dwelling of God, the people down below grow impatient, and with the assistance of Aaron, they construct a golden calf, blasphemously declaring, "These are your gods, Israel, who brought you up out of Egypt" (32:4). Aaron then announces that there will be a "festival to the LORD" (32:5), apparently trying to attach the name of Yahweh ("the LORD") to this calf idol. The entire event is a blatant violation of the first two commandments of the covenant (Exod. 20:3–4). Durham notes that this is not a simple turning away to the idols of foreign countries, but rather an attempt to redefine the representative of and the presence of Yahweh, who had just revealed himself to them at Mount Sinai.[102] They apparently wanted the presence of a more tangible and visible god to lead them,[103] one more like the gods of their neighbors.

The next chapter and a half (Exod. 32:7–33:23) contains some of the most fascinating texts in the OT, as Moses intercedes repeatedly and at length with God on behalf of Israel. Moses then returns to the camp, rallies the Levites, and executes three thousand of the disobedient Israelites who will not side with him and God (32:25–28). He returns to God and confesses to God their sin of making the golden calf idol (32:30–32).

Yet serious consequences for this sin linger. In 33:1–3 God tells Moses to lead the people away from Mount Sinai (where the presence of God had been revealed to them) and to the land he had promised to the patriarchs. God, however, says that *he will not go with them*. Durham states, "Israel has by the sin with the calf destroyed both their right to remain near a place of Yahweh's Presence and also Yahweh's desire to be present in their midst."[104] God says that he will send "an angel" before them to guide them and to help them, but that he himself will not go.[105] The most serious and ongoing punishment for the sin committed in the episode of the golden calf is the loss of God's presence.[106] This is both a punishment and a protective measure with an element of grace, as God states, "I might destroy you on the way" (33:3, 5).[107] God tells the Israelites, "Take off your ornaments" (33:5), an action that

102. Durham, *Exodus*, 121–22.

103. Stuart, *Exodus*, 691.

104. Durham, *Exodus*, 436.

105. This comment by God may provide us with some insight regarding the difference between God's accompanying presence with the patriarchs in Genesis (often involving the angel of the Lord) and his holy and intense presence in Exodus (with fire, clouds, smoke, etc.), a presence associated with his name Yahweh ("the LORD"), as noted in our discussion of Exod. 3 and Exod. 6.

106. Durham notes the loss of everything given to Israel in the preceding chapters: "There will be no special treasure, no kingdom of priests, no holy nation, no Yahweh being their God, no covenant, no Ark, no Tabernacle, no altar, no cloud of Glory" (Durham, *Exodus*, 437).

107. Stuart, *Exodus*, 692.

suggests a nuance of divorce or broken relationship.[108] In 33:4 the people begin to mourn, perhaps implying that they are repentant. At any rate, God leaves the final judgment undetermined at this time, saying, "I will decide what to do with you" (33:5). The fate of Israel as a nation hangs in the balance.[109]

Moses pleads with God once again in 33:12–13, reminding God, "This nation is your people." Now, at last, God backs off of his earlier threat and agrees to continue his presence with Israel, saying, "My Presence will go with you" (33:14). The Hebrew word translated as "Presence" is פָּנַי (*panay*), the word for "face." As mentioned earlier, this word is used frequently as an idiom for the physical presence of someone.

In this context, the request by Moses in Exodus 33:18 that God show him his "glory" seems to be a request that God would actively demonstrate what he has just promised, that his presence will go with Moses and the people. Both the words "glory" and "face" in this context refer to the presence of God, and thus are close synonyms.[110] Moses previously had encountered God's glory within the cloud on the top of the mountain (24:17–18), but apparently he was protected from seeing all of God's glory in its fullness by the cloud itself. In 33:18 Moses may be asking God for a closer, fuller encounter and revelation of God's glory (i.e., his presence). God, however, explains that no one can see his "face" (presence) unveiled and still live (33:20),[111] so God (1) allows his "goodness" to pass by,[112] (2) proclaims his name before Moses, and (3) hides Moses in a rock cleft, covering him with his hand until his glory has passed by, and only then allowing Moses to see his back. This underscores

---

108. Dozeman points to the close connection of "ornaments" and marriage throughout the prophetic literature, noting that the "stripping off of jewelry signifies judgment and even divorce" (Dozeman, *Exodus*, 722–23).

109. Brueggemann, "The Crisis and Promise of Presence," 49.

110. Durham, *Exodus*, 452.

111. The text states that in these conversations between God and Moses, which are apparently taking place in the "tent of meeting" (Exod. 33:7–11), "The Lord would speak to Moses face to face [פָּנִים אֶל־פָּנִים, *panim 'el-panim*], as one speaks to a friend" (33:11). The idiom "face to face" means that Moses and God have a personal encounter, conversing "person to person" without a mediator. It does not imply that Moses was able to look right at the "face/glory" of God. The mention of the cloud in 33:9–10 seems to imply that Moses's encounter with God in the tent of meeting is similar to his encounter with God at the top of Mount Sinai in Exod. 24:15–18. See Stuart, *Exodus*, 699. Wessner argues that the tension between Moses talking to God "face to face" (33:11) and God's statement that no one can see his face and live (33:20) can be resolved by a close scrutiny of the verbs and maintaining the difference between the concepts of actively seeing and passively being seen. That is, Yahweh's "face" can be seen when he takes the initiative and decides "actively" to reveal it (i.e., 33:11), but not when someone else takes the initiative to see God's face, whereby God would be passive (i.e., 33:20) (Wessner, "Moses and the LORD 'Face to Face'").

112. Moberly comments, "The fact that at the supremely critical moment in Israel's existence it is Yahweh's 'goodness' rather than judgment which is brought to the fore is of great theological importance" (Moberly, *At the Mountain of God*, 77).

the ongoing tension between God's immanence (his relatedness) and his transcendence (his otherness). People can know God and have encounters with his presence, talking with him, so to speak, "person to person." On the other hand, he continues to be "beyond human reach and knowledge"[113] even to Moses. Expanding on the notion of his "goodness" (rather than Israel's deserved judgment), God continues in 33:19 by declaring, "I will have mercy on whom I will have mercy, and I will have compassion on whom I will have compassion," no doubt a reference to the fact that he has decided not to destroy Israel for their sin but instead to dwell with them in the tabernacle.

Interestingly, just a few verses later, God "came down in the cloud and stood there with him [Moses] and proclaimed his name, the LORD [*Yahweh*]. And he passed in front of Moses, proclaiming, 'The LORD, the LORD, the compassionate and gracious God, slow to anger, abounding in love and faithfulness, maintaining love to thousands, and forgiving wickedness, rebellion and sin'" (34:5–7). This text underscores the intersection of God's holiness (veiled in the cloud) and the meaning of his name Yahweh and his character (the God who is present and who is gracious and forgiving, but just). Note the strong anthropomorphic terms used of God that stress his close physical presence: he came down (וַיֵּרֶד, *wayyered*), he stood with him (וַיִּתְיַצֵּב עִמּוֹ, *wayyityatseb 'immo* [note that the verb יָצַב (*yatsab*) has connotations of standing firmly or resolutely]), and he passed in front of him (וַיַּעֲבֹר עַל־פָּנָיו, *wayya'abor 'al-panayw*).

The concluding gracious good news is that after the catastrophe of the golden calf and the repeated rounds of pleading by Moses, God's glorious and holy presence is once again with Moses. God can continue with the instructions on how to build the tabernacle, for he has decided to continue with that plan and to come and dwell in the midst of Israel as they travel to the promised land. By the grace of God, the disastrous end of Israel has been averted; his glorious presence will continue to stay with them in the tabernacle.

Leviticus–Numbers

Leviticus and Numbers are closely connected to the book of Exodus.[114] In Exodus 19 God brings his newly redeemed people to Mount Sinai, where

---

113. Moberly, *At the Mountain of God*, 65–66. Hundley observes that there appear to be "three tiers of divine presence in the tabernacle: 1) YHWH himself; 2) the divine glory; and 3) the cloud and fire" (Hundley, *Keeping Heaven on Earth*, 47). The point of these differing portrayals of God's presence, Hundley argues, is that while Yahweh's presence in the tabernacle is ensured, it still retains some enigmatic ambiguity, maintaining the tension between transcendence and immanence.

114. Waltke with Yu, *Old Testament Theology*, 56–57.

he appears to them, enters into covenant relationship with them, and then actually comes to dwell among them in the tabernacle. Israel stays at Mount Sinai throughout the remainder of Exodus, through all of Leviticus, and up until Numbers 10, when Israel finally departs, accompanied by the presence of God in the tabernacle. This "Sinai pericope" thus comprises fifty-eight chapters, approximately 40 percent of the Pentateuch, underscoring the extreme importance of this encounter to the story and theology of the Pentateuch.[115]

Leviticus–Numbers is the natural sequel to the tabernacle narrative of Exodus 25–40.[116] In Exodus, after Moses constructs the tabernacle in strict accordance with the guidelines God gave him (Exod. 25–40), God himself comes in spectacular and dramatic fashion to take up residence in the tabernacle. God in his glory now dwells not in the burning bush or on the top of Mount Sinai but in the tabernacle in the midst of Israel for the purpose of a close, covenant relationship. How can the sinful people of Israel possibly relate to the holy, awesome God of Mount Sinai now that he lives in close proximity to them? How can they worship him or even approach him? What about his holiness? Will that not consume them? Leviticus and Numbers 1–10 address this problem and prescribe the God-given procedures by which Israel can live and relate to the glorious and holy God who now dwells in the tabernacle in close vicinity to them. Then, in Numbers 10, the Israelites leave Mount Sinai and set out for the promised land, accompanied by the presence of God.

The Terminology of Sacrificing in God's Presence

From the opening verses in Leviticus, the presence of God is central. Indeed, Leviticus 1:1–3 sets the tone. "The Lord," whose very name connotes presence (see the discussion on Exod. 3), speaks to Moses from the "tent of meeting" (in Leviticus this refers to the tabernacle; note the proximity of the altar in 1:5), instructing him in how the Israelites are to bring their sacrifices "near" to the presence of God. Terms implying "nearness" and "presence" abound in this passage. In Leviticus 1:2–3 the term *qarab* (קָרַב, to draw near, to cause to draw near) is used four times. This term carries a strong nuance of "being near or in close proximity."[117] Likewise, the derivative noun *qarban*

---

115. Balentine, *The Torah's Vision of Worship*, 120.

116. In Lev. 1–Num. 10 it is assumed that the tabernacle is there with God dwelling within it. See Fretheim, *The Pentateuch*, 123; T. D. Alexander, *From Paradise to the Promised Land*, 237–38; Wenham, *The Book of Leviticus*, 16.

117. B. T. Arnold, "קרב," *NIDOTTE* 3:976. Waltke and Yu explain that this term normally means "to come close enough to the object to see it, to speak to it, or even to touch it" (Waltke with Yu, *Old Testament Theology*, 452).

(קָרְבָּן, that which is brought near), usually translated as "offering," occurs three times. Finally, the phrase *lipne Yahweh* (לִפְנֵי יְהוָה, before the LORD; i.e., in the presence of the LORD), which, as discussed earlier, carries strong connotations of being right in the presence of God, is used as the destination of the sacrifice in 1:3. Thus 1:2–3 reads,

> Speak to the Israelites and say to them: "When anyone among you brings [יַקְרִיב, *yaqrib*, Hiphil of *qarab*] an offering [קָרְבָּן, *qarban*; i.e., "that which is brought near"] to the LORD, bring [תַּקְרִיבוּ, *taqribu*, Hiphil of *qarab*] as your offering [קָרְבַּנְכֶם, *qarebankem*] an animal from either the herd or the flock. If the offering [קָרְבָּנוֹ, *qarebano*] is a burnt offering from the herd, you are to offer a male without defect. You must present it [יַקְרִיבֶנּוּ, *yaqribennu*, Hiphil of *qarab*, with suffix ending "it"] at the entrance to the tent of meeting so that it will be acceptable to the LORD [לִפְנֵי יְהוָה, *lipne Yahweh*, lit. "before the LORD" or "in the presence of the LORD"]."

These terms continue throughout Leviticus, with *qarab* occurring 102 times and *qarban* occurring 80 times. More importantly, the phrase *lipne Yahweh* occurs over 60 times in Leviticus (e.g., 1:5, 11; 3:1, 7, 12) and over 30 times in Numbers (e.g., 3:5; 5:16; 6:16; 14:37), indicating that the sacrifices and other rituals were carried out near or in front of the presence of God in the tabernacle.[118] That is, just about every activity related to worship/ ritual that is prescribed in Leviticus or Numbers is to take place "before the LORD" (i.e., before his indwelling relational presence in the tabernacle). Throughout Leviticus and Numbers, the presence of God is depicted as continuously residing in the tabernacle, and the entire sacrificial system is structured in light of that reality.[119] There is no mention in Leviticus or Numbers of God being up in the heavens with only his footstool in the tabernacle. The Hebrew word for "heavens" does not even occur in Leviticus or Numbers. In regard to worship and relationship, God is residing in the tabernacle.

118. Hartley states, "All activity at the tabernacle took place in Yahweh's presence. The phrase 'before Yahweh,' which runs throughout the sacrificial regulations, not only specified the area in front of the Tent of Meeting, but also recognizes that the various ceremonies were done in the presence of Yahweh" (Hartley, *Leviticus*, lxiv).

119. Fowler writes, "The enduring presence of God is a theological presupposition which pervades the Book of Leviticus. Here the Hebrew idiom occurs 62 times and *every* occurrence refers to the divine presence in the Tabernacle. . . . Because God dwelt in the tent of meeting, the sacrifices carried out before it on the altar are described as being performed 'before the Lord'" (Fowler, "The Meaning of *lipnê* YHWH," 387). See also H. Simian-Yofre, "פָּנִם," *TDOT* 11:609–10; A. S. van der Woude, "פָּנִים," *TLOT* 2:1012, noting that this phrase in Leviticus is a cultic technical term referring to "'before' the locus of God's presence."

Worship and Sacrifice in God's Presence

Just about everything in Leviticus relates to the indwelling, relational presence of God. Mark Rooker points out that Leviticus 1–16 focuses on the role of the priests and the implementation of the sacrificial system, with a main concern or purpose being the "continuance of the presence of God in the midst of the sinful nation," while Leviticus 17–27 specifies the "requirements for holiness for the nation," with a main concern focused on the effect of the presence of God upon the people as he dwells in their midst.[120]

That is, the entire sacrificial system is designed by God so that sinful Israel, both as individuals and as a nation, can approach, worship, and fellowship with him as he dwells right among them in the sanctuary.[121] Numerous scholars have made this point:

> Leviticus is the story of God's instruction for survival in the newly established holy space and holy life of the kingdom of priests. . . . It is comprised of teaching for the priests and the people regarding their responsibilities now that God had come to dwell in their midst.[122]

> The first and most far-reaching belief that underlies the laws of Leviticus is that God is actually present with his people. The regulations for worship, and especially for the offering of sacrifice, are set out as commands which are to be fulfilled in the very presence of God, who is to be found in the tabernacle.[123]

> The presence of the holy God is central to the legislation in Leviticus. . . . All of life, therefore, had to be lived in consciousness of Yahweh's immanent presence.[124]

> The enduring presence of God is one of the theological presuppositions running through the whole book. . . . God is present not only in worship, but at all times, even in the mundane duties of life. . . . The whole of man's life must be lived out in the presence of God.[125]

> The primary theological notion pervading Leviticus is the presence of God.[126]

> The main concerns of the book—as well as of the Bible as a whole—are how God's people were supposed to order their lives now that the holy God dwelled

---

120. Rooker, *Leviticus*, 42. See also Hundley, *Keeping Heaven on Earth*, 173–74.

121. J. Walton argues that the point of the entire sacrificial system was that "it provided a way to decontaminate a sanctuary tarnished by individual and corporate sin and, in so doing, preserve equilibrium in God's presence" (J. Walton, "Equilibrium and the Sacred Compass," 298).

122. Schnittjer, *The Torah Story*, 289. Balentine writes, "The sequel to the erecting of the tabernacle (Exod. 40) is Leviticus" (Balentine, *The Torah's Vision of Worship*, 148).

123. Clements, "Leviticus," 5.

124. Hartley, *Leviticus*, lxiii.

125. Wenham, *Leviticus*, 16–17.

126. Bellinger, *Leviticus, Numbers*, 7.

with them and how they could maintain a relationship with him so that they could enter his presence to worship him.[127]

Likewise, the theme of the presence of God continues to be a central theme throughout Numbers.[128]

The Presence of God and Holiness

Throughout Exodus, Leviticus, Numbers, and Deuteronomy the presence of God is always closely associated with holiness. That is, the presence of God here on earth in the midst of Israel is encircled with holiness, and God's presence emanates holiness outwardly. Recall that as Israel encountered God on Mount Sinai in Exodus 19, one of the first things God told them was that they were to be a "kingdom of priests and a holy nation" (Exod. 19:6). Once God comes to reside in the tabernacle, his holiness projects outward in gradations of holiness—the most holy place, the holy place, the courtyard of the tabernacle, and then the camp of Israel surrounding the tabernacle. Likewise, in approaching God the Israelites (and the priests who represent them) face the need for increasing holiness as they come inward toward God—from the camp, to the courtyard, to the holy place, and then to the most holy place. In addition, God in his holiness cannot continue to dwell in the midst of sinful and impure people. Thus God repeatedly instructs the people, "Be holy, for I am holy" (Lev. 11:44–45; 19:2; 20:26)—that is, they are to be holy so that God can continue to dwell with them. Thus much of Leviticus and Numbers deals with the implications for Israel of God's holiness and his demands for holiness as he dwells among them.[129]

---

127. Ross, *Holiness to the Lord*, 20. Similarly, Morales argues, "The primary theme and theology of Leviticus (and of the Pentateuch as a whole) is *YHWH's opening a way for humanity to dwell in the divine Presence*" (Morales, *Who Shall Ascend the Mountain of the Lord?*, 23). Sommer writes, "The goal of the events at Sinai as P [i.e., the end of Exodus, all of Leviticus, and the first part of Numbers] describes them is divine immanence, and the laws are but the means to that end. . . . P's main concern is not law but the divine presence that observance of the law makes possible" (Sommer, *Revelation and Authority*, 57). Others stressing the centrality of divine presence in the book of Leviticus include Gane, *Leviticus, Numbers*, 32; Rooker, *Leviticus*, 42; F. Gorman, *Divine Presence and Community*, 10–14.

128. Ashley, *The Book of Numbers*, 8.

129. Bellinger, *Leviticus, Numbers*, 7; House, *Old Testament Theology*, 127; T. D. Alexander, *From Paradise to the Promised Land*, 246; Wenham, *Leviticus*, 18–28. Ross writes, "That the LORD God was dwelling among his people and calling them to be a holy nation informs everyone what this book will teach: how the covenant people were supposed to approach the holy LORD, how they were supposed to regulate their lives in light of his presence, and how they were supposed to follow holiness in every aspect of their lives so that they might realize their priestly calling" (Ross, *Holiness to the Lord*, 21). Likewise, Rooker explains, "For God's

At the heart of the sacrificial system is the Day of Atonement in Leviticus 16.[130] According to 16:30, the Day of Atonement is a critical action to purify the nation and the sanctuary "before the LORD" (לִפְנֵי יְהֹוָה, *lipne Yahweh*), thus allowing God to continue to reside in their midst.[131] On the Day of Atonement the high priest is allowed to enter right into the most holy place, the deepest allowable penetration through the multiple gradations of holiness, right into the very presence of God in the most holy place.[132]

On the other hand, the holiness of God emanating out from the most holy place of the tabernacle is extremely dangerous if not respected and if not handled according to God's specific guidelines. This is true for the priests as well as for the people. Thus Aaron obediently initiates the sacrificial system in Leviticus 9, and the glory of the Lord appears to all the people as fire comes out and consumes the burnt offering (vv. 23–24). But in the very next chapter (10:1–3), Aaron's sons, Nadab and Abihu, apparently draw near to the presence of God inappropriately (cf. 16:1) and thus are killed by this same fire from the presence of God. Indeed, disobedience, sin, and impurity, coupled with the defiant refusal of the people of Israel to repent, be cleansed, and become holy, put tension on the resident presence of God. At some point such uncleansed sin could so pollute the sanctuary precincts that the presence of God could be driven away,[133] as actually happens later in Ezekiel 8–11.

The Presence of God and the Covenant

Throughout the patriarchal narratives in Genesis the presence of God is closely associated with the covenant promises that God makes to the patriarchs.

---

presence to remain in the Israelite camp demonstrative holiness among the people was required. This is the main concern of the book and is the justification for the sacrificial rituals" (Rooker, *Leviticus*, 47). Ashley notes that the themes of holiness and the presence of God are central to Numbers as well, but he points out that disobedience and obedience of the people, in the context of God's presence and holiness, become central related themes as well (Ashley, *Numbers*, 8).

130. Numerous scholars note that Lev. 16 is the literary center of Leviticus and that the book of Leviticus is the literary center of the Pentateuch. Thus they argue for viewing Lev. 16 and the Day of Atonement as particularly important. See Morales, *Who Shall Ascend the Mountain of the Lord?*, 23–34; Hartley, *Leviticus*, 217.

131. Morales, *Who Shall Ascend the Mountain of the Lord?*, 31; Milgrom, *Leviticus 1–16*, 51.

132. Morales, *Who Shall Ascend the Mountain of the Lord?*, 32. Note also that the opening verse, Lev. 16:1, references the deaths of Nadab and Abihu, which occurred back in 10:1–2. G. Anderson points out that the text in 16:1 seems to attribute their death to the fact that they came too near to God in an unauthorized manner (G. Anderson, *Christian Doctrine and the Old Testament*, 13). Leviticus 16:1 reads, "The LORD spoke to Moses after the death of two of Aaron's sons when they approached the presence of the LORD [בְּקָרְבָתָם לִפְנֵי־יְהֹוָה, *beqare-batam lipne-Yahweh*] and died" (CSB).

133. Milgrom, *Leviticus 1–16*, 43.

In Exodus this tight connection is likewise stressed. The presence of God, dwelling among his people, is at the heart of the covenant that God makes with Israel at Mount Sinai. Indeed, the covenant relationship in Exodus can be summarized by the tripartite formula statement: "I will be your God; you will be my people; I will dwell in your midst."

Leviticus continues the same tight connection between God's presence and his covenant relationship with Israel. In Leviticus 26:9 God tells Israel, "I will keep my covenant with you." Then in 26:11–13 God cites all of the elements in the tripartite formula, declaring, "I will put my dwelling place among you. . . . I will walk among you and be your God, and you will be my people. I am the LORD your God." At the heart of the covenant relationship are the blessings that Israel will receive due to God's presence. The regulations in Leviticus are not for the purpose of being a legalistic guide; rather, they are the means by which people could respond to the relational God who has entered into covenant relationship with them.[134] The ritualistic regulations in Leviticus are for the purpose of enhancing the covenant relationship between God and Israel based on God's presence in the tabernacle.[135]

Conversely, God warns, if Israel ignores his commands and thus violates the covenant, his presence will become a force to judge them instead of to bless them (26:17, 24–26). Ultimately, God warns Israel of the consequences of violating his commands and breaking the covenant: "I will scatter you among the nations and will draw out my sword and pursue you" (26:33).

The Presence of God in the "Priestly Blessing"

Literarily, Numbers 6:22–27 serves as a concluding benediction to the large bulk of prescriptive material that runs from Leviticus 1 to Numbers 6.[136] The blessing is "a prayer that God would grant his gracious presence and watchcare to his people."[137] The implication of God's presence in this passage can be derived from several factors. First of all, recall that the name Yahweh ("the LORD"), when revealed back in Exodus 3 and 6, carried strong implications of God's presence. In Numbers 6:24–26 the name Yahweh is listed out three parallel times, once in each main verse and blessing. Then in 6:27 God states, "So they [Aaron and his sons] will put my name on the Israelites and I will bless them," closely connecting the name of God (Yahweh) and the blessing. Then note that the term *panim* ("face") is used of God twice in this bless-

---

134. Bellinger, *Leviticus, Numbers*, 12.
135. Wenham, *Leviticus*, 29.
136. Ashley, *Numbers*, 149.
137. Ashley, *Numbers*, 149. Beale states that "the blessing at that time was God's glorious presence" (Beale, *The Temple and the Church's Mission*, 403).

ing, a term used frequently throughout the Pentateuch to represent the presence of God (e.g., Exod. 33:14–15; Deut. 4:37). Numbers 6:25 states, "The LORD make his *face* shine on you," and 6:26 states, "The LORD turn his *face* toward you."[138] Although the phrases "make his face shine" and "turn his face toward" are idiomatic expressions of acceptance, blessing, and favor, the repeated connection throughout Exodus–Deuteronomy between the term *panim* in various grammatical forms and expressions frequently referring to the presence of God in the tabernacle suggests that the usage also connotes that here. Note the stress on the presence of God in the tabernacle throughout the immediate literary context ("before the LORD" in Num. 6:16, 20; 7:3; "to the LORD" in Num. 6:21).

In addition, numerous scholars have noted that Aaron pronounces an unspecified blessing on the people in Leviticus 9:22. Some suggest that in that text he gives the same blessing as Numbers 6:22–27, or at least something similar.[139] Leviticus 9:22 is explicitly embedded in a context that stresses the presence of God in the tabernacle, as 9:21 indicates that Aaron has just been waving a sacrifice "before the LORD," and 9:23–24 states, "And the glory of the LORD appeared to all the people. Fire came out from the presence of the LORD and consumed the burnt offering." Thus the blessing of Numbers 6:22–27 is not a generic blessing to be pronounced in general about God's blessing. It is tied closely to the presence of God in the tabernacle.

Recently, both Jeremy Smoak and Puttagunta Satyavani have argued that this blessing is very much about the presence of God in the tabernacle/temple. Smoak states, "The expression 'may Yahweh make his face shine' conveyed the hope that Yahweh's presence would radiate out from the sanctuary to provide protection and deliverance to those seeking divine aid."[140] Satyavani notes the probable connection to Leviticus 9:22–23 and underscores that right after Aaron delivers the blessing on the people, "the glory of YHWH" appeared to all the people. Thus Satyavani notes that this priestly blessing implies worshiping/experiencing the revealed presence of God. She concludes, "This priestly blessing itself seems a prayer that YHWH/God would grant his gracious presence and watch over his people."[141] It is a prayer to God to look out favorably from his sanctuary and provide blessing and protection.[142]

---

138. Italics have occasionally been added to Scripture quotations for emphasis.

139. Levine, *Numbers 1–20*, 215–16; Budd, *Numbers*, 75; Ashley, *Numbers*, 149.

140. Smoak, *The Priestly Blessing*, 91.

141. Satyavani, *Seeing the Face of God*, 208. Similarly, Ashley argues that this blessing asks "that Yahweh show his benevolent presence to his faithful people. . . . God's gracious presence leads, in the end, to peace" (Ashley, *Numbers*, 152–53).

142. Patrick Miller likewise connects the Numbers 6 blessing to the blessing of Aaron in Leviticus 9:22–23. Miller notes that the overall setting for the Numbers 6 blessing includes "the

The Presence of God in the Ark of the Covenant

Numbers 10:33–36 describes the role of the ark of the covenant in the divine guidance of Israel as they traveled from Sinai. The ark went out before the people, and the "cloud of the LORD" was over them. The presence of God is closely associated with the ark of the covenant. Note how Moses addresses the LORD as present "with" the ark: "Whenever the ark set out, Moses would say: 'Arise, LORD! Let your enemies be scattered, and those who hate you flee from your presence.' When it came to rest, he would say: 'Return, LORD, to the countless thousands of Israel'" (Num. 10:35–36 CSB).[143]

The Presence of God as the Empowering Force for Success in the Conquest

In Numbers 13–14 ten of the twelve spies report that the people in the land of Canaan are too strong for the Israelites to defeat, and the Israelites start to grumble against Moses and Aaron. Joshua and Caleb, however, counter the defeatist attitude of the people and urge that they go in immediately and conquer the land. Joshua and Caleb base this confidence on the empowering presence of God. "If the LORD is pleased with us," they argue, "he will lead us into that land . . . and will give it to us. . . . Do not be afraid of the people of the land, because we will devour them. . . . The LORD is with us" (Num. 14:8–9). As the crisis intensifies, the "glory of the LORD" appears at the tent of meeting, and God threatens to destroy Israel. Once again (cf. Exod. 32) Moses talks God out of it. Moses's primary argument is that God's presence with Israel to deliver and to lead is well known ("You, LORD, are with these people, . . . you go before them in a pillar of cloud by day and pillar of fire by night" [Num. 14:14]); thus, Moses infers, if God destroys the people, then the Egyptians and others will misunderstand. God once again relents from destroying Israel, but he declares that this disobedient generation will wander in the wilderness and never see the promised land. The next day the people appear to repent. However, they think that things are now fine, and they want to go ahead and start the conquest. Moses informs them that this doomed action is foolish because "the LORD is not with" them. Due to their sin, God

---

making of a sanctuary for the presence of God in the midst of his people (Exod. 25–40), the provision of a sacrificial system to enable a sinful people to live in the presence of a holy God (Lev. 1–8), and the establishment and ordination of a priesthood to lead the people in the worship of God." He concludes: "The face of Yahweh indicates the presence of God, but the shining countenance is an emphatically positive presence for help and favor, a sign of the friendly and well-wishing nearness of God" (Miller, "The Blessing of God," 245–46).

143. G. Anderson, "Theology of the Tabernacle," 164.

will not lead them into Canaan with his presence and empower them to be victorious now. The foolish people, however, go to battle on their own without Moses and the ark (the sign of God's presence), and they are defeated soundly (Num. 14:44–45). The presence of God is clearly the critical component in whether or not Israel will be victorious in capturing the promised land.[144]

Deuteronomy

With the presence of God playing such a central role in Exodus, Leviticus, and Numbers, it comes as no surprise to see this central theme continued in Deuteronomy.[145] Indeed, one could summarize Deuteronomy as the terms of the covenant by which Israel, empowered by the presence of God, could conquer the promised land and then live the blessed life with the holy, awesome God in their midst.[146] The expression "before the LORD" (לִפְנֵי יְהוָה, *lipne Yahweh*), used so frequently throughout Leviticus to designate being in close proximity to the presence of God in the tabernacle, is likewise used twenty-five times in Deuteronomy, and in almost every instance it carries the same meaning as in Leviticus, stressing the real and spatial presence of God.[147]

The Presence of God in Israel's History

In the opening chapters of Deuteronomy, as Moses recounts Israel's recent history with God, he stresses repeatedly the central role played by God's presence.[148] In Deuteronomy 1 Moses rebukes the people for their earlier failure to trust in God's presence and to enter the land (Num. 14), declaring, "Then

144. Bellinger summarizes, "Chapters 13 and 14 vividly remind the reading community that the real issue for ancient Israel is not military readiness or even fruitfulness of the land, but the presence of God with them" (Bellinger, *Leviticus, Numbers*, 232).

145. I. Wilson points out that in texts referring back to Horeb/Sinai, percentage-wise, the incidence of "presence" references is higher in Deuteronomy than even in Exodus (I. Wilson, *Out of the Midst of the Fire*, 98).

146. Accordingly, Vogt writes, "Deuteronomy also portrays Yahweh as a God who is present with his people. We have seen that Deuteronomy guards Yahweh's transcendence while at the same time highlighting his presence with his people Israel. The people experienced Yahweh in profound ways at Horeb, but another of Deuteronomy's concerns is to note that his presence will not end when the people enter the land of promise. Rather, they will continue to live out their relationship with Yahweh in the land. Through obedience to Torah, they will be able to experience and actualize Yahweh's presence" (Vogt, *Deuteronomic Theology*, 228).

147. I. Wilson, *Out of the Midst of the Fire*, 131. Knafl states that "it refers to the proximate presence of the deity in a specific site (and not merely his name as a stand in)" (Knafl, *Forming God*, 208–13).

148. McConville notes, "The link between exodus, divine presence and law lies at the heart of Deuteronomy" (McConville, *Deuteronomy*, 105).

I said to you, 'Do not be terrified; do not be afraid of them. The LORD your God, who is going before you, will fight for you, as he did for you in Egypt, before your very eyes. . . . In spite of this, you did not trust in the LORD your God, who went ahead of you on your journey in fire by night and in a cloud by day . . . to show you the way you should go" (Deut. 1:29–33). After their disobedience in Numbers 14, Moses recounts, God stressed to the people that they could not possibly defeat their enemies without his presence (Deut. 1:42). Yet in spite of that disobedience, God has been blessing them and has been with them anyway, as Moses notes: "These forty years the LORD your God has been with you" (Deut. 2:7).

Now, as Moses calls on the Israelites to obey all the commandments of God and to go in and take the land, he reminds them of the very special privilege it is to have God dwelling right among them.[149] Moses then recalls Israel's encounter with the presence of God at Mount Sinai (Horeb): "Remember the day you stood before the LORD [לִפְנֵי יְהוָה, *lipne Yahweh*] your God at Horeb. . . . You came near and stood at the foot of the mountain while it blazed with fire. . . . Then the LORD spoke to you out of the fire. . . . He brought you out of Egypt by his Presence and his great strength" (Deut. 4:10–12, 32–33, 37).

Likewise, in Deuteronomy 9, as Moses reflects back on the episode of the golden calf, he stresses again the dangerous presence of God, noting that the mountain "was ablaze with fire" (v. 15), and that his mediation for them was "before the LORD" (vv. 18, 25). In Deuteronomy 10 Moses also reminds the Israelites that God not only had written the Ten Commandments but also had first proclaimed the commandments to Israel from "on the mountain, out of the fire" (v. 4), stressing God's dangerous and awesome presence.

The Presence of God as the Empowering Force for Conquering the Land

At the beginning of Deuteronomy, one of the reasons that Moses repeatedly stresses how the powerful and relational presence of God has been so involved in their recent past is that Moses wants the Israelites to realize (and to trust) that it is the presence of God who will go before them and defeat their enemies in the promised land. Thus in Deuteronomy 4:37 Moses reaffirms that it was the presence of God who delivered them from Egypt in the recent past, and then he immediately underscores the current purpose of God's delivering presence, "to drive out before you nations greater and stronger than you

---

149. Nelson explains that the comparison with other gods involves "near and far" rather than "true or false" (Nelson, *Deuteronomy*, 65).

and to bring you into their land to give it to you for your inheritance" (4:38).[150] This is a central theme throughout Deuteronomy, as Moses repeatedly tells the Israelites not to be afraid, for God is in their midst and would be the one to drive out the nations in the promised land. Thus Deuteronomy 7:21–22 reads, "Do not be terrified by them, for the LORD your God, who is among you, is a great and awesome God. The LORD your God will drive out those nations before you." Similar statements about God's empowering presence are made in Deuteronomy 9:3; 20:1–4; 31:6, 8.

Transcendence and Immanence: God Is in Heaven Above and on Earth Below

Deuteronomy stresses the immanent presence of God dwelling among the Israelites right in the tabernacle, but it does not neglect the concept of the sovereign God dwelling in heaven. As 4:39 declares, "The LORD is God in heaven above and on the earth below." Yet even this statement comes in a context of stressing God's close and terrifying presence at Horeb/Sinai (4:10–38), where God was speaking to them out of the fire.[151] Peter Vogt points out that Deuteronomy 4 depicts God "as actually present with his people at Horeb and explains the means by which he will continue to be present with them in the near and distant future."[152] That is, this text is in no way minimizing the earthly presence of God in favor of stressing the heavenly. Rather, the text is emphasizing the incredible fact that the awesome God who rules from the heavens actually came down to the earth to encounter Israel at Mount Sinai/Horeb and now dwells in their midst and travels with them.[153] Likewise, Deuteronomy 26:15 ("Look down from heaven, your holy dwelling place") should be taken in light of 4:39, where God is depicted as dwelling both in

150. MacDonald comments, "The mention of YHWH's presence in the exodus acts as an assurance of YHWH's continued presence in the present task of the conquest" (MacDonald, *Deuteronomy and the Meaning of "Monotheism,"* 201).

151. Nelson notes the context in Deut. 4 of stern warning for Israel and suggests that "heaven and earth" in 4:36 and 4:39 harkens back to the warning of 4:26, underscoring "the all-encompassing sphere of Yahweh's jurisdiction" (Nelson, *Deuteronomy*, 70).

152. Vogt, *Deuteronomic Theology*, 135. Vogt points out that 4:10 ("you stood before the LORD your God at Horeb") is a literal reference (p. 121). Likewise, the repeated references to "out of the midst of the fire" throughout Deut. 4–5 (4:12, 15, 33, 36; 5:4, 22, 24, 26) strongly imply that God was considered to be present there. See also I. Wilson, *Out of the Midst of the Fire*, 57–60.

153. McConville notes that Deut. 4 is concerned with the relationship between God's transcendence and his immanence, but he underscores that the immanence of God is "strongly stated," as seen in 4:7 ("near us"), 4:10 ("stood before the LORD"), and 4:11 ("you came near and stood at the foot of the mountain while it blazed with fire") (McConville, "Time, Place and the Deuteronomic Altar-Law," 134–35).

heaven and on earth.[154] It simply maintains the reality of transcendence and immanence at the same time.[155] So while Deuteronomy praises God's sovereign reign as Creator over all the earth, when proclaiming the relational aspects of God and the relational covenant that he makes with Israel, the text focuses on God's immanence, centered on his very presence traveling with them and dwelling in the tabernacle.

Worship and the Place God Will Choose for His Name/Presence to Dwell

In Deuteronomy 12:5–7 Moses declares, "But you are to seek the place the LORD your God will choose from among all your tribes to put his Name there for his dwelling. To that place you must go. . . . There, in the presence of the LORD [לִפְנֵי יְהוָה, *lipne Yahweh*] your God, you and your families shall eat and shall rejoice." Twenty times in Deuteronomy reference is made to the place that God would choose for his name to dwell (with some variations in phraseology).[156]

Influenced by Gerhard von Rad, many OT scholars throughout much of the twentieth century viewed these texts as indicating an evolutionary-type demythologizing shift (or corrective) as the "later" Deuteronomistic writer sought to replace the earlier "primitive" immanence concept of God (and "his glory") dwelling right in the sanctuary with a more sophisticated transcendent understanding that God really dwelt up in the heavens and only a lesser, "hypostatic" essence of God was represented in the sanctuary on earth.[157] This view has often been labeled "name theology."[158] Although this theology was popular for much of the twentieth century,[159] serious and effective rebuttals

154. McConville, "Time, Place and the Deuteronomic Altar-Law," 115.

155. Knafl points out that Deut. 26:15 never states that God is not present in the sanctuary or that God only dwells in heaven, probably reflecting the belief that "YHWH is simultaneously present in heaven and earth" (Knafl, *Forming God*, 213).

156. Block cites the following: Deut. 12:5, 11, 14, 18, 21, 26; 14:23, 24, 25; 15:20; 16:2, 6, 7, 11, 15, 16; 17:8, 10; 26:2; 31:11 (Block, "'A Place for My Name,'" 234).

157. Much of the impetus for this view comes from the source-critical assumption that the "Deuteronomist" writes to the postexilic community, trying to explain the presence of God in light of the destruction of the temple. Clements, a proponent of "name theology," makes this connection explicit in his comments on Deut. 12:5–12: "Clearly this deuteronomic development was conscious of the damaging effect on Israel's theology that had been brought about by the threat to, and eventual destruction of, the Jerusalem Temple at the hands of foreign armies" (Clements, "The Book of Deuteronomy," 385–86).

158. For a history of this view and how it developed, see Richter, *The Deuteronomistic History*, 7–36.

159. An early challenge to "name theology" was Wenham, "Deuteronomy and the Central Sanctuary."

started appearing in the 1990s and have continued into the twenty-first century.[160] Thus this viewpoint has now been rejected by many scholars,[161] or at least seriously modified to stress that God is present simultaneously both in heaven and on earth, combining transcendence and immanence.[162]

That the presence of God in the tabernacle (and the future temple) is the same in Deuteronomy as it was in Exodus and Leviticus is underscored by the repeated use of the same phrase "before the Lord / in the presence of the Lord" (לִפְנֵי יְהוָה, *lipne Yahweh*) throughout Deuteronomy.[163] Furthermore, this phrase is stressed in Deuteronomy 12, particularly in connection with the texts about God choosing the place for his name. For example, the statement in 12:5 "the place the Lord your God will choose . . . to put his Name there for his dwelling" is followed in 12:7 with "There, in the presence of the Lord [לִפְנֵי יְהוָה] your God, you and your families shall eat and shall rejoice." Then again in 12:11, the statement "the place the Lord your God will choose as a dwelling for his Name" is followed quickly in 12:12 with "There rejoice before the Lord [לִפְנֵי יְהוָה] your God."

Yet if Deuteronomy presents God as powerfully and truly present in the tabernacle (without denying his transcendence and his presence in heaven) in a similar fashion to Exodus, Leviticus, and Numbers, why is God's *name* repeated in Deuteronomy in association with the tabernacle/temple? That is, what is the meaning of the repeated emphasis that God will place his *name* to dwell at the place he chooses?

Sandra Richter compares the phraseology associated with God's "causing his Name to dwell there" to other similar usage in the literature of the ancient Near East and argues that the usage in Deuteronomy is a loan adaptation of an Akkadian idiom that stresses ownership. She argues that the fundamental

---

160. McConville and Millar, *Time and Place in Deuteronomy*; I. Wilson, *Out of the Midst of the Fire*; A. S. van der Woude, "שָׁם," *TLOT* 3:1360–62; Richter, *The Deuteronomistic History*; Vogt, *Deuteronomic Theology*; Cook, "God's Real Absence and Real Presence," 121–50.

161. Nelson, *Deuteronomy*, 152–53; Knafl, *Forming God*, 99–109; MacDonald, *Deuteronomy and the Meaning of "Monotheism,"* 193–95; Soulen, *Distinguishing the Voices*, 152–53; Waltke with Yu, *Old Testament Theology*, 474; McConville, *Deuteronomy*, 221–22; Goldingay, *Old Testament Theology*, 2:106; C. Wright, *Deuteronomy*, 162–65; Mayes, *Deuteronomy*, 58–60; W. Kaiser, *The Promise-Plan of God*, 99–100; Kamp, "The Conceptualization of God's Dwelling Place."

162. Hundley writes, "God on earth also remains enthroned above. Thus God's presence on earth carries with it all the connotations of God's presence in heaven" (Hundley, "To Be or Not to Be," 539–40). Likewise, Block explains, "The emphasis on 'the place' highlights the presence and accessibility of the One who actually dwells in heaven (4:39), but who condescends also to reside on earth for the purpose of communing with his people" (Block, "'A Place for My Name,'" 234–35).

163. This is one of the central arguments of I. Wilson (*Out of the Midst of the Fire*, 131) and McConville ("Time, Place and the Deuteronomic Altar-Law," 114–16) against "name theology."

meaning of the idiom is to claim something by putting one's own name on it. Thus God is claiming the conquered promised land as his.[164] Richter affirms the foundational idea that God does indeed dwell in the midst of his people,[165] but she argues that the "name" texts in Deuteronomy actually have little to do with "presence" one way or the other (neither transcendence nor immanence, just possession).

Michael Hundley, on the other hand, concludes that Deuteronomy maintains the close presence of God, but "shrouds that presence in mystery. . . . The Deuteronomist's principal contribution lies not in moving God to heaven but in leaving undefined God's presence on earth. . . . The name serves to simultaneously guarantee YHWH's practical presence and to abstract the nature of that presence."[166]

Indeed, perhaps the best approach for determining the meaning of God's name in Deuteronomy—especially if we are concerned with interconnected, canonical "biblical theology"—is to work within a canonical understanding and context and thus to consider how the name of God (Yahweh) has been used throughout the preceding story, especially in Exodus and Leviticus. If we move away from source-critical presuppositions (trying to understand Deuteronomy in the context of the postexilic situation) and seek to understand Deuteronomy canonically as the words of Moses on the plains of Moab, just prior to Israel entering the promised land, then the dramatic discussions that Moses has had with God himself about God's *name* (i.e., Yahweh) that took place in Exodus 3, 6, and 33 should be the starting point for our understanding of God's *name* in his statements to Moses in Deuteronomy. In our discussions above on God's name in Exodus 3, 6, and 33, we concluded that God's revealed name (Yahweh) is closely related to his saving actions in the exodus and to his close, intense, holy, and dangerous covenantal and relational presence that Moses encountered at the burning bush, which he and Israel encountered on Mount Sinai, and which moved into the tabernacle at the end of Exodus. Similarly, the stress in Leviticus is that God's name is

164. Richter, *The Deuteronomistic History*, 211, 217. In a more recent work, Richter has argued that this phrase is more specifically connected with the establishment of an inscribed monument. She proposes that the construction of the altar on Mount Ebal (Deut. 27) is such an inscribed monument, thus identifying Mount Ebal as "that place," the first central sanctuary (Richter, "The Place of the Name in Deuteronomy").

165. Richter writes, "The theology of the divine presence (the idea that YHWH will dwell among his people) is absolutely fundamental to the faith communicated in the Hebrew Bible. The paradise that was Eden, the paradise that is the Holy of Holies, and the coming paradise which the prophets envision are all characterized by this single concept: YHWH is present" (Richter, *The Deuteronomistic History*, 11).

166. Hundley, "To Be or Not to Be," 552.

holy (20:3; 22:2, 32). In Deuteronomy, God is promising that this same dramatic, relational, yet holy and dangerous, presence will dwell with Israel in the promised land, but only at the one place that God himself would designate. This understanding certainly fits well with the context of Deuteronomy 12, where, as noted above, the statements of God putting his name to dwell in a place are quickly followed by texts stressing God's presence (i.e., 12:5 and 12:7; 12:11 and 12:12).[167] Stephen Cook concludes that Deuteronomy 12:5 "understands the name to be a means of celebration and communion with divine presence. . . . It is placed within Israel to perpetuate and advance God's reputation, identity, and desire for relationship."[168] This conclusion does not necessarily negate Richter's proposal that the "place for God's name to dwell" implies ownership. Throughout Deuteronomy God will state categorically that the land is his to reside in and to give to his vassal Israel.[169] His divine presence in the land is an irrefutable sign of his ownership.

Worship, Ritual, Sacrifice, and the Presence of God

Closely related to the discussion above regarding the meaning of God's "name" in Deuteronomy 12, it should be underscored that Deuteronomy 12 is concerned primarily with sacrifice and worship. The stress on the "one place" to worship God accentuates the importance of God's presence to the kind of worship he desires. That is, God has come down to dwell among his people so that they can have a relationship with him. Personal encounter with him appears to be a very important aspect of how God wants to relate to his people. Daniel Block emphasizes the importance of God's presence in understanding this call to worship: "This text should be seen as a glorious invitation to worship YHWH in his presence. It represents a wonderful provision for the perpetuation of the extraordinary event that happened at Mount Sinai, where YHWH had personally called his people into his presence and invited them to rejoice there."[170] Furthermore, Block notes the connection with Exodus 24:10–11, in which Moses and the elders of Israel ate and drank in the very presence of God. Here in Deuteronomy 12, Block argues, God is

---

167. This connection occurs frequently elsewhere in Deuteronomy. Note, for example, 14:23, "Eat the tithe . . . in the presence of the LORD your God at the place he will choose as a dwelling for his Name"; 16:11, "And rejoice before the LORD your God at the place he will choose as a dwelling for his Name." Cf. 15:20; 16:2, 15–16.

168. Cook, "God's Real Absence and Real Presence," 142.

169. Goldingay, *Old Testament Theology*, 1:517–18.

170. Block, *How I Love Your Torah, O LORD!*, 101. Block also notes that in most of the other passages in Deuteronomy that mention "the place" where God will cause his name to dwell, the context involves worship activities in the presence of the Lord (p. 111).

presenting the provisions for repeating this wonderful blessing indefinitely once they arrive in the promised land, yet this time *all* are invited to the meal, not just the elders and Moses as back in Exodus 24:10–11.[171] Finally, as in Leviticus, the priests in Deuteronomy are depicted as serving in the presence of God (Deut. 17:12; 18:7).

Another important emphasis of Deuteronomy 12 is the joy of the worshiper in the presence of God. Three times this chapter declares that the worshipers and their families will rejoice in the presence of the LORD their God (12:7, 12, 18). When done correctly and in accordance with God's directives, coming into the very presence of God as he dwelt among his people, first in the tabernacle and then later in the temple, was not to be a burdensome or terrifying experience but rather a joyful encounter.

The Presence of God, the Covenant, and the Promise of Land

The book of Deuteronomy is restating the terms of the covenant that God made with Israel back at Mount Sinai/Horeb and is calling Israel to covenant faithfulness. At the heart of the covenant is God's promise to dwell in the midst of his people, and thus the presence of God surfaces frequently in passages that discuss the terms of the covenant. This occurs as Moses reflects back on the covenant made at Mount Sinai/Horeb. In Deuteronomy 4:15–40 the covenant relationship is intertwined with the powerful presence of God, which delivered Israel from Egypt and then spoke to Israel from out of the fire on Mount Sinai/Horeb. Then in the introduction to the Ten Commandments (5:1–5), which forms the heart of the covenant, the encounter that Israel had on Mount Sinai/Horeb with the awe-inspiring presence of God is stressed ("The LORD spoke to you face to face out of the fire" [v. 4]). Then in Deuteronomy 28–30, where the renewal of the covenant is presented along with the blessings for obedience and the curses for disobedience, the presence of God once again forms a critical backdrop. Twice Moses notes that the people are "standing in the presence of the LORD" (29:10, 15) as they are called to follow the terms of the covenant. Finally, the tripartite aspects of the covenant are included in 29:12–15 ("to confirm you . . . as his people, that he may be your God"; "you who are standing here with us today in the presence of the LORD our God").

Likewise, in the warning or "curses" section, several of the most serious punishments are described in terms that relate to the loss of God's presence. One curse is that Israel will be driven out of the promised land and thus away

---

171. Block, *How I Love Your Torah, O LORD!*, 113–14.

from God (28:36, 64–68; 29:28). Climaxing this warning is 31:15–18. Here God appears to Moses once again in a pillar of cloud. God tells Moses that the people will soon turn to other gods and break the covenant (31:15–16). The serious consequence of this broken covenant, God declares, is that he will then "hide his face" from them, an indictment that God mentions twice (31:17–18). The "hiding of God's face" (which we will also encounter in numerous other texts in the OT) describes a breach in the relationship and the loss of God's presence, which then would result in all of the terrible curses described in Deuteronomy 28–30 (see also 32:20).[172] This connection is clearly described in 31:17: "Have not these disasters come on us because our God is not with us?"

Also connected to the covenant and the presence of God is the promise of the land.[173] As God enters into covenant relationship with the Israelites, in which he will dwell among them, the "space" in which they dwell together becomes important. Thus throughout Deuteronomy the theme of the land is ubiquitous. Walter Brueggemann writes, "It will no longer do to talk about Yahweh and his people but we must speak about Yahweh and his people *and his land.*"[174] The "torah," or teaching, of Deuteronomy provides the covenant framework by which Israel can live in the promised land with God in their midst and receive blessings from him.[175] Richter writes that God's perfect plan for them was "the *people* of God in the *place* of God dwelling in the *presence* of God."[176] J. Gordon McConville explains, "The gift of the land is not a thing in itself, but initiates a scenario in which a people lives before their God in covenant faithfulness."[177] Similarly, Brueggemann concludes, "The land for which Israel yearns and which it remembers is never unclaimed space but is always *a place with Yahweh.*"[178]

---

172. Balentine concludes that the phrase "hide the face" in the OT occurs most frequently in judgment texts, and that "the overriding consequence is described as . . . separation from God" (Balentine, *The Hidden God*, 77). Burnett notes that in the OT divine absence "assumes an inherently spatial conceptualization of divine-human relationships" and implies a crisis in the relationship (Burnett, *Where Is God?*, 5, 56, 176).

173. McConville states, "In Deuteronomy, land is not just a place, but an arena of life, the life of Israel in covenant relationship with God" (McConville, "Time, Place and the Deuteronomic Altar-Law," 128–29).

174. Brueggemann, *The Land*, 5.

175. Stressing the tight connection between God's presence and the land is C. Barth, *God with Us*, 176–78. Vogt notes that one of the concerns of Deuteronomy is to assure the people that the presence of God would not end when they entered into the land, but would continue with them in the land (Vogt, *Deuteronomic Theology*, 228).

176. Richter, *The Epic of Eden*, 104.

177. McConville, *Grace in the End*, 132–33.

178. Brueggemann, *The Land*, 5.

Furthermore, there are a number of probable parallels between "the land" in Deuteronomy and the "garden of Eden" in Genesis.[179] That is, numerous scholars observe that the movement of Israel into the bountiful promised land to live with God in their midst is likened to a return to Eden.[180]

Conclusions

The relational presence of God is central to the story in the Pentateuch, driving the theological plot and also functioning as the interconnecting web, providing coherence and interconnectedness to all of the major theological themes in the Pentateuch. The story opens in Genesis with a personal and relational God creating the world and then relating to people in the paradisiacal garden. Because of their disobedience the people are banished from the garden and from God's presence, and thus also from the benefits of God's presence (such as life). The need to return to the "garden" (place where God resides) and to reestablish the close personal relationship with God is a theme that will continue to echo throughout the rest of the OT and into the NT, culminating in the closing chapters of Revelation, where God and his people are once again restored in relationship and living together in the garden.

Throughout the patriarchal narratives of Genesis, the "I will be with you" presence of God is central. Likewise, the concepts of God's presence and God's covenant promises, including the promise of the land, are all inextricably interconnected.

The book of Exodus comes as a first-stage fulfillment of God's promises to the patriarchs and, in particular, as God's action to restore the lost relationship created by the banishment of people from his presence in the garden. God reveals to Moses that the very essence of his name Yahweh means that he will be present with and for his people. Then in what will become the central OT paradigm of salvation, God delivers his people from Egypt and personally leads and guides them to Mount Sinai, where he enters into covenant relationship with them. At the heart of this covenant is the tripartite formula "I will be your God; you will be my people; I will dwell in your midst." Foundational to God's plan for relating to his people and blessing them through his covenant is

179. O. Martin notes the following from Deuteronomy: the land is described as a new paradise, a return to Eden-like bliss; there are numerous references to the creational mandate given to Adam, now passed to Israel; the recurring theme of "life" and the "prolonging of days"; the association of the land with "rest" and the presence of God (O. Martin, *Bound for the Promised Land*, 83–86).

180. Block, "A Place for My Name," 244; Lister, *The Presence of God*, 201; O. Martin, *Bound for the Promised Land*, 83–86.

his close, yet intense, glorious, indwelling presence. Yet if he is to dwell right in their midst, he needs a place in which to stay, so nearly the entire second half of Exodus describes the tabernacle, God's residence. The climactic event comes in Exodus 40 when the powerful and spectacular "glory of the Lord" (God's personal presence) comes to dwell right in the tabernacle.

With the holy and powerful God now dwelling right among the Israelites, their entire way of life needs to change accordingly. Indeed, Leviticus and Numbers 1–10 describe how sinful Israelites can approach the holy God living in their midst and how they can relate to him in worship. Holiness, nearness, and presence are stressed. Everything is done "before the Lord," in his presence. Worship is directed not up to a distant God in heaven but to a very near God living among them right in the tabernacle, underscoring the important interconnection between presence and relationship.

In Deuteronomy the relational presence of God continues to be the central, interconnecting theme. In the opening chapters of Deuteronomy, as Moses recounts the history of Israel, he repeatedly stresses the powerful presence of God leading the Israelites out of Egypt and through the wilderness to Mount Sinai. The worship of God, Deuteronomy stresses, must be carried out in his presence, and at the specific place on earth where he chooses to dwell (i.e., the tabernacle and then the temple). The indwelling presence of God is foundational to the covenant relationship and unites the promises of land and blessing. In summary, Deuteronomy provides the covenant terms by which Israel can find wonderful blessings and life in the promised land with the holy, awesome presence of God living right in their midst to empower them, protect them, and bless them through the relationship.

TWO

The Relational Presence of God in the Historical Books, Psalms, and the Wisdom Books

The Historical Books

Joshua

In the book of Exodus, as a critical part of God's relational covenant with Israel, God's powerful and holy presence comes down into the tabernacle to dwell right among his people. Throughout Israel's journeys from Egypt to the promised land, it is God's close presence that guides and protects Israel. Repeatedly in Exodus, Numbers, and Deuteronomy God promises that his powerful presence will lead and enable Israel to conquer all of their enemies and to enter into the promised land successfully. In the book of Joshua this promise is fulfilled as God's powerful presence leads Israel into the land in dramatic fashion and empowers Israel to achieve spectacular victories over the inhabitants.

In Joshua 1 Moses has died and Joshua is preparing to lead the Israelites across the Jordan into the promised land. As God speaks to Joshua about the upcoming conquest, he opens and closes his instructions with the promise of his empowering presence (1:5, 9). Thus God is reaffirming the continuity of his empowering, relational presence from the era of Moses to the leadership of Joshua and the conquest. In fact, the promise "I will be with you" (אֶהְיֶה עִמָּךְ, 'ehyeh 'immak) in Joshua 1:5 is identical to what God had said to Moses in Exodus 3:12. The people of Israel apparently realize the critical importance of God's presence, for they reaffirm this reality as they pledge to follow Joshua in 1:17, "Just as we fully obeyed Moses, so we will obey you. Only may the LORD your God be with you as he was with Moses." Thus a critical theme in the opening chapter of Joshua is the reassurance of God's empowering presence.[1]

In Joshua 3, as the Israelites cross the river Jordan to enter the promised land, the ark of the covenant, representing the presence of God, goes before them, leading them into the promised land. Joshua points to God's powerful and miraculous intervention of stopping up the Jordan's waters as a reaffirming and encouraging sign of his empowering presence in their midst.[2] Indeed, in several places throughout Joshua the presence of God is implied as he fights for Israel (10:14; 23:3, 10). Throughout the book of Joshua the success of Israel is integrally tied to the powerful presence of God.

Similarly, when Israel ignores God's commands or trivializes him as if he is not there, he withdraws his empowering battle presence, causing Israel to be defeated. This is illustrated in the initial defeat at Ai (Josh. 7).[3] God explains the reason for their defeat in 7:12, connecting it to his warning about withdrawing his presence: "I will not be with you anymore unless you destroy whatever among you is devoted to destruction."

Thus in the book of Joshua it is the presence of God and the empowerment provided by God's relational presence that will enable Israel to carry out God's will and conquer the promised land. This is a central theme that drives the story.

Judges

After the Israelites have a successful beginning to the conquest, described in the book of Joshua as empowered by the presence of God, in Judges they turn away from God to idols, thus losing God's favor and power. Consequently, Judges chronicles how the Israelites spiral downward in a "Canaanization"

---

1. Hubbard underscores the importance of the presence-of-God theme in Josh. 1: "Israel's distinguishing mark is that he [Yahweh] lives only among them. It is the divine presence, and access to God's power, which makes any Israelite undertaking viable. It alone banishes fear" (Hubbard, *Joshua*, 94–95). Butler concurs, noting that the theme of divine presence, stressed here in Josh. 1, "expresses one of the basic roots of Israelite faith, the belief that Yahweh is the God of Israel who accompanies, leads, protects, fights, and goes with the men he has chosen for his work" (Butler, *Joshua*, 12).

2. Ringgren suggests that the meaning of the phrase "the Living God" connotes the active intervention or the "obviously present" nature of God (H. Ringgren, "חָיָה," *TDOT* 4:339). See also Nelson, *Joshua*, 61.

3. Lister, *The Presence of God*, 205.

process.[4] In Judges 1, the transition chapter from Joshua, the narrator states that "the LORD was with" the men of Judah (1:19) and the tribes of Joseph (1:22). Thus they were victorious, even capturing Philistine cities. However, even with the presence of God available to empower them for victory, they do not follow through and complete the conquest as God instructed, and they leave significant regions unconquered. After the first generation dies off, the later generations turn away from God. This starts the cycle that continues throughout much of Judges: the people worship idols; a foreign power invades and oppresses Israel; God raises up a judge to deliver Israel, often empowering that judge through the Spirit of the LORD; then the people turn to foreign gods again. Ryan Lister calls this a cycle of "Presence and Separation."[5]

The Israelites "Did Evil in the Eyes of the Lord"

In Judges 2:10 the narrator states that an entirely new generation grew up "who knew neither the LORD nor what he had done for Israel." This does not mean that they had never heard of God ("the LORD"), but that they had no relationship with God, nor did they worship God.

The indictment in 2:11 that "they did evil in the eyes of the LORD" was also used several times in Deuteronomy (4:25; 9:18; 17:2–3; 31:29), often in warnings of future apostasy. The use of this phrase in Judges 2:11 connects back to Deuteronomy, providing a link from those warnings to the disastrous chapters ahead in Judges where the statement "they did evil in the eyes of the LORD" becomes the repetitive summary of Israel's rebellious and offensive actions before God (3:7, 12; 4:1; 6:1; 10:6; 13:1).[6]

The Hebrew construction translated as "in the eyes of" (בְּעֵינֵי, be'ene) is a common expression in the OT and has two primary possible meanings: (1) viewpoint, opinion, assessment; or (2) presence, eyewitness status, in the visual view of.[7] Thus the phrase "Israel did evil in the eyes of the LORD" can mean (1) what they did, in the opinion of God, was evil; or (2) they did evil right there in view of and in the very presence of God. Either meaning makes sense in the context of Judges (and usage in Deuteronomy as well as in 1–2 Kings). Yet with the covenant stress of "I will dwell in your midst" as a background, and in light of numerous other texts that stress the visual, close location of idolatry as a problem, the nuance of their sinning

---

4. Block, *Judges, Ruth*, 58.

5. Lister, *The Presence of God*, 206.

6. Block, *Judges, Ruth*, 123.

7. E. Jenni, "עַיִן," *TLOT* 2:878; A. M. Harman, "עִין," *NIDOTTE* 3:386. Harman notes that the phrase "in the eyes of" can refer to "actions done right in front of people."

right in close proximity and in the "view" of God seems to be the preferable understanding.

The "Spirit of the LORD" in Judges

Although the "Spirit of the LORD" or the "Spirit of God" is fairly rare in the Pentateuch, which focuses more on the intense presence of God in the tabernacle, it occurs numerous times in Judges (and in 1–2 Samuel), usually in association with the call of someone to a leadership position.[8] Daniel Block notes that in general the use of the phrase "Spirit of Yahweh" ("Spirit of the LORD") in the OT strongly implies the divine presence on earth.[9] He also points out that the authors of the OT historical books, in particular, use references to the "Spirit of Yahweh/God" to refer to God's presence in their midst.[10] In the book of Judges, "the Spirit of the LORD" (Yahweh) comes upon and/or empowers the following: Othniel (3:10), Gideon (6:34), Jephthah (11:29), and Samson (13:25; 14:6, 19; 15:14). These stories in the book of Judges continue to illustrate that the Spirit of God is closely associated with power and with the implementation of his will, but they also underscore the inability of people to control or manipulate God's Spirit, which is unpredictable and uncontrollable by people.[11] The empowering of the Spirit publicly validates their call as leaders, but does not change the character of the judges. It only enables and empowers them to carry out God's will, whether or not they concur.[12] Although not as intense or dramatic as the presence of God in the tabernacle or on Mount Sinai, the Spirit of God upon the judges nonetheless reflects God's presence in validating leaders and empowering them to deliver God's people.

Ruth

While the main story line of the book of Ruth is fairly straightforward and easy to follow, the theology conveyed by the book is not immediately obvious, and there is no consensus among OT scholars even in regard to identifying the main theological point of the book. Much of this debate flows out of the difficulty in dating the composition of the book (preexilic or postexilic), the disagreement over identifying the genre of the book, and the interpretive

8. Firth, "The Spirit and Leadership," 268–69.
9. Block, "The View from the Top," 206. See also MacDonald, "The Spirit of YHWH," 98–99.
10. Block, "Empowered by the Spirit of God," 53.
11. MacDonald, "The Spirit of YHWH," 99–100.
12. Firth, "The Spirit and Leadership," 269, 271, 276–77.

challenge deriving from the various canonical locations throughout history in which the book of Ruth appears (after Judges, after Proverbs, elsewhere in the Writings/Megillot, as the introduction to Psalms).[13] Peter Lau and Gregory Goswell, however, propose that the several major theological themes in Ruth that are derived from the various canonical locations do not each necessarily exclude the others (they prefer a postexilic setting for the composition, viewing Ruth in comparison and contrast with Ezra-Nehemiah).[14] We maintain that studying Ruth from within a biblical theology context of the entire canon (with intertextual allusions and connections to other books) seems to be the preferable approach, rather than tying the theological meaning of Ruth narrowly and specifically to one tight time period and situation (such as a postexilic rebuttal of the foreign marriage prohibitions in Ezra-Nehemiah).[15] We will assume the canonical location of Ruth in the Christian canon, where Ruth serves as a bridge between the chaos and tragedy of Judges and the coming of David.

The Consequences for Leaving the Land and the Presence of God

In its canonical location following Judges and preceding 1–2 Samuel, the book of Ruth is embedded within the Deuteronomistic flow of theological history. Thus in light of the stark and serious covenant disobedience described in the latter chapters of Judges, it does not seem unexpected that a Deuteronomistic warning/curse such as famine (Deut. 28:15–24) would occur (Ruth 1:1). Furthermore, as we discussed in regard to Deuteronomy, the presence of God in the midst of Israel in the land and the blessed life that can be enjoyed by Israel in the land are tightly interconnected. That is, the message of Deuteronomy declared that life in the land would be wonderfully blessed for the people of Israel because God was dwelling among them. Thus the Israelites were not to leave the land! Indeed, leaving the land (and thus being removed from the powerful blessings of the presence of God) was one of the curses warned about in Deuteronomy. So in Ruth 1:1–5, when the family of Elimelek leaves the land, it comes as no surprise—and in keeping with the promises and warnings of the covenant in Deuteronomy—that all the men in the family die and Naomi the widow faces starvation.[16] Naomi correctly assesses the situation: "The Lord's hand has turned against me" (1:13).

13. See the range of views discussed in Lau and Goswell, *Unceasing Kindness*, 159–65; Hawk, *Ruth*, 17–43.

14. Lau and Goswell, *Unceasing Kindness*, 157–65.

15. McKeown states that Ruth could have multiple purposes rather than only one, concluding "that the date of Ruth is uncertain but, thankfully, this does not affect its theological significance" (McKeown, *Ruth*, 4).

16. Lau and Goswell, *Unceasing Kindness*, 74–82; Block, *Judges, Ruth*, 609.

The Presence of God and Finding Blessing Back in the Land

In Ruth 1:6 the narrator explains that Naomi hears word that the LORD (Yahweh) has come to the aid (פָּקַד, *paqad*)[17] of his people. It is significant to note that the book of Ruth consistently uses the covenant name Yahweh,[18] and in this first usage (1:6) the covenantal, relational aspect is further stressed by the addition of the term "his people."[19] After Naomi hears that there is food back in the land of Judah, she (and Ruth) decides to return to the land. Noting the frequent repetition of the term שׁוּב (*shub*, to repent, to turn, to return) throughout this section, Lau and Goswell suggest that Naomi's return to the land is an act of repentance; Naomi is returning to the sphere of God's blessing and to "a right relationship with God and the blessings that follow from that relationship."[20] In essence, the story in the book of Ruth moves from lament to praise.[21]

In keeping with this theme of blessing in the land, Ruth 1:22 notes that Naomi and Ruth arrive in Bethlehem ("the house of bread") right as the barley harvest is starting. Thus it is within the context of harvest (one of the blessings in Deuteronomy that comes from God's presence) that Boaz is introduced as greeting his workers with, "The LORD be with you!" (יְהוָה עִמָּכֶם, *Yahweh 'immakem*), to which they respond, "The LORD bless you!" (יְבָרֶכְךָ יְהוָה, *yebarekka Yahweh*) (2:4).[22] This is an interesting exchange of greetings. A few commentaries assume that this is just a normal greeting that simply means "Hello!" However, as a simple greeting this phrase is not attested anywhere else in the OT.[23] The regular greeting would be "Shalom!" James McKeown points out that if these greetings simply meant "Hello!" it is doubtful the narrator would even have mentioned them.[24] Likewise, Katharine

17. Although the verb פָּקַד has a wide range of meaning, when used with God as the subject and with the object marker אֶת (*'et*) as in this verse, it refers to God's favor, conveying the idea of beneficial, personal attention. See W. Schottroff, "פקד," *TLOT* 2:1024–25; T. F. Williams, "פקד," *NIDOTTE* 3:661.

18. Hubbard, *The Book of Ruth*, 67. The name *Shaddai* ("the Almighty") is also used twice (1:20, 21).

19. Lau and Goswell note that while the characters mention God's name frequently, the narrator mentions God's name only twice, here at the beginning (1:6) and again at the very end (4:13: "The LORD enabled her to conceive"), and that these two statements about the LORD (Yahweh) function as bookends for the story (Lau and Goswell, *Unceasing Kindness*, 102).

20. Lau and Goswell, *Unceasing Kindness*, 81–82, 103–4, 161–62. For a discussion of שׁוּב as a term for "repentance," see Boda, *"Return to Me,"* 24–28.

21. Lau and Goswell, *Unceasing Kindness*, 64–65.

22. Hubbard notes the chiastic structure of the two greetings (יְבָרֶכְךָ יְהוָה / יְהוָה עִמָּכֶם) and posits that the chiasm "affirmed the presence of Yahweh in this scene" (Hubbard, *The Book of Ruth*, 144).

23. Morris, *Ruth*, 271.

24. McKeown, *Ruth*, 41.

Sakenfeld observes, "In this instance, however, the greeting is incorporated into a narrative that is shot through with occasions in which characters invoke divine blessing upon one another (1:8; 2:12; 2:19, 20; 3:10; 4:11). In such a setting, Boaz's greeting should be read with its full theological meaning."[25] Similar phrases do appear in other places, but not as simple greetings. Thus in Joshua 1:17, for example, as Joshua takes over from Moses and prepares for the conquest, the people say, "May the LORD your God be with you!" (יְהִיֶ יְהוָה אֱלֹהֶיךָ עִמָּךְ, *yihyeh Yahweh 'eloheka 'immak*). Perhaps even more relevant is Judges 6:12, when the angel says to Gideon, "The LORD is with you" (יְהוָה עִמָּךְ, *Yahweh 'immekah*).[26]

Likewise, the response of the workers in Ruth 2:4, "The LORD bless you!" (יְבָרֶכְךָ יְהוָה), is remarkably identical to the opening line in the "priestly blessing" of Numbers 6:24, "The LORD bless you!" (יְבָרֶכְךָ יְהוָה), which we discussed in the previous chapter. Coming out of a Deuteronomistic context, a bountiful harvest in the land is directly connected to the blessings provided by God's presence dwelling among his people, and it stands in stark contrast to the suffering situation that Naomi was in while in Moab.[27] Naomi, along with Ruth, has returned to the land of God's presence, and it is here that she (and Ruth) will find blessing.

Indeed, soon after the greeting/affirmation of God's presence and blessing in Ruth 2:4, Boaz will call on God to bless Ruth for seeking the refuge and protection of God's presence. In 2:12 Boaz declares to Ruth, "May you be richly rewarded by the LORD, the God of Israel, under whose wings you have come to take refuge." Boaz, himself the recipient of the blessings of God's presence (2:4), now confers a blessing of God upon Ruth. The use of the Hebrew term כָּנָף (*kanap*, wing) in this context connotes "the image of a bird tenderly protecting its young."[28] Boaz's statement in Ruth 2:12 is very similar to Psalm 91:4, "Under his wings you will find refuge," a verse clearly picturing the care of a bird (91:4a reads, "He will cover you with his feathers").

25. Sakenfeld, *Ruth*, 40–41.

26. Hubbard, noting that the context for both Ruth 2 and Judg. 6 is that of a harvest, wonders if perhaps this greeting was a special "harvest" greeting (Hubbard, *The Book of Ruth*, 144).

27. Hawk concludes, "The declarations of Yahweh's presence and blessing among the people of Bethlehem stand in counterpoint to Naomi's earlier declaration that Yahweh has afflicted her and brought her back empty (1:21). Yahweh is with his people and blesses them" (Hawk, *Ruth*, 78–79).

28. Younger, *Judges, Ruth*, 445. Some scholars propose that the reference to wings refers to the cherubim in the tabernacle/temple, to God as a winged warrior, or to other winged deities. Here in Ruth, however, with no mention of tabernacle of temple, it seems more likely that the reference is to mother birds. Note also that the Hebrew term translated as "wings" (כָּנָף, *kanap*) can also refer to the wing-like appearance of a robe, and it is used in that sense in Ruth 3:9. Thus the usage here in 2:12 sets up the wordplay in 3:9.

Also, as discussed below in regard to Psalms, the term translated as "refuge" pulls together concepts of trust in God with the assurance of God's powerful protective presence.

At the end of the book, now that Naomi and Ruth are safely back in the land enjoying the blessings of the presence of God, the narrator reveals how Ruth (and Naomi) connects to the big picture of theological history: the son produced by Ruth and Boaz is the grandfather of David, the king who will restore the ark and true worship in the presence of God, and the king with whom God will make an everlasting covenant promise.

1–2 Samuel

Through the lives of Samuel, Saul, and David, 1–2 Samuel describes the transition from the time of the judges to the monarchy. The presence of God plays a central role in the life of each and, indeed, drives the story forward.

Samuel and the Presence of God in the Tabernacle

The setting for the opening events of 1–2 Samuel is at the tabernacle, now located at Shiloh. As described in Exodus and Leviticus, the presence of God is now dwelling in the tabernacle, and the language used to describe that reality in 1 Samuel 1–3 is very similar to that used in Exodus and Leviticus.

The presence of God in the tabernacle plays a critical role in the story that introduces Samuel. Thus in 1 Samuel 2:17–18, the sin of Eli's sons "before the LORD" in 2:17 is contrasted with Samuel's ministering "before the LORD" in 2:18 by the repetition of the identical Hebrew phrase: אֶת־פְּנֵי יְהוָה ('et-pene Yahweh). Then the story of Samuel's call in 1 Samuel 3 takes place right in the tabernacle, in very close proximity to the most holy place. The boy Samuel "was lying down in the house of the LORD, where the ark of God was" (3:3). This indicates that Samuel most likely was lying down in the holy place of the tabernacle, just in front of the most holy place. His job probably was to keep the menorah lamp filled with oil and burning continuously throughout the night (cf. Exod. 27:20–21).[29] The intense and powerful presence of God is closely associated with the ark, so the mention of the ark of God here is a reminder that God dwelt right in the most holy place, preparing the reader for the upcoming conversations that Samuel will have with God. Indeed, God calls to Samuel twice, and each time Samuel thinks it is Eli (who probably was sleeping in a tent just outside of the tabernacle). On the third time, however, "The LORD came and stood there [וַיָּבֹא יְהוָה

---

29. Firth, 1 & 2 Samuel, 76.

וַיִּתְיַצַּב, *wayyabo' Yahweh wayyityatsab*], calling as at the other times" (3:10). The word translated as "came" implies movement, and the word translated as "stood there" connotes "to stand firmly." Before he calls Samuel the third time, God apparently comes and positions himself between Samuel and the entrance of the tabernacle. The episode concludes by declaring, "The LORD was with Samuel. . . . The LORD continued to appear at Shiloh, and there he revealed himself to Samuel through his word. And Samuel's word came to all Israel" (3:19–4:1).

The Spirit of God Comes upon God's Chosen King

In 1 Samuel 10 the Spirit of God comes upon Saul. As in the book of Judges, this coming of the Spirit of God is a public validation of God's selected leader. The Spirit of God also empowers Saul, guiding him to a dramatic victory over the Ammonites (1 Sam. 11). Saul, however, disobeys Samuel and God repeatedly. Thus God eventually removes his Spirit from Saul and puts it on David instead (16:13–14). Yet the Spirit of God in David's life is different from how the Spirit is given to Saul and to the judges. Not only is the coming of the Spirit upon David never associated with mighty acts of salvation or valor, but also in 16:13 the text declares that as Samuel anointed David, "the Spirit of the LORD came powerfully on David from that day forward" (CSB). The phrase "from that day forward" implies that the Spirit of God stayed with David throughout his life, and was not removed as it was from Saul.[30] Then several times over the next few chapters it is said of David that "the LORD is with him" (16:18; 18:12, 14, 28). God's presence in David's life protects him and prospers him during times of serious personal crisis.[31]

David and the Bread of the Presence

Throughout the chapters of 1 Samuel describing the early days of David, the fact that God (or the Spirit of God) was with him is mentioned repeatedly, both by the narrator and by characters in the story (16:13; 17:37, 45; 18:12, 28). Thus there is a very interesting dynamic underlying the story in 21:1–9 as David comes to the priests at Nob and eats some of the "bread of the Presence," apparently from the "table of Presence," located in the holy place of the tabernacle (Exod. 25:23–30; Lev. 24:5–9). First Samuel 21:6 stresses the presence of God by describing the bread as the "bread of the Presence" (לֶחֶם

---

30. Block, "Empowered by the Spirit of God," 52; Firth, *1 & 2 Samuel*, 184. Firth also notes in regard to David that "a key aspect of the Spirit's role was to point to Yahweh's presence" (Firth, "The Spirit and Leadership," 279).

31. Bergen, *1, 2 Samuel*, 180–81.

הַפָּנִים, *lehem happanim*) that had been removed "from before the LORD" (מִלִּפְנֵי יְהוָה, *millipne Yahweh*). It is also important not to miss the meaning of the "bread of the Presence" in the tabernacle and its implied connotations in the life of David. Michael Hundley notes that the action of placing the bread on this table in the holy place highlighted the presence of God.[32] The table in the holy place that held the "bread of the Presence" symbolized the fellowshipping and sustaining aspects of God's very presence (Exod. 25:23–30; Lev. 24:5–9). In 1 Samuel 21 David is forced to flee for his life. He is separated even from his good friend Jonathan. Although he seems to have men with him, the narrator keeps them well in the background. Thus when he visits the priests at Nob, "alone" and looking for nourishment, the invitation to eat of the "bread of the Presence," which has come from the very presence of God, is suggestive of connotations of fellowshipping with God and finding strength and protection in his presence.

The Presence of God and the Ark Narratives

Often in the OT the relational presence of God is focused upon, or centered upon, the ark of the covenant. R. E. Clements writes, "The ark is intimately bound up with the presence of God. Where the ark is, Yahweh is."[33] In 1–2 Samuel there are three important narratives that focus on the ark of the covenant (1 Sam. 4:1–7:17; 2 Sam. 6:1–23; 15:24–29), along with an additional reference to the ark made by Uriah in 2 Samuel 11:11. The fact that there are three ark narratives and that these accounts occupy a tremendous amount of narrative space in 1–2 Samuel underscores the extremely important role that the ark, and the associated presence of God, plays in 1–2 Samuel.[34] Indeed, as Patrick Miller and J. J. M. Roberts note in their analysis of the first episode, to label these chapters as the "Ark Narratives" is to miss the point, for the "subject of the narrative is *Yahweh*, not the ark. The issue is not what happens to the ark, but what Yahweh is doing among his people."[35]

In the first episode (1 Sam. 4:1–7:17), without consulting God, the Israelites bring the ark from Shiloh to the battlefield. The narrator reminds the readers of the presence of God associated with the ark by referring to it as "the ark of the covenant of the LORD Almighty, who is enthroned between the cherubim"

---

32. Hundley, *Keeping Heaven on Earth*, 103. See also Longman, *Immanuel in Our Place*, 59.

33. Clements, *God and Temple*, 29. See also Rendtorff, *The Canonical Hebrew Bible*, 523; A. Campbell, *2 Samuel*, 69; G. Anderson, "Theology of the Tabernacle," 165.

34. Gitay posits that "the story of the Books of Samuel revolves around the ark" (Gitay, "Poetics of the Samuel Narrative," 225).

35. P. Miller and Roberts, *The Hand of the Lord*, 79.

(4:4). Presumably, the Israelites remember how the ark had empowered Joshua in his victories, and they assume that they can manipulate God to give them a similar victory once again. Nonetheless, the Philistines defeat them, capture the ark, and carry it out of Israel and back to Philistia as a captured prize (5:1–2). A theological crisis now exists for Israel. First of all, it appears that the Philistines and their gods are more powerful than Israel and their God. Second, at the heart of God's covenant with Israel was the promise that he would dwell among them in their midst. Now, however, he has been carried off, out of the promised land.[36]

God, however, has not been defeated, and in colorful style he "executes" the Philistine god Dagon (5:3–5) and then by himself invades and "conquers" the Philistines, moving city by city, accepting the surrender of each city like a conquering king (5:6–12).[37] Finally the Philistines pay a tribute to him in gold, and he returns to Israel triumphantly (6:1–21).

The point of the narrative is that the powerful presence of God cannot be manipulated or controlled by people in any way. God's presence brings wonderful blessings of peace and prosperity on Israel, but only on his terms. The power of his presence cannot be used inappropriately, nor can it be controlled by anyone in Israel.

The second ark episode is in 2 Samuel 6. David decides to bring the ark, the symbol of God's actual presence among his people, to his new capital in Jerusalem and to establish it there as the center of Israel's worship. At the beginning of the story the theological significance of the ark is stated clearly once again as a reminder: the LORD Almighty sits enthroned "between the cherubim on the ark" (6:2). David's motives may be good, but his method of moving the ark violates God's strict guidelines about how to do so, defined in Numbers 4 (it must be moved by Kohathite Levites, using poles; cf. 1 Chron. 15:11–15). David, along with Ahio and Uzzah, places the ark on a cart, following the pattern used by the Philistines back in 1 Samuel 6:7. When the oxen stumble, Uzzah reaches out and touches the ark, violating God's strict guidelines regarding its holiness, and God strikes him dead. After a three-month delay David then tries again, and this time he moves the ark successfully

---

36. The departure of God from the land is stressed in the episode about Eli's daughter-in-law (4:19–22). Twice she states, "The Glory has departed from Israel" (4:21–22). The term "glory" clearly refers to the presence of God associated with the ark.

37. The "hand of Yahweh" is a central theme in this passage, pointing to a close and personal judgment. It underscores how powerful and dangerous the presence of God is, and how he can easily act alone to defeat his enemies. See Brueggemann, *First and Second Samuel*, 28–33. P. Miller and Roberts conclude, "While the visible symbol of Yahweh's power and presence here is the ark, the invisible manifestation of that same power and presence is *the hand of Yahweh*" (P. Miller and Roberts, *The Hand of the Lord*, 86).

because he follows God's guidelines for handling it.[38] Now as he brings the ark and the presence of God into Jerusalem, David, wearing the linen ephod that normally designated one as a priest, dances before the presence of God (לִפְנֵי יְהוָה, *lipne Yahweh*, before the LORD) in joy and in worship. The phrase "before the LORD" is stressed, occurring five times in this episode (6:14, 16, 17, 21 [twice]). The point of the story is that the presence of God associated with the ark brings blessing upon David, leading him to worship God in joy, but that even David must treat God according to God's guidelines that flow out of his holiness. The message to Israel is that God desires to dwell among them, but he expects them to respect and revere his holiness and worship him and approach him according to his stipulations. Walther Eichrodt writes, "Thus the Ark as the locus of God's presence is not only an object of fear in face of the devastating divine holiness, but also of joy in the divine power and in the promise of his being near at hand to aid."[39]

The last two references to the ark in 2 Samuel (11:11; 15:24–26) are related in subtle irony. In 2 Samuel 11 we see David, the hero of most of 1–2 Samuel, at his sinful worst. In 11:11, as David tries to cover up his rape of Bathsheba by encouraging Uriah to go home for the night and sleep with the now pregnant Bathsheba, Uriah notes that "the ark and Israel and Judah are staying in tents" (i.e., at the siege of Rabbah). This casual reference implies that David has sent the ark, along with the accompanying presence of God, to the battle at the city of Rabbah, while he himself stayed behind in Jerusalem. Thus David was, so to speak, voluntarily (and perhaps disobediently) away from the presence of God. It is perhaps significant to note that it is at this time in David's life that he falls into the most serious sin of his life, one that will have long-lasting negative consequences.

In 2 Samuel 15, but a few short chapters later, as the disastrous consequences of David's sin cause his kingdom to unravel, he is forced to flee Jerusalem. In 15:24–26 Zadok the priest carries the ark out of Jerusalem, prepared to bring the ark with David in his retreat from Jerusalem. David, however, tells Zadok, "Take the ark of God back into the city. If I find favor in the LORD's eyes, he will bring me back and let me see it and his dwelling place again" (15:25). So one of the severe consequences of David's sin against Uriah and Bathsheba is that he is forced to leave the presence of God and the blessings that such close fellowship and presence brought. In contrast to the joy and celebration with which David entered into Jerusalem in 2 Samuel 6

---

38. Firth writes, "This time, the ark was carried on its poles. David thus shifted from a Philistine model of moving the ark to one consistent with Torah, though this is stressed more in 1 Chr. 15:1–15" (Firth, *1 & 2 Samuel*, 377).

39. Eichrodt, *Theology of the Old Testament*, 2:270.

as he accompanied the ark into the city, now David weeps as he flees the city without the powerful and protecting presence of God in the ark (15:30), hoping and praying that one day he will be able once again to rejoice and worship in God's presence. Thus for David the high and low points of his career as king are paralleled by his relationship with the presence of God associated with the ark of the covenant. At the high point of his reign he joyfully and worshipfully brings the ark of God to Jerusalem, soon to be followed by God's covenant promise to him of an eternal dynasty. At the low point of his reign, crippled by guilt from his rape of Bathsheba and murder of her husband, he is now separated from the ark and the presence of God. Yet, unlike Saul, and according to God's covenant promise of 2 Samuel 7:14–15, the repentant David has not been permanently rejected as king, and, as the story plays out, he will be restored to his throne in Jerusalem, although things never quite return to the status of the pre-Bathsheba days.

1–2 Kings

First and Second Kings opens with the death of David and the transfer of the crown to his son Solomon. After consolidating power, Solomon builds a beautiful temple for God, who in dramatic and spectacular fashion moves in to dwell in the temple just as he had dwelt in the tabernacle. Yet God makes it clear from the beginning that his ongoing powerful and holy presence in the temple is contingent upon the covenant obedience of the king and the people. Unfortunately, starting with Solomon, many of the kings, as well as the people, turn away from God and worship idols and other gods. Therefore, first God banishes the Northern Kingdom, Israel, from the land and then later likewise banishes the Southern Kingdom, Judah, from the land, sending them into exile. The book of 2 Kings ends with the Babylonian destruction and plunder of the temple and the banishment of Judah from God's presence (2 Kings 24–25).

The Temple, the Dwelling Place of God

In 1 Kings 5–8 Solomon builds a magnificent temple for God. The temple has the same basic layout and contains the same basic furnishings as were in the tabernacle; only everything in Solomon's temple is bigger. Like the tabernacle, the symbolism in the temple's furnishings and décor suggests a connection to the garden of Eden (cherubim, botanical motifs engraved on the walls and doors, etc.).[40] Like the tabernacle, the increasing value in

---

40. Hurowitz, "YHWH's Exalted House," 87. Merrill notes that these decorative motifs were "reminiscent of the paradisiacal setting of the first holy space, the garden in Eden, where

the gradation of materials (bronze to silver to gold) as one moved from the courtyard to the holy place to the most holy place pointed to the focus on God's presence in the most holy place. Likewise, the table of the "bread of the Presence" highlighted one of the blessings brought by the relational presence of God dwelling right there in the temple. Walter Brueggemann observes, "What interests us beyond the artistry, however, is the theology of Real Presence that is attached to the artistic work. The temple of Solomon did indeed mediate the Real Presence of Yahweh in quite palpable form."[41]

After completing the temple, Solomon has priests and Levites move the ark of the Lord's covenant into the most holy place of the temple (1 Kings 8:1–9).[42] The narrator declares that immediately the presence of God came to fill the temple: "When the priests withdrew from the Holy Place, the cloud filled the temple of the LORD. And the priests could not perform their service because of the cloud, for the glory of the LORD filled his temple" (8:10–11). The reference to the "cloud" and the "glory of the LORD" makes an explicit connection back to Exodus 40:34, which uses the same terminology for the presence of God. Just as the powerful presence of God, as revealed at Mount Sinai, came to dwell in the tabernacle, now the same powerful presence of God comes to dwell in the temple.[43] God has taken up residence in the temple.[44] This intense presence of God dwelling in the temple, right in the midst of the people, underscores the continuation of the covenant promises God made at Sinai ("I will be your God; you will be my people; I will dwell in your midst").

Indeed, as indicated throughout Psalms (as well as in the preexilic prophets), for the next several hundred years the presence of God will be closely associated with the temple, and the worship of God will be directed to his presence in the temple.

---

the Lord had first made his presence known and where he had provided access to those created as his image to enjoy fellowship with him" (Merrill, *Everlasting Dominion*, 433).

41. Brueggemann, *Theology of the Old Testament*, 671.

42. In 2 Sam. 6:12–22, as David brings the ark of the Lord to Jerusalem, he is frequently said to either dance or make sacrifices "before the LORD," stressing his close proximity and his relationship with God. In 1 Kings 8–9, however, Solomon is never said to be "before the LORD," raising perhaps a question about the intimacy of his relationship with God.

43. Brueggemann, *Solomon*, 93; Kamp, "The Conceptualization of God's Dwelling Place," 431–32.

44. Merrill, *Everlasting Dominion*, 443. Leithart underscores the importance of this event, calling it "an event of world-historical importance." He explains, "Yahweh, the creator of heaven and earth, settles in Jerusalem. . . . The temple is the place of Yahweh's enthronement, again pointing to the human temple at the center of the Father's kingdom" (Leithart, *1 & 2 Kings*, 70–71).

Solomon's Relationship with the Presence of God

As discussed above, in 1 Kings 8:10–11 God comes in dramatic fashion to fill the temple. In 1 Kings 8:12–13 Solomon affirms that significant event. In 1 Kings 8:22–53, however, when Solomon dedicates the temple by praying to God, he repeatedly directs his prayer to God in heaven, sometimes adding that heaven is where God does indeed dwell. This is extremely ironic, even strange, in light of the fact that the narrator just stated quite clearly that God's presence has come into the temple to dwell (8:10–11), a point reaffirmed by Solomon himself in 8:12–13.

Within OT scholarship there is no consensus in regard to explaining this anomaly. Complicating the problem are issues of assumed composition (influence of the final redactor), along with conclusions regarding the overall assessment of Solomon being expressed by the narrator. That is, should Solomon be viewed as a model of true worship, one who is informing the audience regarding truth about God and how to worship God? Or is Solomon to be viewed as one who "did evil in the eyes of the LORD" (11:6), even worshiping other gods, and thus whose statements about his relationship with God and his worship of God must be taken with a grain of salt?

Some interpreters view Solomon's statements about God dwelling up in heaven as part of the Deuteronomistic shift to "name theology," a supposed corrective over the earlier concept of divine presence in the temple espoused by the "priestly writer."[45] As we discussed above in relation to Deuteronomy, the evidence such as the frequent use of the phrase "before the LORD" throughout Deuteronomy makes this theory unlikely in Deuteronomy. Thus it is unlikely here as well.

A related view observes the exilic/postexilic context implied by the ending of 1–2 Kings (destruction of Jerusalem and the temple, followed by exile) and posits that Solomon's prayer is directed at readers in the exile, since for them God is no longer in the temple. If so, then this text would be encouraging the exiles by reassuring them that God still reigns up in heaven and still hears their prayers, even though they are in exile outside the land. This view suffers from the fact that throughout the prayer Solomon regularly assumes that the temple *is* still present and operational. That is, he doesn't just say to pray up to God in heaven; rather, he says to pray toward the temple in Jerusalem and that God up in heaven will hear (1 Kings 8:29–30, 31–32, 33–34, 38–39,

---

45. A related view is that this text is comprised of numerous very complex redactional layers and that the redactors did not always smooth out the tensions with earlier forms of the text. For example, Römer sees five different identifiable redactions from five different time periods for this chapter (Römer, "Redaction Criticism," 63–76).

42–43, 48–49). Note also that 1 Kings 8:8 mentions that the poles from the ark of the covenant can be seen "to this day," which mitigates against placing the entire narrative point of view strictly into an exilic or postexilic situation. On the other hand, it is possible that while Solomon's statements imply the existence of the temple as he speaks, the narrator may be citing Solomon's words in a more prophetic sense, with the exiles as the implied audience.

A third view understands the prayer of Solomon as continuing the tension frequently observed in the OT between the immanence and transcendence of God. The OT often holds the transcendence of God (he dwells in heaven and is absolutely sovereign over all the earth) and the immanence of God (he personally dwells in the tabernacle or temple so that he can relate to people) in tension, affirming both at the same time. Likewise, to the ancient readers, it may have been possible to conceive of God residing in both locations at the same time. That is, God was personally present in both throne rooms, the heavenly and the earthly, at the same time. Relatedly, some scholars argue that the earthly throne room was an extension of the heavenly (i.e., the earthly ark of the covenant was the footstool of the heavenly throne). Clements explains that God's presence in his earthly dwelling place in the temple did not preclude that he also dwelt in the heavens, but rather presupposed it. Like the tabernacle, "Yahweh's house in Jerusalem was intended to be a copy, or symbol, of the cosmic 'house' where he had his abode."[46]

While this understanding of the relationship between God's heavenly abode and his earthly abode is correct, it does not entirely remove the tension or conflict in this specific text. The point of God's earthly abode is to enhance God's relationship with his people. If the presence of God comes to the temple specifically to relate to his people and to allow them to worship him there, why does Solomon immediately turn away from it and address God up in the heavens? With the fiery and dangerous God who appeared on Mount Sinai and then dwelt in the tabernacle now clearly present in the temple but a few yards away from Solomon, who is standing nearby in the courtyard, a presence of God so intense that the priests cannot continue their work in the temple (8:10–11), why does Solomon lift his hands toward heaven (8:22) and address God up in heaven? With the promise of "I will dwell in your midst" at the heart of the covenant, and with the dramatic coming of God into the holy of holies ("The glory of the LORD filled the temple") still powerfully fresh as a critical component of that covenant relationship, why does Solomon say, "Will God really dwell on earth?" (8:27)? Solomon then repeatedly stresses that God actually dwells up in heaven. There is nothing like this in Exodus,

46. Clements, *God and Temple*, 65–68.

and the word "heaven" doesn't even occur in Leviticus. Worship and relationship to God in Leviticus is always "before the LORD" and always directed to the presence of God in the most holy place of the tabernacle. In Exodus the powerful and relational presence of God dwelling right in the tabernacle is the affirmation and seal of the covenant relationship. Furthermore, Moses never turns away from the intense presence of God in the tabernacle (or in the burning bush or at Mount Sinai) to lift his hands toward heaven to pray to God in heaven.

Another option for understanding Solomon's prayer in 1 Kings 8 starts with placing the prayer into the full narrative context of the Solomon narratives. In recent years more and more scholars have been noting that the narrator of 1 Kings 1–11 is often criticizing Solomon instead of praising him, even when the text on the surface seems to be praising him. They note that numerous negative features of Solomon's character and actions are presented throughout the narrative[47] and observe that, from the narrator's point of view, Solomon is the one who starts Israel down the path of idolatry that leads to the disastrous ending of 2 Kings. At the heart of this view is the observation that Solomon is seriously violating the prohibitions for the king in Deuteronomy 17:14–17 (where the king is forbidden to accumulate large quantities of horses, silver and gold, and wives).[48]

Likewise, the final verdict on Solomon comes in 1 Kings 11:6: "Solomon did evil in the eyes of the LORD." Underscoring the unthinkably blasphemous idolatry of Solomon, 11:7–8 states that he builds numerous pagan worship sites nearby, east of the temple (probably right across the Kidron Valley, on the Mount of Olives, in clear view of the temple, which has doors that open to the east).[49]

---

47. Jeon concludes that this is perhaps the majority view, acknowledging several variations within the view (Jeon, "The Retroactive Re-evaluation Technique," 20). Jeon lists the following sources that espouse the "negative assessment" view: Provan, *1 and 2 Kings*; Walsh, "The Characterization of Solomon"; Bimson, "1 and 2 Kings"; Eslinger, *Into the Hands of the Living God*, 123–82; Wiseman, *1 and 2 Kings*, 82; Gray, *I & II Kings*, 114; Nelson, *First and Second Kings*, 30; Brueggemann, *The Land*, 85–86; Gunn and Fewell, *Narrative in the Hebrew Bible*, 169; Olley, "Pharaoh's Daughter, Solomon's Palace, and the Temple," 368; J. D. Hays, "Has the Narrator Come to Praise Solomon or to Bury Him?"

48. J. D. Hays, "Has the Narrator Come to Praise Solomon or to Bury Him?," 169. Generally agreeing with this conclusion, yet with some qualifications, is Seibert, *Subversive Scribes and the Solomonic Narrative*, 38–40.

49. Note the continuing wordplay on the "eyes" of God. In 8:29 Solomon prays, "May your eyes be open toward this temple night and day," and in 9:3 God declares, "I have consecrated this temple. . . . My eyes and my heart will always be there." Then in 11:6 the narrator proclaims, "Solomon did evil in the eyes of the LORD," the "evil" described clearly in the verses that follow: Solomon builds worship sites for pagan gods just to the east of Jerusalem.

So if the final verdict on Solomon in 1 Kings 11 is negative because his heart is turned away from God, then perhaps we should take the words of Solomon in 1 Kings 8 with caution, as the words of a theologically questionable character in the story who is not walking closely with God.[50] If Solomon is building high places for the gods Chemosh and Molek nearby (or making plans for such), and likewise worshiping Ashtoreth and other gods nearby (11:4–8), he may be more comfortable with Yahweh, the God of Israel, dwelling up in the heavens and not dwelling right there within view of the king's pagan worship sites. Or perhaps Solomon's stress on God being up in heaven rather than in the temple simply reflected his lack of an intimate relationship with God. The point of God's presence on earth was to facilitate relationship with his people. Interestingly, other than one brief mention in 8:28 and the brief references in 8:62–66 at the end of the dedication ceremonies (and the parallel passage in 2 Chron. 7:4), Solomon is never said to have served, worshiped, or prayed "before the LORD"—that is, in God's close presence, as Moses, the priests and Levites in Leviticus, and David did with regularity.

In conclusion, it is not entirely clear how best to resolve the tension between the narrator's description of the "cloud" and the "glory" of God coming to fill the temple in dramatic fashion as in the tabernacle (1 Kings 8:10–11) and Solomon's repeated statements in 8:22–53 that downplay God's real powerful and glorious presence in the temple and instead locate God's presence up in the heavens. While it is plausible to view this as another instance of tension between God's immanence and transcendence, the evidence seems stronger that Solomon, in his less than stellar obedience and worship of God, is intentionally shifting his focus away from God's immanent and monotheistically demanding relational presence in the temple and trying to place God at a more comfortable distance (for Solomon with his numerous pagan worship sites nearby) up in the heavens. The consequences of this royal shift away from God's relational presence and toward pagan worship will be played out tragically throughout the rest of 1–2 Kings, ending with the destruction of the temple and the exile.

Hezekiah, Josiah, and the Presence of God

In contrast to Solomon, those later kings throughout the rest of 1–2 Kings who do have a close relationship with God are said to approach and address

---

50. In discussing the prayer of Solomon in 1 Kings 8:22–53, Japhet comments that "nowhere is God's presence in the Temple mentioned!" She continues by noting, "Not explicitly, but rather by means of omission, the prayer succeeds in distancing the divine presence from the Temple" (Japhet, *The Ideology of the Book of Chronicles*, 53).

God in the temple (using the phrase לִפְנֵי יְהוָה, *lipne Yahweh*, before the LORD). For example, in 2 Kings 19:14 Hezekiah took the threatening Assyrian letter and "went up to the temple of the LORD and spread it out before the LORD [לִפְנֵי יְהוָה]"—that is, before the presence of God. Likewise, Hezekiah addresses God as "LORD, the God of Israel, enthroned between the cherubim" (19:15), a clear and direct reference to the presence of God dwelling in the most holy place of the temple. Similarly, "before the LORD" is used of Josiah, another king who has a good relationship with God and who relates to God dwelling in the temple, not to God up in the heavens (2 Kings 22:19; 23:2–3).[51]

The Banishment of Israel and Judah from the Presence of God

Before Solomon even finishes the temple, God warns him that the divine indwelling presence is contingent upon faithful obedience (1 Kings 6:11–13). Then in 9:6–7 God warns, "If you or your descendants turn away from me . . . and go off to serve other gods and worship them, then I will cut off Israel from the land I have given them and will reject this temple."[52] Of course, in light of 1 Kings 11:1–8, where Solomon not only worships foreign gods but even builds worship centers for them, the warnings of God are ominous. Indeed, in contrast to the spectacular description of the temple construction in 1 Kings 5–8, the rest of 1–2 Kings records the dismantling of that same temple (1 Kings 14:26; 2 Kings 16:17; 18:16; 24:13; 25:9, 13–17).[53]

In 2 Kings 13:23, however, the text states that because of God's compassion and his concern for his covenant with Abraham, Isaac, and Jacob, that in spite of Israel's sin, God has been unwilling to destroy them "or banish them from his presence [וְלֹא־הִשְׁלִיכָם מֵעַל־פָּנָיו, *welo'-hishlikam me'al panayw*]." This verse underscores once again the close connection between God's relational covenant promises and his presence.

---

51. In this context of comparing Josiah and Solomon, it is interesting to note that part of Josiah's reform was specifically to remove the high places that Solomon had built for Ashtoreth, Chemosh, and Molek on the Hill of Corruption (i.e., the Mount of Olives, just across the Kidron Valley from the temple) (2 Kings 23:13).

52. In 9:7 the Hebrew phrase translated by NIV (also CSB) as "I will reject this temple" (אֲשַׁלַּח מֵעַל פָּנַי, *'eshallah me'al panay*) is unusual. Literally, the verse states, "I will send away [שָׁלַח, *shalah*] from my presence this house which I have sanctified for my name." The ESV, NRSV, and NASB translate the phrase as "cast out of my sight." The Hebrew term שָׁלַח normally carries an idea of "sending away" (which makes sense when used of the Israelites going into exile, as in 2 Kings 13:23; 24:20), but it can also refer to ending a relationship or sending away as a divorce. Perhaps that is the implication here. God's presence has made the temple holy, but he will end that relationship, separate it from his presence, and allow it to be destroyed. Burnett quips, "The Babylonian destruction makes Jerusalem and its temple the center of divine absence instead of divine presence" (Burnett, *Where is God?*, 177).

53. Nelson, *First and Second Kings*, 47.

Yet their sin continues. God's patience with them runs out, and three times in 2 Kings 17 the narrator mentions that God removed the Israelites (the Northern Kingdom) "from his presence" (17:18, 20, 23). God and the narrator use similar terminology later regarding the removal of the Southern Kingdom, Judah (2 Kings 23:26–27; 24:3). Then in the climactic statement of 2 Kings 24:20, the narrator summarizes the consequences for Judah using similar language: "And in the end he thrust them from his presence." So in 2 Kings the exile is regularly described in terms of being banished ("sent away") from the presence of God.

1–2 Chronicles

First and Second Chronicles covers much of the same historical period that 1–2 Samuel and 1–2 Kings cover, but the focus and emphasis of 1–2 Chronicles are slightly different. In the Deuteronomistic History running from Joshua to 2 Kings, the narrator is demonstrating that even though God graciously established his covenant and came to dwell in the midst of his people in order to bless them and relate to them, Israel and Judah both rejected him and failed to keep the covenant and to worship God alone. Thus they were banished or driven away from the land and from God's presence. The narrator of 1–2 Chronicles assumes that its readers know this material. Written in the postexilic period, however, 1–2 Chronicles emphasizes not hindsight, seeking to explain the why of the exile, but foresight, looking forward.

There are several important themes in 1–2 Chronicles, but three of the most central and interrelated themes are driven by the presence of God: (1) the temple (mentioned over 175 times in 1–2 Chronicles), including God's presence associated with the ark of the covenant and the relational worship that should take place there; (2) the Davidic dynasty, especially in relation to the temple and to God's covenant promises (the covenant promises and the concept of kingship are closely interconnected with God's presence);[54] and (3) retribution, the warning of banishment from God's presence if the people do not repent and turn back to faithfully worship God.

---

54. Tuell points out, "What *does* interest the Chronicler is the temple and its worship. David as the founder of the temple's liturgy, and Solomon, as the temple's builder, are therefore of primary importance. Later kings are praised or blamed for their actions regarding the temple: hence, the special attention given to Hezekiah (2 Chr. 29–32) and Josiah (2 Chr. 34–35). The Davidic kings are important for their roles in establishing and preserving the temple, but it is the temple and its liturgy that primarily concern the Chronicler" (Tuell, *First and Second Chronicles*, 5). Selman notes that in Chronicles there are two central blessings stressed that flow out of the covenant relationship Israel had with God: Israel's presence in the promised land and God's presence with his people (Selman, *1 Chronicles*, 57–58).

David and the Presence of God

David dominates much of the narrative in 1 Chronicles. In 1 Chronicles 11 the Chronicler moves the story to Jerusalem and describes David's capture of the city (vv. 4–9). The point of capturing Jerusalem is not so much that it will be the capital for David's reign but that it will be the location of the temple and the dwelling place of God.[55] At the conclusion of this account, and summarizing the basic cause for David's success, the Chronicler states, "And David became more and more powerful, because the LORD Almighty was with him" (1 Chron. 11:9). The terminology used for this empowering presence of God connects David back to Moses and Joshua, where similar terminology was used: "As I was with Moses, so I will be with you [Joshua]" (Josh. 1:5).

Then later in the story, as God gives the explanation to the prophet Nathan regarding the Davidic promises, God revisits his relationship with David by remembering, "I have been with you wherever you have gone" (1 Chron. 17:7–8). After Nathan reports this word from God to David, the king immediately went in and "sat before the LORD [לִפְנֵי יְהוָה, *lipne Yahweh*]" (17:16) and prayed. David is depicted as constantly being in the presence of God.

The Ark of the Covenant and the Presence of God

The ark of the covenant plays a critical role in the Chronicler's account of David and Solomon. The majority of the forty-six references to the ark in 1–2 Chronicles occur either in the story of David's transfer of the ark to Jerusalem (1 Chron. 13–16) or in the story of Solomon's placement of the ark in the completed temple (2 Chron. 5–6).[56] The significance of the ark in both stories is that it represents the very presence of God.[57] In 1 Chronicles 13:6 the narrator makes the presence of God quite clear: "David and all Israel went . . . to bring up from there the ark of God the LORD, who is enthroned between the cherubim—the ark that is called by the Name." Then in 13:8 David and the people are described as making music and celebrating "before God" (לִפְנֵי הָאֱלֹהִם, *lipne ha'elohim*). In fact, it is the holy presence of God associated with the ark that made the manner of moving it so important. Even King David has to honor and respect the holiness of the presence of God and move the ark exactly as God prescribed.[58]

---

55. Selman, *1 Chronicles*, 48.
56. Begg, "The Ark in Chronicles," 134.
57. Japhet, *The Ideology of the Book of Chronicles*, 59.
58. Tuell, *First and Second Chronicles*, 59.

The transfer of the ark (and thus the presence of God) to Jerusalem is precisely what gives significance to the city,[59] interconnecting the themes of blessing through God's presence,[60] the establishment of the Davidic dynasty by God's power, and the worshiping relationship that David and the Israelites will have with God (1 Chron. 16).

Likewise, after Solomon completes the construction of the temple, it is the formal, ceremonial relocation of the ark into the most holy place of the temple (2 Chron. 5:2–14) that is the climax of the entire temple narrative, underscored by the cloud and the glory of God coming to fill the temple. Ralph Klein notes that the ark clearly "signifies Yahweh's presence with his people in the temple."[61]

David, Solomon, and Worship in the Temple

Closely interconnected to the ark of the covenant is the narrative of David's planning for the future temple and Solomon's construction of the temple. Indeed, one of the central criteria that the Chronicler uses in assessing the kings of Judah is how they interact with the temple.[62] Thus one of David's important contributions in Chronicles is his planning for the construction of the temple (1 Chron. 22; 28–29). Likewise, Solomon's major contribution is the actual construction of the temple (2 Chron. 2–5).

The presence of God is closely connected to his desire for a relationship with his people. That is, God dwells among his people so that he can relate to them. A critically important component of that relationship is worship. Interestingly, as important as the construction of the temple is, the Chronicler is even more interested in the *worship* of God that was to take place in the temple. Sara Japhet writes, "Chronicles is concerned primarily with the form Temple ritual took, with its organization and implementation, and not with the structure that housed the worship."[63] Thus David's major contribution, according to Chronicles, is his organization and implementation of worship designed for God's presence in the temple. Numerous texts throughout 1–2 Chronicles describe the way in which worship was to be conducted (1 Chron. 9:29–32; 23:28–32; 2 Chron. 5:12–13; 7:5–6; 8:12–13; 13:10–11;

---

59. Klein notes, "Just as Jerusalem was the home for the Davidic king, David made sure that Yahweh's dwelling place would be there as well" (Klein, *1 Chronicles*, 330).

60. Note that the household of Obed-Edom the Gittite is blessed throughout the three months during which the ark resides with them (1 Chron. 13:12–14), underscoring the blessing relationship with the presence of God in the ark.

61. Klein, *2 Chronicles*, 80.

62. Cudworth, *War in Chronicles*, 3–4.

63. Japhet, *The Ideology of the Book of Chronicles*, 177.

23:18). Likewise, a large amount of 1–2 Chronicles is dedicated to the identity and the hierarchy of those Levites and priests leading in worship (1 Chron. 23–26; 2 Chron. 8:14–15).[64] Throughout the texts describing the worship of God are frequent references to his presence, either there with the ark or in the temple.[65]

Within the broader context of worship, the Chronicler is particularly interested in music, especially choral music.[66] John Kleinig makes a compelling argument that one of the central features of this choral music performed near the ark or in the temple precincts was its close association with the presence of God.[67] He concludes, "By proclaiming the LORD's name, the singers evoked the LORD's glory, hidden in a cloud in the temple, and revealed his veiled presence verbally to his people there in their song of praise. They led the people in responding with awe, gratitude and jubilation to the LORD's acceptance of them and their sacrifice to him."[68]

Furthermore, the Chronicler also frequently stresses the joy of the worshipers at the conclusion of the major religious celebrations that he describes.[69] Texts that mention the joy of the worshipers include 1 Chronicles 15:16, 25; 16:10, 27, 33; 29:9, 17, 22; 2 Chronicles 7:10; 15:15; 20:27; 23:18; 29:36; 30:21–26. Clearly, the Chronicler is interested not only in stressing the presence of God in the temple but also in underscoring the relational implications of that presence. As in Exodus and Leviticus, the joyful worship of God is inextricably interconnected with his presence in the midst of his people and the wonderful blessings that his presence brings to them.

The Presence of God Comes to Reside in the Temple

After Solomon completes the construction of the temple, as the climactic event he places the ark of the covenant in the most holy place of the temple (2 Chron. 5:2–10). At this point God's presence manifests itself in the temple in a dramatic way that was visible both to the priests and to the people. That

---

64. Japhet, *The Ideology of the Book of Chronicles*, 175.

65. Hill comments that in Chronicles "the call to worship is an invitation, a summoning of the assembly of the faithful into God's presence" (Hill, *1 & 2 Chronicles*, 40–41). On the important role of the priests in Chronicles, Lynch concludes, "Through sacrificial acts before Yhwh, hymnic praise at the ark and in battle, the priests bear witness to Yhwh's presence and power over Israel's enemies" (Lynch, *Monotheism and Institutions in the Book of Chronicles*, 207).

66. Kleinig notes the following texts that relate to liturgical music in Chronicles: 1 Chron. 6:31–47; 9:14–16, 33; 15:1–16, 43; 23:2–5, 24–32; 25:1–31; 2 Chron. 5:11–14; 7:1–6; 8:12–15; 20:18–30; 23:12–13, 18; 29:25–30; 30:21–22; 31:2; 34:12–13; 35:15 (Kleinig, *The Lord's Song*, 14).

67. Kleinig makes this point throughout *The Lord's Song* (e.g., 133, 144–47, 157, 187).

68. Kleinig, *The Lord's Song*, 190.

69. Williamson, *1 and 2 Chronicles*, 31; see also Dirksen, *1 Chronicles*, 20–21.

is, God comes to dwell in the newly built temple. The Chronicler mentions this twice (2 Chron. 5:13–14; 7:1–3) in an inclusio that preludes and concludes the long prayer of Solomon in 2 Chronicles 6.[70] The description clearly alludes back to similar events in Exodus, when the presence of God came down first on Mount Sinai and then again came to dwell in the tabernacle (cf. 2 Chron. 5:13b–14 and 7:1–3 with Exod. 19:17–18 and 40:34–38).[71] Japhet writes, "The experience at Sinai is unparalleled in its physical and psychological immediacy and its impact on the entire people. It is this experience that the Chronicler superimposes on the dedication of Solomon's temple. From his point of view, God's presence in the Temple is very real, and all the people of Israel are eye-witnesses to YHWH's entry into His house."[72] Then immediately after God's presence comes to fill the temple (2 Chron. 7:1–3), the Chronicler notes in 7:4 that the king and all the people offered sacrifices "before the LORD" (לִפְנֵי יְהוָה, lipne Yahweh), again stressing the presence of God in the temple.[73] The temple now contains God's presence in the midst of his people.

70. This prayer of Solomon is analyzed above as part of the discussion on 1 Kings 8. The two prayers are similar, and the issues are similar in both. With God's powerful presence recently descended into the most holy place, Solomon repeatedly addresses God up in the heavens. Here in Chronicles, however, there are two important differences. First, as noted above, the dramatic descent of God's powerful presence into the temple serves as an inclusio, being stressed both before and after the prayer of Solomon. Second, in the Chronicles account Solomon wraps up his prayer to God up in the heavens by saying, "Now arise, LORD God, and come to your resting place, you and the ark of your might" (2 Chron. 6:41), perhaps implying that Solomon ends his prayer by calling on God to enter into the most holy place, where the ark is, a call that is indeed answered by God in 2 Chron. 7:1–3. So in Chronicles Solomon doesn't seem to leave God up in heaven as firmly as he does in 1 Kings. Also, in general, the Chronicles account of Solomon is more positive in its assessment of Solomon and does not stress his idolatry as 1 Kings does. Thus the narrative presentation of Solomon's prayer does not carry the ominous shadow of idolatry that the account in 1 Kings seems to reflect. On the other hand, Jeon maintains that Solomon's disobedience of Deut. 17 is still clearly evident in 2 Chron. 8, and he concludes that the Chronicler is arguing that God will honor and fulfill his covenant promise to David through Solomon in spite of Solomon's faults and disobedience of Deut. 17 (Jeon, *Impeccable Solomon?*, 220–21). In regard to Solomon's prayer (in both 1 Kings 8 and 2 Chron. 6), Japhet posits that Solomon is indeed downplaying God's presence in the temple, a shortcoming that the Chronicler addresses with Jehoshaphat's prayer in 2 Chron. 20, where the presence of God in the temple is stressed (see below) (Japhet, *The Ideology of the Book of Chronicles*, 54–55). Likewise, as mentioned above, it is also possible that the Chronicler, like the narrator of 1–2 Kings, is indicating that God does reside both in heaven and on earth at the same time. Neither place can contain him. Yet for relationship with his people, God comes down into the temple to reside among his people.

71. Japhet, *The Ideology of the Book of Chronicles*, 58–59.

72. Japhet, *The Ideology of the Book of Chronicles*, 59.

73. Selman underscores the important connection between the temple and God's presence, noting that the temple as the place of God's name is identical in meaning to "the place where God himself was to be found" and "is closely associated with the temple as an expression of God's presence among his people" (Selman, "Jerusalem in Chronicles," 49–50).

The Kings of Judah, the Temple, and the Presence of God

In 2 Chronicles the kings of Judah who follow Solomon are evaluated by the way they honor and respect the temple and the worship of God in the temple.[74] Closely interrelated with this are constant references to the presence of God. That is, those kings who are evaluated positively (Asa, Jehoshaphat, Jotham, and Hezekiah) all relate positively to the presence of God.[75]

Thus the Spirit of God speaks to Asa through the prophet Azariah, telling him, "The LORD is with you when you are with him" (2 Chron. 15:2). The rest of the chapter stresses the importance of "seeking the LORD," a concept common in Chronicles,[76] sometimes a broad concept of piety and faithfulness to God, but more often a reference to worshiping God in the temple.[77]

The account of Jehoshaphat is filled with references about God being with him or of him being "before the LORD" (2 Chron. 17:3; 20:9, 13, 17, 18). In 20:5–12 Jehoshaphat offers up a prayer to God that starts off similarly to the prayer of Solomon back in 2 Chronicles 6, asking, "Are you not the God who is in heaven?" (20:6). Yet Jehoshaphat quickly shifts the focus back to God's presence in the temple, declaring, "They . . . have built in it a sanctuary for your Name, saying, 'If calamity comes upon us, we will stand in your presence before this temple that bears your Name and cry out to you'" (20:8–9). Japhet argues that this is an important intentional contrast to the prayer of Solomon: "To stand before the house is to stand before God. Here we find the element missing from the body of Solomon's prayer: YHWH's presence in the Temple. . . . The Temple does not function as a channel through which prayers pass upward to heaven, where they are heard by God; rather, prayers are said in the Temple because God hears them *in the Temple*."[78] While in the Jehoshaphat narrative God's residing presence for prayer and worship is clearly seen to be in the temple, as Jehoshaphat and his army go out to battle,

---

74. Throughout 2 Chronicles this often involves the way in which each king either repaired the temple, reestablished proper temple worship, or removed pagan idols (Asa, 15:18; Jehoshaphat, 17:3–6; Jotham, 27:3; Hezekiah, 29:3–36).

75. Likewise and in contrast, those kings who are disobedient and unfaithful are described as being in a negative relationship with the temple (e.g., 2 Chron. 24:18, "they abandoned the temple of the LORD"; 2 Chron. 26:21, "King Uzziah . . . [was] banned from the temple of the LORD"; 2 Chron. 28:24, "Ahaz . . . shut the doors of the LORD's temple").

76. Williamson, *1 and 2 Chronicles*, 95.

77. Tuell writes, "Seeking the Lord is a persistent theme in Chronicles, and refers specifically to worship before the temple" (Tuell, *First and Second Chronicles*, 169).

78. Japhet, *The Ideology of the Book of Chronicles*, 54–55. Japhet also underscores that the Chronicler makes "no real distinction between building a house for God and building a house for His name" (p. 55). She concludes that God's real presence in the temple is seen through his glory, his name, and his ark (pp. 54–59).

God's presence goes with them to ensure their victory (2 Chron. 20:17, 21).[79]
Then, after the victory, they return to the temple to rejoice, worship, and
praise God (2 Chron. 20:27–28).

In the brief positive account of Jotham, the Chronicler notes that "Jotham
grew powerful because he walked steadfastly before the LORD [לְפָנֵי יְהוָה,
lipne Yahweh] his God" (2 Chron. 27:6). Likewise, the success of Hezekiah
is clearly associated with the presence of God. Hezekiah "opened the doors
of the temple of the LORD and repaired them" (29:3). He reestablishes proper
worship led by the Levites and priests, reminding them, "The LORD has chosen you to stand before him and serve him, to minister before him and to
burn incense" (29:11). He also tries to bring the northern tribes back to a
relationship with God, inviting them to worship God faithfully in the temple.
Hezekiah exhorts the northern tribes, "Return to the LORD. . . . Come to
his sanctuary. . . . He will not turn his face from you if you return to him"
(30:6–9). Likewise, the positive assessment of Hezekiah in 31:20–21 underscores his faithful obedience and temple worship in God's presence: "This is
what Hezekiah did throughout Judah, doing what was good and right and
faithful before the LORD [לְפָנֵי יְהוָה, *lipne Yahweh*] his God."

The Exile as the Loss of God's Presence

One of the central themes in Chronicles is that of divine retribution, the
warning and then the implementation of banishment from God's relational
presence as a result of disobedience and sin.[80] The exile is depicted in terms
of being removed from God's presence. Interconnected with this theme of
the banishment of people from God's presence is the recurrent theme of the
dismantling and destruction of the temple, God's residence and the focal
location of his presence. For example, shortly after Solomon dedicates the
temple, God warns, "If you turn away and . . . go off to serve other gods . . . ;
then I will uproot Israel from my land, which I have given them, and will reject
this temple I have consecrated for my Name. . . . This temple will become
a heap of rubble" (2 Chron. 7:19–21). As noted above in our discussion of

---

79. Lynch notes that in 2 Chron. 20:21 the Levitical singers are appointed to "praise him
for the splendor of his holiness as they went out at the head of the army." He suggests that
the unusual phrase translated as "splendor of his holiness" (cf. Ps. 29:2, 9) is a reference to a
theophany of God; that just as the ark represented the presence of God at the head of the army
in the conquest of Joshua, now the Levitical singers signal God's special presence at the head
of the army as well (Lynch, *Monotheism and Institutions in the Book of Chronicles*, 174–79).
See also Kleinig, *The Lord's Song*, 177.

80. Chronicles also calls for repentance and a restoration of relationship. Boda observes that
in Chronicles repentance "is relational, typified by the key word 'seek (God's face)'" (Boda,
"Return to Me," 143).

1 Kings 9:7, the similar Hebrew phrase here in 2 Chronicles 7:20, translated by the NIV as "I will reject this temple" (אֲשַׁלַּח מֵעַל פָּנָי, *'eshallaḥ me'al panay*), is a reference to banishment away from God's presence. Translated more literally it would read, "I will send away from my presence this house that I have sanctified for my name."

The Davidic Covenant, the Temple, and Hope for the Future

As noted above, 1–2 Chronicles is written in the postexilic era and reflects a forward-looking orientation.[81] Two of the central themes of the book, God's promise to David regarding a royal dynasty and God's presence in the temple, along with the associated proper worship of God, form the basis for the hope emerging from 1–2 Chronicles.[82] That is, the Davidic covenant and the temple are vital to God's provision for the future restoration.[83] Note also that the promises regarding the Davidic covenant and the promises regarding the future temple are closely interrelated with each other and likewise interconnected with the presence of God. Recall that in the Davidic covenant God promised not only that a royal descendant of David would rule but also that a descendant would build the "house of God" (i.e., the temple), a place where God will dwell.[84]

The final verses of 1–2 Chronicles interconnect all of these themes. Throughout the final chapter of 2 Chronicles the temple and its demise are mentioned repeatedly (36:7, 10, 14, 15, 17, 18, 19). In addition, the prophet Jeremiah is mentioned several times (35:25; 36:12, 21, 22). Then the closing two verses declare:

> In the first year of Cyrus king of Persia, in order to fulfill the word of the LORD spoken by Jeremiah, the LORD moved the heart of Cyrus king of Persia to make a proclamation throughout his realm and also to put it in writing: "This is what Cyrus king of Persia says: 'The LORD, the God of heaven, has given me all the kingdoms of the earth and he has appointed me to build a temple [lit. 'house']

81. Kelly, *Retribution and Eschatology in Chronicles*, 236–41. Kelly stresses the central role that the Davidic covenant plays in the Chronicler's positive hope for the future (pp. 156–67). Furthermore, he notes the interconnection between the Davidic covenant and the temple, concluding, "The temple also testifies to the covenant, and the two 'houses' of the theocracy are shown to be mutually related" (p. 185).

82. Tiño, *King and Temple in Chronicles*, 150–51.

83. Selman, *1 Chronicles*, 62; Waltke with Yu, *Old Testament Theology*, 761.

84. Also noting the interconnection in Chronicles between the temple as the place of God's presence, the dual meaning of "house" as both temple and dynasty, and the strongly implied promise of a coming Davidic ruler even as the rebuilt temple is mentioned at the end of Chronicles is Dempster, *Dominion and Dynasty*, 226–27.

for him at Jerusalem in Judah. Any of his people among you may go up, and may the LORD their God be with them.'" (2 Chron. 36:22–23)

This ending to 1–2 Chronicles (and also to the Hebrew canon) is quite intriguing. Since David and the Davidic covenant are not explicitly mentioned, some assume that those promises are not part of the Chronicler's closing message.[85] On the other hand, Scott Hahn argues convincingly that the repeated reference to Jeremiah in earlier verses (35:25; 36:12, 21), along with the statement in 36:22 "in order to fulfill the word of the LORD spoken by Jeremiah," strongly implies that texts and prophecies beyond just the seventy-year prophecy of Jeremiah must be in mind. Hahn proposes that in light of the central role that the Davidic covenant plays throughout Chronicles, the allusion here to fulfilling Jeremiah's prophecies probably includes the many prophecies in Jeremiah about the future Davidic king (especially Jer. 23:3–6; 33:14–16).[86]

Whether or not the promises to David are clearly in view, the closing in Chronicles is hopeful, and the restoration of the temple is clearly in view. That is, the future hope of the Chronicler centers on rebuilding the temple. Martin Selman underscores that throughout 1–2 Chronicles the temple is the place where God resides and where his presence is known. Likewise, the temple and the presence of God are tightly interconnected with the fulfillment of God's promises and prophecies.[87]

Finally, note that the final verse in 2 Chronicles contains all three aspects of the familiar tripartite covenant formula ("I will be your God; you will be my people; I will dwell in your midst"), which we have seen throughout the OT: "Any of *his people* ["You will be my people"] among you may go up, and may the LORD *their God* ["I will be your God"] *be with them* ["I will dwell in your midst"]" (36:23). So Chronicles ends with a reminder of God's covenant promises, a call to restore the temple in Jerusalem (the place for God's presence), and a proclamation of God's relational presence with his people.

Ezra-Nehemiah

There is a wide consensus that the books of Ezra and Nehemiah were originally combined into one book and should be studied together. Ezra-Nehemiah tells the story of the exiles who returned to Jerusalem during the

---

85. See, for example, Braun, *1 Chronicles*, xxvii.
86. Hahn, *The Kingdom of God as Liturgical Empire*, 187–89.
87. Selman, "Jerusalem in Chronicles," 49–51.

Persian era and how they struggled to rebuild the temple, the city of Jerusalem, and the community. The reconstruction of the temple (Ezra 1–6) is an important theme, and it serves as a fitting introduction to the remaining part of the book: establishing the community (Ezra 7–10), rebuilding the walls of Jerusalem (Neh. 1–7), and the dedication of the walls (Neh. 8–10).[88]

Back in the Land, but . . .

In Ezra-Nehemiah the hand of God and his sovereign actions working through various Persian monarchs underscore that God is watching over his people even in exile and helping them to overcome obstacles and to return to the land. On the other hand, the resulting situation described in Ezra-Nehemiah seems to be a far cry from the glorious return and restoration under a Davidic king that was prophesied in the prophets and implied in the Davidic covenant of 2 Samuel 7. Indeed, the text of Ezra-Nehemiah (as in Haggai and Zechariah) repeatedly stresses that Persian monarchs, not Davidic kings, rule over Judah.[89] Douglas Nykolaishen notes the "strangeness" of Israel being back in the land with a temple but still under Persian rule. He comments that the point, especially of Ezra 1–6, is that "God will make a way for them to have a faithful relationship with him even under these strange circumstances."[90] So Ezra-Nehemiah is demonstrating that the promised restoration has begun (at God's initiation and empowerment), but that "the promised restoration has not yet fully arrived."[91] There are two critically important things missing in the reestablished community in Jerusalem that highlight the "not yet" situation: (1) there is no Davidic king on the throne (quite to the contrary, Persian kings rule); and (2) God's intense, relational, powerful presence is not in the temple.

God Does Not Return to the Second Temple

Ezra 1:2–3 is practically identical to the final verse in 2 Chronicles (36:23). The following chapters in Ezra 1–6 then describe the return of some of the exiles and the reconstruction and dedication of the temple. While God's sovereign intervention and empowerment behind the scenes are evident, what is glaringly absent from this account is any mention of God's actual return to take up residence in this rebuilt temple as he did earlier in the tabernacle

---

88. Klein, "The Books of Ezra & Nehemiah," 676.
89. Klein, "The Books of Ezra & Nehemiah," 680.
90. Nykolaishen and Schmutzer, *Ezra, Nehemiah, and Esther*, 73–74.
91. Nykolaishen and Schmutzer, *Ezra, Nehemiah, and Esther*, 8. Williamson describes it as a sense of "Now, and not yet" (Williamson, *Ezra, Nehemiah*, liii).

and in the temple. That is, when Moses completes the tabernacle, the coming
of God into that sanctuary is dramatically proclaimed (Exod. 40:34: "Then
the cloud covered the tent of meeting, and the glory of the LORD filled the
tabernacle"). Likewise, when Solomon completes the construction of the
temple, God comes to fill the temple in similar spectacular fashion (1 Kings
8:10–11: "The cloud filled the temple of the LORD. And . . . the glory of the
LORD filled his temple"; see also 2 Chron. 5:13–14; 7:1–2). After the completion of the reconstructed temple in Ezra 6, however, and in stark contrast,
there is no mention at all of the presence of God, either his cloud or his glory,
coming to fill the new temple. Neither is there any reference to the ark of the
covenant, the focal point of God's presence in the earlier sanctuaries. In light
of the repeated strong emphasis seen in earlier texts on how God comes to
fill these sanctuaries with his glorious and holy presence, the silence in Ezra 6
is startling and certainly highlights the contrast. The presence of God does
not return to the postexilic, rebuilt temple of Ezra 6.

Not only is this a glaring absence when Ezra 6 is compared with Exodus
40, 1 Kings 8, and 1 Chronicles 5 and 7,[92] but also the silence concerning any
entrance of God into the sanctuary as part of the temple dedication is quite
noticeable and significant when the account is placed in its ancient Near
Eastern literary context. Victor Hurowitz has analyzed numerous literary
accounts of temple building and dedication ceremonies from other cultures
throughout the ancient Near East as well as in biblical texts, and he has
argued convincingly that all of them follow a remarkably similar literary
pattern, describing similar events in parallel order.[93] The Exodus account
of the tabernacle and the 1 Kings and 2 Chronicles accounts of Solomon's
temple follow this standard pattern as well. When compared with this standard literary pattern of the ancient Near East describing temple building
and dedication, however, the account in Ezra 6 matches the other accounts
in all aspects *except in regard to any mention of the deity coming into the
temple*. Lisbeth Fried comments, "Except for the induction of the god into the
completed temple, all the components of a typical Mesopotamian building
story are present in Ezra 1–6."[94] Hurowitz concludes, "Ezra 6.17–22 reports
the dedication of the rebuilt temple, but contains no reference to the crucial

---

92. Interestingly, but not convincingly, Blenkinsopp maintains that the temple account in
Ezra 1–6 is written as a fulfillment of Ezekiel's temple account in Ezek. 40–48 (Blenkinsopp,
Judaism, 132–33). Curiously, however, even though he discusses the return of God's presence
to take up residence in the temple in Ezek. 44:1–4, he does not discuss (or even mention) that
unlike in Ezekiel, in Ezra-Nehemiah the glory of God never returns to the temple.

93. Hurowitz, *I Have Built You an Exalted House*.

94. Fried, "Temple Building in Ezra 1–6," 338.

event of God's entry into the temple, or to the installation in the temple of any symbol of divine presence."[95]

Not only is the text silent in Ezra 1–6 about any return of God's real presence into the rebuilt temple, but also throughout the rest of Ezra-Nehemiah this absence of God's intense presence in the temple is implied by the terminology used of those worshiping and praying to God. Although in Ezra-Nehemiah there are descriptions of numerous dedications, prayers, and sacrifices that take place in the temple vicinity, nowhere in Ezra-Nehemiah does the phrase "before the LORD" (לִפְנֵי יְהוָה, *lipne Yahweh*) occur.[96] For example, when Ezra confesses the sin of the people, he is in the temple area, but the narrator simply says that he is "before the house of God" (10:1, 6). This would be a very peculiar switch in terminology from earlier usage if God is indeed present in the temple. Yet if God is not present in the temple, as indicated in our discussion above, then this type of terminology is to be expected. Likewise in Nehemiah 8, when Ezra gathers the people to read the Torah of Moses to them, the people are said to be "before the Water Gate," not "before the LORD" (vv. 1, 3). Furthermore, in Nehemiah 10, when the people make a written promise to support the temple, the text repeatedly says that they will bring wood, firstfruits, firstborn, and tithes "to the house of our God" (vv. 34, 35, 36, 38) rather than "before the LORD," as is the norm in Leviticus (e.g., 1:5, 11; 3:1, 7, 12; 4:4, 6, 7, 15, 18; 6:7, 14, 25).

Thus it seems clear that God has not returned to the rebuilt temple to dwell there as he did previously in the tabernacle and in the first temple. The people

95. Hurowitz, *I Have Built You an Exalted House*, 268. Fried makes this same comparison and likewise comments, "What we are completely missing, however, is . . . the element in which the god takes up residence in this temple" (Fried, "The Torah of God as God," 288). Fried goes on to argue from Neh. 12 that the Torah scroll becomes the physical manifestation of the presence of God (p. 298). Relatedly, Becking proposes that the temple vessels which are returned to the temple serve as a "symbolic presence" of God (Becking, "Silent Witness," 267–78). Neither Fried's proposal nor Becking's suggestion is convincing, but both concur that the presence of God is missing in the rebuilt temple, and that such an absence poses a problem. Their two different proposals are attempts to address the problem of God's apparent absence in the rebuilt temple.

96. Although "before the LORD" (לִפְנֵי יְהוָה) is never used by the narrator or by any of the characters in Ezra-Nehemiah, there are three passages that do use "before" (לִפְנֵי) in connection with Elohim (God). Two of these usages occur while Ezra and Nehemiah are still in Babylonia (Ezra 8:21; Neh. 1:4–6). While perhaps indicating that God is still very much "with" the exiles in Babylonia in an "accompanying" presence kind of way (as likewise indicated in Ezek. 1 in the prophet's vision of God while still in Babylonia), these references clearly are not referring to God's return to the rebuilt temple in the intense-presence fashion seen earlier in the tabernacle and in the temple. The third usage is in Ezra's prayer of confession in Ezra 9:15 ("Here we are before you in our guilt"). While this text could be taken as evidence of God's presence in the temple, it is more likely that Ezra is using "before you" in the same sense here as he used "before our God" in Ezra 8:21, while he was still in Babylon.

are back in the land, and the temple has been rebuilt. However, things have not gone back to the way they were before the Babylonian exile. The promised restoration has started, but it is far from being fulfilled. As the historical account of the OT draws to an end, two momentous promises of God remain unfulfilled: the establishment of a Davidic king on the throne and the return of the intense, empowering, relational presence of God dwelling in the midst of his people.

Esther

It is well known that God is not mentioned at all in Esther (neither Elohim nor Yahweh occurs). On the other hand, many scholars note that throughout the book God does seem to be providentially working behind the scenes. The point of Esther seems to be that "God graciously extends his providential protection also to the Jews who refuse to return to the Land."[97] The "hand of God" is at work here (as in Ezra-Nehemiah), even though it is not explicitly mentioned.[98] The watching-over and protecting "I am with you" kind of presence is strongly implied, even for these disobedient Jews who remained in exile, but clearly they do not experience the intense and relational presence of God that was experienced by their ancestors (or promised by the prophets), and the complete absence of any reference to God in the book of Esther is a reminder that they are still in exile, separated from the blessings and protection that the relational presence of God would bring.

Psalms

The book of Psalms deals with Israel's worship and praise of God; thus it should come as no surprise to find the presence of God surfacing as a central theme running throughout the book.[99] Indeed, as was the case for worship in Leviticus, one of the central dynamics of worship in Psalms is the encounter with the presence of God.[100] In his *Old Testament Theology*, Gerhard von

97. Waltke with Yu, *Old Testament Theology*, 549.

98. Schmutzer writes, "Even though no person mentions God—even in expected places like 4:14—God is present and working, rather creatively" (Nykolaishen and Schmutzer, *Ezra, Nehemiah, and Esther*, 206). See also Reddit, "Esther," 145–46.

99. Of the 150 psalms, over 90 of them refer to the presence of God. In their commentary on Psalms, Brueggemann and Bellinger mention the presence of YHWH or "the divine presence" over 100 times (Brueggemann and Bellinger, *Psalms*). Likewise, one of Terrien's longest chapters in his book on the theme of divine presence in the Bible is entitled "The Psalmody of Presence" (Terrien, *The Elusive Presence*, 278–349).

100. Bellinger, *Psalms*, 144. Longman notes that the primary setting for many of the psalms was in the sanctuary, because that was where God was present, particularly for the purpose of

Rad entitles the chapter on the theology in Psalms "Israel before Yahweh."[101] Jerome Creach argues that the whole point of the prayers in Psalms, their hope and the "destiny of the righteous," is to be able to come near (into the presence of) God himself.[102] Likewise, at the heart of the call throughout Psalms to trust in God is the declaration that his divine presence is an assurance for Israel in the face of every threat.[103]

Obviously, the book of Psalms is complex and diverse, and proposed approaches to studying Psalms have likewise been diverse. In recent years numerous scholars have adopted a somewhat "eclectic" approach that combines (or at least recognizes as helpful) aspects of three main approaches to Psalms: (1) form-critical analysis, (2) canonical-development analysis (sometimes called "editorial criticism"), and (3) thematic analysis. That is, many scholars still recognize the importance of Hermann Gunkel's classification of the psalms by form, although sometimes qualifying his rubric slightly by moving toward Claus Westermann's focus on "lament" and "praise" as the two central types of psalm.[104] Without abandoning this form-critical classification, however, numerous scholars have come to the conclusion that the canonical development and organization of the Psalter was quite intentional, a conclusion that has hermeneutical and theological implications.[105] In addition, as scholars study Psalms in the context of form and flow, there is a fairly broad recognition of central themes, such as worship, praise, the reign of God, and refuge, sometimes interwoven throughout the Psalter and sometimes located within one or more of the five books of Psalms.[106]

---

relationship (dialogue). The psalms themselves, he argues, are a kind of literary sanctuary, "an intimate expression of personal dialogue with God" (Longman, "Psalms," 248–49; Longman, "From Weeping to Rejoicing," 224–25).

101. Von Rad, *Old Testament Theology*, 1:355. Kraus concurs with von Rad's title but adds qualification to it. While it is true that Psalms reflects Israel's response to God's actions (creation, deliverance, etc.) and presence, Kraus notes that Israel was never an equal partner in the dialogue, but was always separated by a "chasm" of God's holiness. That is, they experienced and praised the great "steadfast love" (חֶסֶד, *hesed*) of God's presence only with great astonishment (Kraus, *Theology of the Psalms*, 11–12).

102. Creach, *The Destiny of the Righteous*, 42–52.

103. Brueggemann and Bellinger, *Psalms*, 71 (commenting on Ps. 11).

104. Gunkel, *The Psalms*; Westermann, *Praise and Lament in the Psalms*.

105. Particularly influential in this development was G. Wilson, *The Editing of the Hebrew Psalter*.

106. Recent works that summarize the history of Psalms studies and then gravitate toward the inclusion of two or all three of these approaches, especially the form critical and the canonical flow approaches, include Bellinger, *Psalms*, 15–36; Bullock, *Psalms*, 1:1–13; deClaissé-Walford, Jacobson, and Tanner, *The Book of Psalms*, 13–45; McCann, "The Book of Psalms," 643–65; Limburg, *Psalms*, xiv–xvii; Hossfeld and Zenger, *Die Psalmen I*; Hossfeld and Zenger, *Psalms 2*; Hossfeld and Zenger *Psalms 3*; Brueggemann and Bellinger, *Psalms*, 1–8. Bucking the trend and remaining skeptical of the canonical flow approach is Longman, *Psalms*, 34–35. Stressing

The relational presence of God plays a central role across all three of these approaches. That is, as one seeks to develop biblical theology out of Psalms through the "eclectic" approach described above, the relational presence of God emerges as pervasively central to almost every theological aspect that the Psalter addresses. Throughout Psalms, the focused, intense presence of God and his approachability in the temple are indeed foundational to the most critical relational aspects between God and his people, as discussed below.

The Worship of God and the Presence of God in the Temple

Foundational to the worship and praise expressed in Psalms is the under-standing that God himself dwelt in the temple in Jerusalem prior to the de-struction of Jerusalem by the Babylonians. This is the dominant image of the divine presence in Psalms.[107]

Worship in the Psalter is not directed toward some kind of nebulous spirit up in the heavens but rather is focused directly toward God dwelling in the temple. Hans-Joachim Kraus declares, "If we approach the OT Psalms with the question where one should look for and find the God of Israel whom the hymns and songs of thanksgiving glorify, on whom the laments call, and whom all the songs and poems involve, the unanimous, never doubted, and ceaselessly expressed answer is: Yahweh Sebaoth is present in the sanctuary in Jerusalem. Zion is the place of God's presence."[108]

Furthermore, W. H. Bellinger argues that throughout the Psalter worship is a response of God's people specifically to his divine presence and the blessings derived from that presence. Thus the psalms of praise "celebrate the life-giving presence of God."[109] Not only that, but at the heart of worship in Psalms is the encounter between the worshiping community and God's presence. This wor-ship encounter between the community and the presence of God brought about renewal, enabled wholeness in life, and gave instruction for faithful, obedient living.[110] It also demanded a behavior change on the part of the worshipers, because only the righteous could dwell in the holy presence of God (Pss. 15:1–2; 11:7). Related to this is the observation by Creach that coming into the presence of God is often depicted in Psalms as the "reward" for the righteous ones. The wicked perish apart from God, but the righteous live in his presence.[111]

---

and focusing on the canonical flow approach are Robertson, *The Flow of the Psalms*; Snearly, *The Return of the King*.

107. J. Hamilton, "Divine Presence," 116; Kraus, *Psalms 1–59*, 68.

108. Kraus, *Psalms 1–59*, 68.

109. Bellinger, *Psalms*, 108, 144–45.

110. Bellinger, *Psalms*, 89, 108, 144–45.

111. Creach, *The Destiny of the Righteous*, 5, 42–52.

Likewise, the powerful emotions expressed by the psalmists in worship are driven by the encounter with the presence of God. Daniel Estes writes, "From tearful laments to jubilant shouts of praise, the psalms reflect the emotions of Old Testament believers as they approached Yahweh."[112] The psalms of praise reflect the joy experienced due to God's presence.[113] For example, Psalm 16:11 declares, "You make known to me the paths of life; you will fill me with joy in your presence."

The Face of God

As discussed earlier, the Hebrew term *panim* (פָּנִים; plural of the word for "face") is a central term used extensively for the presence of God throughout the OT. In the Psalter various forms of *panim* occur 133 times in 126 verses. In 84 of these verses the reference is to God, usually to Yahweh ("the LORD") but also occasionally to Elohim ("God").[114] Many of these texts are in contexts that reflect God in the temple, and most of these texts are in reference to God's intense personal presence. The sheer number of these texts is an indication of the important role that the presence of God plays in the book of Psalms. Kraus, for example, observes that in Psalms the "face of Yahweh" is a reference to the reality of God's presence in the temple sanctuary. In fact, Kraus underscores that the imagery related to the "face of Yahweh" is *the* characteristic expression for God's presence in Israel's worship.[115]

Numerous other scholars have also noted the relationship between the use of *panim* and God's presence in Psalms. For example, in discussing Psalm 11:7 ("The upright will see his face") Walter Brueggemann and W. H. Bellinger note that this is an offer of "Real Presence," situated in the temple. For those qualified, this face-to-face encounter in the temple provides the gift of life, providing safety (refuge [11:1]) in a world of threat.[116] Ernest Lucas notes that in several places in Psalms (e.g., 24:6; 27:4; 42:1–2) "seeking" or "beholding the face of Yahweh" is an expression referring to God's presence experienced

---

112. Estes, *Handbook on the Wisdom Books and Psalms*, 141. In discussing the theology of Psalms, Estes observes that one of the central emphases is that "Zion is the site of Yahweh's presence as he dwells in the Holy of Holies in the temple," and that the people of Israel "are suffused with a profound sense of living in the presence of Yahweh" (pp. 150–51).

113. Bellinger, *Psalms*, 79.

114. Using MT verse notations, these include 4:7; 9:4, 20; 10:11; 11:7; 13:2; 16:11; 17:2, 15; 18:7; 19:15; 21:7, 10; 22:25, 28, 30; 24:6; 27:8, 9; 30:8; 31:17, 21; 34:17; 38:4; 41:13; 42:3; 44:4, 25; 45:13; 50:3; 51:11, 13; 56:14; 61:8; 62:9; 67:2; 68:2, 3, 4, 5, 9; 69:18; 76:8; 79:11; 80:4, 8, 17, 20; 85:14; 86:9; 88:3, 15; 89:16; 90:8; 95:2, 6; 96:6, 9, 13; 97:3, 5; 98:6, 9; 100:2; 102:1, 3, 11, 29; 104:29; 105:4; 114:7; 116:9; 119:58, 135, 169, 170; 139:7; 140:14; 141:2; 142:3; 143:2, 7; 147:17.

115. Kraus, *Theology of the Psalms*, 39.

116. Brueggemann and Bellinger, *Psalms*, 70–71.

in the worship in the temple.[117] James Hamilton explains that to be in the presence of God is to be before his face.[118]

In recent years several scholars have observed that the "priestly blessing" of Numbers 6:24–26 ("The LORD bless you and keep you; the LORD make his face shine on you") echoes repeatedly throughout Psalms.[119] O. Palmer Robertson suggests that the "priestly blessing" of Numbers 6:24–26 is ritually pronounced at least ten times in Psalms.[120] Jeremy Smoak concludes that in Psalms the motifs of "seeking the face of God" and "seeing the face of God" are references to visiting the temple and receiving blessings from the presence of God there. Likewise, he argues that the expression "May God make his face shine" conveyed the concept of God's presence "radiating" out from the sanctuary to provide protection and deliverance.[121] Similarly, Brueggemann and Bellinger posit that the "face of YHWH" refers to the cultic presence of God in the temple, the source of blessing and life.[122]

Lament and Praise, from Absence to Presence

Although most scholars recognize several form-critical "types" of psalms, there is a general consensus that the two major and most common types are "lament" (or "complaint") and "praise."[123] Likewise, it is commonly noted that within many of the individual lament psalms, the author often moves from lament early in the psalm to end the psalm with praise. Indeed, J. Clinton McCann states that the two are so frequently in juxtaposition to each other that in Psalms they are often theologically inseparable; the lament ends in praise.[124]

The presence of God is critical to understanding this interconnection between lament and praise, for the lament psalms speak of the absence of God while the praise psalms rejoice in the restored presence of God.[125]

117. Lucas, *The Psalms & Wisdom Literature*, 56.

118. J. Hamilton, "Divine Presence," 117.

119. Smoak, *The Priestly Blessing*, 90–110; Robertson, *The Flow of the Psalms*, 43–44; J. Hamilton, "Divine Presence," 117; Satyavani, *Seeing the Face of God*, 229. Chavel even suggests that the three repeated "may the LORD" blessings of Num. 6:22–27 correspond to the three stages of a pilgrimage to worship God in the temple (Chavel, "The Face of God," 18–19).

120. Robertson cites Pss. 4:6; 31:16; 37:6; 67:1; 80:1, 3, 7, 19; 94:1; 104:15; 118:27; 119:135; 139:12 (Robertson, *The Flow of the Psalms*, 43).

121. Smoak, *The Priestly Blessing*, 90–91.

122. Brueggemann and Bellinger, *Psalms*, 70.

123. Westermann, *Praise and Lament in the Psalms*; Bullock, *Psalms*, 1:2; Limburg, *Psalms*, xiv.

124. McCann, "The Book of Psalms," 669.

125. Bellinger, *Psalms*, 146; Burnett, *Where Is God?*, 135–49.

Tightly interconnected to the lament psalms is the concept of "crying out to God in distress." Personal disaster is a central theme in Psalms, often related to a sense of isolation, of being "cut off from family and friends, distant from temple and community, and often far removed from God himself."[126] Yet frequently throughout the Psalter when the psalmist cries out in distress to God (sometimes directed to God in the temple [e.g., 3:4; 18:6]) because of this separation, God responds by delivering the one who cries out and becoming present again. Thus the movement within the lament psalms from lament to praise is a movement from divine absence to divine presence.[127]

Some scholars have also noted that generally many of the lament psalms are located early in the Psalter (most of Book I is lament), while many of the praises are located later in Psalms (especially in Book V). Thus in the final canonical collection they see movement from lament to praise,[128] a movement that can also be described as a movement from divine absence to restored presence.[129]

Refuge in the Presence of God

Jerome Creach has argued that the motifs "Yahweh as refuge" and the "destiny of the righteous" are two of the most central themes in Psalms, with both themes instrumental in the ordering and structuring of the Psalter.[130] The word חָסָה (hasah), which the NIV often translates as "to take refuge," occurs in the Hebrew Bible 58 times (including the noun form), with 37 of these occurrences in Psalms. The basic meaning of the word is "to hide in" or "to hide with," but with strong connotations of "to trust." In the lament psalms this word is often used in a "formula of trust" statement (Pss. 7:1; 11:1; 16:1; 25:20; 31:1; 57:1; 71:1; 141:8).[131] Thus it is closely associated with the word בָּטַח (batah, to trust).[132] In referring to "refuge" the psalmist is speaking of God's protective power that comes with his presence, particularly his powerful presence emanating from the temple on Zion.[133] Creach points

---

126. Johnston, "The Psalms and Distress," 66.

127. Burnett, *Where Is God?*, 137.

128. Limburg, *Psalms*, xvii; G. Wilson, "The Structure of the Psalter," 246. Crutchfield presents a helpful chart that illustrates the shift from Book I (4 psalms of praise, 19 psalms of lament) to Book V (13 psalms of praise, 4 psalms of lament) (Crutchfield, "Psalms," 347–48).

129. Burnett, *Where Is God?*, 149.

130. Creach, *Yahweh as Refuge*; Creach, *The Destiny of the Righteous*.

131. E. Gerstenberger, "חסה," *TLOT* 2:464–65.

132. Creach, *Yahweh as Refuge*, 32.

133. W. Brown states, "Zion is the geographical embodiment of 'refuge'" (W. Brown, *Seeing the Psalms*, 19–26).

out that חָסָה (*hasah*, to take refuge in) relates to virtually every aspect of devotion to God in the Psalter. That is, taking refuge in the presence of God becomes synonymous with trusting in God.[134]

Psalm 18 is particularly instructive. This is a royal thanksgiving psalm attributed to David.[135] After declaring his trust in God as his strength and refuge in verses 1–2, the psalmist tells of the reason for his praise. In verses 4–5, using the typical language of lament, he recalls his close encounter with Sheol, the realm of the dead.[136] He calls out to God, who hears his voice, "from his temple" (v. 6). God then parts the heavens and comes down (v. 9), much as he did at Mount Sinai in the exodus (v. 12). William Brown suggests that "Sheol" and similar conceptual terms (e.g., "the pit") serve as the "symbolic opposite or counter metaphor" of "refuge." That is, "refuge" in the presence of God is closely associated with life, while the antithesis, the absence of God, is associated with death. The language of lament, Brown continues, is often set between pit and refuge, death and deliverance, divine absence and divine presence. As we noted above, once again we see the movement from lament to praise as paralleling the movement from divine absence to divine presence.[137] These images imply not only trust and the concept of standing firm but also relationship between God and the one who prays.[138]

The "wing" metaphor is used in connection with God numerous times in Psalms (17:8; 36:7; 57:1; 61:4; 63:7; 91:4). Some scholars suggest that this term evokes the image of the winged cherubim of the tabernacle or temple. Others point out that winged gods and goddesses show up frequently in the iconography of the ancient Near East, perhaps providing a point of reference for the usage in the OT. Others posit that it may metaphorically picture God as a winged warrior, an imagery also not uncommon in the ancient Near East.[139] In Psalms, however, as in Ruth 2:12, the reference to the wings of God does seem to refer metaphorically to the refuge and protection that birds provide for their young. This is clear in Psalm 91:4: "He will cover you with his feathers, and under his wings you will find refuge."

134. Creach, *Yahweh as Refuge*, 48.
135. This psalm is repeated in 2 Sam. 22.
136. Brueggemann and Bellinger, *Psalms*, 97.
137. W. Brown, *Seeing the Psalms*, 26–27.
138. W. Brown, *Seeing the Psalms*, 19.
139. See discussion by Hawk, *Ruth*, 81–82; Kwakkel, "Under YHWH's Wings." Kwakkel leans toward the "protecting bird gathering her young" view of the metaphor but concedes that the evidence is inconclusive and that two or more other possibilities are plausible, or even a combination of interinfluential background understandings (pp. 162–63).

Remembering the Powerful Presence of God Who Led Israel in the Exodus

There are numerous direct references and allusions to the exodus event in the Psalter. Kraus writes, "Whenever the Psalms speak of Israel's beginnings or of the beginnings of God's coming to Israel, we find the theme of the exodus. The patriarchs . . . are also mentioned . . . , but in Psalms the basic event is always the exodus, the deliverance from Egypt." It was during the exodus that God came to dwell among Israel, transforming Israel into God's sanctuary.[140] Psalm 68, for example, tracks the history of God's presence with Israel, starting with the exodus and culminating with the establishment of his sanctuary in Zion.[141] Likewise, Psalm 77:14–20 recalls the powerful presence of God as he led Israel through the Red Sea as a shepherd leads a flock.[142]

Canonical Ordering, the Location of God's Presence, and Eschatological Hope

Although the image of God dwelling in the temple and ruling from his throne in Zion is the most dominant portrayal of the divine presence in Psalms, the depiction of God enthroned and ruling from the heavens is also frequent. For example, Psalm 2:4 declares, "The One enthroned in heaven laughs," and 11:4 states, "The LORD is on his heavenly throne." Other texts include 14:2; 18:9–10; 20:6; 33:13–14; 53:2; 57:3–5; 68:33–34; 73:25; 80:1, 14; 102:19; 103:19; 113:5; 115:3; 123:1; 144:5; 148:1–2; 150:1.

There are, however, two important considerations to keep in mind in regard to the image of God enthroned and ruling from heaven. First is the historical context. After the Babylonians destroy Jerusalem in 587/586 BC, there is no temple, and consequently no presence of God in the temple. As discussed below, Ezekiel 8–10 describes the departure of the presence of God from the temple just prior to that event. Thus for psalmists describing current reality in the exilic and postexilic times, God's presence is not in the temple but only in the heavens. While there is no consensus regarding the dating of many of the psalms—complicated by the issues of initial composition, canonical

---

140. Kraus, *Theology of the Psalms*, 51–52.

141. Bullock, *Psalms*, 1:512–13. Brueggemann and Bellinger write, "Psalm 68 portrays God as the one who comes to deliver and then is present to bless the community from Zion. . . . The poem celebrates in liturgy this life-giving YHWH, who has taken a remarkable journey from Sinai through the wilderness and on to the throne in Zion" (Brueggemann and Bellinger, *Psalms*, 295, 298).

142. Niehaus discusses numerous allusions to the exodus event in Psalms. This indicates, he concludes, that the "so-called Sinai theology and the so-called Zion theology are closely related" (Niehaus, *God at Sinai*, 283–87).

placement, stitching, editing, and superscription headings—nonetheless several of the psalms listed above addressing God up in the heavens seem to reflect exilic or postexilic situations. The historical setting for many psalms can be multifaceted, because they may have been initially composed in the preexilic era but later edited in the exilic or postexilic time. For example, C. Hassell Bullock suggests that while Psalms 3–41 (most of Book I) were composed and edited in the preexilic era, Book II (Pss. 42–72), Book III (Pss. 73–89), and Book IV (Pss. 90–106) were edited in the exile. Book V (Pss. 107–150), he argues, was edited after the exiles returned.[143]

Thus it is possible, perhaps even probable, that the final editing and arrangement of Psalms 42–150 (Books II, III, IV, V) was done after the temple was destroyed. Within this block of psalms, and in the exilic/postexilic period, some were not only edited but also composed. For example, Psalm 102:19, one of the psalms that depicts God as residing up in the heavens, declares, "The LORD looked down from his sanctuary on high, from heaven he viewed the earth." This psalm is clearly exilic or postexilic, for note the statement in 102:16: "For the LORD will rebuild Zion and appear in his glory."[144] Many of the psalms of Book V (Pss. 107–150) are often dated to the postexilic period. Although dating of the psalms can be speculative and indeterminate, it is instructive to note that of the eight psalms cited above from Books IV and V that depict God as ruling from heaven, seven of them (Pss. 102; 103; 115; 123; 144; 148; 150) are often dated to the exilic or postexilic era.[145] The dating of Psalm 80 (from Book III) is less than clear, with no scholarly consensus, although the repeated plea to God to "restore us" (80:3, 7, 19), along with the cry "return to us" (80:14), may imply an exilic/postexilic setting.[146]

Numerous scholars stress the importance of the fall of Jerusalem and the exile to the canonical ordering and structure of the psalms.[147] The distinction between the two very different historical contexts (preexilic versus exilic/postexilic) is likewise an important distinction to recognize in studying the presence of God. In the preexilic era God dwells in the temple, and normal worship activities as reflected in many of the psalms focus on his presence there. Israel relates to God primarily through his presence in the temple. In the exilic and postexilic time, however, Israel has lost the indwelling presence of God. As in the exilic and postexilic prophetic literature, the psalmists who

143. Bullock, *Psalms*, 1:7–11.

144. Kraus, *Psalms 60–150*, 284, 286; Limburg, *Psalms*, 345.

145. Kraus, *Psalms 60–150*, 284, 290, 378, 437, 542, 562, 570.

146. Tate, *Psalms 51–100*, 313; Bullock, *Encountering the Book of Psalms*, 65.

147. McCann, "The Book of Psalms," 660, citing G. Wilson, *The Editing of the Hebrew Psalter*, 213.

write (and edit) during the exilic/postexilic era move their focus from the temple (which is in ruins) to the heavenly residence and throne room of God, who rules over all the earth as they cry out to God in pain and yet reaffirm their faith in his sovereign control. Zion, the place so closely associated with God's presence in the temple as well as with the king he establishes and rules through, takes on an eschatological orientation.

On the other hand, several of the texts that depict God as residing or ruling from heaven also portray God as residing or ruling from the earthly temple, all in the same psalm.[148] For instance, Psalm 18:9–10 depicts God as coming down from the heavens: "He parted the heavens and came down; dark clouds were under his feet. He mounted the cherubim and flew; he soared on the wings of the wind." Yet this heavenly response came because God heard the psalmist's cry "from his temple" (18:6)—that is, the earthly temple in Jerusalem. Thus the depiction is that God heard the psalmist's cry from his residence in Jerusalem and then responded by coming down from the heavens.

In similar fashion, Psalm 68:33–34 extols God "who rides across the highest heavens" and "whose power is in the heavens," and then declares in the next verse, "You, God, are awesome in your sanctuary" (68:35), a reference to God residing in the temple. So this psalm depicts God as both in the heavens and in the temple. Bullock notes that this psalm presents a condensed history of God's presence with Israel, from the dramatic deliverance from Egypt brought about by his powerful presence to his residence in the sanctuary on Mount Zion in Jerusalem.[149] Similarly, Psalms 11, 14, and 18 appear to present God as being both immanent (present in the temple) and transcendent (present in the heavens) at the same time.[150]

As discussed earlier, there are several interrelated conceptual ways to view these two simultaneous realities. One view is to understand the earthly tabernacle and temple as copies of the heavenly "cosmic" house in which God resides.[151] This seems to be the implication of Exodus 25:9, 40; 26:30.[152] Hebrews 9:23–24

---

148. Robertson, *The Flow of the Psalms*, 58–59. Robertson notes that this concept is presented in the introductory Ps. 2: "Psalm 2 anticipates a significant theme that runs throughout the Psalter by referring to Zion as the Lord's dwelling place, while recognizing that his throne is simultaneously in heaven. Integral to the basic elements of the Davidic covenant as developed in the Psalter is the Lord's residing in the midst of his people. Yet he never relinquishes his sovereign rule from the exalted heights of heaven."

149. Bullock, *Psalms*, 1:512–13.

150. Craigie argues that the combination of immanence and transcendence is the point of Ps. 11:4. Yahweh is very much with the psalmist, present with him in his crisis, but also very much universally transcendent, and thus able to project his power anywhere; thus he has control of the chaos of the psalmist's crisis (Craigie, *Psalms 1–50*, 133).

151. Clements, *God and Temple*, 65.

152. Kraus, *Theology of the Psalms*, 26.

explains that the tabernacle (and by extension, probably the temple as well) was a copy of the heavenly court. Hebrews 8:5 notes that the tabernacle was not only a copy but also a shadow of the heavenly court. A related view is to see "the temple as an earthly manifestation of a heavenly reality."[153] In this view the most holy place of the temple served as an interconnected extension of the heavenly throne room. Sometimes the imagery for this concept portrays the most holy place or the ark of the covenant as the earthly footstool for God's heavenly throne (Pss. 99:5; 132:7; also 1 Chron. 28:2).[154] Many scholars present this image (the throne of God in heaven and the ark of the covenant as his footstool) as the primary way that God was envisioned.[155] Yet note that this image is used only a few times, and the metaphoric imagery of how God's dual presence in the temple and in heaven is to be viewed is fluid, within certain parameters. Thus besides the image of the heavenly throne with earthly footstool, God's throne is also depicted as being the ark of the covenant itself.[156] Thus statements describing God as "enthroned between the cherubim" (Ps. 80:1) could be envisioning him as in the most holy place of the temple, seated between the two cherubim that formed part of the ark or, perhaps, seated above the ark between the two large free-standing cherubim that flanked the ark in the most holy place.

Also note that in one of the "footstool" references (Ps. 132:7), the text is actually stressing the presence of God in the temple, not in the heavens. The verse reads as follows: "Let us go to his dwelling place [לְמִשְׁכְּנוֹתָיו, le-mishkenotayw], let us worship at his footstool [לַהֲדֹם, lahedom]." The term "dwelling place" (מִשְׁכָּן, mishkan) is a clear reference to the temple, where God is dwelling. This is made clear in 132:13–14: "For the LORD has chosen Zion, he has desired it for his habitation [לְמוֹשָׁב, lemoshab]: 'This is my resting place forever; here I will reside [אֵשֵׁב, 'esheb], for I have desired it'" (NRSV). Thus the term "footstool" is referring to the ark of the covenant, and in this text it clearly represents the place of God's presence.[157] The use of the term "footstool" may imply the heavenly throne, but the presence of God in this text is not projected as being in heaven but rather as being there in the most holy place with the ark.

Part of our problem with this issue is that we as modern thinkers tend to view the heavenly throne room as a "place," and, in particular, as a different

---

153. Longman, *Psalms*, 91.

154. Note that in Isaiah's encounter with Yahweh in the temple he reports that "the train of his robe filled the temple" (Isa. 6:1). This would fit with the image of the temple being God's footstool.

155. J. Hamilton, "Divine Presence," 116.

156. Von Rad, *Old Testament Theology*, 1:237.

157. Kraus, *Psalms 60–150*, 480–81.

"place" than the temple. On the other hand, Jon Levenson points out that the heavenly temple is "beyond localization."[158] Likewise, Hans-Joachim Kraus observes that in the temple "the dimensions of space are broken through and transcended."[159] Thus it may be incorrect to view the temple and the heavenly throne room as separate "places."

It is important to keep in mind that the temple on Mount Zion in Jerusalem was viewed as the dwelling place (i.e., the residence) of God. As clearly established in Exodus and in 1 Kings, when God comes to dwell in the tabernacle and then in the temple, this is not mere symbolic imagery but the real, powerful, and awesome presence of God, residing and ruling right in the temple. It is this presence of God that is so important in the relationship between God and his people. That is, God makes himself known to his people, and his presence is a critical part of that revelation.[160] It is this "I will dwell in your midst" presence that is essential to the covenant and that provides such covenant blessings as protection, refuge, sustenance, and even joy.[161] Kraus writes, "The basic experience of the Psalms is that Yahweh speaks in the sanctuary (Pss. 60:6; 108:7)."[162] It is in the presence of God in the temple that the psalmists confess, lament, pray, and rejoice, for this is God dwelling in their midst.

Yet the psalmists never limit God to the earthly temple, especially when they reflect on his sovereign reign over all the earth. They repeatedly affirm that he is not confined to the temple; he is neither regional nor even earthbound.[163] God is the Creator of the world and the King over all the earth and all nations; thus in this sense he rules from the heavens. When the psalmists (and Israel) relate to God through praise, prayers, petitions, or sacrifice, however, they interact with his relational presence in the temple.

The Reign of God, Covenant, Messianic Hope, and the Flow of Psalms

Although there is no consensus among those who seek to track theological movement across the five books of the Psalter, most studies recognize the significance of the reign of God and the reign of his appointed representative, the king, especially as formulated in the Davidic covenant. Thus numerous

158. Levenson, *Sinai and Zion*, 140.
159. Kraus, *Theology of the Psalms*, 76.
160. Kraus, *Theology of the Psalms*, 32.
161. J. Hamilton writes, "The people of Israel enjoy the benefits of Yahweh's presence among them because they are in covenant relationship with him. The corollary is that if the covenant is broken, Yahweh's presence will be withdrawn" (J. Hamilton, "Divine Presence," 118).
162. Kraus, *Theology of the Psalms*, 33.
163. Clements, *God and Temple*, 67.

scholars recognize the importance of Psalm 89 and its placement at the end of Book III (Pss. 73–89), at the seam between Book III and Book IV. It is in Psalm 89 that the psalmist connects the fall and destruction of Jerusalem with (humanly speaking) the apparent end and failure of the Davidic covenant (see especially 89:38–51).[164] Starting with Psalm 90 and reflected in the "The LORD reigns" psalms (Pss. 93–100), Book IV then presents a response to the loss of Jerusalem and the Davidic monarchy.[165] Book IV stresses confidence in the sovereign reign of God over all the nations and is a "theological affirmation of Yahweh's kingship over against the failed Davidic dynasty."[166] In Book V there is a stress on restoration, both of Israel itself and of its worship of God its king.[167] Furthermore, in Book V the restoration is closely interconnected with messianic expectation; the restoration of God's rule will come via his chosen Davidic (messianic) king.[168]

Recall that in 2 Samuel 6 David brings the ark of the covenant, the focal point of God's presence (and reign), to Jerusalem (Zion), and in 2 Samuel 7 God promises the Davidic covenant. Later, Solomon, the son of David, will build the temple in which the presence of God will reside, still associated with the ark. This close association between the Davidic covenant, Zion, and the

164. Bullock, *Psalms*, 1:8–10; McCann, "The Book of Psalms," 659–61; Tate, *Psalms 51–100*, xxv–xxvii; Robertson, *The Flow of the Psalms*, 142–46; Snearly, *The Return of the King*, 99–101.

165. Some scholars see a similar overall purpose to Book III as well. Burnett, for example, suggests that "the Elohistic Psalter [Pss. 42–83] was most likely created with a view to the desired rebuilding and restoration of the Jerusalem temple. . . . As an integral component of the two-part Davidic psalm book resulting in Pss 2–89, a psalm book dominated by laments and culminating in a call for a restoration of the Davidic dynasty (Ps 89), the Elohistic Psalter presents a plea to the divine for the reestablishment of David and Zion" (Burnett, "A Plea for David and Zion," 113).

166. Bullock, *Psalms*, 1:10. Several scholars note that in the context of the collapsed Davidic monarchy, Book IV seeks to ground the reaffirmation of Israel's faith in the premonarchial Mosaic traditions associated with the exodus (Tate, *Psalms 51–100*, xxvii; McCann, "The Book of Psalms," 662; Creach, *The Destiny of the Righteous*, 70–71). Recall that at the heart of those exodus traditions was the powerful and awesome presence (glory) of God, who delivered Israel, came down to dwell in their midst in the tabernacle, and then traveled with them, protecting and sheltering them in the wilderness.

167. While remaining somewhat tentative, Ross explains the thematic flow as follows: "Books I and II lay out the foundation of God's program in the Davidic monarchy, Book III reflects the failure of the monarchy and was shaped with the exile in mind, and Books IV and V present the restoration and the hope for the future with the LORD as king" (Ross, *A Commentary on the Psalms*, 54). For a similar understanding of the five books, see deClaissé-Walford, Jacobson, and Tanner, *The Book of Psalms*, 38.

168. Snearly writes, "Essentially the Psalter teaches that there is a heavenly king who has appointed an earthly vice-regent to establish his kingdom in a world of unruly kings. This program is not abandoned in Psalm 89, as is often assumed; the sorry state of the Davidic line is lamented, but hope in Yahweh's earthly vice-regent has not been forsaken" (Snearly, *The Return of the King*, 4).

presence of God residing with the ark in the temple is reflected repeatedly in Psalms.[169]

In an interesting and compelling synthesis, Robertson argues that the reign of God in Zion and the reign of his anointed one (the Messiah) in Zion unite together eschatologically into one kingdom in Psalms; indeed, he posits, this is critical to the structure of Psalms. Robertson writes, "This all-embracing decree regarding the reign of God and his Anointed One from their united thrones in Zion sets the stage for the full development of the Psalter. . . . Eventually, Messiah's kingship must merge with God's kingship so that the kingdoms of earth and heaven, of time and eternity, are one. This merger of the two kings and the two kingdoms permeates the theology of the Psalter."[170] This is not just a conceptual or spiritual kingdom, Robertson notes, but one still very much grounded in the idea of a "place" that God choses for his name to dwell (connecting back to the exodus), that place being both Zion and the heavenly throne room simultaneously. The dual themes of "dynasty" and "dwelling place," central realities of the Davidic covenant promise yet expanded upon in the Psalter, permeate the psalms and play a central role in the theological development of the Psalter.[171] At the heart of the "dwelling place" theme is the presence of God and/or his anointed Messiah. Thus the messianic hope in the psalms is not just for a restored king and a restored reign but for a restored presence of God. This restored relational presence certainly includes the restored reign, but also restored refuge (safety, security, deliverance, *shalom*) as well as restored worship and joyful relationship.

Related to this is the observation that in the postexilic collections of Books IV–V, after the loss of God's presence in Jerusalem in 587/586 BC, the psalmist does not abandon the focus on God residing among his people in his sanctuary. That is, the psalmist never turns to a spiritualizing concept of only visualizing God as up in the heavens (or in people's hearts), but rather maintains an eschatological outlook with continuing depictions of worshiping and enjoying God's presence in a very "preexilic" style of presence in the temple. For example, coming toward the end of the Psalter, the Psalms of Ascent (Pss. 120–134) stress the presence of God in the temple of Jerusalem (122:9; 125:1–2; 128:5; 132:5–14; 133:3; 134:2–3), often as if in a preexilic context. Then in the Psalter's final psalm (Ps. 150), while reference is made to God's presence both in the heavens and in his earthly sanctuary, the description of

---

169. Murphy, *The Gift of the Psalms*, 54–55; Lucas, *The Psalms & Wisdom Literature*, 55–56; Mays, *Psalms*, 31.
170. Robertson, *The Flow of the Psalms*, 15.
171. Robertson, *The Flow of the Psalms*, 48–49.

how to praise him appears to reflect the earthly cultic context of the temple.[172] Thus the Psalter does seem to look forward to an eschatological time of a new, enhanced presence of God that unites temple presence and royal rule.

The Wisdom Books: Proverbs, Job, Ecclesiastes, and Song of Songs

The wisdom books are not merely guidelines for practical living; they are also theological in nature, complementing the biblical theology of the rest of the OT. While the wisdom books do not focus on the salvation-history story of Israel, they certainly assume it. They add to the biblical theology of presence that we have been studying by explicating a slightly different angle of how people can relate to the presence of God. In a sense, wisdom plays a role as mediator between God and humanity. Wisdom's concern is not just to transmit practical knowledge for living but to assist God's people in building a close relationship with him.[173] Wisdom is both the result of a relationship with God and the means to building upon that relationship.[174]

Proverbs

Wisdom, Relationship, and "the Fear of the LORD"

Proverbs 1:7 declares, "The fear of the LORD is the beginning of knowledge," and Proverbs 9:10 echoes, "The fear of the LORD is the beginning of wisdom." These verses form a thematic inclusio for Proverbs 1–9, and indeed the fear of the LORD as the beginning of wisdom is the motto for the entire book of Proverbs,[175] as well as for biblical wisdom instruction in general.[176] The concept conveyed by "the fear of the LORD" is more than just "respect" or even "awe" and is perhaps best understood as "the sense of standing before the God who created everything, including humans whose very existence

---

172. Brueggemann and Bellinger, *Psalms*, 618–19. They note that the Psalter concludes by summoning the entire worshiping community "to full-throated praise around the presence of God."

173. Von Rad writes, "Still, the most important thing is that wisdom does not turn towards man in the shape of an 'It,' teaching, guidance, salvation or the like, but of a person, a summoning 'I.' So wisdom is truly the form in which Jahweh makes himself present and in which he wishes to be sought by man" (von Rad, *Old Testament Theology*, 1:444).

174. Longman, *The Fear of the Lord Is Wisdom*, 62. Melton writes, "The sages sought wisdom as a means to experience divine presence and favour over against answers or simply to obtain wisdom for wisdom's sake. As a result, at times, God and Wisdom are referred to interchangeably" (Melton, "'O, That I Knew Where I Might Find Him,'" 206).

175. Van Leeuwen, "Proverbs," 173; Ansberry, "Wisdom and Biblical Theology," 185–86.

176. Birch et al., *Theological Introduction to the Old Testament*, 376.

depends on him."[177] Thus "at its foundation wisdom is a theological category, through and through. . . . Wisdom requires a relationship with Yahweh."[178]

Creation, Wisdom, and the Presence of God

Wisdom in general, and the book of Proverbs in particular, places a strong emphasis on God as Creator and on the miracle and spectacle of creation. Creation becomes the "overarching horizon of wisdom's worldview."[179] Yet while creation often stresses the sovereign transcendence of God, sometimes in Proverbs (as in Gen. 1–2) the immanence of God and his personal appearance and involvement are stressed when recounting the creation.[180] For example, as in Genesis 1–2, Proverbs 8:22–31 presents God as intimately and personally present and involved in creation.[181] What is different is that in Genesis 1:2 the Spirit of God is involved, hovering over the water, and in Proverbs 8:22–31 the personified Wisdom is involved, witnessing everything side by side with God, and in 8:30–31, wisdom is "rejoicing in his presence" (מְשַׂחֶקֶת לְפָנָיו, *mesaheqet lepanay*) and delighting over the world and mankind.

Woman Wisdom and the Presence of God

One of the most intriguing features of Proverbs 1–9 is the extensive use of a female personification of wisdom (1:20–33; 3:13–20; 4:1–9; 7:4; 8:1–36; 9:1–6), referred to by many scholars as Woman Wisdom.[182] Indeed, Woman Wisdom plays a central role in the theology of Proverbs 1–9. Proverbs 8:22–24 declares that she was "brought forth," "formed," "given birth" even before the creation, and she appears to assist God in the creation, rejoicing over the

---

177. Longman, *The Fear of the Lord Is Wisdom*, 12. Lucas suggests that the "fear of the LORD" had its origin in the spectacular encounters Israel had with God such as at Mount Sinai. For example, similar language is used in Exod. 14:10, 31; 20:18–20. Likewise, the phrase "fear the LORD" is used for the awe-inspired, devotional obedience called for in Deut. 10:12–13, 20 (Lucas, *The Psalms & Wisdom Literature*, 109–10).

178. Longman, *The Fear of the Lord Is Wisdom*, 14.

179. Ansberry, "Wisdom and Biblical Theology," 176. See also the discussion by Boström, *The God of the Sages*, 48–89.

180. In regard to Proverbs, see the discussion on God's transcendence and immanence in Waltke, *The Book of Proverbs*, 69–72.

181. Boström, *The God of the Sages*, 89. After spending an entire chapter analyzing the transcendence and sovereignty of God in Proverbs, and another chapter analyzing the immanence (personal relational aspects) of God in Proverbs, Boström concludes by affirming that in Proverbs God is both sovereign/transcendent and intimately connected to the world and individuals in a personal relationship (240–41).

182. See Longman, *The Fear of the Lord Is Wisdom*, 14–24; Waltke, *The Book of Proverbs*, 83–86; Perdue, *Proverbs*, 8–9. Goldingay creatively refers to her as "Ms. Insight" (Goldingay, *Old Testament Theology*, 1:48–49).

creation at the end (8:30–31). There is strong evidence in Proverbs 8 that she is closely connected to God himself in some way. John Goldingay notes that she is closely related to God, sometimes with him, but sometimes separate—"like God's daughter."[183] Commenting on Proverbs 8:35, where Woman Wisdom declares, "For those who find me find life," Gerhard von Rad states, "Only Jahweh can speak in this way. And yet, wisdom is not Jahweh himself; it is something separate from him."[184] Terence Fretheim suggests that Woman Wisdom can be identified as "the personification of a reality that has been divinely embedded in the creation and suffuses its structures and life. . . . Wisdom is a dynamic, relational reality within creation that is personified."[185] Tremper Longman goes so far as to suggest, "Woman Wisdom is not simply a personification of God's wisdom but actually represents Yahweh himself." Furthermore, Longman argues, the point of the Woman Wisdom personification is to stress the personal relationship that God wants with his people through wisdom. That is, the relationship with God that Proverbs calls for is depicted by Woman Wisdom. The point of Proverbs is not just to give practical advice but to lead people to a close and proper relationship with God.[186] Woman Wisdom is the metaphor for that close relationship. Indeed, some argue that Woman Wisdom is the mediator for that personal relationship, and she connects people with the presence of God in a personal relationship.[187] Likewise, Longman notes, "One cannot be called wise unless one has a proper relationship with Yahweh."[188]

In light of the unique status of Woman Wisdom and the role she plays in mediating the relationship between people and God, as well as the strong connection of wisdom to creation, Proverbs 3:13–18 is particularly relevant to our study. This unit opens and closes with an inclusio using the term "blessed"

183. Goldingay, *Old Testament Theology*, 1:48–49. He also points out that in 8:30, when Wisdom says, "*I was* constantly at his side. *I was* filled with delight day after day," twice the term אֶהְיֶה (*'ehyeh*, I am) is used. Goldingay suggests that this is a subtle connection back to God's repeated use of "I am" and "I will be with you" when he speaks to Moses in Exod. 3:12–14.

184. Von Rad, *Old Testament Theology*, 1:444.

185. Fretheim, *God and World*, 207.

186. Longman, *The Fear of the Lord Is Wisdom*, 21–25. Waltke and Yu write, "The sage represents wisdom as a unique woman who wears the mantle of a prophet, carries the scrolls of wise men, and wears the goddess-like diadem. The prophetic, sapient, and divine components of her characterization so interpenetrate one another that she emerges as a unique personality whose only peer is Jesus Christ" (Waltke with Yu, *Old Testament Theology*, 85). Indeed, they suggest that Woman Wisdom foreshadows Christ (pp. 85, 127–33).

187. Perdue states, "Woman Wisdom is the divine teacher mediating between God and humanity" (Perdue, *Wisdom Literature*, 52). See also Melton, "'O, That I Knew Where I Might Find Him,'" 214.

188. Longman, *The Fear of the Lord Is Wisdom*, 25.

(אַשְׁרֵי, *'ashre*) in regard to the one who finds/holds wisdom. But in the climax
of this passage, the text states of Woman Wisdom that "all her paths are
peace. She is a tree of life to those who take hold of her" (3:17b–18a). The
mention of the "tree of life" seems to be a clear reference back to the tree of
life in Genesis 2–3.[189] Ironically, while it was the unauthorized and disobedient desire for knowledge that resulted in the banishment of Adam and Eve
from the garden, the tree of life, and the presence of God in Genesis 2–3, in
Proverbs God offers a way back to the garden, to his presence, and to the tree
of life, through Woman Wisdom.[190] Once again we see the important role of
Woman Wisdom in mediating and facilitating the relationship between people
and the presence of God.

Job

While theodicy is obviously a central issue in Job, creation theology
is also present, as in Proverbs. Yet underlying all of this and tying it together is the basic concept of wisdom and relating to God through wisdom.
Tremper Longman underscores three basic lessons to be gleaned from Job:
(1) "The source of wisdom is God"; (2) "The proper human response to
God's wisdom is submission"; and (3) "The book's emphasis on the idea
that the fear of the Lord is the proper response to God's wisdom again
demonstrates that wisdom is fundamentally the result of a relationship
with God."[191] Because God's relationship with Job is one of the central,
driving themes of the book, it is no surprise to find that the presence of
God plays a highly significant role, especially in the dramatic conclusion
and climax of the book.

In his book *Old Testament Wisdom*, James Crenshaw entitles his chapter
on Job "The Search for Divine Presence."[192] Indeed, as the story unfolds,
in the middle chapters of dialogue between Job and his friends, Job boldly
states repeatedly that he wants an audience with God so that he can present
his case face-to-face with God (Job 13:1–28; 23:1–17). Job considers God's

189. Waltke, *The Book of Proverbs*, 259–60; Garrett, *Proverbs, Ecclesiastes, Song of Songs*,
82; Hurowitz, "Paradise Regained." Hurowitz notes that besides the "tree of life" terminology,
the passage also uses the term *'adam* (אָדָם) repeatedly (pp. 56–61). Likewise, he suggests that
the double use of דֶּרֶךְ (*derek*, way, path, road) in 3:17, prefacing the mention of the tree of
life in 3:18 alludes back to the final words of Gen. 3:24, where the cherubim are to guard "the
way [דֶּרֶךְ] to the tree of life."

190. Hurowitz, "Paradise Regained," 60–61.

191. Longman, *The Fear of the Lord Is Wisdom*, 61–62. Longman also notes that the book
of Job is not so much about suffering as it is about wisdom. See Longman, *Job*, 31–32.

192. Crenshaw, *Old Testament Wisdom*, 88–115.

absence/silence as part of the punishment he is enduring ("Why do you hide your face and consider me your enemy?" [13:24]). Frustrated with his failure to encounter God, he bemoans the fact that God does not set office hours (24:1). He thinks that if only he could get a chance to have a personal meeting with God, he would be able to clear things up through his strong rational argumentation.

In Job 38:1 God does show up, personally and powerfully, for a meeting with Job ("Then the LORD spoke to Job out of the storm"). This is a theophany—a personal, powerful, awe-inspiring appearance of God. Note also the shift in terminology used of God. While the name Yahweh ("the LORD") was used by the narrator in Job 1–2, the characters (Job and his friends) refer to God primarily as Elohim ("God") and El Shaddai ("the Almighty"). There is only one mention of Yahweh (12:9) in chapters 3–37. Yet when God shows up in chapters 38–41, the narrator regularly refers to him as Yahweh. As we have noted earlier, Yahweh is not only the name associated with the covenant and God's great deliverance in the exodus but also the name particularly associated with God's personal and relational presence.[193] Thus God's powerful presence will dominate the ending of the book, and his speeches to Job will provide the climactic denouement to the story.

Of course, Job's encounter with God in chapters 38–41 is not at all what he was expecting. Also the story takes an interesting twist in that God seems unconcerned with answering any of Job's specific questions about his justice. On the other hand, "the fact of God's presence entirely satisfies Job's deepest longings, while the reminder that God is not bound to human views of justice effectively answers Job's pursuit of litigation."[194] Tremper Longman underscores the importance of the restored relationship: "Yahweh's speeches are intended not to give Job an answer to the question of why he suffers but to reestablish the proper relationship between God and his human creature. Job . . . 'repents.' . . . He no longer seeks an answer to the question of his suffering: he simply bends the knee to God in submission."[195]

Job's final words reverberate with the impact of his encounter with the presence of God: "My ears had heard of you but now my eyes have seen you" (42:5). Job's repentant (toward his challenge of God's justice) and submissive acceptance of God's rule over creation have paved the way for reestablishing his relationship with God. Longman concludes, "His relationship with God

---

193. Quite a number of scholars note the shift in Job 38 in the terminology used for God. See, for example, Murphy, *The Tree of Life*, 33; Alden, *Job*, 38; L. Wilson, *Job*, 4.

194. L. Wilson, *Job*, 16.

195. Longman, *Job*, 65. Hartley comments, "God's presence authenticates Job, drawing him out of his self-love to focus his affection on God" (Hartley, *The Book of Job*, 50).

has gone through the flames and has emerged stronger."[196] Yet it was the personal presence of God encountering Job that reestablished his relationship with God and restored Job.

Ecclesiastes and Song of Songs

Although there is disagreement on how to read and interpret Ecclesiastes, it probably is best, following Tremper Longman (and others) to see two voices in Ecclesiastes. One is that of Qohelet (1:12–12:7), which is evaluated and critiqued by the other voice, that of the "frame narrator" (or father), who provides the introduction (1:1–11) and the conclusion (12:8–14), along with the critique of Qohelet as he instructs his son "concerning the dangers of speculative, doubting wisdom in Israel."[197] The conclusion of this frame narrator (or father) is as follows: (1) Qohelet's wisdom can be helpful (with discernment), but it is severely limited, especially in regard to the big questions of life; and (2) the answer is to "fear God," which, as in Proverbs, is the beginning of wisdom and is critical for relating to God.

Indeed, the entire point of the book is summarized and synthesized in the final chapter, where the frame narrator concludes, "Here is the conclusion of the matter: Fear God and keep his commandments" (12:13). While there is no direct reference to the presence of God in Ecclesiastes, it is perhaps implied by the connotation of relationship. As mentioned in our discussion of Proverbs above, the exhortation to "fear the Lord" (or, here, in Eccles. 12:13, to "fear God") is evoking the understanding in Proverbs that the fear of the Lord is the beginning of wisdom and implies the establishment of a right relationship with God.[198]

Song of Songs is often included with the wisdom books, although many scholars limit the wisdom books to Proverbs, Job, and Ecclesiastes.[199] Throughout

---

196. Longman, *The Fear of the Lord Is Wisdom*, 60–61. Janzen suggests that the book of Job ultimately "corresponds to the shape of the Christian canon, which begins with an idyllic creation story suffused with light and charged with blessing (Gen. 1–2), moves through catastrophe . . . and arrives finally at an end imaginatively envisaged as a transformed version of its beginning (Revelation 21–22)" (Janzen, *Job*, 4).

197. Longman, *The Book of Ecclesiastes*, 38; Longman, *The Fear of the Lord Is Wisdom*, 27–30. Disagreeing with the "two voices" theory and advocating a unified voice of Qohelet is Daniel Fredericks in Fredericks and Estes, *Ecclesiastes & The Song of Songs*, 36–41.

198. Longman, *The Fear of the Lord Is Wisdom*, 40. Bartholomew connects "Fear God and keep his commandments" in 12:13 with "Remember your Creator" in 12:1 and notes that the concluding point of Ecclesiastes is "in ironic exposure of a way of knowing that depends upon reason and experience alone, as opposed to an approach that starts with remembering one's Creator, with faith and obedience" (Bartholomew, "Ecclesiastes," 184).

199. Clarke argues that Song of Songs is a wisdom book, connected to the wisdom tradition in Israel. She points out numerous "shared characteristics" between the woman in Song of

history Christians and Jews have interpreted Song of Songs in a wide variety of ways, often allegorically. Many of the allegorical interpretations view the love affair in Song of Songs as reflecting the love that God has for Israel or that Jesus has for his church.[200] In this case, the intimate and relational presence of God is a significant theme and part of the central theology of the book. Most recent OT scholars, however, interpret Song of Songs as a celebration of intimate love between a man and a woman within the bounds of marriage. Following this understanding, which is to be preferred, the topic is one that does not directly involve the presence of God.

Conclusions

The Historical Books

God's presence is with Joshua as it was with Moses. Focused in the ark of the covenant, God's presence empowers Israel to cross into the promised land and to defeat the inhabitants. Yet during the time of the judges, Israel squanders the blessings from the presence of God, turning to idols and doing evil in the presence of God. Thus God limits his powerful blessings, allowing Israel to be overrun by foreign oppressors. Yet in his grace he sends his Spirit to empower judges to deliver his wayward people. The book of Ruth describes the devastating consequences of leaving the land where the blessings of God's presence are. Likewise, as Ruth and Naomi return to the land, the place of God's presence, they find blessing and provide hope for the future.

The call of Samuel in 1–2 Samuel underscores the important reality that the all-powerful God himself dwells in the tabernacle. Likewise, God's presence is associated with the ark of the covenant, and in the ark narratives of 1 Samuel 4–6 God demonstrates that his powerful and holy presence cannot be manipulated by anyone. God in his immanence in the ark remains completely sovereign and independent of any caretakers. The story of David,

---

Songs and the two women (Woman Wisdom and Woman Folly) in Proverbs. She summarizes the wisdom of Song of Songs: "Follow the example of the idealized Solomonic wisdom-seeker, by seeking a wise woman and making her your bride" (Clarke, "Seeking Wisdom in the Song of Songs," 112).

200. See the discussion of the interpretive history and interpretive approaches of Song of Songs by Daniel Estes in Fredericks and Estes, *Ecclesiastes & The Song of Songs*, 275–86. The allegorical approach has a long pedigree, including Augustine, Calvin, and Luther. Interestingly and more recently, although not convincingly, J. Hamilton notes allusions in the book to the Davidic monarchy and to the garden of Eden and concludes that the book, while not allegorical, is definitely prophetically messianic. He concludes, "In the music of the Song of Songs, the messianic remnant of Israel got a glimpse of the one they hoped would arise to restore them to Eden" (J. Hamilton, "The Messianic Music of the Song of Songs," 345).

which dominates 1–2 Samuel, is driven by David's relationship with God, especially God's intense presence associated with the ark and in the tabernacle. At the height of David's career he joyfully and worshipfully brings the ark (and the presence of God) into Jerusalem, establishing this city as the residence of God. At the low point of his career he is separated from the presence of God.

In 1–2 Kings and 1–2 Chronicles Solomon builds the temple, and the glorious, holy presence of God comes in dramatic, spectacular fashion into the temple to reside there. This provides incredible blessings for Israel and Judah so long as they worship God correctly. But as they turn to idols, worshiping them right in God's presence, he warns of banishing them away from his presence and from the land. Indeed, they do continue to disobey and worship idols. Thus both Israel and Judah are driven from God's presence, and judgment falls on the land and on Jerusalem. Even the temple is destroyed. Israel is now away from the land, and, implied here but clarified in Ezekiel 8–11, so is God.

First and Second Chronicles underscores that Israel's worship is directed at the indwelling presence of God in the temple. In addition to sacrifice, an important component in the relationship that the presence of God establishes with his people through worship is music. Another feature of 1–2 Chronicles is that these books stress the tight interconnection between God's presence (associated with the temple), the Davidic covenant, and hope for a future restoration.

In Ezra-Nehemiah some of the exiles return to the land and rebuild the temple and the city of Jerusalem. While this seems to be a good start toward the restoration, two critical things are still lacking. Instead of a Davidic king, the Persians rule. Equally serious, God's intense and powerful presence does not come back to the temple. Thus two main forward-looking promises remain unfulfilled: the promise of a righteous, Davidic king and the return of God to the temple.

Psalms

The presence of God clearly plays a critical, central role in Psalms, and it can be summarized as follows: (1) The worship of God is described as an encounter between God's people and the presence of God; the joy of the believer in Psalms is a result of that privileged encounter. (2) Terms relating to the "face of God" are used both of encountering God's presence in the temple and of requesting that God's presence radiate out from the temple to provide protection, deliverance, and blessing. (3) The laments/complaints are rooted in the loss of God's presence, especially the protective, refuge-providing, and blessing aspects of his presence; the movement from lament to praise reflects a restoration of God's relational presence. (4) Those who are righteous take refuge in the presence of God; taking refuge in the presence of God, often preceded by crying out to God, is synonymous with trusting in God. (5) The psalmists often allude back to the exodus; frequently the point of this allusion is to reaffirm faith by remembering how the powerful and dramatic presence of God personally led his people out of Egypt, into covenant relationship at Mount Sinai, and on through the wilderness to the land. (6) The reign of God, the Davidic covenant, and the messianic hope in Psalms are all integrally interconnected with Zion and the presence of God; God reigns over the world from his heavenly throne room, but the psalmists (and Israel) approach him and relate to him through his sanctuary on Zion. (7) For the enemies of God and his people, his presence is to be feared, for he personally brings judgment on those who do evil and oppose him. (8) When the canonical ordering of Psalms is placed within the context of Israel's history, especially the fall of Jerusalem in 587/586 BC and the end of the Davidic dynasty in Judah, the absence and the restored presence of God in Zion become a significant part of the eschatological and messianic hope emerging out of the Psalter.

The Wisdom Literature

Once we recognize the important role of God's relationship with people that is reflected in the Wisdom literature, it comes as no surprise to see interconnected concepts of God's presence. God's relationship with his people and God's presence among his people are tightly interconnected. Likewise, the Wisdom literature also reflects nuances of both God's transcendence and his immanence, an interaction that we have noted frequently throughout the rest of the OT. The Wisdom literature presents the transcendence of God when it depicts him as Creator of all and providential Judge of all. Yet the immanence of God, and thus his presence, is also stressed, especially in the central metaphor of "Woman Wisdom" in Proverbs and in God's personal dialogue with Job at the climactic end of the book. Thus even in the Wisdom literature God's presence plays a central and highly significant role.

THREE

The Relational Presence of God
in the Prophets

Isaiah

The presence of God and how God relates to his people through his presence drive the "story" in the book of Isaiah. Initially God, the "Holy One of Israel," dwells in the temple. The sin of Israel, however, committed right in God's presence, threatens to rupture the covenant relationship, and God warns that without their repentance he will banish them from his presence. But God promises that in the future he will return to dwell once again in the midst of his people. He will restore them and their relationship to him in a new exodus through a messianic Davidic king who is closely connected to God himself.

The Holy One of Israel Dwells in the Temple

While the book of Isaiah affirms God's omnipresence (6:3) and his sovereign reign over all creation from his high and exalted throne in heaven, it is also clear that during the historical times of Isaiah, from the reign of Uzziah to that of Hezekiah (1:1), God is presented as actually dwelling in the temple.[1] This is a continuation of the biblical story in which God first comes to dwell

---

1. Vriezen writes, "The Temple of God in Jerusalem is indeed a great privilege, but it is still more a cause for great responsibility; for it means that the living, holy God dwells in Jerusalem. This is the reason for the importance of Zion: its value is founded in him only. In Isaiah it is neither the political situation nor the pretension of the cult that dominates his spiritual life, but the certitude of the real presence of God" (Vriezen, "The Theology of Isaiah," 130–31).

in the tabernacle and then later comes to dwell in the temple. In Isaiah this reality is reflected in several ways as the themes of presence, holiness, and power intersect.

Thus throughout Isaiah 1–39 the reality of God dwelling in the temple (or in Jerusalem, or on Mount Zion) is assumed and alluded to several times.[2] Examples include 8:18, "We are signs and symbols in Israel from the LORD Almighty, who dwells [הַשֹּׁכֵן, hashoken] on Mount Zion";[3] and 31:9, "'Their stronghold will fall because of terror . . . ,' declares the LORD, whose fire is in Zion, whose furnace is in Jerusalem." Likewise in 37:14, after the Assyrian king Sennacherib sends him a threatening letter, Hezekiah "went up to the temple of the LORD and spread it out before the LORD [לִפְנֵי יְהוָה, lipne Yahweh, in the presence of the LORD]."[4]

Likewise, one of the central concerns of Isaiah is the holiness of God. This is indicated by Isaiah's repeated use of the phrase "the Holy One of Israel" throughout the book (10 times in Isa. 1–39, 12 times in Isa. 40–66).[5] The construct form "Holy One *of Israel*" implies not only the relationship between God and Israel[6] but probably also the presence of God dwelling in Israel.[7]

Foundational to Isaiah's understanding and proclamation of the holiness of God is his encounter with God in the temple (Isa. 6).[8] Although there

2. J. Hamilton, "God with Men in the Prophets," 181.

3. Blenkinsopp observes that the reference in 8:18 to God dwelling on Mount Zion connects with Isa. 6 (Isaiah's encounter with God in the temple) as an inclusio (Blenkinsopp, *Isaiah 1–39*, 223–24).

4. Mettinger cites this text as an example of the fact that "the notion of the royal presence of God on the cherubim throne in the Jerusalem Temple" was characteristic and normative (Mettinger, *The Dethronement of Sabaoth*, 24–25). Likewise, the ensuing answer from God and the action taken by the "angel of the LORD" are presented as if God were in Jerusalem, hearing the insults of the Assyrians ("because your insolence has reached my ears" [37:29]). God then refers to "this city" (אֶל־הָעִיר הַזֹּאת, 'el-ha'ir hazz'ot) in three consecutive verses (37:33, 34, 35) as if Jerusalem were in direct view. Then, in ironic judgment, since Sennacherib had sent his messengers (הַמַּלְאָכִים, hammale'akim) to Jerusalem with his threats, God now sends his messenger (מַלְאַךְ יְהוָה, mal'ak Yahweh) out (וַיֵּצֵא, wayyetse') to kill 185,000 Assyrians (37:36). The implied imagery of וַיֵּצֵא (he went out) is that the "angel of the LORD" went out of Jerusalem, from God to the Assyrians. See Tull, *Isaiah 1–39*, 536.

5. House, *Old Testament Theology*, 274; Roberts, "Isaiah in Old Testament Theology," 131–33; Gammie, *Holiness in Israel*, 74–101; B. Anderson, "The Holy One of Israel"; Goldingay, *Isaiah*, 7–8.

6. Goldingay, *Isaiah*, 15.

7. Roberts, "Isaiah in Old Testament Theology," 132–33. Blenkinsopp notes that the phrase "Holy One of Israel" is associated with the sanctuary and the "holy city," where God sits enthroned and rules (Blenkinsopp, *Isaiah 1–39*, 108–9).

8. Oswalt writes, "The vision of 6:1–8 is fundamental to the entire course of Isaiah's ministry and shape of his book. The glory, the majesty, the holiness, and the righteousness of God became the ruling concepts of his ministry" (Oswalt, *The Book of Isaiah: Chapters 1–39*, 176).

might be some ambiguity about whether Isaiah is actually in the physical temple in Jerusalem or having a heavenly vision, the use of common terms for the temple (הֵיכָל, *hekal* [6:1]; בַּיִת, *bayit* [6:4])[9] along with references to the doorposts and especially to the altar (מִזְבֵּחַ, *mizbeah* [6:6]) strongly imply that the vision at least begins in the Jerusalem temple, or is partially "grounded" in the Jerusalem temple.[10] That is, Isaiah seems to be in the temple as the vision begins, but he is quickly shown that the presence of God, while it completely fills the temple, is nonetheless much larger than the physical temple and actually fills all the earth. Brevard Childs concludes, "The imagery is initially that of the Jerusalem temple—doorposts, smoke, altar—but these are shortly transformed into a heavenly scene."[11] Hans Wildberger cautions against drawing too sharp a distinction between the earthly sanctuary and the heavenly sanctuary: "To try to distinguish between an earthly and a heavenly sanctuary attempts to make a distinction which the ancient person would never have attempted. God dwells in heaven, but he is also present in the sanctuary."[12]

Note also that the punishment that God declares to Isaiah during this vision uses near/far imagery by employing the use of רָחַק (*rahaq*, to be far, to

9. The word הֵיכָל (lit. "palace") occurs 80 times in the OT. The vast majority of these usages refer to the earthly temple in Jerusalem (59 times). There are only 3 occurrences where the reference is clearly to the "heavenly temple." In three other texts it is unclear whether the heavenly temple or the earthly temple is in view. Other usages refer to the palaces of human kings (13 times) and the tabernacle (2 times). Ottosson doesn't even mention the "heavenly temple" option in his discussion (M. Ottosson, "הֵיכָל," *TDOT* 3:382–88). Likewise בַּיִת (lit. "house") is used to refer to the temple in Jerusalem hundreds of times. Jenni notes that there is "perhaps" one possible time when בַּיִת is used to refer to a heavenly temple (Ps. 36:9) (E. Jenni, "בַּיִת," *TLOT* 1:236).

10. Scholars who maintain that Isaiah's vision occurs in the Jerusalem temple, either completely or at least initially, include Goldingay, *Isaiah*, 58; G. Tucker, "The Book of Isaiah 1–39," 102; Tull, *Isaiah 1–39*, 139; B. Anderson, "The Holy One of Israel," 7; Gentry, "The Meaning of 'Holy,'" 409–10; Beuken, "The Manifestation of Yahweh," 76; Childs, *Isaiah*, 55; Wildberger, *Isaiah 1–12*, 263; Seitz, *Isaiah 1–39*, 54; Levenson, *Sinai and Zion*, 122–23; O. Kaiser, *Isaiah 1–12*, 74–75. Those favoring the view that it is primarily a heavenly vision include G. Smith, *Isaiah 1–39*, 187; Brueggemann, *Isaiah 1–39*, 58; Chisholm, *Handbook on the Prophets*, 25.

11. Childs, *Isaiah*, 55.

12. Wildberger, *Isaiah 1–12*, 263. Drawing from texts such as 2 Sam. 6:2 ("the LORD Almighty, who is enthroned between the cherubim on the ark"), various views have been put forward regarding the connection between the ark of the covenant, the cherubim, and the throne of God. Some argue that the ark serves as the throne of God and the most holy place as his royal courtroom. Others posit that the imagery is of God seated in heaven with the ark serving as his footstool (1 Chron. 28:2; Ps. 99:1–5). See the discussion in Clements, *God and Temple*, 28–39; Haran, *Temples and Temple-Service*, 246–59. Agreeing with Wildberger, Mettinger writes, "The heavenly and earthly may not be regarded as two opposed poles in a field of tension: rather, heaven and earth become one in the sacred space of the sanctuary" (Mettinger, *Dethronement of Sabaoth*, 31).

distance [6:12]), a term that normally connotes spatial distance. Isaiah asks, "How long?" and God answers, "Until the LORD has sent everyone far away" (וְרִחַק יְהוָה אֶת־הָאָדָם, *werihaq Yahweh 'et-ha'adam*).

The Israelites Have Forsaken God, Who Dwells in Their Midst

Isaiah's encounter with the presence of God, the Holy One, in the temple (Isa. 6) forms the backdrop for Isaiah's extensive message of warning and judgment on Israel. The sin of Israel, abandoning God and his gracious law to practice idolatry and social injustice, particularly in such close proximity to God's holy and relational presence, is presented as especially offensive, dishonoring, and upsetting to God, who dwells right there on Mount Zion in the temple.

This theme runs throughout the opening indictment presented in Isaiah 1. In 1:3 the use of the term "my people" alludes back to the covenant formulation "I will be your God; you will be my people; I will dwell in your midst." Allusions to family ties also run throughout this passage, and the imagery is that of God in close proximity to the people, being dishonored and abandoned. The Israelites "have forsaken [עָזְבוּ, *'azebu*] the LORD; they have spurned [נִאֲצוּ, *ni'atsu*] the Holy One of Israel and turned their backs [נָזֹרוּ אָחוֹר, *nazoru 'ahor*] on him" (1:4). All three terms imply a willful rejection of the close relationship they once had with God, and conceptually the terms carry spatial connotations as well as connotations of breaking the basic covenant relationship the Israelites had with God. The word עָזַב (*'azab*) means "to abandon, to leave"; נָאַץ (*na'ats*) connotes "to disdain, despise, treat disrespectfully," suggesting that they violated God's holiness in particular by despising him; נָזֹרוּ אָחוֹר (*nazoru 'ahor*) means "to end the relationship and become a stranger" (cf. ESV and NRSV: "who are utterly estranged"). "Israel walked away from the confines of what it had called home and where it lived under protecting care."[13]

Then in Isaiah 1:10–17 God explains that the sacrifices brought to the temple into his very presence by the Israelites are meaningless, even annoying, since their worship is insincere and they are characterized by serious and consistent social injustice. The imagery that God uses is that of him residing in the temple from where he can hear and see the hypocritical sacrifices and festivals outside, which offend him. "When you come to appear before me [לֵרָאוֹת פָּנָי, *lera'ot panay*, lit. "to see my face"], who has asked this of you, this trampling of my courts?" (1:12). In 1:13–16 God

---

13. Mettinger, *Dethronement of Sabaoth*, 26.

seems to be tired or "beat down" from all these sacrifices right before him (e.g., "I cannot bear your worthless assemblies" [1:13]).[14] Other examples include 3:8 and 29:13. These verses summarize the offenses to the holiness of the presence of God, an offense that ultimately will lead to his departure and absence.[15]

Judgment as Separation from the Presence of God

Just as one of the blessings of being in covenant relationship with God was his divine presence in the midst of Israel ("I will dwell in your midst"), one of the central aspects of the judgment that falls on Israel for disobeying God and dishonoring his holy presence in their midst is the loss of his special intense presence as was manifested in the temple. That is, at the heart of the judgment that Isaiah proclaims is Israel's banishment from God's presence. One of the ways this is expressed is through the terminology of abandonment, banishing, and exile. The conceptual world created by many of the terms used for judgment is one with strong frequent overtones of spatial separation (i.e., away from the presence of God).[16] Certainly the concept of exile is also related to being away from "the land of Israel," but the land is generally connected very closely to Jerusalem and Mount Zion—that is, the place where God dwells. Two aspects of separation are involved in the use of this terminology. First, Israel is banished from the land, the place given to them by God as a gift where they can be blessed with him living in their presence. Second, God also abandons the land of Israel, leaving the temple in Jerusalem, personally coming after the disobedient Israelites in judgment, and then returning to heaven, no longer residing "in their midst" in the temple.[17] This separation and abandonment strongly imply the end of the Mosaic covenant ("I will be your God; you will be my people; I will dwell in your midst").

God Hides His Face from Israel in Judgment

Not only does God banish Israel from the land and away from his presence, but also he himself actually turns away from them, removing his presence from

---

14. On the burdening and wearying of God, see Fretheim, *The Suffering of God*, 127–48.

15. Brueggemann, "Presence of God," 682.

16. For example, the term נדח (*nadah*) means "impel, thrust, drive away, banish" (Isa. 8:22; 11:12; 27:13; 56:8). Likewise, the word נטש (*natash*) means "forsake, leave unattended/unprotected" (Isa. 2:6) and carries a fundamental notion of separation.

17. Goldingay writes, "Yhwh abandoned Judah in 587. One could picture that in terms of the people being thrown out of Yhwh's land or of Yhwh leaving the land, but either way the children and the parent are no longer living in the same house" (Goldingay, *Old Testament Theology*, 2:363).

them. This is expressed several times through the idiom of God hiding (סָתַר, *satar*) his face or himself from them (Isa. 8:17; 54:8; 59:2; 64:7).

Several helpful works have been written dealing with the absence or hidden-ness of God in the OT.[18] Samuel Balentine underscores that in the prophets in general, and in Isaiah in particular, God's hiding is a direct response to Israel's corporate sin and rebellion. Balentine concludes that within the prophetic material the consequences of God's hiding result in separation, "a separation that results from God's not hearing, seeing, or answering; a separation that is implicit in the threat of death; a separation effected by God's abandonment of Jerusalem." Perhaps the most emphasized consequence of God's hiding is the destruction of Jerusalem and the Babylonian exile.[19]

Joel Burnett writes that these references to divine absence "assume an inherently spatial conceptualization of divine-human relationships."[20] That is, when God was dwelling there in the temple of Jerusalem in Israel's midst, there was a close relationship between God and Israel, but in the exile the distance between Israel and God (who now dwells back in heaven) underscores the frayed and distant current relationship.[21] This is clear especially in Isaiah 63:7–64:12. This prophetic psalm (or lament) first recalls those wonderful days of the exodus when God's presence delivered Israel from Egypt (63:9) and led them in the wilderness (63:11–14).[22] After stressing the close personal presence of God with them in the exodus ("The angel of his presence saved them"; "he

18. The classic work is Balentine, *The Hidden God*. A more recent discussion, which includes extensive ancient Near Eastern background material, is Burnett, *Where Is God?* In his discussion of Isa. 45:15 Goldingay also provides a lengthy discussion of the "absence" or "hiddenness" of God (Goldingay, *The Message of Isaiah 40–55*, 85–88).

19. Balentine, *The Hidden God*, 68. Burnett adds, "Biblical reflection on divine absence reaches perhaps its greatest proportions in consideration of the exile, in which the Babylonian destruction makes Jerusalem and its temple the center of divine absence instead of divine pres-ence" (Burnett, *Where Is God?*, 177).

20. Burnett, *Where Is God?*, 176. Burnett argues that Israel's understanding of divine pres-ence/absence is rooted in their encounter with God in the exodus. He writes, "Throughout the Hebrew Bible, Israel's identity is intimately bound with the memory of its first encounters with its God and an understanding of various relational foundations for continuing divine presence (p. 5).

21. Simian-Yofre writes, "Yahweh's hiding of his face ([*panim*] often with *min* + personal obj.) is not simply a punishment: it signifies a radical disruption of the relationship with God" (H. Simian-Yofre, "פָּנִים," *TDOT* 11:603).

22. God's personal presence is stressed: "The angel of his presence [מַלְאַךְ פָּנָיו, *mal'ak panayw*] saved them"; "he who brought them through the Sea"; "he who set his Holy Spirit among them, . . . who led them through the depths"; "They were given rest by the Spirit of the LORD"; "how you guided your people to make for yourself a glorious name" (63:9–14). Oswalt observes that "the angel [of his presence] is the Lord himself as visibly present" (Oswalt, *The Book of Isaiah: Chapters 40–66*, 607). Childs notes that "spirit" in 63:11 and 63:14 refers specifically to the holy presence of God (Childs, *Isaiah*, 524). Likewise, Block concludes that

who set his Holy Spirit among them"; "They were given rest by the Spirit of the LORD"), this psalm then acknowledges the difference in the current state of affairs.[23] God is not currently present with them but is absent from them and dwelling up in heaven, leaving them defenseless against their enemies. It calls on God to return from heaven and reestablish his powerful presence among his people as he did in the time of Moses.[24] "Look down from heaven and see. . . . Where are your zeal and your might?" (63:15). "Why, LORD, do you make us wander from your ways . . . ? Return for the sake of your servants" (63:17). "For a little while your people possessed your holy place, but now our enemies have trampled down your sanctuary" (63:18). "Oh, that you would rend the heavens and come down. . . . Come down to make your name known to your enemies" (64:1–2).[25] "No one calls on your name or strives to lay hold of you; for you have hidden your face from us" (64:7). "Oh, look on us, we pray, for we are all your people" (64:9). "Our holy and glorious temple, where our ancestors praised you, has been burned with fire" (64:11). "After all this, LORD, will you hold yourself back?" (64:12).

This is not just a call on God to intervene. It is a call for God to come back down as he did at Mount Sinai and to once again establish a close covenant relationship with Israel through his powerful presence.

God's Presence in Judgment

Eventually the patience of God runs out. The disrespect and the blatant violation of his holiness as he dwells right there in the temple, in their midst, result in a terrifying change in the state of affairs as the presence of God seems to come out of the temple and to actually attack and hunt down the Israelites as their enemy.[26] Bernhard Anderson notes, "Living in the presence of the holy God means to be exposed to God's judgment from which there is no escape."[27] John Goldingay stresses that just as God's relationship with Israel is close and personal, so, too, his wrath against them for disrespecting

---

"spirit" (רוּחַ, *ruah*) in 63:7–14 is a synecdochic expression for God himself (Block, "The View from the Top," 180–81).

23. Arguing that this passage should be viewed as an exilic lament is Williamson, "Isaiah 63,7–64,11."

24. Note the use of "father" and "redeemer," family terms with covenant connotations. See Niskanen, "Yhwh as Father, Redeemer, and Potter."

25. Seitz observes that the call for God to tear open the heavens and come down refers to his self-manifestation at Sinai (Seitz, "The Book of Isaiah 40–66," 529).

26. For a discussion of this phenomenon in other biblical texts of the OT, see especially chap. 3, "God Is an Enemy: The Wars against Unfaithful Israel," in Longman and Reid, *God Is a Warrior*, 48–60.

27. B. Anderson, "The Holy One of Israel," 19.

and dishonoring that relationship is close and personal.[28] In Isaiah 1:24–31 God declares a huge shift in the relationship as he moves from protector to enemy, declaring, "I will turn my hand against you."[29] The theme of God's hand outstretched in judgment against Israel is stressed especially in 9:12–10:4, with the fourfold repetition of "Yet for all this, his anger is not turned away, his hand is still upraised" (9:12, 17, 21; 10:4). His presence now becomes terrifying for Israel. The "burning fire" that they experience (9:19) is "the fire of Yahweh's fury."[30] Other texts stressing God's personal presence in judgment include Isaiah 2:6–22; 8:13–15; 26:17; 29:1–4.

The New Exodus, Restored Presence, and Restored Covenant Relationship

The promise of a future restoration after the judgment, while concentrated in Isaiah 40–66, is a theme that runs throughout the book of Isaiah. At the heart of this future restoration is the restored presence of God. Just as the sin of Israel resulted in God's departure from Jerusalem and their banishment from the land, now in the coming messianic time of restoration God will personally come, defeat Israel's enemies, lovingly regather his people and return them to the land, and reestablish his presence among them on Mount Zion, where not only Israel but also the nations of the world will acknowledge his presence and worship him.[31] The implication of this restoration is that it is a reestablishment of the covenant relationship, as seen in its tripartite formulation: "I will be your God; you will be my people; I will dwell in your midst."

---

28. Goldingay, *Old Testament Theology*, 2:288–92. Goldingay notes that the wrath of God in the OT reflects "the strong feelings that emerge from God's passionate involvement with the world and with Israel" (p. 288). Regarding the judgment on Israel, he comments, "So none of this happens without Yahweh's personal involvement" (p. 290).

29. B. Anderson, "'God with Us,'" 242–43.

30. B. Anderson, "'God with Us,'" 242–43. Brueggemann notes the ironic contrast in the use of "his hand is still upraised" in Isa. 9:12–10:4 in judgment of Israel and the similar use of this imagery in Exod. 6:6, where the hand of God is outstretched to deliver Israel (Brueggemann, *Isaiah 1–39*, 87–88). B. Anderson notes the significance of placing the 'Immanuel' (God with us) promise of Isa. 6–8 right in the middle of oracles dealing primarily with judgment on God's unrepentant people. He concludes that the presence of God ("the Holy One of Israel") simultaneously brings about judgment on the unrepentant and redemption on those to be restored (B. Anderson, "'God with Us'").

31. Merrill argues convincingly that Isaiah combines the theme of "second exodus" with the theme of pilgrimage and procession (Merrill, "Pilgrimage and Procession," 268–69). That is, in the restoration, the people of Israel—indeed, even people from all the world—will come to God in Jerusalem. This traveling is viewed as another great exodus deliverance, with God protecting and delivering his people, but also as a great pilgrimage, with the people of Israel and the world streaming to God to worship him.

Yet throughout the restoration passages there are frequent indications and hints that the new, coming restored covenant relationship will be different, even better, than the old one, particularly in regard to God's presence and his relationship with his people.

Thus Isaiah 2:2–3 portrays God as once again dwelling in his temple on Mount Zion in Jerusalem, but this time all the nations and many peoples will stream to the temple to worship him. Isaiah 4:2–6 likewise looks to the future ("in that day") and presents a picture of God once again present on Mount Zion. This text uses terminology that clearly connects it to Israel's encounter with the presence of God on Mount Sinai during the exodus. Yet while the imagery of smoke and fire is similar to earlier experiences with the presence of God, there are significant differences that point to the fact that the future restoration is not merely a return to the status quo of the old covenant but is the inauguration of something bigger and better. *All* Mount Zion and *all* who have assembled there are covered with the cloud and fire. Brevard Childs writes, "The sign of God's gracious presence is no longer confined to the Holy of Holies with its access only to the high priest, but the entire mountain is overshadowed as a sacred sanctuary."[32] Drawing similar conclusions, Donald Gowan states, "The promise of a cloud by day and a fire by night in Isaiah 4 is clearly a promise of the permanent presence of God himself in the midst of his people. . . . It is thus the certain, never failing, all-sufficient, caring, and protecting presence of God."[33]

In Isaiah 12:6, as the prophet concludes chapters 1–12 and looks to the future restoration ("in that day" [12:1, 4]), he declares, "Shout aloud and sing for joy, people of Zion, for great is the Holy One of Israel among you" (or "in your midst," בְּקִרְבֵּךְ, *beqirbek*).[34] The phrase "among you" or "in your midst" is a clear reference to the presence of God once again dwelling among them. Otto Kaiser writes, "Thus the aim of history, which through every judgment is moving towards its consummation, is the presence of

32. Childs, *Isaiah*, 37. Childs continues by noting the trajectory of this eschatological theme throughout Isaiah down to Isa. 60:19–20, and culminating in Rev. 21:22–27, where "the presence of God now replaces the temple and provides the light rather than the sun and the moon." Likewise making a connection between Isa. 6:4–6 and Rev. 21 are O. Kaiser, *Isaiah 1–12*, 57; G. Smith, *Isaiah 1–39*, 158.

33. Gowan, *Eschatology in the Old Testament*, 12–13. Others noting that the terminology used in this passage stresses the returned presence of God include Brueggemann, *Isaiah 1–39*, 43; Williamson, *Isaiah 1–27*, 1:313–14; Seitz, *Isaiah 1–39*, 41–42; O. Kaiser, *Isaiah 1–12*, 56–57; G. Smith, *Isaiah 1–39*, 158.

34. The use of the phase "Holy One of Israel" suggests that 12:6 is an inclusio paralleling 1:4. The contrast of this opening and closing is stark. In 1:4 it is the Holy One of Israel who is judging them; here in 12:6 the Holy One of Israel is blessing them so much that they break out in song. See O. Kaiser, *Isaiah 1–12*, 169.

God."[35] In the future God will once again dwell among his people, thus indicating a reestablishment of the tripartite covenant ("I will be your God; you will be my people; I will dwell in your midst").

Isaiah 40:1–11 opens the second half of Isaiah (chaps. 40–66) with a proclamation of comfort to the exiles because God will return to Jerusalem and bring them with him. The passage reverberates with connections to the exodus, but while there are similarities to the exodus, what God intends here in this "new exodus" is nonetheless a "qualitatively new event," something even more spectacular.[36] At the heart of this "good news" is the return of God's presence.

Recall that the tripartite formula for God's covenant relationship with Israel that he established at Mount Sinai during the exodus was "I will be your God; you will be my people; I will dwell in your midst." Isaiah 40:1 opens by connecting back to this covenant formula, "Comfort, comfort *my people*, says *your God*."[37] Then the verses that follow describe the coming of God to dwell among them again.

Isaiah 40:5 declares, "The glory of the LORD will be revealed, and all people will see it together." As mentioned earlier, the "glory of the LORD" often refers to the presence of God himself, or as Childs describes it, "that aspect of the divine image which is made visible to human perception."[38] The reference to the revelation of God's glory in 40:5 may allude back to Isaiah's vision in chapter 6[39] or back to the revelation of God's accompanying glory during the exodus,[40] or perhaps even to both. What is especially new and unique in this text is that the revelation of God's glory will be to all people. The glory (presence) of God will be revealed not just to Moses or to Isaiah, or even just to the Israelites returning from exile, but to everyone in the world. This indicates "the inbreaking of a new age of salvation,"[41] the "realization of God's saving purpose for the whole world."[42] "Here is your God" is the

---

35. O. Kaiser, *Isaiah 1–12*, 169.

36. Goldingay, *Isaiah 40–55*, 21.

37. Childs, *Isaiah*, 297; Goldingay, *Isaiah 40–55*, 12; Oswalt, *The Book of Isaiah: Chapters 40–66*, 49; North, *The Second Isaiah*, 72–73.

38. Childs, *Isaiah*, 299.

39. Childs, *Isaiah*, 299–300.

40. Goldingay, *Isaiah 40–55*, 21.

41. Childs, *Isaiah*, 299.

42. Oswalt, *The Book of Isaiah: Chapters 40–66*, 52. Goldingay writes, "This event is one of ultimate importance. It is significant for the whole world. The restoration of the exiles and of Jerusalem is to be the occasion and the means of Yhwh's universal self-revelation" (Goldingay, *Isaiah 40–55*, 22). North concurs, "Clearly what is anticipated is the coming of God himself, a theophany compelling in its majesty, which is to mark the beginning of a new era for all mankind" (North, *The Second Isaiah*, 77).

good news to be proclaimed in Zion (40:9), for God in all of his glory and power has arrived in Jerusalem via his royal highway, carrying his people with him like captured plunder, but tenderly as a shepherd would carry the lambs of his flock (40:10–11).

Several passages in Isaiah describe the return of God to Zion (35:1–10; 40:1–11; 52:7–12).[43] Goldingay writes, "The most terrible element in the nightmare is Yhwh's abandonment of Israel. The crucial center of any vision for the future must be Yhwh's return."[44] This return of God to Zion is thus a critical development in the restoration of the covenant relationship between God and Israel, reversing God's departure from the temple described in Ezekiel (see below).[45]

In Isaiah 35:2 both parallel phrases "the glory of the LORD" and "the splendor of our God" suggest the presence of God in person.[46] The return of God in 35:1–2 impacts the land, restoring the devastated desert land to a beautiful and productive garden. The implications are that the return of God's presence is directly connected to the restoration of nature (as well as to the new creation).[47] The return of God's presence in 35:3–10 also directly affects the people, as a highway is built to allow all those whom God has rescued and healed to enter into Zion (where he now again resides) and celebrate with singing.[48]

Isaiah 52:8 proclaims that the "watchmen" in Zion will see God with their own eyes when he returns to Zion. The idiom translated by the NIV as "with their own eyes" (lit. "eye to eye," עַיִן בְּעַיִן, *'ayin be'ayin*) probably connotes "to see close up."[49] Just as Ezekiel sees the departure of God, so the watchmen

---

43. There are numerous similarities between Isa. 35:1–10 and 40:1–11. Both speak of God's return, mention the revelation of his glory, describe the special highway prepared for his return, and address people in Zion (along with God) who are singing or shouting joyfully. Isaiah 52:7–12 likewise proclaims God's return to Zion, calling on Jerusalem (implied people) to sing joyfully. Goldingay suggests that 52:7–12 forms an inclusio with 40:3–11 around the theme of God's return to Zion (Goldingay, *Isaiah 40–55*, 456). Childs likewise notes the similarities between 52:7–12 and 40:1–21 (Childs, *Isaiah*, 406).

44. Goldingay, *Old Testament Theology*, 2:361. See also Moltmann, *The Coming of God*, 24.

45. Goldingay, *Isaiah 40–55*, 20; North, *The Second Isaiah*, 74.

46. Goldingay, *Isaiah 40–55*, 20.

47. Fretheim, *God and World*, 194–98. On the theme of the future transformation of nature in the OT, see Gowan, *Eschatology in the Old Testament*, 97–120. On connecting the presence of God with the transformation of nature, see Middleton, *A New Heaven and a New Earth*, 105–7.

48. Goldingay, *Old Testament Theology*, 2:363.

49. North, *The Second Isaiah*, 222. Modern translations handle this phrase in various ways: "before their very eyes" (NLT); "in plain sight" (NRSV); "eye to eye" (ESV); "every eye" (HCSB). In light of the reference to God's vanguard and rearguard in 52:12, it is interesting to note the use of this same idiom in Num. 14:14: "They have already heard that you, LORD, are with these people and that you, LORD, have been seen face to face [lit. "eye to eye"], that your cloud stays

in Jerusalem will witness the visible return of God. As in the other texts, the return of God to Jerusalem signals the return of the exiles to Jerusalem as well. Isaiah 52:12 pictures the returning exiles as under the close watch and protection of the presence of God himself, who both goes before them and behind them, as the pillar, fire, cloud, and angel of God did in the exodus (Exod. 13:21–22; 14:19–20; Num. 14:14; Deut. 1:33).

As in numerous earlier chapters in Isaiah, chapter 58 likewise centers Israel's hope for the future on the restored presence of God.[50] Once again using the imagery of the exodus, God declares, "The glory of the LORD will be your rear guard. . . . The LORD will guide you always" (58:8, 11). Likewise, in contrast to the judgment and the corresponding absence of God, in this future time the protecting presence of God will be with them: "You will cry for help, and he will say, 'Here am I'" (58:9).

The Messianic Davidic King and the Presence of God

Playing a central role in the restoration and the return of God's presence is the coming messianic Davidic king. The book of Isaiah will connect the Messiah very tightly with the presence of God. Thus in Isaiah 7–9, chapters connected by the theme of a coming "child," the sign of a child to Ahaz in the context of the Syro-Ephraimite war (chap. 7), apparently fulfilled in "near view" fulfillment by a child born to Isaiah (chap. 8), also merges into the future messianic Davidic king (chap. 9).[51] Although the interrelationship between these three chapters and the interpretation of them are complex, the NT (Matt. 1:22–23) connects the ultimate fulfillment of these prophecies to the Messiah, Jesus Christ. What is significant to our study is the close connection between the presence of God and the coming Messiah. The term "Immanuel" ("God with us") not only is given as the name of the coming child (Isa. 7:14) but also is repeated twice in Isaiah 8 (vv. 8, 10). Isaiah 8:10 proclaims that the foreign hostile nations will be shattered, for "God is with us" (עִמָּנוּ אֵל, 'immanu 'el). That is, the presence of God will once again defeat their enemies (as he did in the exodus). Then in 9:6 the "child" (and connections back to 7:14 are implied) is called "Wonderful Counselor, Mighty

---

over them, and that you go before them in a pillar of cloud by day and a pillar of fire by night." Goldingay and Payne suggest that the idiom implies seeing and then "hastening to witness, on the basis of a real personal revelation of God" (Goldingay and Payne, *Isaiah 40–55*, 2:267).

50. Childs, *Isaiah*, 479–80. Childs notes that Isa. 58:1–7 is answering the question of why the salvation of God is delayed, while 58:8–14 actually describes that salvation (p. 475).

51. For an overview discussion of how these three chapters relate in regard to the "child" and the coming Davidic king, see J. D. Hays, *The Message of the Prophets*, 110–12; Chisholm, *Handbook on the Prophets*, 32–34; Seitz, *Isaiah 1–39*, 60–75; G. Smith, *Isaiah 1–39*, 201–5, 235–43.

God, Everlasting Father, Prince of Peace." The term "Mighty God," used of God himself clearly in 10:21, strongly suggests that this coming messianic Davidic king will be closely identified with God.[52]

Likewise, the coming Davidic king described in Isaiah 11 appears to be a continuation and expansion of the "Davidic" child prophecy of Isaiah 9.[53] Once again, while this prophecy points to a coming messianic Davidic king, there is clearly something very special about this king in regard to the presence of God, for the "Spirit of the LORD" (רוּחַ יְהוָה, *ruah Yahweh*) will rest on him (11:2). Although it is far from clear exactly what the "Spirit of the LORD" refers to,[54] this phrase probably is a reference to the presence of God.[55] Yet, this coming Davidic king with "the Spirit of the LORD" gathers the exiles and nations to himself (11:10–16), an act normally associated with God. Then he appears to reside on Mount Zion. The statement that "his resting place will be glorious" (11:10) is most likely an allusion to the abode of the regathered people on Mount Zion, "glorious" because God is dwelling in their midst, as described in 4:2–6.[56]

God's Presence and God's Spirit

Although the use of the phrase "Spirit of the LORD" in Isaiah 11:2 is not clear in regard to whether it refers to the actual presence of God or not, the use of the word "Spirit" (רוּח, *ruah*) in 32:15 and 44:3, along with concepts of pouring out (עָרָה, *'arah* [32:15]; יָצַק, *yatsaq* [44:3]), does seem to indicate the actual presence of God.[57] Notice also that the "pouring out" of God's Spirit

---

52. G. Smith writes, "By itself, this name does not automatically mean that this son is a divine person, because many names include the name of God in them. But the later use of this same name to describe God himself in 10:21 demands that this son be identified with God in a very close manner. No other person ever has God's name and God is never called Moses, Abram, David, or Jeremiah, so there must be something very special about this son that causes him to have God's name" (G. Smith, *Isaiah 1–39*, 241).

53. G. Smith, *Isaiah 1–39*, 268; Seitz, *Isaiah 1–39*, 96–104; Childs, *Isaiah*, 102.

54. Marlow concludes that the "spirit of the LORD" in Isa. 11:2 validates the coming Davidic ruler just as the presence and absence of the "spirit of the LORD" signaled the rise of David and the fall of Saul in 1 Sam. 16. Furthermore the "spirit of the LORD" serves to empower the coming ruler as it empowered Moses, Elijah, and Elisha (Marlow, "The Spirit of Yahweh," 225–26). Note also the use of wisdom-related terms also associated with "spirit," apparently in parallel in Isa. 11:2.

55. Block, "The View from the Top," 180, 206–7. In this passage the "Spirit of God" is more commonly understood as a special empowering or "superhuman element granted to God's chosen vessel" (Ma, *Until the Spirit Comes*, 68).

56. Childs, *Isaiah*, 106.

57. Chisholm, on the other hand, argues that רוּח in Isa. 32:15 should not even be rendered as "spirit" but rather as "vigor" or "life" (Chisholm, *Handbook on the Prophets*, 78). Thus he would not concur that this is a reference to the presence of God. Most scholars, however, do

is on all the people and not just on selected empowered leaders; thus Isaiah seems to be prophesying of something different from what has happened in the past.[58] Likewise, given the descriptions in the verses that follow each text, the outpouring apparently results in a complete transformation of the people, a transformation that implies the reversal of the covenant curses that Israel had experienced.[59] Indeed, Daniel Block argues convincingly that all four OT texts in which God's Spirit is poured out (Isa. 32:15; 44:3–4; Ezek. 39:29; Joel 2:28) are in covenant contexts, and the pouring out of God's Spirit serves to restore the tripartite covenant relationship between God and his people ("I will be your God; you will be my people; I will dwell in your midst").[60] This outpouring of God's Spirit thus inaugurates the restoration.[61] Block further notes that the pouring out of God's Spirit is the definitive act by which God claims and seals restored Israel as his own people.[62]

The "I Am with You" Presence of God

Throughout Isaiah the image of the future restoration is one of God returning to once again dwell in the midst of Israel. Yet much of the imagery also describes the journey, the trip, the "new exodus" as God defends, protects, and gently leads his people back to Zion to be in his presence. Thus there is a sense of God's presence that assists, protects, and defends his people even before his return to take up residence again in Zion. It is in this context that the repeated phrase "I am with you" occurs (Isa. 41:10; 43:2, 5). God is pointing out that he is with the exiles "as" he restores them or "in order to"

---

understand the "spirit" in Isa. 32:15 as referring to the Spirit of God. See Beyer, *Encountering the Book of Isaiah*, 129; Oswalt, *The Book of Isaiah: Chapters 1–39*, 587; Childs, *Isaiah*, 241; Brueggemann, *Isaiah 1–39*, 258; Blenkinsopp, *Isaiah 1–39*, 434; Waltke with Yu, *Old Testament Theology*, 620–21; Hildebrandt, "Spirit of Yahweh," 753; Routledge, "The Spirit and the Future," 353; VanGemeren and Abernethy, "The Spirit and the Future," 333.

58. Ma, *Until the Spirit Comes*, 101.

59. H. M. Wolff, "Covenant Curse Reversals," 323.

60. Block, "The View from the Top," 202–3. Note the reference to "my people" in Isa. 32:18. Brueggemann writes, "'My people' will now be situated, not in a contested, risky political place, but in a habitation of *shalom*, a place of restful confidence and serene trustfulness. All of the old covenant blessings are now offered as God enacts the new age of well-being" (Brueggemann, *Isaiah 1–39*, 258).

61. Ma, *Until the Spirit Comes*, 102. Blenkinsopp suggests that the "spirit of God" in Isa. 32:15 is the agent of transforming the natural order, a theme that will be expanded upon and given a cosmic context in the "apocalyptic projection of new heavens and new earth (65:17; 66:22)" (Blenkinsopp, *Isaiah 1–39*, 434).

62. Block, "The Prophet of the Spirit," 47; M. V. Van Pelt, W. C. Kaiser, and D. I. Block, "רוּחַ," *NIDOTTE* 3:1077. Also noting the connection between the outpouring of God's Spirit and the restoration of the covenant are Hildebrandt, "Spirit of Yahweh," 753–54; Routledge, "The Spirit and the Future," 353–56.

restore them. That is, his "I am with you" presence is not something to be experienced only after the restoration and his return to Zion but rather is something to draw courage from because his accompanying presence is what will protect them even now in the exile and be with them as the restoration unfolds. This promise of accompanying and protecting presence seems to be different from the "intense" presence of God dwelling in the temple on Mount Zion. This "I am with you" presence is patterned on the exodus experience as far as protection and power go, but it does not seem to include the imagery of clouds and fire, the imagery that normally comes with the revelation of God's glory. That will come later, when God returns to Zion.

Jeremiah

The theme of the presence of God in Jeremiah is similar to the theme in Isaiah, although some points of emphasis as well as a few of the details are different.

God's Presence Is Offended by Sin Right in Front of Him

As in Isaiah, prior to the Babylonian destruction of Jerusalem, the book of Jeremiah presupposes the presence of God dwelling in the temple and reigning from his throne located there. Also as in Isaiah, Jeremiah underscores that the sin of Judah, especially their idolatry, injustice, and hypocritical worship, is especially offensive to God, since he actually dwells right there in the temple. That is, Jeremiah (and often God in first person) will stress the fact that this sin and disrespect are carried out right before or in the presence of (לִפְנֵי, *lipne*) God. There are numerous texts that portray this (e.g., 2:22; 4:1; 23:11; 32:33–34), but it seems to be particularly stressed in the temple sermon of Jeremiah 7. The blatant sinful behavior of the people of Judah, carried out in the temple right in front of God himself, accompanied by hypocritical "worship," is one of the things that especially angers God, who declares, "Will you steal and murder, commit adultery and perjury, burn incense to Baal and follow other gods you have not known, and then come and stand before me in this house [לְפָנַי בַּבַּיִת הַזֶּה, *lepanay babbayit hazeh*] which bears my Name, and say, 'We are safe'—safe to do all these detestable things? Has this house, which bears my Name, become a den of robbers to you? But I have been watching!" (Jer. 7:9–11).[63] Note that God is especially angry at the fact

63. It is highly improbable that Jeremiah's use of "name" in these texts implies a later, more transcendent "name theology" that replaced the earlier, more immanent "*kabod* (glory) theology." First of all, the argument that in the Deuteronomistic History a "name theology" stressing transcendence replaced the earlier "glory theology" stressing immanence has been

that the Judahites think they can blatantly sin before him but then come to the temple for safety, like robbers who hide in a den from the authorities. He is stressing the point that it is he himself dwelling in the temple whom they should fear. Thus, as R. E. Clements writes, "The conquest of Jerusalem and the destruction of the temple were not a denial of the presence of God in Israel's midst, but a confirmation of it, because the events that happened were the consequences of his wrath."[64]

Judgment as Banishment from God's Presence

The language of judgment in Jeremiah is similar to that of Isaiah, filled with terms and concepts carrying connotations of separation from God.[65] Jeremiah stresses two primary concepts of the coming separation. First, God will drive the people of Judah and Jerusalem from his presence and from the land into exile. Second, he himself will leave.

One of the terms used that is particularly ironic (and Jeremiah loves irony and wordplay) is עָזַב ('azab). The NIV frequently translates this as "forsake," but it can also carry strong nuances of "leaving, being left behind, abandoning."[66] God declares that Judah first abandoned or left (עָזַב) him, especially to go worship other gods; thus he will abandon or leave (עָזַב) them. Numerous passages accuse the people in Judah and Jerusalem of leaving or abandoning (עָזַב) God (1:16; 2:13, 17, 19; 5:7, 19; 9:13; 16:11; 17:13; 19:4; 22:9). In 5:19 God connects their abandonment of him directly and ironically

---

seriously (and convincingly) challenged by I. Wilson, *Out of the Midst of the Fire*; Vogt, *Deuteronomic Theology*; Richter, *The Deuteronomistic History*; and, more recently, Cook, "God's Real Absence and Real Presence." Regarding Jer. 7, Mettinger writes, "Jeremiah does not contest the presence of God in his Temple sermon (Jer. 7:1–15). He does not replace it with a sort of Name theology. . . . What Jeremiah does is to impose a *condition* on the presence of God: the obedience of the people to God's will (Jer. 7:9)" (Mettinger, *Dethronement of Sabaoth*, 65). Terrien concurs, "The question was no longer whether God would continue to dwell (*shaken*) in the *hagios topos*, but rather whether he would allow worshippers who are devoid of morality to remain there" (Terrien, *The Elusive Presence*, 205).

64. Clements, *God and Temple*, 101.

65. Besides עָזַב ('azab, to abandon), discussed above, the other words that Jeremiah uses frequently that imply spatial separation include נָטַשׁ (natash, to cast off, throw away, abandon, leave [e.g., 7:29; 23:39]), נָדַח (nadah, to impel, thrust, drive away, banish [e.g., 8:3; 24:9; 27:10, 15; 29:18]), and שָׁלַח (shalah, to send, send away, divorce [e.g., 3:1, 8; 9:16; 15:1]).

66. This meaning can be seen clearly in several nontheological usages of עָזַב in Jeremiah. "All the towns *are deserted*; no one lives in them" (4:29); "Even the doe in the field *deserts* her newborn fawn because there is no grass" (14:5); "Does the snow of Lebanon ever *vanish* from its rocky slopes?" (18:14). Gerstenberger notes that the basic meaning when used with inanimate objects is "to leave." In regard to persons (or God), "this sort of turning away or separation also generates juridical, economic, political, and emotional considerations" (E. Gerstenberger, "עָזַב," *TDOT* 10:586).

to their exile: "And when the people ask, 'Why has the LORD our God done this to us?' you will tell them, 'As you have forsaken me [עֲזַבְתֶּם אוֹתִי, *'azabtem 'oti*] and served foreign gods in your own land, so now you will serve foreigners in a land not your own." R. L. Alden notes that עָזַב is a "covenantal term used to denote the act of breaking the covenant."[67] It is noteworthy that a term with a basic meaning of "to leave" in a spatial sense is used theologically (and somewhat figuratively) to refer to rupturing the covenant relationship. God uses the term as well, declaring in 12:7, "I will forsake [עָזַבְתִּי, *'azabti*] my house, abandon [נָטַשְׁתִּי, *natashti*; see discussion below on נָטַשׁ, *natash*] my inheritance; I will give the one I love into the hands of her enemies."[68] Thus Thomas Raitt concludes, "At the onset of the full destructive power of the Exile's punishments, God was understood to have ended his relationship with his people and to have left them."[69]

Yet the judgment vocabulary in Jeremiah is rich, and there are numerous other words and concepts also used to convey the idea of forced separation from God's presence into exile. For example, in 10:18 God states, "At this time I will hurl out [הִנְנִי קוֹלֵעַ, *hineni qolea'*] those who live in this land." The word קָלַע (*qala'*) is also used for "slinging" a rock as a weapon (Judg. 20:16; 1 Sam. 17:49). In 16:13 God uses the word טוּל (*tul*, throw, hurl), a term also used for "throwing" spears (1 Sam. 18:11; 20:33): "So I will throw you out [וְהֵטַלְתִּי, *wehetalti*] of this land into a land neither you nor your ancestors have known." Nuances of "scattering" are conveyed with the word פּוּץ (*puts*), used in 18:17: "Like a wind from the east, I will scatter them [אֲפִיצֵם, *'apitsem*] before their enemies; I will show them my back and not my face."[70]

---

67. R. L. Alden, "עָזַב," *NIDOTTE* 3:365. Stähli also notes that עָזַב is very frequently used in covenant contexts, presenting the abandonment of God or his covenant. Jeremiah, he observes, uses the term "to characterize the abandonment and thus the disruption of the covenant relationship" (H.-P. Stähli, "עָזַב," *TLOT* 2:868).

68. The word "house" can refer to the people (J. Thompson, *The Book of Jeremiah*, 357) or, more likely, to the temple. See Lundbom, *Jeremiah 1–20*, 653; J. D. Hays, *Jeremiah and Lamentations*, 82. "Inheritance" in this verse probably refers to both the land and the people. "The one I love" refers to the people. See Lundbom, *Jeremiah 1–20*, 654.

69. Raitt, *A Theology of the Exile*, 66.

70. Note the idiom of God now showing the people his back rather than his face. Lundbom sees this as a striking and ironic anthropomorphism: the people have been turning their backs to God (Jer. 2:27; 7:24; 32:33), and now God turns his back to them in a fitting punishment (Lundbom, *Jeremiah 1–20*, 823). Yet note that throughout this study we have seen a close connection between the term for "face" (פָּנִים, *panim*) and God's presence. So when God turns his back to them rather than his face, it signals the loss of his powerful and protective presence. Longman captures this imagery: "By showing them his back rather than his face, he indicates that he will depart from them during the day of their disaster, when the punishment comes. They will see his back as he walks away from them to let them suffer the consequences in his absence" (Longman, *Jeremiah, Lamentations*, 141).

God also uses פוץ to refer to the exile in 9:16; 13:24; 30:11. Finally, God uses the Hiphil of סור (*sur*, clear away, get rid of, remove) in 32:31: "From the day it was built until now, this city has so aroused my anger and wrath that I must remove it from my sight [לְהָסִירָהּ מֵעַל פָּנַי, *lahasirah me'al panay*]." Note also that the word translated by the NIV as "my sight" is פָּנַי (*panay*, my face), the term often used of God's presence. This nuance is captured by the CSB: "I will therefore remove it from my presence."[71]

God Personally Fights against Jerusalem

As in Isaiah, one of the most terrifying images in Jeremiah, as the prophet warns of the coming judgment, is that of God himself personally fighting against Jerusalem and Judah. So not only will God withdraw his presence from the temple, from where he was protecting the people of Judah, but also his presence will actually fight against them. Texts that present this terrifying judgment include Jeremiah 4:26;[72] 9:16; 21:5,[73] 10; 33:5;[74] 44:11.

God Will Return to His Throne in Zion, a Throne without the Ark

Although the first twenty-nine chapters of Jeremiah focus on judgment, there are several significant texts describing the spectacular future time of restoration. Jeremiah 3:16–18 is one of those important texts:

> "In those days when your numbers have increased greatly in the land," declares the LORD, "people will no longer say, 'The ark of the covenant of the LORD.' It will never enter their minds or be remembered; it will not be missed, nor will another one be made. At that time they will call Jerusalem the Throne of the LORD, and all nations will gather in Jerusalem to honor the name of the LORD. No longer will they follow the stubbornness of their evil hearts.

71. The same idiomatic phrase is used in 2 Kings 23:27 (אָסִיר מֵעַל פָּנַי, *'asir me'l panay*) and 24:3 (לְהָסִיר מֵעַל פָּנָיו, *lehasir me'l panayw*) in clear reference to the exile.

72. McKane comments, "The townships lie in ruins and this is not simply the blind cruelty of natural or historical disaster. It is the deliberate action of Yahweh" (McKane, *Jeremiah*, 1:107). Longman notes that this imagery connects to the theme of God as a divine warrior who has come to punish (Longman, *Jeremiah, Lamentations*, 51).

73. The pronoun "I" is emphatic (וְנִלְחַמְתִּי אֲנִי אִתְּכֶם, *wenilhamti 'ani 'ittekem*). Lundbom states, "It is Yahweh himself who is taking up the fight against his covenant people" (Lundbom, *Jeremiah 21–36*, 102). Longman calls it a "reverse holy war" (Longman, *Jeremiah, Lamentations*, 154).

74. Regarding this verse, Goldingay writes, "It is not merely Babylonian missiles that are hitting the fabric and the people of Jerusalem. Yhwh is hitting them" (Goldingay, *Old Testament Theology*, 2:359).

In those days the people of Judah will join the people of Israel, and together they will come from a northern land to the land I gave your ancestors as an inheritance."

The phrase "In those days" implies that the future will be different and will have important discontinuities with the past.[75] "When your numbers have increased greatly" envisions the future restoration, when God's people are back in the land, fruitfully multiplying. What is rather shocking about this vision of the future is that there is no ark of the covenant in Jerusalem.[76] Since the construction of the tabernacle during the exodus, and continuing into the time of the temple in Jerusalem, the ark of the covenant had been the central focal point for the presence of God dwelling in Israel's midst. Also, the ark often was associated with the throne of God, viewed either as the throne itself or as the footstool of his throne (2 Kings 19:15; 1 Chron. 28:2; Ps. 99:1). Even more shocking is the fact that no one misses it or tries to replace it.[77] The reason that no one misses it or tries to replace it is given in 3:17: "They will call Jerusalem the Throne of the LORD." Thus the city of Jerusalem will replace the ark as God's throne.[78] Jeremiah describes a time when the presence of God has returned, but his imagery is not that of God returning to the temple to dwell in the holy of holies enthroned on the ark as in the past. In the future, the entire city of Jerusalem will be the throne of God, who now seems to dwell in the city.

In the second half of 3:17 the NIV reads, "and all nations will gather [or "will be gathered"—the stem is Niphal] in Jerusalem to honor the name of the LORD." Furthermore, the NIV has assumed the connotation of "to honor," but the text actually says only that they will be gathered "to the name of the LORD, to Jerusalem" (לְשֵׁם יְהוָה לִירוּשָׁלָ͏ִם, *leshem Yahweh lirushalaim*).[79] As discussed earlier, however, the "name of the LORD" is another way of referring to his presence, and this is the probable meaning here, as the NRSV and ESV translate ("and all nations shall gather to it, to the presence of the LORD in

---

75. Lundbom, *Jeremiah 1–20*, 314.

76. The statement "People will no longer say, 'The ark of the covenant of the LORD'" seems to imply that the phrase "the ark of the covenant of the LORD" was being used as an oath, like the oath "This is the temple of the LORD" in 7:4. See McKane, *Jeremiah*, 1:73; Lundbom, *Jeremiah 1–20*, 314.

77. Recall that the ark of the covenant symbolized several extremely important theological realities. Not only did it serve as the throne of Yahweh, but also it served as the "mercy seat" for the Day of Atonement, and it contained the "torah," the law of God. It underscored the holiness of God and the difficulty of sinful people approaching the holy God.

78. Lundbom, *Jeremiah 1–20*, 314; McKane, *Jeremiah*, 1:73.

79. Lundbom, *Jeremiah 1–20*, 315. Note, however, that the entire phrase "to the name of the LORD, to Jerusalem" is lacking in the LXX, replaced by the simple "to her."

Jerusalem").[80] The presence of God seems to pervade the entire city,[81] with the nations of the world gathered around.[82] So Jeremiah 3:16–18 describes a time in the future when the presence of God will be in the city of Jerusalem, ruling from his throne, but not the throne associated with the ark of the covenant. Indeed, the entire city will be considered his throne.

God Regathers His People as a Shepherd Gathers His Flock

As in Isaiah, in Jeremiah God promises to be personally involved in the restoration of his people, regathering them like a caring shepherd gathers his sheep (Jer. 23:3). Likewise, as in Isaiah (and especially in Ezekiel), the image of God as the loving shepherd and that of the coming messianic figure whom he raises up as shepherd sometimes overlap or merge. Thus in Jeremiah 23:3–6 God says that he himself will regather the flock, but also that he will place shepherds over them and raise up a righteous and just Davidic king to rule over them.

God's Restored Presence Is at the Center of the New Covenant

Jeremiah 30–33 is filled with repeated language of how God will personally regather and restore his scattered people. This regathering is driven by the powerful, purposeful presence of God, and it leads to the new covenant. Jeremiah 30:11, for example, reads, "For I am with you, says the Lord, to save you" (NRSV) (כִּי־אִתְּךָ אֲנִי נְאֻם־יְהוָה לְהוֹשִׁיעֶךָ, *ki-'ittka 'ani ne'um-Yahweh lehoshi'eka*).[83] Tremper Longman states that this declaration ("I am with you") indicates a restoration of God's presence and thus a restoration of the covenant that had been disrupted by the sin of the people.[84] That the covenant is being restored is made certain by 30:22, where God declares the

80. Terrien notes that a number of commentators translate the phrase as "to the *presence* of Yahweh in Jerusalem" (Terrien, *The Elusive Presence*, 207).

81. Allen, *Jeremiah*, 58; Longman, *Jeremiah, Lamentations*, 43. Weinfeld writes, "All Jerusalem is, as it were, the abode of God" (Weinfeld, "Jeremiah and the Spiritual Metamorphosis," 20). Harrison explains, "The divine presence in Zion will overshadow the ark and other cultic objects by its majesty, making the use of such symbols of God's reality unnecessary" (Harrison, *Jeremiah and Lamentations*, 66).

82. Jeremiah 16:19–21 is similar in regard to depicting the nations as coming to God in the future: "Lord, . . . to you the nations will come from the ends of the earth. . . . 'Therefore I will teach them . . . my power and my might. Then they will know that my name is the Lord.'"

83. "I am with you to save you" (NRSV, ESV, NASB) captures the Hebrew grammatical sense better than the NIV's "I am with you and will save you." Note that Jer. 30:11–12 is lacking in the LXX but reappears almost identically in Jer. 46:27–28. God will promise "I am with you" to Jeremiah several times (1:8, 19; 15:20). The construction in 15:20 (כִּי־אִתְּךָ אֲנִי לְהוֹשִׁיעֶךָ, *ki-'itteka 'ani lehoshi'aka*) is very similar to that in 30:11 and 46:27–28.

84. Longman, *Jeremiah, Lamentations*, 200.

rest of the tripartite formula of the covenant: "So you will be my people, and I will be your God."[85] Stating the three aspects of this tripartite covenant formula ("I will be your God; you will be my people; I will dwell in your midst") indicates that a "new" covenant is being promised, one with a restored presence of God; indeed, Jeremiah will spell out the details of the new covenant in the next chapter (Jer. 31).

Thus the opening verse of Jeremiah 31 restates the "I will be their God; they will be my people" formula. Then 31:6 envisions the restoration of God's presence back in Zion: "Come, let us go up to Zion, to the LORD our God." Then in the verses that follow (31:7–14) God is once again depicted as personally regathering his flock like a shepherd and restoring them to their land. In 31:23 the "sacred mountain" refers to Zion (cf. 31:6), the Temple Mount, which lies at the center of the blessings bestowed on the returned exiles,[86] again implying that it is God's presence there that brings this blessing.

In Jeremiah 31:31–33 God declares explicitly that he will make a "new covenant" with Israel and Judah because they broke the old one made at Sinai. This "new covenant" seems to be right at the heart of the restoration. Allusions back to the exodus and to the old covenant made during the exodus at Mount Sinai are strong. Just as a new exodus had been promised in 16:14–15, so now a new covenant to go with the new exodus is promised.[87] In 31:33 a clear connection is made to the tripartite covenant formulation. Jeremiah 31:33 repeats two of the elements in their typical formulation: "I will be their God, and they will be my people." The third aspect, God's presence ("I will dwell in their midst"), undergoes a surprising modification, for Jeremiah 31:33 declares, "I will put my law [תּוֹרָתִי, *torati*] in their midst [בְּקִרְבָּם, *beqirbam*] and write it on their hearts."

Note that *torah* means not only "law" but also "teaching" or "instruction." It is frequently associated with the revelation of God's will, and in Jeremiah it normally refers to "commandments, statutes, and words that must be heeded."[88] Second, this text has several connections back to Jeremiah 7 and 11 (the broken covenant),[89] as well as to 3:16–18, where the future restoration (time of the new covenant) is described and the ark of the covenant, a central feature of the old covenant, is explicitly said to be absent but not missed.[90]

---

85. Longman, *Jeremiah, Lamentations*, 203; J. D. Hays, *Jeremiah and Lamentations*, 220; Allen, *Jeremiah*, 339.

86. Longman, *Jeremiah, Lamentations*, 209.

87. Allen, *Jeremiah*, 355.

88. Keown, Scalise, and Smothers, *Jeremiah 26–52*, 134.

89. Allen, *Jeremiah*, 355.

90. Keown, Scalise, and Smothers, *Jeremiah 26–52*, 133.

There was a strong tradition that placed the *torah* of God in or next to the ark (Deut. 31:26; Exod. 25:16). Just as God would not be returning to the ark as his throne and localized place of his presence (Jer. 3:16–18), so also God will renew dramatically both the location of the *torah* (placed in their midst, written on their hearts) and their ability to obey it. The result of this *torah* (teaching) in their midst is given in 31:34: "They will all know me, from the least of them to the greatest," indicating a widespread restored relationship between God and his people.[91]

Ezekiel

Numerous scholars have noted that the central theological movement of the book of Ezekiel can be tracked through three major visions of Ezekiel, all of which relate to the presence of God: (1) Ezekiel sees God on his mobile throne with the exiles in Babylon (1:1–3:15); (2) Ezekiel sees God leave the temple in Jerusalem (8:1–11:25); and (3) Ezekiel sees God come back into the new, future temple (40:1–48:35).[92] These three units are also tightly connected by the use of the phrase "glory of the LORD" (כְּבוֹד־יְהוָה, *kebod-Yahweh*), a phrase that refers to the presence of God and that occurs numerous times in these texts.[93] Also, throughout the book the word פָּנֶה (*paneh*, face, presence) occurs (in various grammatical forms) over 150 times. Likewise, Ezekiel opens with a vision of God's presence and then closes with this statement: "And the name of the city from that time on will be: THE LORD IS THERE" (48:35). Without doubt, the presence of God (his departure and return) is a central theme, if not *the* central theme, in the book of Ezekiel.[94]

91. Leene points out the similarities between Jer. 31:31–33 and Jer. 24:5–7. In 24:5–7 God speaks of the restoration of Israel, likewise using the covenant formula "They will be my people, and I will be their God" (24:7), and promising to give them a "heart" to know him, that he is Yahweh (Leene, "Ezekiel and Jeremiah," 161–62).

92. McConville, *A Guide to the Prophets*, 87, 99–100; Blenkinsopp, *A History of Prophecy in Israel*, 168–69; Petersen, *The Prophetic Literature*, 140. Some scholars add the fourth vision in Ezek. 37:1–14 (the valley of dry bones) into this breakdown by vision. See, for example, Darr, "The Book of Ezekiel," 1089. Kutsko suggests that the book revolves structurally around the Jerusalem temple and the divine כָּבוֹד (*kabod*, glory = presence). He organizes the flow of thought in chiastic form: A—From Divine Presence to Divine Absence (1:1–11:25); B—Preparation for Destruction (12:1–24:27); C—Oracles against the Nations (25:1–32:32); B'—Preparation for Restoration (33:1–39:29); A'—From Divine Absence to Divine Presence (40:1–48:35) (Kutsko, *Between Heaven and Earth*, 1–2, 9).

93. Tooman, "Covenant and Presence," 156.

94. House, *Old Testament Theology*, 327–29. House entitles his chapter on Ezekiel "The God Who Is Present."

Ezekiel Encounters the Presence of God While in Exile

Ezekiel's first encounter with the presence of God occurs in 1:1–3:15.[95] As with Isaiah's encounter with God in Isaiah 6, Ezekiel's encounter with God serves as the prophet's special prophetic "call" or "commissioning." While there are several similarities between Ezekiel's engagement with God and Isaiah's engagement with God, there are important differences as well.[96] The most obvious difference, of course, is the location. Isaiah encounters God in the temple, where God normally dwelt. Ezekiel encounters the presence of God while in exile in Babylonia. So while Isaiah's encounter stresses the holiness of God as the starting point for his call, Ezekiel's encounter stresses the mobility of God and his sovereign power to show up even in Babylonia to call and to empower his prophet among the exiles. Also, while in Isaiah the scene is one of worshiping God seated peacefully up on his throne in the temple, in Ezekiel the glory of God (1:28) comes in the "windstorm" on a fiery chariot accompanied with lightning flashes, more in keeping with how he appeared back in the exodus.[97]

The phrase "glory of the LORD" is used frequently in Ezekiel.[98] It is a clear reference to the presence of God.[99] Walther Zimmerli writes, "No vague presence of deity passed him by, but Yahweh, the God of Israel, in the glory of the כְּבוֹד־יְהוָה met him as he had met with Israel in the great events of the wilderness period."[100]

Another very significant feature in Ezekiel's vision that differs from Isaiah's is the important and pervasive role that the "Spirit/spirit" plays. Indeed, the word רוּחַ (*ruah*, spirit, wind, breath) occurs eight times in this opening call narrative (1:4, 12, 20, 21; 2:2; 3:12, 14, 24). This introductory usage plays an important role in setting the stage for the frequent use of רוּחַ throughout the book of Ezekiel. Indeed, Daniel Block calls Ezekiel "The Prophet of the Spirit."[101]

95. Kutsko remarks, "Indeed, Ezek 1:1–3:15 and 8:1–11:25 contain the most graphic portrayals of the divine presence in the Hebrew Bible" (Kutsko, *Between Heaven and Earth*, 88).
96. See the comparison of the two visions in Zimmerli, *Ezekiel 1*, 108–10.
97. Zimmerli, *Ezekiel 1*, 109. The picture of God riding on his fiery storm-chariot, along with the ominous burning coals, is a terrifying vision that brings connotations of judgment and wrath, a dominant theme in the early years of Ezekiel's ministry. See C. Wright, *The Message of Ezekiel*, 53; Block, *The Book of Ezekiel: Chapters 1–24*, 108–9.
98. The "glory of the LORD" or "the glory of the God of Israel" occurs in Ezek. 1:28; 3:12, 23; 8:4; 9:3; 10:4, 18, 19; 11:22, 23; 43:2, 4, 5; 44:4.
99. Eichrodt, *Ezekiel*, 58; Zimmerli, *Ezekiel 1*, 124; Block, *The Book of Ezekiel: Chapters 1–24*, 105; Kutsko, *Between Heaven and Earth*, 12.
100. Zimmerli, *Ezekiel 1*, 124.
101. Block, "The Prophet of the Spirit," 27–49.

In Ezekiel 1:4 the term רוּחַ refers to a windstorm. In 1:12, however, even though the NIV translates with a lowercase *s* ("Wherever the spirit would go, they would go"), the use of רוּחַ in this verse is best understood as the "Spirit" coming from the one seated on the throne, God himself.[102] Likewise in 1:20 the first reference to רוּחַ ("wherever the Spirit would go") should be understood as the רוּחַ (Spirit) coming from God. Less clear is the later reference in 1:20, repeated in 1:21, to the רוּחַ הַחַיָּה (*ruah hahayah*), translated by the NIV as "the spirit of the living creatures." This is the "spirit" that enlivens the wheels themselves and gives them motion and direction. Although the NIV takes the singular term הַחַיָּה ("the life" or "the living one") as a collective for all four living creatures, a number of scholars have argued that the word should be rendered just as "life" and the phrase translated as "the Spirit of life," a reference back to the same Spirit in 1:12 and 1:20 that emanates from God seated on his throne, who controls all movement of the creatures, wheels, and throne.[103]

In Ezekiel 1:28 the prophet falls on his face before the glory of God. In 2:1 God tells him to stand up, and then in 2:2 Ezekiel states that "the Spirit came into me and raised me to my feet." At this point God explains to Ezekiel the task ahead. After God is finished speaking to Ezekiel, the Spirit lifts Ezekiel up (3:12) and then takes him away (3:14). In 3:22–24 Ezekiel has an experience similar to that in 2:1–2: he sees the glory of God; he falls down on his face; the Spirit lifts him up; and God gives him instructions.

It is interesting to note that although the book of Isaiah uses the term רוּחַ fifty-one times, there is no mention of the Spirit at all in Isaiah's vision of God in the temple (Isa. 6). When Isaiah speaks of the Spirit in association with God, it is generally in passages describing the future restoration. Ezekiel, on the other hand, uses the term רוּחַ extensively in describing his encounters with God. Throughout the call of Ezekiel (1:4–3:27) the Spirit (רוּחַ), apparently closely associated with God himself and emanating from him, plays an important role in moving the chariot and in moving Ezekiel.

So does the repeated use of רוּחַ in the opening call narrative of Ezekiel convey anything special or alert us to some introductory theological point? While acknowledging the complexity of the term and the wide semantic range

102. Zimmerli, *Ezekiel 1*, 130; Block, "The Prophet of the Spirit," 36; Cooper, *Ezekiel*, 67; Allen, *Ezekiel 1–19*, 32; Greenberg, *Ezekiel 1–20*, 45–46; Eichrodt, *Ezekiel*, 57; C. Wright, *The Message of Ezekiel*, 50; R. Alexander, "Ezekiel," 757; Schuele, "The Spirit of YHWH," 21–22. Thus the CSB translates, "Wherever the Spirit wanted to go, they went."

103. Block, *The Book of Ezekiel: Chapters 1–24*, 101; Block, "The Prophet of the Spirit," 36–37; Zimmerli, *Ezekiel 1*, 130; C. Wright, *The Message of Ezekiel*, 50; Allen, *Ezekiel 1–19*, 34; Cooper, *Ezekiel*, 69; Levison, *Filled with the Spirit*, 97–98.

of usage, Daniel Block nevertheless comes to some general conclusions about the term in Ezekiel. In understanding the רוּחַ of God, he concludes, "We should think first and foremost of the divine presence on earth. . . . The *rwḥ* [רוּחַ]is the power of God at work among humankind. It is his creating, animating, energizing force. The *rwḥ* [רוּחַ] can hardly be identified as one other than God himself."[104]

Recently Andreas Schuele has proposed that in Ezekiel רוּחַ functions as "another layer to the manifestation of God's presence." That is, the רוּחַ is a powerful and fluid wind-like force that surrounds the intense "glory of the LORD" presence. Unlike the "glory of the LORD," Schuele maintains, "the free-flowing *rûaḥ* draws humans into the aura of the divine presence; and while even this is still a forceful and not entirely 'safe' encounter with God, the *rûaḥ* is seen as that part of the divine aura that connects with the human world and becomes a power of transformation and change."[105]

God Dwells in the Temple and Is Offended by Idolatry There

As in Isaiah and Jeremiah, and prior to the departure of God from the temple in Ezekiel 8–11, God is depicted as dwelling in the temple in Jerusalem, from where he is particularly offended by the idolatrous practices of the people of Judah right in and around the temple itself. The book of Ezekiel frequently points out this particular offense against God's holy presence.[106] The reason for this, according to John Kutsko, is that idolatry is an "illegitimate expression for God's presence."[107] In a book that focuses on the presence and absence of God, therefore, it is not surprising that one of the subthemes is Israel's faith in the false presence of the pagan gods.[108]

104. Block, "The Prophet of the Spirit," 48–49.

105. Schuele, "The Spirit of YHWH," 21–22. Schuele also proposes that the *kabod* and *ruah* seem to reflect the graded holiness associated with the temple and the tabernacle (i.e., most holy place, holy place, courtyards, camp/city). Regarding the unique and central role that the "spirit" plays in Ezekiel, Levison notes that not only does the spirit give life, but it gives movement and vitality to that life (Levison, *Filled with the Spirit*, 97–98). MacDonald likewise observes the centrality of the "spirit" in Ezekiel's encounters with God, especially in his call as a prophet (MacDonald, "The Spirit of YHWH").

106. Kutsko, *Between Heaven and Earth*, 25–29. Ezekiel is also unique in that he does not use the term אֱלֹהִים (*'elohim*) to refer to the idols, but rather uses the derogatory term גִּלּוּלִים (*gillulim*), which carried connotations of "excrement" or "dung balls." See the discussion by Kutsko, *Between Heaven and Earth*, 32–35; Barrett, "Idols, Idolatry, Gods," 354.

107. Kutsko, *Between Heaven and Earth*, 25–76.

108. Kutsko writes, "Ezekiel purposefully mocks idolatry in order to offer the exiles a theological proposition: the physical presence of idols indicates their powerlessness, and the absence of God's presence indicates God's power" (Kutsko, *Between Heaven and Earth*, 75).

In Ezekiel 8 God will take Ezekiel on a tour back in Jerusalem (where God is dwelling) through the temple, pointing out numerous areas where idolatry is occurring right in the temple gates and in the temple courtyards. In 8:6 God asks Ezekiel, "Do you see what they are doing—the utterly detestable things the Israelites are doing here, things that will drive me far from my sanctuary?" It is not just the temple grounds that are defiled. It is the holy presence of God in the temple that is offended, and this blatant defilement is encroaching dangerously close.[109] This theme is repeated with slight variation in 23:36–39.

Judgment as Separation from the Presence of God

As in Isaiah and Jeremiah, in Ezekiel the judgment coming on Israel/Judah often is described in terms relating to separation from God, and thus also the loss of his protective and blessing presence in Jerusalem. In Ezekiel 7:22, for example, God states, "I will turn my face away from the people, and robbers will desecrate the place I treasure." The phrase "I will turn my face" describes a separation between God and people. It is often used of God's abandonment of Jerusalem and the consequent destruction of Jerusalem,[110] a meaning that it seems to carry here in this verse. Although "the place I treasure" could refer to the entire land or to the city of Jerusalem, it probably refers to the temple. God will abandon the temple, and the invading Babylonians will defile it.[111] In 39:23–24 the semantic equivalent "I hid my face from them" is used twice. As mentioned above, this phrase implies the removal of God's presence and an abandonment by God leading to a separation between God and his people.[112]

Likewise, and similar to the pattern seen in Isaiah and in Jeremiah, in Ezekiel not only does God separate himself from Jerusalem and Judah in judgment, but also he separates the people from him and from the land by driving them into exile. For example, in Ezekiel 22:15 he declares, "I will disperse you among the nations and scatter you through the countries."

God Finally Departs from the Temple

One of the most significant events in Ezekiel and central to his theology of divine presence is his vision of the departure of God from the temple in

---

109. Block states that this activity has alienated God from his own sanctuary. These practices present "a direct challenge to Yahweh's presence. Either Yahweh alone is Israel's God (cf. v. 4) or he is not their God at all" (Block, *The Book of Ezekiel: Chapters 1–24*, 287–88).

110. Balentine, *The Hidden God*, 17, 68.

111. Eichrodt, *Ezekiel*, 104; Zimmerli, *Ezekiel 1*, 212.

112. Balentine, *The Hidden God*, 68.

Ezekiel 8:1–11:25.[113] In 8:3 the Spirit lifts Ezekiel up and takes him in a vision to the temple in Jerusalem. There, as discussed above, he witnesses the terrible extent to which Israel was practicing idolatry right before God in the temple complex. Indeed, God tells him that these things will drive him far from his sanctuary (8:6). In Ezekiel 9 the prophet sees the "glory of the LORD" move to the threshold of the temple, where God decrees judgment (death) on all in the city of Jerusalem who do not mourn over the detestable things occurring in the temple. This judgment is to start right there at the sanctuary (9:6). The judgment on the city thus begins at the very time God abandons his temple, and at his instigation.[114] In this vision it is not the Babylonians who are the attackers of Jerusalem; it is God himself who has become Jerusalem's enemy.[115] Then again in Ezekiel 10, as in Ezekiel 1, the prophet sees "the glory of the LORD" on his chariot throne accompanied by four "living creatures." Now that Ezekiel sees this vision and these creatures at the temple in Jerusalem, he is able to identify them as cherubim, heavenly creatures that serve as attendants and guardians of God's presence.[116] In Ezekiel 10 the prophet sees God and his chariot throne emerge from the temple and stop at the east gate. In 11:1 the Spirit once again lifts Ezekiel up and takes him to the east gate. From there he sees the "glory of the LORD," the presence of God, depart from the temple and move to the Mount of Olives to the east (11:22–23),[117] after which the Spirit lifts Ezekiel up again and takes him back to Babylonia. Implicit from the context is that God is leaving the temple because of the accumulated and consistent sin of the people, especially their idolatry. Paul House notes the irony: "By not acknowledging the Lord's presence in proper ways the people have exchanged protective presence for a terrible, punishing force."[118] God's departure is an abandonment of the temple and of Jerusalem, leaving the inhabitants to be finished off by the coming Babylonians.[119]

---

113. Block notes that while the theme of God leaving his people occurs in both Isaiah and Jeremiah, it is Ezekiel who develops "the theme of Yahweh's abandonment of his temple and his city most fully" (Block, *The Book of Ezekiel: Chapters 1–24*, 274–75). Clements states, "This vision drama is the pivotal center of the entire book of Ezekiel's prophecies" (Clements, *Ezekiel*, 34).

114. Allen, *Ezekiel 1–19*, 167.

115. Clements, *Ezekiel*, 41.

116. See J. D. Hays, *The Temple and the Tabernacle*, 106.

117. The movement of God ends with him above the Mount of Olives, just east of the temple. There is no indication of whether or not he continues on to Babylonia. See House, *Old Testament Theology*, 333. Note that in 43:1–5 the presence of God will return to the temple "from the east."

118. House, *Old Testament Theology*, 333.

119. Zimmerli, *Ezekiel 1*, 253.

So in a very real sense, the presence of God leaves the temple in Jerusalem.[120] At this point one wonders if this signals the end of the old covenant, as expressed in the tripartite formula: "I will be your God; you will be my people; *I will dwell in your midst.*"[121] Certainly the blessings for covenant obedience in Deuteronomy 28:1–12 depart with God, and the curses for covenant disobedience, already underway, start to escalate (Deut. 28:15–68).[122]

God Personally Fights against Jerusalem

As in Isaiah and Jeremiah, in Ezekiel God not only withdraws his protective and blessing covenant presence from Jerusalem but also becomes their enemy. God himself uses graphic language that depicts him as personally fighting against them. His presence is no longer a comfort and blessing; now it terrorizes in judgment.[123] For example, in numerous texts God is depicted as brandishing a sword against Israel (often Jerusalem) (5:17; 6:3; 11:8; 12:14; 14:17; 21:3–5; 33:2).[124]

Likewise, the phrase "I am against you" (הִנְנִי עָלַיִךְ, *hineni 'alayik*) occurs numerous times in Ezekiel, with either Jerusalem or the foreign nations usually as the target of God's opposition (5:8; 13:8, 20; 26:3; 28:22; 29:3, 10; 30:22; 34:10; 35:3; 38:3; 39:1). There is a fairly strong argument for viewing the phrase "I am against you" as a formula that "constituted the cry by which one person would challenge another in man-to-man combat."[125] Thus it implies that God has become Jerusalem's enemy and is intent on personally

---

120. Raitt summarizes, "God separates himself from his people, rejects the dispensation of the temple which formerly made him accessible, and initiates an annihilatory judgment which is understood as an outpouring of his wrath" (Raitt, *A Theology of Exile*, 74).

121. Raitt states, "Ezekiel stands in substantial continuity with Hosea and Jeremiah in preaching a suspension in the election status of Judah within the framework of the Exodus-Sinai tradition" (Raitt, *A Theology of Exile*, 74).

122. Block writes, "When God abandons his people, they lose all right to his favor and his protection. From Ezekiel's perspective, the turning point in Israel's history came not with the accession of Zedekiah or even the Babylonian capture of Jerusalem, but with the departure of the glory of the King of heaven from his temple" (Block, *The Book of Ezekiel: Chapters 1–24*, 360).

123. Terrien observes, "Jeremiah and Ezekiel 'saw' in the catastrophe, not the sign of Yahweh's absence, but, on the contrary, the manifestation of his presence in judgment" (Terrien, *The Elusive Presence*, 262).

124. While we obviously view the image of God with drawn sword as an anthropomorphic figure of speech (perhaps metonymy), O. Kaiser reminds us that "where we sense an abstract generalization, the ancient Israelite, at least in form of expression, clung to the specific and concrete" (O. Kaiser, "חֶרֶב," *TDOT* 5:162). Likewise, the image of God as a warrior fighting against Israel as an enemy is a well-documented one. See Longman and Reid, *God Is a Warrior*, 48–60; P. Miller, *The Divine Warrior*, 170–75.

125. Block, *The Book of Ezekiel: Chapters 1–24*, 201–2; Zimmerli, *Ezekiel 1*, 175. The original case for this view was developed by Humbert, "Die Herausforderungsformel 'hinnenî êlékâ.'"

fighting against it. Furthermore, "I am against you" is the exact opposite of the covenant statement of protecting presence, "I am with you."[126]

The terrifyingly direct and personal encounter with God in judgment is likewise expressed with the phrase "face to face" (פָּנִים אֶל־פָּנִים, *panim 'el-panim*) in 20:35: "I will bring you into the wilderness of the nations and there, face to face, I will execute judgment upon you." "Face to face" recalls how Moses used to meet with God (Exod. 33:11; Deut. 34:10), but this time the point of such a meeting will not be intimate relationship (as with Moses) but instead terrifying judgment. There will be no cloud or mediator to protect Israel from the intense and dangerous presence of God.[127] In fact, in alluding to the exodus, this text in Ezekiel seems to be reversing the great story of God's deliverance to create an "antitype." Rather than encounter the powerful and terrifying presence of God in the wilderness in deliverance and in covenant relationship, now in the wilderness Israel will encounter the terrifying presence of God in unmediated judgment—quite a reversal.[128]

Covenant, Presence, and Spirit in the Future Restoration

In Ezekiel 36:24–28 God speaks of the future restoration (God speaks similarly in 11:17–20). First God speaks of regathering his people from all the countries (36:24). Then he declares, "I will give you a new heart and put a new spirit in you; I will remove from you your heart of stone and give you a heart of flesh. And I will put my Spirit in you and move you to follow my decrees and be careful to keep my laws. Then you will live in the land I gave your ancestors; you will be my people, and I will be your God" (36:26–28). The promise of God's Spirit ("I will put my Spirit in you") is much different from merely an inner transformation of the human heart.[129] That is, the transforming cause of the "new heart" and the "new spirit" is the Spirit of God living in the midst of his people.[130] That is, people's hearts will be transformed, but they will be transformed by the presence of

---

126. Block, *The Book of Ezekiel: Chapters 1–24*, 202; C. Wright, *The Message of Ezekiel*, 90.

127. Block, *The Book of Ezekiel: Chapters 1–24*, 651.

128. Allen, *Ezekiel 20–48*, 15–16; Kutsko, *Between Heaven and Earth*, 94–95; Zimmerli, *Ezekiel 1*, 416.

129. Leene compares the "inner renewal" in Ezek. 36 with that in Jer. 31, arguing that Jeremiah is dependent upon Ezekiel, rather than Ezekiel upon Jeremiah. Yet Leene stays with terms of "inner renewal" and does not address the implications of God's Spirit, not just the "new heart" and "new spirit," within them (Leene, "Ezekiel and Jeremiah," 150–75).

130. Note also how this is restated clearly at the conclusion of Ezek. 1–39: "I will no longer hide my face from them, for I will pour out my Spirit on the people of Israel" (39:29).

God's Spirit that he will put within them. Thus Block argues that the "new spirit" mentioned in 36:26 is God's רוּחַ (the Spirit of God),[131] the "divine presence on earth."[132]

Ezekiel's vision of the valley of dry bones in 37:1–14 connects to 36:26 and expands on it,[133] indicating that the Spirit of God will play the critical role in reviving the life of Israel. Nathan MacDonald observes that Ezekiel 37 is about the revivification of Israel and also about the return of God's gracious presence.[134] Then at the end of Ezekiel 37 God speaks of making a "covenant of peace," an "everlasting covenant" (37:26). A critical part of this "restored" or "new" covenant is the presence of God, for he proclaims, "I will put my sanctuary among them forever. My dwelling place will be with them; I will be their God, and they will be my people" (37:26–27).

These passages (Ezek. 11:17–20; 36:24–28; 37:14, 24–28) are closely interconnected around the related themes of restoration, the Spirit of God as presence, and the formation of a "new" or "restored" covenant. Likewise, the language and terminology used in Ezekiel imply a close relationship with Jeremiah 31:31–33 as well.[135] Note the frequent reference in these passages to the tripartite covenant formula, "I will be your God; you will be my people; I will dwell in your midst," using various ways of describing the third category:

> I will make a new covenant. . . . I will put my law in their minds [*torah* in their midst] and write it on their hearts. I will be their God, and they will be my people. (Jer. 31:31–33)

> I will give them an undivided heart and put a new spirit in them. . . . They will be my people and I will be their God. (Ezek. 11:19–20)

131. Block, *The Book of Ezekiel: Chapters 25–48*, 356; Block, "The Prophet of the Spirit," 39; Tooman, "Covenant and Presence," 178.

132. Block, "The Prophet of the Spirit," 48; Robson, *Word and Spirit in Ezekiel*, 270. Eichrodt notes that this activity of the spirit is "the central point of God's renewal of his people in the new age. The spirit of God permeates each individual member of the people of God so as to carry out an inward transformation. . . . The human will is fully united with the will of God through being brought into permanent contact with the might of his spirit, which gives man power to shape his life in accordance with God's commandments" (Eichrodt, *Ezekiel*, 500). Tooman observes that 36:23c–38 introduces the idea that "the divine presence" is "the solution to permanent covenant obedience and the pathway to full national restoration" (Tooman, "Covenant and Presence," 178).

133. Block, *The Book of Ezekiel: Chapters 25–48*, 356, 373, 382.

134. MacDonald, "The Spirit of YHWH," 115.

135. Blenkinsopp, *Ezekiel*, 168–69; Tooman, "Covenant and Presence," 175–79; Block, "The Prophet of the Spirit," 39; Waltke with Yu, *Old Testament Theology*, 621; House, *Old Testament Theology*, 341.

I will give you a new heart and put a new spirit in you. . . . And I will put my Spirit in you. . . . You will be my people, and I will be your God. (Ezek. 36:26–28)

Then you, my people, will know that I am the LORD. . . . I will put my Spirit in you. (Ezek. 37:13–14)

I will make a covenant of peace with them; it will be an everlasting covenant. . . . I will put my sanctuary among them forever. My dwelling place will be with them; I will be their God, and they will be my people. (Ezek. 37:26–27)

Although Jeremiah focuses on the infusion of God's *torah* while Ezekiel focuses on the infusion of God's Spirit, it certainly seems as if they are referring to the same event, the renewal of the covenant relationship.[136] At the heart of this covenant renewal, enabling the obedience of God's people and heightening the intimate relationship, is the new way in which God will dwell in their midst.

William Tooman sums up the relationship between these texts insightfully:

The central concern of Ezekiel's visions is restoration of the Temple and the divine presence. The central concern of the deliverance oracles is restoration of the covenant. The two themes, though, are not entirely separate. . . . These oracles associate the restoration of the divine presence with the giving of a new covenant, a covenant of peace, making the conditions for restoration of the covenant coextensive with conditions for the restoration of the divine presence. . . . In the future, the presence of the divine spirit within the people would be the remedy for their ills and the guarantee of their eternal acceptance. Thus, covenant and presence go hand in hand.[137]

Ezekiel 1–39 contains one more reference to "Spirit" and presence. In the concluding verse of Ezekiel 1–39 (and serving as the introduction to chaps. 40–48),[138] God declares, "I will no longer hide my face from them, for I will pour out my Spirit on the people of Israel" (v. 29). As mentioned above, the hiding of God's face is related to his separation from Israel, and his abandonment of Jerusalem in particular, leading to the destruction of the city (cf. 39:23).[139] This text implies that the reverse of God hiding his face is that

136. Block, "The Prophet of the Spirit," 39.
137. Tooman, "Covenant and Presence," 175, 179.
138. While Ezek. 39:25–29 serves primarily as the conclusion to Ezek. 38–39 (concerning Gog), it also serves as a transition or introduction to Ezek. 40–48. C. Wright comments, "The way is at last clear for God to dwell among his people in renewed worship and eternal fellowship—which is what follows in chapters 40–48" (C. Wright, *The Message of Ezekiel*, 324).
139. Balentine, *The Hidden God*, 68–69.

he pours out his Spirit on the people, thus endowing them with his presence in a special way.[140]

God's Presence, the Coming Shepherd, and the Covenant

As in Isaiah and Jeremiah, in Ezekiel God describes himself as personally and intimately involved in the regathering and restoration of his people. Likewise similar to Isaiah and Jeremiah, one of God's favorite images in this regard is that of the shepherd (see especially Ezek. 34).[141] As in Isaiah, the image of God as the great deliverer and shepherd overlaps and/or merges into that of a Davidic figure, here called "my servant David," also described as a shepherd (34:23–24).[142] In 34:24 God declares, "I the LORD will be their God, and my servant David will be prince among them [בְּתוֹכָם, *betokam*, in their midst]." Block points out the covenant formula connections in this verse ("I will be their God . . . בְּתוֹכָם") and suggests that the Davidic Messiah is depicted as symbolizing the presence of God in the midst of the people.[143] God climaxes this regathering of sheep with a promise of a "covenant of peace" (34:25) and then closes the oracle with a restatement of the tripartite covenant formula: "Then they will know that I, the LORD their God, am with them and that they, the Israelites, are my people, declares the Sovereign LORD. You are my sheep, the sheep of my pasture, and I am your God, declares the Sovereign LORD" (34:30–31). Block writes, "Ezekiel declares Yahweh's true goal in his salvific activity: that the family of Israel might realize the presence of God among them, and the reestablishment of the covenant relationship between them and their God."[144]

---

140. See the discussion of various views on what "I will pour out my Spirit" means in this verse in Robson, *Word and Spirit in Ezekiel*, 93, 252–53. Block maintains that "pouring out" the Spirit in 39:29 is different than "giving the Spirit" in 36:27. He argues that "pouring out the Spirit" in 39:29 serves as a sign and seal of the covenant (Block, *The Book of Ezekiel: Chapters 25–48*, 488). Robson disagrees and argues that the two verses are essentially saying the same thing and are referring to the bestowal of God's presence (Robson, *Word and Spirit in Ezekiel*, 93, 252–53). Both views have merit, for it seems that God does sign and seal the people in covenant relationship through his renewed presence, and thus the reestablishment of the covenant is indicated by the tripartite formula.

141. Zimmerli notes the similarities between Ezek. 34 and Jer. 23 (Zimmerli, *Ezekiel 2*, 218).

142. C. Wright comments, "Here Ezekiel is certainly not contrasting the two, but binding them together as two dimensions of the same overall rule. The coming ruler will embody all that the rule of God himself implies. Like the equally mysterious Immanuel figure, his presence will embody the presence of God himself and all that comes with it" (C. Wright, *The Message of Ezekiel*, 280).

143. Block, *The Book of Ezekiel: Chapters 1–24*, 301.

144. Block, *The Book of Ezekiel: Chapters 1–24*, 306. Tooman states that "restoration of the divine presence is explicitly linked with restoration of covenant" (Tooman, "Covenant and

God Returns to His Future Temple and Dwells There

Ezekiel's final vision (Ezek. 40–48) is longer and more complex than his earlier visions, but it still is directly connected to them. In Ezekiel 8–11 the prophet saw God abandon the temple, an event with tumultuous implications, not only for Jerusalem but also for God's relationship with his people.[145] Now God no longer dwells in the midst of Israel, and Israel no longer dwells in the land but rather in exile. In Ezekiel's glorious final vision, however, both of these separations are reversed, for God will return to dwell in his temple, once again in the midst of his people.[146] While Ezekiel 40–48 contains several themes (the new temple, the sacrificial system, the division of the land), we will focus on the "high point" of his vision: the return of God to the temple.[147]

In Ezekiel 40–42 the prophet is given a tour of the new temple, but it is still empty of the presence of God (Ezekiel and his guide even take measurements in "the Most Holy Place" [41:4]).[148] Then in 43:1–7 Ezekiel describes God's return to this temple. In 43:2–3 the prophet identifies the "glory of God" in this vision as the same "glory of God" he had seen earlier in Ezekiel 1 and 8–11. In 43:4–5 Ezekiel states, "The glory of the LORD entered the temple through the gate facing east. Then the Spirit lifted me up and brought me into the inner court, and the glory of the LORD filled the temple." As mentioned earlier, the phrase "the glory of God" is a clear reference to the presence of God.[149] In reverse order from how God departed in Ezekiel 10–11, God now comes from the east, passes through the very gate from which he had departed (10:19; 11:1, 23), and then enters the temple. Recall that both the tabernacle and Solomon's temple had an eastward orientation of the gates and entryways to the courtyard, the holy place, and the holy of holies.[150]

As in Ezekiel's earlier visions of God's presence, in 43:5 the Spirit plays a role in physically moving Ezekiel so he can see and understand the vision (2:2;

Presence," 168). Both Block (pp. 303–5) and Tooman (pp. 166–67) point out the many close connections between Ezek. 34:25–31 and Lev. 26.

145. Commenting from the context of Moses's conversation with God in Exod. 33 regarding God's presence, C. Wright states, "Without the presence of Yahweh dwelling in their midst, Israel might as well stay in the wilderness. Now, centuries later, that awful prospect was a reality: Israel was in the wilderness of exile, and Yahweh had abandoned his dwelling-place" (C. Wright, *The Message of Ezekiel*, 327).

146. Block, *The Book of Ezekiel: Chapters 25–48*, 494; Joyce, "Temple and Worship in Ezekiel 40–48," 154–55.

147. C. Wright, *The Message of Ezekiel*, 328.

148. Joyce observes that there is no furniture mentioned at all except the "wooden altar . . . the table that is before God" (41:22), probably the incense altar (Joyce, "Temple and Worship in Ezekiel 40–48," 150).

149. Block, *The Book of Ezekiel: Chapters 25–48*, 578.

150. Block, *The Book of Ezekiel: Chapters 25–48*, 578–79.

3:12–14, 24; 8:3; 11:1, 5, 24). Thus the Spirit is once again closely associated with the "glory of God," particularly as God's presence comes into contact with people. In similar fashion to Isaiah's encounter with God in Isaiah 6, in Ezekiel 43:5 the prophet, apparently standing in the courtyard right in front of the entrance to the temple itself, states that the glory of God filled the temple. From inside the temple, God speaks to him. In contrast to their last conversation at the temple, when God pronounced judgment on the people of Jerusalem and announced that their terrible sins committed right in the temple would drive him away (8:6, 17–18; 9:1, 4–7), now God tells Ezekiel, "This is the place of my throne and the place for the soles of my feet. This is where I will live among the Israelites forever" (43:7).[151] There is no mention of the ark of the covenant, often associated with the throne of God, a situation similar to that described in Jeremiah 3:16–17, when the ark would be gone but Jerusalem would serve as the throne of God.[152] Walther Zimmerli suggests that God's words in 43:7 ("I will live among the Israelites forever") are more focused on his dwelling in Israel's midst than on dwelling in the temple. God concludes this short speech with a similar statement in 43:9: "I will live among them forever."[153]

Furthermore, the boundaries and the extent of the graded levels of holiness associated with the tabernacle and the Solomonic temple seem to have changed dramatically, as 43:12 declares: "All the surrounding area on top of the mountain will be most holy." Paul Joyce suggests that this moves the emphasis off the inner room of the temple (the most holy place) as the location of God's holy presence and broadens the extent and impact of the holiness of his presence.[154]

In Ezekiel 47 the prophet is taken once more to the temple, where he now sees a life-giving river flowing out of the temple (where the presence of God now dwells) and down to the Dead Sea, which is made fresh and productive by this river. The cause of this life-giving freshwater flow is clearly the presence

---

151. The phrase "the place of my throne and the place for the soles of my feet" envisions a royal throne with a footstool, common in the ancient Near East. The footstool is an extension of the throne and carries connotations of dominion and rule. This parallel phrasing "the place of my throne" (מְקוֹם כִּסְאִי, *meqom kis'i*) with "the place for the soles of my feet" (מְקוֹם כַּפּוֹת רַגְלַי, *meqom kappot raglay*) is very similar to Isa. 60:13, where "the place of my sanctuary" (מְקוֹם מִקְדָּשִׁי, *meqom miqdashi*) is paralleled to "the place of my feet" (מְקוֹם רַגְלַי, *meqom raglay*). See discussion by Block, *The Book of Ezekiel: Chapters 25–48*, 580–81; Zimmerli, *Ezekiel 2*, 415–16.

152. Block, *The Book of Ezekiel: Chapters 25–48*, 581; Zimmerli, *Ezekiel 2*, 415; C. Wright, *The Message of Ezekiel*, 334. Joyce notes the many points of connection between Ezek. 43 and Jer. 3:15–18 (Joyce, "Temple and Worship in Ezekiel 40–48," 150–54).

153. Zimmerli, *Ezekiel 2*, 416. On the other hand, the rest of the vision in 40–48 certainly seems focused on the temple.

154. Joyce, "Temple and Worship in Ezekiel 40–48," 156–57.

of the glory of God in the temple.[155] This image carries strong allusions to the river that watered the garden of Eden in Genesis 2:10–14, a place where God's presence was likewise manifest (Gen. 3:8).[156] Thus with the garden imagery this vision seems to suggest a recapturing of the Edenic situation of blessing and the presence of God in the garden.

Finally, the book of Ezekiel closes with a description of a city (a new, renamed Jerusalem) and its gates (48:15–35), concluding with "The name of the city from that time on will be: THE LORD IS THERE" (v. 35). This stresses the abiding presence of God dwelling with his people in this new city. The new name implies that the character of the city itself is connected to God's presence, which emanates from the temple and pervades the entire city.[157]

Daniel

The powerful, holy, and relational presence of God departed from Jerusalem in Ezekiel 8–11, the Babylonians destroyed the temple, and the people of Judah were banished from God's presence into exile in Babylonia, later to come under Persian control. The book of Daniel is an encouragement to these people (and to those who come later), proclaiming in chapters 1–6 that God is more powerful than the kings of Babylon and Persia, and declaring in chapters 7–12 that God will judge evil and establish his eternal world kingdom, a kingdom greater than any human kingdom. The climactic event in the establishment of God's world kingdom is the arrival of the Son of Man to receive authority, glory, and power from the Ancient of Days (Dan. 7).

The Exile, Angels, and the Transcendence of God

An intriguing feature of the book of Daniel is that there is no "And the word of the LORD came to Daniel" (as it did to Jeremiah and Isaiah). Instead, God regularly speaks to Daniel through the mediation of angels, as is the norm for apocalyptic visions. Yet in the Daniel narratives God also uses angels to intervene and deliver. For example, in explaining his deliverance from the lions'

155. Blenkinsopp, *Ezekiel*, 230.
156. Blenkinsopp, *Ezekiel*, 358; Fishbane, *Text and Texture*, 118–19; Zimmerli, *Ezekiel 2*, 510; Clements, *Ezekiel*, 204; Clements, *God and Temple*, 71–72, 107; Blenkinsopp, *Ezekiel*, 231; C. Wright, *The Message of Ezekiel*, 358; Beale and Kim, *God Dwells among Us*, 20–21. Clements notes that there was a widespread belief in the connection between the presence of God and a fertilizing river flowing through or from Zion to bless the land (Clements, *God and Temple*, 71). He cites Ps. 46:4 as an example: "There is a river whose streams make glad the city of God, the holy place where the Most High dwells."
157. Block, *The Book of Ezekiel: Chapters 25–48*, 739–40.

den, Daniel states, "My God sent his angel, and he shut the mouths of the lions" (6:22). Likewise, in light of Daniel's explanation in that verse, there is a strong case to view the fourth man in the fiery furnace, who "looks like a son of the gods," as likewise being an angel (3:25).[158] In fact, Daniel has the most developed angelology in the OT.[159] This appears to be related to the fact that God has departed from the temple (Ezek. 8–11) and no longer dwells in the midst of his people. Thus there is a certain "distancing" of God, with a shift from his intense relational immanence in the temple to his more distant (yet still all-powerful) transcendence in the heavens, now relating to people through angelic intermediaries and also using angels to intervene and protect.[160]

This phenomenon seems to be similar to the situation in Exodus 32–33 when God tells Moses that he will send an angel with Moses and the people to empower them in the conquest but that he himself ("the LORD") will not go with them (32:33–33:3). Thus the people would have a powerful angelic intermediary but not the intense and covenantal, relational presence of God. God was threatening to distance himself from them because of their sin with the golden calf. Of course, Moses strenuously objects, and God eventually agrees to come and dwell in the midst of the people in the tabernacle and to accompany them with his powerful indwelling, relational presence.

Similarly, the relational name Yahweh ("the LORD"), which often is associated with the presence of God, is used in Daniel only in the penitential prayer in chapter 9, where its usage stands in strong contrast to the absence of God's covenant-relational name in the rest of the book.[161] Elsewhere Elohim ("God") is used, and several times God is referred to as "the God of heaven" (2:18, 19, 28, 37, 44), perhaps stressing his sovereignty but also likely underscoring that he is not dwelling in the midst of exiled Israel.

The Ancient of Days and the Coming Son of Man

Daniel 7 is arguably the climactic chapter of the book.[162] After Daniel's vision of the four beasts (7:1–8) he is given a vision of the Ancient of Days

---

158. Very few scholars interpret the fourth man in the furnace as the preincarnate Christ; the vast majority of scholars, in light of 6:22, understand this person to be an angel. See Lucas, *Daniel*, 92; J. Hamilton, *With the Clouds of Heaven*, 142.

159. Lucas, "Daniel: Book of," 122.

160. Meier, "Angels, Messengers, Heavenly Beings," 29; Schöpflin, "God's Interpreter," 201. Newsom observes that the role of angels definitely increases in the exilic and early postexilic biblical literature, with references to angels becoming quite common in the literature of Second Temple Judaism. She notes that this increase in angels seems to be related to the fall of Jerusalem but concludes that the reason is unclear (Newsom, "Angels," 250–52).

161. Goldingay, "Daniel in the Context of Old Testament Theology," 643, 647.

162. W. S. Towner, *Daniel*, 91.

(undoubtedly God himself) coming to sit on his throne and hold court. While many scholars assume that this scene takes place in heaven as the regular "heavenly council," John Goldingay argues rather convincingly that this scene takes place on earth.[163] There are several additional observations that strengthen Goldingay's argument. The vision starts not with an ongoing heavenly court but with the establishment of the court. That is, the opening verse (7:9) is not so much a picture of God already sitting on his throne as it is of God taking his seat on his throne. Furthermore, 7:9 states that "thrones were set in place,"[164] implying that this event is not in a permanent throne room but probably is similar to that of a conquering king setting up his throne in captured territory as proof of his victorious conquest.[165] Also, the description in 7:9 of the throne as "fiery" and with "wheels" connects this theophany rather directly to those of Ezekiel 1 and 10,[166] and thus it appears to underscore the mobility of God's chariot-like throne, as in Ezekiel. Recall that Ezekiel sees God on this same wheeled and fiery chariot throne departing from the temple in Ezekiel 10. The numerous connections of Daniel 7:9–14 with Ezekiel 1 and 10 suggest that Daniel's vision is similar, but in contrast it depicts God returning to earth to sit on his throne on earth and to carry out judgment here on earth.[167]

Likewise, the description of the messianic Son of Man coming with the clouds of heaven is a picture not of ascent to heaven, but rather of descent

---

163. Goldingay, *Daniel*, 164–65. Goldingay argues that (1) elsewhere in the OT God normally carries out judgment here on the earth and not in heaven; (2) there is no indication in the text of a scene change from 7:1–8 (clearly on earth) and 7:9; and (3) in 7:22, when referring back to the throne room scene in 7:9, the text reads "until the Ancient of Days *came* and pronounced judgment," indicating a perspective from the earth.

164. The Aramaic word used here, רְמָא (*rema'*), can refer to "setting up," but it can also mean "to cast down" or "to throw down," and it is used frequently in Dan. 3 and 6 to refer to "throwing something downward," either Daniel into the lions' den or his friends into the fiery furnace (3:6, 11, 15, 20, 21, 24; 6:7, 12, 16, 24 (BDB, s.v. "רְמָא"). As such, the usage in 7:9 could easily refer to throwing/casting thrones down to earth and then sitting on them.

165. This would be similar to the famous Assyrian wall relief of the siege and capture of Lachish, which depicts the Assyrian king Sennacherib seated on his throne just outside the city, being fanned by his attendants, reviewing captured wealth, and rendering judgment on the defeated people, who are on their knees bowing down before him. See also Jer. 49:38, where God proclaims judgment on Edom by declaring, "I will set my throne in Elam."

166. Some scholars contend that Daniel's vision is of the same "heavenly council" scene that Micaiah describes in 1 Kings 22:19. Micaiah, however, doesn't mention a throne "flaming with fire" with "its wheels all ablaze" and with a "river of fire" flowing out from the throne, as Daniel does in 7:9–10. The two visions seem to be quite different.

167. Lacocque stresses the significance of noting the allusions/connections to Ezek. 1 and 8–11. He argues that this connection, in association with the references to the temple in Dan. 9:20–27, also implies a temple setting for Dan. 7:9–14 (Lacocque, *The Book of Daniel*, 125, 143).

from the heavens across the earthly landscape to the mobile throne room of the Ancient of Days.[168] G. R. Beasley-Murray underscores that nowhere in the OT (or even in Jewish or talmudic literature) are clouds used in describing "heavenly" scenes, but they are regularly used when a heavenly being is moving from hiddenness to appearance, from transcendence to immanence.[169] Note also that in Ezekiel clouds are associated with the prophet's visions of God in 1:4 (God comes in a cloud to Ezekiel in Babylon) and in 10:3–4 (clouds fill the temple to veil the glory of God). So the scene described in Daniel 7 probably is referring to the presence of God (first the Ancient of Days, then the closely associated divine/human Son of Man) coming back to earth to deliver the "holy people of the Most High" (7:21–22), to defeat evil empires (7:15–27), and to establish God's eternal kingdom, which his people will possess and enjoy (7:18, 22, 27).[170] In this sense, the apocalyptic vision in Daniel 7 seems to be similar to (yet perhaps preceding) the return of God described at the end of Ezekiel (chaps. 43–48).[171] At the climax of history the presence of God returns to earth. At the heart of this climactic event is the coming to earth of the Son of Man, who is clearly identified as Jesus Christ in the NT. The return of the presence of God is at the heart of the message of Daniel.

168. Goldingay points to Isa. 19:1 ("the LORD rides on a swift cloud and is coming to Egypt") and Ps. 18:10–13 as similar examples of God coming to earth powerfully in judgment, and he concludes that Dan. 7:13 most likely describes a movement from heaven to earth (Goldingay, *Daniel*, 167). Likewise, S. Miller interprets the text as describing the Son of Man coming from heaven to earth (S. Miller, *Daniel*, 207). Longman points out that the "cloud" imagery often accompanies God's appearance here on earth—as a pillar of cloud in the exodus (Exod. 13:21), as a cloud covering Mount Sinai (Exod. 19:16), and as a cloud filling the tabernacle (Lev. 16:2) (Longman, *Daniel*, 187). Lacocque notes that of over a hundred references to clouds in the OT, over 70 percent are connected either to the Mount Sinai encounter or to the temple/tabernacle (Lacocque, *The Book of Daniel*, 146).

169. Beasley-Murray, "The Interpretation of Daniel 7," 48–49. Lucas questions the earthly identification and concludes that the most one can say is that it is "mythic space" (Lucas, *Daniel*, 181). Pate points out, however, that one of the characteristics of apocalyptic literature is that heaven and earth "are not hermetically sealed compartments." There is a certain amount of parallel and merging of the two images because there is a "heavenly counterpart to the historical story of Israel. . . . Israel's story in heaven overlaps with Israel's story on earth" (Pate, *Interpreting Revelation and Other Apocalyptic Literature*, 102–3).

170. Note that both the Son of Man and the "holy people of the Most High" seem to possess the kingdom. For a discussion of the options for identifying the "holy people" and how they relate to the Son of Man, see Lucas, *Daniel*, 191–92; Goldingay, *Daniel*, 176–78.

171. Ezekiel 43:3 underscores that Ezekiel's vision of God returning to the temple is similar to the vision that Ezekiel saw in chapters 1 and 10; that is, it includes the fiery mobile throne with wheels (as in Dan. 7:9: throne, fire, wheels). In Dan. 7:10 a river of fire flows out from before the throne (in judgment), and in Ezek. 47:1–12 a river of fresh water flows out from the temple (in restoration).

The Book of the Twelve

Scholars throughout the twentieth century typically analyzed the "Minor Prophets" as individual books, often grouping and discussing them along with the "Major Prophets" in historical order (i.e., the Assyrian-period prophets: Jonah, Amos, Hosea, Micah, Isaiah, etc.). In recent years, however, the trend has been to recognize the entire Book of the Twelve (Hosea through Malachi) as a literary unit (while still, of course, acknowledging the same kind of diversity that one sees in a book like Jeremiah).[172] Speaking very generally, there is some movement or shift in emphasis across the canonical arrangement of the Book of the Twelve, breaking down into three main sections: Hosea through Micah (warnings about God); Nahum through Zephaniah (the judgment of God); and Haggai through Malachi (the restoration of God).[173] Since the postexilic setting of the final section (Haggai through Malachi) does give that unit a special uniqueness, we will discuss the Book of the Twelve in two parts: (1) Hosea through Zephaniah; and (2) Haggai through Malachi.

Hosea through Zephaniah

Not surprisingly, the theme of God's presence occurs in Hosea through Zephaniah in much the same manner and emphasis as in Isaiah, Jeremiah, and Ezekiel.

Jonah and the Presence of God

The book of Jonah is quite different from most of the other prophetic books, and thus we will treat Jonah separately from the rest of the Book of the Twelve. Unlike most of the other prophets, Jonah preaches to those in Nineveh and not to those in Jerusalem or Israel.[174] Yet Jonah's interactions with God throughout the book reveal that the presence of God is active and playing a central role in Jonah's unusual story too. In 1:2 God tells Jonah to go to Nineveh and preach against it "because its wickedness had come up before me [לְפָנָי; *lepanay*]." While not without ambiguity, this statement seems to envision God up on his heavenly throne, exercising his sovereignty over all

---

172. Nogalski and Sweeney, *Reading and Hearing the Book of the Twelve*; Seitz, *Prophecy and Hermeneutics*; J. D. Hays, *The Message of the Prophets*, 260–63.

173. House, "The Character of God in the Book of the Twelve"; J. D. Hays, *The Message of the Prophets*, 262.

174. At least within the story line of the book, he preaches to the Ninevites. The overall literary message is directed to those in Israel. See J. D. Hays, *The Message of the Prophets*, 301.

of the nations. This is in strong (and rather ironic) contrast to 1:3, in which Jonah seeks to flee from the presence of God. The phrase "from the presence of God" (מִלִּפְנֵי יְהוָה, *millipne Yahweh*) is stated twice (chiastically) in this one verse,[175] underscoring its importance to the story. The implication is that Jonah seems to view God as restricted to his dwelling place in the temple in Jerusalem,[176] and he seems to infer that if he could just get far enough away and out of God's reach, then God would no longer call on him to go to Nineveh. Numerous scholars discuss the problematic implications of Jonah's actions, some of them maintaining that the OT belief in the omnipresence of God was so prevalent that it would be unlikely that Jonah could have actually believed he could escape the presence of God.[177] On the other hand, as noted above, the most prevalent and central concept of Israel concerning God was that he dwelt in the temple in Jerusalem. Jonah himself seems to reflect this understanding as he later mentions God's holy temple (הֵיכַל קָדְשֶׁךָ, *hekal qodsheka*) twice in his prayer from the fish (2:4, 7). Likewise, as we have noted earlier, there are frequent references in the prophets (as well as elsewhere)[178] to God banishing people from his presence. So the concept of moving away from the presence of God is not foreign to the OT, although it is usually God himself who implements this banishment from his presence as a punishment for sin. This underscores the irony of Jonah's flight. Most of the prophetic literature speaks of God's banishing of the disobedient Israelites or Judahites from his presence due to their violation of the covenant. Jonah, on the other hand, tries to leave the presence of God voluntarily, in order to escape carrying out God's command. God, however, hunts Jonah down, forces him back into his presence, and compels Jonah to indeed carry out God's will in calling on the Ninevites to repent.

Furthermore, the tension between Jonah's actions in 1:3 and the implied universal sovereignty of God in 1:2 is integral to the plot development of the story. Billy Smith and Frank Page point out that לִפְנֵי (*lipne*) can stress the relational aspect of presence and not just physical locational presence. Thus

---

175. The chiasm of this verse is recognized by numerous writers. See, for example, Trible, "The Book of Jonah," 494; B. Smith and Page, *Amos, Obadiah, Jonah*, 226; Youngblood, *Jonah*, 51. Usually credit for first noting this is given to Lohfink, "Jona ging zur Stadt hinaus (Jona 4,5)," 200–201.

176. Likewise seeing the temple implied in this phrase is Bruckner, *Jonah, Nahum, Habakkuk, Zephaniah*, 42.

177. Jonah seems to acknowledge this in 1:9: "I worship the LORD, the God of heaven, who made the sea and the dry land."

178. Youngblood cites Cain's banishment from God's presence in Gen. 4:16 as well as the banishment from his presence of those who attempt holy offerings while ritually impure (Youngblood, *Jonah*, 62–63).

they propose that what Jonah is seeking to do when he flees the presence of God (מִלִּפְנֵי יְהוָה, *millipne Yahweh*) is to end his relationship with God as prophet, rebelliously refusing to serve God.[179]

At any rate, as the narrator makes clear, God's power and presence are not restricted to Jerusalem, and subsequently he personally hurls a storm directly against the ship that carries the prophet. Continuing the irony, just before they throw Jonah overboard, the sailors cry out to God from the boat in the midst of the storm, as if God were their patron deity of the sea and present right there in the storm, and God responds by halting the storm right after Jonah lands in the water. The sailors then offer a sacrifice and vows to God, apparently carried out from the ship while in the middle of the sea. In the ancient Near East both sacrifices and vows normally were carried out at or near temples (i.e., in sacred space), because that was where the gods were thought to reside. This action by the sailors ironically implies recognition not only of God's power but also of God's presence there in the sea as deity of the sea.[180]

Ironically, Jonah also eventually calls out in distress to God, from whom he had been fleeing. From "the realm of the dead [שְׁאוֹל, *she'ol*]" he calls out (2:2). Although he had been trying to flee from God and the word of God, fortunately for Jonah, he has been unable to do so. Thus God answers him and delivers him.

While in the fish, Jonah describes his descent toward death by saying, "I have been banished from your sight [מִנֶּגֶד עֵינֶיךָ, *minneged 'eneka*]" (2:4), a phrase implying the loss of God's presence. That is, to experience death is described as a movement away from God's presence. Belatedly, Jonah finally cries out to God. Interestingly, as noted above, although Jonah is in the sea and even in the fish, he still prays toward God in the temple, mentioning God's "holy temple" twice, chiastically (2:4, 7). The strong implication is

---

179. B. Smith and F. Page, *Amos, Obadiah, Jonah*, 226–27. Youngblood, *Jonah*, 57–58, concurs, stating that Jonah was trying to "escape the revelation of God experienced in the particular place where YHWH chose for his name to dwell. . . . Jonah, however, abandoned his station, wishing to renounce the prophetic distinction of standing in the presence of the deity in the divine council" (Youngblood, *Jonah*, 57–58). For a similar understanding, see Fretheim, *The Message of Jonah*, 80–81.

180. Brody notes that Canaanite and Phoenician sailors normally would make sacrifices in temples prior to and after voyages. Yet he also points out that they would also often offer sacrifices at sea as they passed near sacred promontory points of land that were dedicated to their gods of the sea. Often these promontory points held shrines. Then he explains that sailors would also cry out to their deities for help while at sea if they were facing storms or an upcoming battle. Thus Brody concludes that the sailors in Jon. 1:16 offer both sacrifices and vows while at sea in recognition of God as their "new" patron deity of the sea (Brody, "*Each Man Cried Out to His God*," 78–82).

that Jonah's petition reaches God in the temple.[181] Hans Walter Wolff sees this prayer "finding admittance" at the place of God's presence, in his holy temple. He concludes, "The power of Yahweh's presence in the sanctuary allows even the cry from the far-off depths of the sea to arrive at its goal."[182] The point seems to be that God is dwelling in his holy temple in Jerusalem, but still he has the power to speak, punish, and deliver outside the boundaries of Israel, indeed, even in the depths of the sea (and even in Nineveh, as Jon. 3–4 underscores).[183]

Dwelling in the Temple, God Is Offended by the Sin Right before Him

As in Isaiah, Jeremiah, and Ezekiel, the presence of God dwelling in the temple is an assumed reality in the Book of the Twelve prior to the exile (e.g., Hosea 11:9; Joel 1:14; Mic. 6:6). Even the false prophets and the apostasizing leaders assume that God dwells in the temple; in fact, as in the book of Jeremiah, they think that God's presence in the temple will protect them (Mic. 3:11). Yet, as in Jeremiah, for the leaders to assume that God's presence in the temple would protect them against their enemies while they disregard his *torah* and blatantly offend him with their idolatry is a huge and ironic mistake, as Micah 3:12 graphically points out. Indeed, the book of Micah opens with a proclamation that God himself bears witness against both Judah and Samaria from the temple: "Hear, you peoples, all of you, listen, earth and all who live in it, that the Sovereign LORD may bear witness against you, the Lord from his holy temple " (1:2).[184] Likewise, in Hosea 7:2 God refers to the sins of his people as being right before him.

The portrayal of God ruling from the heavens is not absent from the Minor Prophets, and this image is used particularly when God's sovereign reign over all the nations of the earth is being stressed. Thus Amos 9:6 declares, "He builds his lofty palace in the heavens and sets its foundations on the earth." Yet note that even here the text portrays God's palace as having its foundations on the earth. That is, his presence and rule are not either in heaven or in the temple but are in both simultaneously.[185]

181. Youngblood, *Jonah*, 108.

182. H. W. Wolff, *Obadiah and Jonah*, 137.

183. Timmer, *A Gracious and Compassionate God*, 86–87.

184. The royal residence of God is called "holy" because it is sanctified by his presence. While "his holy temple/palace" occasionally can refer to God's heavenly dwelling (Ps. 11:4), here it probably refers to his dwelling in Jerusalem. See Mays, *Micah*, 40.

185. Recall the advice that we cited from Wildberger regarding Isa. 6: "To try to distinguish between an earthly and a heavenly sanctuary attempts to make a distinction which the ancient person would never have attempted. God dwells in heaven, but he is also present in the sanctuary" (Wildberger, *Isaiah 1–12*, 263).

God Personally Fights against the Israelites and Judahites

As in Isaiah, Jeremiah, and Ezekiel, God in his judgment shifts from being present to bless and protect to being present as a terrifying warrior fighting against Israel and Judah. In Joel 2:10–11 God is depicted as the warrior/king at the head of his army,[186] an enemy army that has come to attack Israel. In Amos the image of God fighting personally against his "former people" as an enemy warrior/king appears several times (4:12–13;[187] 5:16–17;[188] 9:1–4). Likewise, in Micah 1:3–7 God is portrayed as a divine warrior/king coming personally to punish his covenant-breaking people.[189]

The book of Zephaniah uses similar imagery, portraying God as personally coming to judge disobedient and unfaithful Judah and Jerusalem: "I will stretch out my hand against Judah and against all who live in Jerusalem" (1:4); "At that time I will search Jerusalem with lamps and punish those who are complacent" (1:12). Indeed, judgment on Jerusalem is described throughout Zephaniah 1, while the presence of God is stressed in 1:7: "Be silent before the Sovereign LORD, for the day of the LORD is near."

God Will Regather His People and Once Again Dwell in Their Midst

As in Isaiah, Jeremiah, and Ezekiel, several of the Minor Prophets prophesy a time in the future when God will regather his scattered people and once again dwell in their midst. For example, using the term שָׁכַן (*shakan*, to dwell, pitch a tent), with its strong connotations of recalling how God came to dwell among Israel in the tabernacle in the exodus tradition,[190] the final unit in Joel (3:17–21 [4:17–21 MT]) opens and closes with the future picture of God dwelling in Zion: "Then you will know that I, the LORD your God, dwell in Zion, my holy hill" (3:17); "The LORD dwells in Zion!" (3:21).[191] His presence on Mount Zion makes the entire hill, as well as Jerusalem itself, "holy" (3:17). Aspects of the tripartite covenant formula are present. The traditional designation of God's people Israel as "the sons of Israel" is used in 3:16,[192] and God is referred to as "your God" in 3:17. The additional closing stress in 3:21 that

---

186. H. W. Wolff, *Joel and Amos*, 47–48. Stuart explains that there are "two levels of invasion imagined concurrently: symbolically, the locusts, and literally, the divine army" (Stuart, *Hosea–Jonah*, 251).

187. Stuart, *Hosea–Jonah*, 339–40.

188. Stuart suggests Lev. 26:6 as the linguistic background, which depicts the sword passing right through the land (Stuart, *Hosea–Jonah*, 350).

189. Barker and Bailey, *Micah, Nahum, Habakkuk, Zephaniah*, 50.

190. Garrett, *Hosea, Joel*, 394.

191. Note the similarity between the ending of Joel and the ending of Ezekiel, stressing the presence of God.

192. Crenshaw, *Joel*, 196–97.

God "dwells" (שֹׁכֵן, *shoken*) among them completes the covenant formula and closes the book with a strong future promise of covenant restoration, centered on the restored presence of God.[193] Likewise, his restored presence is closely associated with the renewal of the land itself (3:18), with a fountain of water flowing out of God's temple, as in Ezekiel 47:1–12.[194]

Zephaniah 3:14–20 ends the book of Zephaniah with a depiction of the future restoration that likewise focuses on God's presence. The stress is not on the restored land, however, but rather on the restored relationship between God and his people. All three elements of the tripartite covenant formula are likewise present. The "my people" aspect is reflected in the intimate terms used of relating to God in 3:14 ("Daughter Zion" and "Daughter Jerusalem"). "The LORD *your God*" is mentioned in 3:17. The restored presence described as God "in your midst" (בְּקִרְבֵּךְ, *beqirbek*) is stated twice (3:15, 17). Likewise, God's love (אַהֲבָה, *'ahabah*) mentioned in 3:17, carries strong covenant connections.[195] God is no longer a warrior/king personally fighting against them as an enemy; he is now king and warrior (3:15, 17) saving them, protecting them, and rejoicing over them.

Covenant, Presence, and Spirit

In a manner similar to Isaiah and Ezekiel, Joel 2:18–32 (2:18–3:5 MT) combines the themes of restored (or renewed) covenant, restored presence of God, and the pouring out of God's Spirit. First of all, note that all three elements of the tripartite covenant are present in 2:18–27. In 2:18 God takes pity on "his people," and in 2:26 he refers to them as "my people." He tells the people of Zion to "rejoice in the LORD *your God*" (2:23), and he says that they "will praise the name of the LORD *your God*" (2:26). Then 2:27 contains all three elements ("I will be your God; you will be my people; I will dwell in your midst"): "Then you will know that I am in Israel [בְּקֶרֶב יִשְׂרָאֵל אָנִי, *beqereb yisra'el 'ani*], that I am the LORD *your God*, and that there is no other; never again will *my people* be shamed."[196] Indeed, God's presence is essential to the covenant relationship.[197]

193. Noting various covenant components of this passage are Allen, *The Books of Joel, Obadiah, Jonah, and Micah*, 121; H. W. Wolff, *Joel and Amos*, 81; Stuart, *Hosea–Jonah*, 270.

194. Allen, *The Books of Joel, Obadiah, Jonah, and Micah*, 122–24. Allen writes, "Yahweh's presence in Zion was the key to the blessing of the whole land" (p. 122).

195. P. J. J. S. Els, "אהב," *NIDOTTE* 1:279.

196. Those noting the strong covenant elements in this passage include Allen, *The Book of Joel, Obadiah, Jonah, and Micah*, 96; Crenshaw, *Joel*, 159; Stuart, *Hosea–Jonah*, 260. Likewise, VanGemeren notes that Joel 2:27 "is the climactic affirmation of Yahweh's covenant presence" (VanGemeren, "The Spirit of Restoration," 83).

197. Crenshaw, *Joel*, 159.

Yet while in 2:19–26 the blessings of God's renewed covenant presence are described as restored agricultural bountifulness of the land, in 2:28–32 the blessing is presented as the outpouring of God's own Spirit. As in Isaiah and Ezekiel, the promise that God would pour out his Spirit on all people reflects a new era in the relationship. Leslie Allen comments that the pouring out of God's Spirit in 2:28–32 reveals that the promise of presence in 2:27 will be even more abundantly filled.[198]

As we noted earlier in the discussion of Isaiah and Ezekiel, the term רוּחַ (*ruah*, Spirit/spirit) in the context of God pouring out his Spirit is used as a synecdoche for God himself, representing the presence of God on earth.[199] As in Isaiah 32:15 and 44:3–4, as well as in Ezekiel 39:29, the pouring out of God's Spirit in Joel 2:18–32 serves to restore the covenant between God and his people in a "bigger and better" manner.[200] As in Jeremiah's "new covenant" when all, from the greatest to the least, will know God (Jer. 31:34), here in Joel 2:28–29 the Spirit of God will be poured out on all people, men and women alike.

Haggai through Malachi

Both Haggai and Zechariah open in the second year of King Darius of Persia (520 BC). As described in Ezra-Nehemiah, a small group of exiles has returned to Judah and Jerusalem, but their situation—still few in number, struggling, under Persian domination—hardly seems to fit the glorious restoration depicted by the earlier prophets.[201] A group is back in the land, so in some sense the promised regathering appears to have been started; however, the Persians still rule, and God's powerful presence has not returned. The restoration seems to be still in the future. Indeed, the people back in the land still seem to be experiencing covenant curses to some extent, including the loss of God's presence.[202]

God Does Not Return to Dwell in the Second Temple

In the preexilic prophets God repeatedly threatens to stop dwelling "in the midst" of Israel in the temple, and in Ezekiel 11 he actually departs just prior to the Babylonian capture and destruction of Jerusalem. In the postexilic era

198. Allen, *The Books of Joel, Obadiah, Jonah, and Micah*, 98–99.

199. Block, "The View from the Top," 180, 206–7.

200. Routledge suggests that the pouring out of God's Spirit denotes a new intimacy with God (Routledge, "The Spirit and the Future," 356).

201. Exploring the "failure of the restoration" within the context of the geopolitical domination of the Persians is Albertz, "The Thwarted Restoration."

202. Patrick, "Time and Tradition in the Book of Haggai," 51. Tollington writes, "Taken as a whole Zech 1:12 indicates that the community ought to see its present experience as part of an ongoing period of judgment and punishment from Yahweh beginning with the exile and the destruction of the temple" (Tollington, *Tradition and Innovation in Haggai and Zechariah*, 187–88).

a small group of exiles has returned and rebuilt the temple, albeit on a much smaller scale (Hag. 1:12–2:5). Earlier in Israel's history, at the completion of the tabernacle (Exod. 40:34–38) and again after the completion of the first temple (1 Kings 8:10–11), the glory of God had filled the holy sanctuary in dramatic, spectacular fashion, stressing that the entire point of the facility was that it was the place where God himself dwelt. After the postexilic construction of the second temple, however, there is no description in any of the texts (Haggai, Zechariah, Ezra-Nehemiah) of the glory of God coming to fill the temple.[203] The absence of this event is huge. R. E. Clements writes, "The temple was rebuilt, and no miraculous return occurred." Postexilic life was restored in Judea, but the "crowning promise, that the presence of God would be in Israel's midst remained in the realm of eschatological hope."[204] The return of God to the temple was still in the future.[205]

The Enabling Presence of God Is with the Postexilic Community

Nonetheless, as the preexilic prophets looked to the future, they often depicted an enabling "I am with you" presence of God that would help the exiles

203. As mentioned above for Ezra-Nehemiah, Fried points out that the temple construction account in Ezra 6 basically follows the standard ancient Near Eastern literary pattern for temple construction. What is glaringly missing, she stresses, is the central element: a description of the god entering the temple to take up residence (Fried, "The Torah of God as God," 287–88). In discussing the construction of the second temple in Haggai, Kessler also notes the unusual absence of any text describing the "ceremonial inauguration" or "fresh manifestation of the divine presence" in Haggai. The reason for this, Kessler argues unconvincingly, is that in other ancient temple reconstructions the return of the deity was never certain, but that in Haggai's case God had already promised to "take pleasure" in the temple (Hag. 1:8). Thus Kessler implies that since the return of the deity was not in question, it would not be so much of an event that it would need recording (Kessler, "Temple Building in Haggai," 378–79). In light of the tremendous importance placed on the entry of God into both the tabernacle in Exodus and the temple in 1 Kings, however, it seems unlikely that this entrance could merely be inferred from the promise of God's approval in Hag. 1:8. Likewise, if God's presence had returned to the rebuilt temple, the question in Hag. 2:3 would be insultingly strange: "Does it [the rebuilt temple] not seem to you like nothing?"

204. Clements, *God and Temple*, 125–26. Clements notes that a sense of the unfulfilled promise of God's return to the rebuilt temple is well reflected in the rabbinic literature. A doctrine developed in the rabbinic literature that there were five things in the first temple that were lacking in the second temple. Two of these, and arguably the most vital aspects, are the Shekinah (the rabbinic concept of the divine presence) and the Holy Spirit (in rabbinic thinking connected to canonical prophecy). See Abelson, *The Immanence of God*, 261–67; Fried, "The Torah of God as God," 284. Also note that both Josephus and the Mishnah give extensive and detailed descriptions of many parts of the second temple, but neither of these sources mentions either the ark of the covenant or the presence of God as being in the holy of holies.

205. Patrick writes, "There is no king, no economic prosperity, foreign rule, and a meager population. Thus, the current plight of the Yehudites resembles a continuation of the curses from the exilic period of judgment. . . . YHWH has yet to return to his people" (Patrick, "Time and Tradition in the Book of Haggai," 55).

to return to Judah. In Haggai 1:12 the remnant back in the land "obey the voice of God" and "the message of the prophet Haggai." This is immediately followed in 1:13–14 by God's declaration of his enabling presence: "I am with you." He stirs up the spirits of the leaders and the people, and they begin reconstruction of the temple. Indeed, throughout the exilic and postexilic periods God's powerful and holy presence does not return to the temple to reestablish his covenant, but God does continue to provide his "I am with you" presence to comfort and to protect his people, even while in exile. This "I am with you" presence is similar to how the patriarchs in Genesis experienced God's presence. It was empowering and protecting, but not the intense, glorious, fiery, and holiness-emanating presence that came to dwell with Israel in Exodus.

In the Future God Will Once Again Dwell in the Temple in Jerusalem

Both Haggai and Zechariah look back at the exile as a past event and now look forward to what God is going to do in the new era of salvation. The restored presence of God will play a central role in this new era of salvation. In summarizing Haggai and Zechariah, Mark Boda writes, "For Haggai and Zechariah the restoration was multidimensional. Fundamentally, it involved the return of God's presence. . . . These two prophets complement each other. Both announce an imminent restoration inaugurated by the return of God dependent on repentance of the people. . . . For both the ultimate goal is the return of the presence and blessing of God to his people in order to transform the cosmos."[206] Haggai focuses on the reconstruction of the temple as a prerequisite for God's return. Zechariah focuses on repentance and ethical reform of the people as a prerequisite for God's return. Both of these factors seem to be required, and while Haggai and Zechariah present God's return as imminent, the failure of the returned exiles to turn completely to God in obedience leaves the coming return of God still just out of reach on the future horizon.[207]

In Haggai 2, in response to the disappointment the people feel at the scaled-down and sparse temple that they have just reconstructed, God declares, "In a little while I will once more shake the heavens and the earth. . . . I will fill this house with glory. . . . The glory of this present house will be greater than the glory of the former house" (Hag. 2:6–9). In light of the clear allusion to the exodus in Haggai 2:5, the phrase "once more" in 2:6 undoubtedly connects back to the dramatic and frightening "shaking" that occurred when God descended at

---

206. Boda, *Haggai, Zechariah*, 47–48.
207. See Ackroyd, *Exile and Restoration*, 200–217; Delkurt, "Sin and Atonement in Zechariah's Night Visions," 251; Kashlow, "Zechariah 1–8 as a Theological Explanation," 402; Boda, "From Fasts to Feasts," 405; Gowan, *Theology of the Prophetic Books*, 168.

Mount Sinai (Exod. 19:16–19).[208] In a context where silver and gold are specifically mentioned (Hag. 2:8), some scholars view the promise of filling the house with "glory" (כָּבוֹד, *kabod*) as a reference to the physical wealth that will flow into the temple from the nations.[209] On the other hand, theophany traditions from Mount Sinai are also integral to the context, and כָּבוֹד is used frequently in the OT (and especially in the exodus tradition) in reference to God's presence in the tabernacle and temple; thus other scholars see the reference to "glory" filling the temple as a reference to God's personal return to the temple.[210]

Note also that along with filling the temple with glory, in Haggai 2:9 God promises to give שָׁלוֹם (*shalom*, peace) as well. John Durham has argued convincingly that שָׁלוֹם often is associated with the presence of God. He argues that in about 65 percent of the usages of שָׁלוֹם in the OT the reference is not so much to "peace" as it is to "fulfillment." In these cases שָׁלוֹם "describes a completeness, a success, a maturity, a situation which is both prosperous and secure—withal, a state of well-being which is a direct result of the beneficent PRESENCE of God. This beneficent PRESENCE is at the very least either assumed or implied in the context of each of these images of שָׁלוֹם, and it is mentioned in some specific way in nearly fifty separate passages."[211] Similarly, Gerhard von Rad underscores that frequently שָׁלוֹם "denotes a relationship rather than a state." Tightly connected to the concept of relationship, von Rad continues, is the close association between שָׁלוֹם and covenant.[212] In Haggai 2, with allusions within the context to God's theophanic appearance on Mount Sinai (where he first established the Mosaic covenant), accompanied by references to his "Spirit" (2:5), to his "glory," and to his house, the observation that שָׁלוֹם frequently is associated with God's presence and his covenant fits well with the context. The return of God to dwell in the temple restores the covenant and brings שָׁלוֹם.

Within the eight "night visions" of Zechariah 1:7–6:8 God makes several promises to return and to dwell in the temple in Jerusalem. The specific

208. Boda, *Haggai, Zechariah*, 123. Boda notes the clear allusion back to the exodus in 2:5 (pp. 122–23).

209. Kessler, "Tradition, Continuity and Covenant," 27; Petersen, *Haggai and Zechariah 1–8*, 68–70.

210. Boda, *Haggai, Zechariah*, 124–27. Boda argues for a view that includes both. The word "glory" can refer to wealth as well as to God's presence. A wordplay is perhaps in use implying that in the future the temple would be adorned with the physical wealth of the nations symbolizing the more important "glory" that represented the presence of God.

211. Durham, "שָׁלוֹם and the Presence of God," 276–77. Likewise noting the frequent (two-thirds) occurrences in which שָׁלוֹם describes the state of fulfillment as the result of God's presence is G. L. Carr, "שָׁלוֹם," *TWOT* 2:931.

212. G. von Rad, "שָׁלוֹם: B. שָׁלוֹם in the OT," *TDNT* 2:402–3.

timing of this event, however, is not entirely clear. David Petersen concludes that the verbs in 1:16 are ambiguous, somewhat matching the ambiguity regarding time in the entire unit of the eight night visions.[213] He proposes that Zechariah's visions "stand somewhere between purely mundane concerns and an utopian vision of renewal," conveying a sense of "inbetweenness" or "somewhere in between."[214] Petersen's helpful suggestion for viewing restoration fulfillment in Zechariah 1–8 as "somewhere in between" is similar in many regards to the NT "already but not yet" understanding of the kingdom of God.

The future nature of the promised restoration is more obvious in Zechariah's third vision (2:1–13 [2:5–17 MT]). In 2:4 the angel tells Zechariah that Jerusalem will be a city without walls. Then God explains why no walls are needed: "I myself will be a wall of fire around it, . . . and I will be its glory within" (2:5). The view of Jerusalem presented here is clearly eschatological.[215] Stone walls for defense will be quite superfluous if God himself is present defending the city. "Fire" is often associated with God's presence (e.g., the burning bush in Exod. 3:2–4; the pillar of fire in Exod. 13:21–22), and "glory" is a major designation of God's presence.

Likewise, the restoration of God's presence is promised in Zechariah 2:10–13 (2:14–17 MT). The promise "For I am coming, and I will live among you" (2:10) reflects standard terminology of God's restored presence. The repeated covenantal language used here implies that when God returns and his presence is restored, many nations will be added to the covenant relationship.[216] There is also a stress in this passage on the profound holiness that God brings to everything in his presence. Peter Ackroyd comments, "The implication is that with God himself being present in his Temple in Zion, the whole land—the actual ground itself—becomes holy."[217]

Echoing the promise of the return of God's presence in Zechariah 1:16 and 2:10–11 is Zechariah 8:2–8. Relational and covenantal aspects run throughout the text as all three portions of the tripartite covenant formula are stated: "I will return to Zion and dwell in Jerusalem. . . . I will bring them back to live in Jerusalem; they will be my people, and I will be faithful and righteous to them as their God."[218]

---

213. Petersen, *Haggai and Zechariah 1–8*, 156.

214. Petersen, "Zechariah's Visions," 198–202. See also Kashlow, "Zechariah 1–8 as a Theological Explanation," 393.

215. Meyers and Meyers, *Haggai, Zechariah 1–8*, 155.

216. Boda, *Haggai, Zechariah*, 238.

217. Ackroyd, *Exile and Restoration*, 181.

218. As in Zech. 1:16, the verbs used in Zech. 8:3 (NIV: "I will return . . . and dwell") are perfect tense (*qātal*) (שַׁבְתִּי, *shabti*, and שָׁכַנְתִּי, *shakanti*). Here in 8:3, as in 1:16, scholars

Although scholars differ on the time frame on some of the texts in Zechariah 1–8, there appears to be a consensus on the future eschatological orientation of Zechariah 8:18–23, or at least of 8:20–23, the closing oracle/oracles of Zechariah 1–8, signaled especially by the phrase "in those days" (8:23).[219] This final section of Zechariah 1–8 describes the pilgrimage of many peoples and nations to Jerusalem to seek God. Indeed, it is the dwelling presence of God that is drawing these people to Jerusalem. The powerful figure of speech presented is that of foreign peoples grabbing the hems of Jews' robes and pleading, "Let us go with you [to Jerusalem], because we have heard that God is with you" (8:23).

Likewise, the eschatological, even apocalyptic, orientation of Zechariah 9–14 is widely accepted. Central to this unit is the return of God to Jerusalem to rule as king over his kingdom, now a universal kingdom that includes the nations.[220] Yet, unlike in the visions of God's return in the preexilic prophets, in Zechariah 11:4–17 the people appear to reject the return and rule of God (and/or his appointed shepherd), thus resulting in another time of judgment before the final establishment of God's rule.[221]

In Zechariah 9:1–8 God appears as the divine warrior, defeating Israel's traditional enemies before returning to dwell in and defend his temple in Jerusalem.[222] As in some of the preexilic texts, in Zechariah 9:9–10 the return of God blurs with the establishment of a Davidic, messianic king.[223] In the closing sections of Zechariah (12:9–14:21) the theme of the return of God to rule as king in Jerusalem is closely intertwined with themes of judgment,

---

take differing views regarding whether God's return has already occurred (Meyers and Meyers, *Haggai, Zechariah 1–8*, 413) or whether his return is a future event (Boda, *Haggai, Zechariah*, 380). Boda writes, "It is clear that for Zechariah this return of Yahweh's presence still lies in the future and . . . that its delay is attributed to enduring sin among the restoration community" (Boda, *The Book of Zechariah*, 480). Gowan notes that with the temple rebuilt, the conditions were ripe for God's return, and that Zech. 8 "represents a fairly complete example of the eschatology of the Old Testament." On the other hand, Gowan continues, "Complete fulfillment still remained out of reach" (Gowan, *Theology of Prophetic Books*, 168). Meyers and Meyers split Zech. 8:2–8 into five different oracles. While they understand 8:3 as having already occurred, they conclude that 8:7–8 must be in the eschatological future (Meyers and Meyers, *Haggai, Zechariah 1–8*, 428–30). Yet note the close parallel between 8:3 and 8:8. In 8:3 God states, "I will return to Zion and dwell in Jerusalem [וְשָׁכַנְתִּי בְּתוֹךְ יְרוּשָׁלָ͏ִם, *weshakanti betok Yerushalaim*]." In 8:8 he states, "I will bring them back to live in Jerusalem [וְשָׁכְנוּ בְּתוֹךְ יְרוּשָׁלָ͏ִם, *weshakenu betok Yerushalaim*]."

219. See, for example, Meyers and Meyers, *Haggai, Zechariah 1–8*, 435–45; Petersen, *Haggai and Zechariah 1–8*, 117–20.

220. Chisholm, *Handbook on the Prophets*, 468.

221. Chisholm, *Handbook on the Prophets*, 468; Boda, *Haggai, Zechariah*, 458.

222. Boda, *Haggai, Zechariah*, 409–10.

223. Boda, *Haggai, Zechariah*, 414–17. See also Boda, *Zechariah*, 564–65.

forgiveness, purification, holiness, and covenant renewal ("I will say, 'They are my people,' and they will say, 'The LORD is our God'" [13:9]). The closing unit (14:16–21) depicts the nations streaming to Jerusalem to worship God there. In this final scene the holiness normally associated with utensils within the temple itself has now expanded, not only to the pots throughout Jerusalem and Judah but also to the bells on horses, traditionally an unclean animal (Lev. 11:1–8). Thus the presence of God dwelling in Jerusalem makes that which was unclean to be clean and holy, eliminating every distinction between holy and profane, including the distinction between Jews and the nations.[224]

Likewise, Malachi describes a future time when God would personally return to the temple (3:1). In response to the people's disobedient question in 2:17 ("Where is the God of justice?"), Malachi points to the future "day of his coming" (3:2) and declares that God himself will return to the temple (3:1) and bring about justice (3:5). In 3:1 God first states that he will send a messenger to "prepare the way before me [לְפָנַי, *lepanay*]," a phrase with probable connotations of presence. Then "the Lord you are seeking will come to his temple," undoubtedly a reference to God himself.[225] This promise/announcement that God is coming to the temple strongly implies that he is not already there and that his return to the temple is part of the future "day of the LORD."

Conclusions

In the prophetic literature, including Daniel, the presence of God is at the very center of both the historical story and the theological story. The presence of God, for example, is tightly and inextricably connected to the entire concept of covenant and God's relationship with his people. The tripartite formula "I will be your God; you will be my people; I will dwell in your midst" is cited or alluded to repeatedly throughout the prophetic literature and the reality of this presence (or its absence) drives the story. In addition, this relational presence of God is the web that connects the major themes in the prophets

---

224. R. Smith, *Micah–Malachi*, 293; Boda, *Haggai, Zechariah*, 528.

225. Those identifying the one returning to the temple as God include Clements, *God and Temple*, 125–26; R. Smith, *Micah–Malachi*, 328; Chisholm, *Handbook on the Prophets*, 481–82; Verhoef, *The Books of Haggai and Malachi*, 288–89; Baker, *Joel, Obadiah, Malachi*, 268–69; Malone, "Is the Messiah Announced in Malachi 3:1?," 218–19; Goswell, "The Eschatology of Malachi," 635. Malchow goes so far as to declare, "In spite of an awareness by some that this could refer to a messenger, virtually all modern exegetes agree that the 'Lord' is Yahweh" (Malchow, "The Messenger of the Covenant," 253).

such as holiness, glory, name, power, worship, deliverance, sin and separation, exile, restoration, kingdom, judgment, blessing, *shalom*, and spirit.

The presence of God dominates the OT story in the prophets. The exodus tradition of encountering God at Mount Sinai, who then comes to dwell in Israel's midst, is assumed by the prophets. Thus throughout the preexilic prophets God is depicted as dwelling in the temple in Jerusalem. His heavenly reign is acknowledged, as is his sovereignty over all nations and all of the earth. But in regard to the relational story of God and his people, the nearly constant point of reference, both literally and figuratively, is upon God dwelling in the temple. Because of God's holiness emanating from the temple, and due to his close proximity to everyone in Jerusalem and Judah, sin and apostasy (abandoning God for idols) are particularly offensive. God warns repeatedly of this offense, pleading with the people and warning them to repent and return to a true worship worthy of his holy presence, before it is too late. He warns them that if they disregard the holy demands of his presence and continue to dishonor him and sin against him, then the blessings of his personal presence will be replaced with terror as he will leave his temple and personally fight against them as a powerful and enraged warrior. Judgment will result in the loss of God's presence. The separation between the people and God not only will involve his departure from the temple but also will include his banishment of them from the land.

Yet in the future, God promises, he will bring his people back to the land, personally caring for them and enabling them to return by his accompanying "I am with you" presence. This will be followed by a spectacular return of the "glory" of God to his temple, where his regathered people, along with all the nations, will come faithfully to worship him. Their experience of God's presence in the temple (and emanating throughout Jerusalem and Judah) will be enhanced by the pouring out of his Spirit upon them. All of these various streams of enhanced presence will signal the establishment of a new and wonderful covenant relationship between God and his people, with him once again dwelling in their midst.

Historically, a sad and tragic reality follows God's many warnings. Israel and Judah do not repent and return to God. His warnings are ignored. The sin and idolatry of Judah become so great that God does indeed depart from his temple, signaling the end (or at least the serious disruption) of the covenant defined by "I will dwell in your midst." God departs from the temple, and the people are thrown out of the land and driven into exile away from his presence.

Yet God enables a group to return to the land, and his "I am with you" presence empowers them to rebuild the temple, albeit in an extremely scaled-down version. In this postexilic situation, however, the powerful and spectacular presence ("glory") of God does not enter the rebuilt temple like he did into the tabernacle and the first temple. He does not come and reestablish a new Davidic kingdom centered on the temple, as promised by the preexilic prophets. Some of the people are back in the land and the temple is rebuilt, indicating that the conditions are ripe for the restoration to at least begin. But there is no indication that the "glory" of God is dwelling in the most holy place. Indeed, Judea is under foreign (Persian) domination still, and the people continue to struggle with sin and disobedience. The wonderful restoration of God and his powerful presence promised by the prophets are still future, and this promise of God's future return connects the OT to the NT. Indeed, the temple stays empty of God's presence and without a Davidic king until Jesus Christ (Immanuel) arrives.

FOUR

The Relational Presence of God in Matthew, Mark, and Luke-Acts

The primary focus of the Synoptic Gospels and Acts is that Jesus Christ comes to us as the one who manifests God's relational presence in a unique and powerful way. Here we continue to lay out our case that in God's relational presence we come face-to-face with the driving force and ultimate goal of the whole biblical story, the very center of biblical theology. This chapter surveys Mark's and Matthew's portrayals of God's relational presence in terms of Jesus's identity, his mission, and his community (along with the resulting conflict), as well as his eschatological and sustaining presence. Then, we turn our attention to the story as advanced in Luke-Acts to see the presence theme appear in Luke's presentation of God's plan, Jesus himself, the Holy Spirit, the people of God, and Christ's promised return.

The Synoptic Gospels and Acts show that Jesus himself manifests God's personal presence as the incarnate Son of God, that the kingdom of God is rooted in the reality of God's relational presence, and that presence lies at the heart of kingdom righteousness and discipleship to Jesus. In addition, we see that presence is the goal of the cross and resurrection as God seeks to bring people back to a healthy relationship with himself so they may experience his presence for eternity. What Jesus began to do during his earthly ministry recorded in the Gospels, he continues to do by his Spirit, as Acts details. The presence-filled experience of Pentecost provides the foundation and motivation not only for the mission of God's people but also for God's promise of his eschatological presence to come.

Matthew and Mark

Jesus's Identity

Mark: "Jesus Christ, the Son of God"

Mark begins his Gospel with a bold proclamation of Jesus's identity: "The beginning of the gospel of Jesus Christ, the Son of God" (1:1 CSB). He supports this announcement with a composite citation of Isaiah 40:3 and Malachi 3:1 (a reworking of Exod. 23:20) to show that John the Baptist's role is to prepare for Jesus, the one through whom God's personal presence is made known.[1] Thus the focus is not on the messenger or the people but on the "way of the Lord," and Rikk Watts rightly concludes, "Whatever else, for Mark Israel's Lord is, in some mysterious and unparalleled sense, present in Jesus."[2] Mark's opening emphasis on God's presence in Jesus continues in 1:8 as John the Baptist promises that the coming, more powerful one will "baptize you with the Holy Spirit" (1:8), a startling declaration, since the clear OT expectation was that Yahweh ("the LORD") himself would pour out his Spirit in the last days (e.g., Isa. 32:15; 44:3; Ezek. 36:26–27; 39:29). Thus for Mark, "the coming of Jesus *is* the eschatological coming of God."[3]

Jesus experiences his baptism in trinitarian fashion (Mark 1:10–11). The heavens are "torn open" (σχιζομένους, *schizomenous*) and the Spirit descends "on him" (εἰς αὐτόν, *eis auton*) like a dove, probably an echo of Isaiah 64:1, where the prophet prays that God would tear open the heavens and make his presence known. Ben Witherington notes the parallel and observes, "Jesus is anointed by the very presence and power of God, such that wherever Jesus goes and whatever he does, the presence and power of God dwells in him and empowers his words and deeds."[4] Then, in Mark 1:11, God's voice from heaven declares, "You are my Son, whom I love; with you I am well pleased" (cf. Gen. 22:2; Ps. 2:7; Isa. 42:1). The OT citations highlight Mark's high Christology and signify Jesus as the beloved and Spirit-empowered Son-Servant, who will inaugurate and announce the good news of the kingdom. Only in Mark 1:11 and 9:7 (and parallels) do we encounter divine direct discourse in the Synoptics, and both times God refers to Jesus as "my Son." This baptismal pronouncement serves as the "keystone in the life and ministry of Jesus" and

---

1. See Watts, "Mark," 113–20. In the LXX Isa. 40:3 ends with "for our God" (τοῦ θεοῦ ἡμῶν, *tou theou hēmōn*), but Mark replaces this phrase with "for him" (αὐτοῦ, *autou*) in 1:3c, allowing the Christian reader to understand "the Lord" (κυρίου, *kyriou*) of 1:3b to refer to Jesus. See France, *Mark*, 64.
2. Watts, "Mark," 120.
3. France, *Mark*, 70.
4. Witherington, *Mark*, 75.

enables Jesus "not only to speak and act *for* God but *as* God," demonstrated by his subsequent work that includes forgiving sins, healing the sick, driving out demons, calling the disciples, and teaching with authority.[5] James Edwards astutely observes, "What Jesus does as God's servant ultimately has meaning only because of who he is as God's Son."[6] All that Jesus does, he does as the one who reveals God's presence.

In addition to setting a high christological tone for his work in the opening (1:1–13), Mark uses several major titles throughout to stress Jesus as the revelation of God's relational presence. The most prominent title is "Son of God," since, as we have seen, this is how God identifies Jesus right from the start (1:11; cf. the other "my Son" in 9:7 at Jesus's transfiguration). The parable of the tenants in 12:1–12 echoes Jesus's identity as the Son of God using similar language. The landowner, who represents God in the story, only has "one left to send, a son, whom he loved" (v. 6). The shift from servants to a beloved son recalls the Father's earlier identification and emphasizes Jesus's true identity as the Son of God.

At Jesus's trial before the Sanhedrin in 14:53–65, when the high priest asks Jesus if he is "the Messiah, the Son of the Blessed One" (v. 61; cf. 1:1), Jesus answers in a way that, according to R. T. France, represents the "christological climax of the gospel."[7] Jesus replies, "I am" (Ἐγώ εἰμι, *Egō eimi*), echoing the self-revelation of God in Exodus 3:14, and then adds: "And you will see the Son of Man sitting at the right hand of the Mighty One and coming on the clouds of heaven" (v. 62; cf. Ps. 110:1; Dan. 7:13), signifying his future role as their eschatological judge. The reaction of the high priest and the events that follow demonstrate that Jesus was put to death for claiming to be the very presence of God in their midst, both now and on the last day.

The "Son of God" of 1:1 also forms an inclusio with the centurion's statement in 15:39: "Surely this man was the Son of God!"[8] The first human in this Gospel to confess Jesus as God's Son does so after watching him suffer and die on the cross. Ironically, while God's presence in Jesus was rejected by the religious leaders and not yet fully recognized by his own disciples, it was affirmed by a Roman soldier. The ripping of the sky in 1:10 is matched

---

5. Edwards, *Mark*, 38.

6. Edwards, *Mark*, 38.

7. France, *Mark*, 610.

8. Garland notes that the two "my Son" declarations of 1:11 and 9:7 are bracketed by the broader inclusios of "Son of God" in 1:1 and 15:39 (Garland, *A Theology of Mark's Gospel*, 228). Grammatically speaking, although the Greek phrase in 15:39 lacks the definite article, Mark still intends *the* Son of God rather than *a* Son of God, since a definite predicate nominative omits the article when it comes before the verb. Thus, as Edwards notes, "Mark's use of 'Son of God' in 15:39 is meant in the full Christian sense" (Edwards, *Mark*, 480).

with the ripping of the temple curtain in 15:38 as this Gospel comes to a high christological conclusion.[9]

The title "Messiah" ("Christ") is applied to Jesus by others, most famously by Simon Peter in his confession in 8:29.[10] In this turning-point pericope, Peter confesses Jesus as "the appointed agent of God whose coming marks the fulfillment of the divine promise and the realization of Israel's hopes."[11] Although Jesus doesn't reject the title, he doesn't prefer it, and even Mark qualifies it quickly in 1:1 by adding, "Jesus the Messiah, the Son of God" (cf. 14:61).

Jesus refers to himself often as the "Son of Man,"[12] primarily against the backdrop of Daniel 7.[13] The expression allows Jesus the flexibility to infuse it with meaning through his own words and actions: the Son of Man has authority to forgive sins (2:1–12), to exercise authority over the Sabbath (2:23–28), to suffer and die and be raised (8:31; 9:9, 12, 31; 10:33–34, 45; 14:21, 41), and to be exalted and to return in glory (8:38; 13:26–27; 14:62). As Simon Gathercole notes, the narrative pattern in Mark weaves together the Son of Man sayings to communicate the authoritative figure revealed, rejected, and vindicated.[14] All phases of Christ's work—incarnation, crucifixion (cf. 10:45: a ransom for many with a view to future relationship), resurrection, and second coming—point to God's relational presence as the ultimate goal and outcome.

Finally, Mark also uses the title "Lord" (κύριος, *kyrios*) numerous times to link Jesus to the God of Israel. Many of these instances appear intentionally ambiguous in order to show that both God and Jesus share the identity of "Lord."[15] For example, the quotation in 1:2–3 (attributed to Isaiah, where "Lord" certainly refers to God) shifts the focus to Jesus as he enters the story in 1:9 (see also 5:19; 11:3; 12:11; 13:20, and also 11:9, where Jesus also shares

9. The only two uses of "tear" (σχίζω, *schizō*) in Mark occur in 1:10 and 15:38. In 15:38 the temple curtain is ripped in two from top to bottom. Whether the ripping of the curtain signifies God's judgment on the temple as the locus of his presence or whether the work of Christ now makes available direct access to God, both interpretations highlight divine presence.

10. The related title, "Son of David," is rarely used in Mark's Gospel because of its political baggage, but it does appear (10:47–48; 12:35; cf. 11:10).

11. Lane, *Mark*, 291.

12. The background of the title "Son of Man" has been notoriously difficult to pin down. See Hurtado and Owens, *"Who Is This Son of Man?"*

13. Gathercole, "The Son of Man in Mark's Gospel."

14. Gathercole, "The Son of Man in Mark's Gospel," 372. R. Hays observes, "The suggestion that Mark actually depicts the man Jesus as *the embodied presence of the God of Israel* has rarely been considered," but he goes on to affirm *"Jesus' identity with the one God of Israel"* (R. Hays, *Echoes of Scripture*, 46, 62).

15. See Johansson, *"Kyrios* in the Gospel of Mark." *Kyrios* occurs in Mark 1:3; 2:28; 5:19; 7:28; 11:3, 9; 12:9, 11, 29 [2x], 30, 36 [2x], 37; 13:20, 35. For more on Mark's Christology, see Hurtado, *Lord Jesus Christ*; Bauckham, *Jesus and the God of Israel*.

God's name). Following the citation of the Shema (Deut. 6:4) in 12:29 with its monotheistic emphasis, Mark uses Psalm 110:1 with its two uses of "lord" (κύριος twice in 12:36) to highlight how God and Jesus share this title. Thus, Mark characterizes Jesus throughout his Gospel as authoritatively united to God's way, God's work, and God's person.[16] In other words, Jesus uniquely manifests God's relational presence to humanity.

Matthew: "Immanuel . . . God with Us"

Matthew begins his Gospel with a direct focus on "Jesus the Messiah the son of David, the son of Abraham" (1:1). The opening phrase, "this is the genealogy" (βίβλος γενέσεως, *biblos geneseōs*), evokes for the reader a connection with the creation story in Genesis 1:1 and aligns "God's presence in the beginning of heaven and earth with his presence in the new beginning in Jesus."[17] But Matthew is just getting started. The inclusion of a detailed genealogy links Jesus solidly to the Jewish people and God's relationship to them. "Jesus was not an afterthought to Judaism," says Craig Keener, but rather "was the goal to which Israel's lovingly remembered history pointed."[18]

As Matthew begins his birth narrative proper in 1:18–25, he emphasizes how Jesus's very identity and mission are intertwined with God's presence. David Kupp observes that "*every character and event* of these episodes is in some way subject to the extraordinary sense of YHWH," whether through the action of the Spirit, angels, dreams, heavenly messages, or the prophetic voice of God.[19]

The child is named "Jesus, because he will save his people from their sins" (1:21).[20] His salvific mission will fulfill the prophetic word of Isaiah 7:14. While much scholarly ink has been spilled over the meaning of "virgin" in the first part of the quotation, Matthew's primary purpose centers on 1:23b: "and they will call him Immanuel (which means 'God with us')."[21] Richard Hays refers to 1:23 (and its citation of Isa. 7:14) as "a major keynote of his Gospel: Israel's God is now present to his people precisely in the person of Jesus."[22] The "God with us" of Matthew 1:23 forms an inclusio with the "I

---

16. Edwards, *Mark*, 28.

17. Kupp, *Matthew's Emmanuel*, 54.

18. Keener, *Matthew*, 77.

19. Kupp, *Matthew's Emmanuel*, 54.

20. For a recent discussion of the significance of 1:21 to Matthew's Gospel, see Greer, "A Key to Matthew's Gospel."

21. Matthew changes the prophet's singular to a plural: "they will call," perhaps looking ahead to what the redeemed community will eventually learn to say about Jesus: in him, God is with us. See France, *Matthew*, 58.

22. R. Hays, *Echoes of Scripture*, 165.

am with you" promise of 28:20, showing that the theme of divine presence envelops Matthew's entire Gospel as a guiding framework. The first part of this guiding inclusio links Jesus's mission in 1:21 (Savior) with his core identity in 1:23 (God with us). Notice the linguistic grouping:

> 1:21: "and you will call his name Jesus"—καὶ καλέσεις τὸ ὄνομα αὐτοῦ Ἰησοῦν (*kai kaleseis to onoma autou Iēsoun*)
>
> 1:23: "and they will call his name Immanuel"—καὶ καλέσουσιν τὸ ὄνομα αὐτοῦ Ἐμμανουήλ (*kai kalesousin to onoma autou Emmanouēl*)
>
> 1:25: "and he called his name Jesus"—καὶ ἐκάλεσεν τὸ ὄνομα αὐτοῦ Ἰησοῦν (*kai ekalesen to onoma Iēsoun*)

Kupp describes this connection as "inextricably interdependent," such that every time "Jesus" is mentioned throughout Matthew's Gospel, the reader would be reminded of "God with us," a particularly reassuring thought for a predominantly Jewish-Christian audience.[23]

In light of the framing inclusio and the high Christology throughout this Gospel, Matthew intends for his readers to think of Jesus as "God with us" in the fullest sense: "Jesus as God's Son is also God himself with his people, effecting their deliverance. This is the ultimate manifestation of God's presence."[24] Thus Kupp is right to see the redeemed community as recognizing Jesus himself in this context as "the ultimately personal mode of YHWH's presence."[25] The Immanuel declaration in 1:23 certainly sets the stage for Matthew to pursue the theme of divine presence throughout his Gospel.

Jesus's Mission

Mark: Kingdom Teaching, Discipleship, and Mighty Works

Kingdom Teaching. While Mark's focus is squarely on Jesus's identity and mighty works, he does emphasize divine presence within the dedicated teaching segments. He begins in 1:14–15 with Jesus proclaiming the "good news of God," before defining the nature of this good news in 1:15: "The time has come. . . . The kingdom of God has come near. Repent and believe the good news!" God's kingdom "has come near" both temporally and spatially in the person of Jesus. God's personal presence has invaded history. Most

---

23. Kupp, *Matthew's Emmanuel*, 57.
24. D. Turner, *Matthew*, 73.
25. Kupp, *Matthew's Emmanuel*, 58. Osborne finds a parallel with John's portrayal of Jesus in John 1:14 as God's Shekinah presence so that in Jesus, God is once again walking planet Earth (Osborne, *Matthew*, 79).

importantly, the arrival of the presence of God incarnate in Jesus of Nazareth constitutes and embodies the arrival of the kingdom (1:1, 10–11). In a theological sense, God's relational presence precedes, creates, and signifies the kingdom—no presence, no kingdom.

The parables of Mark 4 connect receiving God's word (an extension of his presence) with the kingdom. In the parable of the sower in 4:1–20, the Markan sandwich of the parable proper (vv. 3–9) and its explanation (vv. 14–20) draws attention to the central section (vv. 10–13), especially Jesus's statement "The secret of the kingdom of God has been given to you [his disciples]" (v. 11). Only in relationship to the presence of Jesus will the truths of the kingdom make sense. The three shorter parables in 4:21–34 continue this same theme of hearing. Also, in the first of these stories (vv. 21–25), the Greek grammar indicates that the "lamp" (v. 21) should be understood as subject rather than object (i.e., "Does *the lamp come* in order to be placed under the bowl or the bed?"), signifying that Jesus is the lamp who shines the light of God's presence in this world.[26] The figure of a lamp often was used in the OT as a metaphor for God's presence (e.g., 1 Sam. 3:3; 2 Sam. 22:29) or that of the Davidic Messiah (e.g., 2 Kings 8:19; Ps. 132:17). Elsewhere in the NT Jesus as the lamp of God becomes even more explicit (e.g., John 8:12; Rev. 21:23).[27]

In the parable of the tenants in Mark 12, Israel is compared to God's vineyard (see Isa. 5:1–7), and the beloved son is the one sent by the father (cf. Mark 1:11; 9:7), an implicit identification of Jesus as the Son of God. The rejected stone will become the most important stone in God's new living temple (see Ps. 118:22).[28] The final phrase, "the Lord has done this" (Mark 12:11; cf. Ps. 118:23), points to God as the one who has made his presence known in Jesus.

Discipleship. Jesus's invitation to the four fishermen in Mark 1 captures the essence of discipleship as a matter of presence: "Come, follow me" (1:17; cf. 2:14).[29] At its core, discipleship entails experiencing the personal presence of Jesus (cf. 1:18; 2:14; 8:34; 10:21, 28). Whereas the primary devotion of rabbinic disciples was to the Torah, Jesus calls his followers first and foremost

---

26. Lane, *Mark*, 165–66; Edwards, *Mark*, 139. Stein notes that "the term 'come' (ἔρχεται, *erchetai*) is frequently associated in Mark with the coming of Jesus, the coming of the kingdom of God as well as the parousia (1:7, 14, 24, 29, 39; 2:17; 3:20; 8:38; 10:45; 11:9–10; 13:26, 35, 36; 14:62" (Stein, *Mark*, 224).

27. Ryken, Wilhoit, and Longman, *Dictionary of Biblical Imagery*, 486.

28. Cf. Luke 20:17; Acts 4:11; Rom. 9:33; 1 Cor. 3:10–17; 2 Cor. 6:16; Eph. 2:19–22; 1 Pet. 2:6–8.

29. The expression δεῦτε ὀπίσω μου (*deute opisō mou*, come after me) in 1:17 is best translated, "Come, follow me." The term ἀκολουθέω (*akoloutheō*, follow) is included in 1:18; 2:14–15; 8:34; 10:21, 28.

to himself.[30] Robert Gundry observes that Jesus's call differs significantly from the prophetic pattern, which typically finds the prophet calling people to follow God. Gundry concludes, "Jesus stands not merely in the place of the Law [or the Prophets], but in place of God."[31]

Likewise, when Jesus chose the Twelve, the first expressed purpose was that they "be with him" (3:14). While this could simply refer to a summons to accompany him on his travels (e.g., 3:7; 5:24; 10:52), it probably carries more theological weight here as a call to companionship, allegiance, and participation in the mission.[32] Edwards writes, "The simple prepositional phrase 'to be with him' has atomic significance in the Gospel of Mark. Discipleship is a relationship before it is a task, a 'who' before a 'what.'"[33] Even before the disciples were sent out to fish for people or preach or drive out demons, they were called to be with Jesus. Presence lies at the heart of discipleship and provides the foundation for the extension of Jesus's ministry through his followers.

We see the defining role of presence in discipleship also in 8:27–9:1, the climactic pivot of Mark's Gospel. Here Jesus sets forth the demands of discipleship in a manner that highlights the centrality of relational presence: "Whoever wants to be *my* disciple must . . . follow *me*. . . . Whoever loses their life for *me* . . . If anyone is ashamed of *me* and *my* words . . ." (8:34–38). The multiple references to the person of Jesus emphasize that discipleship centers on Jesus's personal presence. The call to discipleship is fundamentally a call into a relationship with God's presence manifested in Jesus.

Against this backdrop of viewing discipleship as an experience of and commitment to the relational presence of Jesus, we see how the disciples' failures should be viewed primarily as violations of presence. Mark's unflattering portrayal of the disciples has been well documented, and explanations abound as to why Mark would plot this course.[34] What is often overlooked is the relational nature of these failures and how they constitute rejections of the very presence of Jesus.

After calming the storm, Jesus asks the disciples, "Why are you so afraid? Do you still have no faith?"—that is, "no faith *in me*?" (4:40). Their follow-up question, "Who is this?" (4:41), suggests a failure to grasp the presence

---

30. Edwards, *Mark*, 49–50, characterizing "being with Jesus" as "the essential prerequisite for the active ministry which follows" (cf. Luke 10:38–42; Acts 1:21).

31. Gundry, *Mark*, 70.

32. France, *Mark*, 159.

33. Edwards, *Mark*, 113.

34. For a helpful summary of the discussion, see Witherington, *Mark*, 54–56, and especially the appendix "Mark's Perspective on the Disciples" (pp. 421–42). We agree with Witherington that the term "disciples" refers primarily to the Twelve but also extends beyond that group to include others.

of Jesus as the one who calms the seas. Following Peter's confession, Jesus finds it necessary to rebuke Peter for thinking more like Satan than like God (8:31–33). Peter's offense amounts to a rejection not just of redemptive plans but of the presence of the Redeemer. Jesus's follow-up instruction confirms the violation of presence that has just occurred (note the multiple first-person singular pronouns in 8:34–38). He concludes with a powerful warning about the eschatological consequences of violating presence by rejecting discipleship: "If anyone is ashamed *of me and my words* in this adulterous and sinful generation, the Son of Man will be ashamed *of them* when *he comes* in his Father's glory with the holy angels" (v. 38).

In Mark 9, after the majority of the Twelve fail to drive out a demon from a boy, Jesus tells them, "This kind can come out only by prayer" (9:29), implying that they had attempted an exorcism apart from a reliance on God's powerful presence. Jesus goes on to define greatness in the kingdom using the object lesson of a child (9:36–37). Since little children function here as a symbol for fellow disciples, Jesus is connecting his very presence ("my name") with his followers in the strongest possible way (cf. similar statements in 9:41–42).

We see most clearly how the disciples' failures are violations of presence in the betrayal of Judas and the denials of Peter. Judas's betrayal, at its core, is the giving up or handing over of a person and, as such, proves to be the ultimate violation of presence. Peter's denials are seen as rejections of relational presence: Jesus's "You yourself will disown *me* three times" versus Peter's "Even if I have to die *with you*, I will never disown *you*" (14:30–31). Later, in the courtyard of the high priest, Peter's denials are specifically related to disowning the person of Jesus: "I don't know this man you're talking about" (14:71).

The final word related to discipleship and presence, however, is not failure but rather loyalty and restoration.[35] Mark's female disciples are generally portrayed in a much more positive light, chiefly because they prove loyal in this matter of relational presence. They serve Jesus and the Twelve (1:29–31; 16:1–7), exercise faith and humility (5:25–34; 7:24–30), and express unashamed devotion (14:3–9), most notably at the cross and the tomb (15:40–41, 47; 16:1–8). The women attend to the priority of relational presence in a manner that begs for scriptural recognition, although 16:8 indicates that fear paralyzed them into (what was most likely a temporary) silence.

Regarding restoration, the angel's message to the women is that Jesus has risen and they should "go, tell his disciples and Peter, 'He is going ahead of you into Galilee. There you will see him just as he told you'" (16:7; cf. 14:28).

35. See Garland, *A Theology of Mark's Gospel*, 433–36.

In other words, resurrection makes possible forgiveness and the restoration of relational presence. Even if Peter is mentioned specifically because he had yet to rejoin the others, we still see the role of presence in restoring community.

Mighty Works. Mark records Jesus's mighty works for the purpose of revealing his identity as the one who manifests God's presence in this world. The theme of presence runs strongly through the healing and nature miracles in Mark. As Jesus heals the paralyzed man in Capernaum, he pronounces his sins forgiven (2:1–12). France concludes, "To claim to do what only God could do, and to constitute himself God's spokesman in declaring sins forgiven, was to infringe the divine prerogative."[36] And notice that Jesus doesn't just pronounce or declare the sins forgiven, but indeed does the forgiving himself, as if he were God.[37]

Likewise, Jesus makes God's presence known by healing on the Sabbath (3:1–6), thus demonstrating that he is "Lord even of the Sabbath" (2:28). Against the backdrop of the repeated references in the OT to the Sabbath belonging to Yahweh ("the LORD") (e.g., Exod. 16:25; 20:10; 31:13; Lev. 19:3, 30; Deut. 5:14; Ezek. 20:12–13), Jesus now claims to make God's presence known as Lord of the law.[38] As a result, "the righteous purpose of God as manifested in the Torah can be recovered and fulfilled only in relation to Jesus, who is its Lord."[39]

In the episode of the raising of Jairus's daughter and the healing of the bleeding woman in 5:21–43, the emphasis falls upon how Jesus's presence calls for faith (5:34, 36), seeks relational as well as physical healing (5:32–34), and turns death into a temporary sleep (5:39). That Jesus does his mighty work directly without appealing to God suggests that Jesus incarnates the powerful presence of God.

On Jesus's visit to the Decapolis and his healing of the deaf man (7:31–37), two items deserve special attention. First, the term translated as "could hardly talk" (μογιλάλος, *mogilalos*) used in verse 32 is a rare term that occurs elsewhere in the Greek Bible only in Isaiah 35:6, a passage that celebrates God as the one who will come to heal the deaf. Mark probably alludes to the Isaiah 35 context in order to show that "the promised intervention of God took place in the ministry of Jesus."[40] Second, the comment about Jesus doing all things

---

36. France, *Mark*, 126.

37. France, *Mark*, 129. This falls in line with the common OT expectation that God's presence brings healing and forgiveness (e.g., Exod. 15:26; Deut. 32:39; 2 Chron. 7:14; Ps. 130:3–4).

38. Stein, *Mark*, 150. Garland has shown that throughout Mark, Jesus presents himself as the "final arbiter of the intention of the law" (Garland, *A Theology of Mark's Gospel*, 308–12). As God incarnate, Jesus pronounces what God's intention is concerning the law.

39. Edwards, *Mark*, 97.

40. Lane, *Mark*, 266.

well in verse 37 echoes Genesis 1:31 ("God saw all that he had made, and it was very good") and equates God's good work in creation with Jesus's mighty works of healing. As Jesus travels through Jericho, blind Bartimaeus cries out for healing from "Jesus, Son of David" (10:47, 48), a title likely carrying messianic overtones and most certainly pointing to Jesus as the one through whom the man would experience God's healing presence.[41]

The nature miracles in Mark also display the presence theme in particularly convincing ways. When Jesus calms the storm in 4:35–41, he taps into the Jewish belief that only the God of Israel could control nature (e.g., Pss. 65:7; 89:9; 93:3–4; 107:29), a power that God demonstrated dramatically in taming the Red Sea in the exodus (Exod. 14:21). The disciples' response of fear and awe (cf. Mark 4:41 with Exod. 14:31; also Jon. 1:10) demonstrates that Jesus can do what only God can do. In Jesus's calming of the sea the disciples encounter the very presence of God: "They were terrified and asked each other, "Who is this? Even the wind and the waves obey him!" (4:41).

We see a similar connection to divine presence in the feeding of the five thousand in 6:30–44 and of the four thousand in 8:1–9. In Mark 6, just prior to the feeding episode, we read that Jesus "saw a large crowd" and "had compassion on them, because they were like sheep without a shepherd" (6:34). This allusion to Numbers 27:17 shows that "for Mark, in some mysterious way the great shepherd Yahweh is himself present in Jesus."[42] The miracle of the provision of food in the desert connects Jesus with God, who provided manna in the wilderness. In these episodes we see again that as the incarnate presence of God, Jesus can do what only God can do.[43]

The miracle of walking on the water in 6:45–52 provides several significant indications of divine presence. First, the expression "walking on the lake" in verse 48 points to a supernatural act of walking on top of the water, something only God can do.[44] Second, we are told that Jesus was "about to pass by them" (v. 48), a phrase signaling a self-revelation of God: passing by Moses (Exod. 33:19, 22), by Elijah (1 Kings 19:11), and especially by Job in the parallel in Job 9 ("He alone stretches out the heavens and treads on the waves of the sea. . . . When he passes me, I cannot see him; when he goes by,

---

41. For more on the title "Son of David" and whether it should be understood to carry messianic significance, see Hurtado, *Mark*, 174–75.

42. Watts, "Mark," 161.

43. In addition, Stein notes verbal similarities between the two feeding accounts and the Last Supper, suggesting that all three experiences foreshadow the coming messianic banquet (Stein, *Mark*, 370).

44. See Job 9:8; 38:16; Ps. 77:19; Isa. 43:16; 51:10; Hab. 3:15; Sir. 24:5–6; *Odes of Solomon* 39:10.

I cannot perceive him"; vv. 8, 11).[45] Third, the one who walks on the sea now makes himself known to the terrified disciples: "Take courage! It is I [ἐγώ εἰμι, egō eimi]. Don't be afraid" (Mark 6:50). While the "It is I" or "I am" could simply be a statement of identification, the context favors a theophanic understanding in connection with God's "I am that I am" self-revelation to Moses (Exod. 3:14; cf. Deut. 32:39; Isa. 41:4; 43:10; 46:4; 51:12). All in all, there is little more that Jesus could have done in this encounter to make God's presence known to his closest followers.

Jesus's work through the cross and the resurrection stands as the greatest mighty work of all. Prior to the cross, Jesus spoke of himself as the bridegroom and predicted a time when the bridegroom would be "taken" (ἀπαρθῇ, aparthē) from the guests (Mark 2:20). A closely related verb for "taken" is used in Isaiah 53:8 to speak of the death of the suffering servant. Jesus here refers to the day when his incarnational presence would conclude. Yet his use of the bridegroom image, one used frequently in the OT to refer to Yahweh ("the LORD") as the bridegroom of Israel (e.g., Isa. 54:5–6; 62:4–5; Hosea 2:14–20), points to a sustaining presence extending beyond death to a future eschatological presence.

The crucifixion event itself shines the spotlight on the theme of presence in several substantial ways. First, the ironic accusations that Jesus couldn't destroy and rebuild the temple in three days (Mark 15:29–30; cf. 14:58) are countered by his death, subsequent resurrection, and ongoing presence among his people, which constitutes the building of a holy temple (e.g., 2 Cor. 6:16; Eph. 2:21–22; 1 Pet. 2:5). Second, we see in Jesus's "My God, my God" cry from the cross (Mark 15:34) the ultimate breaking of relational presence for the purpose of securing a permanent experience of this same divine presence for his followers. Third, at his death, the tearing of the temple curtain signals the end of the Jerusalem temple as the locus of divine presence as Jesus replaces the temple. Last, the soldier's confession of Jesus as the Son of God represents one of the high christological peaks in this Gospel (15:39; cf. 1:1; 8:29). Whether the soldier was aware of the significance of his statement is unclear, but surely Mark intends his readers to understand Jesus as the incarnate Son of God, especially since the designation "Son of God" brackets the entire Gospel (1:1; 15:39; cf. 1:11).

Even Jesus's three passion predictions, which play such a crucial role in Mark's Gospel (8:31; 9:31; 10:34), emphasize a restoration of presence at

45. Edwards, *Mark*, 198–99. The term "pass by" (παρέρχομαι, parerchomai) is used often in the LXX as a technical term for divine epiphany: Exod. 12:23; 33:19, 22; 34:6; 1 Kings 19:11; Job 9:11; Isa. 26:20 (God's wrath).

his coming resurrection. Just as there is a coming crucifixion, so there is a coming reversal in the resurrection and an implied reunion of Jesus with his disciples. Jesus's resurrected presence guarantees reunion, even for Peter (16:7). Mark's short resurrection narrative serves as a reminder that presence creates community.

Matthew: Fulfillment, Discipleship, and Righteousness

Jesus, the Fulfillment of the Promise of Yahweh's Presence. Matthew's focus on the theme of fulfillment is well established,[46] but what is not always appreciated adequately is his emphasis on Jesus as the personal fulfillment of the promise of divine presence. Matthew isn't content to stress the fulfillment of predictive prophecy or of various historical patterns or intertextual connections, as important as these may be; he's keen on calling our attention to Jesus as the incarnation of God's relational presence, as we've already seen in the Immanuel announcement in 1:22–23.[47]

The fulfillment of God's presence among his people centers on Jesus, the one in whom the kingdom of heaven "has come near" (ἤγγικεν, *ēngiken*) (3:2; 4:17). God's rule and reign have arrived precisely in the person and ministry of Jesus of Nazareth. The long-standing promise of Yahweh to dwell among his people would be realized only "through a transcendent and supernatural work of God himself," and this occurs in and through Jesus, the Immanuel Messiah and Son of God.[48] As Jesus proclaims the good news, heals the sick, casts out demons, and even raises the dead—mighty works all—people experience the relational presence and reign of God (4:23–25). Notice the very same pattern when Jesus authorizes his disciples in 10:1, 7–8 to perform such mighty works as they proclaim the arrival of the kingdom.

Along with Mark, Matthew also underscores Jesus's mighty works as a demonstrative fulfillment of God's presence. In the episode of the calming of the storm in Matthew 8:23–27, Jesus does what only God can do (e.g., Ps. 89:8–9; 107:29). Also related to the sea, Jesus walks on the water and identifies himself to his terrified disciples as "I am" (14:27: ἐγώ εἰμι, *egō eimi*), words that surely evoke an earlier promise from Yahweh ("the LORD") to Moses (Exod. 3:14 LXX). The disciples' response certainly leaves that impression: "Then those who were in the boat worshiped him, saying, 'Truly you are the

---

46. See, for example, T. Schreiner, *The King in His Beauty*, 433–41. Schreiner traces the fulfillment theme, paying particular attention to its christological implications.

47. The fulfillment theme should not be restricted to the ten or so specific instances of the fulfillment formula but instead must be painted in broader strokes to include theological concepts.

48. T. Schreiner, *The King in His Beauty*, 443.

Son of God'" (14:33; cf. Job 9:8). When the imprisoned and desperate John the Baptist sends his followers to ask Jesus if he really is the expected Messiah, Jesus points to his messianic words and mighty deeds as evidence that he is God's anointed one (11:4–6). Jesus's answer echoes prophecies such as Isaiah 35:5–6 and 61:1, texts that describe "the blessings which will accompany the coming of God himself to judge and save."[49]

In Matthew 12:22–29 we see that Jesus, the stronger one, has arrived and by the Spirit of God is binding the strong man, driving out demons, and reclaiming God's rightful possessions—all sure indicators that Yahweh's presence and kingdom are being manifested in Jesus. Jesus was conceived by the power of the Spirit (1:18, 20), empowered by God's Spirit at his baptism (3:16–17), and later would baptize his people "with the Holy Spirit and fire," or the fiery presence of God (3:11; cf. Zech. 13:9; Mal. 3:2–3). Consequently, his endowment with the Spirit (12:18–21; cf. Isa. 42:1–4) to perform mighty works (12:28) is yet another indication that God is making his promised presence known in Jesus. Blaine Charette rightly concludes, "By virtue of this unique endowment of the Spirit, Jesus, who is appointed to be Emmanuel, becomes the particular locus of God's presence on earth."[50]

Matthew shows how Jesus fulfills the promise of Yahweh's presence among his people in at least three additional ways: Jesus as the shepherd, as the one greater than Moses, and as the new temple (we treat this later). Volumes have been written on each of these topics, but we mention them briefly to stress their role in Matthew's presentation of the theme of God's relational presence.

Matthew portrays Jesus as shepherd (e.g., 2:4–6; 9:35–36; 14:14; 15:32; 18:12–14; 26:31). In 2:6 Matthew combines the first part of Micah 5:2 with 2 Samuel 5:2 to announce Jesus as the one who fulfills the role of the ultimate Davidic king, the one who will do what Israelite kings have failed to do: perfectly embody God's shepherding presence among his people. Grant Osborne rightly hears an echo of Ezekiel 34:11–16 here, "where God himself will become the shepherd of his people."[51]

Scholars have also stressed Matthew's understanding of Jesus as the new Moses.[52] But Matthew's primary point is that Jesus is far more than a new Moses; he is the one who manifests God's personal presence and power inherently. Jesus sovereignly interprets and fulfills the law (e.g., 5:17–20; 19:3–12), miraculously feeds the multitudes (14:13–21; 15:32–39), and stands as the

---

49. France, *Matthew*, 424.
50. Charette, *Restoring Presence*, 125.
51. Osborne, *Matthew*, 89. See also Baxter, *Israel's Only Shepherd*.
52. Allison, *The New Moses*.

central figure in the preview of God's glorious presence at the transfiguration, where Moses is present (17:1–8).[53] The writer of the book of Hebrews makes the superiority of Jesus explicit (3:3, 6; 8:6; 9:24–26). Jesus makes known God's presence in ways that far surpass anything seen in Moses.

Jesus's Call to Discipleship and Righteousness. Michael Wilkins concludes his significant study on discipleship in this Gospel by touching on the importance of presence: "Matthew's Gospel is just that: 'the good news' that Messiah has come to be with his people and will be with them always. Peter and the disciples are historical examples of what Jesus, with his people, can accomplish."[54] God's relational presence among his people plays out in a variety of ways in this Gospel under the umbrella of Jesus's call to discipleship and righteousness.[55] We will touch on only a few high points in our overview.

To begin with, discipleship is fundamentally a call to follow a person: "Follow me" (4:19; 8:22; 9:9; 10:38; 16:24; 19:21, 27–28). Wilkins rightly surmises that "allegiance to his person is *the* decisive act."[56] It's impossible to even imagine discipleship or righteousness, as Jesus conceives it, apart from relational presence. Throughout his Gospel Matthew uses the pronoun "of me" (ἐμοῦ, *emou*) to highlight the vital necessity of relating to Jesus personally (e.g., "because of me," "on account of me," "acknowledge me," "worthy of me").[57] Such demands of discipleship call for faithfulness and prepare Jesus's followers to suffer. In 5:10–11 Jesus says, "Blessed are those who are persecuted *because of righteousness*. . . . Blessed are you when people insult you, persecute you . . . *because of me*" (5:10–11), showing how discipleship to Jesus lies at the heart of kingdom righteousness, and how presence lies at the heart of both. When disciples are brought before governing authorities on his account, Jesus assures them they will be able to rely on the Father's Spirit to speak through them (10:20; cf. 3:11). Here Jesus anticipates his postresurrection departure and the coming of the Spirit to indwell his community, and

---

53. T. Schreiner, *New Testament Theology*, 173–75.

54. Wilkins, *Discipleship in the Ancient World*, 224.

55. Except for Luke's use of the term "righteousness" (δικαιοσύνη, *dikaiosynē*) in a hymn in Luke 1:75, Matthew alone uses the term among the Synoptic Gospels. By this term, Matthew emphasizes the notion of ethical conduct, which dovetails nicely with his emphasis on discipleship. The noun for "disciple" (μαθητής, *mathētēs*) occurs more than 70 times in Matthew, much more than in the other Synoptics, and the verb μαθητεύω (*mathēteuō*) is found only in Matt. 13:52; 27:57; 28:19 among all four Gospels—all of this signifying the importance of this theme in Matthew. See Hagner, "Matthew," 266.

56. Wilkins, *Matthew*, 179.

57. Note "because of me" in 5:11; 10:18, 22, 39; 19:29; 16:25; 24:9; "acknowledges me" in 10:32, 33; "worthy of me" in 10:37 (2x); "with me" in 12:30 (2x); "from me" in 15:8; 25:41; "in my name" in 18:5; 24:5. There are many additional important uses of this personal pronoun as a theological marker in Matthew.

he offers a window into a trinitarian way of thinking that is spelled out more explicitly in John 13–16 (cf. Matt. 28:19).[58]

The Sermon on the Mount provides the clearest encapsulation of Jesus's teachings in Matthew on discipleship and righteousness. The sermon begins with the familiar beatitudes, or blessings, and two elements stand out immediately: (1) in the opening and closing beatitude the kingdom belongs to the disciples presently (5:3, 10), yet also (2) the majority of God's promised blessings are eschatological blessings. Disciples are included as members and participants of the kingdom now, the kingdom that has arrived in the person of Jesus, but the consummation of their blessedness awaits the day when they are with their Lord. This "already but not fully" aspect of kingdom discipleship illustrates how ethics and eschatology are joined in Jesus. As Robert Guelich puts it, "Instead of ethics swallowing up eschatology in Matthew, we have just the reverse. The implicit attitudes and conduct of the Beatitudes as well as the demands of 5:20–48 are only intelligible in light of that new eschatological moment between God and humanity established by Jesus's person and ministry."[59]

There are additional elements of the Sermon on the Mount that call attention to God's relational presence. In 5:14 Jesus tells his disciples, "You are the light of the world." Jesus himself is the great light who has entered the world (4:16, citing Isa. 9:2), and now Jesus's people become that light (cf. Isa. 42:6). David Turner notes that if the reference to "city" in Matthew 5:14 alludes to Jerusalem, which is likely, then this implies "that God's illuminating presence in the world flows from Jesus's disciples" rather than from a particular place.[60]

In 5:17 we read that Jesus came not to abolish the law and the prophets but to fulfill them, or to bring them to their intended goal. As the incarnation of God's presence among his people, Jesus fleshes out God's communication of himself. In Jesus, the true intent of the Scriptures is now made known.

At the very heart of the Sermon on the Mount, both structurally and theologically, lies the model prayer—Jesus's teachings on how disciples should commune with their Father (6:9–13). The form of address ("our Father") and the individual elements within the prayer bear a distinctly relational tone. The "name" evokes the very presence of God. "Kingdom" and "will" allude to the arrival of God's ruling presence. "Bread," "forgiveness," and "deliverance"

---

58. See France, *Matthew*, 393. France admits that there is no formal theology of the Trinity at this point but observes that "such apparently unplanned collocations are the stuff of which later trinitarian theology was made."

59. Guelich, *The Sermon on the Mount*, 111.

60. D. Turner, *Matthew*, 155.

point to God meeting his children's physical, relational, and spiritual needs as a loving Father. At the very core of Jesus's teaching on discipleship and righteousness stands a warm invitation to experience the intimate presence of the living God through what is affectionately known as the Lord's Prayer.

Our brief tour of the Sermon on the Mount closes with Jesus's conclusion in 7:21–23. It is not the one who merely says "Lord, Lord" who will enter the kingdom, but rather the one who obeys the Father's will (7:21). Such obedience is further explained in 7:22–23 as being known by Jesus rather than simply performing religious deeds (cf. 25:12). Jesus's knowledge of his genuine disciples is a relational knowledge, and those not known by him are sent away from his presence (7:23).[61] Entering the kingdom, living as a genuine disciple, and having a righteousness that surpasses that of the Jewish religious leaders all come down to an authentic experience of God's relational presence.

Community and Conflict

Matthew: Jesus's Identification with His People

We begin with Matthew's emphasis on community. Matthew is the only Gospel to use the word "church" (ἐκκλησία, *ekklēsia* [16:18; 18:17]), a word that connotes a gathered covenant community. It is "my church" that Jesus says he is establishing, a covenant community formed by virtue of their relationship to Jesus personally.[62] Matthew develops this theme of Jesus's presence among his people in several significant ways: through his use of the marriage analogy, his portrayal of the church as a spiritual family, his crucial statement about disciples being gathered in his name (18:20), and his institution of the Lord's Supper (which we treat later). We begin with the marriage analogy.

When John's disciples ask Jesus why they and the Pharisees fast but his disciples do not fast, Jesus responds by equating himself with a bridegroom (9:14–15; cf. 25:1–10). How can the wedding guests (i.e., his disciples) mourn while the bridegroom (Jesus) is "with them" (9:15)? They cannot! Now is the time for celebration. The bridegroom serves as an important metaphor for God in the OT (e.g., Isa. 54:5–6; 62:4–5; Hosea 2:16–23; cf. John 3:29).[63] Granted, Jesus's disciples will fast when the bridegroom is taken "from them"

---

61. For an insightful biblical-theological exploration of what it means to be known by God, see Rosner, *Known by God*.

62. In the phrase "I will build my church" (οἰκοδομήσω μου τὴν ἐκκλησίαν, *oikodomēsō mou tēn ekklēsian*) in 16:18, the pronoun "my" (μου, *mou*) receives emphasis; it is a congregation of those who follow and belong to Jesus—yet another subtle signpost to God's relational presence among his people.

63. Blomberg, *Matthew*, 158; D. Turner, *Matthew*, 255; Hagner, *Matthew 1–13*, 243.

(likely a reference to his coming crucifixion), but his presence among them will continue after his resurrection (28:20). The marriage analogy anticipates the theme of the people of God as the bride of Christ, which is more fully developed in the rest of the NT (e.g., 2 Cor. 11:2; Eph. 5:25–32; Rev. 19:7; 21:1–2, 9; 22:17).

Matthew also features Jesus's use of the image of family to depict his presence among his people. In 12:48–50 Jesus identifies his followers (i.e., his "brother and sister and mother") as his genuine family. The term "brothers" (or "siblings") carries significant weight in Matthew, who defines it (when not referring to biological kin) as members of Jesus's community (see 5:22–24, 47; 7:3–5; 12:48–50; 18:15, 21, 35; 23:8; 25:40; 28:10).[64] Particularly relevant here is the parable of the sheep and the goats in 25:31–46.[65] In this story, the King (Jesus, the Son of Man; see 25:31, 34) judges the righteous worthy of eternal life on the basis of how they have treated "the least of these brothers and sisters of mine" (25:40), since that is in fact how they have treated Jesus himself ("you did for me"). The unrighteous are condemned on the same basis: "Whatever you did not do for one of the least of these, you did not do for me" (25:45). How people treat Jesus, whose presence is tied to his community, becomes the basis for final judgment. This is reinforced in Matthew's use of the term "little ones," which also denotes the community of Jesus's disciples (see μικρός [*mikros*] in 10:42; 11:11; 18:6, 10, 14). In 25:40 the term "least" (τῶν ἐλαχίστων, *tōn elachistōn*), the superlative degree of μικρός, is used.[66] All this is to say that Jesus ties his presence directly to his community of followers.

The reality of Jesus's presence among his people is made especially clear in 18:20, which, along with 1:23 and 28:20, stands as one of the central pillars of the theme of divine presence in this Gospel.[67] In fact, 18:20 and 28:20 and the rest of the emphases on divine presence echo the inaugural statement in 1:23, which in turn echoes the OT theme of God living among his people (e.g., Ezek. 43:7; Joel 2:27; Zech. 2:10–11) and anticipates (from a canonical perspective) the coming Holy Spirit and God's people dwelling with him in the new creation.[68]

In 18:20 Jesus says, "Where two or three gather in my name, there I am with them." When the Jewish leaders "gather" (συνάγω, *synagō*) in Matthew,

---

64. Blomberg, *Matthew*, 107.
65. See Ladd, "The Parable of the Sheep and the Goats."
66. BDAG 314.
67. Kupp, *Matthew's Emmanuel*, 85–88.
68. Hagner, *Matthew 14–28*, 533. Hagner writes, "It is not far from this sense of the divine presence (cf. Joel 2:27; Zech 2:10–11) to the Christology of Paul or of the author of Hebrews."

their assembly is opposed to the will of God.[69] When Jesus's disciples gather, however, they experience Jesus's presence. The immediate context is one of prayer in a discipleship relationship and the assurance of the Father's positive response (v. 19), followed by an explanation ("for" [v. 20]): Jesus's presence among his people makes prayer possible and fruitful. And in light of the parallel between "I am with you" and "it will be done for them by my Father," this presence is God's very presence among his people.[70] Jesus's declaration of deity and assurance of his continuing presence among his people finds significance also in light of the rabbinic saying that when two or three study the law together, the Shekinah (the glorious presence of God) is in their midst.[71] The rest of the NT attests to this continuing presence of Jesus with his people through the Spirit of Christ (e.g., Acts 16:7; Rom. 8:9; Gal. 4:6; Phil. 1:19).

Mark: Conflict with the Demonic and with Religious Leaders

Matthew's emphasis on God's presence with his people is now set in canonical contrast to Mark's emphasis on conflict. Perhaps surprisingly, the theme of divine presence surfaces strongly in Mark in connection with divine judgment and, more specifically, in Jesus's conflicts with the demonic and with religious leaders. Demons are among the first to recognize Jesus's true identity in Mark's Gospel. In 1:21–28 the impure spirits react to Jesus with fearful questions and a compulsory confession: "What do you want with us, Jesus of Nazareth? Have you come to destroy us? I know who you are—the Holy One of God!" (v. 24). Although not the exact title, the connection to "the Holy One," an expression used throughout the OT to refer to Yahweh, is hard to miss. Mark seems to use "the Holy One of God" much like "Son of God" to indicate Jesus's special relationship to God and to designate him as the incarnation of God's personal presence (cf. "You are the Son of God" in 3:11 and "Jesus, Son of the Most High God" in 5:7). In this context, the demons recognize in Jesus the powerful presence of God and fear their impending

69. Kupp, *Matthew's Emmanuel*, 86. See, for example, Matt. 2:4; 22:34, 41; 26:3, 57; 27:17, 62; 28:12.

70. Blomberg, *Matthew*, 281. Blomberg writes, "Jesus implicitly equates himself with God and promises his continuing spiritual presence in the church after his death. Echoes of the Immanuel theme of 1:23 (God with us) reverberate."

71. France, *Matthew*, 699; Osborne, *Matthew*, 688. Keener writes, "An ancient Jewish saying promised God's presence not only for ten males (the minimum prerequisite for a synagogue—b. Ber. 6ab; Meg. 23b; p. Meg. 4:4, §5; . . . 1QS 6.3, 6; CD 13.2–3), but for even two or three gathered to study his law (m. 'Abot 3:2, 6; Mek. Bah. 11.48ff.; cf. m. Ber. 7:3). Here Jesus himself fills the role of the Shekinah, God's presence, in the traditional Jewish saying (which probably predates this saying, since the rabbis would not likely borrow it from Christian sources)" (Keener, *Matthew*, 455–56).

judgment at the hands of God's Holy One (cf. 5:7; Luke 4:34; John 6:69), the stronger one who has come to destroy them (cf. 1:7; 3:27).[72]

The episode of the calming of the storm in Mark 4:35–41 also stresses how God's presence in Jesus brings judgment. The specific commands used for calming the elements read more like an exorcism than a nature miracle (i.e., σιωπάω [siōpaō, "Quiet!"] and φιμόω [phimoō, "Be still!"]; cf. 1:25; 3:12; 8:30, 33; 9:25). In the OT only God can control the turbulent sea and the violent wind.[73] The disciples are encountering in Jesus the very presence of God. The concluding question "Who is this?" in 4:41, although not explicitly answered for a time, calls for a response: this is none other than God in their midst.

When the teachers of the law accuse Jesus of being empowered by Beelzebul (3:22–30), he insists that his ministry of driving out demons entails returning God's possessions to God and reuniting these tortured people with his relational presence. As the "stronger one" (ὁ ἰσχυρότερος [ho ischyroteros] in 1:7), he is able to enter the house of the "strong man" (ὁ ἰσχυρός [ho ischyros] in 3:27), bind him, and take away his possessions (demonized people) and return them to a right relationship with their Creator (cf. Isa. 49:24–26).[74]

Something similar occurs when Jesus delivers the demonized man in Mark 5:1–20. Jesus goes to an unclean area, confronts the impure spirits controlling a man living among the unclean tombs, and drives the demons into unclean animals, which then drown in the sea (the source of the satanic storm?). Jesus's strong presence brings life where there was death, freedom where there was captivity, calm where there was chaos and violence, sanity where there was insanity, and purpose where there was misery and despair. Mark concludes the account with another clue that in Jesus we meet the presence of God. Jesus tells the man, "Go home to your own people and tell them how much *the Lord* [κύριος, kyrios—the word used for Yahweh in the LXX] has done for you, and how he has had mercy on you" (5:19; cf. Luke 8:39: "how much God has done for you"). The man then goes away and begins to "tell in the Decapolis how much *Jesus* had done for him" (5:20).

---

72. Lane notes the marked difference between the forms of address used by the demons (e.g., "Holy One of God" in 1:24; "Son of God" in 3:11; "Son of the Most High God" in 5:7) and those used by ordinary sick people (e.g., "Lord" in 7:8; "Teacher" in 9:17; "Son of David" in 10:47–48; "Master" in 10:51) (Lane, *Mark*, 74).

73. See, for example, Pss. 33:7; 65:7; 89:9; 104:7; 107:29; Prov. 30:4; Job 26:12; 28:25; 38:8; Nah. 1:4; and chiefly, the exodus event.

74. Contra Edwards (*Mark*, 122), who views the "possessions" as demonic spirits, France is correct to conclude, "We should perhaps understand the strong man's σκεύη [skeuē, possessions] here as representing the people rescued (by exorcism) from Satan's oppression" (France, *Mark*, 173).

Interestingly, we see Jesus authorizing the Twelve to extend his ministry of driving out demons in order to return God's possessions to God and restore God's relational presence. He appoints or "makes" (ἐποίησεν, *epoiēsen*; cf. Gen. 1:1 LXX) the Twelve "that they might be with him and that he might send them out to preach and to have authority to drive out demons" (3:14–15). In 6:6–13 Jesus sends out the Twelve two by two "and gave them authority over impure spirits" (6:7). They also extend his liberating presence through preaching repentance and healing the sick (6:12–13).

Jesus's conflict with the religious leaders also highlights Mark's portrayal of the judgment dimension of God's relational presence. In 2:6–12 the leaders accuse Jesus of blasphemy for claiming to forgive sins. Only God can forgive sins, they say (2:7). The inclusio structure of the paragraph identifies the Son of Man with God as the one capable of forgiving sins:

2:7: "Who can forgive sins but *God* alone?"

2:10: "The *Son of Man* has authority on earth to forgive sins."

2:12: "This amazed everyone and they praised *God*, saying, 'We have never seen anything like this!'"

When Jesus announces that "the Son of Man has authority on earth to forgive sins" (2:10), he is boldly proclaiming that God's presence is among them as Jesus, the Son of Man, who speaks and acts for God.[75]

The other divine prerogative that announces Jesus as the manifestation of God's presence is his lordship over the Sabbath (cf. John 5). In Mark 2, when Jesus's disciples are accused of violating the Sabbath by picking grain, Jesus responds with a story of David and his men and concludes, "The Sabbath was made for man, not man for the Sabbath. So the Son of Man [i.e., Jesus] is Lord even of the Sabbath" (vv. 27–28). It is Jesus's very presence as Lord that authorizes a proper recovery and fulfillment of Torah.[76] A similar episode occurs in 3:1–6 in Jesus's healing of the man with the withered hand on the Sabbath.

In Mark 11 the religious leaders raise questions about Jesus's authority: "By what authority are you doing these things? . . . And who gave you authority to do this?" (v. 28). Jesus claims that his authority is from God, but he does so indirectly, using the question about the origin of John's baptism—Is it heavenly or human? It's important to recall that when Jesus was baptized by

---

75. See the insightful excursus "Son of Man" in Edwards, *Mark*, 79–81.

76. Stein notes that in the OT God alone is the Lord of the Sabbath because he instituted and consecrated it (e.g., Gen. 2:3; Exod. 20:8–11; 31:12–17; Lev. 23:3) (Stein, *Mark*, 149).

John, the presence of God was fully displayed, including the Father's voice and the Spirit's descent. Who gave Jesus this authority to forgive sins, heal diseases, drive out demons, restore the Sabbath, enjoy table fellowship with sinners, condemn the temple, and so on? His authority derives from his identity as God incarnate and his words and actions as the one who now manifests God's relational presence.

Jesus's conflict with the religious leaders reaches a climax at his examination before the Sanhedrin in Mark 14. The high priest asks, "Are you the Messiah, the Son of the Blessed One?" (v. 61), and Jesus's response, "I am" (Ἐγώ εἰμι, *Egō eimi*), calls for the high priest to tear his clothes and proclaim, "'You have heard the blasphemy. What do you think?' They all condemned him as worthy of death" (v. 64). The religious leaders clearly understood Jesus to be equating himself with God. In the end, Jesus is crucified for claiming to be the presence of God in their midst.

Eschatological Presence

God's relational presence in the Synoptic Gospels extends beyond Jesus's incarnational presence to his promise of God's future and final presence among his people. Because of the degree of overlap in this section, we will treat both Matthew and Mark under each heading.

Jesus as the New Temple

Mark shows the relational presence of God through Jesus powerfully in chapters 11–16, where, as Larry Hurtado observes, "a claim surfaces again and again [through his direct teaching, his responses to controversy, and his prophetic acts] that Jesus in some way replaces the temple as the central place where God manifests himself."[77] Jesus's words and actions call into question "the very heart of Israel," since "the very presence of God in their midst is at stake. To reject Jesus is to reject the very presence of God." In place of the temple, Jesus has become the "means of true meeting between God and humanity, and thus the means of coming into God's presence."[78] Perhaps we should speak of replacement in the sense of Jesus "fulfilling" the temple.[79]

---

77. Hurtado, *Mark*, 202. Mark uses two different terms for "temple." Prior to the passion narrative, he uses ἱερόν (*hieron*), referring to the whole temple complex. During the passion accounts, he prefers ναός (*naos*), referring to the temple's inner sanctuary. This semantic distinction doesn't have a major impact on the theological point being made throughout.

78. Witherington, *Mark*, 311.

79. We are indebted to P. Schreiner, *The Body of Jesus*, which repeatedly makes this point (e.g., p. 15).

In Mark 11 the cursing of the fig tree (vv. 12–14, 20–21) sandwiches Jesus's clearing of the temple (vv. 15–19) to show that he is actually condemning both the tree and the temple.[80] Not only is the temple being cursed, but also it is being replaced/fulfilled by Jesus himself, since he reminds his followers to "have faith in God" (11:22), a faith that includes prayer and forgiveness (11:24–25). Such realities accompany God's true presence in contrast to the present temple's deceptive and empty rituals (11:15–17).[81]

In Jesus's encounters with the religious leaders in 11:27–12:44 the controversy centers on the nature of his authority and relationship to the Jerusalem temple and its leadership. The presence theme surfaces here at a number of points. Jesus links his authority to God, the implied authority behind John's preparatory ministry (11:29–33). As noted earlier, Jesus implicitly identifies himself as the "son, whom [the father] loved" in the parable of the tenants (12:6; cf. 1:11; 9:7) and the cornerstone of a new temple (12:10; Ps. 118:22; cf. Luke 20:17; Acts 4:11; Rom. 9:33; 1 Pet. 2:6–8). This first episode ends with "The Lord has done this" (12:11; Ps. 118:23), pointing to God as the one who makes his presence known in Jesus. In 12:13–17 Jesus identifies human beings as belonging to God since they bear God's image (Gen. 1:26). In other words, pay taxes to Caesar and give yourselves to God, since you were created to experience his relational presence. In teaching on marriage at the resurrection in 12:18–27 Jesus argues that God's relationship to his people (patriarchs and prophets included) guarantees their future resurrection. Since they are in relationship to the God of the living (v. 27), they must be raised to live in his presence, a presence that conquers the last enemy, death. In 12:28–34 Jesus stresses two interconnected commandments associated with relational presence—loving God and loving one's neighbor—and affirms that these count for more than burnt offerings and sacrifices, rituals associated with the temple. In 12:35–37 Jesus uses Psalm 110:1 to identify himself as the Messiah, God's Son, and David's Lord, who certainly has authority over the temple and its leaders (cf. 14:61–62).

In Mark 13 Jesus predicts the coming destruction of the Jerusalem temple as a result of God's judgment. Much as Jeremiah had predicted the destruction of the temple by Nebuchadnezzar because the people had violated God's dwelling,

---

80. Jesus's condemnation (rather than rehabilitation) of the temple is supported not only by the structural links between the temple and fig tree stories but also by the use of the fig tree imagery in the OT in connection with God's judgment (e.g., Isa. 34:4; Jer. 5:17; Hosea 2:12; Joel 1:7, 12; Amos 4:9; Hab. 3:17).

81. Quite likely, as Hurtado notes, Mark's readers would have made sense of this dramatic act through the Christian teaching that Jesus's resurrection body and the church now stand as the new temple of God (e.g., Mark 14:58; 15:29; 1 Cor. 3:16–17; 12:27) (Hurtado, *Mark*, 183).

name, and presence, so Jesus pronounces coming judgment on the temple (Jer. 7:12–14; cf. Jer. 7:11 in Mark 11:17). As Kent Brower notes, "The very destruction of the temple is confirmation that God's good purposes are now centered in Jesus and the new people of God."[82] In Jesus and the new temple that he is creating, not the Jerusalem temple, we now see the presence of God.

Of special interest here are the repeated accusations that Jesus claimed he would destroy "this temple made with hands and in three days build another, not made with hands" (14:58; 15:29; cf. John 2:19–22; Heb. 9:11, 24). To destroy and to rebuild are parts of the same reality: Jesus's death and resurrection (8:31; 9:31; 10:34).[83] Jesus's resurrection inaugurated the temple of his presence among his people by the Spirit. Sharing in God's eternal presence through Jesus, ironically, was made possible by Jesus refusing to come down from the cross.

The ripping of the temple curtain in 15:38 precisely at Jesus's death and just prior to the centurion's confession in 15:39 shows without a doubt that Jesus's ministry supersedes the temple as the locus of God's relational presence. The inner sanctuary is now laid bare by the death (and coming resurrection) of Jesus, dramatizing that "Jesus has become the new access to God."[84]

In Matthew's Gospel, Jesus certainly fulfills the promise of Yahweh's presence by replacing the Jerusalem temple, the most sacred of Jewish institutions related to divine presence.[85] When confronted by the Pharisees in Matthew 12 for allowing his disciples to pick and eat grain on the Sabbath, Jesus defends his actions by pointing to others (David and the priests) who "violated" the Sabbath in connection with the temple (vv. 1–5). Then Jesus boldly proclaims, "I tell you that something greater than the temple is here" (v. 6). This would have been a shocking pronouncement because the Jerusalem temple stood as the heart of Israel due to its function in mediating God's presence to the people.

Jesus's triumphal entry (21:1–11), his disruption of the temple (21:12–17), and his cursing of the fig tree (21:18–22) all serve as a backdrop to his subsequent teaching, including the parable of the tenants of the vineyard (another national symbol). Jesus concludes this parable by quoting Psalm 118:22–23 and referring to the rejected stone that has now become the cornerstone (21:42). Whether cornerstone or capstone, Jesus, through his coming rejection and his vindication at the resurrection, has become the key component in the new temple (cf. Isa. 28:16; Acts 4:11; 1 Pet. 2:6). It's hard to miss the

---

82. Brower, "'Let the Reader Understand,'" 142.

83. On the pairing of "I will destroy" and "I will rebuild," see Perrin, *Jesus the Temple*, 104–13.

84. Hurtado, *Mark*, 184.

85. On the theme of Jesus as the new temple in the Synoptics, see Beale, *The Temple and the Church's Mission*, 171–92.

temple imagery here in light of the pericope's location in Matthew and the overall thrust of this Gospel.

Jesus as the new temple is also a theme that Jesus's enemies hold against him to the end (e.g., the trial "witnesses" in 26:60–61 and the accusing bystanders in 27:40). Matthew also stresses the ripping of the temple curtain from top to bottom (27:51), an event that "would appear to announce the end of the temple order and suggest . . . that the presence of God which dwelt there has now burst forth from it for good."[86] David Kupp is spot-on in concluding, "Jesus in Matthew has replaced Jerusalem and the Temple as the focus of God's presence and salvation."[87]

The Messianic Banquet

Throughout his ministry, Jesus's table fellowship with sinners and his feeding miracles often foreshadow the coming messianic banquet.[88] Jesus broke bread with sinners and offered them forgiveness in anticipation of the heavenly feast to come (cf. Isa. 25:6–9; 55:1–2; Matt. 8:10–11; Rev. 3:20; 19:6–9). He shares his gracious and forgiving presence with them now in hopes that they will share in his unhindered presence at the consummation of the kingdom. For example, following the episode of the healing/forgiving of the paralyzed man in Mark 2, Jesus calls Levi and enjoys table fellowship with sinners and tax collectors (vv. 15–17). Then, in the next paragraph (vv. 18–20), the bridegroom imagery assumes a future feasting of the groom with the wedding guests following a time of temporary fasting in his absence.

Nowhere is the messianic banquet theme more front and center than at the Last Supper. At the supper Jesus institutes the new covenant of his relational presence. As William Lane observes, "Jesus instituted something new in which the bread and wine of table-fellowship become the pledge of his saving presence throughout the period of time prior to the parousia and the establishment of the Kingdom of God in its fullness."[89] In other words, the fellowship instituted by the supper was "not just a commemoration of his past presence but an experience of his continuing presence with them."[90] The

86. Charette, *Restoring Presence*, 102.

87. Kupp, *Matthew's Emmanuel*, 240. Beale says that the new temple "introduces access for all believers to God's holy presence in a way that was not available in the old creation" (Beale, *The Temple and the Church's Mission*, 190).

88. See, for example, Lane, *Mark*, 106–7. Stein observes, "The feeding of the 5,000 and the 4,000 were probably also understood by the Evangelists as proleptic participations of the Last Supper and the eschatological banquet" (Stein, "Last Supper," 449).

89. Lane, *Mark*, 507–8.

90. Hurtado, *Mark*, 236.

supper, at least in part, may also be viewed as an interim feast anticipating Jesus's future presence with his disciples at the messianic banquet.

This is made explicit in the manner in which Jesus concludes the Last Supper. He promises his future presence in the strongest of terms: "I will not drink from this fruit of the vine from now on until that day when I drink it new *with you* in my Father's kingdom" (Matt. 26:29; cf. Mark 14:25; Luke 22:18).[91] The expression "that day" refers to the parousia and the subsequent marriage of God with his people celebrated by the great wedding feast. Once again Matthew is stressing that Jesus saves his people from their sins (1:21; 26:28) by being "God with us" (1:23). Matthew's addition of "with you" in 26:29 reflects a subtle but powerful expression of the presence theme through the use of "with" (μετά, *meta*) plus a genitive pronoun.[92] Matthew uses this "withness" construction nine times in chapter 26 to remind the disciples of his coming passion (26:18, 20), their future celebration together in the new creation (26:29), and their shared suffering (26:36, 38, 40, 51, 69, 71). The reader of Matthew's Gospel is thereby confronted with divine presence as a personal reality that calls for complete devotion to Jesus's "person, teaching and suffering."[93]

Michael Wilkins sees here a connection to the fourth cup of the Passover, which was associated with God's promise in Exodus 6:7: "I will take you as my own people."[94] Jesus reassuringly promises never to celebrate by partaking in the eschatological meal until his people have persevered through their tribulations in this world and joined him for the heavenly wedding feast. Presence represents the completion of redemption. In a real sense, God's relational presence with his people is the goal of the cross and resurrection. The banquet remains unfinished until the eschaton, and every NT account of the Last Supper refers to this future fulfillment (Mark 14:25; Matt. 26:29; Luke 22:16; 1 Cor. 11:26).[95]

Jesus's Future Return

God's eschatological presence in Jesus culminates in that time and place when and where Jesus will return in glory to defeat evil once and for all, to

---

91. Most scholars rightly see this as another reference to the coming messianic banquet, alluded to numerous times in Matthew (e.g., 5:6; 8:11; 14:20; 15:37; 25:10, 21, 23). Osborne notes how "'with you' (*meth' hymōn*) points back to 1:23 (Immanuel, 'God with us') and means the disciples have a part in the final eschatological blessing" (Osborne, *Matthew*, 969).

92. See Kupp, *Matthew's Emmanuel*, 96–100.

93. Kupp, *Matthew's Emmanuel*, 97.

94. Wilkins, *Matthew*, 837–38. See also Lane, *Mark*, 508–9.

95. Stein, *Mark*, 653. The future messianic banquet is a consistent theme in Scripture (e.g., Isa. 25:6–9; 55:1–2; Matt. 8:11–12; Luke 13:29; Rev. 19:9).

redeem his people, and to inaugurate the new creation. This theme plays a critical role in relation to crucial events as well as in the main teaching sections of Mark's Gospel (parables in chaps. 4 and 12, and the Olivet Discourse in chap. 13).

In the parable of the sower (4:1–20) and the three shorter parables that follow (4:21–34), Jesus hints at his parousia by using the image of the harvest, a common metaphor for the consummation of the kingdom (see 4:8, 20, 29, and likely allusions to the parousia in 4:22, 25).[96] In addition, the entire parable of the tenants in Mark 12 coalesces around the image of the eschatological harvest (12:9; cf. 8:38; 14:62).

In 8:34–9:1 Jesus ties faithful discipleship to his eschatological presence. Most naturally, Jesus is referring in 8:38 not to his ascension/exaltation but rather to his glorious return at the end of the age as Judge and Redeemer (cf. 13:26–27; 14:62; 1 Thess. 4:13–5:11; 2 Thess. 1:6–10).[97] To reassure his followers, Jesus promises, "Some who are standing here will not taste death before they see that the kingdom of God has come with power" (9:1), most likely a reference to the transfiguration that immediately follows. Each Synoptic Gospel follows Jesus's promise with an account of the transfiguration before "some" of the disciples (Matt. 17:1–13; Mark 9:2–13; Luke 9:28–36).[98] The reassurance comes in this way: those who fellowship with Jesus's sufferings now will fellowship with his glorious presence on the last day. Faithfulness to Jesus's relational presence stands as the central priority of kingdom discipleship.

Jesus's transfiguration, among other things, is a foreshadowing of his resurrection and ultimately of his glorious parousia. The setting on a high mountain (recalling the epiphany of God to Moses on Mount Sinai), the cloud symbolizing God's glorious presence throughout Scripture, the transfiguration itself, and the Father's command "Listen to him" (i.e., to Jesus, the incarnation of God's presence) all highlight Jesus's presence. Jesus's body is "transfigured" (μετεμορφώθη, *metemorphōthē*) before them (9:2) and clothed in divine glory (9:3; cf. Dan. 7:9 with reference to the Ancient of Days), a dramatic preview of his coming eschatological glory.[99] Both the Shekinah cloud and the voice in 9:7 represent God's glorious presence (cf. Exod. 16:10; 19:9; 24:16; 33:1). The

96. Ryken, Wilhoit, and Longman, *Dictionary of Biblical Imagery*, 365–67.

97. Stein, *Mark*, 409; Hurtado, *Mark*, 142; Garland, *A Theology of Mark's Gospel*, 257–58; contra France, *Mark*, 342–43.

98. Peter refers to the transfiguration as "the coming of our Lord Jesus Christ in power" (τὴν τοῦ κυρίου ἡμῶν Ἰησοῦ Χριστοῦ δύναμιν καὶ παρουσίαν, *tēn tou kyriou hēmōn Iēsou Christou dynamin kai parousian*) in 2 Pet. 1:16.

99. Lane, *Mark*, 318; Stein, *Mark*, 417.

theophany assures the disciples that Jesus's redemptive path to glory will take him through the valley of the cross. Nevertheless, suffering will not have the final word, since the manifestations of divine presence at the transfiguration foreshadow God's powerful presence to be revealed at Jesus's resurrection and, finally, at his parousia.

In chapter 13 Mark interweaves the destruction of Jerusalem and its temple by the Romans in AD 70 with the Son of Man's return at the end of the age.[100] The near event of God's judgment on the temple forms part of his eschatological judgment to be fully realized at the end of the age.[101] Mark 13:24–27 most certainly relates to the parousia and this final judgment. The shaking of the cosmos in verses 24–25 (cf. Isa. 13:10; 34:4) in preparation for the "newly restored temple-people with whom he will dwell, constituting its new center"[102] forms the backdrop against which Jesus speaks in verses 26–27 of his return. Jesus "riding the clouds" is an allusion to Daniel 7:13 and associates him with the presence and glory of God himself.[103] At Jesus's return he will "gather his elect," assuring the faithful that they will experience his presence in salvation. God's scattered people will at last know his gathering and comforting presence at the coming of Jesus. In the OT God is the one who gathers his people, and at the parousia Jesus will assume this task, signifying that he himself will manifest God's glorious presence on the last day.[104]

Along with 8:38 and 13:26–27, Mark makes an explicit reference to the future coming of the Son of Man in 14:62, when Jesus stands before the Sanhedrin. In response to the high priest's question as to whether he is "the Messiah, the Son of the Blessed One," Jesus answers, "I am," and adds, "And you will see the Son of Man sitting at the right hand of the Mighty One and coming on the clouds of heaven" (14:62; cf. Ps. 110:1; Dan. 7:13). Not only does Jesus identify himself as the Son of Man here, but also he proclaims his enthronement and parousia. On that day the roles will be reversed, and he will come as the eschatological Judge of his accusers.

---

100. See Stein, *Jesus, the Temple, and the Coming of the Son of Man*.

101. Witherington, *Mark*, 342.

102. Watts, "Mark," 227.

103. Adams notes how generally in the OT "it is God who travels with the clouds" (e.g., Exod. 19:9; 34:5; Num. 11:25; 12:5; 2 Sam. 22:12; Pss. 18:11–12; 97:2; Isa. 19:1; Nah. 1:3) (Adams, "The Coming of the Son of Man," 60). More generally, "clouds" in the OT often symbolize the presence and glory of God (e.g., Exod. 14:20; 16:10; 24:15–16; 33:9; Lev. 16:2; Num. 10:34; Ps. 104:3).

104. Bock observes that "gathering was a common image for eschatological deliverance (Isa. 11:12; 27:12–13; 43:5; 49:5; 56:8; 60:1–9; Zech. 2:6; *1 Enoch* 62:13–14; *Psalms of Solomon* 8:28; 11:2–5; 17:26; *4 Ezra* [= 2 Esdras] 13:39–40)" (Bock, *Jesus according to Scripture*, 346). Lane notes how in the OT gathering is attributed to God in texts such as Deut. 30:3–4; Ps. 50:3–5; Isa. 43:6; 66:8; Jer. 32:37; Ezek. 34:13; 36:24; Zech. 2:6, 10 (Lane, *Mark*, 476).

Matthew also highlights Jesus's eschatological presence, as Mark Allan Powell observes: "The mission of Jesus in Matthew's Gospel is fundamentally eschatological."[105] Grounded in Jesus's resurrection as that which inaugurates the "not yet" of the kingdom, Matthew stresses Jesus's promised return, conceives of judgment as separation from God's presence, and affirms eternal reward as a permanent experience of that same presence. We will deal with judgment and reward in the following section.

Jesus promises his future coming in a variety of ways in Matthew. Using the verb ἔρχομαι (*erchomai*, to come), he assures his disciples of his return (10:23; 16:27–28 [followed by the transfiguration, which previews his parousia and perhaps also his resurrection]; 24:30, 42, 44, 46; 25:10 [the bridegroom's arrival]; 25:27 [the master's arrival]; 25:31). Jesus uses the same verb in his lament over Jerusalem when he promises, "You will not see me again until you say, 'Blessed is he who comes in the name of the Lord'" (23:29; cf. Ps. 118:26), likely a reference to his second coming. At the trial scene, in response to the high priest who asks if he is "the Messiah, the Son of God" (26:63), Jesus's answer underscores the significance of presence by referring to his exaltation "sitting at the right hand of the Mighty One" (22:64; cf. Ps. 110:1) and his future return "coming [ἔρχομαι] on the clouds of heaven" (26:64; cf. Dan. 7:13). Matthew also uses the familiar term παρουσία (*parousia*, coming) to reinforce the reality of Jesus's future eschatological presence—in the disciples' question about his coming (24:3) and Jesus's lengthy answer (24:27, 37, 39).[106] And as discussed above, Jesus's reference to his reunion with his disciples at the coming messianic banquet in 26:29 also stresses his eschatological presence, a presence that will mean both judgment and reward.

The Coming Judgment and Reward

Throughout Matthew's Gospel divine judgment is conceived of primarily as the absence of divine presence (e.g., 5:29–30; 7:23; 8:12; 10:28, 33; 13:41–42; 25:30, 41, 46).[107] The presence-destroying aspect of judgment reaches its climax, ironically, on the cross in Jesus's cry of abandonment: "My God, my God, why have you forsaken me?" (27:46). Jesus had already been abandoned by his disciples (26:56), by the leaders of the people and some of the people

---

105. Powell, *God with Us*, 8. See also Hagner, "Matthew's Eschatology."

106. A full exploration of Jesus's Olivet Discourse is beyond the scope of this study but certainly would reinforce the main point being made here.

107. P. Schreiner speaks of "hell" (γέεννα, *geenna*) as the "antonym of the kingdom" in Matthew and understands them as mutually exclusive places (P. Schreiner, *The Body of Jesus*, 33–34). At the heart of this contrast stands the reward of presence versus the loss of God's relational presence. Mark's take on judgment is summarized under the discussion on conflict above.

themselves (26:57–68; 27:39–43), by his executioners (27:27–31), and by his fellow sufferers (27:44). Now he confesses to feeling abandoned by God himself (cf. Ps. 22:1). Jesus's temporary separation from the Father is not the end of the story, of course, but it remains the supreme theological example of how sin sabotages our experience of God's relational presence.

In wonderful contrast, the reward for the righteous centers on divine presence. The idea of a reward of presence begins to surface in the Beatitudes in Matthew 5. Aside from the framing blessings of 5:3, 10 ("for theirs is," present tense of εἰμί), the rest appear to be primarily eschatological blessings ("for they will be," future tense). The predominance of future (divine) passives (5:4, 6, 7, 9) indicates that God himself will provide these blessings (i.e., they will be comforted by God, filled by God, etc.). Yet, in Matthew the kingdom of heaven/God has arrived in the person of Jesus, so the disciples' blessedness has been brought forward into their present experience. Craig Keener compares these blessings to a "*spiritual* down payment," and Donald Hagner to a "manifestation of realized eschatology."[108] These blessings are all associated with experiencing the unhindered presence of God in the new creation—comforted, filled, and shown mercy by God, the inheritance of citizenship, and the privilege of seeing God face-to-face as a child looks on a parent. If God's relational presence is removed from these blessings, they evaporate into meaningless platitudes. God's greatest blessing is himself, and that is precisely what Jesus, using a wealth of relational language, promises.

The realization of rewards can be seen clearly in Matthew 6, where terms for "reward" occur: the noun μισθός (*misthos*) in 6:1, 2, 5, 16, and the verb ἀποδίδωμι (*apodidōmi*) in 6:4, 6, 18. While this concept is sometimes used negatively to describe those who already have their reward or will not receive a reward from the Father (6:1, 2, 5, 16), Jesus uses it positively in 6:4 (giving), 6:6 (prayer), and 6:18 (fasting), each time assuring his followers that "your Father . . . will reward you." Whether realized in the present or reserved for the future kingdom, rewards are inseparably connected to God's presence. The full experience of such rewards must await Jesus's return (16:27).

In Jesus's conversation with the wealthy young man in 19:16–24 and his follow-up teaching of the disciples in 19:25–30, Jesus explains reward in eschatological terms: a sharing in Jesus's future reign (cf. Matt. 25:23; Rev. 2:26–27; 3:21; 20:6) and eternal life itself (cf. Matt. 25:46), certainly meaning life in God's presence.[109] In this way, Jesus answers the man's initial question

---

108. Keener, *Matthew*, 167; Hagner, *Matthew 1–13*, 96.
109. For the spatial significance of 19:28, see P. Schreiner, *The Body of Jesus*, 139–44.

in 19:16 about what he should do to inherit eternal life. The answer boils down to "Come, follow me" (19:21)—follow Jesus in order to spend eternity with him.

In 24:30 we read of "the Son of Man coming on the clouds of heaven," such clouds often being a biblical symbol for God's glorious presence (e.g., Exod. 13:21–22; 40:34–38; Ps. 68:4; Jer. 4:13; Dan. 7:13; Rev. 1:7). He will "gather his elect" from the ends of the earth, and that initiates the reward: being gathered to the Lord for eternal life in his presence. Jesus then warns his listeners to pay attention to signaling events because they will then know that "it is near, right at the door" (24:33), better translated as "he is near" (NRSV, CSB, NET, ESV).

Matthew 25 consists of three longer parables that deal with eschatological issues: the ten bridesmaids (25:1–13), the talents (25:14–30), and the sheep and the goats (25:31–46). In each case the nature of eschatological reward centers on experiencing God's relational presence. In the first story, the bridegroom arrives, and the bridesmaids who are prepared for his coming are escorted "with him to the wedding banquet" (25:10). The unprepared bridesmaids are turned away, and they hear the bridegroom say, "I don't know you" (25:12).

In the second story, when the master returns to settle accounts with his servants, those who have invested wisely hear, "Well done, good and faithful servant! You have been faithful with a few things; I will put you in charge of many things. Come and share your master's happiness!" (25:21, 23), likely an allusion to the messianic banquet and the abundance, celebration, and, above all, intimate fellowship that it will bring (cf. 8:11; 22:2; 25:10; 26:29; Rev. 21:7). The contrasting punishment for the wicked, lazy servant is separation from the master's (Jesus's) joyous presence ("thrown outside, into the darkness" [25:30]).

In the concluding story of Matthew 25, when the Son of Man comes in glory with his angels, the nations are gathered for judgment and separated into contrasting groups: the sheep (righteous) and the goats (unrighteous). The king says to the righteous, "Come, you who are blessed by my Father; take your inheritance, the kingdom prepared for you since the creation of the world" (v. 34). This "eternal life" (v. 46) involves an intimate experience of the unmediated presence of God. Those who have already shared food, drink, shelter, clothing, and a healing and redemptive presence with the corporate Christ will be rewarded with his presence in the new creation, a presence abounding in the very things they were deprived of in this world. Christ says to those who failed to minister to him by their neglect of "the least of these brothers and sisters of mine" (25:40), "Depart from me," and they go to "eternal punishment" (vv. 41, 46).

Sustaining Presence

Among the Synoptic Gospels, Matthew places a premium on Jesus's sustaining presence among his people presently.[110] He does so in two major ways: the presence inclusio of Matthew 1–2 and 27–28, and the promise of Jesus's presence with his people in their co-mission—that is, a shared endeavor by the Spirit of the risen Jesus and his people (28:20).

The Presence Inclusio in Matthew

Matthew's narrative structure supports the theme of divine presence. Ulrich Luz insightfully observes that the "Immanuel motif shows that Matthew's Christology is narrative in character. The presence of God can only be related and testified, not captured in concepts. In Matthew, titular Christological categories are subordinate to narrative ones."[111] Thus, the grand inclusio of Matthew 1–2 and 27:51–28:20 observed by David Kupp shows the significance of the presence theme for Matthew's narrative structure:[112]

ἰδού (*idou*, behold) (1:20, 23; 2:1, 9, 13, 19)	ἰδού (27:51; 28:2, 7 [2×], 9, 11, 20)
angel of the Lord (1:20–2:20)	angel of the Lord (28:2–7)
great joy (birth) (2:10)	great joy (resurrection) (28:8)
special role of women (1:5–20)	special role of women (27:55–28:10)
Jerusalem rejection (2:3–23)	Jerusalem rejection (27:61–66; 28:11–15)
into Galilee (2:22)	into Galilee (27:55, 28:7, 10, 16)
faithful obedience (1:24–2:23)	faithful obedience (27:55–28:16)
ὁράω + προσκυνέω (*horaō*, to see, + *proskuneō*, to worship) (2:2, 8, 11)	ὁράω + προσκυνέω (28:17)
the four women, the magi (1:1–2)	all the nations (1:1–2)
Lord, Holy Spirit, Son (1:18–25)	Father, Son, Holy Spirit (27:54; 28:19)
God commands, directs (1:18–2:23)	Jesus directs, commands (28:16–20)
μεθ' ἡμῶν ὁ θεός (*meth' hēmōn ho theos*, "God with us") (1:23)	ἐγὼ μεθ' ὑμῶν εἰμι (*egō meth' humōn eimi*, "I am with you") (28:20)

In this way, Matthew's story emphasizes Jesus's divine status and his presence among his people as God's presence among them. The bookend texts are

---

110. For insights into Matthew's unique contribution, see the significant study by P. Schreiner, *The Body of Jesus*. While we agree with most of Schreiner's conclusions, his book is limited to Matthew's Gospel, which means that he doesn't deal with the robust pneumatology of the rest of the NT, especially John and Luke-Acts (e.g., the "Spirit of Jesus/Christ" in Acts 16:7; Rom. 8:9; Phil. 1:19; 1 Pet. 1:11).

111. Luz, *The Theology of the Gospel of Matthew*, 32.

112. Kupp, *Matthew's Emmanuel*, 101, with slight modifications.

1:23 with 28:20, where we see the presence of "God with us" now explicitly confirmed as the presence of the risen Jesus with us, fulfilled in time when he sends the Spirit to indwell his people (cf. John 14:16–17, 25–26; 16:7; Acts 16:7; Phil. 1:19). This calls for a more careful look at the climactic expression of divine presence in Matthew, 28:16–20.

The Promise of Jesus's Presence in the Church's Mission

Following his resurrection, Jesus tells the faithful women worshipers to summon the Eleven to Galilee: "Go and tell my brothers to go to Galilee; there they will see me" (Matt. 28:10). They meet him there, interestingly enough, on "the mountain."[113] Their first reaction is hesitant (or puzzled) worship (προσκυνέω, *proskyneō*; cf. 14:31, 33), perhaps bewildered at this new invitation to worship Jesus of Nazareth as Immanuel.[114] Then Jesus "came to them," a spatial alignment that surely takes on added theological meaning in light of Matthew's overall theme. Jesus begins, "All authority in heaven and on earth has been given to me" (28:18), an echo of Daniel 7:13–14, where the Son of Man comes with the clouds of heaven and receives authority, glory, and sovereign power from the Ancient of Days before being worshiped by all nations and peoples. Jesus doesn't bestow divine authority on his disciples but soon will promise that "he himself incarnates that divine authority in their midst" so that the church's mission will continually depend on "his ongoing presence."[115]

The commission proper appears in 28:19–20a and resembles OT commissioning scenes, where divine presence always plays a vital role. God often reassures his inadequate people that his ongoing presence will empower them to complete the assigned task (e.g., Gen. 28:15; Exod. 3:12; 4:12; Josh. 1:5, 9; Judg. 6:16; Isa. 41:10; Jer. 1:8).[116] Now it is the risen Jesus, identified alongside the Father and Holy Spirit, who promises his ongoing empowering presence. The three subordinate Greek participles ("go[ing]," "baptizing," "teaching") support the central imperative verb ("make disciples") to present his followers with their main mission until his return: discipleship to Jesus.

---

113. Note the significance of mountains (or "the mountain") in Matthew: 4:8; 5:1, 14; 8:1; 14:23; 15:29; 17:1, 9, 20; 21:1, 21; 24:3; 26:30; 28:16.

114. For a look at the use of προσκυνέω in Matthew, see Kupp, *Matthew's Emmanuel*, 225–28. His case would be even stronger if his *soft* sense of Jesus's divine presence were understood in the *hard* sense of deity as proposed by Gathercole, *The Preexistent Son*, 75–76. Oddly, Kupp's entire work seems to point to the logical conclusion of Jesus's full deity.

115. Kupp, *Matthew's Emmanuel*, 105.

116. See France, *Matthew*, 1119; Hagner, *Matthew 14–28*, 888.

Matthew concludes his "God with us" Gospel as Jesus, Immanuel, promises his ongoing presence with his followers: "And surely I am with you always,
to the very end of the age" (28:20b). The category most fundamental to Matthew's Christology, according to Luz, is the story of God with his people.[117]
Kupp notes that Jesus's declaration is in "the first-person voice of YHWH's
Emmanuel."[118] Jesus's presence is the presence of God among his people.
This is the truest and fullest meaning of Immanuel, God with us (1:23). The
disciples can only dare to carry out the assigned mission if they experience
it as a co-mission, a shared endeavor by the Spirit of the risen Jesus and
his people. The "God with us" / "I am with you" (1:23; 28:20) reality holds
together this entire gospel as God's relational presence constitutes the heart
and soul of Matthew's message. The last phrase, "to the very end of the age,"
reminds us again of Jesus's vow/promise in 26:29, "I will not drink from this
fruit of the vine from now on until that day when I drink it new *with you*"
at the messianic banquet in the consummated kingdom. Until then, Jesus
himself will be with his sojourning people, a promise no doubt primarily
fulfilled through the coming of the "Spirit of Jesus" at Pentecost (Acts 2:1–4;
cf. John 14:16–17, 25–26; 16:7; Acts 16:7; Phil. 1:19).[119]

Luke-Acts

The richly textured presentation of the theme of God's relational presence
in Mark and Matthew continues in Luke-Acts. Since Luke seeks to tell one
theological story in both his Gospel and the book of Acts, including both
Jesus and the early church, we have opted to treat Luke and Acts together. In
surveying Luke's two volumes for their contribution to the theme of God's
relational presence, five central emphases lead the way: (1) God's purposes
and plan; (2) Jesus: Savior, Lord, and Messiah; (3) the Holy Spirit; (4) the
people of God; and (5) Christ's return.

117. Luz, *The Theology of the Gospel of Matthew*, 31. Luz writes, "If the earthly and
the exalted are one, if God is present in his community in the form of *Jesus*, if the gospel to
be proclaimed by the community is that of *Jesus*, then clearly the story of the earthly Jesus is
already an elementary expression of the *lasting* presence of God in his community" (p. 33).
118. Kupp, *Matthew's Emmanuel*, 105, 236.
119. P. Schreiner rightly observes that Matthew lacks any reference to Jesus's ascension
or his promise of the Spirit, thus "showcasing the presence of the risen Jesus" among his
people (P. Schreiner, *The Body of Jesus*, 27 [see pp. 26–28, 147–50]). While Schreiner affirms the theological importance of Jesus's presence through the Spirit, he stresses Jesus's
identification with his people. Nevertheless, a whole-Bible biblical theology finds room for
both Jesus's oneness with his people, his body, and his sustaining presence among them
through his Spirit.

God's Purposes and Plan to Redeem a People

Darrell Bock rightly declares, "God is the major actor in Luke-Acts."[120] God is at work fulfilling his promises and carrying out his plan to redeem a people for himself. John Squires concludes that the plan of God "functions as the foundational theological motif" for Luke-Acts.[121] Luke makes reference to God's plan in both specific and overarching ways. He uses particular expressions such as "the plan," "foreknown," "foretold," "chosen," "promised," "it is necessary," and "fulfilled" to identify God's work of carrying out the plan.[122] But God's plan moves far beyond individual terms to encompass broader narrative movements and themes.[123] In the end, Luke makes it clear that God desires a permanent and unhindered relationship with his redeemed people, allowing them to experience his relational presence forever.

To begin with, God's plan is rooted in his character as a caring, loving Father (Luke 12:6–7) who gives the kingdom to his children (12:22–34), explained in verse 33 as "treasure in heaven," meaning life in his bountiful presence. He is a missionary God to the core, whose heart is firmly set on seeking and saving the lost (Luke 15).[124] His character is what makes the "withness" of reconciliation possible (e.g., in Luke 15 the father ran to meet the younger son but also "went out and pleaded with" the older son). The Son extends the Father's purposes, as Jesus makes clear when he says of Zacchaeus, "Today salvation has come to this house, because this man, too, is a son of Abraham. For the Son of Man came to seek and to save the lost" (Luke 19:9–10).

Luke also stresses how God's plan means the fulfillment of his covenant promises revealed in Scripture.[125] With the coming of Jesus, the Messiah and Lord, and the pouring out of the Spirit in the last days, God has made good on his covenant promises to Abraham (Luke 1:54–55; Acts 3:24–25), Moses (Acts 3:22; cf. Luke 9:30, 33), David (Luke 1:68–70; Acts 2:29–30), and the prophets (Acts 3:21). God's people, as promised, will now experience the abiding presence of God's Spirit and lasting hope (Acts 26:6–7).

---

120. Bock, *A Theology of Luke and Acts*, 99.

121. Squires, "The Plan of God in the Acts of the Apostles," 23. For the detailed discussion, see Squires, *The Plan of God in Luke-Acts*.

122. Bock, *A Theology of Luke and Acts*, 125, 140–41.

123. The following takes into consideration the list by Bock, *A Theology of Luke and Acts*, 134–48, and Squires, "The Plan of God in the Acts of the Apostles," 23–36.

124. See J. Green, "'Salvation to the End of the Earth.'" He argues for salvation as the dominant theme in Luke-Acts and writes, "Salvation is the coming of the kingdom of God to displace other kingdoms, and entails membership in the new community God is drawing together around Jesus" (p. 89).

125. For more detail on this aspect of God's plan, see Bock, "Scripture and the Realisation of God's Promises."

God's plan centers on Jesus, the Lord and Messiah. Luke stresses this in his Gospel, as do the other Synoptics (e.g., Luke 4:16–21), but he makes it a special point of emphasis in Acts. What happened to Jesus was God's plan: he was anointed, empowered to minister, appointed to suffer, raised from the dead and exalted (e.g., 2:22–36; 3:14–15; 4:10–11; 5:30–32; 7:55–56; 10:40–43; 13:30–37). And because Jesus is Lord and Messiah, the good news of the kingdom will now be preached and people will be invited to experience God's salvation (gentiles included), a salvation that unites them with his healing and delivering presence.

The coming of the Spirit to guide, sustain, and empower God's people also binds them together as one people with a clear mission to Israel and the nations (Acts 1:8). The Spirit, whom Jesus promised in Luke 24:49, comes in power in Acts 2, 8, and 10, equipping God's people to speak a message of good news to all nations, a message often accompanied by mighty works. Bock rightly observes where all this is going for Luke: "Luke's theology paints a picture that focuses on the salvation of a caring, gracious God, who has sent Jesus to transform people's lives through the gift of salvation in the Spirit. God's ultimate desire is to bring people permanently back into healthy relationship with him, to seek and save the lost (Luke 19:10), and to call them to testify to God's goodness in promise (24:44–49)."[126]

God's purpose of seeking a relationship with his people so that they may experience his presence drives his plan at multiple points (e.g., fulfillment of promises, Christology, the good news of the kingdom, the coming of the Spirit, the one people of God, the mission to Israel and the nations). God's relational presence among his people is the end game, the goal of God's multifaceted plan. It is for this reason that God is often praised in Luke-Acts. Zechariah praises God because "he has come to his people and redeemed them" and because he caused the rising sun (cf. Mal. 4:2) "to come to us from heaven" (Luke 1:68, 78). While holding the child Jesus, Simeon praises God: "My eyes have seen your salvation" (Luke 2:30). In Luke 7:11–17, after Jesus raises the widow's son from the dead, the people are filled with awe and praise God with reference to Jesus: "God has come to help his people" (v. 16). God has done what is necessary through the coming of the Son and the giving of the Spirit to make possible an experience of his relational presence.

Jesus: Savior, Risen Lord, and Messiah

The theme of God's relational presence also appears quite strongly in Luke's portrayal of Jesus. Howard Marshall rightly observes that "Luke presents the

126. Bock, *A Theology of Luke and Acts*, 148.

same basic Christology as the other Synoptic Gospels," but we highlight a few aspects with regard to the theme of presence.[127] Luke stresses Jesus's identity as Son of God and Messiah. Jesus bears a unique filial relationship to God, one that is recognized by God (Luke 1:32, 35; 3:22), by Jesus (20:13), by Luke (3:38), and, perhaps most surprisingly, by the demonic as Jesus goes about his healing and delivering work (4:3, 9, 34, 41; 8:28; also as Messiah in 4:41). When Luke emphasizes Jesus's identity as Messiah, it carries the idea of God's salvific presence.[128] When "an angel of the Lord," accompanied by the "glory of the Lord" (both symbols of presence in the OT), announces that "a Savior has been born to you," this Savior is then identified as "Messiah, the Lord" (2:9–11). The unique construction "Messiah-Lord" conveys the idea that Jesus is the Messiah who is the "Lord," a title used exclusively for God in the OT.[129] God has indeed come to his people. The phrase "Messiah of the Lord" or "God's Messiah" is used in 2:26 and 9:20 with much the same effect: God himself has brought salvation to his people (cf. 24:26, 46).

Luke also makes much of Jesus as God's presence among us, especially through his mighty works of healing, forgiving sins, calming the sea, and destroying the demonic (e.g., 4:33–37; 5:8–11, 17–21; 8:22–25; 18:35–43). Nowhere in Luke is this made plainer than in Jesus's inaugural sermon in the Nazareth synagogue in Luke 4:16–21. Jesus applies the Isaiah 61 reading directly to himself when he says, "Today this scripture is fulfilled in your hearing" (v. 21).[130] As a result, Jesus is the bearer of the Spirit of the Lord, and he declares the good news to the poor, freedom to the prisoner, healing to the diseased, and freedom to the oppressed (4:18–19). All the benefits that accompany God's coming, as promised by the prophets, are now made available in the person of Jesus. In his personal presence, deliverance and salvation are offered to all. Indeed, as Jesus says to his sign-seeking generation, "Something greater than Solomon is here. . . . Something greater than Jonah is here" (11:31–32)—namely, the Son of God–Messiah with a greater message of rescue and reconciliation.

The coming of God in Jesus to visit his people is a particularly poignant Lukan theme. Simeon takes the baby Jesus in his arms and praises God as Sovereign Lord for allowing him to see salvation personified, a light to the

127. Marshall, *New Testament Theology*, 146.

128. For a comprehensive study of the concept of the Messiah in Luke-Acts, see Strauss, *The Davidic Messiah in Luke-Acts*.

129. Edwards, *Luke*, 76.

130. As Bock notes, the emphasis falls on the current availability of these promised blessings, since "today" (σήμερον, *sēmeron*) stands at the head of the sentence. "Σήμερον is a key term in Luke's theology and stresses that the opportunity for salvation is this very moment" (Bock, *Luke*, 1:412). See Luke 2:11; 5:26; 12:28; 13:32–33; 19:5, 9; 22:34, 61; 23:43.

gentiles and the glory of Israel (2:28–32; cf. the episode of Zacchaeus in 19:1–10). Luke portrays the coming of Jesus as the coming of God to help his people (e.g., 1:68, 78; 7:16). When Jesus restores a demonized man in 8:26–39, Jesus tells the man, "Return home and tell how much God has done for you," and the man goes away and tells all over the town "how much Jesus had done for him" (v. 39). As Jesus approaches Jerusalem in Luke 19, he weeps over the city and mourns that the city will be destroyed "because you did not recognize the time of God's coming to you" (v. 44). Kavin Rowe concludes, "The visitation of Jesus is the presence of God coming to Jerusalem as κύριος [kyrios, Lord]."[131] Could anything be more tragic than missing the arrival of the very presence of God?

It's not surprising that Luke explicitly identifies the kingdom of God with the presence of Jesus. The transfiguration experience of light, glorious splendor, the cloud of God's presence, and the heavenly voice in 9:28–36 are all introduced in 9:27 as an experience of seeing the kingdom. When Jesus sends out the seventy-two to extend his ministry of healing and teaching, he assures them repeatedly, "The kingdom of God has come near [ἤγγικεν, ēngiken]" (10:9, 11), referring to the redemptive influence of Jesus's presence. In responding to the Pharisees, Jesus announces, "The kingdom of God is in your midst" (17:21). The kingdom of God is right in front of them in the presence of Jesus. Bock describes this verse as a "crux on Luke's view of the kingdom" and concludes that the kingdom "is present in the person of Jesus and his offer of forgiveness and [anticipating Acts] in the community of faith that he spawns and rules."[132]

In Acts 1:1 Luke refers to his former book, where he "wrote about all that Jesus *began* to do and to teach," establishing that Luke-Acts is a single story and we should expect the risen and exalted Christ to continue manifesting his powerful presence to his people.[133] In Acts, as Larry Hurtado mentions, "there is a clear emphasis on Jesus as 'Lord' that associates him in astonishing ways with God."[134] Luke's emphasis on Jesus's ascension and exaltation as Messiah and Lord (e.g., Luke 22:69; 24:49–50; Acts 1:2, 9–11; 2:33; 5:31; 7:55–56) raises the possibility, as Douglas Buckwalter notes, that "he depicts in Acts the exalted Jesus as present within the church in the same way that the OT

131. Rowe, *Early Narrative Christology*, 166.
132. Bock, *Luke*, 2:1414, 1419.
133. Bock identifies five elements that connect Luke and Acts as a single story: the reference to Luke's former book (Acts 1:1), the address in both volumes to Theophilus (Luke 1:3; Acts 1:1), the link in Acts 1:4–5 to John the Baptist (the opening story in Luke), overlapping accounts of the ascension, and the direct connection between Luke 24:47, 49 and Acts 1:2 regarding the instruction to await the Spirit and to witness (Bock, *Acts*, 51–52).
134. Hurtado, *Lord Jesus Christ*, 179.

describes transcendent Yahweh as immanently involved with Israel."[135] In Acts, as in the Synoptic Gospels, Jesus as "the cornerstone" constitutes the beginning of the new temple (4:11).[136] In the OT Yahweh is portrayed as present to his people through his Spirit but also through particular self-manifestations such as the angel of the Lord and God's face, glory, and name.[137]

Luke builds on this background to stress the presence of the exalted Jesus in Acts through the Holy Spirit, through signs and wonders, through angelic messengers and visionary experiences, and through "the name of Jesus." Jesus promised his disciples in Luke 24:49 that he would send what the Father had promised, "power from on high," referring to the Holy Spirit, as Acts 1:4–5, 8 makes clear. Jesus then pours out the Spirit on his followers (Acts 2:33), and the "Spirit of Jesus" subsequently directs their mission (Acts 16:7; cf. Gal. 4:6; Phil. 1:19). We agree with Buckwalter that "the Spirit represents, if not mediates, the exalted Jesus' presence and continued activity among his people."[138] The risen Christ is at work in additional ways, but his work through the Spirit seems to be the primary manifestation of his presence to his people.

Although the risen Christ has been exalted to the right hand of God (Acts 2:33; 5:31; 7:55–56), he continues to make his presence known on earth. Luke portrays Jesus as performing signs and wonders through his apostles (specifically in 4:30; 14:3; and often implied, as in 2:43; 5:12; 8:13). In addition to working miracles, the risen Jesus sends angelic messengers and provides personal visions, usually as a means of directing their witness or mission. R. F. O'Toole surely is correct when he argues that Luke's concept of "witness" often portrays activity of the risen Jesus.[139] On several occasions the risen Jesus appears to Paul—for example, on the Damascus road (9:3–6, 27; 22:6–10; 26:13–18; also to Ananias in 9:10–17); in a vision in Corinth when Jesus assures him, "I am with you" (18:9–10); while he is praying at the Jerusalem temple (22:18–21); and in Jerusalem again when "the Lord stood near Paul," assuring him that his mission wasn't finished (23:11). Jesus also appears to Peter in a vision, instructs him concerning the mission to the gentiles, and sends his rescuing angel to bring him out of prison (10:33; 11:7–9; 12:11, 17). Acts 11:21 sums up the activity of the risen Jesus in Acts when it says with regard to the missionaries to Antioch, "The Lord's hand was with them, and a great number of people believed and turned to the Lord."

135. Buckwalter, "The Divine Saviour," 113.
136. For more on Jesus as the new temple, see Beale, *The Temple and the Church's Mission*, 216, with reference to Acts.
137. Buckwalter, "The Divine Saviour," 113–14.
138. Buckwalter, "The Divine Saviour," 116.
139. O'Toole, "Activity of the Risen Jesus in Luke-Acts," 479–82.

One of the most powerful ways that the risen Jesus makes his presence known to his people in Luke-Acts is through his name. As Buckwalter says, "Luke's use of ὄνομα [*onoma*, name] makes immanent the transcendent Lord who reigns supreme in heaven."[140] Just as in the OT, where the name of Yahweh stands parallel to and substitutes for Yahweh himself, so in Luke-Acts "the name of Jesus signifies the person, the very essence, presence, work and the authority-power of Jesus."[141] This strong interconnection between the person and the name explains why people are saved by believing in or calling on the name of the Lord (Acts 2:21; 10:43; 22:16; cf. 4:12); why they are baptized in the name of Jesus (2:38; 10:48; 19:5; 22:16); why healings (3:6, 16; 4:7, 10), other types of miracles (4:30), and exorcisms (16:18; and the attempted mimic by the sons of Sceva in 19:13–15) occur in the name of Jesus; why the powerful proclamation of the good news is associated with Jesus's name (8:12; 9:15, 27–28); and why those who insist on speaking this good news in Jesus's name (4:17–18; 5:28, 40) could suffer for that same name (5:41; 9:16; 15:26; 21:13). In fact, "all who call on your name" is a synonym for the entire Christian movement in Acts (2:21; 9:14, 21; 15:14, 17; 26:9–10). At times, the name is clearly a synonym for Jesus himself (4:12; 9:16; 19:17; 26:9).

The Holy Spirit as God's Personal Presence

Luke emphasizes the Holy Spirit as God's personal presence in significant ways in his Gospel but even more dramatically in Acts.[142] Max Turner rightly concludes, "The Spirit, in the New Testament writings, is first and foremost the empowering presence and activity of God amongst and alongside his people."[143] Luke's portrayal certainly bears this out, beginning with the birth narratives of Luke 1–2, where the Spirit repeatedly fills people for the purpose of carrying out the divine plan: John the Baptist (1:15), Elizabeth (1:41), Zechariah (1:67), and Simeon (2:25–27). The Spirit is, of course, vitally involved with the miraculous conception of Jesus (1:35), anoints him at his baptism (3:21–22; cf. 4:18; Acts 10:36–38), and empowers him for public ministry (4:18–19), including the time he drives out demons "by the finger of God" (11:20; cf. Matt. 12:28, which says "by the Spirit of God").[144]

---

140. Buckwalter, "The Divine Saviour," 119. See also the discussion in Hurtado, *Lord Jesus Christ*, 197–206.

141. Kim, "How Did Luke Understand 'the Name of Jesus'?," 107.

142. With almost twenty references to the Spirit in Luke (compared to six in Mark and twelve in Matthew) and almost twenty mentions in Acts.

143. M. Turner, "The Work of the Holy Spirit in Luke-Acts," 146.

144. For reasons why Matthew, rather than Luke, explicitly refers to the Spirit in this case, see Bock, *Luke*, 2:1079; Marshall, *Luke*, 475–76.

Most significantly for our purposes, in his Gospel Luke anticipates the coming of the Spirit at Pentecost (3:15–16; 24:49).[145] In 3:16 John explains that while he baptizes with water, Jesus, the more powerful and more worthy one, will baptize "with the Holy Spirit and fire" (cf. Acts 1:5 and 11:16, which omit the reference to "fire," perhaps because the judgment image does not fit the situation of an audience of believers).[146] Here Luke looks forward to the pouring out of the Spirit at Pentecost, fulfilling the promise in Joel 2:28. The personal presence of God will now dwell within individual disciples, a new chapter in salvation history. In Luke 24:49 Jesus instructs his followers to stay in Jerusalem until they "have been clothed with power from on high," the Spirit promised by both the Father and the Son. The story then picks up in the book of Acts.

Acts opens with a repetition of Jesus's instructions "through the Holy Spirit" to the apostles (1:2) to stay in Jerusalem and "wait for the gift my Father promised"—their coming baptism with the Spirit (1:4–5). Pentecost inaugurates this new chapter. Prior to this momentous event the Spirit indwelt a few select people for a particular mission or on a special occasion, but now God's personal presence comes to live within every genuine disciple of Jesus. As Howard Marshall observes, "Reception of the Spirit is evidently the sine qua non of being a Christian and is the clear mark that God has accepted recipients into his people (Acts 15:8)."[147] On this occasion, described in Acts 2, God's ongoing presence becomes individualized and universalized among God's people (vv. 16–18). To be "baptized with the Holy Spirit" at its core means to be indwelt by the presence of God, a presence promised by the Father and now poured out by the exalted Jesus (2:33). Although the Spirit plays a crucial role in empowering believers to carry out Jesus's co-mission (see below), the coming of the Spirit is not purely functional. We agree with Marshall, who concludes, "A one-sided insistence that the Spirit is purely a Spirit of prophecy and mission in Acts is unjustified."[148] Pentecost is a relational experience of God's presence before it is missional. God is fulfilling his longtime promise to live among his people (e.g., Lev. 26:11–12; Ezek. 37:26–28; Zech. 2:10–11).

---

145. Luke's Gospel makes a few additional references to the Spirit's role in the life of a believer: God's good gift of the Spirit to his children (11:13), Jesus's warning of the consequences of blaspheming the Spirit (12:10), and the Spirit's instructions and empowerment for witnessing under duress (12:11–12).

146. Stein, *Luke*, 135.

147. Marshall, *New Testament Theology*, 201. T. Schreiner says, "I conclude, then, that the primary purpose for the granting of the Spirit at Pentecost, to the Samaritans, to Cornelius and his friends, and to the Ephesian twelve is to testify that those who receive the Spirit are members of the people of God" (T. Schreiner, *New Testament Theology*, 458–59).

148. Marshall, *New Testament Theology*, 201.

In the Pentecost event itself the analogies of a violent wind and fire symbolize God's presence much as they did in OT theophanies (e.g., Exod.
19:16–19; 2 Sam. 22:16; 1 Kings 19:9–18; Isa. 66:15; Ezek. 13:13). But, as
G. K. Beale rightly argues, "Acts 2 depicts not merely a theophany but also
the descent of the heavenly end-time temple of God's presence upon his
earthly people. They are constructed to be part of God's temple, not with
physical building materials, but by being included in the descending presence
of his Spirit."[149] The tongues of fire represent the descent of God's presence.[150]
The background of God's life-giving breath may also be in view (cf. Acts
17:25). For instance, in Genesis 2:7 (LXX) God's "breath" brings life,[151] and
the breath or Spirit of Yahweh gives life to the dry bones in Ezekiel's vision
(Ezek. 37:9–14). But Ben Witherington wisely cautions, "The Spirit in Luke's
theology is not just a force or a power or a wind (this is surely why he uses
two different words for wind and for the Spirit), but the living presence of
a powerful God."[152]

Luke then reports that "all of them were filled with the Holy Spirit" (Acts
2:3–4). Luke uses nine verbs to describe the bestowal of the Spirit in Acts.[153]
While the exact nature of these terms and the realities they reflect are debated, they all refer to an experience of God's relational presence. The Jewish-
Christian Pentecost is then extended to the believing Samaritans (8:14–17)
and gentiles (10:44–48) as the Spirit crosses nearly insurmountable social
barriers to unite the church as one body of Christ indwelt by God's relational
presence (cf. 15:8). The uniqueness of Pentecost in its several manifestations
argues against viewing the two-stage pattern as a paradigm of Spirit baptism

149. Beale, "The Descent of the Eschatological Temple, Part 1," 99.

150. Beale notes parallels between Acts 2 and 1 Enoch 14:8–25; 71:5 to show the likelihood
that "the descent of the Holy Spirit at Pentecost 'from heaven' in the form of 'tongues of fire'
is to be conceived as the descent of God's tabernacling presence from his heavenly temple"
(Beale, The Temple and the Church's Mission, 206). Beale also observes a link between the
phrase "tongues of fire" and Isa. 20:27–30, where it certainly indicates "God's theophanic
presence in the temple" (pp. 205–6).

151. Bock, Acts, 97.

152. Witherington, Acts, 132n11.

153. J. Hamilton lists the following: "(1) λαμβάνω [lambanō] ('receive') 2:33,38; 8:15,17,19;
10:47; 19:2. (2) δίδωμι [didōmi] ('give') 5:32; 8:18; 11:17; 15:8. (3) ἐκχέω/ἐκχύννω [ekcheō/
ekchunnō] ('pour out') 2:17–18,33; 10:45–46. (4) βαπτίζω [baptizō] ('baptize') 1:5; 11:16 (cp.
Luke 3:16). (5) ἐπιπίπτω [epipiptō] ('fall upon') 8:16; 10:44; 11:15. (6) ἔρχομαι [erchomai] ('come')
19:6. (7) ἐπέρχομαι [eperchomai] ('come upon') 1:8. (8) πίμπλημι [pimplēmi] ('fill') 2:4; 4:8,31;
9:17; 13:9 (cp. Luke 1:15,41,67). (9) πληρόω [plēroō] ('fill') 13:52" (J. Hamilton, God's Indwelling Presence, 184). These terms can refer to the Christian life as marked by the Spirit or to the
filling with the Spirit for inspired proclamation, but many describe the eschatological gift of
the Spirit—the initial experience for individual Christians of God's personal presence (for these
distinctions, see J. Hamilton, God's Indwelling Presence, 202).

in addition to conversion. Acts 19:1–7 doesn't appear to be an exception, since these people were disciples of John the Baptist rather than followers of Jesus. Hence, their conversion and reception of the Spirit occur simultaneously.[154] The essence of Pentecost is that God has now given himself to his people in fulfillment of his promise that he would one day dwell among them.[155]

The new chapter of God's people experiencing his relational presence individually drives much of what happens in the rest of Acts, meaning that the mission of the church flows from the Pentecost experience. This shows up most clearly in how the Spirit communicates with God's people, equips church leaders, and empowers believers to witness, express and defend the faith, and fulfill their mission through suffering.

The Spirit plays a vital role in communicating with God's people, especially in connection with the Scriptures. In 1:16 Peter sees the Spirit at work communicating through David (cf. Pss. 69:25 [68:26 LXX]; 109:8 [108:8 LXX], quoted in 1:20), and Peter and John make a similar claim in 4:25 (cf. Ps. 2:1–2 LXX). In addition, the Spirit's communication with God's people also applies to what God accomplished in and through Jesus (5:31–32). Many of the teachings of Jesus in John's Gospel regarding the role of the Paraclete as the communicator of truth also play out in Acts (e.g., John 14:25–26; 16:12–15). Later in the Acts narrative Paul tells the Jewish leaders in Rome that the "Holy Spirit spoke the truth to your ancestors" (28:25) through the prophet Isaiah (Isa. 6:9–10 in Acts 28:26–27). God's presence brings an informed knowledge of God and his purposes. In contrast to these positive examples, we also see what happens when people reject the instructing and guiding Spirit: Ananias and Sapphira, who lie to and test the Holy Spirit (5:3, 9), and Stephen's persecutors and their ancestors, who "always resist the Holy Spirit" (7:51).

We also read of the Spirit giving specific direction and assistance to missionaries. The Spirit leads Phillip into a conversation with the Ethiopian official, before later moving Philip to other preaching opportunities (8:29, 39–40). When Peter arrives in Caesarea, Cornelius tells him, "We are all here in the presence of God to listen to everything the Lord has commanded you to tell us" (10:33), suggesting that God's Spirit has arranged this appointment. In the Jerusalem Council's letter to the gentile believers, we read, "It seemed good to the Holy Spirit and to us not to burden you with anything beyond the following requirements" (15:28), meaning that the Spirit in some

---

154. For more on the precise relationship of the Spirit to salvation, see Dunn, *Baptism in the Holy Spirit*; M. Turner, "The Spirit and Salvation in Luke-Acts."

155. D. Peterson, "The Pneumatology of Luke-Acts," 203.

way directed this momentous decision. The Holy Spirit prevented Paul and his companions from preaching the word in the province of Asia (16:6), and the "Spirit of Jesus" prohibited them from entering Bithynia (16:7).

We also see God's personal presence equipping church leaders in a noticeable way in Acts (cf. Jesus "full of the Holy Spirit" in Luke 4:1). In 4:8 Peter, "filled with the Holy Spirit," addresses the rulers and elders of Israel. The seven men of Acts 6 are said to be "full of the Spirit and wisdom" (6:3), and Stephen is singled out as one "full of faith and the Holy Spirit" (6:5) and who speaks with wisdom provided by the Spirit (6:10). Later, while Stephen (again "full of the Holy Spirit") endures the rage of his persecutors, he is rewarded with a heavenly vision of God's glorious presence with the exalted Jesus standing at God's right hand (7:55–56; cf. 2:17). Barnabas is also said to be "full of the Holy Spirit and faith" (11:24), and Saul/Paul is "filled with the Holy Spirit" (9:17; 13:9). Paul also tells the elders of the Ephesian church that the Holy Spirit has made them overseers (20:28). Throughout Acts we see that one important qualification for godly leaders is true spirituality, lives marked by following the Holy Spirit—meaning an obedient responsiveness to God's personal presence.

The Spirit also empowers believers to bear witness to the good news of Jesus, as many of the foregoing examples indicate.[156] John Squires says that Acts 1:8 reinforces "the programmatic role of the Spirit," so that the mention of "witness" throughout Acts is connected to the Spirit although the Spirit is not always mentioned.[157] Those who are filled with the Spirit frequently speak about Jesus or proclaim God's word (e.g., 2:4; 4:8, 31; 5:32; 6:5, 10; 7:55; 11:24; 13:9). This also occurs on a larger scale as the Spirit sets apart missionaries such as Paul and Barnabas to spread the message (9:17; 13:2, 4). For our purposes, it's essential to note that in Acts the presence and power of the Spirit are integral to faithful witness to Jesus.

All too often, the Spirit-empowered witness and mission come at great sacrifice and cost because they occur in the rigors of spiritual warfare. The sheer number of imprisonments, beatings, trials, and sundry hardships bears this out. In addition, we have specific references to God's presence with his people on mission through suffering. The Spirit gives Stephen the wisdom to defend the faith unto death (6:5; 7:54–56) and Saul the power to rebuke Elymas the sorcerer (13:8–11). Paul is compelled by the Spirit to go to Jerusalem even as the Spirit warns him of coming imprisonment and hardships (20:22–23).

156. The Spirit's prophetic role in Acts is well established. See M. Turner, "The 'Spirit of Prophecy.'"
157. Squires, "The Plan of God in the Acts of the Apostles," 23.

The disciples at Tyre "through the Spirit" urged Paul not to go to Jerusalem (21:4), and Agabus the prophet warned that the Holy Spirit said that the Jewish leaders would bind Paul and hand him over to the gentiles (21:10–11).

To sum up: Luke portrays Jesus as operating in the power of the Holy Spirit, anticipating the new era of the Spirit at Pentecost (Luke 3:16; 24:49). God's long-standing promise to pour out his presence on his people is inaugurated when the Spirit comes to dwell within every believer. The church's experience of God's relational presence up close and personal drives the rest of the Acts narrative, as is seen in how God communicates with his people, equips church leaders, and empowers believers to bear witness, express and defend the faith, and fulfill the mission through suffering. Max Turner is correct to conclude, "The Spirit is not mere 'substance' but the presence, empowering and saving activity of the God of Israel himself, the self-revealing extension of his person and vitality into history."[158]

The People of God: New Temple and New Community

God's presence among his people in Luke-Acts takes two complementary paths: the church as the new temple, and the church as the new community. For the most part, we will focus on Acts in this section.

In his study on church and temple in the NT, Howard Marshall concludes that God is present with his people in three ways: (1) his omnipresence in the world, (2) his presence with individuals, and (3) his presence in the Christian ἐκκλησία (*ekklēsia*, church, assembly). He notes, "Both individuals and community can be described as the temple of God."[159] From a canonical perspective, although the motif of church as temple blooms into full flower in Paul's writings, Hebrews, 1 Peter, John, and Revelation, we already see the shift beginning to occur in Luke and certainly in Acts.

The emerging theme of the church as the temple begins early in Luke with the highlighting of the positive reception in the temple of the baby Jesus as the prophesied Messiah (e.g., in connection with Zechariah, Elizabeth, Simeon, and Anna) and the boy Jesus conversing with and amazing the teachers of Israel in the temple courts.[160] Jesus's replacement of the temple had begun. This emphasis continues throughout Luke as it does in the other Gospels—for example, in Jesus's cleansing/condemning of the temple (Luke 19:45–46) and his declaration of the temple's coming destruction (Luke 21:5–6).

---

158. M. Turner, "The 'Spirit of Prophecy,'" 328–29.
159. Marshall, "Church and Temple in the New Testament," 217–18.
160. See J. D. Hays, *The Temple and the Tabernacle*, 170.

Acts opens with what G. K. Beale calls the "theophany at Pentecost," which signals the "irrupting of a newly emerging temple in the midst of the old Jerusalem temple that was passing away."[161] And while the early church continues to meet in the temple courts, most likely for practical reasons, to pray and fellowship and experience God's mighty works, the location also provides a natural setting for preaching about Jesus, the temple's replacement. Luke abandons the subtlety as Acts unfolds, with the temple becoming a major locus of conflict between the early Christian leaders and the temple authorities (e.g., 4:1–3; 5:12–18, 21–26; 21:27–36).

The move from Jesus as the new temple to God's people as his temple becomes official in Acts. Peter highlights Psalm 118:22 in Acts 4:11, a psalm also quoted by Jesus at the conclusion of his parable of the tenants (Luke 20:17; cf. Matt. 21:42; Mark 12:10–11; see also 1 Pet. 2:6–8). Beale observes that Acts 4:11 is "the most direct identification of Christ as the beginning of the new temple in the entire book of Acts."[162] Although Peter's main point is God's response to the leaders' rejection of Jesus, the metaphor makes the most sense when Jesus as "the cornerstone" (i.e., a crucial part of the temple) is understood to imply the existence of a whole new building (i.e., God's people as the true temple).[163]

We also see the idea of church as temple in Acts 15:16–17 when James appeals to Scripture (mainly Amos 9:11–12) to argue that God's people consist of believing Jews *and* gentiles. The "dwelling of David" (v. 16 NRSV) likely refers to the eschatological people of God, a messianic temple or Christian community consisting of redeemed Jews and gentiles.[164] In the last days, inaugurated by the resurrection of Jesus and the coming of the Spirit at Pentecost (cf. Acts 2:17), God has built his end-time temple formed by his people.

Luke also portrays God's relational presence with the church by stressing the richness of its community in a variety of ways. We begin with Luke's use of the terms "church" (ἐκκλησία, *ekklēsia*) and "the Way" (ἡ ὁδός, *hē hodos*). When Luke uses "church" in Acts to refer to a Christian assembly, the unmistakable impression is that of a community energized by the presence of God.

---

161. Beale, *The Temple and the Church's Mission*, 204. For a detailed argument that through his cumulative use of the OT Luke portrays Pentecost as "the decisive time when God first began to build his people into his eschatological temple of the Holy Spirit," see Beale, "The Descent of the Eschatological Temple, Part 2," 84. D. Peterson comments, "Preaching about the centrality of the exalted Christ in God's plans for Israel suggested that he was a replacement for the temple, the law and the whole structure of worship associated with it" (D. Peterson, "The Worship of the New Community," 377).

162. Beale, *The Temple and the Church's Mission*, 216.

163. McKelvey, *The New Temple*, 195–204.

164. Bauckham, "James and the Jerusalem Church," 453–58.

They have a holy reverence for God (5:11; 9:31); respond to God by growing, thriving, and learning (9:31; 11:26; 14:27; 16:5; cf. the term "Christian" in 11:26); pray (12:5); respond to needs (11:22; 14:27; 15:3–4); embrace their gifts and ministry responsibilities (13:1; 14:23; 15:22; 20:17, 28); and along with facing stiff persecution (8:1, 3; 12:1) experience the Spirit's encouragement, both directly and indirectly (9:31; 15:41; 16:5). The expression "the Way" is unique to Luke-Acts as a depiction of God's people. In his Gospel Luke uses it primarily to speak of the way of God through Jesus the Messiah or "the way of the Lord" (1:76, 79; 3:4; 7:27; 20:21), whereas in Acts it designates the Christian community, and especially a people all too familiar with persecution (9:2; 18:25–26; 19:9, 23; 22:4; 24:14).

The concept of a God-indwelt community also comes through strongly in the summaries in Acts 2:42–47 and 4:32–37, which reflect a learning, growing, worshiping, generous, faithful, joyful, and loving people. Here we see a true community of the Spirit, as evidenced by signs and wonders, the praising of God, the Lord adding to their number, a faith anchored in Jesus's resurrection, and God's grace working among them powerfully (2:43, 47; 4:33).

Throughout the rest of Acts three aspects of this God-filled community stand out. First, as noted above, the essential spiritual life of the community is evident to all. They are people who worship the Lord and rejoice in all that he is doing among them (2:47; 5:41; 8:39; 11:18; 13:1–2; 21:20). They support and encourage one another, another sign of God's immanent provision (14:20, 22; 15:30–31, 33; 16:40; 20:1–2; 28:14–15). They are devoted to communing with the Lord through prayer (1:7–14, 23–26; 2:42; 3:1; 10:9–11; 12:5; 13:2–3). Hospitality is abundant and the meeting of practical needs is common, an indication that God's generous grace rests upon his people (2:41–47; 4:32–37; 6:3; 9:19, 27; 11:29–30; 16:15, 33–34; 21:4–9, 16–18; 27:3). The community is also centered in God's word (2:42, 46; 5:42; 6:2, 4; 11:25–26; 15:35; 17:2–3; 18:11; 19:9–10; 20:7–12; 28:30–31).

Second, the community's mission points to the presence of their missionary God among them. Jesus says from the beginning that they will be his "witnesses" (1:8; cf. Isa. 43:10, 12: "'You are my witnesses,' declares the LORD"), signifying that the risen Jesus's relational presence lies at the heart of the church's primary task. Peter and John are given boldness and strength to bring healing to a crippled beggar and to proclaim salvation in Jesus alone by virtue of their relationship to the presence of Jesus (4:13; cf. the "name" of Jesus in 3:16; 4:10, 12). The community's mission centers in preaching or speaking the word of God / the Lord (e.g., 4:29, 31; 6:2, 4; 8:4, 25; 11:1, 19; 13:5, 26, 44, 46; 14:3, 25; 15:35, 36; 16:32; 17:13; 18:11; 19:10). The heart of this message comprises the availability of a reconciled relationship to God through Jesus Christ by virtue of his life, death, and resurrection. As a result of the presence-empowered mission, the word of God or message about Jesus grows and spreads (6:7; 12:24; 13:49; 19:20) as the Lord adds to the number of disciples (2:47; 5:12–13; 6:1, 7; 9:31; 11:25–26; 14:21–23; 16:5, 14–15, 33–34; 17:4, 12, 34; 18:8).

This same pattern of God's presence empowering the mission is clear in Paul's commissioning. The exalted Jesus himself appears to Paul and calls him to proclaim the gospel to the world, gentiles included (Acts 9:1–19; 22:3–16; 26:9–18). Jesus appears to Paul and appoints him as a servant and a witness of what he has seen and will see of Jesus (26:16). When Ananias lays hands on him, Paul is filled with the Spirit, God's indwelling presence (9:17). Ananias says that God has chosen Paul to "know his will and to see the Righteous One and to hear words from his mouth" and to "be his witness" (22:14–15), all relational images. At the heart of Paul's conversion and commissioning lies God's relational presence. In Acts 13:1–3, while the church leaders are worshiping the Lord, the Spirit gives instructions about setting apart Barnabas and Saul for missionary work. Eckhard Schnabel writes, "The fact that Luke relates the words of the Holy Spirit in direct speech, placed between his comment on the worship of the church (v. 2a–b) and the sending off of Barnabas and Saul by the church (v. 3), underscores Luke's emphasis that the initiative for the missionary work of these two missionaries comes from God's Spirit."[165] On several other occasions God speaks to the disciples through heavenly visions or angels (9:10, 12; 10:3, 17, 19; 11:15; 16:9, 10; 18:9), providing guidance in the mission. For example, in the Acts 10 account Luke repeatedly refers to visions and angels as God's means of bringing together the apostle Peter with a captive gentile audience. Brian Rosner notes that although Luke-Acts contains some ninety-five characters, five are major characters: God, Jesus, the Spirit, Peter, and Paul.[166] The Triune God is working both center stage and behind the scenes to extend the good news to all nations so that more people may enjoy his presence forever.

Third, God is present with his people as they suffer. Gamaliel warns the Sanhedrin early on against punishing this new Jesus movement, since it might be "from God" and, if so, they might find themselves "fighting against God" as they persecute God's messianic people (5:34–39). Ironically, they flog the apostles and order them not to speak "in the name of Jesus" before releasing them (5:40). The apostles then rejoice because they have been "counted worthy of suffering disgrace for the Name" (5:41). As we have seen, the "name

165. Schnabel, *Acts*, comments on Acts 13:2, Logos.
166. Rosner, "The Progress of the Word," 223–24.

of Jesus" often is strongly connected to Jesus's presence, meaning that the apostles suffered because of their relationship with the person of Jesus (cf. 9:16).

In Stephen's address to the Sanhedrin he rehearses the history of the presence of God in the midst of his people: the God of glory appeared to Abraham (7:2); God was with Joseph in Egypt (7:9); God appeared to Moses at the flaming bush near Mount Sinai (7:30–33); and the Lord reminded David that "the Most High does not live in houses made by human hands" (7:48).[167] Just before he is martyred, Stephen, full of the Holy Spirit (6:5; 7:55), looks up to heaven and sees the "glory of God" (i.e., God's glorious presence) and Jesus the Son of Man standing at God's right hand (7:55–56).[168] Even in the face of death, as Susan Booth notes, "the first Christian martyr experienced the very real presence of the triune God standing with him."[169]

When Paul is called to be an apostle, he is confronted directly by the risen Jesus. On three occasions Paul repeats (and Luke includes) the exchange that speaks volumes about the role of divine presence in the community (9:3–5; 22:6–8; 26:13–15; cf. Gal. 1:16). Paul speaks about being struck down by a heavenly light blazing down on him and of hearing the voice ask, "Saul! Saul! Why do you persecute me?" He responds, "Who are you, Lord?" The Lord Jesus then answers, "I am Jesus, whom you are persecuting." As Brian Rapske observes, "The 'I am' of the heavenly speaker probably also recalls to a shocked Saul the ineffable name of God."[170] In addition, we note the clear identification of the risen Jesus with his people, what Richard Longenecker sees as an "organic and indissoluble unity that exists between Christ and his own."[171] Jesus's presence was so closely tied to his people that when Paul persecuted the followers of Jesus, he was persecuting Jesus.

The Blessed Hope: Christ's Return

Whether Jesus's disciples were interrogated, beaten, imprisoned, or even martyred, the Lord was with them. And his sustaining presence points to a more positive ending, that of God's eschatological presence among his people.

Luke embraces the "already but not yet" framework of eschatology common in the rest of the NT. In his Gospel Luke emphasizes the "already"

---

167. Booth, *The Tabernacling Presence of God*, 137–38.

168. Bock suggests that Jesus is pictured as standing in order to indicate that he is personally welcoming and receiving Stephen and his testimony and standing in judgment upon the Jewish reaction to him (Bock, *Acts*, 311–12).

169. Booth, *The Tabernacling Presence of God*, 138.

170. Rapske, "Opposition to the Plan of God and Persecution," 239.

171. Longenecker, "The Acts of the Apostles," 371.

dimension as Jesus through his teachings and mighty works initiates the kingdom (e.g., 11:20; 17:21). Jesus inaugurated the "already," but this inauguration did not begin in full "until the Spirit arrived and the rule of God could be enabled from within his people."[172] This becomes clear when we notice the significance of this framework in the opening chapters of Acts (note our added emphases):

1:1: ". . . all that Jesus *began* to do and to teach."

1:4–5: "*Wait* for the gift my Father *promised*, which you have heard me speak about. For John baptized with water, but *in a few days* you will be baptized with the Holy Spirit."

1:6–8: "'Lord, are you *at this time* going to restore the kingdom to Israel?' . . . 'It is not for you to know the times or dates the Father has set by his own authority. But you will receive power *when* the Holy Spirit comes on you.'"

1:11: "This same Jesus, who has been taken from you into heaven, *will come back in the same way* you have seen him go into heaven."

2:17: "*In the last days*, God says, I will pour out my Spirit on all people."

2:18: "I will pour out my Spirit *in those days*."

2:20: ". . . *before the coming of the great and glorious day of the Lord*."[173]

2:34–35: "The Lord said to my Lord: Sit at my right hand until I *make* your enemies a footstool for your feet."

2:39: "The *promise* is for you and your children and for all who are far off—for all whom the Lord our God will call."

With the coming of Jesus and now the sending of the Spirit, the promised "already" has arrived and the "not yet" has been launched. But Luke clearly anticipates Jesus's future return (e.g., Acts 1:11), where God's plans and promises will be consummated. God is not content with anything less than perfect, unhindered fellowship with his people throughout eternity. The reality of God's relational presence drives the eschatological plan toward its final fulfillment.

The central event in the consummation of God's "already but not yet" plan is the return of Jesus Christ. Matthew and Mark feature one major discourse on the return of Christ (Matt. 24–25; Mark 13), while Luke includes two (Luke

---

172. Bock, *A Theology of Luke and Acts*, 391.

173. This part of the Joel quotation anticipates the final eschatological event of the day of the Lord. As Witherington notes, "The coming of the Spirit is an eschatological event, indeed the inauguration of those end times, with more events to follow" (Witherington, *Acts*, 143).

17:20–37; 21:5–36). All the Synoptic accounts converge at the coming of the Son of Man (Matt. 24:29–31; Mark 13:24–27; Luke 21:25–28), and Luke's version emphasizes presence in two specific ways. First, Luke says in 21:27 that Jesus will come "in a cloud" and "with power and great glory" (both symbols of presence; cf. Luke 9:26), an event that Peter will later characterize (quoting Joel) as "the coming of the great and glorious day of the Lord" (Acts 2:20). As Darrell Bock notes, "The image of riding the clouds is reserved in the OT for God or as a description of pagan gods" and certainly indicates the arrival of God's powerful presence at the parousia of Jesus.[174] Luke adds in Acts 1:11 that Jesus "will come back in the same way you have seen him go into heaven," meaning not only a visible, public, bodily return to the earth but also one that is "enveloped in the cloud of divine presence and glory."[175]

Second, Luke adds a note of reassurance for the disciples: "When these things begin to take place, stand up and lift up your heads, because your redemption is drawing near" (Luke 21:28; cf. 21:31, 36). This hopeful reassurance is based on the coming salvation of God in its full relational sense—eternal life in God's presence. F. F. Bruce sees the interval between Jesus's exaltation and parousia as a time when the "presence of the Spirit would keep his people in living union with their risen, glorified, and returning Lord," yet he also notes that Jesus's ascension means that "his abiding presence and energy fill the whole book of Acts, and the whole succeeding story of his people on earth."[176]

The return of Christ also constitutes the arrival of judgment, a time for punishing the wicked and rewarding the righteous. Luke stresses the reality of coming justice for all (Luke 18:8; Acts 17:31; 24:25; cf. 10:42). He defines judgment in terms of the reward of presence for the faithful versus the punishment of removal from presence for evildoers (Luke 17:30–35). The wicked will be thrown into hell, disowned before the angels of God, and told to depart from his presence (12:5, 9; 13:27). They will faint from terror at Jesus's return and the shaking of the cosmos (21:26). In contrast, the righteous will be acknowledged before the angels of God, be able to stand before the Son of Man, and take their place at the great feast in the kingdom of God (12:8; 21:28, 36; 13:29). Whatever one makes of the story of the rich man and Lazarus in Luke 16:19–31, with its many interpretive issues, it certainly depicts how divine judgment relates to the theme of presence. In the end, Lazarus is carried to "Abraham's side" (v. 22) and experiences comfort in God's presence

174. Bock with Simpson, *Jesus according to Scripture*, 447.
175. Longenecker, "The Acts of the Apostles," 259.
176. Bruce, *Acts*, 39.

(v. 25), while the rich man is in Hades, a place of torment and agony (vv. 23, 25). The righteous and the wicked are then permanently separated by a great chasm (v. 26).

Luke stresses the relational presence of God in the consummated kingdom in a colorful way using the image of the messianic wedding feast. There are several places where a fellowship meal or celebration, whether explicitly or implicitly, anticipates the eschatological meal: Jesus's table fellowship with sinners (e.g., with Levi in Luke 5:29–35), the feast celebration at the return of the prodigal son and his reunion with the father (Luke 15:23–24), the meal in the Emmaus story when Jesus breaks bread and gives thanks and is then recognized by the disciples (Luke 24:30–32).

There are, however, definitive references to the messianic wedding banquet. More generally, in the parable of the great feast in Luke 14:15–24, the story revolves around who will actually accept the invitation and attend the banquet (note also the attendees from every direction coming to the feast in 13:29). More specifically, we see this emphasis in two important texts. First, the parable on being prepared for the master's return (Luke 12:35–36) is followed by a blessing on those who wait faithfully (12:37–38). Jesus tells them that their reward will include the privilege of intimate table fellowship in the master's presence, where, surprisingly, the master himself will serve them (v. 37; cf. 22:27). The wedding banquet in the story looks forward to the eschatological wedding feast.

Second, at his final Passover meal with his disciples Jesus points to the heavenly supper. While taking the meal, he tells them plainly, "I will not eat it again until it finds fulfillment in the kingdom of God" (22:16), and "I will not drink again from the fruit of the vine until the kingdom of God comes" (22:18). At the point where Jesus appoints them to extend the kingdom mission, he says, "I confer on you a kingdom, just as my Father conferred one on me, so that you may eat and drink at my table in my kingdom and sit on thrones, judging the twelve tribes of Israel" (22:29–30). God's relational presence (and all the privileges and responsibilities that it brings) lies at the heart of the consummated kingdom. James Edwards writes, "The ultimate goal of the redemptive work of Christ is not simply to save sinners, but to transform them to become servants of Christ, and as servants to be made siblings who rule for and *with Christ*."[177]

The blessed hope of Christ's return also brings resurrection and restoration for God's people, and both realities are tied to God's relational presence. The resurrection of the righteous involves reward from the Lord

177. Edwards, *Luke*, 636 (emphasis added).

(Luke 14:14) as they find ultimate identity in their relationship to God: "They are God's children, since they are children of the resurrection" (Luke 20:36; cf. 6:35). This eternal family relationship has been secured by the resurrection from the dead. In Acts Luke also speaks of hope as the "hope of resurrection of the dead" (23:6; 24:15). The Messiah himself has pioneered the way forward—the hope of resurrection leading to life in God's presence (2:25–28; cf. Ps. 16:8–11). This same hope is what God promised Israel (26:6–8; 28:20).

Christ's return also brings restoration. When the disciples ask in Acts 1:6 whether it is time for Jesus to "restore [ἀποκαθιστάνεις, *apokathistaneis*] the kingdom to Israel," he tells them that their task is not to establish the eschatological calendar but rather to be his witnesses not only in Israel but also to the ends of the earth (1:8). In Peter's speech in Solomon's Colonnade in Acts 3, he refers to the final restoration: "Heaven must receive him until the time comes for God to restore [ἀποκαταστάσεως, *apokatastaseōs*] everything, as he promised long ago through his holy prophets" (v. 21). At his return, Jesus not only will resurrect his people but also will restore creation for the purpose of living among his people forever. Revelation 21–22 paints this final picture of God among his people in much finer detail.

Even as we wait for the return of Christ and the resurrection and restoration that it brings, Jesus promises God's presence in the interim. The repentant thief hanging next to Jesus at his crucifixion asks that Jesus remember him when he comes in his kingdom, likely a reference to the parousia (Luke 23:42). The man's request is far exceeded when he is promised a place in Jesus's exalted presence in the immediate future: "Truly I tell you," Jesus says, "today you will be with me in paradise" (23:43). As David Garland notes, Luke is convinced that Jesus is the first to enter paradise and indeed opens the gates of paradise (Rev. 2:7; *Testament of Levi* 18:10), suggesting that the criminal will be "hosted by Jesus in the highest heaven."[178]

Stephen's testimony at his death points in the same direction, as the account of his death highlights images of divine presence (e.g., Spirit, glory, right hand). Moments before his martyrdom Stephen declares that the transcendent presence of God, the Most High, cannot be confined to handmade houses (Acts 7:48; cf. 1 Kings 8:27; 2 Chron. 2:6). Then, full of the Holy Spirit, Stephen looks to heaven and sees the glory of God and Jesus exalted to God's right hand (7:55–56). As they are stoning him, he prays that Jesus

---

178. Garland, *Luke*, 926–27. Bock writes, "Jesus' reply also suggests that the criminal will be in some conscious, intermediate state until the resurrection, though this conclusion is implied, rather than explicit" (Bock, *Luke*, 2:1858).

will receive his spirit, meaning that he will continue living in the presence of
Jesus (7:59; cf. Luke 23:46).

Conclusions

The theme of God's relational presence continues to drive the theological plot
in the Synoptic Gospels and Acts by providing coherence and interconnectedness to the story. Once again, we see that it stands as the cohesive center of the
biblical theology for this chapter of the biblical story. Our theme is grounded
in Jesus's identity as the one through whom Yahweh's personal presence is
made known: "Immanuel . . . God with us." Jesus's mission as God among us
reinforces the theme of relational presence in many ways. Through his presence and teaching we see that the kingdom of God has come near. Disciples
are called to follow him so that they may be with him and may partner with
him in the mighty works of manifesting God's healing and delivering presence. Jesus replaces the temple as the primary place where God's presence
is made known. Now through Jesus's death and resurrection the temple of
God's presence among his people by his Spirit is inaugurated. The church is
born through the coming of the Holy Spirit, God's empowering presence, to
indwell individual believers. Even as God's people struggle in their pilgrimage, their battle mirrors the greater war of God's presence confronting the
powers of darkness. They are sustained by God's presence in the interim. The
story moves toward a magnificent conclusion, with a powerful emphasis in
the Synoptics and Acts on God's eschatological presence. The "already" has
arrived and is also a "not fully," anticipating the fullness yet to come. Jesus's
return precedes the great wedding of Jesus the bridegroom and his people the
bride. This much-anticipated union is celebrated by the messianic wedding
feast followed by eternal reward in God's presence. Much of what we have seen
in the Synoptics and Acts will surface again in the rest of the New Testament.

FIVE

The Relational Presence of God in Paul's Letters and in Hebrews and the General Letters

In this chapter we will explore how the theme of God's relational presence provides a unifying center not only in Paul's writings but also in the book of Hebrews and the General Letters.[1] The presence theme occurs in a number of major overlapping movements in both groups of writings: God's revelatory presence, incarnational presence, presence in achieving and providing salvation, presence in our union with Christ and through the person and work of the Holy Spirit, presence in and among his people, and sustaining and eschatological presence. God's relational presence also honors the narrative or story structure of the biblical material by providing the conceptual key around which the story coheres.[2] It is the story of how God acts to be dynamically and relationally present with his people.

Paul's Letters

While many are optimistic that one can write a theology of Paul, the enthusiasm fades considerably when it comes to the possibility of finding a center to

1. We subscribe to the traditional view of the Pauline authorship of all thirteen letters.
2. In this way we see our work as complementary to the massive contribution of N. T. Wright, with his emphasis on the metanarrative of exile and restoration. See especially N. T. Wright, *Paul and the Faithfulness of God*. See also the concise application of Wright's framework to the entire NT in Eskola, *A Narrative Theology of the New Testament*. Our emphasis on God's relational presence gets at the heart and soul of the biblical narrative.

Paul's theology.[3] This long-debated question is situated in the larger context of the unity and diversity of the apostle's thought. The lingering question is how Paul's Letters can feature coherence of thought while simultaneously addressing diverse local situations. Although the trend toward emphasizing diversity continues, the stubborn issue of the unity simply won't go away.[4] For this reason, many such centers have been proposed (e.g., God, Christ, salvation history, justification by faith, reconciliation, the apocalyptic triumph of God, union with Christ, God's glory, the cross, the story of Israel, the gospel, covenant).

Most of the suggestions for a center to Paul's thought seem too narrow and inflexible, and they fail to do justice to the breadth and depth of Paul's writings. While they rightly highlight an important Pauline theme (e.g., reconciliation, justification), they come up short in capturing the overall theological coherence of his letters. Occasionally, a center is too broad and doesn't clarify the apostle's thought (e.g., God). We need an organizing center that appreciates the diverse emphases in his letters but coheres through their contingent circumstances.[5] We believe that God's relational presence offers the most promising center of Paul's theology.[6]

Our proposal stands closest to that of Douglas Moo ("God's act in Christ"), Thomas Schreiner ("God in Christ"), Richard Bauckham ("christological monotheism"), and Constantine Campbell ("union with Christ"), but we contend that God's relational presence offers an even more comprehensive and unifying center. David Capes, Rodney Reeves, and E. Randolph Richards opt for Bauckham's christological monotheism as the "key concept that organizes and makes sense of all Paul's theology," but they define the concept in a manner that closely resembles God's relational presence: "So the coherence of Paul's theology seems to us to be Christological monotheism. . . . It is not a principle; it is a person. It is not a big idea; it is a relationship with God through Christ."[7]

3. Porter, "Is There a Center to Paul's Theology?" See also the historical overview in Hasel, *New Testament Theology*, chap. 3.

4. Thielman writes, "Even scholars who are unhappy with talk of a 'center' or 'core' for Paul's thought often find themselves eventually speaking of a basic principle around which Paul's theology is organized" (Thielman, *Theology of the New Testament*, 231). Thielman opts for "God's graciousness toward his weak and sinful creatures" as the center (p. 232).

5. The coherence-contingency framework remains an important contribution. See Beker, *Paul the Apostle*, 7.

6. See Moo, "Paul," 138; T. Schreiner, *Paul*, chaps. 1–2; C. Campbell, *Paul and Union with Christ*, chap. 13.

7. Capes, Reeves, and Richards, *Rediscovering Paul*, 357.

God's Revelatory Presence

God's words are extensions of his personal presence. Or, as Timothy Ward puts it, "*Communication* from God is therefore *communion with* God, when met with a response of trust from us."[8] Through his words—his *revelatory presence*—"God draws people into union with Christ and into relationship with himself."[9] God, through his words, intends to enter into relationship with human beings, thereby allowing them to experience his divine presence. Ward continues, "When we speak of Scripture as a mode of God's presence, we are asserting that it is in the *speech acts* of Scripture that God reveals himself by being semantically present to us, as he promises, warns, rebukes, reassures and so on."[10] In this section we will draw together some of Paul's explicit statements about God revealing himself to his people and how they are significant for our understanding of God's relational presence.

In the opening chapters of Romans Paul repeatedly emphasizes how God has spoken. In the past, God revealed himself through the created order, including his creation of human beings (1:18–20). More specifically, God spoke to his people Israel, giving them his words/law (3:2, 20; 9:4–6; 10:19–21). They have been "entrusted with the very words of God," Paul says (3:2).

More recently, God has spoken the good news of Christ to the world. (We will say more about Paul's gospel below, but here we note how the gospel is God's revelation to bring people into relationship with himself.) Paul refers to the "mystery hidden for long ages past" but now "revealed and made known through the prophetic writings by the command of the eternal God" (Rom. 16:25–26; cf. 1 Cor. 4:1). The gospel comes as a result of God's revelation (Gal. 1:11–12; Eph. 3:3–5; cf. 2 Cor. 12:1–9) and is a proclaimed gospel (1 Cor. 15:1–2, 11; Gal. 1:11; 2:2; 2 Tim. 1:11; Titus 1:1–3). This gospel "mystery" has been preached to gentiles, allowing them to be coheirs with Israel, members of one body, and sharers together in the promise in Christ Jesus (Eph. 3:1–12). In a complementary passage in Colossians Paul defines the mystery—once hidden but now disclosed to God's people—as "Christ in you [relational], the hope of glory [presence]" (1:27). God's word of good news comes to humanity for the purpose of calling forth a response of faith (Rom. 10:17) and providing salvation and eternal life (1 Thess. 2:13–16; Titus 1:1–3).

God's revelatory presence becomes practical and specific as God instructs his people through his apostles and prophets (e.g., 1 Cor. 14:24–33). God's people are to "let the message of Christ dwell among [them] richly as [they]

---

8. Ward, *Words of Life*, 32. See also Ward's earlier work, *Word and Supplement*.
9. Ward, *Words of Life*, 52.
10. Ward, *Words of Life*, 66.

teach and admonish one another with all wisdom" (Col. 3:16). Paul viewed his instructions to the churches as coming ultimately from the Lord (1 Thess. 4:1–2), and those who reject his instructions are not rejecting a human being but rather are rejecting God—"the very God who gives you his Holy Spirit" (1 Thess. 4:7–8). God's instructions through his apostles and prophets are directly tied to God's personal presence.

God's revelatory presence also includes the Scriptures. Paul opens and closes Romans with a reference to the Scriptures. The gospel that Paul proclaims had been "promised beforehand through his [God's] prophets in the Holy Scriptures regarding his Son . . . : Jesus Christ our Lord" (1:2–4). This gospel, Paul says in conclusion, reveals the mystery once hidden but now "revealed and made known through the prophetic writings [Scriptures] by the command of the eternal God, so that all the Gentiles might come to the obedience that comes from faith" (16:25–26). Here we see that the Scriptures serve God's purposes related to his relational presence. Later, Paul reminds Timothy of "how from infancy [he has] known the Holy Scriptures," the teachings that are able to make him "wise for salvation through faith in Christ Jesus" (2 Tim. 3:15; cf. 2 Pet. 1:20–21). "All Scripture," Paul writes, is "God-breathed" (2 Tim. 3:16), meaning that "God speaks through these words," that he "breathed life and meaning and truth into them all."[11] Through Scripture God has prepared Timothy and others like him for ministry, a ministry that centers in experiencing the relational wholeness that God intended for his people.[12]

God's Incarnational Presence

Much like in the Gospels, God's incarnational presence in Jesus continues to play a major role in Paul's thought. Jesus Christ, the Son of God, came into this world as a flesh-and-blood human being, died a physical death, and was bodily raised from the dead. God extends his personal presence to us in the person of his Son.

Paul repeatedly alludes to Jesus's incarnation, usually in connection with the achieving of salvation for humanity. Jesus, a descendant of David (Rom. 1:3; 2 Tim. 2:8), "appeared in the flesh" (1 Tim. 3:16) and testified "before Pontius Pilate" (1 Tim. 6:13).[13] Christ the Savior was "born of a woman" and

---

11. Witherington, *Letters and Homilies for Hellenized Christians*, 1:360.

12. Paul's reference to being "taught by God" in 1 Thess. 4:9 is likely an indirect reference to the Thessalonian Christians' knowledge of the Scriptures. See Fee, *The First and Second Letters to the Thessalonians*, 160.

13. Paul and other NT writers use the term φανερόω (*phaneroō*, appear) to refer to Jesus's incarnation (e.g., 2 Tim. 1:10; Heb. 9:26; 1 Pet. 1:20; 1 John 1:2; 3:5, 8).

"born under the law" in order to redeem and offer adoption into God's family (Gal. 4:4–5). In this Savior, God's grace has "appeared," offering salvation to all people (2 Tim. 1:10; Titus 2:11; 3:4–7).[14]

Paul tells the Corinthians that for their sakes Jesus "became poor, so that [they] through his poverty" might become enriched spiritually (2 Cor. 8:9). Here the poverty image likely refers to Jesus's incarnation.[15] This poverty entailed Christ "taking the very nature of a servant, being made in human likeness," and "being found in appearance as a man" (Phil. 2:7–8).[16] Jesus was the "one man" through whom God's grace gift came to the world (Rom. 5:15, 17, 19). This "one mediator between God and mankind, the man Christ Jesus" (1 Tim. 2:5) "came into the world to save sinners" (1 Tim. 1:15). The term "mediator" (μεσίτης, *mesitēs*) points to Jesus as the "go-between God,"[17] who brings God and people into a new relationship that could be described using a host of metaphors (e.g., covenant, reconciliation, adoption).[18] God's presence mediated through Jesus is fundamentally relational.[19]

In Jesus's body, God's very presence dwells. Jesus was sent "in the likeness of sinful flesh" to condemn sin "in the flesh" (Rom. 8:3) and to offer salvation through his "body" and "blood" (1 Cor. 11:23–26). We read in Colossians that the Son is the "image of the invisible God" and that "God was pleased to have all his fullness dwell in him" (1:15, 19). In Christ, "all the fullness of the Deity lives in bodily form" (2:9). In Jesus Christ we see the visible, tangible presence of God incarnate. In Ephesians Paul begins to build the bridge between the physical body of Jesus and the church, the body of Christ, when he says that Jesus set aside "in his flesh" the law with its regulations, created "in himself" one new humanity, and "in one body" reconciled Jews

---

14. The noun ἐπιφάνεια (*epiphaneia*, appearing) and the verb ἐπιφαίνω (*epiphainō*, appear) are used primarily in the Pastoral Epistles to refer to Jesus's incarnation (2 Tim. 1:10; Titus 2:11; 3:4) or his parousia (1 Tim. 6:14; 2 Tim. 4:1, 8; Titus 2:13). Outside the Pastoral Epistles, see Luke 1:79; Acts 27:20; 2 Thess. 2:8.

15. Harris writes, "Christ himself chose to exchange his royal status as an eternal inhabitant of heaven for a slave's status as a temporary resident on earth. . . . He surrendered all the insignia of divine majesty and assumed all the frailty and vicissitudes of the human condition" (Harris, *The Second Epistle to the Corinthians*, 579).

16. Although the exchange imagery as used in 2 Cor. 8 does not exactly parallel what Paul is saying in Phil. 2, where the "form of God" is not exchanged for but is displayed in the "form of a slave." See Harris, *The Second Epistle to the Corinthians*, 579.

17. Fee, *1 and 2 Timothy, Titus*, 65. Hebrews speaks of Jesus as the mediator of a new covenant (8:6; 9:15; 12:24).

18. P. Towner, *The Letters to Timothy and Titus*, 181.

19. See the masterful work by Tilling, *Paul's Divine Christology*.

and gentiles to God (2:14–16).[20] In Jesus Christ, God incarnate, we meet the relational presence of God in person.

God's incarnational presence was also manifest in Jesus's death on the cross. Paul's theology of the cross runs extensively through his writings, so our summary here focuses on the cross as incarnational presence. Michael Gorman refers to the "revelatory crucifixion of Jesus the Messiah" as one of the most significant dimensions of his death: "Jesus' death on the cross *reveals* the faithfulness, love, and (paradoxically) power of God."[21] Multiple references in Paul's writings attest to Jesus's physical death on a cross: the Lord of glory was crucified (1 Cor. 2:8); Christ, the Passover lamb, was sacrificed (1 Cor. 5:7); the Lord Jesus was killed (1 Thess. 2:15); Jesus became obedient unto death on a cross (Phil. 2:8). Jesus's entry into our world and physical death on a criminal's cross became a central element in early Christian tradition and preaching. Of "first importance," Paul says, is "that Christ died for our sins according to the Scriptures, that he was buried, that he was raised on the third day according to the Scriptures" (1 Cor. 15:3–4).

Jesus's physical death effected lasting relational change between God and humanity. Paul speaks of Christ's death securing our rescue or redemption (Gal. 1:4; Col. 2:13–15; 1 Tim. 2:5–6), and this redemption came with the promise of the Spirit, God's personal presence (Gal. 3:13–14). The cross demonstrated God's love (Rom. 5:8), a love from which nothing can separate us (Rom. 8:31–39). Jesus's death established the new covenant, thereby uniting God and his people in an everlasting relationship (1 Cor. 11:23–26). The purpose of the cross was that "we might become the righteousness of God" (2 Cor. 5:21), likely a reference to a right standing before God and a right relationship with him. Believers have now been reconciled to God through the cross (Eph. 2:15–16). God's people have been "brought near by the blood of Christ" (Eph. 2:13), and they now "belong to the Lord" (Rom. 14:8–9). They are "his very own" people (Titus 2:14). They now "have access to the Father" through Christ's work on the cross and constitute God's holy temple, "a dwelling in which God lives by his Spirit" (Eph. 2:18–22). Looking to the future, Jesus's blood secured redemption that anticipates a final, future redemption of "God's possession" (Eph. 1:14). Paul comforts the Thessalonian Christians with the assurance that "whether we are awake or asleep, we may live together with him" (1 Thess. 5:10).

---

20. Schnackenburg asserts, "So close is the connection of the Church to Christ that she already appears in the Cross as a New Creation, the one redeemed humanity" (Schnackenburg, *Ephesians*, 117).

21. M. Gorman, *Apostle of the Crucified Lord*, 135. See also M. Gorman, *Cruciformity*.

The crucified Jesus is also the resurrected Jesus (Rom. 1:4; 1 Cor. 15:4; 2 Cor. 5:15; Gal. 1:1; 2 Tim. 2:8). And Jesus's bodily resurrection serves as yet another verification of God's incarnational presence among us. Jesus was raised from the dead and is now at the right hand of the Father, interceding for us, his body (Rom. 8:34; Eph. 1:19–20). He is Lord of both the dead and the living (Rom. 14:8–9). Shortly after his resurrection Jesus appeared to many of his followers (1 Cor. 15:5–8). And his resurrection has present and future implications for how believers experience God's presence. In the present, we have been raised with Christ and participate in his resurrection spiritually (e.g., Col. 2:12; 3:1; Phil. 3:10). In the future, with Jesus as the firstfruits of those who have died and been raised, Jesus's resurrection guarantees our bodily resurrection at the end of the age (1 Cor. 6:14; 15:20–21; 1 Thess. 1:8–10).

Just as God was present with Israel, so now God is present in Christ with his people, the church. The foundation of God's presence with his people in Christ has been laid with an emphasis on the incarnation of Jesus, the Son of God: his becoming a real human being, his physical death on the cross, and his bodily resurrection.

God's Presence Communicated through the Gospel

Paul stresses throughout his letters that God's relational presence lies at the heart of his work to provide salvation. Paul himself was dramatically transformed and redirected through a personal encounter with the risen Lord Jesus on the Damascus road (Acts 9:1–19; 22:3–16; 26:9–18). As a result, Paul the missionary theologian/preacher proclaims a gospel that centers on divine presence using a variety of metaphors and images. Whether Paul is speaking of justification or reconciliation or adoption or new creation, we see God's commitment to be in relationship with and live with his people rising to the surface.

The gospel of God's relational presence begins with God's love and mercy. Often Paul's addressees are described as those whom God loves (e.g., Rom. 1:7; 1 Thess. 1:4; 2 Thess. 2:13; Col. 3:12; Eph. 1:4–5; 2:4–5; Titus 3:4–5). Out of his love and mercy God provides salvation as a grace gift. At the very heart of this gift is the person and work of Jesus Christ: Paul writes to the Corinthians, "Thanks be to God for his indescribable gift!" (2 Cor. 9:15), likely referring to the "life, death, and resurrection of Christ."[22]

---

22. Barclay, *Paul and the Gift*, 1. Barclay observes, "Grace is everywhere in Second Temple Judaism. But it is the incongruous grace that Paul traces in the Christ-event and experiences in the Gentile mission that is the explosive force" (p. 572).

The gospel of God's gracious gift of himself in Jesus Christ appears throughout the Pauline Letters in a variety of ways. We will briefly discuss four and their connection to God's relational presence. First, the gospel of Christ sets forth God's righteousness and allows sinners to be justified by grace through faith (e.g., Rom. 1:17; 3:21–22, 26; 2 Cor. 5:21; Gal. 2:15–16; Phil. 3:9). The meaning of "righteousness" and "justification" in Paul's thought is one of the most hotly contested topics in Pauline theology.[23] N. T. Wright speaks of four key aspects to justification: (1) the work of Jesus, the Messiah of Israel; (2) the covenant that God made with Abraham, the purpose of which was to bring salvation to the world; (3) the divine law court, where God as Judge acquits those who believe in Jesus Christ; and (4) eschatology, or the vision of God's future for the whole world and for his people.[24] At the risk of oversimplifying: the justification debates center on which aspect should be primary and which ones secondary. The thread that runs through all four is relationship.[25] As a result, we take the phrase "God's righteousness" to refer to God's character, chiefly his covenant faithfulness to fulfill his promises, while "justification" refers to the relational status that God graciously bestows on those who put their faith in Christ. Believers are declared to be "in the right," or in right relationship with God. In terms of the effect on a repentant sinner, we view justification as primarily relational with ethical and eschatological implications (e.g., Rom. 3:21–26; 5:1–2, 15–19; 10:4–13; Gal. 2:15–21; Eph. 2:4–10).

Paul's summary statement in Romans 5:1–4 sums up Romans 1–4 and provides a foundation for Romans 5–8. This brief text also provides a window through which to see God's relational presence in Paul's teaching about justification:

> Therefore, since we have been justified through faith, we have peace with God through our Lord Jesus Christ, through whom we have gained access by faith into this grace in which we now stand. And we boast in the hope of the glory of God. Not only so, but we also glory in our sufferings, because we know that suffering produces perseverance; perseverance, character; and character, hope.

Justification is activated by (though not based upon) faith (v. 1). The result is "peace with God" through Jesus Christ (v. 1), which Douglas Moo

---

23. For a clear and helpful overview, see C. Campbell, *Paul and Union with Christ*, chap. 11.

24. N. T. Wright, *Justification*, ix–x.

25. An emphasis marshaled by Tilling, *Paul's Divine Christology*, 256. Tilling concludes that "the Pauline Christ-relation is a divine Christology expressed as relationship."

understands not as "an inner sense of well-being, or 'feeling at peace' . . . , but the outward situation of being in a relationship of peace *with* God."[26] Consequently, having gained "access" to God's grace by faith, believers now "stand" in this grace (v. 2). One of the chief blessings of justification is the ongoing enjoyment of God's grace, which certainly cannot be separated from God's person. Leon Morris notes that "grace is not something apart from God, but is God giving himself to us in his graciousness."[27] Our boast or confidence, then, becomes "the hope of the glory of God" (cf. Rom. 3:23; 8:17–18, 21, 30), meaning the hope of an eschatological experience of God's glorious presence. Paul's gospel reveals that God has already begun to make his glorious presence known to his people through the "face" or person of Christ (2 Cor. 4:6; 1 Tim. 1:11). God has started to call his people into an experience of his relational presence (1 Thess. 2:12; 2 Thess. 2:14).

The second way in which God's gracious gift appears in Paul's writings centers on the redemption/rescue/freedom theme. Through Jesus's gift of himself on the cross, believers are liberated from evil powers and receive forgiveness of sins, enabling them to enter into a new relationship with God (Rom. 3:24–25; 1 Cor. 1:30; Eph. 1:7; Col. 1:13–14). Redemption leads to adoption (Gal. 4:5), and the purpose of redemption is that God's people might receive the "blessing given to Abraham" and "the promise of the Spirit [God's personal presence]" (Gal. 3:14).

Third, the gospel of Jesus Christ brings relational reconciliation and adoption into God's family.[28] Through the work of Christ, those who put their faith in him are reconciled to God or put into right relationship with him (Rom. 5:10–11; 2 Cor. 5:16–21). Through Christ, God reconciles people to himself for the purpose of presenting them "holy in his sight, without blemish and free from accusation" (Col. 1:22; cf. 1:19–20). While the law-court context of Colossians 1:22 gets the attention of many commentators, we shouldn't miss the relational reunion that takes center stage: God's people will be presented "before him" (κατενώπιον αὐτοῦ, *katenōpion autou*), or in his glorious presence (cf. Eph. 1:4: "before him"; Jude 24: "before his glorious presence"). Through the work of Christ believers are "brought near" to God's people and to God himself (Eph. 2:13, 16–18). They now have "access to the Father by one Spirit" (v. 18), meaning that they have entered into a close relationship with God and may enter his presence through worship and prayer (cf. Eph. 3:12). Believers are now God's children in full relationship with him, and as

26. Moo, *The Epistle to the Romans*, 299.
27. Morris, *The Epistle to the Romans*, 219.
28. On the theme of reconciliation, see the classic work by R. Martin, *Reconciliation*.

family members they may enter God's presence crying out, "Abba, Father" (Rom. 8:14–16; Gal. 3:26; 4:4–6).

Fourth, the gospel brings the promise of the Spirit and life. Conversion is the initiatory experience of the eternal life that God has brought to light through the gospel of Jesus (1 Tim. 6:12; 2 Tim. 1:1, 10; Titus 1:1–3). We are made alive with Christ (Col. 2:13). God graciously gives his Spirit to his children (Rom. 8:9–10; 2 Cor. 5:5; Gal. 3:14; Eph. 1:13–14), and the Spirit guarantees that they will receive the final inheritance of eternal life with God. The children are then heirs, having the hope of eternal life (Rom. 8:14–17; Gal. 3:29; 4:7; Eph. 3:6; Titus 3:4–7). God's salvation in Christ means that ultimately we will live in his presence: "For God did not appoint us to suffer wrath but to receive salvation through our Lord Jesus Christ. He died for us so that, whether we are awake or asleep, we may live together with him" (1 Thess. 5:9–10; cf. 4:17). If the Spirit is a foretaste of God's glorious presence, then we may assume that our inheritance will be nothing less than life in the very presence of the Lord himself.

God's Presence through Our Union with Christ

In Paul's writings the theme of God's relational presence often features distinctly participationist language (e.g., in, into, with, and through Christ). Presence doesn't get any more intimate than this. In his comprehensive study *Paul and Union with Christ*, Constantine Campbell uses the four terms "union, participation, identification, incorporation" to summarize what Paul means when he speaks of a believer's union with Christ:[29]

> *Union* gathers up faith union with Christ, mutual indwelling, trinitarian, and nuptial notions. *Participation* conveys partaking in the events of Christ's narrative. *Identification* refers to a believer's location in the realm of Christ and their allegiance to his lordship. *Incorporation* encapsulates the corporate dimensions of membership in Christ's body. Together these four terms function as "umbrella" concepts, covering the full spectrum of Pauline language, ideas, and themes that are bound up in the metatheme of "union with Christ."[30]

Truly, Paul's union-with-Christ language occurs extensively throughout his letters and represents a pillar of his thought and teaching on God's relational presence. Campbell describes union with Christ as quite possibly "a key to

29. C. Campbell, *Paul and Union with Christ*, 29, 413.
30. C. Campbell, *Paul and Union with Christ*, 413.

Paul's theology" or the "webbing that holds it all together."[31] We see union with Christ highlighting God's relational presence in at least four main ways.

First, through union with Christ, a believer experiences new life. This new life has its source in participation with Christ in his death, burial, and resurrection. Believers have died with Christ (Rom. 6:8; Col. 2:20), and through their identification with Christ at baptism they participate in his death (Rom. 6:3–5). Death does not have the final word, however, since they also participate in Christ's resurrection: "We were therefore buried with him through baptism into death in order that, just as Christ was raised from the dead through the glory of the Father, we too may live a new life. For if we have been united with him in a death like his, we will certainly also be united with him in a resurrection like his" (Rom. 6:4–5; cf. Eph. 2:5; Col. 2:12–13).

In addition to participating in Christ's death and resurrection, believers have also been seated "with him in the heavenly realms" (Eph. 2:6). Their life is now "hidden with Christ in God" and will one day be revealed at Christ's return and their bodily resurrection (Col. 3:3–4; cf. Rom. 6:8; 1 Cor. 15:22). Because of all that has happened, Paul can describe a believer as a new creation (2 Cor. 5:17). Christ lives in believers (Gal. 2:20). He dwells in their hearts through faith, and as they know his love they are "filled to the measure of all the fullness of God" (Eph. 3:16–19). They experience God's presence as new life—new spiritual life now in their union with Christ and new physical life at his parousia. As Paul tells the Corinthians, "There is but one God, the Father, from whom all things came and for whom we live; and there is but one Lord, Jesus Christ, through whom all things came and through whom we live" (1 Cor. 8:6). Union with Christ first means new life.

Second, believers participate in a new relationship with God through Christ. To begin with, Paul sees himself and his coworkers as Christ's ambassadors, preaching that God wants to reconcile the world to himself through Christ (2 Cor. 5:18–20). God made Christ, who had no sin, to be sin for us, "so that in him we might become the righteousness of God" (2 Cor. 5:21; cf. Phil. 3:8–9). In union with Christ believers enter into a right relationship with God; that is, they become the righteousness of God. As N. T. Wright concludes, this is more than status, and it moves into the area of a reconciled relationship: "It is the covenant faithfulness of the one true God, now active through the paradoxical Christ-shaped ministry of Paul, reaching out with the offer of reconciliation to all who hear his bold preaching."[32] Those who enter into a new relationship with God through Christ belong to Christ

---

31. C. Campbell, *Paul and Union with Christ*, 440–42.
32. N. T. Wright, *Pauline Perspectives*, 73.

(Rom. 7:4). They have been adopted as God's children through Christ (Rom. 8:14–17; Eph. 1:5). And, as children, they are "heirs of God and co-heirs with Christ," sharing in both Christ's suffering and his glory (Rom. 8:17). Union with Christ brings a new relationship with God and a host of resulting benefits and blessings: "It is because of him that you are in Christ Jesus, who has become for us wisdom from God—that is, our righteousness, holiness and redemption" (1 Cor. 1:30) (see also the spiritual blessings in Christ detailed in Eph. 1:3–14).

Third, believers share in a new relationship with Christ's body. This happens on at least two levels, the individual and the corporate. On the individual level, Paul insists in 1 Corinthians 6:15 that, as Gordon Fee puts it, "the believer's physical body is to be understood as 'joined' to Christ's own 'body' that was raised from the dead."[33] This joining occurs through the Spirit, as the immediate context makes clear (1 Cor. 6:17). But it is nevertheless a real experience of Christ's presence through union with Christ. Paul's entire argument not to engage with prostitutes rests upon this union with the Lord. Paul also later speaks of the spiritual communion with Christ that occurs during the Lord's Supper as believers share in the body and blood of the Lord (1 Cor. 10:16–17). This also serves as a deterrent to participating in the idolatrous pagan feasts.

On a corporate level, union with Christ brings believers into a new relationship with Christ's body, the church. In Christ, believers "form one body, and each member belongs to all the others" (Rom. 12:5). They are all one in Christ Jesus (Gal. 3:28), forming "one new humanity" in Christ (Eph. 2:15). Christ is the head of his body, the church (Eph. 1:22–23; 4:15–16). Using a different metaphor, Paul likens the church to a building or a temple: "In him the whole building is joined together and rises to become a holy temple in the Lord. And in him you too are being built together to become a dwelling in which God lives by his Spirit" (Eph. 2:21–22). This one new humanity created in Christ, all reconciled to God, is indwelt by God's presence as God's new temple.

The body and the temple metaphors overlap in a couple of key texts that emphasize the believer's new relationship with Christ's body. In Ephesians 1:22–23 Paul writes, "And God placed all things under his feet and appointed him to be head over everything for the church, which is his body, the fullness of him who fills everything in every way" (cf. Eph. 3:19). Clinton Arnold rightly identifies the background here as the OT description of the "divine presence and manifestation of God in the temple."[34] God's

---

33. Fee, *The First Epistle to the Corinthians*, 258.
34. C. Arnold, *Ephesians*, 118.

glory—"the essence, power and presence of God"—filling the temple shows up in LXX passages such as 2 Chronicles 7:1 (ἔπλησεν, *eplēsen*), Ezekiel 43:5 (πλήρης, *plērēs*) and 44:4 (πλήρης), and Isaiah 6:1 (πλήρης), using the verb or adjective forms of Paul's noun for "fullness" (πλήρωμα, *plērōma*) from Ephesians 1:23. They all portray God's glorious presence filling the temple.[35] The term πλήρωμα, Arnold contends, "becomes coextensive with the presence of God."[36] In Colossians 2:9–10 Paul makes a complementary statement: "For in Christ all the fullness of the Deity lives in bodily form, and in Christ you have been brought to fullness. He is the head over every power and authority" (cf. Col. 1:19). Douglas Moo also sees the OT emphasis on God dwelling in the temple as the background to this text: "God in his fullness has not taken up residence in and therefore revealed himself in a building but in a body. Characteristic of the new covenant administration is the replacement of the Temple with Christ as the focus for God's presence and as the nucleus of God's people. . . . In him, and in him alone, God has decisively and exhaustively revealed himself. All that we can know or experience of God is therefore found in our relationship with him."[37] We will give more attention below to Paul's emphasis on how God's relational presence is experienced corporately.

Fourth (and this aspect will be developed more extensively in the next section), believers begin a new relationship with God's Spirit in connection with their union with Christ. We've already seen the Spirit's role in connection with the people of God as the temple. Constantine Campbell notes that "the people of God constitute the 'location' in which God dwells, and in that sense they have replaced the function of the temple of old."[38] When people are incorporated into Christ, they are indwelt by the Holy Spirit (Eph. 1:13–14). The Spirit is the one who "effects the presence of Christ in believers."[39] So much so that the phrases "in Christ" and "in the Spirit" often are virtually synonymous theologically in Paul's writings (e.g., Rom. 8:9–10; Eph. 3:16–19).[40] The Spirit is God's personal presence who allows believers to experience and live out their union with Christ (see Eph. 2:17–18).

---

35. C. Arnold, *Ephesians*, 118.

36. C. Arnold, *Ephesians*, 118. M. Barth observes, "*Pleroma* may therefore be considered a synonym of the name, the glory, the Spirit, or the *shekina* of God" (M. Barth, *Ephesians*, 205).

37. Moo, *The Letters to the Colossians and to Philemon*, 193–95.

38. C. Campbell, *Paul and Union with Christ*, 290.

39. C. Campbell, *Paul and Union with Christ*, 360–61.

40. C. Campbell, *Paul and Union with Christ*, 361. Campbell notes how Michael Gorman highlights an implicit trinitarianism in Paul's thought when he says that "in Christ" is shorthand for "in God/in Christ/in the Spirit" (p. 367). See M. Gorman, *Inhabiting the Cruciform God*, 4.

God's Presence through the Holy Spirit

Paul's theology of the Spirit begins with the foundational reality that God indwells his people by his Spirit in fulfillment of the OT prophecies that he would return to live among his people (e.g., Jer. 31; Ezek. 36–37; Joel 2). God's promise to indwell his people again comes to fulfillment at Pentecost (Acts 2). Gordon Fee concludes, "The Spirit is none other than the fulfillment of the promise that God himself would once again be present with his people."[41]

Consequently, Paul can tell the Roman Christians that only those who have the Spirit belong to Christ (Rom. 8:9–10)—no Spirit, no Christian, according to Paul. It is not outward circumcision that brings a person into relationship with God but rather the "circumcision of the heart, by the Spirit" (Rom. 2:29). The new heart and new spirit God promised in Ezekiel 36–37 have become reality. God has given his Holy Spirit, his personal presence, to his people through Jesus Christ (1 Thess. 4:8; Titus 3:5). Again, for Paul, it is foundational that God's Spirit comes to live within a believer and effects a radical relational change. Paul's emphasis on God's relational presence through the Holy Spirit can be seen in (1) the central Pauline images of the church, (2) the Spirit's mighty works within and among believers, and (3) the Spirit as God's personal guarantee that believers will spend eternity in his presence.

The three major images of the people of God in Paul's Letters highlight the Spirit as God's personal presence: God's family, God's temple, and the body of Christ.[42] Because God has given his people his Spirit, they have become his children. "Because you are his sons," Paul tells the Galatians, "God sent the Spirit of his Son into our hearts, the Spirit who calls out, 'Abba, Father.' So you are no longer a slave, but God's child" (Gal. 4:6–7). In a similar passage in Romans 8, Paul writes, "For those who are led by the Spirit of God are the children of God. . . . The Spirit you received brought about your adoption to sonship. And by him we cry, 'Abba, Father.' The Spirit himself testifies with our spirit that we are God's children" (vv. 14–16). Because they have received the Spirit, they have been adopted as God's children. Because the Spirit dwells within their hearts, they cry out, "Abba, Father." Paul tells the gentile believers in Ephesus that they are no longer strangers and foreigners but are "fellow citizens with God's people and also

---

41. Fee, *God's Empowering Presence*, 845. See Fee's insightful discussion on the usage of important terms such as πνεῦμα (*pneuma*) and πνευματικός (*pneumatikos*) in Paul's writings (pp. 14–36).

42. Fee, *God's Empowering Presence*, 873–76.

members of his household" (Eph. 2:19; cf. 1 Tim. 3:15). Inclusion in God's family is made possible by Christ, through whom they now have "access to the Father by one Spirit" (Eph. 2:18). Access to the family comes with the Spirit's indwelling presence.

In the OT God's temple in Jerusalem, especially the inner sanctuary or holy of holies, constituted the place where God lived among his people.[43] As we have seen previously, Jesus Christ replaced the Jerusalem temple as the locus of divine presence. With his ascension and the coming of the Spirit at Pentecost, the people of God now form the temple of the Spirit of God. Paul tells the Corinthians that they are "God's building" (1 Cor. 3:9). Paul had preached the gospel of Jesus Christ crucified and risen and, in doing so, had laid the only proper foundation for this God-building or temple. Building upon this foundation, builders must avoid the cheap materials of this world system and instead use the lasting, eternal materials appropriate to the gospel (1 Cor. 3:10–15). The "gold, silver, costly stones" imagery is taken from the building of Solomon's temple (1 Chron. 29:2; 2 Chron. 3:6).[44] Paul concludes with a rhetorical question and a warning: "Don't you know that you yourselves are God's temple and that God's Spirit dwells in your midst? If anyone destroys God's temple, God will destroy that person; for God's temple is sacred, and you together are that temple" (1 Cor. 3:16–17). The presence of the Spirit in their midst constitutes God's dwelling place or temple among them.

Paul later warns the Corinthians about sexual immorality and idolatry on the basis of who they are as the temple of God's Spirit (1 Cor. 6:13–20). He cautions them not to unite their bodies with prostitutes, since they have been united with the Lord—whoever is united with the Lord "has become one S/spirit with him" (6:17).[45] The Corinthian believers are to "flee sexual immorality," because they know (or should know) that their "bodies are temples of the Holy Spirit, who is in you, whom you have received from God" (6:19). In a similar passage in 2 Corinthians 6 Paul tells them not to be "yoked together with unbelievers," since there is no agreement between righteousness and wickedness, light and darkness, or "the temple of God and idols" (vv. 14–16). They should live differently, because they are "the temple of the living God," as God said: "I will live among them and walk among them, and I will be their God, and they will be my people" (2 Cor. 6:16; cf. Lev. 26:12; Jer. 32:38; Ezek. 37:27).

43. For more on the temple in biblical theology, see T. D. Alexander and S. Gathercole, *Heaven on Earth*; Beale, *The Temple and the Church's Mission*.
44. Fee, *God's Empowering Presence*, 874.
45. Fee, *God's Empowering Presence*, 133, for this translation.

Ephesians 2:18–22 summarizes Paul's teaching on the people of God as the temple of the Spirit (note our added emphases):

> For through him we both have *access to the Father by one Spirit*. Consequently, you are no longer foreigners and strangers, but fellow citizens with God's people and also members of his household, built on the foundation of the apostles and prophets, with Christ Jesus himself as the chief cornerstone. In him *the whole building* is joined together and rises to become a *holy temple in the Lord*. And in him you too are being built together to become *a dwelling in which God lives by his Spirit*.

God's people have access to God's presence by the Holy Spirit within them and among them. They are not simply allowed to enter the holy of holies; they themselves are now the holy of holies. God now dwells among his people. Fee concludes,

> Here, then, is how one is to understand all the "indwelling" terminology in Paul: by the indwelling of the Spirit, both in the individual and in the community, God (or Christ) indwells his people. Here is the ultimate fulfillment of the imagery of God's presence, begun but lost in the Garden, restored in the tabernacle in Exodus 40 and in the temple in 1 Kings 8. It is God's own presence among us that marks us off as the people of God. . . . So not only do we have access to the presence of God (v. 18), but God himself by the Spirit has chosen to be present in our world in the gathered church.[46]

The last of the three major images of the people of God in Paul's Letters is that of the body of Christ. Here we will note briefly the importance of the Spirit's role in connection with this image. In 1 Corinthians 12 Paul says, "We were all baptized by one Spirit so as to form one body [of Christ] . . . and we were all given one Spirit to drink" (v. 13). It is the Spirit, and only the Spirit, who can take different members and make them into one body. Their reception of the Spirit allows them to experience together the "fellowship of the Holy Spirit" (2 Cor. 13:14). There is one body of Christ and one Spirit, who binds the diverse members together in peace (Eph. 4:3–4). Believers are to "stand firm in the one Spirit, striving together as one for the faith of the gospel" (Phil. 1:27). According to Philippians 2:1–2, the "common sharing in the Spirit" constitutes a vital part of the basis for unity in the church. The Holy Spirit, who indwells members of Christ's body, and the resulting unity within the body provide an intense experience for believers of God's relational presence.

46. Fee, *God's Empowering Presence*, 689–90.

A second way Paul emphasizes God's relational presence through the Holy Spirit can be seen in the Spirit's mighty works within and among believers (e.g., gifting, empowering, sanctifying). There are at least five major ways in which the Spirit conveys God's presence to his people. First, the Spirit conveys God's love and life to his people. God's love has been "poured out into our hearts through the Holy Spirit" (Rom. 5:5; cf. 8:16). In addition to helping believers realize and experience God's love demonstrated in Christ, the Spirit also gives eternal life to God's people (Rom. 8:2, 6, 10–11; 2 Cor. 3:3, 6; Gal. 5:25; 6:8). This life brings with it a glorious freedom (Rom. 8:2, 15–18; cf. 2 Cor. 3:17). Believers are no longer obligated to keep the law. Rather, when they keep in step with the Spirit, they fulfill the law and please God (Rom. 8:4; Gal. 5:16, 22–26; 6:1–2).

Second, the Spirit helps us know God. In Ephesians 1 Paul prays that the Father would give the Ephesians "the Spirit of wisdom and revelation," so that they may "know him better" (v. 17). This renewed reception of the Spirit would enable them to know God more adequately, including the hope of his calling, the wealth of his glorious inheritance in God's people, and his great power for those who believe (vv. 18–19). Simply put, the Spirit grants "wisdom and understanding" so that God's people may know his will (Col. 1:9). The Spirit enables believers to grasp what God has done, is doing, and will do in their lives. The knowledge of God and his will includes God's past and present work in their lives: "What we have received is not the spirit of the world, but the Spirit who is from God, so that we may understand what God has freely given us" (1 Cor. 2:12; cf. Eph. 3:4–5). Believers have "the mind of Christ" because of the Spirit's presence within them (1 Cor. 2:16). But God also reveals to his people what he has prepared for them long-term, and the Spirit is the one who reveals these things (2:9–10).

Third, the Spirit gives what is necessary for spiritual life and health. Paul praises God for blessing his people "with every spiritual blessing in Christ" (Eph. 1:3). Fee rightly argues that "spiritual" should be interpreted to mean "Spirit blessings" or "blessings that pertain to the Spirit," blessings spelled out in more detail in Ephesians 1:4–14.[47] The Holy Spirit makes these blessings real in the believer's experience. The Spirit's blessings are also highlighted throughout Paul's Letters as yet more evidence of his powerful presence at work in the church. The Spirit gives power (Rom. 15:13; Eph. 3:16), help in time of need (Phil. 1:18–19), the ability to wait in hope (Gal. 5:5; cf. Rom. 15:13), joy in adverse conditions (1 Thess. 1:6), joyful gratitude in worship (Eph. 5:18–20; Col. 3:16), and unity in the common mission (Phil. 1:27; 2:1–2),

47. Fee, *God's Empowering Presence*, 666–67.

to name just a few. Through it all, the indwelling Spirit himself helps believers in their weakness by interceding for them according to the will of God (Rom. 8:26–27). Here we see God's relational presence at its deepest: the Holy Spirit within knows the saints perfectly and prays God's will for them with "wordless groans" (v. 26). Douglas Moo surely is correct when he says that these groans likely refer to the Spirit's rather than the believer's groans: "the Spirit's own 'language of prayer,' a ministry of intercession that takes place in our hearts (cf. v. 27) in a manner imperceptible to us."[48] The Holy Spirit meets God's people in the midst of their weakness and expresses their deepest heart struggles to God. Paul summarizes how the Spirit's presence ministers life to the believer when he says, "The kingdom of God is not a matter of eating and drinking, but of righteousness, peace and joy in the Holy Spirit" (Rom. 14:17).

Fourth, the Spirit provides empowerment for living the Christian life. As Paul tells the Corinthians, "The kingdom of God is not a matter of talk but of power," and the Spirit is the source of such power (1 Cor. 4:20; cf. 1 Thess. 1:5). Paul gets right to the point with Timothy when he reminds him to "fan into flame the gift of God, which is in you through the laying on of my hands," likely a reference to the "Spirit God gave us," who does not foster timidity but "gives us power, love and self-discipline" (2 Tim. 1:6–7). The Holy Spirit present within Timothy will give him the strength and power needed to carry out the task. In fact, there are times when the term "power" ($\delta\acute{\upsilon}\nu\alpha\mu\iota\varsigma$, *dynamis*) is virtually synonymous with "Spirit": God "is able to do immeasurably more than all we ask or imagine, according to his power that is at work within us" (Eph. 3:20; cf. 1:19–20; 3:16).

More generally, the Holy Spirit is the sanctifying Spirit. People are "saved through the sanctifying work of the Spirit and through belief in the truth" (2 Thess. 2:13). As the gospel goes out, people who respond in faith become an offering acceptable to God, "sanctified by the Holy Spirit" (Rom. 15:16). Paul's description to the Corinthians masterfully captures the Spirit's role in the sanctifying process: "We all, who with unveiled faces contemplate the Lord's glory, are being transformed into his image with an ever-increasing glory, which comes from the Lord, who is the Spirit" (2 Cor. 3:18). When people come to the Lord, the veil that covers their hearts is removed, Paul says, and they enter a relationship with the Lord, who is (or is experienced as) the Spirit (2 Cor. 3:15–17). This is reminiscent of Moses's glimpse of God's glory upon entering his presence (Exod. 34:34–35), only radically different since Christians now behold God's glory with faces

---

48. Moo, *The Epistle to the Romans*, 525–26.

forever uncovered.[49] The Lord's Spirit brings freedom and a new experience of God's glorious presence (2 Cor. 3:17–18). As believers contemplate the Lord's glory, they are being transformed into Christ's image more and more, that is, with "ever-increasing glory." This all "comes from the Lord, who is the Spirit." The Holy Spirit transforms believers in such a way that they experience God's glorious presence more fully in this life in anticipation of an experience of final glory.

The Spirit also sanctifies believers in their battle with the flesh. The righteous requirement of the law is fully met by those who live not according to the flesh but according to the Spirit (Rom. 8:4). As believers live "by the Spirit" they will "put to death the misdeeds of the body" and experience life (Rom. 8:13). Those who get their life from the Spirit and walk by the Spirit will never gratify the flesh but will keep in step with the Spirit and, as a result, bear the fruit of the Spirit and reap eternal life (Gal. 5:16–6:10).

Fifth, the Spirit provides empowerment for ministry to others. Since God's nature is that of a self-giving God, we are not surprised to hear that believers experience the Spirit's presence in part as empowerment for service. The Spirit gifts God's people individually for the building up of the body of Christ (1 Cor. 1:7; 7:7): "To each one the manifestation of the Spirit [e.g., wisdom, knowledge, faith, healing, miraculous powers, prophecy] is given for the common good" (1 Cor. 12:7). The Spirit forms God's people into one body and distributes to each person empowering abilities to edify the other members (1 Cor. 12:11–13). In Ephesians 4:3–13 Paul attributes this gifting of God's people to Christ with the same end goal in mind: "to equip his people for works of service, so that the body of Christ may be built up" (v. 12).

Serving in the new way of the Spirit (Rom. 7:6; Phil. 3:3) means boasting only in what Christ has accomplished through a person while relying on the power of the Spirit for ministry (Rom. 15:18). This entails serving others with integrity (2 Cor. 12:18; 1 Thess. 1:5) and a genuine concern to do what is best for them (Gal. 6:1–2). Paul highlights the priority of living and proclaiming the gospel in the power of the Spirit (versus worldly rhetoric alone in 1 Cor. 2:4–5), since the true gospel of Jesus Christ is firmly associated with the Holy Spirit (2 Cor. 11:3–4; Eph. 1:13; Phil. 1:27; 1 Thess. 1:5).

The theme of God's relational presence through the Spirit in Paul's writings also includes an eschatological element: the Spirit as guarantee of eternal life in God's presence. Paul uses three key terms to convey the Spirit's role in linking the now with the not yet. To begin with, Paul tells the Roman Christians, "We

---

49. Harris, *The Second Epistle to the Corinthians*, 313. He concludes that the "Lord" probably refers to God, who is now experienced as the Spirit (p. 318).

ourselves, who have the firstfruits of the Spirit, groan inwardly as we wait eagerly for our adoption to sonship, the redemption of our bodies" (Rom. 8:23).[50] Here, "firstfruits" identifies a ministry of the Spirit, as "both the *beginning* of a process and the unbreakable *connection* between its beginning and the end."[51] And this connection is supremely personal and present for believers. In the expression "firstfruits of the Spirit," τοῦ πνεύματος (*tou pneumatos*) is likely an epexegetic or appositional genitive pointing to the Spirit himself, God's personal presence within believers, as the guarantor of eternal life in God's presence (cf. Gal. 6:8).

The other two terms that Paul uses to describe the Spirit's eschatological presence among his people work together in both Corinthians and Ephesians: the verb "seal" (σφραγίζω, *sphragizō*) and the noun "deposit" (ἀρραβών, *arrabōn*). These two commercial terms reassure God's people that the Spirit is God's promise now of eternal life in his presence in the age to come. Presence now guarantees presence then. Paul reminds the Corinthians that God has anointed his people and "set his seal of ownership" on them (2 Cor. 1:22). When they believed in Christ, he tells the Ephesians, they were "marked in him with a seal, the promised Holy Spirit" (Eph. 1:13). They have been "sealed for the day of redemption," and this "seal" is the Spirit himself (Eph. 4:30). Clinton Arnold notes the significance of this concept: "In the new covenant era, the one true God has marked all of his people as belonging to himself by means of a seal. This seal is the eschatological fulfillment of the promised gift of the Holy Spirit. The presence of the Holy Spirit in the life of a believer is a firm indication that the person is possessed by God."[52]

The complementary term "deposit" explicitly shows that the seal of the Spirit has positive eschatological consequences. Paul tells the Corinthians that God "put his Spirit in our hearts as a deposit, guaranteeing what is to come" (2 Cor. 1:22), and again, that God "has given us the Spirit as a deposit, guaranteeing what is to come" (2 Cor. 5:5). To the Ephesians Paul says that the seal is "the promised Holy Spirit, who is a deposit guaranteeing our inheritance until the redemption of those who are God's possession—to the praise of his glory" (Eph. 1:13–14). The term "deposit" occurs frequently in ancient papyri to express the sense of "down payment" or "earnest money" in a business context.[53] The Spirit is God's pledge or promise that believers

---

50. Compare in 1 Cor. 15:20, 23 the risen Christ as the "firstfruits" of believers who have died and will be resurrected at his return. The "Spirit" and "firstfruits" also occur together in 2 Thess. 2:13 in connection with the Spirit's work of sanctification.

51. Moo, *The Epistle to the Romans*, 519–20.

52. C. Arnold, *Ephesians*, 93.

53. C. Arnold, *Ephesians*, 93.

will experience a final redemption in the future, and, even more, that this final experience of God's presence has already begun in the present through the indwelling of the Holy Spirit.

God's Presence among His People, the Church

Faith in Jesus the Messiah places a person in the community of the Messiah, the church. These people *belong* to Jesus (Rom. 1:6; 7:4; 8:9; 14:8; 1 Cor. 15:23; Gal. 3:29; 5:24). They are Christ's people, called and set apart as a holy people to the Lord (e.g., Rom. 1:7: "To all in Rome who are loved by God and called to be his holy people"; cf. 1 Cor. 1:2; Col. 3:12; Titus 2:14). They experience God's relational presence as members of this community. While Pauline ecclesiology has not always received the attention it deserves, Paul's doctrine of the church reveals how central God's relational presence is to the center of his thought. "When we read Paul in his own terms," N. T. Wright contends, "we find that for him the one, single community is absolutely central. The community of Christ, in Christ, by the Spirit, is at the very heart of it all."[54] We see God's presence in the way Paul describes the nature of the church, both through the term ἐκκλησία (*ekklēsia*, church, assembly) and through key images, in the way Jesus is present with his people in worship, and in matters related to the unity of the church.

Paul's use of the term for "church" (ἐκκλησία) falls into three categories: (1) individual congregations or assemblies in specific geographical locations (e.g., Gal. 1:2: "the churches in Galatia"; Col. 4:15: "Nympha and the church in her house"), (2) the one, universal church consisting of all Christians on earth or in heaven (e.g., 1 Cor. 10:32; 11:22: "the church of God"), and (3) the local representatives of God's universal church (e.g., Rom. 16:4: "all the churches of the Gentiles"; 1 Thess. 2:14: "God's churches in Judea").[55] These three categories are attempts to specify the nuances of the relationship between God's people and their place, but as George Ladd puts it, "The local church is not part of the church but is *the church* in its local expression."[56] These people are bound to Christ, and hence they gather with one another. They meet because they have been "called into fellowship with his Son, Jesus Christ our Lord" (1 Cor. 1:9). They have a "common sharing in the Spirit" (Phil. 2:1) and are part of the "fellowship of [created by] the Spirit" (2 Cor. 13:14). Apart from God's relational presence, attempts to define "church" biblically become meaningless. Presence produces church, and we see this

---

54. N. T. Wright, *Pauline Perspectives*, 410.
55. Harris, *Second Epistle to the Corinthians*, 132–33; BDAG 303–4.
56. Ladd, *A Theology of the New Testament*, 582.

even in its basic definition: the people in whom God is present, and therefore a people with shared beliefs and practices who gather in community.

Paul also uses key images of the church to highlight the relational presence of God. We've already discussed the images of family, temple, and body under the section above on the Holy Spirit. Here we note how these three central images stress God's presence specifically in relation to God and Christ. The family imagery even begins with how Paul identifies believers as "brothers and sisters" (e.g., Rom. 8:29; 14:10–21; 1 Cor. 5:11; Eph. 6:23; 1 Tim. 6:2—i.e., places where ἀδελφός [adelphos] in context refers to both men and women). Believers are family members by virtue of their relationship with God through Christ.

The family metaphor takes a complementary turn when Paul speaks of Christ as the husband of the church. Against the background of God as the husband of Israel (e.g., Isa. 54:5; Jer. 3:14; 31:32; Ezek. 16:8), Jesus is portrayed as the husband or bridegroom of the church (e.g., Matt. 9:14–15; Rev. 21:2). Paul tells the Romans that they have died to the law through the physical body of Christ crucified that they "might belong to [or "be joined to"] another, to him who was raised from the dead" (Rom. 7:4). In the marital context of Romans 7:2–3, we know that Paul is comparing the new relationship believers have with their Lord to a marriage, with Christ as the husband. In 2 Corinthians Paul writes, "I am jealous for you with a godly jealousy. I promised you to one husband, to Christ, so that I might present you as a pure virgin to him" (11:2). And Christ as husband to his church comes to the forefront in Ephesians 5:25–32, where we hear that "Christ loved the church and gave himself up for her to make her holy, cleansing her by the washing with water through the word, and to present her to himself as a radiant church, without stain or wrinkle or any other blemish, but holy and blameless" (vv. 25–27). He feeds and cares for his body, the church (v. 29). This "profound mystery" regarding "Christ and the church" is likely God's hidden plan now revealed in Christ (cf. Eph. 1:9; 3:3, 4, 9; 6:19), but with a sharpened focus on the ultimate goal of the plan: the relationship of love between the Triune God and his people and his plan that they live in his presence forever. The husband-wife relationship provides the most intense illustration of this grander purpose. The ultimate purpose of the gospel is that God's people experience and enjoy his relational presence beginning now and extending throughout eternity.

Paul's second key image, the temple, takes us back to the whole point of the tabernacle and later the temple in the first place: God dwelling among his people (e.g., Exod. 25:8; 33:9–10). Yet, even when Solomon dedicates the temple, he acknowledges that no earthly building can contain God's glorious presence: "But will God really dwell on earth? The heavens, even the highest heaven, cannot contain you. How much less this temple I have built!" (1 Kings 8:27–30). The tension between God's universal presence and his presence among his people is eased a bit when we speak of the church as "the temple of the living God" (2 Cor. 6:16). Heaven and earth have drawn closer together in anticipation of God's people living in God's presence in the new creation. Paul's "new-Temple ecclesiology," as N. T. Wright puts it, begins now with the church.[57]

God's building is rising up to "become a holy temple in the Lord. . . . being built together to become a dwelling in which God lives by his Spirit" (Eph. 2:21–22; cf. 1 Cor. 3:9). As Mark Bonnington observes, Paul's ethical/pastoral concern to spur on his readers to holy living explains why he uses the temple imagery, but holy living makes sense only if the grounding image itself is rooted in the reality of God's holy (and relational) presence.[58] Paul's theology of a holy God in the midst of his people (i.e., presence) reflected in his temple theology is the ultimate driving force of his ethics.

Paul's use of the image of the body of Christ may stem from his own experience on the Damascus road, where Christ is explicitly identified with his persecuted people: "Saul, Saul, why do you persecute me?" (Acts 9:4). This experience certainly would have made a deep impression on Paul. Throughout his writings Paul identifies the church as Christ's body: "So in Christ we, though many, form one body, and each member belongs to all the others" (Rom. 12:5). This is much more than saying that the church is a group or body of believers. They are united to Christ in such a way as to be described as "the body of Christ," where each person is a part of it (1 Cor. 12:27). Christ is distinct from his body, yet the church is intimately connected to Christ. Believers are "members of his body" (Eph. 5:30) or "parts of his body" (1 Cor. 12:12, 20). As the "head" of the body (Eph. 1:22; 4:15; Col. 1:18) or even the "Savior" of the body (Eph. 5:23), Christ enables the unity and nourishment and growth of the body (Eph. 4:15; 5:29–30; cf. Col. 2:19). The entire image is infused with the encounter of God's relational presence in Christ.

We also see God's presence among his people in the way Jesus is present with his church in worship. As Howard Marshall puts it, "If the congregation is the place of God's presence, then God is active in it," and here is where Paul "develops his idea of the spiritual gifts or charismata that are manifested in the congregation through the various activities of the Spirit in different

57. N. T. Wright, *Pauline Perspectives*, 412.
58. Bonnington, "New Temples in Corinth." Bonnington writes, "The Temple is about divine presence and ownership, divine holiness and the existence of centred-bounded sacred space, all of which demand of God's people individually and collectively holy purity" (p. 159).

individuals."[59] Paul makes this explicit in Ephesians 4:1–13, where we see that the risen Christ has gifted his body with gifted leaders "to equip his people for works of service, so that the body of Christ may be built up until we all reach unity in the faith and in the knowledge of the Son of God and become mature, attaining to the whole measure of the fullness of Christ" (vv. 12–13). The goal of spiritual gifts is Christlikeness—a mature demonstration of the presence and character of Christ in the life of the believer (cf. Eph. 3:19). When such gifts are properly exercised, it leads ultimately to the conversion of unbelievers as described in 1 Corinthians 14:24–25. The climax of their conversion is the confession "God is really among you!" (v. 25). This saying likely reflects Isaiah 45:14: "They will bow down before you and plead with you, saying, 'Surely God is with you, and there is no other; there is no other god'" (cf. Zech. 8:23). Paul seems to be suggesting that through the church (originally Israel in the Isaiah text) God will accomplish the conversion of outsiders.[60] Through their experience of God's presence among his people unbelievers will come to faith in Christ. Presence fuels evangelism.

Worship also includes prayer and praise as well as the celebration of the Lord's Supper, all of which are experiences of God's relational presence. Throughout Paul's Letters prayer, intercession, petition, thanksgiving, and praise make up a significant element in early Christian worship.[61] Through prayer and praise believers have access to God, relate to and respond to God, discern and submit to God's will, and experience his relational presence in a variety of ways. Since worship often occurred in a home setting in the early church, the sharing of a meal was transformed into sharing the bread and cup of the Lord's Supper, symbolizing Christ's sacrificial death and the establishment of the new covenant.[62] Whatever else the Lord's Supper is, it certainly is a participation (κοινωνία, koinōnia) in the body and blood of Christ (e.g., 1 Cor. 10:16–17; 11:20–34). In some way—the exact nature of this has been debated throughout Christian history—partaking of the bread and cup brings an experience of the Lord's presence in worship. To narrow this participation only to the benefits of Christ's death seems too restrictive. As Ben Witherington says, "There seems to be some sort of real spiritual communion with Christ."[63] In 1 Corinthians 10:18–22 Paul warns against joining in the idol feasts precisely because of the danger of a real spiritual communion with demons.

---

59. Marshall, *New Testament Theology*, 456.
60. Ciampa and Rosner, "1 Corinthians," 743.
61. For example, Rom. 1:8; 1 Cor. 1:4; 14:16; 2 Cor. 1:3; Eph. 1:3, 17; 3:14; 6:18. See Hurtado, *Lord Jesus Christ*.
62. Marshall, *New Testament Theology*, 457.
63. Witherington, *Conflict and Community in Corinth*, 225.

Finally, we see God's presence in the way Paul urges believers to maintain the unity of the church. This aspect of presence is closely related to God's presence in worship described above. The one body with many members is nevertheless one body in Christ (Rom. 12:4–5). The cup of thanksgiving is a participation in the blood of Christ, and the bread is a participation in the body of Christ with the many as one body all sharing the one loaf (1 Cor. 10:16–17). All who have been baptized by one Spirit form one body because all have been given the one Spirit to drink (1 Cor. 12:13). All who were baptized into Christ have been clothed with Christ, and all are one in Christ (Gal. 3:26–28). Through Christ those who were far away have been brought near and given access to the Father by one Spirit; they are fellow citizens with God's people and members of his household (Eph. 2:17–19). As N. T. Wright says, "Wherever you look in Paul, you see him arguing for, and passionately working for, the unity of the church."[64] Unity is always linked to a shared experience of God's relational presence at its core. For this reason, Jesus is also present among his people as the one who disciplines. We see this clearly when Paul says that he has already judged a rebellious man "in the name of our Lord Jesus," and when he charges the congregation to discipline the man when "the power of our Lord Jesus is present" (1 Cor. 5:3–5). Similarly, those who eat the bread and drink the cup of the Lord "in an unworthy manner" are "guilty of sinning against the body and blood of the Lord," and as a result, those "who eat and drink without discerning the body of Christ eat and drink judgment on themselves" (1 Cor. 11:27–32).

Much more could be said about how we experience God's relational presence as members of the community of Jesus the Messiah, but we have hit the high points. Paul's basic definition of church rests upon a shared experience of God's presence resulting in shared beliefs and practices. The apostle uses the central images of the church as a family, a temple, and a body to emphasize how God's presence proves foundational to the identity and purpose of the people of God. We also see God's presence among his people in their worship experience as God works among them and through them in the world.

God's Sustaining Presence

God's sustaining presence shows up in Paul's writings in three interrelated ways: (1) God's presence brings initial life to the believer; (2) God's presence offers ongoing grace, mercy, and peace; and (3) God's presence strengthens and empowers believers in life and ministry. God sustains first through bringing

---

64. N. T. Wright, *Pauline Perspectives*, 410.

people into his life through fellowship with Jesus Christ. God has been faithful to call believers into "fellowship with his Son, Jesus Christ our Lord" (1 Cor. 1:9). This relational language led David Garland to translate κοινωνία (*koinōnia*) as "common-union," since Paul is speaking of their "sharing in Christ (objective genitive)."[65] So, initially at conversion, believers experience God's sustaining presence through his gift of spiritual life. Paul makes this explicit in 1 Corinthians 8:5–6: "For even if there are so-called gods, whether in heaven or on earth (as indeed there are many 'gods' and many 'lords'), yet for us there is but one God, the Father, from whom all things came and for whom we live; and there is but one Lord, Jesus Christ, through whom all things came and through whom we live."

Those who experience God's life are bound to him by his love demonstrated through Jesus Christ. Nothing in all creation will be able to separate God's people from his love that is in Christ Jesus (Rom. 8:35–39). James Dunn notes that Paul's final words in this dramatically powerful section of Romans 8 "sum up in most emphatic tone Paul's confidence in the *faithfulness* of God to those whom his love has thus embraced and sustains."[66] Those who respond to God's love with a reciprocal love are "known by God" (1 Cor. 8:3), and being "known by God" provides yet another building block in the foundation of God's sustaining presence (Gal. 4:9; 2 Tim. 2:19).[67]

God's sustaining presence offers ongoing grace, mercy, and peace to the believer. Paul repeatedly reminds his Christian readers that they receive God's life not just at conversion but throughout their spiritual journey, as they experience his ongoing grace, mercy, and peace. We see this chiefly through the unique way Paul opens and closes his letters. These theologically loaded phrases go beyond mere standard letter convention to reflect the heart of God's relationship with his people. Paul's modified Greek greeting of χάρις (*charis*, grace) and the common Jewish greeting of *shalom* (presented as εἰρήνη, *eirēnē*, peace) appear in all of his letters (Rom. 1:7; 1 Cor. 1:3; 2 Cor. 1:2; Gal. 1:3; Eph. 1:2; Phil. 1:2; Col. 1:2; 1 Thess. 1:1; 2 Thess. 1:2; 1 Tim. 1:2; 2 Tim. 1:2; Titus 1:4; Philem. 3). In 1–2 Timothy he adds "mercy" (ἔλεος, *eleos*) to the greeting.

Likewise, Paul closes his letters with a prayer that God or one of God's enabling gifts such as grace or peace would be with his readers. "The God of

65. Garland, *1 Corinthians*, 35. Similarly, Fee, *The First Epistle to the Corinthians*, 45.
66. Dunn, *Romans 1–8*, 508.
67. The underlying reality of "knowing" in a biblical sense implies a level of intimacy that our common English usage fails to capture. As Thiselton notes, "An authentic Christian process of **knowing** . . . is inextricably bound up with **loving**" (Thiselton, *First Epistle to the Corinthians*, 626). Knowing and being known by God imply much more than acquaintance or factual knowledge. God's people belong to him in the deepest relational way possible.

peace be with you all," he tells the Christians in Rome (Rom. 15:33). A chapter later Paul promises that "the God of peace will soon crush Satan under your feet" before concluding with the prayer "The grace of our Lord Jesus be with you" (Rom. 16:20). He elsewhere uses a similar prayer that the grace of the Lord Jesus would be with his readers (1 Cor. 16:23; 2 Cor. 13:14; Gal. 6:18; Eph. 6:24; Col. 4:18; 1 Thess. 5:28; 2 Thess. 3:18; 1 Tim. 6:21; 2 Tim. 4:22; Titus 3:15; Philem. 25). He briefly expands the "grace be with you" prayer on a few occasions: "May the grace of the Lord Jesus Christ, and the love of God, and the fellowship of the Holy Spirit be with you all" (2 Cor. 13:14); and "Grace to all who love our Lord Jesus Christ with an undying love" (Eph. 6:24). He also regularly prays that the grace of the Lord or the Lord Jesus Christ would "be with your spirit" (Gal. 6:18; Phil. 4:23; 2 Tim. 4:22; Philem. 25), likely a way of personalizing the same prayer. Ronald Fung notes that Paul's desire for his readers is that they may experience "the gracious indwelling presence of the Lord Jesus Christ."[68] To pray that God's grace, love, and peace be with you is to say, "God be with you"; God gives his sustaining and empowering self to believers.[69] Again, often Paul will simply pray that God will be with his readers: "And the God of love and peace will be with you" (2 Cor. 13:11); "And the God of peace will be with you" (Phil. 4:9); "May God himself, the God of peace, sanctify you through and through" (1 Thess. 5:23); "Now may the Lord of peace himself give you peace at all times and in every way. The Lord be with all of you" (2 Thess. 3:16). The theologically careful way Paul concludes his letters reflects a bold confidence in God's sustaining presence with these congregations. It's as if Paul's entrusting them to God's sustaining care is a vital part of his apostolic ministry.

Because of Paul's "thorn in the flesh" (2 Cor. 12:7), God's gift of his sustaining grace remained immanently personal to him: "Three times I pleaded with the Lord to take it away from me. But he said to me, 'My grace is sufficient for you, for my power is made perfect in weakness'" (2 Cor. 12:8–9). God's gracious presence supports Christians especially in times of trial and suffering (e.g., 2 Cor. 8:1–5). These experiences serve as testimonial results of "standing" in God's sustaining grace (Rom. 5:2). Closely related to living in God's grace is the final category of how God sustains believers with his presence—how God's presence strengthens and empowers believers in life and ministry.

According to Paul, God's ever-present help for his people appears in the way he strengthens and empowers his people, provides for them, comforts

---

68. Fung, *The Epistle to the Galatians*, 315.
69. Fung, *The Epistle to the Galatians*, 315.

and encourages them, and protects them. These interrelated aspects of God's sustaining presence must also be seen alongside Paul's robust emphasis on the present help of the Spirit noted above. First, God strengthens and empowers his people. Paul closes Romans with a doxology that characterizes God as "him who is able to strengthen [στηρίζω, *stērizō*] you according to my gospel and the proclamation of Jesus Christ" (16:25 NRSV). We see similar prayers that God would provide strength on several occasions in the Thessalonian correspondence: "May he strengthen your hearts" (1 Thess. 3:13); "May our Lord Jesus Christ himself and God our Father . . . encourage your hearts and strengthen you in every good deed and word" (2 Thess. 2:16–17); "But the Lord is faithful, and he will strengthen you and protect you from the evil one" (2 Thess. 3:3). Commands to be strong in the Lord or thanksgiving for the strength God or the Lord Jesus provide also frequently appear in Paul's Letters: "Be strong in the Lord and in his mighty power" (Eph. 6:10); "I can do all things through him who gives me strength" (Phil. 4:13); "I thank Christ Jesus our Lord, who has given me strength" (1 Tim. 1:12); "But the Lord stood at my side and gave me strength" (2 Tim. 4:17).

Paul's testimony about God's sustaining strength in his own life is something he prays his readers will also experience, especially when it comes to spiritual warfare. The apostle can alert the Corinthians that he fights spiritual battles not with the weapons of this world but with weapons having "divine power to demolish strongholds" (2 Cor. 10:4). And he also reminds the Ephesians that they have the "full armor of God" available for standing against the devil's schemes (6:10–11, 13). God's sustaining strength is not just an apostolic privilege; rather, it is available now to all believers in a multitude of ways: truth; righteousness; the gospel of peace; faith; the certainty of salvation and the Spirit's sword, which is God's word; and prayer (6:14–18). More generally, Paul insists that God is always powerfully at work among his people: "In all things God works [συνεργέω, *synergeō*] for the good of those who love him" (Rom. 8:28); "his incomparably great power for us who believe" (Eph. 1:19; cf. Col. 1:29).

We also see God's sustaining presence in the way he provides for his children. The one who "did not spare his own Son, but gave him up for us all" will also "graciously give us all things" (Rom. 8:32). Douglas Moo notes that the "all things" here should not be restricted to salvation but includes "all those blessings—spiritual and material—that we require on the path toward that final salvation."[70] Paul reminds the Corinthians, "God is able to bless you abundantly, so that in all things at all times, having all that you need,

70. Moo, *The Epistle to the Romans*, 541.

you will abound in every good work" (2 Cor. 9:8), and he emphasizes that God will supply their seed and enlarge their harvest so that they are enriched and enabled to give generously to others (9:9–11). He plainly tells the Philippians, "God will meet all your needs according to the riches of his glory in Christ Jesus" (Phil. 4:19). Gordon Fee summarizes, "Thus, the final word in the body of the letter proper is this one, 'every need of yours in keeping with the wealth that is his in glory made available to you in Christ Jesus.' This says it all; nothing more can be added."[71] We see here a clear connection between God's glorious presence ("according to the riches of his glory") and how God's sustaining presence meets our every need in Christ Jesus. Paul's confidence in God as provider also comes through in his instructions to his coworkers: "Command those who are rich in this present world not to be arrogant nor to put their hope in wealth, which is so uncertain, but to put their hope in God, who richly provides us with everything for our enjoyment" (1 Tim. 6:17). God's sustaining provision permeates the life and ministry of the apostle Paul.

God's sustaining presence means also that God comforts and encourages his people. This comes through most noticeably in 2 Corinthians, where "comfort" is a major emphasis.[72] God is the "Father of compassion and the God of all comfort, who comforts us in all our troubles" (2 Cor. 1:3–4). This comfort that originates with the Father "abounds through Christ" (2 Cor. 1:5). Later, in chapter 7, Paul describes God as the God "who comforts the downcast" (v. 6). In this case, Paul experienced God's comfort through the return of Titus and through the comfort that the Corinthians had bestowed upon this coworker. Paul begins his magnificent Christ hymn in Philippians 2 with the foundational protasis: "Therefore if you have any encouragement from being united with Christ, if any comfort from his love, if any common sharing in the Spirit, if any tenderness and compassion" (v. 1). Union with Christ brings encouragement and comfort from his sustaining love. As is often the case for Paul, comfort stands in contrast to the sufferings and trials of this world (cf. Phil. 1:29–30). Paul also prays that his readers will experience God's encouragement and comfort: "May the God who gives endurance and encouragement give you the same attitude of mind toward each other that Christ Jesus had" (Rom. 15:5); "May our Lord Jesus Christ himself and God our Father, who loved us and by his grace gave us eternal encouragement and good hope, encourage your hearts and strengthen you in every good

71. Fee, *Paul's Letter to the Philippians*, 454–55.
72. In 2 Corinthians the noun παράκλησις (*paraklēsis*) and the verb παρακαλέω (*parakaleō*) together are used multiple times to refer to God's or Christ's "comfort" given to believers.

deed and word" (2 Thess. 2:16–17). These are merely a few examples of how Paul highlights believers' experience of God's encouragement and comfort through Jesus Christ.

God's sustaining presence also includes his protection and deliverance of his people. This can refer to God's initial rescue of people when they become disciples of Jesus, as in Colossians 1:13: "For he has rescued us from the dominion of darkness and brought us into the kingdom of the Son he loves." It can also refer to God's sustaining protection in the pursuit of the mission of the gospel. In this sense, sometimes Paul speaks about physical rescue, as in the opening of 2 Corinthians: "He has delivered us from such a deadly peril, and he will deliver us again. On him we have set our hope that he will continue to deliver us, as you help us by your prayers" (1:10–11). Or when he says to Timothy, "You, however, know all about my teaching, my way of life, my purpose, faith, patience, love, endurance, persecutions, sufferings—what kinds of things happened to me in Antioch, Iconium and Lystra, the persecutions I endured. Yet the Lord rescued me from all of them" (2 Tim. 3:10–11). And, at other times, Paul speaks about a deliverance that is spiritual in nature. In the closing of 2 Timothy Paul alludes to both physical and spiritual rescue: "But the Lord stood at my side and gave me strength, so that through me the message might be fully proclaimed and all the Gentiles might hear it. And I was delivered from the lion's mouth. The Lord will rescue me from every evil attack and will bring me safely to his heavenly kingdom. To him be glory for ever and ever. Amen" (4:17–18). As in these verses, the reference to future spiritual deliverance often points to God's eschatological presence. Also, in the opening of 1 Thessalonians, as Paul is encouraging his readers about the public impact of their faith in Christ, he mentions "Jesus, who rescues us from the coming wrath" (1:10). Before we explore the eschatological presence of God in more detail, we note one additional way that God protects his people: both the Spirit and Jesus intercede for them from heaven: "And he who searches our hearts knows the mind of the Spirit, because the Spirit intercedes for God's people in accordance with the will of God. . . . Christ Jesus who died—more than that, who was raised to life—is at the right hand of God and is also interceding for us" (Rom. 8:27, 34).[73]

God's Eschatological Presence

For the apostle Paul, the conclusion to God's great story runs like a powerful river through his teachings. Paul is thoroughly eschatological in his thinking,

---

73. Jesus's intercessory role is further developed in Hebrews with its portrait of him as high priest (e.g., 7:25; 9:24).

because he believes what God has done in Christ will also have significant future repercussions. The ultimate result of God's incarnational presence in Jesus is that God's people can expect a glorious future with God in a new creation. Jesus's life, death, and resurrection inaugurated this beautiful ending to the story that is anything but an ending. In Paul's Letters God's eschatological presence includes emphasis on the final redemption or salvation, Christ's return and the bodily resurrection of believers, the last judgment (loss of presence or eternal life in God's presence), and believers' future and final experience of God's glorious presence.

In his two great summary letters, Romans and Ephesians, Paul stresses the finality of redemption and salvation in a way that highlights God's relational presence. In Romans 8 he speaks of how believers "wait eagerly for our adoption to sonship, the redemption of our bodies" and how this "hope" carries the confident expectation of receiving something we do not yet have (vv. 23–24; cf. Col. 1:5). This expectation is of a transformed, resurrection body fit for eternal life in God's presence. In Ephesians 1 Paul mentions the Spirit as the relational connection between this age and the age to come: "the promised Holy Spirit, who is a deposit guaranteeing our inheritance until the redemption of those who are God's possession—to the praise of his glory" (vv. 13–14). Later in Ephesians he writes about "the Holy Spirit of God, with whom you were sealed for the day of redemption" (4:30). Believers are "God's possession" in the sense that they have been "adopted as sons [and daughters] through Jesus Christ *for himself*" (1:5 CSB; cf. Exod. 19:5; Deut. 14:2; Mal. 3:17; 1 Pet. 2:9). They are in relationship with God through Jesus Christ made effective by the Spirit. One day they will be completely and perfectly redeemed, meaning that God will take permanent possession of those who already belong to him. They will live in his glorious presence forever.

Paul can also refer to salvation in the future tense theologically. In Romans 13 he notes the arrival of the hour for believers to awake from their slumber "because our salvation is nearer now than when we first believed. The night is nearly over; the day is almost here" (vv. 11–12). In this context he uses the eschatological certainty of future salvation to call his readers to holy living in the present. It's hard not to see in the expression "the day" an allusion to the "day of the Lord" in OT theology—a time of future judgment and salvation. Paul often alludes to this important event (e.g., Rom. 13:12–13; 1 Cor. 1:8; 5:5; 2 Cor. 1:14; Phil. 1:6, 10; 2:16; 1 Thess. 5:2, 4; 2 Thess. 1:10; 2:2; 2 Tim. 1:12, 18; 4:8). This is the day when believers "will be saved" (Phil. 1:28), when they will "obtain the salvation that is in Christ Jesus, with eternal glory" (2 Tim. 2:10).

Final salvation comes with "eternal glory," meaning that God's glory, majesty, and splendor—his glorious presence—will be experienced in the eternal state. As we have mentioned before, "glory" is often a synonym for God's presence. In Romans 5:2 Paul speaks of boasting "in the hope of the glory of God," likely a reference to Christ making it possible for Christians to "share in the glorious life of God himself (cf. 1 Pet. 5:10)."[74] As believers contemplate the Lord's glory in this life, they are in the process of "being transformed into his image with ever-increasing glory, which comes from the Lord, who is the Spirit" (2 Cor. 3:18). Gordon Fee notes the significance of this process: "In the freedom that the Spirit provides, we have seen the glory of God himself—as it is made evident to us in the face of our Lord Jesus Christ—and we have come to experience that glory, and will do so in an ever-increasing way until we come to the final glory."[75] Believers one day will appear with Christ, who is their life, in glory (Col. 3:4). They will share in the glory of the Lord Jesus Christ (2 Thess. 2:14). They will share in the Lord's presence.

Christ's return and the bodily resurrection of believers form a central part of God's eschatological presence in Paul's writings. Believers are waiting for "the blessed hope—the appearing of the glory of our great God and Savior, Jesus Christ" (Titus 2:13). Simply put, they are waiting for the glorious return of Christ to earth (1 Cor. 1:7; Phil. 3:20; 1 Thess. 1:10; 2:19; 3:13; 4:16). At his coming, believers will receive final salvation rather than receiving God's coming wrath (1 Thess. 1:10; 5:9). The purpose of Christ's return is to gather his people to himself and live with them forever: "For the Lord himself will come down from heaven, with a loud command, with the voice of the archangel and with the trumpet call of God, and the dead in Christ will rise first. After that, we who are still alive and are left will be caught up together with them in the clouds to meet the Lord in the air. And so we will be with the Lord forever" (1 Thess. 4:16–17; cf. 2 Thess. 2:1). The image of being caught up in the "clouds" brings to mind the image of clouds as a "regular feature of biblical theophanies," says F. F. Bruce.[76] In the OT God's divine glory often resides in and shines forth from clouds (e.g., Exod. 19:16; 40:34; 1 Kings 8:10–11; Dan. 7:13), and we see the clouds of God's presence appear also at Jesus's transfiguration and ascension (Mark 9:7; Acts 1:9). Whereas unbelievers will be "shut out from the presence of the Lord and from the glory of his might" (2 Thess. 1:9), believers will be

---

74. Fitzmyer, *Romans*, 396.
75. Fee, *God's Empowering Spirit*, 319.
76. Bruce, *1 and 2 Thessalonians*, 102.

found "blameless and holy in the presence of our God and Father" (1 Thess. 3:13) at Jesus's coming (cf. 1 Thess. 5:23; 1 Cor. 1:7–8; Phil. 1:10; 1 Tim. 6:14). So, whether alive or asleep in the Lord, believers will always live together with their Lord (1 Thess. 5:10). Return ultimately brings eternal reunion for the faithful.

Between return and eternal reunion stands the bodily resurrection of believers. As believers have shared in Christ's death, they will also share in his resurrection (Rom. 6:5). In Philippians Paul anticipated attaining to the resurrection from the dead (3:10–11), a time when our lowly bodies would be transformed into a glorious body like that of our resurrected Lord (3:20–21). Paul develops his case for the nature of the resurrection body more fully in 1 Corinthians 15. In Christ "all will be made alive," he says (v. 22), and this will happen in an instant: "We will not all sleep, but we will all be changed—in a flash, in the twinkling of an eye, at the last trumpet. For the trumpet will sound, the dead will be raised imperishable, and we will be changed" (vv. 51–52). Paul's firm conviction is that "the one who raised the Lord Jesus from the dead will also raise us with Jesus and present us with you to himself" (2 Cor. 4:14). This hope to be "present in the presence" of the Lord at his coming *with* the people he ministered to constitutes a major motivation for Paul (1 Thess. 2:19).[77] Back to reunion with the Lord: resurrection will mean an eternal experience of God's presence.

· Sadly, there is a negative side to Jesus's return, and Paul does not shy away from proclaiming the reality of the coming judgment and the loss of God's presence for unbelievers. Paul speaks of a coming "day of God's wrath, when his righteous judgment will be revealed" (Rom. 2:5). To those who persist in doing good, God will give eternal life, but upon the self-seeking who reject truth and follow evil, God will bring his wrath and anger (Rom. 2:7–8). This will take place "on the day when God judges people's secrets through Jesus Christ" (Rom. 2:16). All will stand before God's judgment seat, and every knee will bow and every tongue acknowledge God (Rom. 14:10–12). When Jesus returns, he will "bring to light what is hidden in darkness and will expose the motives of the heart" (1 Cor. 4:5). The disobedient will have no inheritance in the kingdom of Christ and of God and will suffer the wrath of God (Eph. 5:5–6). In 2 Thessalonians Paul describes God's coming judgment specifically in terms of the loss of presence: "This will happen when the Lord Jesus is revealed from heaven in blazing fire with his powerful angels. He will

---

77. The expression "present in the presence" is taken from Fee, *The First and Second Letters to the Thessalonians*, 108. Bruce notes that the term παρουσία (*parousia*) used to describe the return of Christ occurs six times in the Thessalonian letters (1 Thess. 2:19; 3:13; 4:15; 5:23; 2 Thess. 2:1, 8) and only in 1 Cor. 15:23 elsewhere in Paul's Letters (Bruce, *1 and 2 Thessalonians*, 57).

punish those who do not know God and do not obey the gospel of our Lord Jesus. They will be punished with everlasting destruction *and shut out from the presence of the Lord and from the glory of his might* on the day he comes to be glorified in his holy people and to be marveled at among all those who have believed" (1:7–10). Paul is alluding here to Isaiah 2:10, 19, 21, where on the day of the Lord the wicked are commanded to hide in caves "from the fearful presence of the Lord and the splendor of his majesty."[78] Jeffrey Weima concludes, "Therefore, the persecutors of the Christians in Thessalonica . . . will be forever separated from this glorious and powerful presence of Christ— a sharp contrast to the fate of the Thessalonian believers, who will 'always be with the Lord' (1 Thess. 4:17; cf. 5:10)."[79]

While unbelievers will experience the Lord's condemnation, God's people will be rescued from this coming wrath (1 Thess. 1:10). God will bring praise and reward to his people. When the Lord comes, "each will receive their praise from God" (1 Cor. 4:5). This reward will be an "inheritance" (Col. 3:24). Using OT inheritance language, Paul taps into this notion that God's people will inherit the land promised by God. But in the NT the "inheritance" is often associated with the kingdom of God (e.g., Matt. 25:34; 1 Cor. 6:9–10; 15:50; Gal. 5:21), and even the King himself. The OT background supports this reading. We are told in Deuteronomy 10:9 that the "Levites have no share or inheritance among their fellow Israelites; the LORD is their inheritance." God's people inheriting God's very presence as their portion is not uncommon in the OT (e.g., Num. 18:20; Ps. 16:5; Jer. 10:16; 51:19). This "heritage prize" that Paul refers to is relational to the core. He tells the Philippians that he presses on "toward the goal to win the prize for which God called me heavenward in Christ Jesus," which he earlier defines as taking hold "of that for which Christ took hold of me" (Phil. 3:12–14). Christ took hold of Paul, and now Paul will take hold of Christ, his portion and inheritance. In Ephesians 1:18 Paul looks at the same reality from a slightly different angle when he talks about knowing "the hope to which he has called you, the riches of his glorious inheritance in his holy people" (cf. Col. 1:12). Jesus will rescue him from every evil work, he tells Timothy, and bring him safely into his heavenly kingdom (2 Tim. 4:18). Paul also uses the more familiar Johannine

---

78. Weima, "1–2 Thessalonians," 885.

79. Weima, "1–2 Thessalonians," 885. G. Green notes that *"the presence of the Lord* is associated in a number of texts in the OT and the book of Revelation with the judgment of God (Num. 16.46; Judg. 5.5; Pss. 34.16 [33.17]; 96.13 [95.13]; Jer. 4.26; Ezek. 38.20; Rev. 6.16; 20.11)." He also rightly concludes that in 2 Thess. 1:9 Paul conveys "not merely that the disobedient will be excluded from the Lord's *presence* but that from this *presence* the *everlasting destruction* comes forth" (G. Green, *The Letters to the Thessalonians*, 293).

expression "eternal life" to describe his heavenly inheritance (e.g., Rom. 2:7; 6:22–23; 1 Tim. 1:16; 6:12; Titus 3:7).

Paul's eschatology climaxes in portraying believers sharing in God's glorious presence in the new creation. The "blessed hope" is the "appearing of the glory of our great God and Savior, Jesus Christ" (Titus 2:13). When "Glory" personified appears on the final day with Jesus's parousia, our hope will be perfectly realized. As children and heirs of God, sharing in Christ's sufferings means also sharing in his glory, likely referring to enjoying his glorious presence for eternity (Rom. 8:17; cf. 8:30; 9:23; 2 Cor. 4:17; Col. 1:27; 1 Pet. 4:13; 5:1). Because of this future sharing in God's glorious presence, believers can say with Paul that whether they live or die, they belong to Christ and will be with Christ forever (Rom. 14:8; cf. 1 Cor. 15:23; Phil. 1:21–24; 2 Tim. 2:11).

Hebrews and the General Letters

This collection of works presents us with "valuable, indeed indispensable witnesses to the richness of theological thought in the early church."[80] While these letters maintain diverse emphases (e.g., Christ's priesthood in Hebrews, ecclesiology in 1 Peter, the practicality of faith in James, eschatology in 2 Peter and Jude), their central understanding of the Christian faith stands together beautifully. As the following discussion will demonstrate, the theme of God's relational presence runs through these letters in a powerful and unifying way. A careful study of the texts reveals categories of divine presence similar to those used by Paul in his letters. This section surveys God's relational presence through the incarnation and high priesthood of Christ, his revelation of himself and provision of salvation, his sustaining presence among his people, the presence of the Holy Spirit, and God's eschatological presence.

God's Incarnational Presence

Hebrews opens with a powerful statement about Jesus as God's incarnational presence among us: "In the past God spoke to our ancestors through the prophets at many times and in various ways, but in these last days he has spoken to us by his Son" (1:1–2). The Son is the "radiance of God's glory and the exact representation of his being" (1:3). He is the ultimate expression of God's Word to his people. George Guthrie observes how

---

80. Marshall, *New Testament Theology*, 704. Marshall has a helpful overview of the theological contribution of these letters (chap. 30).

the chiastic structure of Hebrews 1:2b-4 itself draws attention to Christ as God's Word to us:

A God has appointed Christ as heir   *enthronement*
   B Through him he created the world   *cosmic action*
      C He is the radiance of God's glory   *relation to God*
      C' He bears God's stamp   *relation to God*
   B' He governs the universe   *cosmic action*
      (having made purification for sins)   (incarnation)
A' He sat down at God's right hand   *enthronement*[81]

The Son is the radiance (rather than a mere reflection) of God's glory. He reveals the very substance or essential nature (ὑπόστασις, *hypostasis*) of God.[82] As God's Word to us, Jesus is the "manifestation of the person and presence of God."[83] God has spoken, and he has spoken through his Son, the Word made flesh.

Another emphasis in Hebrews gets to the heart of the matter regarding God's incarnational presence: how the Son shares in our humanity. He is the Word made flesh, meaning the Word made like us (i.e., fully human), so that we might experience the full benefit and blessing of God's presence. "Since the children have flesh and blood," the writer of Hebrews says, Jesus also "shared in their humanity" so that through his death he might break the power of the devil and set free those enslaved by sin and death (2:14–15). He continues, "For this reason he had to be made like them, fully human in every way, in order that he might become a merciful and faithful high priest in service to God, and that he might make atonement for the sins of the people" (2:17). The one who makes holy and those made holy are "of the same family" (2:11). The will of God for Jesus entailed Jesus becoming fully human (10:5: "A body you prepared for me"; cf. Ps. 39:7 LXX).[84] Doing the Father's will meant taking on full humanity (10:5, 7, 9; cf. Ps. 39:6–8 LXX). The incarnational presence of God in Jesus provides the foundation for the remainder of God's salvific actions in Christ.

---

81. Guthrie, *Hebrews*, 55. Guthrie modifies the structure proposed by Ellingworth, *The Epistle to the Hebrews*, 95.

82. BDAG 1040; Louw and Nida, *Greek-English Lexicon of the New Testament*, 584.

83. Guthrie, *Hebrews*, 48. See also Luke 9:32; John 1:14; 2:11; 17:5; Rom. 8:17; 1 Cor. 2:8; Phil. 3:21; 2 Thess. 2:14.

84. Lane observes that the writer uses σῶμα (*sōma*) in 10:5 rather than σάρξ (*sarx*), which normally is used when describing Jesus's human body (e.g., Heb. 2:14; 5:7), in order to show that Jesus's death was "qualitatively superior to the offerings prescribed by law" (Lane, *Hebrews 9–13*, 262).

The incarnate Son's suffering and death also highlight God's incarnational presence in a powerful way. Hebrews 2:10 says, "In bringing many sons and daughters to glory, it was fitting that God, for whom and through whom everything exists, should make the pioneer of their salvation perfect through what he suffered." That is, through Jesus's many sufferings and culminating in his sacrificial death, God perfected the Son "in his vocation as the 'Pioneer of his people's salvation.'"[85] And through the Son's death, God brought "many sons and daughters to glory"—to their ultimate destiny of enjoying God's final approval and living in his glorious presence forever. Glory is the goal of Jesus's death on the cross; presence is the ultimate purpose of the incarnation. Craig Koester writes, "'Glory' was used in the LXX and Jewish and Christian writings for divine power and presence. Those who entered glory entered the sphere where God's presence was manifest. . . . Entering glory would mean life everlasting in the presence of God (Rom. 2:7; 5:2; 1 Cor. 15:42–43; Eph. 1:18; 1 Pet. 1:21; 5:10)."[86] Jesus, the pioneer, through his "incarnation, death, entrance into God's presence, and session at God's right hand" has prepared the way for many children to follow to the "glory of the heavenly homeland prepared for them."[87] Peter may hint at this in 1 Peter 1:11, where he mentions "the sufferings of the Messiah and the glories that would follow," likely referring to Jesus's resurrection, ascension, exaltation, and perhaps future return in glory to receive his people (cf. 1 Pet. 4:13; 5:4).

Jesus's incarnational presence meant his tasting death for everyone (Heb. 2:9; cf. 9:15–17). As the Lamb of God, Jesus was "chosen before the creation of the world, but was revealed in these last times" (1 Pet. 1:19–20). He "appeared once for all at the culmination of the ages to do away with sin by the sacrifice of himself" (Heb. 9:26). He is the mediator of a new covenant, and his sprinkled blood "speaks a better word than the blood of Abel," a word we dare not refuse (12:24–25). Ironically, the Lamb is also "the Great Shepherd of the sheep," who appeared once to provide salvation (13:20; cf. 7:27; 9:26), and will appear a second time to bring salvation for those waiting for him (9:28).

Peter also highlights Jesus's incarnational presence but does so more indirectly than the author of Hebrews. Peter speaks of "the grace that was to come to you" in connection with the "sufferings of the Messiah" (1 Pet. 1:10–11). Jesus's earthly presence also supplies one aspect of his redemptive work (1 Pet. 1:18–19; 3:18; 4:1) and foreshadows his eschatological presence (1 Pet. 1:20). When Peter emphasizes Jesus's bodily resurrection, he assumes

85. Cockerill, *The Epistle to the Hebrews*, 138.
86. Koester, *Hebrews*, 228.
87. Cockerill, *The Epistle to the Hebrews*, 137–38.

his incarnational presence (1 Pet. 1:3, 21; 3:18, 21). In addition, when Peter refers to the powerful experience of witnessing Jesus's transfiguration, the incarnational presence is assumed (2 Pet. 1:16–18).

Christ's Priestly Presence

The writer of Hebrews boldly states that believers have "a great high priest who ascended into heaven, Jesus the Son of God" (4:14; cf. 2:17; 3:1; 6:19–20; 8:1).[88] Jesus has entered the inner sanctuary on behalf of God's people by becoming their high priest forever, in the order of Melchizedek (5:6, 10; 6:18–20).[89] George Ladd observes that "the central theme in the Christology of Hebrews is the High Priesthood of Christ."[90] It becomes clear when reading Hebrews carefully that the incarnational presence of God in Jesus, the Son, becomes the "indispensable qualification" for his high priestly presence.[91] God with us becomes God for us.

Jesus's priestly status makes possible his sacrifice of atonement. He became fully human in order that he might be our high priest "and that he might make atonement for the sins of the people" (2:17). He entered the most holy place, the place of God's presence, by his own blood (9:12). This was a once for all sacrifice of the body of Jesus for the sins of the people (7:27; 9:26). He became the "source of eternal salvation for all those who obey him" (5:9).

Having finished his work he sat down in the presence of God, exalted to his right hand (10:12). The effect of Jesus's high priestly sacrifice of himself, as Howard Marshall says, is that people are drawn "into the presence of God without fear" (see 10:19) and they "now have a positive relationship with God that can be described in terms of coming into his presence—a present anticipation of that future consummation."[92]

Believers now participate in a new and superior covenant (8:6, 8; 9:15). In Hebrews 8 we find a quotation of Jeremiah 31:31–34, the longest OT quotation in the NT. Here the focus is on the "new" covenant established by Jesus's sacrificial death, by which people can enter into a relationship with God: "I

---

88. The theme of Christ's priestly presence is featured solely in Hebrews. The General Letters emphasize different aspects of Christ's salvific work.

89. Marshall, *New Testament Theology*, 622–23. Marshall notes that the author uses Melchizedek to show that "there can be a priesthood distinct from that of the tribe of Levi but yet perfectly legitimate in its function and in a sense superior to that of Levi. The priesthood of Christ, who came from Judah and not Levi, can be seen as falling into the same category." See also Hurst, "Priest, High," 964–66.

90. Ladd, *A Theology of the New Testament*, 625.

91. Marshall, *New Testament Theology*, 621.

92. Marshall, *New Testament Theology*, 625.

will put my laws in their minds and write them on their hearts. I will be their God, and they will be my people. No longer will they teach their neighbor, or say to one another, 'Know the Lord,' because they will all know me, from the least of them to the greatest" (8:10–11).

The primary result of this new-covenant relationship is the forgiveness of sins, which leads to permanent access into God's presence (8:12; 10:16–17). God for us (Christ's priestly presence) leads to us with God (eschatological presence). Because of our faithful high priest, believers may "approach God's throne of grace with confidence, so that we may receive mercy and find grace to help us in our time of need" (4:16). The forerunner high priest Jesus has entered the inner sanctuary behind the curtain on behalf of his people (6:19–20). He has "sat down at the right hand of the throne of the Majesty in heaven" and serves his people from this exalted location (8:1–2). He now appears in heaven in God's presence on behalf of believers (9:24). In 10:19–22 the writer clearly summarizes the implications of Jesus's high priestly work: "Therefore, brothers and sisters, since we have confidence to enter the Most Holy Place by the blood of Jesus, by a new and living way opened for us through the curtain, that is, his body, and since we have a great priest over the house of God, let us draw near to God with a sincere heart and with the full assurance that faith brings, having our hearts sprinkled to cleanse us from a guilty conscience and having our bodies washed with pure water." Jesus not only paves the way for God's people to enter God's presence but also intercedes for them to secure their salvation (7:24–25; cf. Rom. 8:34). He is their advocate before God, praying that God would sustain them and secure their eschatological salvation.[93] With consciences cleansed and access into God's presence secured, God's people may now "serve the living God" without fear (Heb. 9:14).

Believers do not have a high priest "who is unable to empathize with our weaknesses"; rather, we have one "who has been tempted in every way, just as we are—yet he did not sin" (4:15). This merciful and faithful, fully human high priest has triumphed over the grave and ascended into heaven (4:14). As a result, believers may "approach God's throne of grace with confidence" (4:16). We see then that Christ's priestly presence, among other things, also serves as the basis for God's sustaining presence.

God's Sustaining Presence

As the "Shepherd" and "Overseer" of their souls, the Lord cares for and sustains his people on their wilderness journey (Heb. 13:20; 1 Pet. 2:25). They

93. Lane, *Hebrews 1–8*, 190.

once were like sheep going astray but now have returned to the Lord. In Isaiah 40:10–11 (LXX) God himself is the Shepherd of his people: "He will tend his flock like a shepherd and gather lambs with his arm and comfort those that are with young" (v. 11 NETS). As Karen Jobes notes, Ezekiel 34:11–12 LXX joins both the shepherding and overseeing roles as part of God's sustaining presence: "I will search for my sheep and watch over them. Just as the shepherd seeks his flock . . . , so will I seek out my sheep and drive them away from every place, there where they were scattered" (NETS).[94] In Hebrews and 1 Peter as in the Gospels, especially John 10, Jesus Christ, the great high priest, also plays the role of the great Shepherd.

Yet, as mentioned earlier, Christ's priestly presence remains foundational to God's sustaining presence. We read in Hebrews 4:14–16, "We have a great high priest . . . , Jesus the Son of God. . . . Let us then approach God's throne of grace with confidence, so that we may receive mercy and find grace to help us in our time of need." The other bookend, Hebrews 10, makes a similar point: "Since we have a great high priest over the house of God, let us draw near to God with a sincere heart and with the full assurance that faith brings" (10:21–22). This idea of "drawing near" (προσέρχομαι, *proserchomai* [see Heb. 4:16; 7:25; 10:1, 22; 11:6; 12:18, 22; 1 Pet. 2:4]) indicates, as George Guthrie observes, that those once prohibited from ever entering God's presence may now enter the very presence of God continually and regularly as part of their relationship with God.[95] Biblical faith involves coming to God believing that he "rewards those who draw near to him" (Heb. 11:6). The Lord's eyes are "on the righteous and his ears are attentive to their prayer" (1 Pet. 3:12, quoting Ps. 33:16 LXX [34:15 ET]).

These passages also suggest that God's people will commonly experience his sustaining presence through the particular means of spiritual growth he has provided. Hebrews 4 mentions approaching God's throne of grace with confidence, likely pointing to prayer and worship as the means of accessing God's presence. Hebrews 10 alludes to additional avenues to God's presence such as faith, forgiveness, hope, love, and a healthy and consistent involvement in the local community (see vv. 19–25).[96] In Hebrews 13 the writer urges believers to keep their lives free from the love of money and cultivate contentment precisely because God has promised his abiding presence: "Never will I leave you; never will I forsake you" (13:5, quoting Deut. 31:6, 8; cf. Gen. 28:15; Josh. 1:5; 1 Chron. 28:20). As a result, believers may

94. Jobes, *1 Peter*, 198.
95. Guthrie, *Hebrews*, 176.
96. Guthrie, *Hebrews*, 348.

say with confidence, "The Lord is my helper; I will not be afraid. What can mere mortals do to me?" (13:6, quoting Ps. 118:6–7). The benediction at the end of Hebrews calls for the God of peace, who raised Jesus from the dead, to equip believers with everything to do his will, and for God to "work in us what is pleasing to him, through Jesus Christ" (13:21). William Lane concludes, "It is God who strengthens the heart with grace (13:9), who fills and supports the heart with charismatic gifts (2:4; 6:5; 13:9), so that it neither wavers nor suffers a deficiency but possesses the capacity to do the will of God."[97] This is indeed God's sustaining presence at work—that is, "working" (present participle ποιῶν, *poiōn*).

Hebrews also highlights God's sustaining presence using the concept of a promised rest. In the OT God promised a rest for his pilgrim people as the goal of their journey through the wilderness to the land. Although one generation rebelled and was prohibited from entering God's rest (Heb. 3:7–11, quoting Ps. 95:7–11), and although Joshua later led Israel into the promised land, the author of Hebrews offers hope to his readers that the promise to enter God's rest still remains (4:1, 6, 7–11). "Today," they are told, "if you hear his voice, do not harden your hearts," but "make every effort to enter that rest" (4:7, 11). The writer concludes, "There remains, then, a Sabbath-rest for the people of God" (4:9). While the focus of God's promised rest lies in the future (see eschatology below), there is an "already" aspect to God's rest. The emphasis on "today" supports this conclusion, and as Guthrie observes: "If the concept of rest as discussed in Hebrews 4 has an entirely future orientation, all of the members of the community are short of achieving it at present."[98] Hebrews 4:3 makes the "already" aspect to rest explicit: "Now we who have believed enter that rest."

God's "Sabbath-rest" for his people is a spiritual reality that may be entered into and experienced now (Heb. 4), while simultaneously having a promised future fulfillment. Harold Attridge articulates well the meaning of rest: "Thus the imagery of rest is best understood as a complex symbol for the whole soteriological process that Hebrews never fully articulates, but which involves both personal and corporate dimensions. It is the process of entry into God's presence, the heavenly homeland (11:16), the unshakeable kingdom (12:28), begun at baptism (10:22) and consummated as a whole eschatologically."[99] If God's Sabbath-rest is primarily an eschatological hope, then entering that rest now surely refers to entering into a relationship with God now and

97. Lane, *Hebrews 9–13*, 564.
98. Guthrie, *Hebrews*, 151–52.
99. Attridge, *The Epistle to the Hebrews*, 128.

experiencing his gracious and sustaining presence for the remainder of the wilderness journey. Jesus's words provide an appropriate parallel: "Come to me, all you who are weary and burdened, and I will give you rest" (Matt. 11:28), especially if Jesus is alluding to Exodus 33:14: "My Presence will go with you, and I will give you rest" (cf. Jer. 6:16).[100]

James uses the attribute of "wisdom" to emphasize God's sustaining presence. "Wisdom is for James, at least in part, what faith is for Paul, what love or life is for John, and what hope is for Peter."[101] God's sustaining presence is not a "tempting to do evil" kind of presence (James 1:13–14) but rather a "willing to give wisdom" kind of presence (1:5–7). "If any of you lacks wisdom," James writes, "you should ask God, who gives generously to all without finding fault, and it will be given to you" (1:5). God's wisdom is available for those who ask in faith without doubting (1:6). As Dan McCartney observes, "The wisdom of James is not just skill at life, however, but the divinely given ability to live in a godly way (as will be developed in James 3) and to endure testing."[102] God gives such wisdom "generously" (ἁπλῶς, haplōs), which is more likely understood as "simplicity" or "integrity" or "single-mindedness" in contrast to the double-mindedness of the doubter mentioned in verses 6–8.[103] God is undivided in his intention to give his people his guiding and sustaining wisdom to live well in this broken world.

In 1 Peter 2:2–3 Peter uses the metaphor of a nursing baby craving pure milk to describe God's sustaining work in the life of a believer: "Like newborn babies, crave pure spiritual [λογικός, logikos] milk, so that by it you may grow up in your salvation, now that you have tasted that the Lord is good." Most commentators equate milk with God's word because Peter uses λογικός, translated as "spiritual" (NIV), instead of the expected term πνευματικός (pneumatikos [2:5]), to clarify that milk refers to God's word (λόγος, logos).[104] Jobes proposes a broader interpretation of the milk metaphor, pointing toward God's sustaining presence as the referent.[105] She concludes, "God in Christ alone both conceives and sustains the life of the new birth. They are to crave the Lord God for spiritual nourishment." This becomes more likely in light of the last part of verse 3: "now that you have tasted that the Lord is good"

---

100. The likely allusion to Exod. 33:14b is noted by D. Turner, *Matthew*, 305.

101. McKnight, *The Letter of James*, 86, quoting Mayor, *The Epistle of St. James*, 38.

102. McCartney, *James*, 88.

103. McKnight, *The Letter of James*, 88; also Moo, *The Letter of James*, 59.

104. For example, see T. Schreiner, *1, 2 Peter, Jude*, 99–100. Schreiner concludes, "Spiritual growth is not primarily mystical but rational, and rational in the sense that it is informed and sustained by God's word."

105. Jobes, *1 Peter*, 130–41.

(cf. Ps. 33:9 LXX [34:8 ET]: "O taste, and see that the Lord is kind"), which points to the Lord himself as the Sustainer.[106]

God's Revelatory-Salvific Presence

In Hebrews and the General Epistles God's revelatory presence points to his provision of salvation through his Son, Jesus Christ, all in hopes of God living among his people in the new creation (see eschatological presence below). Hebrews opens with a declaration that God has "spoken to us by his Son" (1:2). And this divine speech brings salvation, a salvation that was initially announced by the Lord as "God also testified to it by signs, wonders and various miracles, and by gifts of the Holy Spirit distributed according to his will" (Heb. 2:4). This is a shared salvation, a faith "once for all entrusted to God's holy people" (Jude 3). Hebrews says that every effort should be made to enter this relationship with God ("Sabbath-rest"), "For [γάρ, *gar*] the word of God is alive and active. Sharper than any double-edged sword, it penetrates even to dividing soul and spirit, joints and marrow; it judges the thoughts and attitudes of the heart" (4:12). God's penetrating and discerning presence comes to his people through his word (e.g., as the exposition of Ps. 95:7–11 in Heb. 4:1–11 illustrates). One of the final warnings in this letter includes this admonition: "See to it that you do not refuse him who speaks" (12:25), reminding the readers that listening to the Lord speak is not a trivial matter (cf. 2:1–4).

As with the author of Hebrews, both Peter and James connect God's word to the God-sent salvation provided through Jesus, both aspects of his revelatory presence. The prophets once spoke of the coming grace of God through the Messiah and "the glories that would follow" (1 Pet. 1:10–11), a grace finally announced by those who "preached the gospel to you by the Holy Spirit sent from heaven" (1:12). Peter calls on the believers to live godly lives and to love one another deeply because they "have been born again, not of perishable seed, but of imperishable, through the living and enduring word of God" (1:23). The "word" here probably refers to the gospel that had been proclaimed to them and had transformed them into the people of God. His quotation of Isaiah 40:6–8 (LXX) likely taps into the larger context of Isaiah 40, as D. A. Carson notes:

> Yet Peter apparently is claiming something more. If he is expecting his readers to bring the content of Isa. 40 along with the actual lines quoted, then the word preached to them is doubtless the word promising the visitation by Yahweh,

106. Jobes, *1 Peter*, 140. Michaels likewise concludes, "The milk itself is more appropriately interpreted as the sustaining life of God given in mercy to his children" (Michaels, *1 Peter*, 89).

the promised worldwide theophany—manifested in the gospel itself and still to be fulfilled at the end of the age. Precisely because God's word is reliable, Peter's readers can rest assured that the fulfillment that has not yet taken place will come—and "this is the word that was preached to you."[107]

God's revelatory presence through this word of salvation brings new life, eternal life, to his people. In his second letter Peter makes a similar point when reminding his readers that the holy prophets (along with the Lord through his apostles [2 Pet. 3:2]) have provided a reliable word in contrast to the heresy of the false teachers. "Above all," Peter says, "you must understand that no prophecy of Scripture came about by the prophet's own interpretation of things. For prophecy never had its origin in the human will, but prophets, though human, spoke from God as they were carried along by the Holy Spirit" (2 Pet. 1:20–21). Paying attention to this word is like paying attention to a life-giving light shining in a dark place (1:19).

James too stresses how God's revelatory presence brings his salvific presence: the "Father of heavenly lights . . . chose to give us birth through the word of truth" (James 1:17–18). God, both Creator and Father, brought these believers into new life and relationship with himself through the proclaimed word. A few verses later James admonishes his readers to "get rid of all moral filth and the evil that is so prevalent and humbly accept the word planted in you, which can save you" (1:21). The "word planted in you" likely also refers to the gospel message received and acted upon by the hearers. The ability of this received message to "save you" probably refers ultimately to an experience of God's eschatological presence, but an experience that begins here and now (cf. James 4:12; see also Eph. 1:13–14).

God's Presence among His People, the Church

Throughout history God has often made his presence known to and through his people. Hebrews and the General Epistles speak to this aspect of God's relational presence in a variety of ways: believers as the people of God; the church as God's flock, house (or temple), and family; and the various ways God makes his presence known through the practical life of the community.

Individuals become part of the people of God by becoming sharers or participants (μέτοχος, *metochos*) in Christ (cf. Paul's "in Christ"): "We have come to share in Christ, if indeed we hold our original conviction firmly to the very end" (Heb. 3:14). They join a people that finds itself in continuity with faithful Israel. James even addresses his audience as "the twelve tribes

---

107. Carson, "1 Peter," 1022.

scattered among the nations" (James 1:1; cf. 2:21: "our father Abraham"), a phrase that echoes the OT designation of God's people and his faithful presence with them during their exodus and subsequent pilgrim experience. Peter likewise labels his audience as "scattered" or "dispersed exiles" (1 Pet. 1:1). As Howard Marshall observes, these descriptions show that "they regarded themselves as the true successors of the Old Testament people of God."[108] Because of the historical context of the exhortation, Hebrews qualifies (but still retains) this continuity. Kevin Giles comments,

> Although Hebrews appeals primarily to the OT to make its case, it envisages a radical breach with Israel. The old covenant has been replaced by the new (Heb. 8:6–13); the Jewish priesthood and the office and work of the High Priest have come to an end (Heb. 7:11–14, 23–28); and Jesus in offering himself has made obsolete the old sacrificial system (Heb. 9:25–28; 10:11–15). As a consequence the author views the Christian community as new Israel in all but name. The Christians have taken the place of the historic people of God, assuming their distinctive titles and privileges.[109]

Yet, Hebrews can speak of followers of Jesus being "surrounded by such a great cloud of witnesses" (12:1), likely referring to the faithful mentioned in Hebrews 11 and others like them, who have persevered and now bear witness to God's faithful presence through it all. Later, in chapter 12, the author says that these believers have come not to Mount Sinai but to "Mount Zion, to the city of the living God, the heavenly Jerusalem. You have come . . . to the church of the firstborn. . . . You have come to God, the Judge of all, to the spirits of the righteous made perfect, to Jesus the mediator of a new covenant" (vv. 22–24). As the "church of the firstborn" (ἐκκλησία πρωτοτόκων, *ekklēsia prōtotokōn*), a phrase loaded with OT allusions to Israel (e.g., Exod. 4:22–23 LXX), God's people now stand in continuity with the "spirits of the righteous made perfect," a reference to the godly dead who now enjoy God's presence in the heavenly city.[110] Giles notes that Hebrews uses a number of descriptions of the new-covenant people of God that "were originally the prerogative of historic Israel" (e.g., people of God, children of God, saints, God's house).[111]

---

108. Marshall, *New Testament Theology*, 640. Giles sees these descriptions of believers in 1 Pet. 1:1–2 as an explicit identification as the new Israel: "exiles of the dispersion," "chosen and destined by God," "sanctified by the Spirit and . . . sprinkled with his blood" (1 Pet. 1:1–2). See Giles, "Church," 198–99.

109. Giles, "Church," 198.

110. Lane, *Hebrews 9–13*, 470–71.

111. Giles, "Church," 198.

The letter that speaks most directly and forcefully of the church as God's people is 1 Peter. Although it never uses the term ἐκκλησία, "it is more interested in theologically defining the Christian community, the church, than is any other NT writing."[112] Certainly a key text is 1 Peter 2:9–10: "But you are a chosen people, a royal priesthood, a holy nation, God's special possession, that you may declare the praises of him who called you out of darkness into his wonderful light. Once you were not a people, but now you are the people of God; once you had not received mercy, but now you have received mercy." By alluding to Exodus 19:6, Isaiah 43:20–21, and Hosea 2:25, Peter reminds his readers that they are a people belonging to God, who has come after them to rescue them. They now have special access to God as priests. God has established his covenant with them and given them an eternal place in his presence. They are indeed God's special possession. Those once called "Not my people" are now called "My people," and they respond, "You are our God" (Hosea 2:23). Peter is giving his readers a primary identity of being in relationship with God, the God who is always with them.

God's presence among his people also appears through use of images such as God's flock, house (or temple), and family. Peter continues his emphasis on the church by describing it as "God's flock" in 1 Peter 5:2. The prophets commonly describe God's people as his flock (e.g., Isa. 63:11; Jer. 13:17; 31:10; 50:17; Ezek. 34:11–24; Mic. 2:12; 7:14; Zech. 9:16; 10:3). And Jesus is described as the "Shepherd and Overseer" (1 Pet. 2:25), the "Chief Shepherd" (1 Pet. 5:4), and the "great Shepherd" (Heb. 13:20) (cf. John 10:11, 14; Rev. 7:17). The image of the shepherd with the flock speaks of God's care for his people—searching for, gathering, securing, protecting, providing.

God's people are also described as his "house" or temple. In Hebrews 3 the author says that Moses was faithful "in all God's house" (vv. 2, 5; cf. Num. 12:7), meaning that Moses was a faithful servant on behalf of God's people. Jesus, by contrast, is "faithful as the Son over God's house. And we are his house" (3:6). Not only does this stress that Jesus is superior to Moses, but also it emphasizes God's people as God's temple or dwelling place. God's presence lives among his people (cf. 1 Tim. 3:15, and also temple language in 1 Cor. 3:16–17; Eph. 2:19–21; 1 Pet. 2:4–5). Peter compares God's people to a "spiritual house" composed of living stones: "As you come to him, the living Stone—rejected by humans but chosen by God and precious to him—you also, like living stones, are being built into a spiritual house to be a holy priesthood, offering spiritual sacrifices acceptable to God through Jesus Christ" (1 Pet. 2:4–5). By "spiritual" (πνευματικός, *pneumatikos*), the author doesn't

112. Giles, "Church," 198.

primarily mean religious but rather related to or in line with the Holy Spirit, God's empowering presence. God's people are also God's temple.

The final image that merits comment is God's people as God's family. God used Jesus's suffering to bring "many sons and daughters to glory" (Heb. 2:10). Both Jesus and his followers "are of the same family" (2:11), and Jesus is not ashamed to "call them brothers and sisters" (2:11–12; cf. Ps. 22:22), since they are also God's children (2:13).[113] As Craig Koester notes, people normally leave their inheritance to their children, and in this case, Jesus is intent on bringing many sons and daughters to glory through his suffering (2:10).[114] Glory in this context most likely refers to divine presence. The ultimate goal of the family relationship is to be together as family, as God's people experience eternal life in his presence (cf. Rom. 5:2; Eph. 1:18; 1 Pet. 5:10). Koester observes that Hebrews also depicts the destiny of God's people as "divine rest (Heb. 4:10), entering the sanctuary (10:19), and arriving at Mt. Zion (12:22)," all images of experiencing God's eternal presence.[115] In Hebrews 12, when considering the topic of God's discipline, the writer also speaks of God's people as his family. God is the "Father" (12:5–7, 9), and believers are his children (12:6–8). As the Father, God disciplines his children as a loving father—loving, accepting, correcting, wanting what is best; he disciplines his sons and daughters so they might "live" and "share in his holiness" (12:9–10), an indication that God plans for them to live eternally in his presence.

Finally, we see that God makes his presence known through the practical life of the community. God's people are to meet together consistently for worship (Heb. 2:12). The writer of Hebrews confronts those who are abandoning their worship gatherings and challenges them not to give up meeting together but to continue encouraging one another in community (10:24–25). It is in the worship of the community that they will experience God's powerful presence and be encouraged to persevere in the faith. James contrasts their common worship practice, where they "praise our Lord and Father," with their unhealthy pattern of cursing human beings made in God's image (James 3:9). Jude laments that false teachers have become "blemishes at your love feasts" (Jude 12), likely an indirect reference to the community meals where the Lord's Supper would be celebrated. Prayer also marks one aspect of the community where they experience the Lord's presence. Peter calls on his readers to "be alert and of sober mind so that you may pray" in light

---

113. The plural of ἀδελφός (adelphos) is used multiple times in Hebrews and the General Epistles to speak of God's people as "brothers and sisters" or family: Heb. 2:11, 12; 3:1, 12; 10:19; 13:22; James 1:2, 16, 19; 2:1, 5, 14; 3:1, 10, 12; 4:11; 5:7, 9, 10, 12, 19; 2 Pet. 1:10.

114. Koester, Hebrews, 227–28.

115. Koester, Hebrews, 228.

of the nearness of the end (1 Pet. 4:7). Those in trouble or sick, James says, should call on the church leaders to pray over them and they will experience God's forgiveness and healing (James 5:13–16).

Along with worship and prayer, believers experience God's presence through loving and serving one another. Peter instructs his readers to "love one another deeply, because love covers over a multitude of sins" (1 Pet. 4:8; cf. 1:22) and to "offer hospitality to one another without grumbling" (4:9). Hebrews urges believers to "consider how we may spur one another on toward love and good deeds" (10:24). This encouragement happens in large part in the gathered community. Peter also alludes to the proper exercise of spiritual gifts as another way to build up the church. Gifts (χάρισμα, *charisma*) should be used to serve others (1 Pet. 4:10). Gifts ultimately flow from God's grace (χάρις, *charis*), so those who speak should do so "as one who speaks the very words of God," and those who serve should do so "with the strength God provides" (1 Pet. 4:11). God is honored and glorified as God's people experience his presence through ministry to others. We see the contrasting scenario in the string of exhortations in James 4:6–10, where God's grace leads him to oppose the proud and favor the humble. As a result, God's people should submit to God, resist the devil, "come near to God," repent of their sin, and purify their hearts, so that as they humble themselves before the Lord, he will "come near to" them and exalt them. Coming near to God and God coming near to his people in this context likely refers to a restoration of fellowship with the Lord for a repentant believer.[116] God's presence is also linked to the restoration of relationships within the community of God's people that result from doing God's will.[117]

God's Presence through the Holy Spirit

In Hebrews the ministry of the Holy Spirit is closely related to God's revelatory-salvific presence mentioned above. God's Spirit speaks to his people (3:7, followed by a citation from Ps. 95:7–11), reminding them to pay close attention to Christ's voice. The Spirit is very involved in the establishment of the new covenant, including the forgiveness of sins (see 10:15–16, where Jer. 31:31–34 is cited). The Spirit, also through Scripture, warns that before Christ there was "no effective, unhindered or universally available access into God's

---

116. Moo, *The Letter of James*, 193; McKnight, *The Letter of James*, 350; R. Martin, *James*, 153.

117. McKnight suggests that the "language of drawing near to God and God drawing near to us reminds one of the powerful covenant formula of the OT: 'I will be your God and you will be my people' (e.g., Gen. 17:2, 4, 6–8; Exod. 6:2–8)" (McKnight, *The Letter of James*, 350).

presence" (9:8).[118] The people's sin had broken the old covenant, and those who reject God's provision of salvation have "insulted the Spirit of grace" (10:29). The Spirit is the one who brings the believer into an experience of God's grace, and apart from the Spirit there will be no experience of Christ and his new-covenant work.

But the author of Hebrews is convinced of better things in the case of his readers, things that accompany salvation (6:9). At Pentecost believers had received a distribution of the Spirit, God's personal and empowering presence: "God also testified to it [the salvation secured by Christ] by signs, wonders and various miracles, and by the gifts of the Holy Spirit distributed according to his will" (2:4). Although this could refer to the gifts of the Spirit, the term "gifts" is not mentioned, and "distributions of the Holy Spirit" (πνεύματος ἁγίου μερισμοῖς, *pneumatos hagiou merismois*) more likely refers to receiving the Holy Spirit himself.[119] One sure sign that one has membership in the covenant community is "sharing" (μετόχος, *metochos*) in the Holy Spirit (6:4). As Alan Hodson notes, "The presence of the Holy Spirit with a people authenticates them as new-covenant people."[120] Or, as Thomas Schreiner puts it, "Sharing in the Spirit is *the* mark of new life, the prime indication that believers are Christians."[121] Whereas the blood of sacrificial animals proved unable to sanctify, "the blood of Christ, who through the eternal Spirit offered himself unblemished to God," is able to cleanse the conscience "from acts that lead to death, so that we may serve the living God!" (9:13–14). The "eternal Spirit" is another way of speaking of the Holy Spirit, perhaps emphasizing his role in the Christ event that secured eternal redemption and permanent access into God's presence (9:12). Believers are now free to worship (λατρεύω, *latreuō*) the living God without the need for a human priest as mediator (cf. 12:28).

The book of 1 Peter has more frequent references to the Holy Spirit than do most of Paul's Letters.[122] The Spirit's role falls into four main categories, and each touches on our topic of God's relational presence. First, the Spirit plays a direct role in God's revelation of himself. The "Spirit of Christ" (cf. Rom. 8:9) revealed to the OT prophets the sufferings and glories of the coming Messiah, a message reinforced by those who "preached the gospel to you by the Holy Spirit send from heaven" (1 Pet. 1:10–12). The Holy Spirit

118. Hodson, "Hebrews," 229.
119. Hodson, "Hebrews," 234–35.
120. Hodson, "Hebrews," 236.
121. T. Schreiner, *New Testament Theology*, 492.
122. Dubis, *Messianic Woes in First Peter*, 125. Dubis shows how the frequencies of occurrence of πνεῦμα (*pneuma*) compare (using percentages for the number of occurrence of πνεῦμα in relation to the total number of words of each book): Romans (.45%), 1 Peter (.42%), 2 Corinthians (.33%), 1 Thessalonians (.30%), Philippians (.27%).

reveals the prophetic message and empowers those who proclaim the gospel. Peter makes a similar point in 2 Peter 1:21: "Prophecy never had its origin in the human will, but prophets, though human, spoke from God as they were carried along by the Holy Spirit." The Spirit is the revelatory Spirit who has always communicated to God's people what they need to know in order to have a relationship with God and spend eternity in his presence.

Second, the Spirit consecrates God's people: "God's elect, exiles scattered . . . , who have been chosen according to the foreknowledge of God the Father, through the sanctifying work of the Spirit, to be obedient to Jesus Christ and sprinkled with his blood" (1 Pet. 1:1–2). The Spirit is vitally involved in a believer's conversion. Karen Jobes notes that the Holy Spirit is "the instrument, or agency, by which God makes his electing foreknowledge operative in the lives of those who come to faith in Christ."[123] The phrase "to be obedient . . . and sprinkled" probably should be understood as a hendiadys (a single idea expressed by two words) against the background of the covenant ceremony in Exodus 24, where the people of God would vow their obedience (vv. 3, 7) and then be sprinkled with the blood of sacrifice (v. 8).[124] This context, according to Jobes, refers to God's covenant relationship with his people, a people indwelt by God's personal and empowering presence, the Holy Spirit, leading them to live a whole new life in light of Christ's sacrifice.[125]

Third, and very much related to the previous role, is how the Spirit provides life. Peter writes that Christ himself was "put to death in the body but made alive in [or "by"] the Spirit" (1 Pet. 3:18). The Spirit is the one who raised Jesus from the dead and the one who also provides life for the believer. The gospel was preached to those who are now dead, Peter says, that they may ultimately "live according to God in regard to the spirit" (4:6). In this verse, we take πνεύματι (*pneumati*) as a dative of means; that is, believers will experience new life by means of the Holy Spirit (versus the "flesh" [σαρκί, *sarki*]).[126] The Spirit is the life-giving Spirit.

Fourth, the Spirit empowers God's people to suffer as an expression of their faith. Believers are blessed when they are insulted because of the name of Christ, "for the Spirit of glory and of God rests on you" (1 Pet. 4:14 [lit. "the of-glory and the of-God Spirit is resting upon you"]). If the two phrases are considered separately, the "of-glory" would then be identified with God's Shekinah presence, resulting in an epexegetical relationship: "the Presence

---

123. Jobes, *1 Peter*, 69–70.
124. Jobes, *1 Peter*, 72.
125. Jobes, *1 Peter*, 72. See also Davids, *The First Epistle of Peter*, 48.
126. T. Schreiner, *1, 2 Peter, Jude*, 209.

of the Glory, yes the Spirit of God."[127] Isaiah 11:2 promises that the Spirit of the Lord will rest upon the coming messianic figure. Peter draws on this text to remind his readers that the same Spirit who rested upon Christ now rests upon them, fulfilling God's long-standing promise to one day dwell within his people (e.g., Isa. 32:15; Ezek. 39:29; Joel 2:28–29; Zech. 12:10). The Spirit's empowering presence remains even during times of suffering. Here Peter is speaking of the "constant presence of the divine Glory-Spirit with afflicted Christians, inspiring and endowing them permanently."[128] Peter may be saying something similar with his references to "God's power" (1 Pet. 1:5) or "divine power" (2 Pet. 1:3), a power that provides everything God's people need to live a godly life and shields them until their final salvation is revealed.

Although James prefers to use wisdom language when speaking of God's sustaining presence, he does quite possibly mention the Holy Spirit in 4:5: "Or do you think Scripture says without reason that he jealously longs for the spirit he has caused to dwell in us?" This much-debated verse with all its interpretive options leaves open the possibility that God longs for the Holy Spirit he has caused to dwell within his people. In any case, God deeply desires that his people reject friendship with the world and walk in a close relationship with him.

In his short letter Jude mentions the Holy Spirit twice. In verses 19–20 he writes, "These are the people who divide you, who follow mere natural instincts and do not have the Spirit. But you, dear friends, by building yourselves up in your most holy faith and praying in the Holy Spirit, keep yourselves in God's love." Jude first characterizes the false teachers as people who "do not have the Spirit" or as unbelievers (v. 19). They may be full of the world (unspiritual, worldly, ψυχικοί, *psychikoi*), but they lack the presence of God in their lives, the indwelling Holy Spirit (cf. Rom. 8:9; 1 Cor. 2:14). In contrast, true believers are exhorted to keep themselves in the love of God by building themselves up in the faith, praying in the Holy Spirit, and eagerly awaiting the return of the Lord Jesus Christ (vv. 20–21). In this trinitarian formulation, praying in the Holy Spirit provides an intimate connection to God's presence and assistance (cf. Rom. 8:15–16, 26–27; Gal. 4:6; Eph. 6:18).

God's Eschatological Presence

Hebrews and the General Epistles have a richly developed eschatology with four primary emphases when it comes to God's relational presence: hope,

---

127. Schafroth, "1 and 2 Peter," 241. Compare the NET: "the Spirit of glory, who is the Spirit of God, rests on you"; and the NRSV: "the spirit of glory, which is the Spirit of God, is resting on you."
128. Schafroth, "1 and 2 Peter," 242.

inheritance, Christ's return, and judgment. Christian hope finds its source in the resurrection of Jesus Christ and the salvation it brings. Peter begins his first letter with this bold pronouncement: "Praise be to the God and Father of our Lord Jesus Christ! In his great mercy he has given us new birth into a living hope through the resurrection of Jesus Christ from the dead" (1 Pet. 1:3). Although the source of hope lies in the past with Jesus's bodily resurrection, it is very much a "living hope" because it promises a future for God's people with the Lord. (We discuss below the new inheritance as part of God's promise.) Karen Jobes writes, "Christian hope is everliving because Christ, the ground of that hope, is everliving. The present reality of the Christian's life is defined and determined by the reality of the past—the resurrection of Jesus Christ—and is guaranteed into the future because Christ lives forevermore."[129] The author of Hebrews comes to much the same conclusion using the image of Christ's permanent priesthood: "Now there have been many of those priests, since death prevented them from continuing in office; but because Jesus lives forever, he has a permanent priesthood. Therefore he is able to save completely those who come to God through him, because he always lives to intercede for them" (7:23–25).

The goal of hope is that God's people will live in his presence. God made the pioneer of salvation perfect through suffering in order to "bring many sons and daughters to glory" (Heb. 2:10). The reference to "glory" here points to life in God's presence in the new creation. Believers are also portrayed as God's house if they hold firmly to their confidence and the hope in which they boast (Heb. 3:6). God's "house" could refer to God's household in the sense of family, or it could be a reference to God's sanctuary or temple.[130] Whether household/family or temple, the image points to God's people living in his presence as the final destination of their hope. The doxology in Jude sums it up well, although the term hope is never used: "To him who is able to keep you from stumbling and to present you before his glorious presence without fault and with great joy—to the only God our Savior be glory, majesty, power and authority, through Jesus Christ our Lord, before all ages, now and forevermore! Amen" (vv. 24–25). Richard Bauckham says that "his glory" is a "reverential periphrasis for God himself," which focuses the great eschatological hope as that of coming into God's glorious presence.[131] Peter

129. Jobes, *1 Peter*, 85.
130. Koester, *Hebrews*, 247. Israel was referred to as God's "house" (e.g., Exod. 16:31; Hosea 8:1; Heb. 8:8), as is the church in 1 Tim. 3:15. God's "house" can also be a sanctuary (e.g., Exod. 23:19; 34:26; Ps. 27:4), and the church is also referred to as a temple (e.g., 1 Cor. 3:16–17; Eph. 2:19–21; 1 Pet. 2:4–5).
131. Bauckham, *2 Peter, Jude*, 122. Davids notes that "glory" is a typically Jewish way of referring to God, as in, for example, Tobit 12:12; *1 Enoch* 27:2; 63:5; 102:2 (Davids, *The Letters of 2 Peter and Jude*, 111).

Davids observes that this is a "festival in the presence of God, a sea of people singing, praising, and dancing in joyous celebration in the very presence of the God they had served on earth."[132] These authors are challenging their readers to persevere to the end so that their hope may be "fully realized" (Heb. 6:11). God's relational presence for eternity is worth the perseverance.

The significance of hope lies in the way it serves to encourage and anchor the soul: "We who have fled to take hold of the hope set before us may be greatly encouraged. We have this hope as an anchor for the soul, firm and secure. It enters the inner sanctuary behind the curtain" (Heb. 6:18–19). The believer's hope moves into the heavenly dwelling place of God, giving them access now to God's presence. Such access reinforces and stabilizes the believer's faith (Heb. 11:1). This hope, of course, rests upon Jesus's entry into God's presence as the great high priest (Heb. 6:20).[133] And in this priest, as the author of Hebrews plainly says in 7:19, "a better hope is introduced, by which we draw near to God" (see also 4:16; 10:22; 12:22). As a result, believers must "hold unswervingly to the hope" they profess because God is faithful as the promise-maker (10:23).

The second eschatological emphasis centers on the concept of inheritance. Hebrews refers multiple times to God's people inheriting what God has promised (e.g., 6:11–12, 17; 9:15; 10:34–37; 11:39–40). Gareth Cockerill says that the promises of God are "richly manifold" and "charged with the language of covenant and Promised Land."[134] God's people inherit his presence, fulfilling the repeated OT promise that God would live among his covenant people in a place of abundant blessing (Exod. 25:8; Lev. 26:12; Jer. 32:38; Ezek. 37:27). Peter and James describe the inheritance as "a blessing" (1 Pet. 3:9), "eternal glory" (1 Pet. 5:10), "the crown of life" (James 1:12), and "the kingdom" (James 2:5). Occasionally the authors specify that believers will inherit "salvation" (Heb. 1:14; 1 Pet. 1:3–5; 2 Pet. 3:15). Peter says that this inheritance "can never perish, spoil or fade" and is "kept in heaven for you, who through faith are shielded by God's power until the coming of the salvation that is ready to be revealed in the last time" (1 Pet. 1:4–5). The inherited salvation made fully available at Christ's return is protected and eternal, and it will bring believers into God's presence as full-fledged citizens of his heavenly kingdom, no longer scattered exiles (1:1). They will finally be truly at home in his presence.

132. Davids, *The Letters of 2 Peter and Jude*, 111.

133. In 6:19 the participle εἰσερχομένην (*eiserchomenēn*) modifies the relative pronoun ἥν (*hēn*) and therefore describes the action of hope (ἐλπίς, *elpis*) in 6:18, which is the antecedent of that relative pronoun.

134. Cockerill, *The Epistle to the Hebrews*, 284.

Hebrews uses several powerful images to portray believers receiving their inheritance. To begin with, believers enter into God's rest (3:11, 18; 4:1, 3, 5, 10–11). Earlier we discussed the "already" aspect of rest as a present spiritual experience of God's sustaining presence, but "rest" also carries a strong eschatological dimension in Hebrews. Rest refers to spiritual realities for God's people that "have been inaugurated but have yet to be consummated."[135] Rest is a promise that can still be missed (4:1). It has been (or is being) entered (4:3) but is also yet to be entered (4:11), at which point labors will cease (4:10). Canaan, the "promised land," is certainly not the final destination, since those who journeyed there were still searching for a heavenly homeland (11:13–16). David deSilva surely is on target when he concludes, "Entering the rest can be no other than entering that divine realm . . . with entrance into 'glory,' into the place 'behind the curtain,' into the 'unshakable kingdom,' into the 'abiding' and 'coming city' that exists beyond any earthly locale."[136] Rest is life in the presence of God.

Inheritance also means coming into God's presence in the heavenly sanctuary, an image also connected to rest (e.g., Ps. 132:8, 13–14). Christ entered this inner, heavenly sanctuary of God's glorious presence by the sacrifice of himself once to take away sins (Heb. 9:24–26). Christ died once but "will appear a second time, not to bear sin, but to bring salvation to those who are waiting for him" (Heb. 9:28). This delivery of final salvation connects in a deep way to Jesus pioneering the way for God's people to enter his presence eternally. In this sense, Christian hope "enters the inner sanctuary behind the curtain, where our forerunner, Jesus, has entered on our behalf" (Heb. 6:19–20). In the same context where the author of Hebrews talks about our present "confidence to enter the Most Holy Place by the blood of Jesus" (10:19) and the privilege of drawing near to God through faith (10:22), believers are urged to "hold unswervingly to the hope we profess, for he who promised is faithful" (10:23) and to continue meeting together as we "see the Day approaching" (10:25). As Craig Koester concludes, "Listeners can already approach God through prayer (4:14–16), but at the end of this present time they will follow Christ their forerunner completely into God's presence (6:19–20; 10:19)."[137]

The final image used to portray inheritance is arrival at the eternal city of God. Although Abraham journeyed to the promised land, he was still "looking forward to the city with foundations, whose architect and builder is God" (Heb. 11:10). These faithful pilgrims "were longing for a better country—a

135. Guthrie, *Hebrews*, 152.
136. DeSilva, *Perseverance in Gratitude*, 160.
137. Koester, *Hebrews*, 103.

heavenly one," and God has indeed "prepared a city for them" (11:16). This city to come is "Mount Zion, . . . the city of the living God, the heavenly Jerusalem" (12:22). George Guthrie wisely sees how the author balances seven dynamics related to Mount Sinai in 12:18–21 with seven related to Mount Zion in 12:22–24, and many of these are eschatological.[138]

William Lane comments on how the characteristics of Mount Zion point to the relational presence of God:

> Every aspect of the vision provides encouragement for coming boldly into the presence of God (cf. 4:16). The atmosphere at Mount Zion is festive. The frightening visual imagery of blazing fire, darkness, and gloom fades before the reality of the city of the living God, heavenly Jerusalem. The cacophony of whirlwind, trumpet blast, and a sound of words is muted and replaced by the joyful praise of angels in a festal gathering. The trembling congregation of Israel, gathered solemnly at the base of the mountain, is superseded by the assembly of those whose names are permanently inscribed in the heavenly archives. An overwhelming impression of the unapproachability of God is eclipsed in the experience of full access to the presence of God and of Jesus, the mediator of the new covenant.[139]

While full access is granted now, final access awaits arrival at the heavenly city, when believers inherit "a kingdom that cannot be shaken" (12:28), an enduring "city that is to come" (13:14). The eternal celebration begins only when all God's people gather in his presence on "the Day" (cf. Mark 14:25).

The third eschatological emphasis focuses on Christ's return to win the final battle against his enemies and to bring final salvation to his people, which includes a host of rewards with connections to divine presence. As the great high priest, Christ has offered one sacrifice for sins once for all and now sits in God's presence, interceding for his people and waiting for "his enemies to be made his footstool" (Heb. 10:12–13; cf. Ps. 110:1) (see Heb. 7:25; 9:24; Rom. 8:34; 1 John 2:1).[140] Nevertheless, these authors continue to stress the impending "nearness" of Jesus's coming (Heb. 10:25, 37; James 5:8; 1 Pet. 4:7). When "the Day" arrives (Heb. 10:25; 1 Pet. 2:12; 2 Pet. 1:19; 3:10), a day that God has delayed due to his patience and desire for many to repent (2 Pet.

---

138. Guthrie, *Hebrews*, 417–19: (1) the heavenly Jerusalem, the city of the living God; (2) thousands upon thousands of angels in joyful assembly; (3) the church of the firstborn, whose names are written in heaven; (4) God, the Judge of all people; (5) the spirits of the righteous made perfect; (6) Jesus, the mediator of a new covenant; (7) the sprinkled blood that speaks better than the blood of Abel.

139. Lane, *Hebrews 9–13*, 464–65.

140. Below we will say more about how the final judgment plays into the presence theme.

3:8–9; cf. James 5:7), Jesus will appear in glory (1 Pet. 4:13; Jude 14). The kingdom will have arrived (James 2:5). Believers will receive a full experience of God's grace (1 Pet. 1:13).

When Jesus brings final salvation (Heb. 1:14; 1 Pet. 1:5, 9), the faithful will be "richly rewarded" (Heb. 10:35; cf. 11:26). This begins with the resurrection of the righteous dead (Heb. 11:35; 1 Pet. 4:6; 5:6). At Christ's return they will receive "the crown of life" or the crown that is resurrection life (James 1:12; cf. Rev. 2:10: "I will give you life as your victor's crown").[141] Resurrection life for an eternity in God's presence is the returning Lord's first gift to his people.

Peter favors "joy" and "glory" imagery as he describes the results and rewards of this final salvation. His readers' faith will be refined by fire so that it may "result in praise, glory and honor when Jesus Christ is revealed" (1 Pet. 1:7), likely referring to what God bestows on his servants. But glory can also be a synonym for divine presence, as we see in 4:13: "But rejoice inasmuch as you participate in the sufferings of Christ, so that you may be overjoyed when his glory is revealed." When Christ's glory is revealed, believers will "share in the glory to be revealed" (5:1) and will "receive the crown of glory that will never fade away" (5:4). Here, as with "the crown that is life" in James 1:12, we have a Greek epexegetical genitive: "the crown that is glory" (τὸν στέφανον τῆς δόξης, *ton stephanon tēs doxēs*). The strong connection between glory and presence leads to the conclusion that the primary reward for believers is the Lord himself and eternal life in his presence (Jude 21). Peter later calls his readers' attention to the reliability of the prophetic message; they should pay attention to it as they would to a light in a dark place, until "the day dawns and the morning star rises in your hearts" (2 Pet. 1:19). Christ certainly is the "morning star," and his rising in the hearts of believers most likely refers to the spiritual effect of Christ's return: his glorious presence radiates through the whole person. Gene Green notes that the rising of the Lord's glory appears elsewhere in Scripture (e.g., Isa. 60:1; Luke 1:78).[142] Paul uses similar imagery in 2 Corinthians 4:6 when he refers to God making "his light shine in our hearts to give us the light of the knowledge of God's glory displayed in the face of Christ." Christ's return will result in his people seeing the Lord (Heb. 12:14) and living together with him in the new heaven and new earth, a world fully immersed in the will of God (2 Pet. 3:13).

The fourth eschatological emphasis relates to the place of God's presence in judgment. This literature makes repeated statements about the fact of the

141. McCartney notes that the phrase "the crown of life" in James 1:12 and Rev. 2:10 likely represents a Greek epexegetical genitive—that is, "the crown that is life" (McCartney, *James*, 101).

142. G. Green, *Jude and 2 Peter*, 228–29.

coming judgment. People die once and after that face judgment (Heb. 9:27). The Judge of all is God himself (Heb. 12:23, 26–27). The "day of the Lord" or the "day of God" will arrive like a thief to render judgment (2 Pet. 3:10, 12; Jude 6, 14–15). Judgment is a coming certainty (1 Pet. 4:17–18; 2 Pet. 2:9).

Judgment also involves experiencing God's presence, but potentially in a wrathful, condemning way. James says that "the Judge is standing at the door!" (5:9). As Hebrews says, "Nothing in all creation is hidden from God's sight. Everything is uncovered and laid bare before the eyes of him to whom we must give account" (4:13). Noting God's judgment in Deuteronomy 32:35–36, the writer concludes that in judgment unbelievers "fall into the hands of the living God" (Heb. 10:31). Peter describes it as coming before "the face of the Lord" (1 Pet. 3:12), or as giving "account to him who is ready to judge the living and the dead" (1 Pet. 4:5).

Judgment ultimately means separation from God's relational presence. The images and metaphors used in Hebrews and the General Epistles to portray judgment could be interpreted to support either an eternal conscious torment or an annihilationist view, but always they involve an exclusion from God's presence. Judgment is described variously as a land that is cursed (Heb. 6:8), as a fire that consumes (Heb. 10:27; 12:29; 2 Pet. 3:7; Jude 7, 23), as destruction (Heb. 10:39; 2 Pet. 2:1, 3, 12; 3:7, 10, 12, 16; Jude 5, 10), as condemnation (2 Pet. 2:3; Jude 4), and as blackest darkness (2 Pet. 2:17; Jude 13). Very often, usually in the larger flow of the letter, judgment is juxtaposed with salvation, exclusion from presence contrasted with the eternal experience of presence (e.g., throughout Hebrews but summarized in Heb. 10:39; 1 Pet. 4:17–18; 2 Pet. 3:12–13; Jude 21).

Conclusions

The New Testament Letters find their theological center in the theme of God's relational presence. In Paul's Letters, Hebrews, and the General Letters we see virtually the same thematic pattern: God's revelatory presence; his incarnational presence; his presence centered in the gospel of salvation; his presence through the Holy Spirit and his people, the church; his sustaining presence; and his eschatological presence. We also see a special emphasis in Paul through his union-with-Christ theme and in Hebrews through the motif of Christ's priestly presence. Both adapt God's relational presence in powerful ways for their readers.

Paul stresses God's revelatory presence through his words and the message of the gospel in particular. So many of Paul's famously loaded theological

terms—such as justification by faith, righteousness, redemption, reconciliation, and adoption (to name a few)—are rooted in the gospel of God's relational presence made known in Jesus Christ. At the heart of Paul's Damascus-
road experience we find a relational confrontation with the risen Christ, a
relationship that goes a long way toward explaining Paul's emphasis on union
with Christ throughout his writings.

Hebrews and the General Letters likewise stress God's incarnational presence in Christ, and this God-with-us theme leads to a God-for-us high priestly
emphasis especially in Hebrews. We now participate in a new and better covenant through the sacrifice of Jesus Christ, our great high priest.

God's relational presence through the Holy Spirit and his people, the
church, occupies a central place in this section of the New Testament. The
Spirit as God's empowering presence among us fulfills God's long-standing
promise to live among his people permanently. The Spirit's work leads naturally to the reality of the people of God, the church. Paul's leading metaphors
for church (family, temple, and body) reflect the mighty work of the Spirit.
We find a similar emphasis in 1 Peter with Peter's focus on the people of God
as a "spiritual house," a "royal" and "holy priesthood," "a holy nation," and
"God's special possession" (1 Pet. 2:5, 9).

Both in Paul and in Hebrews and the General Letters, God's sustaining
presence stands strong. Paul conceives of God's sustaining presence in the life
of the believer and the community in straightforward and encouraging terms
(i.e., strengthening; comforting; offering grace, mercy, and peace), while the
writer of Hebrews speaks of receiving grace and finding Sabbath-rest. James
stresses the sustaining power of God's wisdom practiced in community.

God's eschatological presence plays a crucial role in this section as well.
Paul's eschatological gospel features the return of Christ, the resurrection of
believers, the reality of judgment and reward, the full realization of salvation, and life in the new creation. God's inheritance is his people; the blessed
hope is Christ coming for his people. Eschatology dominates Paul's theology.
Hebrews and the General Letters, especially 1 Peter, also stress God's eschatological presence. In 1 Peter such a presence features a living hope, and in
Hebrews access to God's presence anchors faith. The promise of eternal rest
describes life in God's presence. Christ's return full of glory and joy brings
final salvation to his people. In contrast, these letters also stress the reality of
separation from God's presence through judgment for unbelievers. But the
focus remains on hope.

We turn now to trace the theme of God's relational presence through
the remainder of the New Testament literature: John's Gospel, Epistles, and
Apocalypse.

SIX

The Relational Presence
of God in John's Gospel,
Epistles, and Apocalypse

The Johannine corpus offers a magnificent vantage point from which to survey God's relational presence among his people.[1] Whether it is God's incarnational presence through the Word made flesh or God's sustaining presence through the ministry of the Paraclete, God's helping presence and discipleship to Jesus or God's eschatological presence as both a present and future reality, God's relational presence in John's Gospel takes center stage. As in his Gospel, John communicates the theme of God's relational presence in his Epistles through a complex and dynamic interweaving of themes. Knowing God and being born of God relate to eternal life, which connects to God's eschatological presence, which ties to believing God and keeping his commands, both of which relate to the role of the Holy Spirit, and so on. Discerning the details is much like trying to identify the various strands of color in a rushing river in full sunlight—beautifully complex. Last, we turn our attention to the many ways in which God's relational presence surfaces in John's Apocalypse: trinitarian, prophetic, incarnational, sustaining, and eschatological. Holding true to the final chapter of the story, this section unveils the final fulfillment of God's long-standing promise to live among his people forever in the new creation.

1. We attribute authorship of the Gospel of John, the Letters of John, and Revelation to the apostle John.

John's Gospel

God has revealed himself as Creator, Communicator, Father, and Sender. He reveals himself in order to establish a personal relationship with his people. God goes to the relational extreme with his incarnational presence in Jesus Christ, the Son. Quite literally, God has spoken in Jesus (i.e., the Word made flesh), and especially through Jesus's signs and "I am" sayings. Jesus as the Son sent by the Father and as the new temple makes God's presence immediately available. Jesus also comforts and encourages his disciples through teaching about God's sustaining presence, made available through the coming ministry of the Holy Spirit and the present community of disciples. Eschatologically speaking, God's life-giving presence as both a present and a future reality shines through. Disciples can begin to experience eternal life in Jesus, and one day they will live with him in God's presence in the place prepared for them.

God's Elusive Yet Revealed Presence

In John's Gospel "God remains hidden, his presence elusive."[2] His only spoken words are found in John 12:28: "I have glorified it, and will glorify it again." Nevertheless, God makes his relational presence known throughout this Gospel in dramatic ways. First, God is the Creator. He creates all things through his Word, bringing light and life to humanity (1:1–3; cf. Gen. 1:1–3), allowing human beings to become his children and experience his presence (1:12–13). With more subtlety than Paul, John depicts a theology of new creation, and, again, as Jeannine Brown observes, "The cumulative effect of these [new creation] motifs indicates that John intends to communicate that in Jesus, the Messiah, the completion and renewal of God's creative work have arrived."[3] God is indeed bringing his light and life-giving presence to the world.

Second, God is the Communicator. Whether through God's word (Israel's Scriptures), the Word (Jesus Christ), or the Holy Spirit, God makes himself known to humanity.[4] God reveals himself in order to rid creation of darkness and death and make possible a relationship through Jesus Christ. The primary point of God's communication of himself and his will is that human beings experience his relational presence.

2. Koester, *The Word of Life*, 25. See also M. Thompson, *The God of the Gospel of John*.
3. J. Brown, "Creation's Renewal in the Gospel of John," 290. See also the extensive discussion in Köstenberger, *A Theology of John's Gospel and Letters*, 336–54.
4. On these three avenues of communication, see Koester, *The Word of Life*, 26–30.

Third, God is the Father. Jesus refers to God as his Father throughout John's Gospel.[5] God is portrayed as the Father of Jesus, with Jesus referring to God as "my Father" (almost 40 times) or "the Father" (more than 80 times). All that Jesus does, he does as the Son of the Father. The Father offers his love and life to humanity through the Son. What's more, God is called the Father of believers, but not until after the resurrection of Jesus: "I am ascending to my Father and your Father, to my God and your God" (20:17). The Father's aim is that people will respond to him in faith and become his beloved children (1:12–13; 3:3–8).

Lastly, God is the Sender. God sends John the Baptist, Jesus, and the Spirit, and this sending represents an act of presence, as Craig Koester notes: "We find that as God sends others, he goes with them. God does not send others into the world in order that he might remain comfortably absent from it. God is in the middle of things, so that even in the face of conflict Jesus can affirm that the 'one who sent me is with me; he has not left me alone' (8:29; 16:32). Sending is an action of the God who is present, not a God who is absent."[6] John identifies the Father as the one who sent Jesus, or the Son as the one sent by the Father or by God.[7] Sometimes the Father is identified primarily as the one who has sent the Son (5:23, 24, 37; 6:44, 57; 7:29; 8:18, 26, 42; 10:36; 11:42; 17:25). At other times the focus is on Jesus's works as originating from the Father (3:17; 4:34; 5:36; 6:29, 38–39; 9:4). Jesus speaks the words of God, meaning that his teachings come from the Father (3:34; 7:16, 28; 12:49; 14:24; 17:8), and what is needed is to believe in or know the one whom the Father has sent (5:38; 12:44; 13:20; 15:21; 17:3, 21, 23). Jesus pleases the Father (5:30; 8:16, 29), clearly reflects the Father (12:45), and is returning to the Father (7:33; 16:5). All in all, this theme of the Son sent by the Father provides a richly textured emphasis on God as the one who reveals his presence primarily in the person of Jesus Christ.

Even from this brief survey of the character of God in John's Gospel—God as Creator, Communicator, Father, and Sender—we come away with a picture of God as one who makes known his presence for the purpose of relationship. The Father gives his one and only Son (3:16) so that the world may have

---

5. The term πατήρ (*patēr*, father) is used 136 times in John's Gospel, and in most of those instances (120 or so) the term refers to God. No other New Testament book comes anywhere close.

6. Koester, *The Word of Life*, 33.

7. He does so primarily using the terms πέμπω (*pempō*, about 24 times) and ἀποστέλλω (*apostellō*, about 17 times). For πέμπω, see 4:34; 5:23, 24, 30, 37; 6:38, 39, 44; 7:16, 28, 33; 8:16, 18, 26, 29; 9:4; 12:44, 45, 49; 13:20 (2x); 14:24; 15:21; 16:5. For ἀποστέλλω, see 3:17, 34; 5:36, 38; 6:29, 57; 7:29; 8:42; 10:36; 11:42; 17:3, 8, 18, 21, 23, 25; 20:21. See the excursus "The Two Johannine Words for Sending," in Köstenberger, *The Missions of Jesus and the Disciples*, 97–106.

"eternal life"—that is, to "know the only true God and Jesus Christ whom he has sent" (17:3). God the Creator communicates through his tabernacling Word so that all who believe might become children of God (i.e., experience his relational presence).

God's Incarnational Presence

The primary way God makes his presence known in John's Gospel is through his Son, Jesus Christ. As Jesus tells Philip, "Anyone who has seen me has seen the Father" (14:9). This emphasis begins early on in John, as the prologue concludes with this bold pronouncement: "No one has ever seen God, but the one and only Son, who is himself God and is in closest relationship with the Father, had made him known" (1:18). The Greek term for "made known," ἐξηγήσατο (exēgēsato), from which we derive the term "exegesis," strongly communicates what Richard Bauckham calls "the most distinctive aspect of John's Christology: the incarnation as revelation of God."[8] This "incarnational-revelatory Christology of John," Bauckham says, "provides the most all-encompassing theological framework for reading Jesus's story, in all the Gospels, as the story of God with us."[9]

God reveals himself by speaking in a supremely personal and tangible way: "In the beginning was the Word, and the Word was with God, and the Word was God" (1:1). And this Word of God, who was with God in the beginning and through whom God created all things, became flesh (σάρξ, sarx) and made his dwelling (σκηνόω, skēnoō) among us (1:1–3, 14). Andreas Köstenberger reminds us that John's theology of the Word is deeply rooted in the OT portrayal of the word of God as God's self-expression or speech. This explains why John's prologue links creation to incarnation as prime examples of God's revealing presence.[10]

This "word" moves past bare-bones information to personal encounter.[11] Interestingly, Revelation uses the same term for "shelter" or "tabernacle over" (σκηνόω) to picture God's presence among his people. In Revelation 7:15 God shelters the great multitude in heaven "with his presence" (σκηνώσει ἐπ' αὐτούς, skēnōsei ep' autous). In 13:5–6 the beast blasphemes God and slanders his name and his dwelling place or tabernacle (σκηνή, skēnē), meaning his people, people with heavenly citizenship. And in 21:3 we see God's dwelling place (σκηνή) among the people as he dwells (σκηνόω) with them. The only

---

8. Bauckham, *Gospel of Glory*, 198.
9. Bauckham, *Gospel of Glory*, 201.
10. Köstenberger, *A Theology of John's Gospel and Letters*, 338–41.
11. Koester, *The Word of Life*, 27.

use of the verb σκηνόω outside of Revelation appears in John 1:14, where God's incarnational presence takes center stage.[12]

John concludes 1:14 with his first mention of "glory": "We have seen his glory [δόξα, *doxa*], the glory of the one and only Son, who came from the Father, full of grace and truth." In the NT δόξα can mean either "honor, prestige, reputation" or "visible splendor" in the sense of glorious presence.[13] The second meaning is in view here. People not only heard the Word; they saw and touched him (1 John 1:1–3). As one of us (Danny) wrote, "The whole point of building the tabernacle is to create a proper place for the presence of God to dwell in the midst of his people and to travel with them. The climax of the tabernacle story in Exodus is the actual occupation of the tabernacle by God (Exod. 40:34–38)."[14] The same occurs at the completion of Solomon's temple (1 Kings 8:10–11), yet God's occupation of the latter is much more cautious. What could not be accomplished through the tabernacle or the temple is fulfilled in Jesus. At last, the fiery, glorious presence of God, barely glimpsed by Moses and kept hidden in the tabernacle and temple, has now become visible in Jesus, fulfilling passages like Isaiah 40:5: "And the glory of the Lord will be revealed, and all flesh [σάρξ] will see the salvation of God, because the Lord has spoken" (LXX, our translation). Also, the connection to the Shekinah glory of God's presence that covered God's people during their wilderness journey is hard to miss (e.g., Exod. 13:21–22; 33:7–11; 40:34–38). John makes it clear that God's glorious presence is now revealed personally and powerfully to all the people, allowing them to see the face of God in Jesus.[15] Jesus is God's Shekinah.[16]

We also see God's incarnational presence manifested through Jesus's "signs":

- changing water into wine—"the first of these signs through which he revealed his glory" (2:1–11);
- healing the official's son—"Your son will live" (4:46–54);
- healing the lame man on the Sabbath—"'My Father is always at work to this very day, and I too am working.' . . . He was even calling God his own Father, making himself equal to God" (5:2–18);

12. See Koester, *The Dwelling of God*, 102. Koester argues that the verb σκηνόω is a play on words that embraces both "flesh" and "glory," and he concludes that "tabernacle imagery is uniquely able to portray the person of Jesus as the locus of God's Word and glory among humankind."

13. Bauckham, *Gospel of Glory*, 43–62, 72–74.

14. J. D. Hays, *The Temple and the Tabernacle*, 59.

15. So Koester, *The Word of Life*, 25. Koester observes that "in the crucified and risen Jesus, they [readers] are called to see the face of God."

16. Frey, "God's Dwelling on Earth," 97.

- feeding the five thousand—"I am the bread of life" (6:2–15, 35);
- healing the blind man on the Sabbath—"I am the light of the world" and "the light of life" (9:1–12, 39; 8:12);
- raising Lazarus—"I am the resurrection and the life" (11:1–45);
- resurrection of Jesus—"Jesus performed many other signs in the presence of his disciples, which are not recorded in this book. But these are written that you may believe that Jesus is the Messiah, the Son of God, and that by believing you may have life in his name" (20:1–31).

Glory, healing, life, provision, light, resurrection—all signposts to God's presence. These miracles point beyond the obvious act of power to something greater, to the glorious presence of God at work in the person of Jesus.

Closely related to Jesus's signs are his seven "I am" sayings (statements featuring the phrase ἐγώ εἰμι, *egō eimi*).[17] The phrase, of course, is an allusion to the Old Testament revelation of Yahweh, the God who is personally present. There are the more familiar "I am" sayings followed by predicates: "I am the bread of life" (6:35, 48), "the light of the world" (8:12; 9:5), "the gate for the sheep" (10:7, 9), "the good shepherd" (10:11, 14), "the resurrection and the life" (11:25), "the way and the truth and the life" (14:6), and "the true vine" (15:1). In addition, there are seven absolute "I am" sayings without a predicate:

Then Jesus declared, "I, the one speaking to you—*I am he*." (4:26)

But he said to them, "*It is I*; don't be afraid." (6:20)

"I told you that you would die in your sins; if you do not believe that *I am he*, you will indeed die in your sins." (8:24)

"When you have lifted up the Son of Man, then you will know that *I am he* and that I do nothing on my own but speak just what the Father has taught me." (8:28)

"Very truly I tell you," Jesus answered, "before Abraham was born, *I am*!" (8:58)

"I am telling you now before it happens, so that when it does happen you will believe that *I am* who I am." (13:19)

"Jesus of Nazareth," they replied. "*I am he*," Jesus said. . . . When Jesus said, "*I am he*," they drew back and fell to the ground. Again he asked them, "Who

17. See the discussion in Bauckham, *The Testimony of the Beloved Disciple*, 243–50.

is it you want?" "Jesus of Nazareth," they said. Jesus answered, "I told you that *I am he*." (18:5–8)

While it's possible to read several of these as normal statements of identification (i.e., "Hey, it's me"), given John's penchant for double meanings and the significance of the number seven in his writings, it also makes good sense to take all seven as a second set of "I am" sayings loaded with christological significance. While the signs reveal God's glory in Jesus, the two sets of sayings seem to make explicit the significance of the signs.[18] According to Richard Bauckham, these two sets of sayings express divine identity, where Jesus is "unambiguously identifying himself with the one and only God, YHWH, the God of Israel."[19] Jesus is the one who can reveal God's relational presence to the world.

John stresses God's incarnational presence in Jesus in various other ways. Two deserve special mention: Jesus as the Father's agent sent to carry out his work, and Jesus as the new temple.[20] We have already mentioned that Jesus is the Son sent by the Father, and this speaks volumes about God's character as Sender (see above). Also, Jesus's explicit "I have come" remarks remove any doubt about his incarnational purpose. He has come from God (8:42; 16:28) or "in my Father's name" (5:43), meaning that he has come as God's authorized representative.[21] Theologically speaking, Jesus serves as God's representative in the sense that he incarnates God's divine presence. Jesus has come to do the Father's will, by giving eternal or resurrection life to all who believe (6:38–40; 10:10), through healing and restoring (9:39), by bringing light and salvation to those in darkness (12: 46), and by bearing witness to the truth (18:37).

The allusion to glory in the prologue prepares the reader for John's portrayal of Jesus throughout his Gospel as the new temple of God's presence. Marianne Thompson writes, "Insofar as it understood Jesus to be the manifestation of God's glory and presence, early Christianity validates 'sacred space,' while nevertheless 'relocating' it and rendering it metaphorically. The symbols of Judaism that are used to explicate his identity [chiefly, temple] are therefore taken up into the person of Jesus, the Messiah of Israel."[22] God had promised to dwell among his people in a new temple (e.g., Ezek. 37:26–28; 43:7–9; Zech. 2:10–11), and John sees this promise fulfilled initially in Jesus,

18. Bauckham, *The Testimony of the Beloved Disciple*, 250.
19. Bauckham, *The Testimony of the Beloved Disciple*, 247.
20. For an overview of temple symbolism in John, see Coloe, *God Dwells with Us*.
21. Keener, *The Gospel of John*, 660.
22. M. Thompson, *The God of the Gospel of John*, 217.

ironically, against the backdrop of the destruction of the Jerusalem temple in AD 70. The following passages point to John's portrayal of Jesus as the new temple:[23]

- The Word became flesh and "made his dwelling" among us (1:14).
- Jesus will rebuild the temple in three days, the temple of his body (2:19, 21).[24]
- True worshipers are not tied to a physical location but rather will worship "in the Spirit and in truth" (4:23–24; cf. 14:6, 9–11).
- In connection with the Feast of Tabernacles and while teaching in the temple courts, Jesus announces that he is the source of living water and the light of the world, images connected to the temple (7:37–38; 8:12; 9:5).
- In the context of the Feast of Dedication, Jesus claims to give eternal life to his followers and to be one with the Father, thus claiming to be God's Son (10:27–38).
- Jesus claims that the Father is in him rather than indwelling the Jerusalem temple, implying that he is the new temple of God (10:38; 14:10–11, 20; 17:21).

God now communicates his relational presence through Jesus, the new temple, a presence no longer restricted to a physical location but now embodied in a person.[25] Jesus becomes the new center of worship, and the coming of the Spirit to followers of Jesus extends the imagery of the new temple beyond his death and resurrection (see below).

God's incarnational presence in Jesus is painted in bright colors through John's Gospel, so that "salvation is construed primarily as knowing God, as participation in God's life, and as having fellowship with God through the one in whom God's presence became embodied in this world."[26] Nevertheless, as Jesus said to his disciples after Mary had anointed his body for burial, "You will always have the poor among you, but you will not always have me" (12:8). Later he refers again to his coming absence: "I will be with you only a little longer. You will look for me, and just as I told the Jews, so I tell you now: Where I am going, you cannot come" (13:33). Against the

23. For more discussion of these and other texts, see Köstenberger, *A Theology of John's Gospel and Letters*, 425–31.
24. See Perrin, *Jesus the Temple*, 80–113.
25. Walker, *Jesus and the Holy City*, 168.
26. M. Thompson, *The God of the Gospel of John*, 240.

backdrop of God's powerful incarnational presence in Jesus and prior to Jesus's eschatological presence, what provision has God made for his people to experience his presence?

God's Sustaining Presence

John's Gospel also speaks of God's sustaining presence and does so in two complementary ways: discipleship to Jesus, including the role of community; and the ongoing work of the Holy Spirit. These two interrelated emphases function almost like two perspectives on the same reality: the one from above (the Spirit) and the other from below (discipleship). We begin with the work of the Holy Spirit.

Sustaining Presence through the Holy Spirit

In John's Gospel the Holy Spirit plays a significant and varied role in sustaining God's people. The Spirit enables people to enter a relationship with God to begin with (1:33; 3:4–8, 34), facilitates true worship (4:23–24), and brings life (6:63; 7:37–39). The Spirit's sustaining presence figures even more prominently in the second half of the Gospel. Jesus's identification of the Spirit as "another παράκλητος" (*paraklētos*), or another (of the same kind) "helping Presence," suggests that "the Spirit's presence with the disciples will replace Jesus' encouraging and strengthening presence with them while on earth"[27] (cf. 14:18 ["*I* will not leave you as orphans; *I* will come to you"]; 16:7).

As "another helping Presence," the Spirit will be with Jesus's disciples forever in an intimately personal way by living not just *with* them but *in* them (14:16–17). Although Jesus is leaving them to prepare a dwelling place (μονή, *monē*) for them (14:2–3), he assures them that he and the Father will come and make their home (μονή) with them (14:23), surely referring to the indwelling of the Spirit. And this is a permanent personal presence: the Spirit will "be with you forever," Jesus says (14:16). The Spirit will testify about Jesus, remind the disciples of his teachings, guide them into all truth, and disclose what is to come (14:26; 15:26; 16:13). The Spirit certainly functions as the presence of Jesus among his people, especially with regard to teaching and revealing God's word.

Perhaps surprisingly, the Spirit also manifests the Father's presence to the disciples: testifying to Jesus (15:26–27), glorifying Jesus (16:14), sustaining

---

27. Köstenberger, *A Theology of John's Gospel and Letters*, 396. We're indebted to Köstenberger for his translation of παράκλητος as "helping Presence."

the disciples (14:17), convicting the world of judgment (16:8–11), and teaching (14:26; 16:13)—all functions also associated with the Father. Thompson rightly contends, "The primary conception of the Spirit that runs throughout the Gospel is that of the Father's life-giving power that has been granted to and is conferred through the Son. . . . The 'theological' coloring of the Spirit both precedes and undergirds the 'Christological' shaping."[28]

The final reference to the Spirit in John features Jesus empowering his disciples for the mission ahead by "breathing" (ἐνεφύσησεν [*enephysēsen*] has no direct object here) and then telling his disciples to "receive the Holy Spirit" (20:22)—most likely a symbolic act anticipating the full outpouring of the Spirit soon to come at Pentecost.[29] Jesus is, in a real sense, telling his disciples that God's powerful presence that has been at work in him will soon continue that work through them. In sum, the Spirit's role is to make God's presence known to the community of Jesus's disciples between the ascension of Jesus and his second coming. As Craig Koester notes, although the Spirit does not take Jesus's place (e.g., no incarnation, no crucifixion), the risen Christ does make his sustaining presence known to the community of faith through the presence of the Spirit.[30]

Sustaining Presence through Discipleship to Jesus

Whereas God sustains his people through his Holy Spirit, from a more ecclesiological perspective God also manifests his relational presence through discipleship to Jesus, a theme that surfaces repeatedly in John's Gospel. At the heart of discipleship to Jesus stands a relational encounter with the presence of Jesus. "Follow me" opens and closes the entire book (1:43; 21:19, 22). As Koester observes, when it comes to discipleship, John provides no list of vices or virtues, no detailed set of exhortations, no comprehensive discipleship manual. Rather, he hones in on the love relationship between the Lord and his followers.[31] This is borne out in Jesus's relationships with individuals such as Nicodemus, the Samaritan woman, Mary and Martha, Mary Magdalene, and Peter, but also through powerful images of new community: the shepherd

---

28. M. Thompson, *The God of the Gospel of John*, 186. See also M. Thompson, *John*, 318–22.

29. Köstenberger, *A Theology of John's Gospel and Letters*, 400. Köstenberger notes that the exact same form of the verb for "breathe" (ἐνεφύσησεν, *enephysēsen*) is used in LXX Gen. 2:7, where God breathes his Spirit into Adam at creation, thus closing the circle "from creation in John 1:1 to new creation in 20:22."

30. Koester, *The Word of Life*, 148, 150. Morris writes, "The Spirit is the divine presence when Jesus' physical presence is taken away from his followers" (Morris, *Jesus Is the Christ*, 159).

31. Koester, *The Word of Life*, 188.

and the flock (10:1–42), the love command and the footwashing (13:1–17, 34–35; 15:12, 17), and the vine and the branches (15:1–17).

Images of a New Community. The image of the shepherd and the flock expresses relational presence in a number of ways: (1) the sheep know the shepherd's voice as he leads them by name and they follow (10:3–4, 16, 27); (2) the shepherd provides nourishment, protection, and abundant life (10:9–10); (3) the personal relationship between the good shepherd and the sheep is grounded in the intimate relationship between the Father and the Son (10:14–15);[32] (4) the shepherd gives his life for the sheep and eternal life to the sheep (10:15, 28); (5) the Son (shepherd) and the Father provide eternal security for the sheep (10:28–29); and (6) there is one flock and one shepherd (10:16). Relational presence lies at the heart of this captivating image.

On the evening of the Lord's Supper Jesus becomes not just the guest but also a slave as he takes up the towel and washes his disciples' feet. When Peter strongly objects to participating in this embarrassing act, Jesus warns him, "Unless I wash you, you have no part with me" (13:8), likely meaning that a failure of discipleship here would result in a failure to share in Jesus's eschatological presence (cf. 14:1–3; 17:24). Jesus then issues his love command, symbolized powerfully by the footwashing: "You also should wash one another's feet" (13:14), and "As I have loved you, so you must love one another" (13:34) (cf. 15:12, 17). This image, along with the love command that it illustrates, speaks of the transformative power of presence, both in the life of the disciple and in the community of loving servants.

Perhaps more than any other, the metaphor of the vine and the branches (15:1–17) portrays the "organic unity between Jesus and his disciples."[33] This viticulture image stresses an interchange of presence in almost every verse: "Remain in me, as I also remain in you" (v. 4). To "remain" (μένω, *menō*) is "to be present with and for someone" and points to a "wholeness in relationship."[34] Thompson notes that abiding features a receptivity or an "openness and responsiveness to Jesus' life-giving presence."[35] Being united to Jesus's presence results in bearing fruit, obedience to Jesus's teachings, and love within the community.

Responding to Jesus Individually. Along with John's emphasis on the corporate experience of God's relational presence through key community

---

32. Carson, *The Gospel according to John*, 387.
33. Köstenberger, *A Theology of John's Gospel and Letters*, 503. Köstenberger notes that the image of the vine and the branches in John comes close to the Pauline "body of Christ" metaphor.
34. Koester, *The Word of Life*, 195.
35. M. Thompson, *John*, 325.

images, he also stresses the individual's experience of God's presence. John employs a variety of terms and expressions to highlight this aspect of discipleship.[36] Individuals are challenged to follow Jesus by engaging in specific *actions*:

- believing in Jesus and his message (e.g., 3:15–18, 36; 6:35, 40, 47; 7:37–38; 11:25–26; 12:44; 14:12)
- believing the Father, who sent Jesus (e.g., 5:24)
- coming to Jesus (e.g., 6:37)
- loving Jesus (e.g., 14:21, 23–24)
- accepting/obeying Jesus's word or teachings (e.g., 3:33; 8:51; 14:21)
- following Jesus (e.g., 8:12)
- living by the truth (e.g., 3:21)
- doing the will of God (e.g., 7:17)
- serving Jesus (e.g., 12:25–26)

Individuals are also challenged to follow Jesus through actions associated with specific metaphors:

- being born again / from above (3:3, 5)
- drinking living water (4:13–14; 7:37)
- eating the bread of life (6:35, 51, 54–58)
- walking in the light (8:12; 12:46)
- entering through the gate that is Jesus (10:9)
- remaining in Jesus (15:5–6)

The *results* of these actions of faithful discipleship point clearly to God's relational presence:

- have eternal life (e.g., 3:15–16, 36; 4:14; 5:24; 6:40, 47, 54, 57–58; 11:25; 12:25)
- never experience spiritual death (e.g., 8:51–52; 11:26)
- experience light (e.g., 3:21; 8:12)
- not stay in darkness (e.g., 12:46)

36. See the significant chapter by Bauckham on individualism in *Gospel of Glory*, 1–19. Bauckham identifies sixty-seven sayings in five different grammatical forms that draw attention to the individual believer's relationship to Jesus.

- experience salvation rather than condemnation (e.g., 3:18; 10:9)
- be loved by God (e.g., 14:21, 23)
- experience the kingdom of God (e.g., 3:3, 5)
- know God's self-revelation (e.g., 14:9, 21)
- receive the Holy Spirit (e.g., 7:37–39)
- be spiritually satisfied (e.g., 4:13–14; 6:35)
- have a fruitful life (e.g., 14:12; 15:2, 5)
- have a secure relationship with Jesus rather than abandonment (e.g., 6:37; 14:18)
- have an enduring relationship with Jesus (e.g., 6:56)
- be honored by the Father (e.g., 12:26)
- live in a place in God's home prepared by Jesus (e.g., 14:23)
- be with Jesus (e.g., 12:26)
- experience resurrection on the last day (e.g., 6:40, 44)

These results characterize a thriving relationship: life (versus death), love and a secure relationship (versus abandonment), light (versus darkness), knowing God (versus rejection), spiritual satisfaction and fruitfulness, honor, enduring personal presence, and resurrection. This is relational language at its deepest and richest.

Thus far in John's Gospel we have noted the presence of God the Father, God's incarnational presence in Jesus, and God's sustaining presence manifested in the Holy Spirit and discipleship to Jesus, both communally and individually, and now we conclude with a survey of God's eschatological presence.

God's Eschatological Presence

Near the end of John's Gospel Jesus prepares the disciples for his departure. Earlier he had told the Jewish leaders that he was going away and that they would be unable to find him or follow him (7:33–34; 8:21). In contrast, he now informs his disciples that he is going away (13:33, 36a), but he quickly assures them that he is going to prepare a place for them and will come back and take them to be with him (13:36b; 14:2–3). Then in chapter 17 Jesus prays, "Father, I want those you have given me to be with me where I am, and to see my glory" (v. 24). Jesus's departure provides the occasion for his teaching about last things, and divine presence plays a crucial role.

Even a cursory reading of John's Gospel has led many interpreters to focus on his realized or inaugurated eschatology, the view that the blessings of the age to come are available now to Jesus's disciples.[37] The assumption has been that John has adopted the temporal framework of the Synoptic Gospels and is simply collapsing the future into the present. But a closer reading suggests that John's thought is a bit more nuanced.

Marianne Thompson rightly proposes that John's eschatology is a function of his Christology and, ultimately, of his theology.[38] The primary implication is that in John's eschatology what is present is more than the future; it is the "life-giving presence of the living God."[39] John is making the point that "the knowledge and presence of God are manifested through and made accessible in the presence of Jesus Christ."[40]

In one sense, the future has indeed invaded the present, and future eschatology remains alive and well in John's Gospel. But the "future" is often defined in terms of experiencing God's relational presence. In the person of Jesus Christ end-time blessings such as eternal life are available now for those who are, by faith, rightly related to Jesus.[41] John commonly portrays this new eschatological reality using contrasting images: light versus darkness, salvation instead of condemnation, life rather than death, and so on. He very often casts this invasion in the language of relational presence.

Eternal life provides the dominant benefit or blessing of John's eschatology, and this life begins now for those who have put their faith in the Son (3:16–18).[42] They experience salvation rather than condemnation (3:16–17). They have crossed from death to life (5:24), a life fundamentally defined by encounter with God's presence. Knowing the only true God and Jesus Christ, whom he sent, *is* eternal life (17:3; cf. 1 John 5:20), and this knowledge moves beyond mere intellectual assent to include trust, relationship, and communion. Eternal

---

37. Traditionally championed by Dodd, *The Interpretation of the Fourth Gospel.*
38. M. Thompson, *The God of the Gospel of John,* 82.
39. M. Thompson, *The God of the Gospel of John,* 86.
40. M. Thompson, *The God of the Gospel of John,* 86.
41. Köstenberger, *A Theology of John's Gospel and Letters,* 297. Köstenberger also comments, "John likely replaced Jesus' end-time teaching found in the Synoptic Olivet Discourse (Matthew 24 pars.) and the pervasive Synoptic emphasis on the kingdom of God with an eschatology that focused on the experience of eternal life in Jesus through the Spirit already in the here and now."
42. In John's Gospel "eternal life" is defined as a relationship with the one true God through Jesus Christ (17:3). Eternal life is a *present experience.* It is given by the Father and the Son (5:21, 26; 17:2). It is found in the Son rather than in the Scriptures (5:39–40). It involves a transfer from death to life (5:24, 29) and cannot be disrupted by death (8:51). It is available to everyone who believes (3:15–16, 36; 4:14; 5:24; 6:47, 50, 51; 20:31). Jesus as the bread of life given by the Father sustains his followers with life (6:27, 32–33, 54). Jesus as the good shepherd came that his people might have full and abundant life (10:10, 28). But eternal life is also a *future expectation,* especially associated with resurrection. A time is coming when the dead will hear the voice of the Son of God and live (5:25, 28–29). Eternal life is resurrection life (6:40; 11:21–27, 32, 41–44).

life is an overflow of the fellowship that exists between the Father and Son (1:18; 10:30; 14:7; 17:11, 22–23). Believers have been born of the Spirit (3:5, 6, 8), who flows through them like rivers of living water (7:38–39). They are true worshipers in Spirit and in truth (4:23–24). Being in relationship to the one who is the "resurrection and the life" means that they will never die (6:50; 8:51; 11:25–26). The life, death, resurrection, and glorification of Jesus inaugurate this new experience, and Jesus repeatedly says that the hour of his glorification has arrived (12:23, 28, 31–32; 17:1, 3–5). The relational presence of God is brought forward into the personal experience of those who follow Jesus through the ministry of the Spirit, God's helping presence.

Nevertheless, John still finds room to stress futurist eschatology, and he does so in terms of God's relational presence. In 1:51 Jesus tells Nathaniel (and likely the rest of the disciples, given the plural pronoun and verb) that they will see "heaven open, and the angels of God ascending and descending on the Son of Man." Jesus, the Son of Man, is the connection between heaven and earth. In the underlying Genesis 28 story of Jacob's vision, Jacob awakens to the thought that "the LORD is in this place" and so names the place the "house of God" or "gate of heaven" or "Bethel" (vv. 16–17, 19). This means, as Craig Keener puts it, that "Jesus is Jacob's ladder," the one who mediates between heaven and earth.[43] The fact that Jesus is God's house or dwelling place (the personal means of access to God's presence) serves as another reminder that Jesus is the new temple.[44] Jesus's promise is likely fulfilled, as G. R. Beasley-Murray suggests, in the whole sweep of his saving ministry, from heaven opening at his baptism to his glorious parousia.[45]

The balance of the Johannine texts reflecting futurist eschatology make two central points. First, the faithful will experience a future bodily resurrection. "A time is coming," Jesus says, "when all who are in their graves will hear [the voice of the Son of Man] and come out," some to experience life, others to face condemnation (5:28–29). Jesus mentions his return on several occasions (e.g., 14:3; 21:22–23), and at his return he promises to raise his followers from the dead. In his discourse on the bread of life, in John 6, Jesus promises at least four times that he will raise his people on the last day (vv. 39, 40, 44, 54; cf. vv. 57, 58). Present and future eschatology become one reality at the raising of Lazarus, reported in John 11. While Jesus no doubt affirms the Jewish belief in future bodily resurrection, he makes it clear that he himself *is* the

---

43. Keener, *The Gospel of John*, 489.
44. Keener, *The Gospel of John*, 489–90.
45. Beasley-Murray, *John*, 28. Helyer contends that "the eschatological dimension of this saying should be neither minimized nor eliminated" (Helyer, *The Witness of Jesus, Paul and John*, 350).

resurrection and the life (11:25; cf. 5:25). These complementary realities are experienced only in relationship to Jesus (14:19). His presence is what makes resurrection life possible, and death is no threat to that relationship.

The second point of emphasis related to futurist eschatology is that Jesus promises his followers a future home in the presence of God. In John 14 Jesus tells the disciples that he is going to the Father's house to prepare a place for them (vv. 2–3, 28). A misreading of this text has no doubt led many a saint to dream about decorating his or her own mansion in heaven. The "Father's house" likely refers to the presence of God in the sense of the new creation, perhaps even using language of the new temple.[46] In the Father's presence there will be many places to live, an abundance of space for God's entire family.

But the mention of place quickly gives way to the priority of personal relationship. Jesus reassures his disciples, "If I go and prepare a place for you, I will come back and take you to be with me [πρὸς ἐμαυτόν, pros emauton] that you also may be where I am" (14:3). He later prays that his followers will be "with me [μετ' ἐμοῦ, met' emou] where I am," where they can see his glory (17:24). As Craig Koester notes, "Where one would expect Jesus to say, 'I will come again and take you to heaven,' he says, 'I will take you to myself.'"[47] In John's Gospel all eschatological roads lead to an experience of God's presence through a relationship with Jesus Christ.

John's Epistles

The varied themes of John's Epistles all point to God's relational presence and cohere around John's emphasis on the mutual indwelling of God with his people.[48] John's indwelling language takes two main forms. First, he uses the verb "remain" or "live" (μένω, menō) twenty-seven times in 1–3 John, mostly to emphasize God's relational presence.[49] As Stephen Smalley points out, "The use of μένειν [menein] at this point suggests an intensely personal knowledge of God; it presupposes an intimate and committed relationship with him, through Jesus, which is both permanent and continuous."[50] God's people remain in Jesus or God, and God or Jesus remains in him. God's people remain or live in the word of God or truth, in love and in light, and these

---

46. Beale, *The Temple and the Church's Mission*.
47. Koester, *The Word of Life*, 184.
48. Malatesta, *Interiority and Covenant*.
49. This verb is a favorite of John, who uses μένω 40 times in his Gospel, a verb used a total of 118 times in the NT.
50. Smalley, *1, 2, 3 John*, 52.

realities remain in them. John emphasizes the reciprocity or mutuality of the indwelling—not only is God in us, but we are also in God.[51] The people of God experience this mutual indwelling through the Holy Spirit, who remains in them, guaranteeing them eternal life.

The second way John speaks of God's indwelling presence is through his "in" or "with" language, including a good deal of overlap with the verb "remain."[52] God's people are "in the Father/Son," as well as "with him." The Father/Son is "in us," and we are "in him." Whoever loves lives in God, and his love is made complete among us. The Holy Spirit lives within us, and God's truth/word/light lives in us. What is striking again is the mutual or reciprocal nature of these expressions. The rule rather than the exception is that God dwells within his people *and* they dwell in/with God. God's presence in 1–3 John is portrayed as relational to the core.

John visits over and over in these letters several major aspects of God's relational presence: Jesus the incarnate Son and the eternal life, believing the truth, the role of the Holy Spirit, obeying and knowing God, and love. Throughout, John's main concern, as Karen Jobes points out, is that "Jesus Christ, God's Son, has come from God the Father to die as the atoning sacrifice for sin, and on the basis of his self-sacrifice, to create for God a new covenant people who will both know him and enjoy eternal life with him."[53]

Jesus, the Incarnate Son and the Eternal Life

Jesus, the Incarnate Son of God

In language reminiscent of the prologue to John's Gospel, 1 John begins with a straightforward pronouncement of God's incarnational presence in Jesus (1:1–4): we have seen, heard, and touched the Word of life, the eternal life, which was with the Father from the beginning and has now appeared. Deceivers and liars and antichrists have failed to acknowledge that Jesus has come in the flesh (2:22; cf. 2 John 7), whereas the true people of God acknowledge that the Son of God "appeared" (ἐφανερώθη, *ephanerōthē*) and did so to take away sins and destroy the devil's work (3:5, 8). The verb "appeared" in 1 John refers to Jesus's making himself known in the incarnation (1:2; 3:5, 8) or at his second coming (2:28; 3:2). Jesus came to bring people into fellowship (κοινωνία, *koinōnia*) with the Triune God and with one another as

---

51. Lieu, *The Theology of the Johannine Epistles*, 44.

52. See 1 John 1:3, 5, 8, 10; 2:1, 5–6, 8, 10, 14, 19, 24, 27–28; 3:3, 5–6, 9, 15, 17, 24; 4:4, 12–13, 15–17; 5:11, 20; 2 John 2–3.

53. Jobes, *1, 2, & 3 John*, 339. Jobes labels this the "preeminent theological point of John's letters" and one that is "consistent with the overarching message of the NT in general."

God's people (e.g., 1:3: "We proclaim to you what we have seen and heard, so that you also may have fellowship with us. And our fellowship is with the Father and with his Son, Jesus Christ"). As a result, God's incarnational presence in Christ is proclaimed so that God's people may share in his relational presence, as Constantine Campbell observes: "The wording . . . hints at the idea of fellowship *within the Godhead* [cf. John 14:10]. . . . God is a God of relationship, and that is why the goal of John's proclamation is fellowship."[54]

God has come to his creation in Jesus (1 John 4:2), and these three testify to Jesus's incarnation: "the Spirit, the water and the blood" (5:6, 8), most likely a reference to Christ's birth or perhaps baptism (water), his death (blood), and the Holy Spirit.[55] The one who embraces the truth that Jesus is the Son of God incarnate is now open to a relationship with God.[56] First John 4:15 states it plainly: "If anyone acknowledges that Jesus is the Son of God, God lives in them and they in God." Acceptance of the gospel of the incarnate Son leads to this mutual indwelling: "As for you, see that what you have heard from the beginning remains in you. If it does, you also will remain in the Son and in the Father" (2:24). God's incarnational presence proves essential to God's work of salvation, since without it the cross becomes meaningless and we are still in our sins. God's incarnational presence in Jesus also makes possible our experience of eternal life in Jesus, yet another aspect of God's presence.[57]

Jesus, the Eternal Life

John emphasizes "life" and "eternal life," a theme that opens and closes his first letter (1:1–2; 5:11–13, 16, 20) and is closely related to God's incarnational presence.[58] The incarnate Son is identified early on in 1 John as "the Word of life," "the life," and "the eternal life" (1:1–2). Life or eternal life is ultimately personal and relational because Jesus *is* "the eternal life," the one who was with the Father and has now appeared (1:2; cf. John 1:4; 5:26; 11:25; 14:6). John says, "God has given us eternal life, and this life is in his Son" (1 John 5:11), a statement that sounds remarkably similar to John 17:3: "Now this is

---

54. C. Campbell, *1, 2 & 3 John*, 25.

55. The traditional view of water as a symbol of new life and the beginning of life at birth makes the most sense because the sacramental view flies in the face of the aorist participle "the one who came" (ὁ ἐλθών, *ho elthōn*) in 5:6, and the "water = Spirit" interpretation fails to give a natural reading of the three witnesses listed in 5:8. See Witherington, *Letters and Homilies for Hellenized Christians*, 542–46. Witherington suggests that this text refers to the incarnation.

56. Jobes writes, "Fellowship with God would not be possible without the historical fact of the incarnation" (Jobes, *1, 2, & 3 John*, 196).

57. Jobes, *1, 2, & 3 John*, 343.

58. See the helpful excursus "A Note on Eternal Life" in Kruse, *The Letters of John*, 184–87.

eternal life: that they know you, the only true God, and Jesus Christ, whom you have sent."

After announcing that the life is in the Son, John declares, "Whoever has the Son has life; whoever does not have the Son of God does not have life" (1 John 5:12). "Having the Son" constitutes having eternal life and involves being "indwelt by the Son,"[59] as John says clearly in 5:20: "And we are in him who is true by being in his Son Jesus Christ. He is the true God and eternal life." Possessing eternal life reflects an ontological experience of a core aspect of God's being and character, his relational presence, his life. This experience entails passing from death to life (3:14) and out from God's judgment (4:16–17). In contrast, not having the Son (i.e., not having eternal life) results in remaining in death or coming under God's judgment (5:12; cf. John 3:16, 36; 5:24, 29; 10:28). John spends much of his first letter unpacking what it means to "have the Son," a reality that relates to believing the truth, being indwelt by the Holy Spirit, obeying and knowing God, and especially loving. As we look more at how the people of God experience this eternal life, one thing remains certain: God's relational presence lies at the center of John's concept of eternal life found in Jesus Christ.

Believing the Truth: Personal and Relational

Because of the threat from the false teachers and those who had left the fellowship, John begins by calling attention to the trustworthy and true gospel message originally entrusted to the community. The concluding purpose statement in 1 John 5:13 explicitly centers on belief in the Son: "I write these things to you who believe in the name of the Son of God so that you may know that you have eternal life" (cf. John 20:31, the purpose statement in John's Gospel, which also features belief). In emphasizing the true gospel, John refers to "the truth" (1 John 1:6, 8; 2:4, 8, 21; 3:19; 2 John 2, 3, 4; 3 John 1, 3, 4, 8, 12), "the word of life" or "[Jesus's] word" or "the word of God" or "the message" (1 John 1:1, 10; 2:5, 7, 14), Jesus's commands (1 John 2:3–4, 7–8; 3:22–24; 5:2–3; 2 John 4, 6), "what you have heard from the beginning" (2:24), and the "teaching of Christ" or "the teaching" (2 John 9–10; cf. "our testimony" in 3 John 12).

What stands out is that this truth is "in us/you" or "not in us/you," depending on a person's relationship to Jesus (1 John 2:8, 23; 4:2–3, 15; 2 John 7). John has no interest in describing an isolated, external truth or word that fails to connect relationally with people. This truth or message is ultimately

---

59. Kruse, *The Letters of John*, 186.

personal and relational. The Word made flesh has appeared, and the proper response, according to John, is to believe in this Jesus-centered message or truth (Jesus's "name" or person in 1 John 3:23; cf. 5:10). Those who do so are born of God, overcome the world, and can rest assured that they have eternal life (5:1, 5, 13). It's the indwelling truth or word, believed and embraced, that gives the people of God the experience of God's relational presence, both now and eternally.

Being Born of, Knowing, and Obeying God

The theme of God's relational presence connects to John's emphasis on the Christian life in even more personal ways. He uses highly relational language such as being "born of God" or "knowing God" to show how God himself personally engages with his children and reorients them to his own life of love, light, truth, purity, righteousness, and so on.[60] Presence lies at the heart of these images.

John speaks of being "born of God" in 1 John 2:29; 3:9; 4:7; 5:1, 4, 18. The birth image reassures believers of their theological conviction about Jesus (5:1) and highlights aspects of their relationship to God. Those who love demonstrate that they have been born of God (4:7), as does everyone who does what is right and refuses to continue in habitual sin (2:29; 3:9; 5:18). Also, those who have been born of God have overcome the world and its false prophets (5:4; cf. 4:4). As Judith Lieu observes, the birth image conveys certainty and security in the relationship: "To be born of God is also to be possessed of a certain assurance. Birth cannot be reversed, neither does it happen by stages or in degrees!"[61] The background is likely the picture of God in the OT as Father to the children of Israel, an image reflecting relational intimacy (e.g., Deut. 32:6; Isa. 63:16; Mal. 1:6).[62] When used of believers, the verb γεννάω (gennaō) appears only in the perfect tense in 1 John, showing that the new birth precedes the practice of righteousness.[63] God draws his people into a spiritual relationship with himself through Christ and implants his very life, the life of his presence, in them, thereby enabling them with the spiritual resources necessary to live abundantly and faithfully.[64]

John's familial imagery continues with the idea of knowing God. When John speaks of knowing God, he intends a personal knowledge of God, as

60. M. Thompson, 1–3 John, 21.
61. Lieu, The Theology of the Johannine Epistles, 34.
62. Smalley, 1, 2, 3 John, 134.
63. T. Schreiner, The King in His Beauty, 535.
64. Marshall, New Testament Theology, 539–40, 546.

Lieu notes: "As in the Fourth Gospel, . . . knowledge [in John's Letters] denotes relationship rather than factual knowledge or perception of reality.
This is equally true in the Old Testament, where knowledge of God involves
acknowledgment, confession and obedience (Jer. 31:33–34)."[65] John writes
to his dear children because they "know the Father" (1 John 2:13–14), and
to the "fathers" in the community because they "know him who is from the
beginning" (2:13). These believers could know that they belong to the truth
and set their "hearts at rest in his presence" because they know God and he
knows them (3:19–20). Although the phrase "in his presence" (v. 19) could
refer to the eschaton, it most likely refers to the believer's life with God in the
here and now. When our hearts condemn us, God is greater than our hearts,
and this knowledge provides the confidence to persuade our hearts to listen
to God rather than the inner voice of accusation. Finally, the reason Jesus
came, John says, was to give his people understanding and enable them to
know him who is true and to be "in him who is true by being in his Son Jesus
Christ" (5:20). Knowing God is personal and relational.

Knowing God also relates directly to truth (see above on believing the
truth). Karen Jobes observes that the concept of truth is "central to both
John's gospel and letters, in which the Greek words for 'truth' and 'knowing' are mentioned almost two hundred times."[66] This truth is "in you"
(1 John 2:8) and "you know the truth" (2:20), John tells his readers. The
truth, he says, "lives in us and will be with us forever" (2 John 2). The
truth is personal and is directly connected to Jesus and a right belief about
Jesus (1 John 4:6), to the Holy Spirit (3:24; 4:2, 6, 13), and to love (4:7–8,
16; 5:2).

Being born of God and knowing God also point us to the notion of obedience to God's commands. Those who have come to know God relationally will
keep his commands, do what is right, purify themselves, and reject habitual
sin (1 John 2:3–5, 29; 3:3, 5–6, 9; 5:2). The commands of God are centered in
Jesus, and a believing obedience remains christocentric (1 John 2:7–8; 3:23;
2 John 4). Keeping God's commands and pleasing him are directly related to
answered prayer (1 John 3:22).

Experiencing God's relational presence means being and living "in God"
(1 John 2:5–6; 4:15–16) or being indwelt by truth (2:8). Such an experience
is genuine for those who obey his word and live as Jesus lived (2:5–6). Along
with belief in Jesus as the incarnate Son of God, the love commands take
center stage among the commands of God.

65. Lieu, *The Theology of the Johannine Epistles*, 32.
66. Jobes, *1, 2, & 3 John*, 340.

God's Love and Divine Presence

Love constitutes one of the main themes of John's Letters. The root form ἀγάπ- (*agap-*) occurs 62 times, with the verb form ἀγαπάω (*agapaō*) appearing 31 times and the noun form ἀγάπη (*agapē*) 21 times. Howard Marshall says that in 1–3 John "love is thematized in a way that is unparalleled elsewhere in the New Testament."[67] Love also connects strongly to the presence theme. For starters, God's love for us demonstrated through Jesus Christ supplies the foundation of any response we might have to God or others (1 John 3:16; 4:9–10). "This is love," John says, "not that we loved God, but that he loved us and sent his Son as an atoning sacrifice for our sins" (4:10). The Father's great love enables us to become "children of God," to become part of God's family (3:1; cf. 5:1). God is love, and "whoever lives in love lives in God, and God in them" (4:16). God's love works "among us," supplying confidence on the day of judgment (4:17). The relational emphasis continues: since love comes from God, everyone who loves "has been born of God and knows God" (4:7), but whoever does not love "does not know God, because God is love" (4:8). God's love for his people provides the foundation for our becoming his children, knowing him, and returning his love.

God's love is to be reciprocated, according to John, who stresses that those who claim to love God will demonstrate their love by obeying his word or commands (1 John 2:5; 5:3; 2 John 6). Believers' love, in other words, flows out of their relationship with God and affects their ethical conduct. They will live like Jesus (1 John 2:6; 4:17). The reverse is true for unbelievers. The love of/for the Father is not found in "anyone who loves the world" (2:15). Those who do "not do what is right" are not God's children; they don't belong to God's family (3:10). God's primary command in the letters is to believe in Jesus and to love one another (3:23). This leads to the final connection between love and divine presence: loving one another.

"We love because he first loved us" (1 John 4:19), John writes, as a way of saying that those who truly love God will love their spiritual siblings as well. Also, "Since God so loved us, we ought also to love one another" (4:11; cf. 2 John 5). The one who believes in Jesus is born of God, and "everyone who loves the father loves his child as well" (5:1), meaning other members of God's family. When people fail to love fellow believers, whom they can see, how can they claim to love God, whom they can't see (4:20)? The relational connection between love for God and love for brothers and sisters in Christ should not be broken, and this connection surfaces repeatedly throughout John's Letters (e.g., 4:21). Whoever loves "lives in the light" (2:10). Those who

67. Marshall, *New Testament Theology*, 538–39.

love have "passed from death to life" (3:14). Everyone who loves "is born of God and knows God" (4:7). When we love one another, "God lives in us and his love is made complete in us" (4:12). Whoever "lives in love lives in God and God in them" (4:16). In contrast, those who refuse to love don't belong to God's family (3:10), don't know God (4:8), and don't love God (4:20); they remain in spiritual death (3:14).

To see the prominence of God's relational presence in the love theme throughout John's Letters, try removing all the touch points to presence from what John says and see what is left. Very little. God's love for his people, their resulting gratitude shown in obedience, and their love for one another are all rooted and grounded in his dynamic and relational presence among his people.

Personal Communion with the Holy Spirit

God's truth, centered in Jesus as the incarnate Son of God, is made real in human experience by the Holy Spirit (1 John 4:6; 5:6).[68] Although John doesn't speak much about the Spirit in his letters, what he does say makes an important contribution to our presence theme. As Edward Malatesta concludes, "Personal communion with the Holy Spirit is a touchstone of Christian interiority."[69] The foundation of the Spirit's work is his endorsement of Jesus as the incarnate Son. We can recognize the Spirit of God as the one who "acknowledges that Jesus Christ has come in the flesh" (4:2). This is indeed the "Spirit of truth" (4:6). The Spirit, along with water and blood, bears witness to Jesus as the incarnate Son of God (5:6, 8). Believers should be comforted by the Spirit's testifying work because the one who is in them (the Triune God effected by the Spirit) is greater than the spirit of the antichrist, which is in the world (4:3–4).

John highlights the Spirit's vital work of assurance in 1 John 2:20, 27. Here he reassures his readers that they "have an anointing from the Holy One," an anointing that is "real, not counterfeit," and one that "remains" in them and "teaches" them about all things. For this reason, John reminds them that they "know the truth," and the desired response is to "remain in him," with "him" referring either to the anointing (possible) or to Jesus (more likely in light of 2:28). The consistent use of the verb "anoint" (χρίω, chriō) in the

---

68. Kruse notes that the primary role of the Spirit is to testify to the tradition (i.e., the gospel of Jesus proclaimed from the beginning) rather than to bring any new revelation as claimed by those who were pulling away from the church in John's context (Kruse, *The Letters of John*, 155). For a fuller treatment of the Spirit in John's writings, see Burge, *The Anointed Community*.

69. Malatesta, *Interiority and Covenant*, 279.

NT points to God as the anointing agent whose medium is the Holy Spirit (Luke 4:18; Acts 4:27; 10:38; 2 Cor. 1:21–22; cf. the metaphorical use in Heb. 1:9).[70] For this reason, most interpreters conclude that the "anointing" in 1 John 2:20, 27 refers to the Holy Spirit. As Gary Burge points out, "One of the chief arguments against the interpretation that sees this anointing as only the word of God or the orthodox kerygma is that this anointing dwells within the believer."[71] John's encouragement in this context also sounds remarkably similar to Jesus's teaching in John 14:26: "But the Advocate, the Holy Spirit, whom the Father will send in my name, will teach you all things and will remind you of everything I have said to you" (cf. John 14:17; 15:26; 16:13). Knowing God and his truth is directly connected to the work of God's presence in the believer made real by the Holy Spirit.

John continues to emphasize the Spirit's role in assuring believers in 1 John 3:11–24, especially verse 24: "The one who keeps God's commands lives in him, and he in them. And this is how we know that he lives in us: We know it by the Spirit he gave us." He adds a parallel in 4:13: "This is how we know that we live in him and he in us: He has given us of his Spirit." One of the Spirit's primary roles is to assure believers of God's presence in their lives and their presence in his. As Stephen Smalley says, "By sharing in the Spirit of God . . . we can receive the assurance of a personal (spiritual) relationship with God himself."[72] The Spirit's presence in the believer is proof of God's presence in the believer. As Colin Kruse observes, this mutual abiding in God involves more than keeping God's commands and suggests a "new and very real spiritual existence" that is "effected through the agency of the Spirit."[73]

We find another likely reference to the Spirit in the puzzling words of 1 John 3:9: "No one who is born of God will continue to sin, because God's seed [σπέρμα, sperma] remains in them; they cannot go on sinning, because they have been born of God." Interpretations of "God's seed" vary widely, and we cannot be dogmatic here, but in our view the Holy Spirit provides the best option. It naturally follows that the birth image echoes Jesus's teachings in John 3, and the connection there is to the Spirit.[74] We conclude with Kruse that the Spirit is the likely referent "in the light of the fact that the new birth is effected by God through the Spirit, and it is

70. Kruse, *The Letters of John*, 103; Jobes, *1, 2 & 3 John*, 127; Schnackenburg, *The Johannine Epistles*, 151; Marshall, *The Epistles of John*, 153.
71. Burge, *The Anointed Community*, 175.
72. Smalley, *1, 2, 3 John*, 250.
73. Kruse, *The Letters of John*, 143.
74. Burge, *The Anointed Community*, 176.

the Spirit who in Johannine theology remains with and in believers."[75] The Spirit's presence in and among disciples plays a significant role in motivating their obedience, a theme that also illustrates God's relational presence among his people.

John's Apocalypse

God's relational presence runs both deep and wide throughout this majestic and mysterious book that is Revelation—the Apocalypse of John. While God's eschatological presence remains most prominent, there are a number of other, extremely significant aspects to God's relational presence: his trinitarian, prophetic, incarnational, and sustaining presence. It's also interesting to see the same theological message of presence wrapped in prophetic-apocalyptic language. We begin with how God has revealed himself as a triune community who extends an invitation to his creation to enter into relationship with the perfect community.

God's Trinitarian Presence

The theme of presence in Revelation is grounded in the very nature and character of the Triune God, who makes himself known. The opening greeting begins with grace and peace being extended from "him who is, and who was, and who is to come, and from the seven spirits before his throne [likely a reference to the sevenfold Holy Spirit], and from Jesus Christ" (1:4–5a). F. F. Bruce notes that the placement of the "seven spirits" between God and Christ, who in Revelation shares many of God's attributes, indicates that "something more than a reference to angels is implied."[76] Richard Bauckham observes that "among early Christian letter-openings, John is unique in giving the standard form of salutation a 'trinitarian' character."[77]

The identification of God as "him who is, and who was, and who is to come" occurs three times in Revelation (1:4, 8; 4:8), and Bauckham notices how John has departed from all other instances of the formula, both Jewish and Greek, in preferring the present participle ("the one who is coming") over the future form ("will be"). In doing so, John stresses not just God's future

75. Kruse, *The Letters of John*, 125. See also Burge, *The Anointed Community*, 176.
76. Bruce, "The Spirit in the Apocalypse," 336.
77. Bauckham, *The Theology of the Book of Revelation*, 24. This is not to read the fully developed patristic theology back into Revelation but merely to observe that John conceives of the divine reality that includes God the Father, Jesus the Son, and the Holy Spirit, an understanding that contributed to the later trinitarian formulation.

existence but his future coming into the world.[78] It's not surprising, then, that the "is to come" element is omitted from the final two instances in the book (11:17; 16:5), since God's presence has already arrived in those contexts. The upshot is that John begins the book by portraying God in a way that stresses not just his eternal nature but also his presence with his creation:

> Thus John interprets the divine name as indicating not God's eternity in himself apart from the world, but his eternity in relation to the world. This is the biblical God who chooses, as his own future, his coming to his creation, and whose creation will find its own future in him (cf. 21:3). Moreover, this interpretation of the divine name is in significant continuity with the meaning of Exodus 3:14 [LXX: Ἐγώ εἰμι ὁ ὤν, *Egō eimi ho ōn*, "I am the one who is"], which most probably is referring not to God's self-existence purely in himself so much as to his commitment to be who he will be in his history with his people. John has characteristically developed that early Israelite faith in God's historical being for his people into the later, eschatological faith in God's final coming to bring all things to fulfilment in his eternal future.[79]

The language of the Almighty, who has cared for his people throughout time and now comes to save and to judge, echoes many OT passages (e.g., Ps. 96:13; Isa. 26:21; 40:10; Mic. 1:2–4; Zech. 14:5) and fits well with Revelation's emphasis on God's final coming (see "God's Eschatological Presence" below).

We see other examples of God's trinitarian presence throughout the book, and usually these also point toward his coming eschatological presence. In Revelation 7 the great multitude that has come out of the great tribulation stands before the throne serving (worshiping) God while being sheltered in his presence (v. 15). They will never again hunger or thirst or face the scorching heat, "for the Lamb at the center of the throne [the Son] will be their shepherd; he will lead them to springs of living water [the Spirit?]. And God [the Father] will wipe away every tear from their eyes" (v. 17). God's people will then experience the caring, protective relational presence of the Triune God. We see a similar reference in 22:1 when the angel shows John the "river of the water of life, as clear as crystal, flowing from the throne of God and the Lamb."

Regarding God's relational nature, Ryan Lister writes, "God's transcendence and immanence both exist because of his Trinitarian nature. The eternal intra-Trinitarian relationship that exists between the Father, Son, and Holy Spirit reveals that God is self-fulfilled relationally and needs nothing outside

---

78. Bauckham, *The Theology of the Book of Revelation*, 29.
79. Bauckham, *The Theology of the Book of Revelation*, 30.

of this fellowship. . . . This intimacy between the members of the Trinity forms the basis of God's immanent relationship with the created order. . . . In other words, the relations between God and the world emanate directly from the relations between the persons of the Trinity."[80] Although it is the least explicit of all aspects of God's relational presence in Revelation, his trinitarian presence provides the basis or grounding for the other aspects of his relational presence.

God's Prophetic Presence

A Prophetic Prologue and Epilogue

As the title of the book states, this is the "revelation" (ἀποκάλυψις, *apokalypsis*) of Jesus Christ (1:1). The Triune God, because his very nature is relational and communicative, makes his presence known. He does so, at least in part, through his prophetic word. To begin with, the prophetic inclusio of the book's opening and closing reaffirms God's intent to make his presence known through revelation. There are at least seven verbal links between the letter's opening and closing, demonstrating how the book is framed by a focus on God's revelation of himself and his plan to his people:

- The revelation originates with God (1:1; 22:6).
- The revelation is to be shown (δείκνυμι, *deiknymi*; 1:1; 22:6, 8) and made known (σημαίνω, *sēmainō*; 1:1).
- The events of the revelation will take place soon (1:1; 22:6).
- The revelation has been mediated through angels (1:1; 22:6, 8, 16) and John (1:1; 22:8–21).
- The revelation is rooted in God's word (1:2–3; 22:6–7, 9–10, 18–19).
- The revelation is a prophetic word written down and communicated to the churches (1:3; 22:6–7, 9–10, 18–19).
- A blessing is pronounced on those who hear and obey this prophetic word (1:3; 22:7, 9).

The revelation from God to Jesus to his angel to John to the churches supplies the primary point of emphasis in the opening and closing of the book. Whatever else the book of Revelation may be, it certainly is a communication from God to his people, an extension of his gracious and truthful presence to people facing the challenge of enduring faithfully.

---

80. Lister, *The Presence of God*, 47.

God's prophetic presence appears throughout the body of the letter as well, especially in connection with John's visionary experiences, the messages to the seven churches, and communicative actions of angels.

John's Visionary Experiences

On numerous occasions John himself has pneumatic, visionary experiences that play a crucial role in communicating God's message to his people. It's interesting that the aorist, active, indicative, first-person, singular form is used 87 times in Revelation, and with few exceptions (usually with Jesus as the subject—e.g., 2:21; 3:9, 21; 22:16) most of these relate that John either "saw" (εἶδον, *eidon*; over 40 times) or "heard" (ἤκουσα, *ēkousa*; almost 30 times) some aspect of the revelation.[81] When you scan these occurrences and their contexts for explicit purpose statements, the results again center on prophetic revelation (e.g., 1:11, 19; 4:1; 5:1–7; 6:9; 10:11; 19:10; 22:8–10, 16).

In addition, on four occasions John is said to be "in the Spirit" (1:10; 4:2; 17:3; 21:10). He is "in the Spirit" on the Lord's day (i.e., during worship), when he receives the vision of the exalted Christ (1:10–18). He hears a loud voice like a trumpet instructing him to write on a scroll what he sees and send it to the seven churches. The visionary journey continues "in the Spirit" as John witnesses and writes about God's throne room (4:2), Babylon the great (17:3), and the new Jerusalem (21:10). Throughout redemptive history God often tells his servants to write down the revelation in order to communicate it to his people (e.g., Exod. 17:14; Isa. 30:8; Jer. 30:2; 36:2). An echo of OT prophetic language, especially from the experience of Ezekiel, also lends weight to John's prophetic authority to pass on a message inspired by the Spirit of the Lord (e.g., Ezek. 2:2; 3:12, 14, 24; 8:3; 11:1, 24; 37:1; 43:5).[82]

John's visionary experiences were prophetic ones in that he heard and saw what God gave him to communicate to his servants. The relational presence of God provides a visionary experience for John and then through John provides an engaging literary and spiritual experience of God's presence for his readers.[83]

---

81. The other occurrences feature different actions by John (i.e., turned around, fell, went, took, ate, was astonished, have seen) or Jesus (have given, have loved, was victorious, sat down, have sent).

82. Beale, *The Book of Revelation*, 203–4.

83. Bauckham writes, "Out of his visionary experience John has produced a work which enables the reader, not to share the same experience at secondhand, but to receive its message transposed into a literary medium" (Bauckham, *The Climax of Prophecy*, 159).

The Messages to the Seven Churches

Key elements within the seven messages highlight the theme of God's prophetic presence. First, the command "write" is repeated in each case and serves at least three purposes: (1) to make the messages accessible for readers living in other places; (2) to make the message definite, emphasizing that the promises will be kept; and (3) to preserve the messages for the future.[84] Second, each message comes from the glorified Christ and serves as part of his "revelation" (1:1–2). Third, many scholars have noted how the messages resemble OT prophetic letters from Elijah and Jeremiah (e.g., 2 Chron. 21:12–15; Jer. 29:4–23, 24–28, 30–32) that feature warnings, encouragement, and promises. Just as God was trying to draw Israel back to himself through the prophets, so Revelation with its seven messages serves the same relational purpose of communicating the holy love of God to his people.[85] Fourth, each letter ends with the statement that whoever has ears should "hear what the Spirit says to the churches." As G. K. Beale notes, "The formula also shows that Christ's words are none other than the words of the Spirit and that Christ dwells among the churches through the Spirit."[86] The admonition to hear what the Spirit says is also reminiscent of Jesus's prophetic call: "Whoever has ears, let them hear" (e.g., Mark 4:9, 23; Matt. 11:15; 13:9, 43; Luke 8:8; 14:35). In Revelation the prophetic word from Christ comes through the Spirit and, perhaps by extension, through Spirit-inspired Christian prophets.[87] A similar emphasis appears in 19:10b, which probably should be translated, "For the witness of Jesus is the Spirit of this prophecy." In other words, God the Spirit is the source of this prophetic message about and from Jesus (i.e., the book of Revelation).[88] Fifth, the letters conclude with eschatological promises to the victors, promises that offer God's eternal presence with all its attendant blessings to those who persevere (2:7, 11, 17, 26–28; 3:5, 12, 21). Although the promises are expressed differently in each letter, they are all versions of the final promise that the victors will enjoy God's relational presence forever (e.g., 21:3, 7; 22:2–4).[89]

---

84. Koester, *Revelation*, 244.

85. See Osborne, *Revelation*, 106.

86. Beale, *The Book of Revelation*, 234.

87. Bauckham concludes, "Thus the Spirit of prophecy speaks through the Christian prophets bringing the word of the exalted Christ to his people on earth, endorsing on earth the words of heavenly revelations, and directing the prayers of the churches to their heavenly Lord" (Bauckham, *The Climax of Prophecy*, 160).

88. Taking μαρτυρία Ἰησοῦ (*martyria Iēsou*) as a plenary genitive, much like ἀποκάλυψις Ἰησοῦ Χριστοῦ (*apokalypsis Iēsou Christou*) in 1:1. See Wallace, *Greek Grammar beyond the Basics*, 119–21.

89. Beale, *The Book of Revelation*, 234.

Communicative Actions of Angels

Apocalyptic literature often features angelic mediators, and Revelation is no exception. Of the 175 uses of the term ἄγγελος (*angelos*) in the NT, 67 occur in the Apocalypse. (The angelic activity is even greater if the elders and living creatures are also considered to be angelic beings.) The emphasis throughout falls on communication. Christ makes known the revelation through his angel to his servant John (1:1; 22:6, 8), the revelation that is a testimony for the churches (22:16). Angels mediate the visions and offer insight into the meaning of the symbols (e.g., 5:2–5; 7:13–14; 10:9; 14:6–7; 17:1, 7, 15–18; 19:9–10; 21:9; 22:1, 6, 9). The revelation, the scroll, the little scroll, the eternal gospel, and the testimony for the churches all revolve around God's grand purpose of judging evil and living among his people in a new creation.

God's Incarnational Presence

Revelation shows that the incarnational presence of God in Jesus Christ stands as a central element of his plan to rescue and live among his people eternally. While Revelation stresses Jesus's exalted and glorified status, it also affirms his incarnation as a significant aspect of God's presence. In chapter 12 we read about a woman who "gave birth to a son, a male child who 'will rule all the nations with an iron scepter'" (12:5; cf. 12:13). The birth of the Christ child signals the beginning of God's incarnational presence. The dominant images for God's incarnational presence are Jesus as the faithful witness, the Lamb, and the firstborn from the dead.

The earliest description of Jesus in Revelation is as "the faithful witness" (1:5). The message to the Laodicean church designates Jesus as "the Amen, the faithful and true witness, the ruler of God's creation" (3:14). Jesus's role as the faithful witness refers both to his mediation of God's revelation and, perhaps more emphatically, to his witness to God's truth through his resulting death.[90] Although the term "witness" (μάρτυς, *martys*) probably was not a technical term to indicate martyrdom in Revelation, μάρτυς and μαρτυρία (*martyria*, testimony) are used consistently in connection with the suffering and death that result from bearing a true and faithful witness (e.g., 2:13; 6:9; 11:3, 7; 12:17; 17:6; 20:4). The God-with-us Jesus is our supreme example of being a faithful witness.

The image of Jesus as the Lamb also communicates God's incarnational presence among his people.[91] Richard Bauckham contends that "the role of

---

90. Mounce, *The Book of Revelation*, 48.

91. "Lamb" (ἀρνίον, *arnion*) is the major title for Jesus in Revelation, which has 29 of the 30 NT occurrences, with all but 13:11 referring to Jesus.

Christ in Revelation is to establish God's kingdom on earth" (cf. 11:15) and that this is "a work of both salvation and judgment."[92] Both aspects are manifestations of God's presence, and the work of salvation centers on the Lamb's sacrificial death. The Lamb is the "slain" Lamb, who shed his blood as a means of defeating everyone and everything opposed to God's rule, once and for all, so that nothing may hinder his relationship with his people (e.g., 5:6, 9, 12; 7:14; 11:8; 12:11; 13:8).

Lastly, the bodily resurrection of Jesus also affirms the incarnational presence of God in Christ. Revelation describes Jesus as the "firstborn from the dead" (1:5); the "Living One," who was dead but is now "alive for ever and ever" (1:18); and the "First and the Last, who died and came to life again" (2:8). Jesus's victory (νικάω [*nikaō*] in 3:21; 5:5) most certainly includes his resurrection. All three images—faithful witness, the Lamb, and the firstborn from the dead—describe God's presence in Jesus: his life, death, and resurrection.

God's Sustaining Presence

Revelation portrays God with his people, and his sustaining presence takes two primary forms in the book: God's presence with the saints in heaven and his presence with the saints on earth.

God's Sustaining Presence in Heaven

God's sustaining presence in heaven can be a bit confusing due to the visionary and apocalyptic nature of Revelation. Should we, for example, view God's presence with the great multitude in chapter 7 or with the 144,000 in chapter 14 as his presence with them during the intermediate state, or should we take these as proleptic visions of the eternal state? The overall emphasis that God is with his heavenly people is clear, regardless of whether we see these as examples of his sustaining or his eschatological presence.

There are a surprising number of references to God's sustaining presence with his heavenly people. When the fifth seal is opened, John sees the souls of martyred believers in heaven (6:9–11). They are located "under the altar" (6:9), a place associated with God's protective presence. They cry out to God (6:10), a reminder that God readily hears and will soon answer their prayers. Each of them is given a white robe, a symbol of purity and victory, and told to "rest" (ἀναπαύω, *anapauō*) until the final resurrection. In other words, they are safely and securely in God's presence.

---

92. Bauckham, *The Theology of the Book of Revelation*, 67.

The great multitude in 7:9–17 stands before the throne of God and before the Lamb (7:9). They also are wearing white robes and holding palm branches, both symbols of victory (7:9), and we later learn that they have "washed their robes and made them white in the blood of the Lamb" (7:14). These who cry out in praise to God and the Lamb (7:10) are subsequently identified as those "who have come out of the great tribulation" (7:14). Most significantly, we are told that they are "before the throne of God and serve him day and night in his temple," and that "he who sits on the throne will shelter them with his presence" (7:15). The heavenly temple is consistently connected with God's presence in Revelation (e.g., 21:3–4, 22; 22:3; cf. Ezek. 37:26–28). And it is God's very presence that is said to "shelter" or "tabernacle over" his people (σκηνώσει ἐπ᾽ αὐτούς, *skēnōsei ep᾽ autous*; cf. John 1:14), an image recalling God's protection and guidance of his people during their wilderness journey when he covered them with the presence of his Shekinah glory (e.g., Exod. 13:21–22; 33:7–11; 40:34–38).[93] Part of what this protective presence includes is spelled out in 7:16–17: "'Never again will they hunger; never again will they thirst. The sun will not beat down on them,' nor any scorching heat. For the Lamb at the center of the throne will be their shepherd; 'he will lead them to springs of living water.' 'And God will wipe away every tear from their eyes.'" The people of God drawn from every nation, tribe, people, and language will experience God's Shekinah presence in the eternal holy of holies that is the new Jerusalem (21:3, 15–18, 22).

In chapter 14 the Lamb is standing with the 144,000 on Mount Zion, a symbol for God's dwelling place. The 144,000 have the Lamb's name and the Father's name written on their foreheads, indicating that God's people belong to him in a secure and permanent relationship. They celebrate God's mighty acts of deliverance with a new song "before his throne"—in his presence (14:3). Joseph Mangina writes, "God is both infinitely worthy of praise and himself harmonious, so that the creature who exists in his presence cannot but break out into song."[94] These "firstfruits to God and the Lamb" (14:4) are safely sequestered in his protective presence.

In close proximity to this glorious portrayal of the Lamb with his people on Mount Zion are three series of judgments in 14:6–11 on those who follow the beast. Then the call goes out for God's people to endure in faithfulness to Jesus (14:12), followed by the second of seven beatitudes in the book: "'Blessed are the dead who die in the Lord from now on.' 'Yes,' says the Spirit, 'they will

---

93. Revelation has a total of seven occurrences of the terms σκηνόω (*skēnoō*) (7:15; 12:12; 13:6; 21:3) and σκηνή (*skēnē*) (13:6; 15:5; 21:3).

94. Mangina, *Revelation*, 172.

rest from their labor, for their deeds will follow them'" (14:13). The Spirit's "yes" shows the importance of the blessing of rest reserved for those who "die in the Lord" (cf. the rest for the martyrs in 6:11). The promise is reminiscent of the Sabbath-rest described in Hebrews 4:1–11. The rest associated with dying "in the Lord" surely includes life in God's presence as they await the final resurrection.

Another example of God's sustaining presence with the saints in heaven occurs just prior to the bowl judgments. We read in chapter 15 about those who had been victorious over the beast, now standing on the sea of glass and holding harps given them by God as they celebrate God's character and mighty acts. The victors' location is significant because the "sea of glass" may recall for readers the bronze "sea" of Solomon's temple used by the priests for ceremonial washing (1 Kings 7:23–44; 1 Chron. 18:8; 2 Chron. 4:2–6). The temple imagery, reflected in the rest of Revelation (e.g., 7:15; 11:19; 14:15–17; 15:5–16:1, 17), portrays the victors as standing in the very presence of God (cf. 4:6).[95]

God's Sustaining Presence on Earth

God's sustaining presence with his people on earth is conveyed by the glorified Christ among the churches, the ministry of the Holy Spirit, and other means such as answers to prayer, spiritual protection, and nourishment.

The Glorified Christ among the Churches. Following the vision of the glorified Christ "among the lampstands" in 1:12–18, we read of Christ communicating God's presence to the churches in chapters 2–3. The expression τάδε λέγει (*tade legei,* these are the words of) is a stock formula common in the LXX when OT prophets introduce sayings from God (τάδε λέγει κύριος: "thus says the Lord"). G. K. Beale concludes that the use of the formula in all seven messages "emphasizes that Christ assumes the role of Yahweh."[96]

The glorified Christ possesses intimate knowledge of the spiritual and relational condition of each congregation. He begins every message by saying, "I know" (οἶδα [*oida*] in 2:2, 9, 13, 19; 3:1, 8, 15), and the object of his knowing includes both their virtues and their vices. The one present among his people is keenly aware of their situation and their actions.

We are told from the start that he "walks among the seven golden lampstands" (2:1; cf. 1:13). As Grant Osborne observes, "The imagery of 'walking' combines the ideas of concern for and authority over the church" so that Christ is present both as one who watches over and one who watches his

---

95. Keener, *Revelation,* 173–74.
96. Beale, *The Book of Revelation,* 229.

people.[97] Christ conveys his sustaining presence most tenderly in the familiar promise to the Laodicean Christians in 3:20: "Here I am! I stand at the door and knock. If anyone hears my voice and opens the door, I will come in and eat with that person, and they with me." When the seven messages are viewed as a unit, the inclusio of 2:1 (walking among the lampstands) and 3:20 (the invitation to table fellowship) reinforces the theme of presence as central to the entire section. Likewise, the closing words to the final letter provide a fitting conclusion to all seven messages. Jesus's persistent initiative to experience table fellowship with wayward believers speaks volumes about his desire to commune with them. No wonder many see the table fellowship imagery of 3:20 as a foretaste of the final messianic banquet (e.g., Rev. 19:6–9).

Oddly, Jesus's "I am coming soon" promises to the churches indicate a kind of absence even in the midst of his sustaining presence (e.g., 2:25; 3:11).[98] We see here an "already but not yet" tension as God's sustaining presence in Christ anticipates the final fulfillment of his eschatological presence.

The Ministry of the Holy Spirit.[99] Christ's sustaining presence among the churches is strongly linked to the ministry of the Holy Spirit. Christ is identified in 3:1 as the one "who holds the seven spirits of God," likely a reference to the sevenfold Holy Spirit (cf. 1:4; 4:5; 5:6; Zech. 4:2, 10).[100] The Zechariah background points to God's work being done not by human might or power but by God's Spirit (Zech. 4:6). Then, at the end of each of the seven messages, which clearly come from the risen Christ, we read the exhortation to "hear what the Spirit says to the churches" (2:7, 11, 17, 29; 3:6, 13, 22)—a reminder that the Spirit and Christ cooperate in making God's sustaining presence known to his people.

In addition, what we might call the Spirit's "location" also reinforces his sustaining presence on behalf of the earthly saints. In Revelation God is seated on the throne (e.g., 4:2; 19:4). Jesus, the Lamb, shares God's throne

---

97. Osborne, *Revelation*, 112.

98. Jesus's promise to come to his people in judgment (e.g., 2:5, 16; 3:3) is treated in a subsequent section.

99. Bauckham accurately notes the references to the Spirit in Revelation to include three categories: the seven spirits (1:4; 3:1; 4:5; 5:6), the phrase ἐν πνεύματι (*en pneumati*, in the Spirit) (1:10; 4:2; 17:3; 21:10), and other references to the Spirit (2:7, 11, 17, 29; 3:6, 13, 22; 14:13; 19:10; 22:17) (Bauckham, *The Climax of Prophecy*, 150). A full-blown study of the Spirit in the book would also include images and concepts that might suggest the presence of the Spirit (e.g., breath of life from God in 11:11 and water of life or living water in 21:6; 22:1, 17).

100. In the phrase "the seven spirits of God and [καὶ] the seven stars," the καὶ is likely connective, as in the NIV and most translations, rather than explanatory (i.e., "the seven spirits who are the seven stars"). Bauckham also observes that "although the term 'spirit' could certainly be used of angels (as frequently in the Dead Sea Scrolls), it rarely has this meaning in early Christian literature and never in Revelation" (Bauckham, *The Climax of Prophecy*, 162).

but also comes to God and takes the scroll from him (e.g., 5:6–7; 22:1, 3). But the Spirit is located "before his [God's] throne" in 1:4. In 4:5 the seven lamps (i.e., the sevenfold Spirit of God) are blazing "in front of the throne." These references indicate that the Spirit's primary role is to make God's powerful presence known in the world, including empowering the church to bear witness to Jesus. In 5:6 the Lamb has seven horns and seven eyes, which are the seven spirits (or sevenfold Spirit) of God "sent out into all the earth." The eyes of Yahweh in the OT, according to Bauckham, "indicate not only his ability to see what happens throughout the world, but also his ability to act powerfully wherever he chooses" (cf. 2 Chron. 16:7–9; Zech. 4:10).[101] Jesus had already told his followers that the Holy Spirit would be sent by the Father and Jesus to carry out their mission in the world (see John 14:26; 15:26; 16:7).

Another possible way the Holy Spirit manifests God's sustaining presence to his people on earth relates to the "seal of the living God."[102] The "seal" (σφραγίς, *sphragis*) (Rev. 7:2, 3, 4, 5, 8; 9:4) stands in contrast to the "mark of the beast." Both marks indicate ownership because they are placed on a person's forehead (e.g., cf. 7:3; 9:4 with 13:16; 14:9; 20:4) and are linked to the names of either God and the Lamb or the beast (cf. 7:3; 22:4 with 13:17; 14:11; 15:2).

In addition to ownership, the seal indicates spiritual protection (see Ezek. 9, where God marks the faithful for protection from divine judgment). Similarly, in Revelation only those who are marked with the seal of the living God can withstand God's coming wrath (e.g., 6:17–7:4; 9:3–4). The seal does not exempt believers from physical persecution or suffering, but it does protect them from spiritual defeat and enables them to remain loyal to Christ. Those who are not sealed, on the other hand, will be deceived by evil forces and will suffer God's wrath (13:7–8; 14:9–11).

The only explicit identification of the seal comes in 14:1: "Then I looked, and there before me was the Lamb, standing on Mount Zion, and with him 144,000 who had his name and his Father's name written on their foreheads." The apostle Paul equates God's seal with the Holy Spirit (2 Cor. 1:22; Eph. 1:13; 4:30), and this may be what John has in mind here also. God's seal indicates that we belong to God and brings assurance that God will protect us spiritually from evil even though we may suffer physical persecution. If the term "seal" is equivalent to the term "name" and name is equivalent to person, then it's hard to draw a strong distinction between God and the Lamb's name/person inscribed on the believer and the Spirit's protective indwelling

101. Bauckham, *The Climax of Prophecy*, 164.
102. See Duvall, *Revelation*, 114.

of the believer. One comes to much the same reality using complementary language.

Throughout history God's Spirit has sustained his people. At the end of history God's Spirit will resurrect the witnessing and willing-to-be-martyred church from the dead, as 11:11 reports: "But after the three and a half days the breath of life from God entered them, and they stood on their feet, and terror struck those who saw them." The "breath of life" (πνεῦμα ζωῆς, *pneuma zōēs*) entered them, likely referring to the Spirit's role in resurrecting God's end-time people—"Spirit of life." The background of Ezekiel 37:1–14 and perhaps Zechariah 4:6 makes this conclusion more likely. The power to resurrect is the ultimate manifestation of God's sustaining power.

God's Sustaining Presence through Other Means. Revelation communicates God's sustaining presence for his people on earth through a variety of other means, including his love and grace, his answers to prayer, his spiritual protection and nourishment, and his presence with his people during persecution.

In the opening of the letter readers are greeted with "grace and peace" (1:4), while in the closing "the grace of the Lord Jesus" is bestowed on (all) God's people (22:21). This bracketing of the entire letter with divine grace reminds the readers that God is present with them as they persevere through hardships and bear faithful witness. Prior to what we might call the "consummation of his grace" stands his sustaining grace in the interim.

Similarly, God reminds his people that they are loved. Christ's past love for his people is stated explicitly in 3:9 when addressing the church in Philadelphia: "I will make those who are of the synagogue of Satan, who claim to be Jews though they are not, but are liars—I will make them come and fall down at your feet and acknowledge that I have loved you." But Christ's past love also surely appears in the multiple references to his sacrificial death on their behalf (e.g., 5:9; 12:11). What's more, Christ's atoning death was but a particular manifestation of his ongoing love for his people so that the opening doxology can speak of "him who loves us" (1:5). Christ's sustaining love as a demonstration of his sanctifying presence appears also in the image of him standing at the door and knocking in hopes of table fellowship to follow (3:20).

God is also present with his people in answer to their prayers. In 5:8; 6:9–11; 8:3–4 the saints cast their requests upon God, asking him to judge evil and, in the case of the martyrs, to avenge their blood (6:10). God hears their cries for justice and answers with judgment fires from heaven (8:3–5). Regarding prayer in Revelation, Joseph Mangina writes, "In the Apocalypse, the commerce between heaven and earth moves both ways. God is the primary agent in the book: therefore the primary thrust of movement is downward, from heaven toward earth. And yet it would be wrong to say that God rules simply by fiat. If the church is called to listen to the word of God, God also listens; the prayers of his people matter to him."[103] And it should be kept in mind that the readers know how this prophecy ends. They see how the prayers will be answered, and this strengthens their belief that God is with them and for them now as they endure in faithfulness.

God's people also experience his sustaining presence through assurance of his protection and nourishment. In the much-discussed verse 3:10 ("I will also keep you from the hour of trial that is going to come on the whole world to test the inhabitants of the earth"), Jesus promises spiritual protection for believers in Philadelphia (and, by application, for all believers; cf. John 17:15). There is a huge difference between experiencing the wrath of God and facing the fury of the dragon, which may result in martyrdom. While believers are never promised exemption from persecution or even death, Revelation does send a clear message that they will be protected spiritually: the sealing of the 144,000 (7:1–8; 14:1–5), the measuring of the temple of God (11:1; cf. Ezek. 40–42), and the protection and nourishment of the woman in chapter 12.[104] The notion of spiritual protection parallels the action of sealing discussed earlier.

Revelation places special emphasis on God's presence with his persecuted people. In chapter 13 the beast "opened its mouth to blaspheme God, and to slander his name and his dwelling place *and* those who live in heaven" and was given power to "wage war against God's holy people and to conquer them" (vv. 6–7). God's "dwelling place" (σκηνή, *skēnē*) refers to the people belonging to God or those with heavenly citizenship, whether they currently reside on earth or in heaven. They stand in contrast to the earth dwellers. The term σκηνή and its cognate verb are used elsewhere to stress God's eschatological presence (7:15; 12:12; 21:3) and may do so here as well.[105] Nevertheless, the point remains: God's tabernacle *is* his people.

While the heavenly nature of God's dwelling place receives emphasis, believers constitute God's dwelling place on earth as well. The outer court of the temple in 11:1, although unmeasured or unprotected from persecution, likely

---

103. Mangina, *Revelation*, 119.

104. The wilderness is a place of trial for God's people but also of protection and provision. In 12:6, 14 the verb τρέφω (*trephō*), translated as "taken care of," means "feed" or "nourish." See BDAG 1014. Also see the excursus "The Desert as a Place of Both Trial and Protection," in Beale, *The Book of Revelation*, 645–46.

105. It's possible, even likely, that the reference in 13:6 is more eschatologically oriented. Whereas the NIV includes an "and" prior to "those who live in heaven," most scholars see it as an appositive: "God's dwelling, that is, those who live in heaven" (e.g., Koester, *Revelation*, 573). This group would include both angelic beings and the redeemed who had died in the Lord.

refers also to the church but from a different perspective—the people of God vulnerable to persecution and martyrdom in this world.[106] In addition, the invading army in 20:9 is said to surround "the camp of God's people [τὴν παρεμβολὴν τῶν ἁγίων, tēn parembolēn tōn hagiōn], the city he loves."[107] Whereas God once walked in the midst of the Israelite camp and revealed his Shekinah or presence among them (Exod. 14:19–20; Deut. 23:14), he now tabernacles among those who follow Jesus Christ, Jewish and gentile believers together. Here, in Revelation 20:9, the camp of the saints and the "city he loves" (cf. 3:9) are synonymous, with both referring to the community of God's people. The point of 20:9 is that God's people are protected from the invading army by his presence.

God's Eschatological Presence

God's Presence in Judgment

Richard Bauckham notes how the whole of Revelation in many ways serves as a vision of the fulfillment of the first three petitions of the Lord's Prayer: "Your name be hallowed, your kingdom come, your will be done" (Matt. 6:9–10).[108] If God's holiness, rule, and will are to be recognized on earth as they are in heaven, the evil powers must be destroyed. So, while it may be surprising at first glance that judgment proves essential to the theme of God's presence, it remains necessary to achieving God's ultimate goal of living intimately and in an unhindered fashion forever among his people.

God's judgment of evil occurs throughout Revelation. The three series of judgment visions (seals, trumpets, bowls) constitute the central part of the book. We read of the defeat of the dragon and his assistants, and part of his judgment includes banishment from God's presence (12:7–9). Revelation 17:1–19:5 portrays the destruction of Babylon—political, religious, economic, and military systems opposed to God. And the final victory described in 19:6–20:15 features judgment as a central component.

Revelation shows that God's judgment ultimately comes from his presence. Each of the three judgment series has some connection to the throne room, suggesting that God is ultimately responsible for judging evil.[109] This

106. Note the NT emphasis on God's people as the temple of God's Spirit (e.g., 1 Cor. 3:16–17; 6:19; Eph. 2:21–22; Heb. 3:6; 1 Pet. 2:5).

107. The term ἅγιοι (hagioi) is used thirteen times to refer to God's people and likely refers to Jewish and gentile Christians together or the church in every instance (5:8; 8:3, 4; 11:18; 13:7, 10; 14:12; 16:6; 17:6; 18:20, 24; 19:8; 20:9).

108. Bauckham, The Theology of the Book of Revelation, 40.

109. Bauckham, The Theology of the Book of Revelation, 41. Bauckham notes that the four living creatures summon the four horsemen (6:1, 3, 5, 7), and that the seven trumpets are blown by the seven angels who stand before God in heaven (8:2, 6).

is especially evident with the bowl judgments when the seven angels come directly from the heavenly temple/tabernacle to unleash their plagues (15:6–7). The temple is said to be "filled with smoke from the glory of God and from his power, and no one could enter the temple until the seven plagues of the seven angels were completed" (15:8), likely indicating that communion with and worship of God (the temple's purpose) "cannot be resumed until the world is actually remade, renewed, and purged of every evil."[110] When the seventh bowl is poured out, a loud voice from the temple and the throne proclaims, "It is done!" (16:17). This declaration is followed by an eschatological storm-earthquake that often accompanies the theophany of God coming in judgment (16:18, 21; cf. 4:5; 8:5; 11:19; Exod. 19:16–18). The final judgment is sometimes vividly portrayed as people coming face-to-face with God. In 6:16 unbelievers seek to hide from God's face (πρόσωπον, *prosōpon*) or presence, which in this context connects directly to his wrath. The same reality occurs in 20:11 at the judgment at the great white throne, where God is described as the one "from whose presence [πρόσωπον] the earth and heavens fled." This is a stark contrast to 22:4, where God's people are comforted by the promise that one day they will see God's face (πρόσωπον).[111]

Judgment not only flows from God's presence but also involves a loss of his presence. The judgment of Babylon begins with a call for the people of God to flee the evil city so as not to share in its sins or receive its punishment (18:4). The overthrow of the wicked city results in the loss of the city's life. Six times the phrase "never again" is used in 18:21–23 to depict what has been taken from the city. James Resseguie notes how the negative language used to describe the overthrow of Babylon contrasts with the "no more" language used to portray what is absent from the new creation: no more sea, tears, death, mourning, crying, or pain (21:1, 4).[112] The absence of all that is good flowing from God's presence contrasts with the absence of all evil from the heavenly city, the place of God's presence.

The final judgment scene, in 20:11–15, portrays in ultimate, final terms the removal of evil from God's life-giving presence once and for all. All of God's enemies suffer the same fate of removal from his presence: beast and false prophet (19:20), Satan (20:10), death and Hades (20:14), wicked humans (20:15; 21:8). Unrepentant sinners will be excluded from the holy city—that

110. Mangina, *Revelation*, 185.
111. The image of God's face as a synonym for God's presence occurs throughout the NT (Matt. 18:10; Acts 2:28; 2 Cor. 4:6; 2 Thess. 1:9; Heb. 9:24; 1 Pet. 3:12); see also the shining of Jesus's face at his transfiguration (Matt. 17:2; Luke 9:29).
112. Resseguie, *The Revelation of John*, 232.

is, from the presence of God (21:8, 27; cf. 2 Thess. 1:5–10).[113] The final vice list (22:15) portrays the wicked as being denied the right to enter the city and eat from the tree of life (22:14–15). Throughout Revelation God's presence is a fire that brings light, comfort, and protection for the faithful but condemnation and banishment for the unfaithful. The common juxtaposition of anathema (e.g., 22:18–19) with *maranatha* (22:20) reminds us that God's presence is not something we should try to domesticate (cf. 21:6–7 with 21:8; see also 1 Cor. 16:22–24); the sacrificial Lamb is also the conquering Ram.[114]

God's Eternal Presence with His People

There is another, more positive aspect to God's eschatological presence: God living among his people in the new creation. In the seven messages in chapters 2–3 all the promises to the victors are eschatological promises: the right to eat from the tree of life in the paradise of God (2:7), immunity from the second death (2:11), hidden manna and a white stone with a new name (2:17), authority over the nations and the gift of the morning star (2:26–28), a white robe and inclusion in the book of life with acknowledgment before the Father (3:5), a permanent place in God's temple and inscription with the name of God, the name of God's city, and Jesus's new name (3:12), and the right to sit with Jesus on his throne (3:21). Believers are instructed to stay faithful until Christ returns (1:7; 2:25; 3:3; 16:15; 22:7, 20), and his parousia serves as the victorious event that ushers in God's eschatological presence.

In keeping with its prophetic-apocalyptic nature, Revelation uses rich and powerful imagery to depict the return of Christ. In 19:11–21 the mighty warrior Christ arrives on a powerful white stallion to judge and wage war against God's enemies. But this warrior image is matched with the preceding scene of the arrival of the wedding supper of the Lamb (19:6–10), an image much more suitable for what Christ's return will mean for his people.

The image of an eschatological wedding celebration best conveys God's final union with his people in the new creation.[115] The language of bride and bridegroom communicates God's perfect love for believers and anticipates our

---

113. The enigmatic verse 14:10 ("They will be tormented with burning sulfur in the presence of the holy angels and of the Lamb") probably refers to the judicial proclamation of judgment that leads to eternal punishment (Osborne, *Revelation*, 541). Revelation differs from the common apocalyptic belief that the wicked would be punished in the presence of the righteous, since the righteous are not included in 14:10 (e.g., *1 Enoch* 48:9; 62:12; 108:14–15) (see Beale and McDonough, "Revelation," 1132).

114. Bruce, "The Spirit in the Apocalypse," 344.

115. See Duvall, *Revelation*, 250–54.

joyous, intimate experience of his personal presence in the new creation. The OT prophets often speak of Israel as the wife of Yahweh (Isa. 49:18; 54:5–6; 62:5; Jer. 2:2; Ezek. 16:15–63; Hosea 2:14–23), and the marriage metaphor regularly portrays God's intimate relationship with his people (e.g., Isa. 54:5–7; Jer. 2:2; Hosea 2:16, 19–20; Matt. 25:1–13). What's more, the metaphor conveys deep emotional security and assurance for Christian readers who are facing persecution. As the divine husband, God has promised his bride a lavish banquet celebrating his defeat of their enemies and his abundant provision (e.g., Isa. 25:6–9).[116] While the wedding supper of the Lamb in Revelation 19:9 likely points forward to the more complete description of the new creation in chapters 21–22, the image strongly anticipates the personal, intimate, joyous time of fellowship that God is preparing for his people.

In the flow of Revelation, at the end of chapter 20 everything seems to have been accomplished: Christ has returned, the saints have been resurrected, God's enemies have been judged, and salvation has been achieved. Why the need for chapters 21–22? Because the goal of salvation is not merely God's deliverance of his people from Satan and sin but also his deliverance of his people *to himself*. Again, the goal of the gospel is not simply salvation or deliverance from evil but also eternal communion with God, the Creator and Redeemer and Sustainer. Consequently, the final vision of Revelation (21:1–22:5) spells out the primary goal and theme not only of the Apocalypse but also of the whole of Scripture: God's relational presence among his people in the new creation. This final vision represents the fulfillment of the promises to those who overcome (chaps. 2–3), the full realization of the worship in the throne room (chaps. 4–5), the answer to the martyrs' prayer (6:9–11), the goal of the judgments (chaps. 6–16), and the outcome of the final conflict with evil (chaps. 17–19). The final vision is actually a doublet: 21:1–8 summarizes what is later explained in more glorious detail in 21:9–22:5.

A brief survey of 21:1–22:5 demonstrates the pervasiveness of the theme of God's relational presence among his people. The opening vision (21:1–8) begins with the place where God will dwell with his people: "a new heaven and a new earth" (21:1, 5), minus any sea, a consistent symbol of evil (12:17–13:1).[117] The place is further described as the holy city and the new Jerusalem, coming down out of heaven from God, prepared as a beautiful bride for her husband (21:2). Notice how the place is also a people, as the holy city resembles a beautifully dressed bride. Bauckham summarizes the three aspects of the

---

116. Jesus also speaks of a wedding banquet in his consummated kingdom (e.g., Matt. 8:11; 22:1–14; 25:1–13; 26:29; Luke 13:29; 14:16–24).

117. For more on the symbolism of the sea in the Apocalypse, see Beale, *The Book of Revelation*, 1042.

new creation as a *place* in which the *people* live in the immediate *presence* of God.[118]

In 21:3 a voice from the throne announces, "Look! God's dwelling place [σκηνή, *skēnē*] is now among the people, and he will dwell with them. They will be his people, and God himself will be with them and be their God." Commenting on this verse, Graeme Goldsworthy says, "This one verse could be said to sum up and to contain the entire message of the Bible. The whole of the history of the covenant and of redemption lies behind this glorious affirmation. Every aspect of the hope of Israel—covenant, redemption, promised land, temple, Zion, Davidic prince, new Eden—is woven into this one simple and yet profound statement: the *dwelling of God is with men* [i.e., among the people]."[119] God now makes good on his long-standing tripartite promise to live among his people, except in Revelation the typical order of the three is reversed because the fulfillment has now arrived (e.g., Lev. 26:11–12; Ezek. 37:26–28; Zech. 2:10–11). God's people will become his permanent tabernacle (cf. the use of σκηνόω [*skēnoō*] in John 1:14 to describe Jesus's incarnation).[120]

Regarding Revelation 21, G. K. Beale makes a strong case for equating the new creation (v. 1), the new Jerusalem (v. 2), and the tabernacling presence of God (v. 3). He writes, "The new creation and Jerusalem are none other than God's tabernacle, the true temple of God's special presence portrayed throughout chapter 21. It was this divine presence that was formerly limited to Israel's temple and has begun to expand through the church, and which will fill the whole earth and heaven, becoming coequal with it. Then the eschatological goal of the temple of the Garden of Eden dominating the entire creation will finally be fulfilled (so Rev. 22:1–3)."[121] Beale rightly concludes that the new heaven and the new earth are described as a temple "because God's goal of universally expanding the temple of his glorious presence will have come to pass."[122]

In 21:4 God is portrayed as a tender, compassionate Father who wipes away every tear from the eyes of his children and whose presence means the

---

118. Bauckham, *The Theology of the Book of Revelation*, 132–43.
119. Goldsworthy, *The Goldsworthy Trilogy*, 313.
120. Mounce observes, "The Greek word for tabernacle (*skēnē*) is closely related to the Hebrew *Shekinah*, which was used to denote the presence and glory of God. In the wilderness wanderings the tabernacle or tent was a symbol of the abiding presence of God in the midst of his people. In the Fourth Gospel, John writes that the Word became flesh and *tabernacled* (*eskēnōsen*) among people so that they saw his glory, the glory of the One and Only (John 1:14). When the Seer writes that the tabernacle of God is with us, he is saying that God in his glorious presence has come to dwell with us" (Mounce, *The Book of Revelation*, 383).
121. Beale, *The Temple and the Church's Mission*, 368.
122. Beale, *The Temple and the Church's Mission*, 369.

absence of all that is evil and disruptive to *shalom*: tears, death, mourning, crying, and pain. Finally, in 21:7 the victors are assured that they will inherit the new creation and will live as God's children in his presence forever. Familial imagery stresses God's relational presence in a manner that plumbs the depths of human emotion.

The second vision, in 21:9–22:5, expands the opening vision (21:1–8), especially in its attention to the holy city itself. John is told to prepare to see "the bride, the wife of the Lamb" and is then carried away in the Spirit to a high mountain and shown "the Holy City, Jerusalem, coming down out of heaven from God" (21:10). Again, the city is the bride; the place is the people. The sacred marriage has occurred, and God and his people will now spend eternity as husband and wife.[123]

The holy city also reflects God's glorious presence (21:11), and it is described with terms such as "shine," "glory," "brilliance," "pure," and "clear." In Revelation the "glory" word group occurs nineteen times, with a range of meaning that includes praise (1:6; 4:9, 11; 5:12, 13; 7:12; 14:7; 15:4; 18:7; 19:1, 7), recognition or acknowledgment (11:13; 16:9), splendor (21:24, 26), and presence (15:8; 18:1; 21:11, 23). Robert Mounce concludes, "In apocalyptic literature the glory of God is a designation for his presence (Ezek. 43:5)."[124] The theme of God's glorious presence continues in subtle ways, as with the mention of jasper. The walls of the city of God are made of "jasper" (21:18), and it is the first of the twelve foundation stones (21:19). Jasper is a translucent stone specifically associated with the light and glory of God, since in 4:3 God himself, seated on his throne, is said to have the appearance of jasper.[125] In other words, the whole of the new creation shines with God's glorious presence.

The city doesn't need the sun or the moon for light, since "the glory [i.e., presence] of God gives it light, and the Lamb is its lamp" (21:23). There are subtle clues that the Holy Spirit joins the Father and Son in showering God's people with his triune presence, clues such as God, the Lamb, and light in 21:23; God, the Lamb, and the water of life in 22:1; and God, the Lamb, and his name in 22:3–4. If this is indeed the case, then references to the Triune God desiring to be present with his people bookend the entire Apocalypse (see 1:4–5).

123. Osborne, *Revelation*, 748.
124. Mounce, *The Book of Revelation*, 390.
125. BDAG 465; Beale, *The Book of Revelation*, 321. Because of the connection between 4:3 and 21:11, 18–19, Mealy concludes that the new Jerusalem is the great white throne of God, the epicenter of reality, God's glorious presence among his people. See Mealy, *After the Thousand Years*, 175.

As is commonly noted, the cube shape of the celestial city reflects the shape of the inner sanctuary of the temple (21:16; cf. 1 Kings 6:20; 2 Chron. 3:8–9), signifying that the entire city is filled with God's presence. And because God's presence fills the entire creation, there is no need for a temple or a special place for God to dwell. Rather, "the Lord God Almighty and the Lamb are its temple" (21:22). Ezekiel's prophetic vision about the restored temple—"THE LORD IS THERE"—has been fulfilled in a wonderfully unexpected way (Ezek. 48:35 to conclude Ezek. 41–48). The cube-shaped holy of holies has been expanded as the Triune God fills the new creation with his presence. God's people will not only observe his Shekinah glory from a distance; they will experience his glorious presence in an intensely personal way.

Finally, in 22:3–4 we read, "The throne of God and of the Lamb will be in the city, and his servants will serve him. They will see his face, and his name will be on their foreheads." In contrast to the high priest wearing the sacred name of God on his forehead and entering God's presence in the holy of holies once a year in the earthly temple, now all of God's people will bear his name and "will see his face." The NT emphasizes both that no one has ever seen God (e.g., John 1:18; 1 John 4:12; 1 Tim. 6:15–16) and that seeing God's face is a firm eschatological hope (e.g., Matt. 5:8; Heb. 12:14; 1 Cor. 13:12; 1 John 3:2). We also see an explicit connection between "face" and God's presence in numerous NT passages (e.g., 2 Cor. 4:6; 2 Thess. 1:9; Heb. 9:24; 1 Pet. 3:12; as well as passages related to Jesus's transfiguration). David Aune writes, "The phrase 'seeing the face of God' is a metaphor in Judaism and early Christianity for a full awareness of the presence and power of God . . . , for worshiping God in the temple, . . . or for seeing God in the context of a prophetic vision."[126] Revelation serves as an example of the first usage, since seeing God's face means experiencing his unmediated presence, whether in judgment (6:16; 20:11) or in worshipful communion (22:4).

Conclusions

In the Gospel of John, God reveals, communicates, and sends in order to make his presence known among his people. His presence gets up close and personal in Jesus, the incarnate Son of God. Jesus, the Word made flesh, tabernacles among us so that we can behold the glorious presence of God like never before (John 1). In Jesus, the new temple and eternal life,

126. Aune, *Revelation 17–22*, 1179.

God's presence has come. The gospel and the resulting Christian life are portrayed through relational images such as being born of God, knowing God, and believing and loving God. God sustains his people with his presence chiefly through the ministry of the Holy Spirit and the community of disciples. God also sustains his people beyond death. In all his writings John features God's eschatological presence, both realized and futurist. God will ultimately judge evil and banish it from his presence, while bringing his people into his eternal presence through resurrection and a permanent home in the new creation.

In 1–3 John, then, we see how multiple themes swirl around the theme of divine presence in a manner similar to John's Gospel. The major difference is that in the Letters we witness John applying the multilayered reality of God's relational presence to the community's life and situation. The realities of presence—the incarnate Son, eternal life, believing the truth, the role of the Spirit, knowing and obeying and loving God—must be wholeheartedly embraced and publicly lived out. God's presence certainly is relational in 1–3 John; we see this in the language of indwelling and the personal images such as being born, knowing, and loving. And God's Spirit himself makes sure that his people experience his presence.

We surveyed multiple aspects of God's relational presence in Revelation: trinitarian, prophetic, incarnational, sustaining (for saints in heaven and on earth), judgmental, and eschatological. What we have seen certainly points us in the direction that God's relational presence supplies the cohesive center of biblical theology:

- the prophetic word that is Revelation comes from the relational Triune God;
- the prophecy is grounded in God's incarnational presence in Christ;
- it communicates God's will for his people and assures them of his sustaining presence as they journey in community toward the new creation;
- it reminds them of the ever-present Holy Spirit and all that he supplies;
- it encourages faithfulness by reminding them of God's judgmental presence;
- most of all, it paints a majestic portrait of what it will mean to live in God's glorious presence in the new heaven and new earth.

Now remains the task of bringing to conclusion the many observations and insights about God's relational presence found throughout the grand story of Scripture.

CONCLUSION

Returning to Our Main Thesis

We return once again to our basic thesis: the Triune God desires a personal relationship with his people and so makes his presence known to establish and cultivate this relationship. In other words, this relational presence of God lies at the heart of the Bible's overall message, at the heart of biblical theology.[1]

God's relational presence forms the cohesive center of biblical theology. By "cohesive center" we are thinking more of a spiderweb than the hub of a wagon wheel.[2] In the web analogy, the main themes of the Bible, like the main threads in the web, connect in one way or the other to the center, sometimes directly and at other times more indirectly. There is a center, but it is not always obvious at first glance how it provides interconnectedness while allowing for flexibility. We believe the relational presence of God serves as this kind of cohesive center for the Bible.

Three Crucial Questions

For a proposed center to carry weight, it must convincingly answer three significant questions.[3] First, does this theme drive the plot of the biblical

---

1. In a recent essay, "Plots, Themes, and Responsibilities: The Search for a Center of Biblical Theology Reexamined," Daniel Brendsel offers abundant wisdom about how we should proceed methodologically before suggesting the following center: "*The triune God is actively engaged in increasing (and incarnating) his presence among his people, a presence that entails for his people the responsibility of worship, in the fourfold story of creation, fall, redemption, and consummation*" (p. 412). We also see the relational presence of God as the driving force and the ultimate goal of the whole biblical story.

2. C. Campbell, *Paul and Union with Christ*, 437–39.

3. See Beale, *A New Testament Biblical Theology*, 168–69. Beale suggests four validation tests for judging one center as better than the others: (1) it should be related to other centers

story from beginning to end? Here we are looking at the narrative impact of the theme throughout salvation history as revealed in the whole Bible. One of the key components in this question is time. A story line differs from a center, but a unifying center should appear consistently as a driving force in the biblical story.

Second, how extensively does this theme appear throughout the Bible? This question addresses the breadth and scope of the theme. G. K. Beale concludes, "The center that is the most comprehensive is to be judged the most probable."[4] Does the theme surface in different types of literature across the biblical canon? For instance, the theme of the kingdom of God appears extensively in the Synoptic Gospels but very few times in Paul's Letters, so it lacks comprehensiveness.

Third, does the proposed center best account for other main themes, or is it also a subcategory? This question probes the depth and connectivity of the theme. Does the proposed center provide cohesion, uniting other pervasive themes into a coherent whole?

God's Relational Presence Provides the Best Answers

From the extensive exegetical work presented, we are confident in concluding that the theme of God's relational presence best answers these three important questions and serves as the cohesive center of biblical theology. To begin with, God's relational presence drives the story line from beginning to end, consistently unifying the story and moving the plot toward its ultimate goal of God living with his people in the new creation. The story begins with the presence of God in creation and in the garden. The Spirit of God hovers over the waters (Gen. 1:1–2). God forms people and enjoys being with them, walking with them in the garden. As John Walton observes, "The presence of God was the key to the garden."[5]

God dwelling among and relating to his people in the garden also concludes the biblical story. Revelation describes the marriage and wedding supper of the Lamb (19:7, 9; 21:2, 9), God comforting his people (21:4), God living among them in the perfected garden (21:3, 7, 22; 22:2, 4), God's people eating freely of the tree of life (22:2, 14) and seeing God's face (22:4)—all (and more) form

---

but have a more overarching focus, and the others should be logical subcategories; (2) it should have a solid textual basis in both the OT and the NT; (3) it should be integrally related to major biblical themes; (4) it should be comprehensive. Our three questions are similar to these four validation tests. See also Beale, "The Eschatological Conception of New Testament Theology," 45.

4. Beale, *A New Testament Biblical Theology*, 168.

5. J. Walton, *Genesis*, 182.

a glorious ending to the story that began in Genesis 1–2.[6] From beginning to end, and in virtually every chapter in between, the relational presence of God unifies and advances the biblical story.

The crisis of the fall of humankind in Genesis 3 is best understood as essentially a loss of access to God's presence and the intimate relationship that it provided. As the story continues, the promise of God's presence constitutes the heart of the covenant. Throughout much of the OT God's covenant relationship with Israel is defined by an often repeated, three-part statement: "I will be your God; you will be my people; I will dwell in your midst." God's deliverance of his people from Egypt, journey with them through the wilderness, and leading of them into the promised land all point to presence. The cloud, the fire, the tabernacle, Mount Sinai, and his going before them into the land all signify divine presence. The building of the temple, the exile and return from exile, and the message of the prophets are all momentous events in Israel's history that find meaning in connection with God's long-standing intention of living among his people. But Ezekiel recounts God's glorious presence leaving the temple, never to return (even in the postexilic rebuilt temple) until Jesus comes into Jerusalem years later.

The coming of Jesus the Messiah makes God's presence known in an intensely personal way: Immanuel, God with us. In Jesus, the incarnate Son of God, the kingdom has come near, the new temple has been revealed, eternal life has been offered. Jesus creates a new community of the Spirit, and with the Spirit's arrival at Pentecost God's empowering presence comes to live within individual believers. This new-covenant community constitutes the temple of the Spirit, the family of God, and the body of Christ—images rooted in divine presence. God continues to sustain his people on their missional journey until Christ's return, when he will raise his people from the dead and reunite them with himself in the new creation, where they will experience eternal, unhindered access to his relational presence.

God's relational presence also answers the second question, about comprehensiveness. This theme appears extensively throughout the Bible. Almost every book (indeed almost every chapter) of Scripture touches on the presence theme, all wrapped in the great presence inclusio of Genesis 1–2 and Revelation 19–22. Because this theme appears across the biblical canon, it also appears throughout the various stages of salvation history. No matter where God is in the process of dealing with his people, the theme of his relational presence stands central.

---

6. See the table in Pate et al., *The Story of Israel*, 271–72, which shows how Revelation concludes what began in Genesis.

God seeking a relationship with his people by making his presence known to them also appears throughout the multiple literary genres and subgenres of Scripture. Whereas some themes are restricted to certain literary types, the presence theme seems to thrive across the genres. Whether historical narrative or prophecy or poetry or Gospel or letter or apocalyptic or whatever, we see God's presence surfacing as a key part of the message.

Presence also appears through all the main theological categories conveyed by Scripture. God's relational presence is central to theology proper, Christology, pneumatology, anthropology, ecclesiology, soteriology, missiology, and eschatology. No other theme unites biblical-theological thought in such a comprehensive yet flexible manner.

God's relational presence as the proposed center of biblical theology also addresses the final question about depth and connectivity. We contend that this theme best accounts for the other main themes and provides a cohesive, web-like center uniting the other themes into a coherent whole. Other proposed centers such as covenant, kingdom, new exodus, salvation, promise, the people of God, history of redemption, justification by faith, reconciliation, new creation, glory, or the "already but not yet" make extremely important contributions and at times overlap with presence, but none proves to be the consistent driving force of the story line like the relational presence of God.

Complementary Themes

While exploring this theme, we often have mentioned the other complementary themes in order to illustrate some aspect of divine presence. For instance, God's covenant relationship with his people, a people indwelt by God's personal and empowering presence, the Holy Spirit, leads them to live a whole new life in light of Christ's sacrifice and enjoy permanent access to his presence. Without presence, covenant becomes meaningless religious ritual. We explored how the kingdom of God is rooted in the reality of God's relational presence, and how presence lies at the heart of kingdom righteousness and discipleship to Jesus. The arrival of the presence of God incarnate in Jesus of Nazareth constitutes and embodies the arrival of the kingdom. God's relational presence precedes, creates, and signifies the kingdom (i.e., the kingdom "has come near" temporally and spatially in Jesus). When Paul speaks about justification or reconciliation or adoption or new creation, God's commitment to be in relationship with and live with his people rises to the surface.

The theme of presence is almost synonymous with "God's glory." Beale concludes that "God's glorious presence is part of the core (new-creational reign)" of his proposed story line.[7] He adds, "God's glory, both his very essence and the glorious praise offered for who he is and what he has done, is the *goal* of the overall storyline that I have formulated. . . . God's glory should be seen as the major point of the storyline, since it is the ultimate goal."[8]

At the conclusion of his thorough study of union with Christ in Paul's writings, Constantine Campbell concludes, "It [union with Christ] is not the centre of his thought, though possibly should be regarded as a key to rediscover the richness and vitality of Paul's theology. Thus, union with Christ is indispensable but not the 'great concern.' Ultimately, it is most likely that Paul's great concern is the glory of God in Christ."[9]

Others have also argued for the glory of God as the center of biblical theology.[10] Early we noted the two primary senses of "glory": (1) honor, prestige, reputation; and (2) visible splendor in the sense of glorious presence.[11] We saw in John's Gospel how Jesus is God's Shekinah.[12] In Revelation the cube-shaped holy of holies is expanded as the Triune God fills the new creation with his presence. All of creation is his temple. God's people not only will observe his Shekinah glory from a distance; they will experience his glorious presence in an intensely personal way. We see glory (in the sense of praise) to be the result of glory (in the sense of presence). Presence precedes praise and makes it possible. Praise is the ultimate result of presence. Praise flows from presence, which makes presence even more central to the Bible's main message.

How It All Fits Together

As the most comprehensive, pervasive, and unifying theme, God's relational presence ties together the whole of biblical theology (see the diagram).

God

What generates this diagram is not simply the story of salvation—creation, fall, redemption, consummation—or the primary categories of systematic theology but rather the theme of God's relational presence. We begin with God. His very name, Yahweh ("the LORD"), implies the promise of divine

7. Beale, *A New Testament Biblical Theology*, 175.
8. Beale, *A New Testament Biblical Theology*, 175, 183.
9. C. Campbell, *Paul and Union with Christ*, 442.
10. Chiefly, T. Schreiner, *New Testament Theology*, 13–14; J. Hamilton, *God's Glory in Salvation through Judgment*, 53.
11. Bauckham, *Gospel of Glory*, 43–62, 72–74.
12. Frey, "God's Dwelling on Earth," 97.

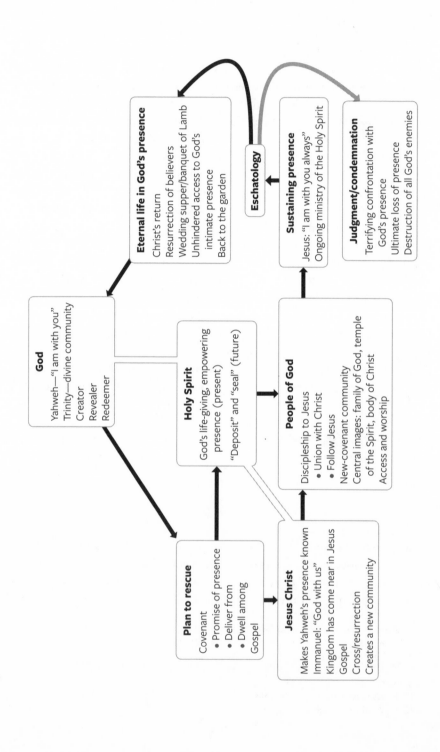

Eternal life in God's presence

Christ's return
Resurrection of believers
Wedding supper/banquet of Lamb
Unhindered access to God's intimate presence
Back to the garden

Sustaining presence

Jesus: "I am with you always"
Ongoing ministry of the Holy Spirit

Judgment/condemnation

Terrifying confrontation with God's presence
Ultimate loss of presence
Destruction of all God's enemies

Eschatology

God

Yahweh—"I am with you"
Trinity—divine community
Creator
Revealer
Redeemer

Holy Spirit

God's life-giving, empowering presence (present)
"Deposit" and "seal" (future)

People of God

Discipleship to Jesus
• Union with Christ
• Follow Jesus
New-covenant community
Central images: family of God, temple of the Spirit, body of Christ
Access and worship

Plan to rescue

Covenant
• Promise of presence
• Deliver from
• Dwell among
Gospel

Jesus Christ

Makes Yahweh's presence known
Immanuel: "God with us"
Kingdom has come near in Jesus
Gospel
Cross/resurrection
Creates a new community

presence: "I am [or "I will be"] with you" (Exod. 3:12, 14). Thus, the primary name for God used throughout the OT connotes his core identity as the God who desires to be personally and relationally present with his people. Given the significance of names in the ancient Near East, this speaks volumes about God being a relational God. When Jesus, the incarnate Son of God, comes on the scene and identifies himself with Yahweh, we meet God's relational presence up close and personal.

God is also triune: Father, Son, Spirit, three in one and one in three, blessed Trinity. God reveals himself as the divine community. However, since the Triune God by his very nature is relational, he extends the opportunity for fellowship with the perfect community to his creation. God's nature as triune, then, provides the basis or grounding for his desire to redeem and draw near to his creation. Fred Sanders writes, "The gospel is Trinitarian, and the Trinity is the gospel. Christian salvation comes from the Trinity, happens through the Trinity, and brings us home to the Trinity."[13]

We also see God's relational presence through his actions as Creator. The Spirit of God hovering over the waters (Gen. 1:2), God forming a man and breathing life into him and then building the woman from the man's rib (2:7, 22), God planting a garden for the couple (2:8, 15), and God walking with Adam and Eve in the garden (Gen. 3:8) all reveal God's desire to be near his people in intimate relationship. These human beings, created in God's "image," are designed to be in an up-close and personal relationship to God.

God not only creates human beings as an extension of his trinitarian, relational self; he also reveals himself to them. When God takes the initiative to reveal himself to and speak to people throughout the story of salvation, God shows himself as Revealer. Throughout the OT we see God revealing himself to key individuals in order to have a closer relationship with his people. In the NT we read that in "these last days" God has spoken in his Son (Heb. 1:2). The Word, who was with God in the beginning and through whom God created, has now been enfleshed and has made his dwelling among us (John 1:1–3, 14). God reveals himself in order to redeem, and he redeems in order to deliver his people from evil and dwell among them forever.

The Rescue Plan

The good news of salvation is that the Triune God has graciously opened his trinitarian life to us.[14] Two words define God's relational rescue plan better than any others: covenant and gospel. Most of Genesis and Exodus is

13. Sanders, *The Deep Things of God*, 10.
14. Sanders, *The Deep Things of God*, 191.

332   *Conclusion*

taken up with recounting how God establishes a covenant relationship with his people, a story told largely through the experience of the patriarchs and Moses. At the epicenter of the covenant is God's promise of his presence (again, "I will be your God; you will be my people; I will dwell in your midst"). If Yahweh is to be the God of his people, he must rescue and redeem them for the purpose of living among them. He must deliver from in order to dwell with. The prophets proclaim this good news to God's people, reminding them of God's original purposes. God even pours out his Spirit in order to restore this tripartite covenant relationship between God and his people (Isa. 32:15; 44:3–4; Ezek. 39:29; Joel 2:28). The people's rebellion temporarily delays God's plan, but future restoration is just over the horizon with the coming Messiah and his gospel.

Jesus Christ

Jesus's coming inaugurates the promised restoration as he announces the "good news" of the kingdom. Jesus is the one through whom Yahweh's personal presence will be made known.

Immanuel, God with us, has arrived. The gospel is embodied and proclaimed by Jesus of Nazareth. Paul articulates this gospel in terms of justification and righteousness, redemption and liberation, reconciliation and adoption, and the arrival of the promised Holy Spirit. John prefers the language of eternal life. This life is in the Son, and everyone who has the Son has life. God's relational presence lies at the center of John's concept of eternal life found in Jesus. Of course, the climax of the Son's mighty works lies in the cross and resurrection, which makes the good news real and available. Jesus then proceeds to create a new-covenant community by calling disciples and building his church.

The People of God

The new-covenant community includes individuals who have answered the call to discipleship to Jesus. The essence of discipleship is to experience the personal presence of Jesus (i.e., "follow me"). These are people united to Christ, participating in his death, burial, and resurrection, with their lives now "hidden with Christ in God" (Col. 3:3–4). Consequently, as part of the new-covenant community, they are identified as God's family, the Spirit's temple, and Christ's body—all images that stress God's relational presence. Jesus is the husband or bridegroom of his bride, the church. God intends for this divine marriage to result in an eternal love relationship between himself and his people. In Christ all individual believers also form one body, with Christ as the head. As the temple of the living God, the church fulfills what the tabernacle and temple attempted to facilitate, though imperfectly: to locate God's presence permanently among his people. The church is now that building in which God lives by his Spirit. As living stones, they are being built into a spiritual house or temple to be a holy priesthood with eternal access to God's presence (1 Pet. 2:4–5). This new humanity, created in Christ, now reconciled to God, is indwelt by God's personal presence. He is the shepherd; we are his flock. He is the vine; we are the branches. As he has loved us, so also we should love one another.

This new relationship with the Triune God grants God's people access to his presence and the opportunity to respond in praise and thanksgiving. Worship includes prayer, praise, celebration of the Lord's Supper, and much more, and believers encounter God's powerful presence in the worshiping community and the exercising of spiritual gifts through loving and serving one another.

The Holy Spirit and God's Sustaining Presence

In the OT the Spirit is poured out in order to restore the covenant relationship of God's promised presence with his people.[15] While God's Spirit is poured out on special leaders such as Saul and David, the OT points forward to a time when God will put his Holy Spirit, his empowering presence, within each member of the covenant community (e.g., Ezek. 36–37). The promised Spirit comes on the day of Pentecost in fulfillment of God's promise to live within and among his people (e.g., Acts 2 fulfilling the promise of Joel 2:28). Before it is a missional experience, Pentecost is a relational experience of God's personal presence. Along with empowering God's people, the Spirit guarantees their future. Using concepts such as "deposit" and "seal," Paul (and perhaps John) stresses the eschatological role of the Spirit in guaranteeing God's people eternal life in his presence. The gift of God's empowering presence secures the promised gift of life with God in the new creation.

Throughout the history of God's people the phrase "I am with you" conveys the sense that God will defend, protect, strengthen, comfort, and guide his redeemed people to an enduring experience of his presence. God's presence sustains his people. Jesus, Immanuel, God with us (Matt. 1:23), promises God's ongoing presence: "I will be with you always" (Matt. 28:20). Christ assumes the role of Yahweh in providing his sustaining presence to the churches

---

15. Block, "The View from the Top," 202–3.

in Revelation 2–3. Christ, our great high priest, has been exalted to God's right hand, where he intercedes for his people so that they may approach God's throne of grace to find grace in time of need (Heb. 4:14–16). Jesus promised his ongoing presence, and this role is fulfilled by the Spirit's indwelling. The Spirit plays the central role in sustaining God's people during their wilderness journey to the heavenly city. Jesus refers to the Spirit as another (of the same kind) "helping Presence" (John 14–16). The Spirit testifies about Jesus, reminds the disciples of his teachings, guides them into all truth, and discloses what is to come (John 14:26; 15:26; 16:13). One of the primary roles of the Spirit, the "anointing from the Holy One" (1 John 2:20, 27), is to assure believers of God's presence in their lives and their presence in his (1 John 3:24). The Spirit is "before the throne" in Revelation, indicating his role in making God's presence known in the world (1:4; 4:5; 5:6).

The Matthean inclusio (Matt. 1:23; 28:20) anticipates the time when Christ will drink the wine new with his people at the messianic banquet (26:29). This brings us to God's eschatological presence.

Eschatology[16]

We see two contrasting future outcomes in how the story concludes, judgment or salvation, and both are best seen in connection with God's presence. When Adam and Eve sinned, the consequence was eviction from the garden and banishment from God's presence. We see loss of presence repeated multiple times in the story: the incident of the golden calf, Israel's exile from the land, the conquest of Jerusalem, the destruction of the temple, God turning his face away (and similar images), the departure of God's presence from the temple, Jesus's opposition to the demonic and the religious leaders, Jesus's disruption of the temple and cursing of the fig tree, Jesus's teachings (especially his parables), and much of the book of Revelation. Paul conceives of the final judgment as the experience of God's wrath (Rom. 2:5) and exclusion from God's presence (2 Thess. 1:7–10). The resulting theological problem of sin for humanity is that they lose access to God's presence and relationship with God.

God's judgment of evil ultimately comes from his presence. As the writer of Hebrews says, "It is a dreadful thing to fall into the hands of the living God" (10:31), and "God is a consuming fire" (12:29). The multiple judgment visions

16. Beale writes, "Eschatology is protology, which means that the goal of all redemptive history is to return to the primal condition of creation from which humankind fell and then go beyond it to a more heightened state, which the first creation was designed to reach but did not" (Beale, *A New Testament Biblical Theology*, 177–78).

in Revelation, concluding with the final judgment scene (20:11–15), portray judgment as the conclusive removal of evil from God's life-giving presence once and for all: Satan and his cohorts, death and all wicked humanity, will be excluded from God's presence—no entry into the heavenly city, no privilege of eating from the tree of life, no eternal experience of God's presence with its attendant blessings. Judgment is first a terrifying encounter with the presence of the Holy God then followed by the loss of his relational presence.

God's salvation stands in stark contrast. The OT promises a restoration of God's presence, but it doesn't happen after the exile, although the people are back in the land and the temple has been rebuilt. There remains the anticipation of the day when God returns to dwell among his people, and this fulfillment is inaugurated with the coming Davidic Messiah, Jesus. The consummation or final fulfillment of God's promised presence occurs with Christ's second coming. Jesus returns, resurrects his people, and gathers them for the wedding supper of the Lamb. This time of intimate table fellowship has been anticipated by Jesus at the first Lord's Supper: "I will not drink from this fruit of the vine from now on until I drink it new with you in my Father's kingdom" (Matt. 26:29). The banquet then remains unfinished until the eschaton.

The eschatological wedding celebration perhaps best conveys God's final union with his people in the new creation. The marriage metaphor expresses the deep relational and emotional significance of life in God's presence. The disciples' eternal reward, their inheritance, is the Triune God and life in his presence. This is the restoration of the kingdom (Acts 1:6). This is the "blessed hope" (Titus 2:13). God's rest is eternal life in his presence. The dwelling of God is now with his people (Rev. 21:3). They are his temple. They are his holy of holies. God's glorious, relational presence now shelters his people forever. God keeps his promises!

Back to the Garden

We've seen how God's relational presence offers the ultimate reason for creation: the self-giving Triune God inviting his people to enjoy perfect community. Presence also lies at the heart of the covenant: "I will be your God; you will be my people; I will dwell in your midst." The fall of humanity is best seen as a loss of presence. Presence incarnate in Jesus Christ and made real by the empowering Spirit makes possible the people of God as his new temple. Presence describes the end result of God's kingdom: eternal communion with the King ("I drink it new with you in my Father's kingdom"). Presence supplies the goal of the gospel: salvation for relationship, for fellowship, and for worship. Presence stands as the final chapter of God's salvation story: a long-anticipated return to the garden. The story moves from walking in the garden to worship in the garden. And the garden is the whole of the new creation, in the shape of the holy of holies, a temple city now indwelt by God's presence. He will wipe away our tears and we will see his face (Rev. 21:4; 22:4). The presence of perfect *shalom* also means the absence of all evil. At the center of it all is God—the Triune God, who has created and redeemed and invited his people to enjoy his relational presence for eternity. That is what the Bible is all about. That is indeed the center of biblical theology.

BIBLIOGRAPHY

Abba, Raymond. "The Divine Name Yahweh." *JBL* 80 (1961): 320–28.

Abelson, Joshua. *The Immanence of God in Rabbinical Literature*. London: MacMillan, 1912. Reprint, Miami: HardPress, 2012.

Ackroyd, Peter R. *Exile and Restoration: A Study of Hebrew Thought of the Sixth Century B.C.* Philadelphia: Westminster, 1968.

Adams, Edward. "The Coming of the Son of Man in Mark's Gospel." *TynBul* 56, no. 2 (2005): 39–61.

Albertz, Rainer. "The Thwarted Restoration." In *Yahwism after the Exile: Perspectives on Israelite Religion in the Persian Era*, edited by Rainer Albertz and Bob Becking, 1–17. STAR 5. Assen: Royal Van Gorcum, 2003.

Alden, Robert L. *Job*. NAC 11. Nashville: Broadman & Holman, 1993.

Alexander, Ralph H. "Ezekiel." In *The Expositor's Bible Commentary*, edited by Frank E. Gaebelein, 6:737–996. Grand Rapids: Zondervan, 1986.

Alexander, T. Desmond. *Exodus*. TTCS. Grand Rapids: Baker Books, 2016.

———. *From Paradise to the Promised Land: An Introduction to the Pentateuch*. 3rd ed. Grand Rapids: Baker Academic, 2012.

Alexander, T. Desmond, and Simon Gathercole, eds. *Heaven on Earth: The Temple in Biblical Theology*. Waynesboro, GA: Paternoster, 2004.

Allen, Leslie C. *The Books of Joel, Obadiah, Jonah, and Micah*. NICOT. Grand Rapids: Eerdmans, 1976.

———. *Ezekiel 1–19*. WBC 28. Dallas: Word, 1994.

———. *Ezekiel 20–48*. WBC 29. Dallas: Word, 1990.

———. *Jeremiah: A Commentary*. OTL. Louisville: Westminster John Knox, 2008.

Allison, Dale, Jr. *The New Moses: A Matthean Typology*. Minneapolis: Fortress, 1993.

Anderson, Bernhard W. "'God with Us'—in Judgment and in Mercy: The Editorial Structure of Isaiah 5–10(11)." In *Canon, Theology, and Old Testament*

Interpretation: Essays in Honor of Brevard S. Childs, edited by Gene M. Tucker, David L. Petersen, and Robert R. Wilson, 230–45. Philadelphia: Fortress, 1988.

———. "The Holy One of Israel." In *Justice and the Holy: Essays in Honor of Walter Harrelson*, edited by Douglas A. Knight and Peter J. Paris, 3–19. Atlanta: Scholars Press, 1989.

Anderson, Gary A. *Christian Doctrine and the Old Testament: Theology in the Service of Biblical Exegesis*. Grand Rapids: Baker Academic, 2017.

———. "Towards a Theology of the Tabernacle and Its Furniture." In *Text, Thought, and Practice in Qumran and Early Christianity*, edited by Ruth A. Clements and Daniel R. Schwartz, 159–94. STDJ 84. Leiden: Brill, 2009.

Ansberry, Christopher B. "Wisdom and Biblical Theology." In *Interpreting Old Testament Wisdom Literature*, edited by David G. Firth and Lindsay Wilson, 174–93. Downers Grove, IL: InterVarsity, 2017.

Arnold, Bill T. *Genesis*. NCBC. Cambridge: Cambridge University Press, 2009.

Arnold, Clinton E. *Ephesians*. ZECNT. Grand Rapids: Zondervan, 2010.

Ashley, Timothy R. *The Book of Numbers*. NICOT. Grand Rapids: Eerdmans, 1993.

Atkinson, David. *The Message of Genesis 1–11: The Dawn of Creation*. TBST. Downers Grove, IL: InterVarsity, 1990.

Attridge, Harold W. *The Epistle to the Hebrews: A Commentary on the Epistle to the Hebrews*. Edited by Helmut Koester. Hermeneia. Philadelphia: Fortress, 1989.

Aune, David E. *Revelation 17–22*. WBC 52C. Dallas: Word, 1998.

Averbeck, Richard E. "Tabernacle." In the *Dictionary of the Old Testament: Pentateuch*, edited by T. Desmond Alexander and David W. Baker, 807–27. Downers Grove, IL: InterVarsity, 2003.

Baker, David W. *Joel, Obadiah, Malachi*. NIVAC. Grand Rapids: Zondervan, 2006.

Balentine, Samuel E. *The Hidden God: The Hiding of the Face of God in the Old Testament*. OTM. Oxford: Oxford University Press, 1983.

———. *The Torah's Vision of Worship*. OBT. Minneapolis: Fortress, 1999.

Barclay, John M. G. *Paul and the Gift*. Grand Rapids: Eerdmans, 2015.

Barker, Kenneth L., and Waylon Bailey. *Micah, Nahum, Habakkuk, Zephaniah*. NAC 20. Nashville: Broadman & Holman, 1999.

Barr, James. *The Concept of Biblical Theology: An Old Testament Perspective*. Minneapolis: Fortress, 1999.

Barrett, R. "Idols, Idolatry, Gods." In *Dictionary of the Old Testament: Prophets*, edited by Mark J. Boda and J. Gordon McConville, 551–55. Downers Grove, IL: InterVarsity, 2012.

Barth, Christoph. *God with Us: A Theological Introduction to the Old Testament*. Grand Rapids: Eerdmans, 1991.

Barth, Karl. *Church Dogmatics* III/1. Edited by G. W. Bromiley and T. F. Torrance. Translated by J. W. Edwards, O. Bussey, and Harold Knight. Edinburgh: T&T Clark, 1958.

Barth, Markus. *Ephesians: Introduction, Translation, and Commentary on Chapters 1–3.* AB 34. Garden City, NY: Doubleday, 1974.

Bartholomew, Craig G. "Ecclesiastes." In *Theological Interpretation of the Old Testament: A Book-by-Book Survey*, edited by Kevin J. Vanhoozer, 179–85. London: SPCK; Grand Rapids: Baker Academic, 2008.

Bauckham, Richard. *The Climax of Prophecy: Studies on the Book of Revelation.* Edinburgh: T&T Clark, 1993.

———. *Gospel of Glory: Major Themes in Johannine Theology.* Grand Rapids: Baker Academic, 2015.

———. "James and the Jerusalem Church." In *The Book of Acts in Its Palestinian Setting*, edited by Richard Bauckham, 415–80. BAFCS 4. Grand Rapids: Eerdmans, 1995.

———. *Jesus and the God of Israel: God Crucified and Other Studies on the New Testament's Christology of Divine Identity.* Grand Rapids: Eerdmans, 2008.

———. *2 Peter, Jude.* WBC 50. Dallas: Word, 1998.

———. *The Testimony of the Beloved Disciple: Narrative, History, and Theology in the Gospel of John.* Grand Rapids: Eerdmans, 2007.

———. *The Theology of the Book of Revelation.* NTT. Cambridge: Cambridge University Press, 1993.

Baxter, Wayne. *Israel's Only Shepherd: Matthew's Shepherd Motif and His Social Setting.* LNTS 457. London: T&T Clark, 2012.

Beale, G. K. *The Book of Revelation: A Commentary on the Greek Text.* NIGTC. Grand Rapids: Eerdmans, 1999.

———. "The Descent of the Eschatological Temple in the Form of the Spirit at Pentecost, Part 1: The Clearest Evidence." *TynBul* 56, no. 1 (2005): 73–102.

———. "The Descent of the Eschatological Temple in the Form of the Spirit at Pentecost, Part 2: Corroborating Evidence." *TynBul* 56, no. 2 (2005): 63–90.

———. "The Eschatological Conception of New Testament Theology." In *Eschatology in Bible and Theology*, edited by Kent E. Brower and Mark W. Elliott, 11–52. Downers Grove, IL: InterVarsity, 1997.

———. *A New Testament Biblical Theology: The Unfolding of the Old Testament in the New.* Grand Rapids: Baker Academic, 2011.

———. *The Temple and the Church's Mission: A Biblical Theology of the Dwelling Place of God.* NSBT 15. Nottingham: Apollos; Downers Grove, IL: InterVarsity, 2004.

Beale, G. K., and Mitchell Kim. *God Dwells among Us: Expanding Eden to the Ends of the Earth.* Downers Grove, IL: InterVarsity, 2014.

Beale, G. K., and Sean M. McDonough. "Revelation." *CNTUOT* 1081–161.

Beasley-Murray, G. R. "The Interpretation of Daniel 7." *CBQ* 45 (1983): 44–58.

———. *John.* WBC 36. Dallas: Word, 2002.

Becking, Bob. "Silent Witness: The Symbolic Presence of God in the Temple Vessels in Ezra and Nehemiah." In *Divine Presence and Absence in Exilic and Post-Exilic*

Judaism, edited by Nathan MacDonald and Izaak J. de Hulster, 267–81. FAT 2/61. Tübingen: Mohr Siebeck, 2013.

Begg, Christopher T. "The Ark in Chronicles." In *The Chronicler as Theologian: Essays in Honor of Ralph W. Klein*, edited by M. Patrick Graham, Steven L. McKenzie, and Gary N. Knoppers, 133–45. JSOTSup 371. London: T&T Clark, 2003.

Beker, J. Christiaan. *Paul the Apostle: The Triumph of God in Life and Thought*. Philadelphia: Fortress, 1980.

Bellinger, W. H. *Leviticus, Numbers*. NIBC. Peabody, MA: Hendrickson, 2001.

———. *Psalms: A Guide to Studying the Psalter*. 2nd ed. Grand Rapids: Baker Academic, 2012.

Bergen, Robert D. *1, 2 Samuel*. NAC 7. Nashville: Broadman & Holman, 1996.

Beuken, Willem A. M. "The Manifestation of Yahweh and the Commission of Isaiah: Isaiah 6 Read against the Background of Isaiah 1." *CTJ* 39 (2004): 72–87.

Beyer, Bryan E. *Encountering the Book of Isaiah: A Historical and Theological Survey*. EBS. Grand Rapids: Baker Academic, 2007.

Bimson, John J. "1 and 2 Kings." In *New Bible Commentary: 21st Century Edition*, edited by D. A. Carson et al., 334–87. Downers Grove, IL: InterVarsity, 1994.

Birch, Bruce C., et al. *A Theological Introduction to the Old Testament*. Nashville: Abingdon, 1999.

Blenkinsopp, Joseph. *Ezekiel*. IBC. Louisville: John Knox, 1990.

———. *A History of Prophecy in Israel*. Rev. ed. Louisville: Westminster John Knox, 1996.

———. *Isaiah 1–39: A New Translation with Introduction and Commentary*. AYB 19. New York: Doubleday, 2000.

———. *Judaism, The First Phase: The Place of Ezra and Nehemiah in the Origins of Judaism*. Grand Rapids: Eerdmans, 2009.

Block, Daniel I. *The Book of Ezekiel: Chapters 1–24*. NICOT. Grand Rapids: Eerdmans, 1997.

———. *The Book of Ezekiel: Chapters 25–48*. NICOT. Grand Rapids: Eerdmans, 1998.

———. "Empowered by the Spirit of God: The Holy Spirit in the Historiographic Writings of the Old Testament." *SBJT* 1 (1997): 42–61.

———. *How I Love Your Torah, O LORD! Studies in the Book of Deuteronomy*. Eugene, OR: Cascade, 2011.

———. *Judges, Ruth*. NAC 6. Nashville: Broadman & Holman, 2002.

———. "'A Place for My Name': Horeb and Zion in the Mosaic Vision of Israelite Worship." *JETS* 58 (2015): 221–47.

———. "The Prophet of the Spirit: The Use of *RWḤ* in the Book of Ezekiel." *JETS* 32 (1989): 27–49.

———. "The View from the Top: The Holy Spirit in the Prophets." In *Presence, Power and Promise: The Role of the Spirit of God in the Old Testament*, edited by David G. Firth and Paul D. Wegner, 175–207. Downers Grove, IL: InterVarsity, 2011.

Blomberg, Craig L. *Matthew*. NAC 22. Nashville: Broadman & Holman, 1992.

Bock, Darrell L. *Acts*. BECNT. Grand Rapids: Baker Academic, 2007.

———. *Jesus according to Scripture: Restoring the Portrait from the Gospels*. Grand Rapids: Baker Academic, 2002.

———. *Luke*. 2 vols. BECNT. Grand Rapids: Baker Academic, 1994–96.

———. "Scripture and the Realisation of God's Promises." In *Witness to the Gospel: The Theology of Acts*, edited by I. Howard Marshall and David Peterson, 41–62. Grand Rapids: Eerdmans, 1998.

———. *A Theology of Luke and Acts: God's Promised Program, Realized for All Nations*. BTNT. Grand Rapids: Zondervan, 2012.

Bock, Darrell L., with Benjamin I. Simpson. *Jesus according to Scripture: Restoring the Portrait from the Gospels*. 2nd ed. Grand Rapids: Baker Academic, 2017.

Boda, Mark J. *The Book of Zechariah*. NICOT. Grand Rapids: Eerdmans, 2016.

———. "From Fasts to Feasts: The Literary Function of Zechariah 7–8." *CBQ* 65 (2003): 390–407.

———. *Haggai, Zechariah*. NIVAC. Grand Rapids: Zondervan, 2004.

———. *"Return to Me": A Biblical Theology of Repentance*. NSBT 35. Nottingham: Apollos; Downers Grove, IL: InterVarsity, 2015.

Bonhoeffer, Dietrich. *Creation and Fall: A Theological Interpretation of Genesis 1–3*. Translated by John C. Fletcher. New York: Macmillan, 1959.

Bonnington, Mark. "New Temples in Corinth: Paul's Use of Temple Imagery in the Ethics of the Corinthian Correspondence." In *Heaven on Earth: The Temple in Biblical Theology*, edited by T. Desmond Alexander and Simon Gathercole, 151–59. Waynesboro, GA: Paternoster, 2004.

Booth, Susan Maxwell. *The Tabernacling Presence of God: Mission and Gospel Witness*. Eugene, OR: Wipf & Stock, 2015.

Boström, Lennart. *The God of the Sages: The Portrayal of God in the Book of Proverbs*. ConBOT 29. Stockholm: Almqvist & Wiksell, 1990.

Braun, Roddy. *1 Chronicles*. WBC 14. Waco: Word, 1986.

Brendsel, Daniel J. "Plots, Themes, and Responsibilities: The Search for a Center of Biblical Theology Reexamined." *Themelios* 35 (2010): 400–412.

Brody, Aaron Jed. *"Each Man Cried Out to His God": The Specialized Religion of Canaanite and Phoenician Seafarers*. HSM 58. Atlanta: Scholars Press, 1998.

Brower, Kent E. "'Let the Reader Understand': Temple & Eschatology in Mark." In *Eschatology in Bible & Theology: Evangelical Essays at the Dawn of a New Millennium*, edited by Kent E. Brower and Mark W. Elliott, 119–43. Downers Grove, IL: InterVarsity, 1997.

Brown, Jeannine K. "Creation's Renewal in the Gospel of John." *CBQ* 72 (2010): 275–90.

Brown, William P. "Manifest Diversity: The Presence of God in Genesis." In *Genesis and Christian Theology*, edited by Nathan MacDonald, Mark W. Elliott, and Grant Macaskill, 3–25. Grand Rapids: Eerdmans, 2012.

———. *Seeing the Psalms: A Theology of Metaphor.* Louisville: Westminster John Knox, 2002.

Bruce, F. F. *The Book of the Acts.* NICNT. Grand Rapids: Eerdmans, 1988.

———. "The Spirit in the Apocalypse." In *Christ and Spirit in the New Testament: In Honour of Charles Francis Digby Moule*, edited by Barnabas Lindars and Stephen S. Smalley, 333–44. Cambridge: Cambridge University Press, 1973.

———. *1 and 2 Thessalonians.* WBC 45. Dallas: Word, 1998.

Bruckner, James. *Jonah, Nahum, Habakkuk, Zephaniah.* NIVAC. Grand Rapids: Zondervan, 2004.

Brueggemann, Walter. "The Book of Exodus." *NIB* 1:677–981.

———. "The Crisis and Promise of Presence in Israel." *HBT* 1 (1979): 47–86.

———. *First and Second Samuel.* IBC. Louisville: John Knox, 1990.

———. *Isaiah 1–39.* WestBC. Louisville: Westminster John Knox, 1998.

———. *The Land: Place as Gift, Promise, and Challenge in Biblical Faith.* 2nd ed. OBT. Minneapolis: Fortress, 2002.

———. "Presence of God, Cultic." *IDBSup* 680–83.

———. *Solomon: Israel's Ironic Icon of Human Achievement.* Columbia: University of South Carolina Press, 2005.

———. *Theology of the Old Testament: Testimony, Dispute, Advocacy.* Minneapolis: Fortress, 1997.

Brueggemann, Walter, and William H. Bellinger Jr. *Psalms.* NCBC. New York: Cambridge University Press, 2014.

Brunner, Emil. *Man in Revolt: A Christian Anthropology.* Translated by Olive Wyon. London: Lutterworth, 1939.

Buckwalter, H. Douglas. "The Divine Saviour." In *Witness to the Gospel: The Theology of Acts*, edited by I. Howard Marshall and David Peterson, 107–23. Grand Rapids: Eerdmans, 1998.

Budd, Philip J. *Numbers.* WBC 5. Waco: Word, 1984.

Bullock, C. Hassell. *Encountering the Book of Psalms: A Literary and Theological Introduction.* Grand Rapids: Baker Academic, 2001.

———. *Psalms.* 2 vols. TTCS. Grand Rapids: Baker Books, 2015–17.

Burge, Gary M. *The Anointed Community: The Holy Spirit in the Johannine Tradition.* Grand Rapids: Eerdmans, 1987.

Burnett, Joel S. "A Plea for David and Zion: The Elohistic Psalter as Psalm Collection for the Temple's Restoration." In *Diachronic and Synchronic: Reading the Psalms in Real Time; Proceedings of the Baylor Symposium on the Book of Psalms*, edited by Joel S. Burnett, W. H. Bellinger, and W. Dennis Tucker, 95–113. LHBOTS 488. London: T&T Clark, 2007.

————. *Where Is God? Divine Absence in the Hebrew Bible.* Minneapolis: Fortress, 2010.

Butler, Trent C. *Joshua.* WBC 7. Waco: Word, 1983.

Campbell, Anthony F. *2 Samuel.* FOTL. Grand Rapids: Eerdmans, 2005.

Campbell, Constantine R. *1, 2 & 3 John.* SGBC. Grand Rapids: Zondervan, 2017.

————. *Paul and Union with Christ: An Exegetical and Theological Study.* Grand Rapids: Zondervan, 2012.

Capes, David B., Rodney Reeves, and E. Randolph Richards. *Rediscovering Paul: An Introduction to His World, Letters, and Theology.* 2nd ed. Downers Grove, IL: InterVarsity, 2017.

Carson, D. A. "Current Issues in Biblical Theology: A New Testament Perspective." *BBR* 5 (1995): 17–41.

————. *The Gospel according to John.* PNTC. Grand Rapids: Eerdmans, 1991.

————. "1 Peter." *CNTUOT* 1015–45.

————. "Systematic Theology and Biblical Theology." *NDBT* 89–104.

Cassuto, Umberto. *From Adam to Noah: A Commentary on Genesis 1–6:8.* Translated by Israel Abrahams. Jerusalem: Magnes, 1978.

Charette, Blaine. *Restoring Presence: The Spirit in Matthew's Gospel.* JPTSup 18. Sheffield: Sheffield Academic, 2000.

Chavel, Simeon. "The Face of God and the Etiquette of Eye-Contact: Visitation, Pilgrimage, and Prophetic Vision in Ancient Israelite and Early Jewish Imagination." *JSQ* 19 (2012): 1–55.

Childs, Brevard S. *Isaiah: A Commentary.* OTL. Louisville: Westminster John Knox, 2001.

————. *Old Testament Theology in a Canonical Context.* Philadelphia: Fortress, 1985.

Chisholm, Robert B. *Handbook on the Prophets: Isaiah, Jeremiah, Lamentations, Ezekiel, Daniel, Minor Prophets.* Grand Rapids: Baker Academic, 2002.

Ciampa, Roy E., and Brian S. Rosner. "1 Corinthians." *CNTUOT* 695–752.

Clarke, Rosalind. "Seeking Wisdom in the Song of Songs." In *Interpreting Old Testament Wisdom Literature,* edited by David G. Firth and Lindsay Wilson, 100–112. Downers Grove, IL: InterVarsity, 2017.

Clements, R. E. "The Book of Deuteronomy." *NIB* 2:271–538.

————. *Ezekiel.* WestBC. Louisville: Westminster John Knox, 1996.

————. *God and Temple: The Idea of the Divine Presence in Ancient Israel.* Reprint, Eugene, OR: Wipf & Stock, 2016.

————. "Leviticus." In *The Broadman Bible Commentary,* edited by Clifton J. Allen, 2:1–72. Nashville: Broadman, 1970.

Clines, D. J. A. "The Image of God in Man." *TynBul* 19 (1968): 53–103.

Cockerill, Gareth Lee. *The Epistle to the Hebrews.* NICNT. Grand Rapids: Eerdmans, 2012.

Coloe, Mary L. *God Dwells with Us: Temple Symbolism in the Fourth Gospel*. Collegeville, MN: Liturgical Press, 2001.

Cook, Stephen L. "God's Real Absence and Real Presence in Deuteronomy and Deuteronomism." In *Divine Presence and Absence in Exilic and Post-Exilic Judaism*, edited by Nathan MacDonald and Izaak J. de Hulster, 121–50. FAT 2/61. Tübingen: Mohr Siebeck, 2013.

Cooper, Lamar Eugene. *Ezekiel*. NAC 17. Nashville: Broadman & Holman, 1994.

Craigie, Peter C. *Psalms 1–50*. WBC 19. Nashville: Thomas Nelson, 1983.

Creach, Jerome F. D. *The Destiny of the Righteous in Psalms*. St. Louis: Chalice, 2008.

———. *Yahweh as Refuge and the Editing of the Hebrew Psalter*. JSOTSup 217. Sheffield: Sheffield Academic, 1996.

Crenshaw, James L. *Joel: A New Translation with Introduction and Commentary*. AB 24C. New York: Doubleday, 1995.

———. *Old Testament Wisdom: An Introduction*. Rev. ed. Louisville: Westminster John Knox, 1998.

Crutchfield, John C. "Psalms." In *What the Old Testament Authors Really Cared About: A Survey of Jesus' Bible*, edited by Jason S. DeRouchie, 336–57. Grand Rapids: Kregel, 2013.

Cudworth, Troy D. *War in Chronicles: Temple Faithfulness and Israel's Place in the Land*. LHBOTS 627. London: Bloomsbury T&T Clark, 2016.

Darr, Katheryn Pfisterer. "The Book of Ezekiel." *NIB* 6:1075–1607.

Davids, Peter H. *The First Epistle of Peter*. NICNT. Grand Rapids: Eerdmans, 1990.

———. *The Letters of 2 Peter and Jude*. PNTC. Grand Rapids: Eerdmans, 2006.

Davies, G. Henton. *Exodus: Introduction and Commentary*. TBC. London: SCM, 1967.

Davies, John A. "A Royal Priesthood: Literary and Intertextual Perspectives on an Image of Israel in Exodus 19:6." *TynBul* 53, no. 1 (2002): 157–59.

deClaissé-Walford, Nancy, Rolf A. Jacobson, and Beth LaNeel Tanner. *The Book of Psalms*. NICOT. Grand Rapids: Eerdmans, 2014.

Delkurt, Holger. "Sin and Atonement in Zechariah's Night Visions." In *Tradition in Transition: Haggai and Zechariah 1–8 in the Trajectory of Hebrew Theology*, edited by Mark J. Boda and Michael H. Floyd, 235–51. LHBOTS 475. London: T&T Clark, 2008.

Dempster, Stephen G. *Dominion and Dynasty: A Biblical Theology of the Hebrew Bible*. NSBT 15. Nottingham: Apollos; Downers Grove, IL: InterVarsity, 2003.

———. "Geography and Genealogy, Dominion and Dynasty: A Theology of the Hebrew Bible." In *Biblical Theology: Retrospect and Prospect*, edited by Scott J. Hafemann, 66–82. Downers Grove, IL: InterVarsity, 2002.

deSilva, David A. *Perseverance in Gratitude: A Socio-Rhetorical Commentary on the Epistle "to the Hebrews."* Grand Rapids: Eerdmans, 2000.

Dirksen, Peter B. *1 Chronicles*. Translated by Anthony P. Runia. HCOT. Leuven: Peeters, 2005.

Dodd, C. H. *The Interpretation of the Fourth Gospel*. Cambridge: Cambridge University Press, 1953.

Dozeman, Thomas B. *Commentary on Exodus*. ECC. Grand Rapids: Eerdmans, 2009.

Dubis, Mark. *Messianic Woes in First Peter: Suffering and Eschatology in 1 Peter 4:12–19*. SBL 33. New York: Peter Lang, 2002.

Dumbrell, William J. *The End of the Beginning: Revelation 21–22 and the Old Testament*. Eugene, OR: Wipf & Stock, 2001.

Dunn, James D. G. *Baptism in the Holy Spirit: A Re-examination of the New Testament Teaching on the Gift of the Spirit in Relation to Pentecostalism Today*. Philadelphia: Westminster, 1970.

———. *Romans 1–8*. WBC 38A. Dallas: Word, 1998.

Durham, John I. *Exodus*. WBC 3. Waco: Word, 1987.

———. "שָׁלוֹם and the Presence of God." In *Proclamation and Presence: Old Testament Essays in Honor of Gwynne Henton Davies*, edited by John I. Durham and J. R. Porter, 272–94. Richmond: John Knox, 1970.

Duvall, J. Scott. "The Beginning and the End." In *The Baker Illustrated Bible Handbook*, edited by J. Scott Duvall and J. Daniel Hays, 29–32. Grand Rapids: Baker Books, 2011.

———. *Revelation*. TTCS. Grand Rapids: Baker Books, 2014.

Duvall, J. Scott, and J. Daniel Hays. *Grasping God's Word: A Hands-On Approach to Reading, Interpreting, and Applying the Bible*. 3rd ed. Grand Rapids: Zondervan, 2012.

Dyrness, William. *Themes in Old Testament Theology*. Downers Grove, IL: InterVarsity, 1977.

Edwards, James R. *The Gospel according to Luke*. PNTC. Grand Rapids: Eerdmans, 2015.

———. *The Gospel according to Mark*. PNTC. Grand Rapids: Eerdmans, 2002.

Eichrodt, Walther. *Ezekiel: A Commentary*. Translated by Cosslett Quin. OTL. Philadelphia: Westminster, 1970.

———. *Theology of the Old Testament*. Translated by J. A. Baker. 2 vols. OTL. Philadelphia: Westminster, 1961.

Ellingworth, Paul. *The Epistle to the Hebrews: A Commentary on the Greek Text*. NIGTC. Grand Rapids: Eerdmans, 1993.

Enns, Peter. *Exodus*. NIVAC. Grand Rapids: Zondervan, 2000.

Eskola, Timo. *A Narrative Theology of the New Testament*. WUNT 350. Tübingen: Mohr Siebeck, 2015.

Eslinger, Lyle. *Into the Hands of the Living God*. BLS 24. Sheffield: Almond, 1989.

Estes, Daniel J. *Handbook on the Wisdom Books and Psalms: Job, Psalms, Proverbs, Ecclesiastes, Song of Songs*. Grand Rapids: Baker Academic, 2005.

Fee, Gordon D. *The First and Second Letters to the Thessalonians*. NICNT. Grand Rapids: Eerdmans, 2009.

———. *The First Epistle to the Corinthians*. NICNT. Grand Rapids: Eerdmans, 1987.

———. *God's Empowering Presence: The Holy Spirit in the Letters of Paul*. Peabody, MA: Hendrickson, 1994.

———. *Paul's Letter to the Philippians*. NICNT. Grand Rapids: Eerdmans, 1995.

———. *1 and 2 Timothy, Titus*. NIBC. Peabody, MA: Hendrickson, 1988.

Firth, David G. *1 & 2 Samuel*. ApOTC 8. Nottingham: Apollos; Downers Grove, IL: InterVarsity, 2009.

———. "The Spirit and Leadership: Testimony, Empowerment and Purpose." In *Presence, Power and Promise: The Role of the Spirit of God in the Old Testament*, edited by David G. Firth and Paul D. Wegner, 259–80. Downers Grove, IL: InterVarsity, 2011.

Fishbane, Michael A. *Text and Texture: Close Readings of Selected Biblical Texts*. New York: Schocken, 1979.

Fitzmyer, Joseph A. *Romans: A New Translation with Introduction and Commentary*. AYB 33. New Haven: Yale University Press, 2008.

Fowler, Mervyn D. "The Meaning of *lip̄nê* YHWH in the Old Testament." *ZAW* 99 (1987): 384–90.

France, R. T. *The Gospel of Mark: A Commentary on the Greek Text*. NIGTC. Grand Rapids: Eerdmans, 2002.

———. *The Gospel of Matthew*. NICNT. Grand Rapids: Eerdmans, 2007.

Fredericks, Daniel C., and Daniel J. Estes. *Ecclesiastes & The Song of Songs*. ApOTC 16. Nottingham: Apollos; Downers Grove, IL: InterVarsity, 2010.

Fretheim, Terence E. "The Book of Genesis." *NIB* 1:321–674.

———. *Exodus*. IBC. Louisville: John Knox, 1991.

———. *God and World in the Old Testament: A Relational Theology of Creation*. Nashville: Abingdon, 2005.

———. *The Message of Jonah: A Theological Commentary*. Minneapolis: Augsburg, 1977.

———. *The Pentateuch*. IBT. Nashville: Abingdon, 1996.

———. *The Suffering of God: An Old Testament Perspective*. OBT. Philadelphia: Fortress, 1984.

Frey, Jörg. "God's Dwelling on Earth: 'Shekhina-Theology' in Revelation 21 and in the Gospel of John." In *John's Gospel and Intimations of Apocalyptic*, edited by Catrin H. Williams and Christopher Rowland, 79–103. London: Bloomsbury T&T Clark, 2013.

Fried, Lisbeth S. "Temple Building in Ezra 1–6." In *From the Foundations to the Crenellations: Essays on Temple Building in the Ancient Near East and Hebrew Bible*, edited by Mark J. Boda and Jamie Novotny, 319–38. AOAT 366. Münster: Ugarit-Verlag, 2010.

————. "The Torah of God as God: The Exaltation of the Written Law Code in Ezra-Nehemiah." In *Divine Presence and Absence in Exilic and Post-Exilic Judaism*, edited by Nathan MacDonald and Izaak J. de Hulster, 283–300. FAT 2/61. Tübingen: Mohr Siebeck, 2013.

Fritsch, Charles T. "God Was with Him: A Theological Study of the Joseph Narratives." *Int* 9 (1955): 21–34.

Fung, Ronald Y. K. *The Epistle to the Galatians*. NICNT. Grand Rapids: Eerdmans, 1988.

Gammie, John G. *Holiness in Israel*. OBT. Minneapolis: Fortress, 1989.

Gane, Roy. *Leviticus, Numbers*. NIVAC. Grand Rapids: Zondervan, 2004.

Garland, David E. *1 Corinthians*. BECNT. Grand Rapids: Baker Academic, 2003.

————. *Luke*. ZECNT. Grand Rapids: Zondervan, 2012.

————. *A Theology of Mark's Gospel: Good News about Jesus the Messiah, the Son of God*. BTNT. Grand Rapids: Zondervan, 2015.

Garrett, Duane A. *Hosea, Joel*. NAC 19A. Nashville: Broadman & Holman, 1997.

————. *Proverbs, Ecclesiastes, Song of Songs*. NAC 14. Nashville: Broadman & Holman, 1993.

Gathercole, Simon J. *The Preexistent Son: Recovering the Christologies of Matthew, Mark, and Luke*. Grand Rapids: Eerdmans, 2006.

————. "The Son of Man in Mark's Gospel." *ExpTim* 115 (2004): 366–72.

Gentry, Peter J. "The Meaning of 'Holy' in the Old Testament." *BSac* 170 (2013): 400–417.

Gentry, Peter J., and Stephen J. Wellum. *Kingdom through Covenant: A Biblical-Theological Understanding of the Covenants*. Wheaton: Crossway, 2012.

Giles, Kevin N. "Church." In *Dictionary of the Later New Testament and Its Developments*, edited by Ralph P. Martin and Peter H. Davids, 194–204. Downers Grove, IL: InterVarsity, 1997.

Gitay, Yehoshua. "Reflections on the Poetics of the Samuel Narrative: The Question of the Ark Narrative." *CBQ* 54 (1992): 221–30.

Goldingay, John. *Daniel*. WBC 30. Dallas: Word, 1989.

————. "Daniel in the Context of Old Testament Theology." In *The Book of Daniel: Composition and Reception*, edited by John J. Collins and Peter W. Flint, 2:639–60. Leiden: Brill, 2002.

————. *Isaiah*. NIBC. Peabody, MA: Hendrickson, 2001.

————. *The Message of Isaiah 40–55: A Literary-Theological Commentary*. London: T&T Clark, 2005.

————. *Old Testament Theology*. Vol. 1, *Israel's Gospel*. Downers Grove, IL: InterVarsity, 2003.

————. *Old Testament Theology*. Vol. 2, *Israel's Faith*. Downers Grove, IL: InterVarsity, 2006.

Goldingay, John, and David Payne. *A Critical and Exegetical Commentary on Isaiah 40–55*. 2 vols. ICC. London: T&T Clark, 2006.

Goldsworthy, Graeme. *The Goldsworthy Trilogy*. Eugene, OR: Wipf & Stock, 2000.

Gorman, Frank H. *Divine Presence and Community: A Commentary on the Book of Leviticus*. ITC. Grand Rapids: Eerdmans; Edinburgh: Handsel, 1997.

Gorman, Michael J. *Apostle of the Crucified Lord: A Theological Introduction to Paul and His Letters*. Grand Rapids: Eerdmans, 2004.

———. *Cruciformity: Paul's Narrative Spirituality of the Cross*. Grand Rapids: Eerdmans, 2001.

———. *Inhabiting the Cruciform God: Kenosis, Justification, and Theosis in Paul's Narrative Soteriology*. Grand Rapids: Eerdmans, 2009.

Goswell, Greg. "The Eschatology of Malachi after Zechariah 14." *JBL* 132 (2013): 625–38.

Gowan, Donald E. *Eschatology in the Old Testament*. Edinburgh: T&T Clark, 1986.

———. *Theology of the Prophetic Books: The Death and Resurrection of Israel*. Louisville: Westminster John Knox, 1998.

Gray, John. *I & II Kings: A Commentary*. OTL. Philadelphia: Westminster, 1963.

Green, Gene L. *Jude and 2 Peter*. BECNT. Grand Rapids: Baker Academic, 2008.

———. *The Letters to the Thessalonians*. PNTC. Grand Rapids: Eerdmans, 2002.

Green, Joel B. "'Salvation to the End of the Earth' (Acts 13:47): God as Saviour in the Acts of the Apostles." In *Witness to the Gospel: The Theology of Acts*, edited by I. Howard Marshall and David Peterson, 83–106. Grand Rapids: Eerdmans, 1998.

Greenberg, Moshe. *Ezekiel 1–20: A New Translation with Introduction and Commentary*. AB 22. Garden City, NY: Doubleday, 1983.

Greer, Jeremy. "A Key to Matthew's Gospel: The Story of Israel in Matthew 1:21." PhD diss., B. H. Carroll Theological Institute, 2014.

Grenz, Stanley J. *The Social God and the Relational Self: A Trinitarian Theology of the Imago Dei*. Louisville: Westminster John Knox, 2001.

Guelich, Robert A. *The Sermon on the Mount: A Foundation for Understanding*. Waco: Word, 1982.

Gundry, Robert H. *Mark: A Commentary on His Apology for the Cross*. Grand Rapids: Eerdmans, 1993.

Gunkel, Hermann. *The Psalms: A Form-Critical Introduction*. Translated by T. M. Horner. FBBS 19. Philadelphia: Fortress, 1967.

Gunn, David M., and Danna Nolan Fewell. *Narrative in the Hebrew Bible*. OBS. Oxford: Oxford University Press, 1993.

Guthrie, George. *Hebrews*. NIVAC. Grand Rapids: Zondervan, 1998.

Hafemann, Scott J. "Biblical Theology: Retrospect and Prospect." In *Biblical Theology: Retrospect and Prospect*, edited by Scott J. Hafemann, 15–21. Nottingham: Apollos; Downers Grove, IL: InterVarsity, 2002.

Hagner, Donald A. "Matthew." *NDBT* 262–67.

———. *Matthew 1–13*. WBC 33A. Dallas: Word, 1998.

————. *Matthew 14–28.* WBC 33B. Dallas: Word, 1998.

————. "Matthew's Eschatology." In *To Tell the Mystery: Essays on New Testament Eschatology in Honor of Robert H. Gundry*, edited by T. Schmidt and M. Silva, 49–71. JSNTSup 100. Sheffield: JSOT Press, 1994.

Hahn, Scott W. *The Kingdom of God as Liturgical Empire: A Theological Commentary on 1–2 Chronicles.* Grand Rapids: Baker Academic, 2012.

Hamilton, James M., Jr. "Divine Presence." In *Dictionary of the Old Testament: Wisdom, Poetry & Writings*, edited by Tremper Longman III and Peter Enns, 116–20. Downers Grove, IL: InterVarsity, 2008.

————. "God with Men in the Prophets and the Writings: An Examination of the Nature of God's Presence." *SBET* 23 (2005): 166–93.

————. *God's Glory in Salvation through Judgment: A Biblical Theology.* Wheaton: Crossway, 2010.

————. *God's Indwelling Presence: The Holy Spirit in the Old and New Testaments.* NACSBT. Nashville: Broadman & Holman, 2006.

————. "The Messianic Music of the Song of Songs: A Non-Allegorical Interpretation." *WTJ* 68 (2006): 331–45.

————. *With the Clouds of Heaven: The Book of Daniel in Biblical Theology.* NSBT 32. Nottingham: Apollos; Downers Grove, IL: InterVarsity, 2014.

Hamilton, Victor P. *The Book of Genesis: Chapters 1–17.* NICOT. Grand Rapids: Eerdmans, 1990.

————. *Exodus: An Exegetical Commentary.* Grand Rapids: Baker Academic, 2011.

Haran, Menahem. *Temples and Temple-Service in Ancient Israel: An Inquiry into Biblical Cult Phenomena and the Historical Setting of the Priestly School.* Oxford: Clarendon, 1978. Reprint, Winona Lake, IN: Eisenbrauns, 1985.

Harris, Murray J. *The Second Epistle to the Corinthians: A Commentary on the Greek Text.* NIGTC. Grand Rapids: Eerdmans, 2005.

Harrison, R. K. *Jeremiah and Lamentations: An Introduction and Commentary.* TOTC. Downers Grove, IL: InterVarsity, 1973.

Hartley, John E. *The Book of Job.* NICOT. Grand Rapids: Eerdmans, 1988.

————. *Leviticus.* WBC 4. Dallas: Word, 1992.

Hasel, Gerhard F. *New Testament Theology: Basic Issues in the Current Debate.* Grand Rapids: Eerdmans, 1978.

Hauge, Martin Ravndal. *The Descent from the Mountain: Narrative Patterns in Exodus 19–40.* JSOTSup 323. Sheffield: Sheffield Academic, 2001.

Hawk, L. Daniel. *Ruth.* ApOTC 7B. Nottingham: Apollos; Downers Grove, IL: InterVarsity, 2015.

Hays, J. Daniel. "Has the Narrator Come to Praise Solomon or to Bury Him? Narrative Subtlety in 1 Kings 1–11." *JSOT* 28 (2003): 149–74.

————. *Jeremiah and Lamentations.* TTCS. Grand Rapids: Baker Books, 2016.

————. *The Message of the Prophets: A Survey of the Prophetic and Apocalyptic Books of the Old Testament.* Grand Rapids: Zondervan, 2010.

————. *The Temple and the Tabernacle: A Study of God's Dwelling Places from Genesis to Revelation.* Grand Rapids: Baker Books, 2016.

Hays, Richard B. *Echoes of Scripture in the Gospels.* Waco: Baylor University Press, 2016.

Helyer, Larry R. *The Witness of Jesus, Paul and John: An Exploration in Biblical Theology.* Downers Grove, IL: IVP Academic, 2008.

Hertog, Cornelis Den. "The Prophetic Dimension of the Divine Name: On Exodus 3:14a and Its Context." *CBQ* 64 (2002): 213–38.

Hildebrandt, Wilf. "Spirit of Yahweh." In *Dictionary of the Old Testament: Prophets,* edited by Mark J. Boda and J. Gordon McConville, 747–57. Downers Grove, IL: InterVarsity, 2012.

Hill, Andrew E. *1 & 2 Chronicles.* NIVAC. Grand Rapids: Zondervan, 2003.

Hodson, Alan K. "Hebrews." In *A Biblical Theology of the Holy Spirit,* edited by Trevor J. Burke and Keith Warrington, 226–37. Eugene, OR: Cascade, 2014.

Hossfeld, Frank-Lothar, and Erich Zenger. *Die Psalmen I: Psalm 1–50.* NEchtB. Würzburg: Echter Verlag, 1993.

————. *Psalms 2: A Commentary on Psalms 51–100.* Edited by Klaus Baltzer. Translated by Linda M. Maloney. Hermeneia. Minneapolis: Fortress, 2005.

————. *Psalms 3: A Commentary on Psalms 101–150.* Edited by Klaus Baltzer. Translated by Linda M. Maloney. Hermeneia. Minneapolis: Fortress, 2011.

House, Paul R. "The Character of God in the Book of the Twelve." In *Reading and Hearing the Book of the Twelve,* edited by James D. Nogalski and Marvin A. Sweeney, 125–45. SBLSymS 15. Atlanta: Society of Biblical Literature, 2000.

————. *Old Testament Theology.* Downers Grove, IL: InterVarsity, 1998.

Houtman, Cornelis. *Exodus.* Translated by Sierd Woudstra. 4 vols. HCOT. Kampen: Kok, 1996.

Hubbard, Robert L. *The Book of Ruth.* NICOT. Grand Rapids: Eerdmans, 1988.

————. *Joshua.* NIVAC. Grand Rapids: Zondervan, 2009.

Humbert, D. Paul. "Die Herausforderungsformel 'hinnenî êlékâ.'" *ZAW* 45 (1933): 101–8.

Hundley, Michael. *Keeping Heaven on Earth: Safeguarding the Divine Presence in the Priestly Tabernacle.* FAT 2/50. Tübingen: Mohr Siebeck, 2011.

————. "To Be or Not to Be: A Reexamination of Name Language in Deuteronomy and the Deuteronomistic History." *VT* 59 (2009): 533–55.

Hurowitz, Victor Avigdor. *I Have Built You an Exalted House: Temple Building in the Bible in Light of Mesopotamian and North-West Semitic Writings.* JSOTSup 115. Sheffield: JSOT Press, 1992.

————. "Paradise Regained: Proverbs 3:13–20 Reconsidered." In *Sefer Moshe: The Moshe Weinfeld Jubilee Volume,* edited by Chaim Cohen, Avi Hurvitz, and Shalom M. Paul, 49–62. Winona Lake, IN: Eisenbrauns, 2004.

———. "YHWH's Exalted House: Aspects of the Design and Symbolism of Solomon's Temple." In *Temple and Worship in Biblical Israel: Proceedings of the Oxford Old Testament Seminar*, edited by John Day, 63–110. LHBOTS 422. London: T&T Clark, 2007.

Hurst, L. D. "Priest, High." In *Dictionary of the Later New Testament and Its Developments*, edited by Ralph P. Martin and Peter H. Davids, 963–67. Downers Grove, IL: InterVarsity, 1997.

Hurtado, Larry W. *The Earliest Christian Artifacts: Manuscripts and Christian Origins*. Grand Rapids: Eerdmans, 2006.

———. *Lord Jesus Christ: Devotion to Jesus in Earliest Christianity*. Grand Rapids: Eerdmans, 2003.

———. *Mark*. UBCS. Grand Rapids: Baker Books, 2011.

Hurtado, Larry W., and Paul L. Owens, eds. *"Who Is This Son of Man?" The Latest Scholarship on a Puzzling Expression of the Historical Jesus*. LNTS 390. London: T&T Clark, 2011.

Isbell, Charles D. "The Divine Name אהיה as a Symbol of Presence in Israelite Tradition." *HAR* 2 (1978): 101–18.

Jacob, Benno. *The Second Book of the Bible: Exodus*. Translated by Walter Jacob. Hoboken, NJ: KTAV, 1992.

Jacob, Edmond. *Theology of the Old Testament*. Translated by Arthur W. Heathcote and Philip J. Allcock. New York: Harper & Row, 1958.

Janzen, J. Gerald. *Job*. IBC. Atlanta: John Knox, 1985.

Japhet, Sara. *The Ideology of the Book of Chronicles and Its Place in Biblical Thought*. Winona Lake, IN: Eisenbrauns, 2009.

Jensen, Philip. "Holiness in the Priestly Writings of the Old Testament." In *Holiness: Past and Present*, edited by Stephen C. Barton, 93–121. London: T&T Clark, 2003.

Jeon, Yong Ho. *Impeccable Solomon? A Study of Solomon's Faults in Chronicles*. Eugene, OR: Pickwick, 2013.

———. "The Retroactive Re-evaluation Technique with Pharaoh's Daughter and the Nature of Solomon's Corruption in 1 Kings 1–12." *TynBul* 62, no. 1 (2011): 15–40.

Jobes, Karen H. *1, 2, & 3 John*. ZECNT. Grand Rapids: Zondervan, 2014.

———. *1 Peter*. BECNT. Grand Rapids: Baker Academic, 2005.

Johansson, Daniel. *"Kyrios* in the Gospel of Mark." *JSNT* 33 (2010): 101–24.

Johnston, Philip S. "The Psalms and Distress." In *Interpreting the Psalms: Issues and Approaches*, edited by David Firth and Philip S. Johnston, 63–84. Downers Grove, IL: InterVarsity, 2005.

Joyce, Paul M. "Temple and Worship in Ezekiel 40–48." In *Temple and Worship in Biblical Israel*, edited by John Day, 145–63. LHBOTS 422. London: T&T Clark, 2005.

Kaiser, Otto. *Isaiah 1–12: A Commentary*. Translated by R. A. Wilson. OTL. Philadelphia: Westminster, 1972.

Kaiser, Walter C., Jr. *The Promise-Plan of God: A Biblical Theology of the Old and New Testaments*. Grand Rapids: Zondervan, 2008.

———. *Toward an Old Testament Theology*. Grand Rapids: Zondervan, 1978.

Kamp, Albert. "The Conceptualization of God's Dwelling Place in 1 Kings 8: A Cognitive Approach." *JSOT* 40 (2016): 415–38.

Kashlow, Robert C. "Zechariah 1–8 as a Theological Explanation for the Failure of Prophecy in Haggai 2:20–23." *JTS* 64 (2013): 385–403.

Keener, Craig S. *The Gospel of John: A Commentary*. 2 vols. Peabody, MA: Hendrickson, 2003.

———. *The Gospel of Matthew: A Socio-Rhetorical Commentary*. Grand Rapids: Eerdmans, 2009.

———. *Revelation*. NIVAC. Grand Rapids: Zondervan, 1999.

Kelly, Brian E. *Retribution and Eschatology in Chronicles*. JSOTSup 211. Sheffield: Sheffield Academic, 1996.

Keown, Gerald L., Pamela J. Scalise, and Thomas G. Smothers. *Jeremiah 26–52*. WBC 27. Dallas: Word, 1995.

Kessler, John. *Old Testament Theology: Divine Call and Human Response*. Waco: Baylor University Press, 2013.

———. "Temple Building in Haggai." In *From the Foundations to the Crenellations: Essays on Temple Building in the Ancient Near East and Hebrew Bible*, edited by Mark J. Boda and Jamie Novotny, 357–79. AOAT 366. Münster: Ugarit-Verlag, 2010.

———. "Tradition, Continuity and Covenant." In *Tradition in Transition: Haggai and Zechariah 1–8 in the Trajectory of Hebrew Theology*, edited by Mark J. Boda and Michael H. Floyd, 1–39. LHBOTS 475. London: T&T Clark, 2008.

Kim, Hak-Chin. "How Did Luke Understand 'the Name of Jesus' and 'in the Name of Jesus'?" *S&I* 3 (2009): 95–117.

Klein, Ralph W. "The Books of Ezra & Nehemiah." *NIB* 3:661–851.

———. *1 Chronicles: A Commentary*. Edited by Thomas Krüger. Hermeneia. Minneapolis: Fortress, 2006.

———. *2 Chronicles: A Commentary*. Edited by Paul D. Hanson. Hermeneia. Minneapolis: Fortress, 2012.

Kleinig, John W. *The Lord's Song: The Basis, Function and Significance of Choral Music in Chronicles*. JSOTSup 156. Sheffield: JSOT Press, 1993.

Klink, Edward W., III, and Darian R. Lockett. *Understanding Biblical Theology: A Comparison of Theory and Practice*. Grand Rapids: Zondervan, 2012.

Knafl, Anne K. *Forming God: Divine Anthropomorphism in the Pentateuch*. Siphrut 12. Winona Lake, IN: Eisenbrauns, 2014.

Koester, Craig R. *The Dwelling of God: The Tabernacle in the Old Testament, Intertestamental Jewish Literature, and the New Testament.* CBQMS 22. Washington: Catholic Biblical Association of America, 1989.

———. *Hebrews: A New Translation with Introduction and Commentary.* AYB 36. New Haven: Yale University Press, 2008.

———. *Revelation: A New Translation with Introduction and Commentary.* AYB 38A. New Haven: Yale University Press, 2014.

———. *The Word of Life: A Theology of John's Gospel.* Grand Rapids: Eerdmans, 2008.

Köstenberger, Andreas. *The Missions of Jesus and the Disciples according to the Fourth Gospel.* Grand Rapids: Eerdmans, 1998.

———. *A Theology of John's Gospel and Letters: The Word, the Christ, the Son of God.* BTNT. Grand Rapids: Zondervan, 2009.

Kraus, Hans-Joachim. *Psalms 1–59: A Commentary.* Translated by Hilton C. Oswald. Minneapolis: Augsburg, 1988.

———. *Psalms 60–150: A Commentary.* Translated by Hilton C. Oswald. Minneapolis: Augsburg, 1989.

———. *Theology of the Psalms.* Translated by Keith Crim. Minneapolis: Augsburg, 1986.

Kruse, Colin G. *The Letters of John.* PNTC. Grand Rapids: Eerdmans, 2000.

Kupp, David D. *Matthew's Emmanuel: Divine Presence and God's People in the First Gospel.* SNTSMS 90. Cambridge: Cambridge University Press, 1996.

Kutsko, John F. *Between Heaven and Earth: Divine Presence and Absence in the Book of Ezekiel.* BJSUCSD. Winona Lake, IN: Eisenbrauns, 2000.

Kwakkel, Gert. "Under YHWH's Wings." In *Metaphors in the Psalms,* edited by Pierre van Hecke and Antje Labahn, 141–66. BETL 231. Leuven: Peeters, 2010.

Lacocque, André. *The Book of Daniel.* Translated by David Pellauer. Atlanta: John Knox, 1979.

Ladd, George E. "The Parable of the Sheep and the Goats in Recent Literature." In *New Dimensions in New Testament Study,* edited by Richard N. Longenecker and Merrill C. Tenney, 191–99. Grand Rapids: Eerdmans, 1974.

———. *A Theology of the New Testament.* Edited by Donald A. Hagner. Rev. ed. Grand Rapids: Eerdmans, 1993.

Lane, William L. *The Gospel of Mark.* NICNT. Grand Rapids: Eerdmans, 1974.

———. *Hebrews 1–8.* WBC 47A. Dallas: Word, 1998.

———. *Hebrews 9–13.* WBC 47B. Dallas: Word, 1998.

Lau, Peter H. W., and Gregory Goswell. *Unceasing Kindness: A Biblical Theology of Ruth.* NSBT 41. Nottingham: Apollos; Downers Grove, IL: InterVarsity, 2016.

Leene, Hendrik. "Ezekiel and Jeremiah: Promises of Inner Renewal in Diachronic Perspective." In *Past, Present, Future: The Deuteronomistic History and the Prophets,* edited by Johannes C. de Moor and Harry F. van Rooy, 150–75. OtSt 44. Leiden: Brill, 2000.

Leithart, Peter. *1 & 2 Kings*. BTCB. Grand Rapids: Brazos, 2006.

Levenson, Jon D. *Sinai and Zion: An Entry into the Jewish Bible*. San Francisco: HarperSanFrancisco, 1985.

Levine, Baruch A. *Numbers 1–20: A New Translation with Introduction and Commentary*. AB 4. New York: Doubleday, 1993.

Levison, John R. *Filled with the Spirit*. Grand Rapids: Eerdmans, 2009.

Lieu, Judith M. *The Theology of the Johannine Epistles*. NTT. Cambridge: Cambridge University Press, 1991.

Limburg, James. *Psalms*. WestBC. Louisville: Westminster John Knox, 2000.

Lister, J. Ryan. *The Presence of God: Its Place in the Storyline of Scripture and the Story of Our Lives*. Wheaton: Crossway, 2015.

Lohfink, Norbert. "Jona ging zur Stadt hinaus (Jona 4,5)." BZ 5 (1961): 185–203.

Longenecker, Richard N. "The Acts of the Apostles." In *The Expositor's Bible Commentary*, edited by Frank E. Gaebelein, 9:207–573. Grand Rapids: Zondervan, 1981.

Longman, Tremper, III. *The Book of Ecclesiastes*. NICOT. Grand Rapids: Eerdmans, 1998.

———. *Daniel*. NIVAC. Grand Rapids: Zondervan, 1999.

———. *The Fear of the Lord Is Wisdom: A Theological Introduction to Wisdom in Israel*. Grand Rapids: Baker Academic, 2017.

———. "From Weeping to Rejoicing: Psalm 150 as the Conclusion to the Psalter." In *The Psalms: Language for All Seasons of the Soul*, edited by Andrew J. Schmutzer and David M. Howard, 219–29. Chicago: Moody, 2013.

———. *How to Read Genesis*. Downers Grove, IL: InterVarsity, 2005.

———. *Immanuel in Our Place: Seeing Christ in Israel's Worship*. GAOT. Phillipsburg, NJ: P&R, 2001.

———. *Jeremiah, Lamentations*. NIBC. Peabody, MA: Hendrickson, 2008.

———. *Job*. BCOTWP. Grand Rapids: Baker Academic, 2012.

———. "Psalms." In *A Complete Literary Guide to the Bible*, edited by Leland Ryken and Tremper Longman III, 245–50. Grand Rapids: Zondervan, 1993.

———. *Psalms: An Introduction and Commentary*. TOTC. Downers Grove, IL: IVP Academic, 2014.

Longman, Tremper, III, and Daniel G. Reid. *God Is a Warrior*. SOTBT. Grand Rapids: Zondervan, 1995.

Louw, Johannes P., and Eugene A. Nida. *Greek-English Lexicon of the New Testament: Based on Semantic Domains*. New York: United Bible Societies, 1996.

Lucas, Ernest C. *Daniel*. ApOTC 20. Leicester: Apollos; Downers Grove, IL: InterVarsity, 2002.

———. "Daniel: Book of." In *Dictionary of the Old Testament: Prophets*, edited by Mark J. Boda and J. Gordon McConville, 110–23. Downers Grove, IL: InterVarsity, 2012.

———. *A Guide to the Psalms & Wisdom Literature*. Vol. 3 of *Exploring the Old Testament*. EB. Downers Grove, IL: InterVarsity, 2003.

Lundbom, Jack. *Jeremiah 1–20: A New Translation with Introduction and Commentary*. AB 21A. New York: Doubleday, 1999.

———. *Jeremiah 21–36: A New Translation with Introduction and Commentary*. AB 21B. New York: Doubleday, 2004.

Luz, Ulrich. *The Theology of the Gospel of Matthew*. Translated by J. Bradford Robinson. NTT. Cambridge: Cambridge University Press, 1995.

Lynch, Matthew. *Monotheism and Institutions in the Book of Chronicles: Temple, Priesthood, and Kingship in Post-Exilic Perspective*. FAT 2/64. Tübingen: Mohr Siebeck, 2014.

Ma, Wonsuk. *Until the Spirit Comes: The Spirit of God in the Book of Isaiah*. JSOT-Sup 271. Sheffield: Sheffield Academic, 1999.

MacDonald, Nathan. *Deuteronomy and the Meaning of "Monotheism."* 2nd ed. FAT 2/1. Tübingen: Mohr Siebeck, 2012.

———. "The Spirit of YHWH: An Overlooked Conceptualization of Divine Presence in the Persian Period." In *Divine Presence and Absence in Exilic and Post-Exilic Judaism*, edited by Nathan MacDonald and Izaak J. de Hulster, 95–119. FAT 2/61. Tübingen: Mohr Siebeck, 2013.

Malatesta, Edward. *Interiority and Covenant: An Exegetical Study of εἶναι ἐν and μένειν ἐν in the First Letter of Saint John*. AnBib 69. Rome: Pontifical Biblical Institute Press, 1978.

Malchow, Bruce V. "The Messenger of the Covenant in Malachi 3:1." *JBL* 103 (1984): 252–55.

Malone, Andrew S. "Is the Messiah Announced in Malachi 3:1?" *TynBul* 57, no. 2 (2006): 215–28.

Mangina, Joseph L. *Revelation*. BTCB. Grand Rapids: Brazos, 2010.

Marlow, Hilary. "The Spirit of Yahweh in Isaiah 11:1–9." In *Presence, Power and Promise: The Role of the Spirit of God in the Old Testament*, edited by David G. Firth and Paul D. Wegner, 220–32. Downers Grove, IL: InterVarsity, 2011.

Marshall, I. Howard. "Church and Temple in the New Testament." *TynBul* 40, no. 2 (1989): 203–22.

———. *The Epistles of John*. NICNT. Grand Rapids: Eerdmans, 1978.

———. *The Gospel of Luke: A Commentary on the Greek Text*. NIGTC. Grand Rapids: Eerdmans, 1978.

———. *New Testament Theology: Many Witnesses, One Gospel*. Downers Grove, IL: InterVarsity, 2004.

Martens, Elmer A. *God's Design: A Focus on Old Testament Theology*. 4th ed. Eugene, OR: Wipf & Stock, 2015.

Martin, Oren. *Bound for the Promised Land: The Land Promise in God's Redemptive Plan*. NSBT 34. Nottingham: Apollos; Downers Grove, IL: InterVarsity, 2015.

Martin, Ralph P. *James*. WBC 48. Dallas: Word, 1988.

———. *Reconciliation: A Study of Paul's Theology*. Rev. ed. Grand Rapids: Zondervan, 1989.

Mathews, Kenneth A. *Genesis 1–11:26*. NAC 1A. Nashville: Broadman & Holman, 1996.

Mayes, A. D. H. *Deuteronomy*. NCB. Grand Rapids: Eerdmans, 1991.

Mayor, Joseph B. *The Epistle of St. James: The Greek Text with Introduction, Notes, Comments and Further Studies*. Reprint, Grand Rapids: Zondervan, 1954.

Mays, James Luther. *Micah: A Commentary*. OTL. Philadelphia: Westminster, 1976.

———. *Psalms*. IBC. Louisville: John Knox, 1994.

McCann, J. Clinton, Jr. "The Book of Psalms." *NIB* 4:641–1280.

McCartney, Dan G. *James*. BECNT. Grand Rapids: Baker Academic, 2009.

McConville, J. Gordon. *Being Human in God's World: An Old Testament Theology of Humanity*. Grand Rapids: Baker Academic, 2016.

———. *Deuteronomy*. ApOTC 5. Leicester: Apollos; Downers Grove, IL: InterVarsity, 2002.

———. *Grace in the End: A Study in Deuteronomic Theology*. Grand Rapids: Zondervan, 1993.

———. *A Guide to the Prophets*. Vol. 4 of *Exploring the Old Testament*. EB. Downers Grove, IL: InterVarsity, 2002.

———. "Time, Place and the Deuteronomic Altar-Law." In *Time and Place in Deuteronomy*, edited by J. G. McConville and J. G. Millar, 89–139. JSOTSup 179. Sheffield: Sheffield Academic, 1994.

McConville, J. G., and J. G. Millar, eds. *Time and Place in Deuteronomy*. JSOTSup 179. Sheffield: Sheffield Academic, 1994.

McDowell, Catherine L. *The Image of God in the Garden of Eden*. Siphrut 15. Winona Lake, IN: Eisenbrauns, 2015.

———. "'In the Image of God He Created Them': How Genesis 1:26–27 Defines the Divine-Human Relationship and Why It Matters." In *The Image of God in an Image Driven Age: Explorations in Theological Anthropology*, edited by Beth Felker Jones and Jeffrey W. Barbeau, 29–46. Downers Grove, IL: InterVarsity, 2016.

McKane, William. *A Critical and Exegetical Commentary on Jeremiah*. 2 vols. ICC. Edinburgh: T&T Clark, 1986.

McKelvey, R. Jack. *The New Temple: The Church in the New Testament*. OTM. Oxford: Oxford University Press, 1969.

McKeown, James. *Genesis*. THOTC. Grand Rapids: Eerdmans, 2008.

———. *Ruth*. THOTC. Grand Rapids: Eerdmans, 2015.

McKnight, Scot. *The Letter of James*. NICNT. Grand Rapids: Eerdmans, 2011.

Mealy, J. Webb. *After the Thousand Years: Resurrection and Judgment in Revelation 20*. JSNTSup 70. Sheffield: JSOT Press, 1992.

Meier, Samuel A. "Angels, Messengers, Heavenly Beings." In *Dictionary of the Old Testament: Prophets*, edited by Mark J. Boda and J. Gordon McConville, 24–29. Downers Grove, IL: InterVarsity, 2012.

Melton, Brittany N. "'O, That I Knew Where I Might Find Him': Aspects of Divine Absence in Proverbs, Job and Ecclesiastes." In *Interpreting Old Testament Wisdom Literature*, edited by David G. Firth and Lindsay Wilson, 205–16. Downers Grove, IL: InterVarsity, 2017.

Merrill, Eugene H. *Everlasting Dominion: A Theology of the Old Testament*. Nashville: Broadman & Holman, 2006.

———. "Pilgrimage and Procession: Motifs of Israel's Return." In *Israel's Apostasy and Restoration: Essays in Honor of Roland K. Harrison*, edited by Avraham Gileadi, 261–72. Grand Rapids: Baker, 1988.

Mettinger, Tryggve N. D. *The Dethronement of Sabaoth: Studies in the Shem and Kabod Theologies*. Translated by Frederick H. Cryer. ConBOT 18. Lund: CWK Gleerup, 1982.

Meyers, Carol L., and Eric M. Meyers. *Haggai, Zechariah 1–8: A New Translation with Introduction and Commentary*. AB 25B. Garden City, NY: Doubleday, 1987.

Michaels, J. Ramsey. *1 Peter*. WBC 49. Dallas: Word, 1998.

Middleton, J. Richard. *The Liberating Image: The Imago Dei in Genesis 1*. Grand Rapids: Brazos, 2005.

———. *A New Heaven and a New Earth: Reclaiming Biblical Eschatology*. Grand Rapids: Baker Academic, 2014.

Milgrom, Jacob. *Leviticus 1–16: A New Translation with Introduction and Commentary*. AB 3. New York: Doubleday, 1991.

Miller, Patrick D., Jr. "The Blessing of God: An Interpretation of Numbers 6:22–27." *Int* 29 (1975): 240–51.

———. *The Divine Warrior in Early Israel*. HSM 5. Cambridge, MA: Harvard University Press, 1973.

Miller, Patrick D., and J. J. M. Roberts. *The Hand of the Lord: A Reassessment of the "Ark Narrative" of 1 Samuel*. Atlanta: Society of Biblical Literature, 2008.

Miller, Stephen. *Daniel*. NAC 18. Nashville: Broadman & Holman, 1994.

Moberly, R. W. L. *At the Mountain of God: Story and Theology in Exodus 32–34*. JSOTSup 22. Sheffield: JSOT Press, 1983.

Moltmann, Jürgen. *The Coming of God: Christian Eschatology*. London: SCM, 1996.

Moo, Douglas J. *The Epistle to the Romans*. NICNT. Grand Rapids: Eerdmans, 1996.

———. *The Letter of James*. PNTC. Grand Rapids: Eerdmans, 2000.

———. *The Letters to the Colossians and to Philemon*. PNTC. Grand Rapids: Eerdmans, 2008.

———. "Paul." *NDBT* 136–40.

Moore, M. S. "Divine Presence." In *Dictionary of the Old Testament: Prophets*, edited by Mark J. Boda and J. Gordon McConville, 166–70. Downers Grove, IL: InterVarsity, 2012.

Morales, L. Michael. *The Tabernacle Pre-Figured: Cosmic Mountain Ideology in Genesis and Exodus*. BTS 15. Leuven: Peeters, 2012.

———. *Who Shall Ascend the Mountain of the Lord? A Biblical Theology of the Book of Leviticus*. NSBT 37. Nottingham: Apollos; Downers Grove, IL: InterVarsity, 2015.

Morris, Leon. *The Epistle to the Romans*. PNTC. Grand Rapids: Eerdmans, 1988.

———. *Jesus Is the Christ: Studies in the Theology of John*. Grand Rapids: Eerdmans, 1989.

———. *Ruth*. TOTC. Downers Grove, IL: InterVarsity, 1968.

Mounce, Robert. *The Book of Revelation*. NICNT. Grand Rapids: Eerdmans, 1977.

Murphy, Roland E. *The Gift of the Psalms*. Peabody, MA: Hendrickson, 2000.

———. *The Tree of Life: An Exploration of Biblical Wisdom Literature*. Rev. ed. with supplement. Grand Rapids: Eerdmans, 2002.

Nelson, Richard D. *Deuteronomy: A Commentary*. OTL. Louisville: Westminster John Knox, 2002.

———. *First and Second Kings*. IBC. Louisville: John Knox, 1987.

———. *Joshua: A Commentary*. OTL. Louisville: Westminster John Knox, 1997.

Newsom, Carol A. "Angels." *ABD* 1:248–53.

Niehaus, Jeffrey J. *God at Sinai: Covenant and Theophany in the Bible and Ancient Near East*. Grand Rapids: Zondervan, 1995.

———. "In the Wind of the Storm: Another Look at Genesis III 8." *VT* 44 (1994): 263–67.

Niskanen, Paul. "Yhwh as Father, Redeemer, and Potter in Isaiah 63:7–64:11." *CBQ* 68 (2006): 397–407.

Nogalski, James D., and Marvin A. Sweeney. *Reading and Hearing the Book of the Twelve*. SBLSymS 15. Atlanta: Society of Biblical Literature, 2000.

North, Christopher R. *The Second Isaiah: Introduction, Translation and Commentary to Chapters XL–LV*. Oxford: Clarendon, 1964.

Nykolaishen, Douglas J. E., and Andrew J. Schmutzer. *Ezra, Nehemiah, and Esther*. TTCS. Grand Rapids: Baker Books, 2018.

Olley, John W. "Pharaoh's Daughter, Solomon's Palace, and the Temple: Another Look at the Structure of 1 Kings 1–11." *JSOT* 27 (2003): 355–69.

Osborne, Grant R. *Matthew*. ZECNT. Grand Rapids: Zondervan, 2010.

———. *Revelation*. BECNT. Grand Rapids: Baker Academic, 2002.

Oswalt, John N. *The Book of Isaiah: Chapters 1–39*. NICOT. Grand Rapids: Eerdmans, 1986.

———. *The Book of Isaiah: Chapters 40–66*. NICOT. Grand Rapids: Eerdmans, 1998.

O'Toole, R. F. "Activity of the Risen Jesus in Luke-Acts." *Bib* 62 (1981): 471–98.

Pate, C. Marvin. *Interpreting Revelation and Other Apocalyptic Literature: An Exegetical Handbook.* Grand Rapids: Kregel, 2016.

Pate, C. Marvin, et al. *The Story of Israel: A Biblical Theology.* Leicester: Apollos; Downers Grove, IL: InterVarsity, 2004.

Patrick, Frank Y. "Time and Tradition in the Book of Haggai." In *Tradition in Transition: Haggai and Zechariah 1–8 in the Trajectory of Hebrew Theology,* edited by Mark J. Boda and Michael H. Floyd, 40–55. LHBOTS 475. London: T&T Clark, 2008.

Perdue, Leo G. *Proverbs.* IBC. Louisville: John Knox, 2000.

———. *Wisdom Literature: A Theological History.* Louisville: Westminster John Knox, 2007.

Perrin, Nicholas. *Jesus the Temple.* Grand Rapids: Baker Academic, 2010.

Petersen, David L. *Haggai and Zechariah 1–8: A Commentary.* OTL. Philadelphia: Westminster, 1984.

———. *The Prophetic Literature: An Introduction.* Louisville: Westminster John Knox, 2002.

———. "Zechariah's Visions: A Theological Perspective." *VT* 34 (1984): 195–206.

Peterson, David G. "The Pneumatology of Luke-Acts: The Spirit of Prophecy Unleashed." In *Issues in Luke-Acts: Selected Essays,* edited by Sean A. Adams and Michael W. Pahl, 211–32. Piscataway, NJ: Gorgias, 2012.

———. "The Worship of the New Community." In *Witness to the Gospel: The Theology of Acts,* edited by I. Howard Marshall and David Peterson, 373–95. Grand Rapids: Eerdmans, 1998.

Peterson, Ryan S. *The* Imago Dei *as Human Identity: A Theological Interpretation.* JTISup 14. Winona Lake, IN: Eisenbrauns, 2016.

Plastaras, James. *The God of Exodus: The Theology of the Exodus Narratives.* Milwaukee: Bruce, 1966.

Porter, Stanley E. "Is There a Center to Paul's Theology? An Introduction to the Study of Paul and His Theology." In *Paul and His Theology,* edited by Stanley E. Porter, 1–19. PSt 3. Leiden: Brill, 2006.

Powell, Mark Allan. *God with Us: A Pastoral Theology of Matthew's Gospel.* Minneapolis: Fortress, 1995.

Preuss, Horst Dietrich. ". . . ich will mit dir sein!" *ZAW* 80 (1968): 139–73.

Propp, William H. C. *Exodus 1–18: A New Translation with Introduction and Commentary.* AB 2. New York: Doubleday, 1999.

Provan, Iain. *Discovering Genesis: Content, Interpretation, Reception.* Grand Rapids: Eerdmans, 2015.

———. *1 and 2 Kings.* NIBC. Peabody, MA: Hendrickson, 1995.

Raitt, Thomas M. *A Theology of the Exile: Judgment/Deliverance in Jeremiah and Ezekiel.* Philadelphia: Fortress, 1977.

Rapske, Brian. "Opposition to the Plan of God and Persecution." In *Witness to the Gospel: The Theology of Acts*, edited by I. Howard Marshall and David Peterson, 235–56. Grand Rapids: Eerdmans, 1998.

Reddit, Paul L. "Esther." In *Theological Interpretation of the Old Testament: A Book-by-Book Survey*, edited by Kevin J. Vanhoozer, 142–47. London: SPCK; Grand Rapids: Baker Academic, 2008.

Rendtorff, Rolf. *The Canonical Hebrew Bible: A Theology of the Old Testament.* Translated by David E. Orton. TBS 7. Leiden: Deo, 2005.

Resseguie, James L. *The Revelation of John: A Narrative Commentary.* Grand Rapids: Baker Academic, 2009.

Richter, Sandra L. *The Deuteronomistic History and the Name Theology.* BZAW 318. Berlin: de Gruyter, 2002.

———. *The Epic of Eden: A Christian Entry into the Old Testament.* Downers Grove, IL: InterVarsity, 2008.

———. "The Place of the Name in Deuteronomy." *VT* 57 (2007): 342–66.

Roberts, J. J. M. "Isaiah in Old Testament Theology." *Int* 36 (1982): 130–43.

Robertson, O. Palmer. *The Flow of the Psalms: Discovering Their Structure and Theology.* Phillipsburg, NJ: P&R, 2015.

Robson, James. *Word and Spirit in Ezekiel.* LHBOTS 447. London: T&T Clark, 2006.

Römer, Thomas. "Redaction Criticism: 1 Kings 8 and the Deuteronomists." In *Method Matters: Essays on the Interpretation of the Hebrew Bible in Honor of David L. Petersen*, edited by Joel M. LeMon and Kent Harold Richards, 63–76. SBLRBS 56. Atlanta: Society of Biblical Literature, 2009.

Rooker, Mark F. *Leviticus.* NAC 3A. Nashville: Broadman & Holman, 2000.

Rosner, Brian S. *Known by God: A Biblical Theology of Personal Identity.* BTL. Grand Rapids: Zondervan, 2017.

———. "The Progress of the Word." In *Witness to the Gospel: The Theology of Acts*, edited by I. Howard Marshall and David Peterson, 215–33. Grand Rapids: Eerdmans, 1998.

Ross, Allen P. *A Commentary on the Psalms.* Vol. 1. KEL. Grand Rapids: Kregel, 2011.

———. *Creation and Blessing: A Guide to the Study and Exposition of the Book of Genesis.* Grand Rapids: Baker, 1988.

———. *Holiness to the Lord: A Guide to the Exposition of the Book of Leviticus.* Grand Rapids: Baker Academic, 2002.

———. *Recalling the Hope of Glory: Biblical Worship from the Garden to the New Creation.* Grand Rapids: Kregel, 2006.

Routledge, Robin. *Old Testament Theology: A Thematic Approach.* Downers Grove, IL: InterVarsity, 2008.

———. "The Spirit and the Future in the Old Testament: Restoration and Renewal." In *Presence, Power and Promise: The Role of the Spirit of God in the*

Old Testament, edited by David G. Firth and Paul D. Wegner, 346–67. Downers Grove, IL: InterVarsity, 2011.

Rowe, C. Kavin. *Early Narrative Christology: The Lord in the Gospel of Luke*. Grand Rapids: Baker Academic, 2009.

Ryken, Leland, James C. Wilhoit, and Tremper Longman III, eds. *Dictionary of Biblical Imagery*. Downers Grove, IL: InterVarsity, 1998.

Sailhamer, John H. *The Pentateuch as Narrative: A Biblical-Theological Commentary*. Grand Rapids: Zondervan, 1992.

Sakenfeld, Katharine Doob. *Ruth*. IBC. Louisville: John Knox, 1999.

Sanders, Fred. *The Deep Things of God: How the Trinity Changes Everything*. Wheaton: Crossway, 2010.

Saner, Andrea D. *"Too Much to Grasp": Exodus 3:13–15 and the Reality of God*. JTISup 11. Winona Lake, IN: Eisenbrauns, 2015.

Satyavani, Puttagunta. *Seeing the Face of God: Exploring an Old Testament Theme*. Carlisle: Langham, 2014.

Schafroth, Verena. "1 and 2 Peter." In *A Biblical Theology of the Holy Spirit*, edited by Trevor J. Burke and Keith Warrington, 238–49. Eugene, OR: Cascade, 2014.

Schnabel, Eckhard J. *Acts*. ZECNT. Grand Rapids: Zondervan, 2012. Expanded digital ed., Logos.

Schnackenburg, Rudolf. *Ephesians: A Commentary*. Translated by Helen Heron. Edinburgh: T&T Clark, 1991.

———. *The Johannine Epistles*. Translated by Reginald Fuller and Ilse Fuller. New York: Crossroad, 1992.

Schnittjer, Gary Edward. *The Torah Story: An Apprenticeship on the Pentateuch*. Grand Rapids: Zondervan, 2006.

Schöpflin, Karin. "God's Interpreter: The Interpreting Angel in Post-Exilic Prophetic Visions of the Old Testament." In *Angels: The Concept of Celestial Beings— Origins, Development and Reception*, edited by Friedrich V. Reiterer, Tobias Nicklas, and Karin Schöpflin, 189–204. Deuterocanonical and Cognate Literature Yearbook 2007. Berlin: de Gruyter, 2007.

Schreiner, Patrick. *The Body of Jesus: A Spatial Analysis of the Kingdom in Matthew*. LNTS 555. London: Bloomsbury T&T Clark, 2016.

Schreiner, Thomas R. *The King in His Beauty: A Biblical Theology of the Old and New Testaments*. Grand Rapids: Baker Academic, 2013.

———. *New Testament Theology: Magnifying God in Christ*. Grand Rapids: Baker Academic, 2008.

———. *Paul, Apostle of God's Glory in Christ: A Pauline Theology*. Downers Grove, IL: IVP Academic, 2006.

———. *1, 2 Peter, Jude*. NAC 37. Nashville: Broadman & Holman, 2003.

Schuele, Andreas. "Made in the Image of God: The Concepts of Divine Image in Genesis 1–3." *ZAW* 117 (2005): 1–20.

————. "The Spirit of YHWH and the Aura of Divine Presence." *Int* 66 (2012): 16–28.

Scobie, Charles H. H. *The Ways of Our God: An Approach to Biblical Theology.* Grand Rapids: Eerdmans, 2003.

Seibert, Eric. *Subversive Scribes and the Solomonic Narrative: A Rereading of 1 Kings 1–11.* LHBOTS 436. London: T&T Clark, 2006.

Seitz, Christopher R. "The Book of Isaiah 40–66." *NIB* 6:309–552.

————. "The Call of Moses and the 'Revelation' of the Divine Name." In *Theological Exegesis: Essays in Honor of Brevard S. Childs,* edited by Christopher Seitz and Kathryn Greene-McCreight, 145–61. Grand Rapids: Eerdmans, 1999.

————. *Isaiah 1–39.* IBC. Louisville: John Knox, 1993.

————. *Prophecy and Hermeneutics: Toward a New Introduction to the Prophets.* STI. Grand Rapids: Baker Academic, 2007.

Selman, Martin J. *1 Chronicles: An Introduction and Commentary.* TOTC. Downers Grove, IL: InterVarsity, 1994.

————. "Jerusalem in Chronicles." In *Zion, City of Our God,* edited by Richard S. Hess and Gordon J. Wenham, 43–56. Grand Rapids: Eerdmans, 1999.

Smalley, Stephen S. *1, 2, 3 John.* WBC 51. Dallas: Word, 1989.

Smith, Billy K., and Frank S. Page. *Amos, Obadiah, Jonah.* NAC 19B. Nashville: Broadman & Holman, 1995.

Smith, Gary. *Isaiah 1–39.* NAC 15A. Nashville: Broadman & Holman, 2007.

Smith, Mark S. *Where the Gods Are: Spatial Dimensions of Anthropomorphism in the Biblical World.* AYBRL. New Haven: Yale University Press, 2006.

Smith, Ralph L. *Micah–Malachi.* WBC 32. Waco: Word, 1984.

Smoak, Jeremy D. *The Priestly Blessing in Inscription and Scripture: The Early History of Numbers 6:24–26.* Oxford: Oxford University Press, 2016.

Snearly, Michael K. *The Return of the King: Messianic Expectation in Book V of the Psalter.* LHBOTS 624. London: Bloomsbury T&T Clark, 2016.

Sommer, Benjamin D. "Conflicting Constructions of Divine Presence in the Priestly Tabernacle." *BibInt* 9 (2001): 41–63.

————. *Revelation and Authority: Sinai in Jewish Scripture and Tradition.* AYBRL. New Haven: Yale University Press, 2015.

Soulen, R. Kendall. *Distinguishing the Voices.* Vol. 1 of *The Divine Name(s) and the Holy Trinity.* Louisville: Westminster John Knox, 2011.

Squires, John T. *The Plan of God in Luke-Acts.* SNTSMS 76. Cambridge: Cambridge University Press, 1993.

————. "The Plan of God in the Acts of the Apostles." In *Witness to the Gospel: The Theology of Acts,* edited by I. Howard Marshall and David Peterson, 19–39. Grand Rapids: Eerdmans, 1998.

Stein, Robert H. *Jesus, the Temple, and the Coming of the Son of Man: A Commentary on Mark 13.* Downers Grove, IL: InterVarsity, 2014.

———. "Last Supper." In *Dictionary of Jesus and the Gospels*, edited by Joel B. Green and Scot McKnight, 445–50. Downers Grove, IL: InterVarsity, 1992.

———. *Luke*. NAC 24. Nashville: Broadman & Holman, 1992.

———. *Mark*. BECNT. Grand Rapids: Baker Academic, 2008.

Strauss, Mark L. *The Davidic Messiah in Luke-Acts: The Promise and Its Fulfillment in Lukan Christology*. JSNTSup 110. Sheffield: Sheffield Academic, 1995.

Stuart, Douglas K. "'The Cool of the Day' (Gen. 3:8) and 'The Way He Should Go' (Prov. 22:6)." *BSac* 171 (2014): 259–73.

———. *Exodus*. NAC 2. Nashville: Broadman & Holman, 2006.

———. *Hosea–Jonah*. WBC 31. Waco: Word, 1987.

Tate, Marvin E. *Psalms 51–100*. WBC 20. Dallas: Word, 1990.

Terrien, Samuel. *The Elusive Presence: The Heart of Biblical Theology*. San Francisco: Harper & Row, 1978.

Thielman, Frank. *Theology of the New Testament*. Grand Rapids: Zondervan, 2005.

Thiselton, Anthony C. *The First Epistle to the Corinthians: A Commentary on the Greek Text*. NIGTC. Grand Rapids: Eerdmans, 2000.

Thompson, J. A. *The Book of Jeremiah*. NICOT. Grand Rapids: Eerdmans, 1980.

Thompson, Marianne Meye. *The God of the Gospel of John*. Grand Rapids: Eerdmans, 2001.

———. *1–3 John*. IVPNTC. Downers Grove, IL: InterVarsity, 1992.

———. *John: A Commentary*. NTL. Louisville: Westminster John Knox, 2015.

Tilling, Chris. *Paul's Divine Christology*. Grand Rapids: Eerdmans, 2015.

Timmer, Daniel C. *A Gracious and Compassionate God: Mission, Salvation and Spirituality in the Book of Jonah*. NSBT 26. Nottingham: Apollos; Downers Grove, IL: InterVarsity, 2011.

Tiňo, Jozef. *King and Temple in Chronicles: A Contextual Approach to Their Relations*. FRLANT 234. Göttingen: Vanderhoeck & Ruprecht, 2010.

Tollington, Janet E. *Tradition and Innovation in Haggai and Zechariah*. JSOTSup 150. Sheffield: JSOT Press, 1993.

Tooman, William A. "Covenant and Presence in the Composition and Theology of Ezekiel." In *Divine Presence and Absence in Exilic and Post-Exilic Judaism*, edited by Nathan MacDonald and Izaak J. de Hulster, 151–82. FAT 2/61. Tübingen: Mohr Siebeck, 2013.

Towner, Philip H. *The Letters to Timothy and Titus*. NICNT. Grand Rapids, Eerdmans, 2006.

Towner, W. Sibley. *Daniel*. IBC. Atlanta: John Knox, 1984.

Trible, Phyllis. "The Book of Jonah." *NIB* 7:463–540.

Tucker, Gene M. "The Book of Isaiah 1–39." *NIB* 6:27–305.

Tucker, W. Dennis, Jr. "The Pentateuch: Divine Will and Human Responsibility." In *The Story of Israel: A Biblical Theology*, by C. Marvin Pate et al., 29–49. Downers Grove, IL: InterVarsity, 2004.

Tuell, Steven S. *First and Second Chronicles*. IBC. Louisville: John Knox, 2001.

Tull, Patricia K. *Isaiah 1–39*. SHBC. Macon, GA: Smyth & Helwys, 2010.

Turner, David L. *Matthew*. BECNT. Grand Rapids: Baker Academic, 2008.

Turner, Max. "The Spirit and Salvation in Luke-Acts." In *The Holy Spirit and Christian Origins: Essays in Honor of James D. G. Dunn*, edited by Graham N. Stanton, Bruce W. Longenecker, and Stephen C. Barton, 103–16. Grand Rapids: Eerdmans, 2004.

———. "The 'Spirit of Prophecy' as the Power of Israel's Restoration and Witness." In *Witness to the Gospel: The Theology of Acts*, edited by I. Howard Marshall and David Peterson, 327–48. Grand Rapids: Eerdmans, 1998.

———. "The Work of the Holy Spirit in Luke-Acts." WW 23 (2003): 146–53.

VanGemeren, Willem A. "The Spirit of Restoration." *WTJ* 50 (1988): 81–102.

VanGemeren, Willem, and Andrew Abernethy. "The Spirit and the Future: A Canonical Approach." In *Presence, Power and Promise: The Role of the Spirit of God in the Old Testament*, edited by David G. Firth and Paul D. Wegner, 321–45. Downers Grove, IL: InterVarsity, 2011.

Van Leeuwen, Raymond C. "Proverbs." In *Theological Interpretation of the Old Testament: A Book-by-Book Survey*, edited by Kevin J. Vanhoozer, 171–78. London: SPCK; Grand Rapids: Baker Academic, 2008.

Verhoef, Peter A. *The Books of Haggai and Malachi*. NICOT. Grand Rapids: Eerdmans, 1987.

Vogt, Peter T. *Deuteronomic Theology and the Significance of Torah: A Reappraisal*. Winona Lake, IN: Eisenbrauns, 2006.

von Rad, Gerhard. *Genesis: A Commentary*. Translated by John H. Marks. OTL. Philadelphia: Westminster, 1972.

———. *Old Testament Theology*. Translated by D. M. G. Stalker. 2 vols. OTL. Louisville: Westminster John Knox, 2001.

Vriezen, T. C. "Essentials of the Theology of Isaiah." In *Israel's Prophetic Heritage: Essays in Honor of James Muilenburg*, edited by Bernhard W. Anderson and Walter Harrelson, 128–46. New York: Harper, 1962.

———. *An Outline of Old Testament Theology*. 2nd ed. Newton, MA: C. T. Branford, 1970.

Walker, Peter W. *Jesus and the Holy City: New Testament Perspectives on Jerusalem*. Grand Rapids: Eerdmans, 1996.

Wallace, Daniel B. *Greek Grammar beyond the Basics: An Exegetical Syntax of the New Testament*. Grand Rapids: Zondervan, 1996.

Walsh, Jerome T. "The Characterization of Solomon in First Kings 1–5." CBQ 57 (1995): 471–93.

Waltke, Bruce K. *The Book of Proverbs: Chapters 1–15*. NICOT. Grand Rapids: Eerdmans, 2004.

———. *Genesis: A Commentary*. Grand Rapids: Zondervan, 2001.

Waltke, Bruce K., with Charles Yu. *An Old Testament Theology: An Exegetical, Canonical, and Thematic Approach*. Grand Rapids: Zondervan, 2007.

Walton, John H. "Equilibrium and the Sacred Compass: The Structure of Leviticus." *BBR* 11 (2001): 293–304.

———. *Genesis*. NIVAC. Grand Rapids: Zondervan, 2001.

Walton, Kevin. *Thou Traveller Unknown: The Presence and Absence of God in the Jacob Narrative*. PBTM. Waynesboro, GA: Paternoster, 2003.

Ward, Timothy. *Word and Supplement: Speech Acts, Biblical Texts, and the Sufficiency of Scripture*. Oxford: Oxford University Press, 2002.

———. *Words of Life: Scripture as the Living and Active Word of God*. Downers Grove, IL: InterVarsity, 2009.

Watts, Rikk E. "Mark." *CNTUOT* 111–249.

Weima, Jeffrey A. D. "1–2 Thessalonians." *CNTUOT* 871–89.

Weinfeld, M. "Jeremiah and the Spiritual Metamorphosis of Israel." *ZAW* 88 (1976): 17–56.

Wenham, Gordon J. *The Book of Leviticus*. NICOT. Grand Rapids: Eerdmans, 1979.

———. "Deuteronomy and the Central Sanctuary." *TynBul* 22 (1971): 103–18.

———. *Genesis 1–15*. WBC 1. Waco: Word, 1987.

———. "Sanctuary Symbolism in the Garden of Eden Story." In *"I Studied Inscriptions from before the Flood": Ancient Near Eastern, Literary, and Linguistic Approaches to Genesis 1–11*, edited by Richard S. Hess and David Toshio Tsumura, 399–404. SBTS 4. Winona Lake, IN: Eisenbrauns, 1994.

Wessner, Mark D. "Toward a Literary Understanding of Moses and the LORD 'Face to Face' (פָּנִים אֶל־פָּנִים) in Exodus 33:7–11." *ResQ* 44 (2002): 109–16.

Westermann, Claus. *Beginning and End in the Bible*. Translated by Keith Crim. Philadelphia: Fortress, 1972.

———. *Genesis 1–11: A Commentary*. Translated by John J. Scullion. Minneapolis: Augsburg, 1984.

———. *Praise and Lament in the Psalms*. Translated by Keith R. Crim and Richard N. Soulen. Edinburgh: T&T Clark, 1965.

Wildberger, Hans. *Isaiah 1–12: A Commentary*. Translated by Thomas H. Trapp. CC. Minneapolis: Fortress, 1991.

Wilkins, Michael J. *Discipleship in the Ancient World and Matthew's Gospel*. 2nd ed. Grand Rapids: Baker, 1995.

———. *Matthew*. NIVAC. Grand Rapids: Zondervan, 2004.

Williamson, H. G. M. *1 and 2 Chronicles*. NCB. Grand Rapids: Eerdmans, 1982.

———. *A Critical and Exegetical Commentary on Isaiah 1–27*. 3 vols. ICC. London: T&T Clark, 2006.

———. *Ezra, Nehemiah*. WBC 16. Waco: Word, 1985.

————. "Isaiah 63,7–64,11." *ZAW* 102 (1990): 48–58.

Wilson, Gerald H. *The Editing of the Hebrew Psalter*. SBLDS 76. Chico, CA: Scholars Press, 1985.

————. "The Structure of the Psalter." In *Interpreting the Psalms: Issues and Approaches*, edited by David Firth and Philip S. Johnston, 229–46. Downers Grove, IL: InterVarsity, 2005.

Wilson, Ian. *Out of the Midst of the Fire: Divine Presence in Deuteronomy*. SBLDS 151. Atlanta: Scholars Press, 1995.

Wilson, Lindsay. *Job*. THOTC. Grand Rapids: Eerdmans, 2015.

Wiseman, Donald J. *1 and 2 Kings*. TOTC. Downers Grove, IL: InterVarsity, 1993.

Witherington, Ben, III. *The Acts of the Apostles: A Socio-Rhetorical Commentary*. Grand Rapids: Eerdmans, 1998.

————. *Conflict and Community in Corinth: A Socio-Rhetorical Commentary on 1 and 2 Corinthians*. Grand Rapids: Eerdmans, 1995.

————. *The Gospel of Mark: A Socio-Rhetorical Commentary*. Grand Rapids: Eerdmans, 2001.

————. *Letters and Homilies for Hellenized Christians*. 2 vols. Downers Grove, IL: IVP Academic, 2006.

Wolff, Hans Walter. *Anthropology of the Old Testament*. Translated by Margaret Kohl. London: SCM, 1974.

————. *Joel and Amos: A Commentary on the Books of the Prophets Joel and Amos*. Edited by S. Dean McBride Jr. Translated by Waldemar Janzen, S. Dean McBride Jr., and Charles A. Muenchow. Hermeneia. Philadelphia: Fortress, 1977.

————. *Obadiah and Jonah*. Translated by Margaret Kohl. CC. Minneapolis: Augsburg, 1986.

Wolff, Herbert M. "The Transcendent Nature of Covenant Curse Reversals." In *Israel's Apostasy and Restoration: Essays in Honor of Roland K. Harrison*, edited by Avraham Gileadi, 319–25. Grand Rapids: Baker, 1988.

Wright, Christopher J. H. *Deuteronomy*. NIBC. Peabody, MA: Hendrickson, 1996.

————. *The Message of Ezekiel: A New Heart and a New Spirit*. TBST. Downers Grove, IL: InterVarsity, 2001.

Wright, N. T. *Justification: God's Plan and Paul's Vision*. London: SPCK, 2009.

————. *Paul and the Faithfulness of God*. COQG 4. 2 vols. Minneapolis: Fortress, 2013.

————. *Pauline Perspectives: Essays on Paul, 1978–2013*. Grand Rapids: Eerdmans, 2013.

Youngblood, Kevin J. *Jonah: God's Scandalous Mercy*. HMSCS. Grand Rapids: Zondervan, 2013.

Younger, K. Lawson. *Judges, Ruth*. NIVAC. Grand Rapids: Zondervan, 2002.

Zimmerli, Walther. *Ezekiel 1: A Commentary on the Book of the Prophet Ezekiel*. Edited by Frank Moore Cross and Klaus Baltzer with Leonard Jay Greenspoon. Translated by Ronald E. Clements. Hermeneia. Philadelphia: Fortress, 1979.

―――. *Ezekiel 2: A Commentary on the Book of the Prophet Ezekiel*. Edited by Paul D. Hanson with Leonard Jay Greenspoon. Translated by James D. Martin. Hermeneia. Philadelphia: Fortress, 1983.

INDEX OF AUTHORS

INDEX OF SCRIPTURE AND
ANCIENT WRITINGS

Old Testament Apocrypha / Deuterocanonical Books

Sirach

Tobit

Old Testament Pseudepigrapha

1 Enoch

4 Ezra (2 Esdras)

Odes of Solomon

Psalms of Solomon

Testament of Levi